IN PRAISE OF

Why I Write

"Asking a novelist why he or she writes is a bit like throwing an egg into an electric fan. The joining of fragility (the writer's ego) to furious torque (also the writer's ego) risks a cloud of splatter. Will Blythe, putting the question to twenty-six well-known American writers, does emerge with a dribble or two of egg on his face. It is worth it. Along with doses of posturing, unhinged prose, kiss-offs and maneuvers, he has elicited shrewd and poignant revelations about the process and the pain."
—Richard Eder, *Los Angeles Times*

"A highly entertaining, candid collection, pleasingly united by unintentionally recurring themes."
—Daphne Uviller, *Time Out New York*

"Blythe envisions this anthology as a counterpoint to the flood of how-to books that assume 'some odd, unspoken consensus that imaginative writing is an activity well worth pursuing.' His larger question, then, is why should anyone write. Ultimately, there's no better answer than the entertaining diversity of the answers we get here, which are various as snowflakes. . . . There's useful advice beneath the inspiration, too: Rick Bass's 'Why the Daily Writing of Fiction Matters' should be required reading in all creative writing workshops."
—*Kirkus Reviews*

"The twenty-six writers featured in this intriguing and moving collection have set out to articulate what it is that drives them to create. . . . Their reasons for writing are as individual as the writers themselves. . . . In describing why they write, many of the contributors end up delving into their core beliefs, experiences, motivations, and feelings—the very things that fuel the creative drive."
—Katherine Wessling, *Speak* (San Francisco)

"One of the delights of this collection is the many unexpected ways the writers approached the question. In all, an eclectic and stimulating collection."
—Mary Paumier Jones, *Library Journal*

Why I Write

Thoughts on the Craft of Fiction

EDITED BY

WILL BLYTHE

LITTLE, BROWN AND COMPANY

Boston   New York   London

FIRST EDITION

Joy Williams's essay, Barry Hannah's essay, and Mark Richard's story
first appeared in *The Oxford American*
David Foster Wallace's essay and Amy Hempel's essay
first appeared in *Fiction Writer*
Richard Ford's essay first appeared in *Granta*

LIBRARY OF CONGRESS CATALOGING-IN-PUBLICATION DATA
Why I write : thoughts on the craft of fiction /
edited by Will Blythe. — 1st ed.
p.   cm.
Twenty-six original essays on writing.
ISBN 0-316-10229-6
1. Authorship.   2. Fiction — Authorship.   I. Blythe, Will.
PN165.W485   1988
808'.02 — dc21   98-21419

10 9 8 7 6 5 4 3 2

MV–NY

Printed in the United States of America

IN HONOR OF

LeGette Blythe
Esther Blythe
Anna Nassif
David Nassif

Contents

Acknowledgments   xi

Introduction by Will Blythe   xiii

At the Point of My Pen   3
     NORMAN MAILER

Uncanny the Singing That Comes from
Certain Husks   5
     JOY WILLIAMS

Where Does Writing Come From?   13
     RICHARD FORD

I Am a . . . *Genius!*   21
     THOM JONES

Some for Glory, Some for Praise   34
     JAMES SALTER

That's What Dogs Do   41
     AMY HEMPEL

Stories   47
     PAT CONROY

Writing and a Life Lived Well: Notes
on Allan Gurganus   61
    ANN PATCHETT

Easing My Heart Inside   69
    TERRY McMILLAN

Why the Daily Writing of Fiction Matters   74
    RICK BASS

Phobia and Composition   84
    RICK MOODY AND
    MARGARET F. M. DAVIS

Secret Agent   98
    DENIS JOHNSON

The Lousy Rider   103
    ELIZABETH GILBERT

Writing   110
    WILLIAM VOLLMANN

For the Money   116
    MARK JACOBSON

Why I Write   124
    STEPHEN WRIGHT

Everything Else Falls Away   128
    LEE SMITH

The Nature of the Fun   140
    DAVID FOSTER WALLACE

Why I Write, or Not   146
    JIM HARRISON

The Wolf in the Tall Grass   155
    MARY GAITSKILL

Rent Retards the Revolution!   164
   DARIUS JAMES

The War We Can't Win, We Can't Lose,
We Can't Quit   171
   BARRY HANNAH

Collecting Myself   182
   TOM CHIARELLA

Why She Writes   188
   JAYNE ANNE PHILLIPS

In Silence   195
   ROBERT STONE

Who Is That Man Tied to the Mast?   198
   MARK RICHARD

Notes on Contributors   222

ACKNOWLEDGMENTS

The editor would like to thank Michael Pietsch and Amanda Murray for, among other qualities, their patience. Thanks also to the writers whose work makes up this book.

Introduction

WILL BLYTHE

F ROM SEA TO SHINING SEA, in bookstores and homes, and even in those Swiss chalet–style condos dotting the purple-mountained majesties, the shelves of America are groaning under the weight of "how-to-write" books. These sprightly, optimistic manuals suggest some odd, unspoken consensus that imaginative writing is an activity well worth pursuing for us Americans, perhaps as a kind of graphomaniacal self-therapy. Evidently, it's no longer enough to read stories; we must write them as well. Everybody in the pool! But given that we all seem to want to know *how* to write, shouldn't we first take a step backward, away from the water's edge, and ask the big question lurking furtively behind the *how*, which is *why* even attempt to write literature in the first place? Why, oh why? That's what this book is about.

Unquestionably, there are many compelling reasons *not* to write. Some are mundane, like having a job, a spouse, a headache. These things can take time and energy away from the creation of literature. So can not having a job, a spouse, and a headache. (In regard to the absence of headache, it must be said that you *can* feel too *good* to write.) There are other mighty rationales for shirking the pen. Not enough money. Too little experience. Bad speller. Not good enough yet. Not good enough compared to García Márquez. Not good enough compared to Shakespeare. Better than Shakespeare but no one seems to agree. Too much ambition. Insufficient ambition. Paranoia. Alcohol. Heroin. Gas pains. Gout. Hay fever.

And of course, there are always powerful metaphysical reasons for not writing. For instance, deep existential dread. The distortions of solitude. The ravages of time. Black holes. The eventual death of the solar system. Being adrift in a meaningless universe in which everything is floating away from everything else. The temptation of silence. By this, I mean that sometimes silence seems more articulate, more full of possibility than language itself; it is the realm of the vision, of the masterfully unwritten, of astounding books that will forever be undiminished by their narrowing in reality.

Wait, there's more. Back here in the brawling American marketplace, it's easy to feel that this is a society in which literature all too often gets shoved behind the traffic barricades by the beefy cops of hype while the clamorous parade of mass culture goose-steps triumphantly down the avenue. "Get over to the cultural margins, you losers," the police yell, vexed by such unglamorous duties. As Don DeLillo has said of his fellow novelists, "We're one beat away from becoming elevator music."

Plus — and I think this is widely known — a writer with a capacity for composing novels and short stories can usually make more money slaving away for the movies and TV. So, really, why does anyone write fiction?

This is evidently a question that has been occurring to people (mainly writers) for quite some time, and for good reason, it seems. I remember the first moment it occurred to me, way back in the balmy spring of 1968. I was soldiering through the fifth grade at Glenwood Elementary School in Chapel Hill, North Carolina. One sunny afternoon in Miss Farrior's reading class, in between casting frequent and admiring glances at my new desert boots and sending the same sort of looks over my shoulder toward the lovely Patty Midgette and Mitzi Cherry, I came across an article in my *Weekly Reader* about the mortality rates of various professions (in retrospect, this study seems altogether too wonderfully morbid for the *Weekly Reader* — might it have actually appeared in that brutal, unsparing *Scholastic* magazine?). Right *down* there with lumberjacks and stock-car drivers in terms of suffering early death were professional writers. Now, I could understand buying the farm by chopping down a tree on top of yourself, or by spinning into a concrete wall at 165 miles an hour. Death loves the woods and the racetrack. But what precisely were the risk factors associated with sitting quietly at a desk, scribbling onto a sheet of paper?

Those statistics seemed inconceivable to me at the time (sadly, a little less so now) because my grandfather LeGette Blythe was a writer, and he was one of the happiest people I've ever known. I'm not talking about spritzy, bubbly, lick-your-face happiness; no, I mean the deep, underground-river kind that makes a person steady and content and a boon to his fellows. Unless you are family or from a certain generation of North Carolina readers, mostly died out now, you probably haven't heard of my grandfather. He was born in 1900 in the tiny town of Huntersville, North Carolina. As a child, he won a pair of shoes in an essay contest sponsored by the Mecklenburg County Fair. I always thought it was his first pair of shoes, but I'm now told that it wasn't; it wouldn't have been unlike my grandfather, honest though he was, to embellish a story ever so slightly. (There are a few overly literal-minded members of my family who say I've inherited this tendency from him.)

He eventually became a newspaperman in Charlotte, famous among his peers for not taking notes and not playing poker. He published several books while still a reporter, including one novel, *Bold Galilean*, that became a best-seller for the University of North Carolina Press. When the editors of the *Charlotte Observer* wouldn't give him a leave of absence to write a new novel, banking on their suspicion that he couldn't afford to give up employment, he called their bluff and quit. He was fifty years old, with a wife, three children, and bills to pay. Over the next four decades, he paid those bills, turning out plays, biographies, history, and fiction (including several biblical novels), some twenty-nine works in all.

The citizens of the Bible were as real to him as his family and neighbors. The story is often told in my family of how he once drove up to the edge of Lake Norman, where he was mistaken for a game warden by several locals who were fishing without the benefit of a license. "How y'all doing?" he said. "Catching anything?" "No sir, no sir," they insisted, pretending to be unaware of the poles bobbing in front of them. (In truth, no one could have been further from a game warden. My grandfather's sympathies tended entirely toward the underdog. He evinced a mild truculence toward improperly or heavily asserted authority, having as a young reporter been bashed into unconsciousness by a hired thug outside a textile mill in Gastonia during the strike of 1929.)

The fishermen relaxed that day by the lake only when my grandfather, apparently oblivious to the discomforting effect he was having, began telling them how Lake Norman was the exact size of the Sea of Galilee, and how the location of the grand town of Cornelius corresponded precisely to that of the Judean city of Capernaum. "Is that right?" the fishermen said, sensing that this might indeed be a day of deliverance, not to mention free fish. It wasn't so much that Pappy, as we called him, saw the Holy Land superimposed on the local map in a kind of geographical allegory. Instead, Mecklenburg County *was* the Holy Land. Who needed Jerusalem when you had Caldwell Station? Over the years, he defied every chance he had to actually visit the dry landscape of his waking dreams. If you were openhearted and sympathetic, history was here now. For my grandfather, it was a mere quirk of chronology that Paul and Judas (the subjects of two of his novels) were not there beside him on the clay banks of Lake Norman, admiring the view.

For as much as the world-at-large intrigued him, no part of it fascinated him more than his home, Mecklenburg County, in western North Carolina. He lived just a hundred yards or so away from the house he had been born in. He knew the night skies, the vegetation, the fields, the creek beds, the old homesteads, even the cats that lived (because he fed them) in the woods behind the house. He knew the citizens of Huntersville as if they were kin, and if you *were* kin . . . well, either way you had better be prepared to talk for a while when you saw him coming. Many was the noontime when my grandmother had to drag him away from the informal gatherings on the lawn after church. "Come on, Gette," she'd bark, being made of sterner stuff than he. It was a hopeless task. He could ask you questions until your head spun, as my father's frequently did when he tried to explain to Pappy some obscure point about sodium transfer in the kidneys. Pappy liked to keep abreast of things. Some days late in his life, he would stand at the window of the house he built for his family in 1928, counting the cars that rolled by on the highway. This wasn't some senile arithmetical mania so much as another way of proudly determining how much his hometown had grown. He had never acquired the antidevelopment bias that is understandably rampant late in this century. He would return from one of his walks shaking his head in delighted, open-eyed wonder at the establishment of a Dairy Queen in some old, kudzu-ridden pasture.

Although he always made himself available to his seven grandchildren, being forever willing to take us out to the garden or bend our ears with family history, he wrote very hard until near the end of his life. He kept deadlines, his own and others', disappearing into his cluttered study (books, old shoes, a reel-to-reel tape recorder, a hornet's nest) for a few hours almost every day, when we heard his typewriter clattering as he pecked away with two fingers, like the old-fashioned reporter he had been. In the closet of his study, he brewed homemade wine that occasionally detonated when the fermentation became too extravagant for its container. There was also, I think, an extra bit of fermentation, of vim, of force, in my grandfather when he wrote — a kind of bottled intensity that ended up on the page. Photographs of him at the typewriter reveal Pappy in a light we rarely witnessed at close range — lost to us, to the world, deep in concentration, utterly elsewhere. And yet he made the process of composition sound maddeningly simple. I once asked him how he wrote his books. "Well," he said, "if you know the beginning of your story, and you know the end, all you have to do is get from one to the other."

For Pappy, writing was part and parcel with the rest of his life, not an extreme quest requiring a hermit's hut in the desert. No, several hours a day upstairs in that maze of a study would do. He was no literary naïf: he wanted to make money, as his deal-making letters to agents and editors confirm, sometimes poignantly. And he was aware that he wasn't exactly famous in the way of, say, F. Scott Fitzgerald. I remember his reading *The Great Gatsby* at the beach one summer. After he finished, he pronounced it a "pretty fine book," which was high praise since he was not a florid man. "I guess he did pretty good, didn't he?" my grandfather said of Fitzgerald. "But I don't believe he had a happier life than I've had. No, I don't think I would trade with him." He died on Halloween afternoon, 1993. He had asked my grandmother if his dying would be all right with her. She probably told him to hush.

Why did he write? His life is emblematic of fiction writers in that he wrote, in part, because he was good at it. He got paid for it (not an insubstantial thing); he made a name for himself with it. And as with other fiction writers, making stories put him in contact with otherwise inaccessible regions, in his case, the Holy Land. I also think that writing was his gift, as it is the gift of the authors who have contributed to this book, and that a gift avoided and unexercised is deep trouble indeed. My grandfather would surely have seen the Old Testament story of the talents applying here. He located his motivation somewhere between the customs of a trade and the dictates of compulsion. Not every novelist dives deep under the ocean of existence, nor does every one wield an ax with which to strike the frozen sea within. Would my grandfather have been a better writer if he'd been an unhappier man? Perhaps, though unhappiness takes its toll, and what it offers in the way of insight, it can take away in energy and conviction. Anyway, he had his sadnesses and disappointments, mind you, and he felt the pain of many beyond himself. It's not as if any of us escapes sorrow for long. My grandfather's virtues were not exactly simple. Goodness never is.

* * *

As with the heart and most criminal defendants, writers always have their reasons.

There are, actually, dozens of reasons, as the following essays attest. And that's the way it's been through the ages, apparently: a myriad of private compulsions, a welter of incontestable desires. In his midtwenties, Franz Kafka, insurance man, remarked, "God doesn't want me to write, but I must write." E. M. Cioran proposed that "a book is a postponed suicide." Jorge Luis Borges scribbled to "ease the passing of time."

Other writers betray evidence of a bloody psychic shootout between misanthropy and altruism. William Gass creates literature, he says, "because I hate. A lot. Hard." He also asserts that the "aim of the artist ought to be to bring into the world objects which do not already exist there, and objects which are especially worthy of love." Samuel Johnson famously proclaimed that "no man but a blockhead ever wrote except for money." (Mark Jacobson, in his apologia on page 116, asserts the same.) But Johnson also declared that the "only end of writing is to enable readers to better enjoy life or better . . . endure it."

These are large, compassionate sentiments, their enormity the province of philosophers, who are willing to make the sort of grand pronouncements about art that most fiction writers shy away from. The latter's capacities are more often for the specific at the expense of the general, for the exception rather than the rule; they are well aware of the psychological burdens that come with grandiosity, with overclaiming for one's work. In fact, let's allow a philosopher, the Spaniard Ortega y Gasset, to step in where fiction writers fear to tread. "The possibility of constructing human souls," he wrote, "is perhaps the major asset of future novelists."

Now, constructing human souls is a pretty big responsibility. In fact, it used to be God's job. If writers had to think of salvation every time they sat down to type . . . well, they might as well be preachers. It's not that literature doesn't save souls; I suspect it has a better record in that department than the church. But God help the writer who pulls up to his desk with soul-saving in mind. Not that many American writers could acknowledge such an impetus for their own work, so great is their inherent modesty or their inherent fear of seeming immodest.

That said, I'm convinced that writers, in spite of themselves, do preserve souls, even make them. It's a little embarrassing to say this, because I'm not even sure I really believe in the soul — not, at least, in the spooky little ghost-aura that goes with us like a shadow, that might, like a parasite abandoning a dead host, fly out of us when we die. By soul, I mean a certain depth, an inwardness, a watchfulness. Detachment, solitude, stillness.

You might find it in a man sitting in his backyard on a summer night, clinking the ice in his gin and tonic. Staring into the window of his own house, watching his wife watch the Atlanta Braves on the Superstation. He's trying to remember exactly what passionate love feels like, the difference between eternity and boredom.

You might encounter it in a securities lawyer. She is supposed to be working this weekend but instead stares moonily out the window at the Woolworth Building, thinking to herself how peculiar it is to be alive at four o'clock on a Saturday afternoon. Just strange. She can't quite get over the oddness of it all.

You'd also be likely to discover soul in someone quietly reading. I can almost guarantee it. And indeed, the corollary to the question of why one writes is the question of why one reads. Among the functions of literature in general, and of fiction in particular, is the way they sharpen the ear and open the heart. The poet Joseph Brodsky once suggested, not altogether in jest, that the world's leaders might be better chosen for their views on Dickens and Stendhal and Cervantes rather than for their analyses of foreign policy and domestic affairs.

The very act of reading literature, the anticommunalism of it, the slow drift into reverie, the immersion into the charismatic black-and-white grids of the page — all of this emphatically unplugs us from that other grid, that beeping, noisome electronic grid that attempts to snare us in a web of reflex, of twitch and spasm. Does this make the pursuit of literature a Luddite maneuver, with all of the shadowings of melancholy and futility attendant on such rebellions? I suspect that to the contrary, passionate reading will become a form of permanent opposition, as vigorous and rooted and abiding as the great religious movements that we have seen rekindled in the last few decades. It often strikes me that one of the few moves left for the literary avant-garde (which is looking plain tuckered out these days — it's been a busy century) would be to plant a woody glade, dense with bamboo and shade and silence, in the midst of the roaring city of news and corporate blather, away from the tiring intimations of hipness trotted out by tireless marketeers. Anybody who's ever danced to rock 'n' roll knows how much fun mass-cult. can be, but it's getting increasingly difficult to forget how uniform are its tastes, how deadly is its ubiquity, and how ugly it is in its monotony.

In the spirit of my grandfather, then, this book is about the happiness of writing, about writing as an antidote to boredom and monotony and uniformity. It tells you from a variety of points of view — some acerbic, some rhapsodic, some as straightforward as a recipe — why writing (and its common-law husband, reading) are worth doing, why they're absolutely fun and pleasurable (except when they're not) and essential, whether you're Fitzgerald, or whether you're just you.

A few final notes. Why, to begin with, did I select twenty-six *fiction* writers, as opposed to poets or journalists, for this collection? Simple. I'm partial to the form. More often than not, fiction, with its beautiful deceptions and its artful lies, reveals far more than fact ever will. We breathe in air, we exhale stories: who we saw on our way to the laundromat, why we didn't get in until six in the morning, how we fell in love with a voice that came in the window off a darkened street. In this sense, we—all of us—every day, in one way or another, write fiction.

Nonfiction, by contrast, still strikes me as a slightly less exalted genre (though, as always, the question is not so much *what* a piece of writing is as whether it's any good). To the extent that journalists over the last thirty-five years or so have asserted a greater claim to making literature — and I think they have — it's largely due to their having borrowed the techniques and license of novelists and short-story writers. In the interest of their work, these nonfiction writers have had to submit to the philosophical proposition that reality is largely created by the observer, which makes it an awful lot like, well, fiction.

As for poetry (and its practitioners' exclusion from these pages): call me a rube or a philistine, but I, for one, have never felt that the rhythms of fiction, its buried music, are one lick less glorious than those of poetry. In fact, I suspect that the elements of sound and meter that go into making a compelling fictional voice are, partly because they're not foregrounded, trickier to deploy in prose than in verse. Stories must not only advance through time (which a poem need not do), they must also sound right. Prose, too, lives and dies by the beat.

Now, I don't want to start a sectarian feud here. I like poetry and even a couple of poets. And these days, poets have a tougher row to hoe than fiction writers — not too many people want to buy the effete little vegetables they're raising in those lonely gardens. No, poetry's fine. It's just that for far too long, fiction, with its greater proximity to ordinary speech, has gotten a bum rap for being a more primitive form of language. No sir, I just can't take it anymore, watching poetry climbing solo up Mount Olympus to the evolutionary peak of language, with fiction the faithful Sherpa trudging far behind, lugging the tent and the cookstove and the freeze-dried goodies and the satin pillows to make poetry cumfy through the icy night.

Clearly, then, this is an anthology dedicated to the partisan notion that writing fiction is — I won't say this too loudly, because some writers may feel I'll jinx things by admitting it — a form of happiness, of supreme awareness that, once experienced, can be given up only with the greatest reluctance. In the end, reading the wonderfully varied essays in *Why I Write* will be worth your while, particularly if you are a student of writing, because the book is a lodestone, a talisman, a collection of spells, the most obstreperous and cranky magic manual you will ever read. It places you in the accident-prone midst of the creative process, with all of its flukes and capriciousness, and yes, its occasional grandeur. *Why I Write* is an act of literary cosmology — twenty-six superb writers working their way back to the Big Bang of narrative fiction, trying to get at origins that can never, fortunately, be precisely traced. It's the story of their stories, where their fiction came from (to the extent that anyone can really say; remember, this is magic we are talking about), where it goes. The accounts here evoke the strange miracle — and miracle is not too strong a word — through which fiction is conjured into being.

When you read these essays, you will realize that there is no Interstate running directly from the writer's imagination to a finished piece of fiction. And if that seems a little daunting to those who like their road maps emblazoned with the most efficient route by Triple A, it's also a liberation. Forget the how-to manuals; assembled within this book are the real methods, the genuine genealogies of creation: this is the real story of writing. Writers can get where they're going by just about any route — overland, underground, through the air, in their dreams. The way is open.

WHY I WRITE

At the Point of My Pen

NORMAN MAILER

I MAY NOT TELL YOU why I write — it could be too complicated for my mind — but I can tell you about my dear friend, my
oldest friend, Jean Malaquais, and why he writes.

I remember how it was with him forty years ago when he was in
his midforties and was working on a novel, *The Joker*. He would
spend fourteen hours a day at his desk. Since he was punctilious
about literary virtue to the point of vice, he would, what with dele-
tions, corrections, and revisions, manage to advance his narrative
two or three hundred words. One page a day for fourteen hours of
horrendous labor. Since his powers of concentration were intense, it was, indeed, a labor for which no other adjective applied.
Fourteen hours. Horrendous. I, a more self-indulgent writer, used
to complain that a thousand words in three or four hours was
hardly a fair bargain for me.

I asked him once, "Why do you insist on remaining a writer?
With your intelligence, with your culture, you could be success-

ful at so many things. Writing may not be a normal activity for you."

He happened to agree. "You are absolutely right," he said. "I am not a natural writer. There are even times when I detest this torture. I achieve so little of my aims."

His aims, needless to say, were immense. They were exactly at the center of the problem. "All right," I said, "why not do something else?"

"Never," he said.

"Never? Tell me why."

"The only time I know the truth is when it reveals itself at the point of my pen."

I have been thinking of Jean Malaquais's answer for forty years. I could go on at length about how I write to convey my anger at all that I think is wrong in this world, or I could speak of the mystery of the novelist's aesthetic — ah, to be able to create a world that exists on the terms one has given it! — or I could even, unlike Jean Malaquais, be able to say, "When it's a matter of making a living, you can't beat the hours." But finally, I subscribe to his reply. For me, it has the advantage of being incontestably true. The only time, right or wrong, that I feel a quintessential religious emotion — that the power of the truth is in me — comes on occasion when I write, no, even better: the only time I know the truth is at the point of my pen.

Uncanny the Singing That Comes from Certain Husks

JOY WILLIAMS

IT'S BECOME FASHIONABLE these days to say that the writer writes because he is not whole: he has a wound, he writes to heal it. But who cares if the writer is not whole? Of course the writer is not whole, or even particularly well. There's something un-wholesome and self-destructive about the entire writing process. Writers are like eremites or anchorites — natural-born eremites or anchorites — who seem puzzled as to why they went up the pole or into the cave in the first place. Why am I so isolate in this strange place? Why is my sweat being sold as elixir? And how have I become so enmeshed with words, mere words, phantoms?

Writers when they're writing live in a spooky, clamorous silence, a state somewhat like the advanced stages of prayer but without prayer's calming benefits. A writer turns his back on the day and the night and its large and little beauties, and tries, like some half-witted demiurge, to fashion other days and nights with words. It's absurd. Oh, it's silly, dangerous work indeed.

A writer starts out, I think, wanting to be a transfiguring agent, and ends up usually just making contact, contact with other human beings. This, unsurprisingly, is not enough. (Making contact with the self — healing the wound — is even less satisfactory.) Writers end up writing stories — or rather, stories' shadows — and they're grateful if they can, but it is not enough. Nothing the writer can do is ever enough.

E. M. Forster once told his friend Laurens van der Post that he could not finish a story that he had begun with great promise, even brilliance, because he did not like the way it would have to finish. Van der Post wrote, "The remark for me proved both how natural stories were to him and how acute was his sense of their significance, but at the same time revealed that his awareness was inadequate for the task the story imposed upon it."

I like van der Post's conception of story — as a stern taskmaster that demands the ultimate in awareness, that indeed *is* awareness. The significant story possesses more awareness than the writer writing it. The significant story is always greater than the writer writing it. This is the absurdity, the disorienting truth, the question that is not even a question, this is the koan of writing.

Malcolm Muggeridge wrote in an essay on Jesus, "When a person loses the isolation, the separateness which awareness of the presence of God alone can give, he becomes irretrievably part of a collectivity with only mass communications to shape its hopes, formulate its values and arrange its thinking."

Without the awareness of separateness, one can never be part of the whole, the nothingness that is God. This is the divine absurdity, the koan of faith.

Jean Rhys said that when she was a child she thought that God was a big book. I don't know what she thought when she was no longer a child. She probably wished that she could think of a big book as being God.

A writer's awareness must never be inadequate. Still, it will never be adequate to the greater awareness of the work itself, the work that the writer is trying to write. The writer must not really know what he is knowing, what he is learning to know when he writes, which is more than the knowing of it. A writer loves the dark, loves it, but is always fumbling around in the light. The writer is separate from his work but that's all the writer is — what he writes. A writer must be smart but not too smart. He must be dumb enough to break himself to harness. He must be reckless and patient and daring and dull — for what is duller than writing, trying to write? And he must never care — caring spoils everything. It compromises the work. It shows the writer's hand. The writer is permitted, even expected, to have compassion for his characters, but what are characters? Nothing but mystic symbols, magical emblems, ghosts of the writer's imagination.

The writer doesn't want to disclose or instruct or advocate, he wants to transmute and disturb. He cherishes the mystery, he cares for it like a fugitive in his cabin, his cave. He doesn't want to talk it into giving itself up. He would never turn it in to the authorities, the mass mind. The writer is somewhat of a fugitive himself, actually. He wants to escape his time, the obligations of his time, and, by writing, transcend them. The writer does not like to follow orders, not even the orders of his own organizing intellect. The moment a writer knows how to achieve a certain effect, the method must be abandoned. Effects repeated become false, mannered. The writer's style is his doppelgänger, an apparition that the writer must never trust to do his work for him.

Some years ago I began writing essays. They were strident, bitter pieces on topics I cared about deeply. I developed a certain style for them that was unlike the style of my stories — it was un-elusive and rude and brashly one-sided. They were meant to an-noy and trouble and polarize, and they made readers, at least the kind of readers who write letters to the editors of magazines, half nuts with rage and disdain. The letter-writers frequently mocked my name. Not only didn't they like my way with words, my rea-soning, my philosophy, they didn't believe my name. My morbid attitude, my bitter tongue, my anger, denied me the right to such a name, my given name, my gift, signifier of rejoicing, happiness, and delight.

But a writer isn't supposed to make friends with his writing, I don't think.

The writer doesn't trust his enemies, of course, who are wrong about his writing, but he doesn't trust his friends, either, who he hopes are right. The writer trusts nothing he writes — it should be too reckless and alive for that, it should be beautiful and menac-ing and slightly out of his control. It should want to live itself somehow. The writer dies — he can die before he dies, it happens all the time, he dies as a writer — but the work wants to live.

Language accepts the writer as its host, it feeds off the writer, it makes him a husk. There is something uncanny about good writ-ing — uncanny the singing that comes from certain husks. The writer is never nourished by his own work, it is never satisfying to him. The work is a stranger, it shuns him a little, for the writer is really something of a fool, so engaged in his disengagement, so self-conscious, so eager to serve something greater, which is the writing. Or which could be the writing if only the writer is good enough. The work stands a little apart from the writer, it doesn't want to go down with him when he stumbles or fails or retreats.

The writer must do all this alone, in secret, in drudgery, in confusion, awkwardly, one word at a time.

The writer is an exhibitionist, and yet he is private. He wants you to admire his fasting, his art. He wants your attention, he doesn't want you to know he exists. The reality of his life is meaningless, why should you, the reader, care? You don't care. He drinks, he loves unwisely, he's happy, he's sick . . . it doesn't matter. You just want the work — the Other — this other thing. You don't really care how he does it. Why he does it.

The good piece of writing startles the reader back into Life. The work — this Other, this other thing — this false life that is even less than the seeming of this lived life, is more than the lived life, too. It is so unreal, so precise, so unsurprising, so alarming, really. Good writing never soothes or comforts. It is no prescription, neither is it diversionary, although it can and should enchant while it explodes in the reader's face. Whenever the writer writes, it's always three o'clock in the morning, it's always three or four or five o'clock in the morning in his head. Those horrid hours are the writer's days and nights when he is writing. The writer doesn't write for the reader. He doesn't write for himself, either. He writes to serve . . . something. Somethingness. The somethingness that is sheltered by the wings of nothingness — those exquisite, enveloping, protecting wings.

There is a little tale about man's fate and this is the way it is put. A man is being pursued by a raging elephant and takes refuge in a tree at the edge of a fearsome abyss. Two mice, one black and one white, are gnawing at the roots of the tree, and at the bottom of the abyss is a dragon with parted jaws. The man looks above and sees a little honey trickling down the tree and he begins to lick it up and forgets his perilous situation. But the mice gnaw through the tree and the man falls down and the elephant seizes him and hurls him over to the dragon. Now, that elephant is the image of death, which pursues men, and the tree is this transitory existence, and the mice are the days and the nights, and the honey is the sweetness of the passing world, and the savor of the passing world diverts mankind. So the days and nights are accomplished and death seizes him and the dragon swallows him down into hell and this is the life of man.

This little tale with its broad and beastly strokes seems to approximate man's dilemma quite charmingly, with the added caveat that it also applies to the ladies ("she" being "he" throughout here, the writer's woes not limited by gender; like Flannery O'Connor's Misfit, the writer knows there's no enjoyment to be had in this life). This is the story, then, pretty much the story, with considerable latitude to be had in describing those mice, those terrifying mice. But it is not for the writer to have any part in providing the honey — the passing world does that. The writer can't do better than that. What the writer wants to do, to be, is to be the consciousness of the story, he doesn't want to be part of the distraction; to distract is ignoble, to distract is to admit defeat, to serve a lesser god. The story is not a simple one. It is syncretistic and strange and unhappy, and it all must be told beautifully, even the horrible parts, particularly the horrible parts. The telling of the story can never end, not because the writer doesn't like the way it must end but because there is no end to the awareness of the story which the writer has only the dimmest, most fragmentary awareness of.

Why do I write? Writing has never given me any pleasure. I am not being disingenuous here. It's not a matter of being on excellent terms with my characters, having a swell time with them, finding their surprising remarks prescient or amusing. That would seem to be a shallow pleasure indeed. Rewriting, the attention to detail, the depth of involvement required, the achievement and acknowledgment of the prowess and stamina and luck involved — all these should give their pleasures, I suppose, but they are sophisticated pleasures that elude me. Writing has never been "fun" for me. I am too wary about writing to enjoy it. It has never fulfilled me (nor have I fulfilled it). Writing has never done anyone or anything any good at all, as far as I can tell. In the months before my mother died, and she was so sick and at home, a home that meant everything and nothing to her now, she said that she would lie awake through the nights and plan the things she would do during the day when it came — she would walk the dog and get birdseed and buy some more pansies, and she would make herself a nice little breakfast, something that would taste good, a poached egg and some toast — and then the day would come and she could do none of these things, she could not even get out the broom and sweep a little. She was in such depression and such pain and she would cry, If I only could do a little sweeping, just that. . . . To sweep with a good broom, a lovely thing, such a simple, satisfying thing, and she yearned to do it and could not. And her daughter, the writer, who would be the good broom quick in her hands if only she were able, could not help her in any way. Nothing the daughter, the writer, had ever written or could ever write could help my mother who had named me.

Why does the writer write? The writer writes to serve — hopelessly he writes in the hope that he might serve — not himself and not others, but that great cold elemental grace which knows us.

A writer I very much admire is Don DeLillo. At an awards ceremony for him at the Folger Library several years ago, I said that he was like a great shark moving hidden in our midst, beneath the din and wreck of the moment, at apocalyptic ease in the very elements of our psyche and times that are most troublesome to us, that we most fear.

Why do I write? Because I wanna be a great shark too. Another shark. A different shark, in a different part of the ocean. The ocean is vast.

Where Does Writing Come From?

RICHARD FORD

> Our brains are dulled by the incurable mania of
> wanting to make the unknown known.
>
> ANDRÉ BRETON, *The Surrealist Manifesto*

I'VE OFTEN BEEN GUILTY of trying to answer the question above. I've done it on public stages after readings, in panel discussions with dozing colleagues, standing before rows of smirking students, for cruel and cynical journalists in hotel rooms at home and abroad. And I believe I can honestly say that I would never spontaneously have asked myself this question had not someone else seemed interested, or had my financial fortunes not seemed (correctly or incorrectly) tied to such speculation. I either knew the answer, I suppose, or thought I didn't need to know it. Yet once the question was asked, I admit that over these years I've taken an interest in the answers I've come up with — which is to say, dreamed up — much in the way I take interest in the progress of any piece of fiction I'm writing. This, after all, is what one does, or what I do, anyway, when I write fiction: pick out something far-fetched or at least previously unthought of by me, something I feel a kind of languageless yen for, and then see what I can dream up about it or around it that's interesting or amusing to me, in the hope that by making it make sense in words I'll make it interesting and important to someone else.

Plenty of writers for plenty of centuries have furrowed their brows over this question — where does it come from, all this stuff you write? "All good poetry is the spontaneous overflow of powerful feelings" was an important part of Wordsworth's answer. And I've seen no reason I shouldn't just as well get my two cents down, on the chance I might actually get to or near the bottom of the whole subject and possibly help extinguish literature once and for all — since that seems to be where the inquiry tends: let's get writing explained and turned into a neat theorem, like a teasing problem in plasma physics, so we can forget about it and get back to watching *Seinfeld*. And failing that, I might at least say something witty or charming that could make a listener or a reader seek out the book I really do care about — the one I've just written and hope you'll love.

It may be that this investigation stays alive in America partly because of that principally American institution, the creative-writing course — of which I am a bona fide graduate, and about which Europeans like to roll their eyes. The institution has many virtues — time to write being the most precious. But it also has several faults, one of which is the unproven good of constantly having like-minded colleagues and compatriots around to talk about what one is doing, as if companionship naturally improved one's important work just when one is doing it. How we do what we do, and why we do it, may just be a subject a certain kind of anxious person can't help tumbling to at a time in life when getting things written at all is a worry, and when one's body of work is small and not very distinguishable from one's private self, and when one comes to find that the actual thing one is writing is not a very riveting topic of conversation over drinks. Among dedicated novices, the large subject of provenance may be all we have in common, and all that will pass for artily abstract speculation of a disinterested kind.

Though clearly another socioliterary force that keeps the topic alive is that among many people who are *not* writers, there's occasionally a flighty belief that writers are special people, vergers of some kind, in charge of an important interior any person would be wise to come close to as a way of sidling up to a potent life's essence. Questions about how, why, etc., become just genuflections before the medium. And writers, being generally undercharged in self-esteem and forever wanting more attention for their work, are often quite willing to become their work's exponent if not its actual avatar. I remember an anecdote about a male writer I know who, upon conducting an interested visitor to his desk overlooking the Pacific, is reported to have whispered as they tiptoed into the sacred, sun-shot room, "Well, here it is. This is where I make the magic."

Again, nothing's new here: just another instance of supposing an approach upon the writer will reveal the written thing more fully, more truly; or, if not, then it's the old mistake of confusing the maker with the made thing — an object that may really have some magical pizzazz about it, who knows?

Considering an actual set of mechanical connections that might have brought a piece of writing from nowhere, the "place" it resided before I'd written it, to its final condition as the book I hope you'll love, actually impresses upon me the romantic view that artistic invention is a kind of casual magic, one that can't be adequately explained the way, say, a train's arrival in Des Moines can be nicely accounted for by tracing the tracks and switches and sidings and tunnels all the way to its origin in Paducah.

You can — and scholars do — try to trace some apparent connections back from the finished work to the original blank mind and page and even to before that (he used his father's name for the ax-murderer . . . hmmm; she suffered glaucoma just like the jilted sister who became a Carmelite nun, so how can you argue the whole damn story isn't about moral blindness?). But of course such procedures are famously unreliable and even sometimes downright impertinent, since in the first place (and there need not be a second) such investigations start at and take for granted the existence of Des Moines, whereas for the writer (and I mean to abandon this train business), Des Moines is not just a city but a name that has to be not merely found, but conjured. In fact the name may not even have been Des Moines to begin with — it may have been Abilene or Chagrin Falls — but *became* Des Moines because the writer somehow slipped up and let Abilene slip his mind, or because Des Moines had that nice diphthong in it and looked neat and Frenchy on the page, whereas Abilene had those three clunky syllables, and there was already a dopey country song about it. Anyway, there are at least two Abilenes, one in Texas and another one in Kansas, which is confusing, and neither has rail service.

You can see what I mean: the true connections could never really be traceable because they exist only in that murky, silent, but fecund interstellar night where impulse, free association, instinct, and error reign. And even if I were faithfully to try explaining the etiological connections in a piece of writing I'd done, I still might lie about them, or I might just be wrong because I forgot. But in any case I'd finally have to make something up pretty much the way a scholar does — though not exactly like a writer, who, as I said before, always starts with nothing.

I remember a complimentary reviewer of a book I'd written once singling out for approval my choice of adjectives, which seemed to him surprising and expansive and of benefit to the story. One sentence he liked contained a phrase in which I'd referred to a character's eyes as "old": "He looked on her in an old-eyed way." Naturally, I was pleased to have written *something* that *somebody* liked. Only, when I was not long afterward packing away manuscripts for the attic, my eyes happened to fall upon the page and the very commended phrase, "old-eyed," etc., and I noticed that somehow in the rounds of fatigued retyping that used to precede a writer's final sign-off on a book in the days before word processors, the original and rather dully hybridized "cold-eyed" had somehow lots its c and become "old-eyed," only nobody'd noticed since they both made a kind of sense.

This is my larger point writ, admittedly, small, and it calls to mind the joke about the man from Alabama who couldn't understand how a thermos could keep cold things cold and hot things always hot, and expressed his wonder in a question akin to the title of this very essay: "How do it know?"

Anyone who's ever written a novel or a story or a poem and had the occasion later to converse about it with an agitated or merely interested reader knows the pinchy feel that comes when the reader tries to nail down the connections *linking* the story to some supposed "source," as a way either of illuminating the procedures that transform life to shapely art, or else of just plain diminishing an act of creation to some problem of industrial design.

In my case, this inquiry often centers on the potent subject of children, and specifically writing about children, and more prosecutorily on how it is I can write about children to such and such effect without actually having or having had any myself.

It's frequently surprising to whomever I'm speaking to that I can write persuasively about children; although the surprise is often expressed not as pure delight but in a kind of blinkingly suspicious tone whose spirit is either that I *do* have children (in another county, maybe) and don't want to admit it, or else that somebody in a position of authority needs to come down and take a closer look at my little minor inventions to certify if they're really as finely drawn as they seem.

Myself, I try to stay happy about such questioning. Some stranger, after all, *has* or *seems to have* read at least a part of some book I've written and been moved by it, and I'm always grateful for that. He or she could as easily have been watching *Seinfeld*, too. And so mostly I just try to smile and chuckle and mumble-mutter something about having been a child once myself, and if that doesn't work I say something about there being children pretty much everywhere for the watchful to study, and that my Jamesian job is to be a good observer. And finally, if that still isn't enough, I say that if it were so hard to write about children, I of all people wouldn't be able to do it, since I'm no smarter than the next guy.

But the actual truth — the one I know to be true and that sustains my stories — is that even though I was once a child myself, and even though there is a God's own slew of bratty kids around to be studied like lab rats, and even though I'm clearly not the smartest man in the world, I still mostly write about children by making them up. I make them up out of language bits, out of my memories, out of stories in the newspapers, out of overheard remarks by my friends and their kids, out of this and out of that, and sometimes out of nothing at all but the pleasurable will to ascribe something that might be interesting on the page to a child instead of to an adult or a spaceman or a horse, after which a *child*, a fictive child, begins to take shape on the page as a willed, moral gesture toward the reader. "'All I want for Christmas is to know the difference between *that* and *which*,' said little Johnny, who was just ten years old but already beginning to need some firmer discipline." Behold: a child is born.

⸺Occasionally, if pushed or annoyed, I'll come right out and say it: *I make these little buggers up, that's what. So sue me.* But an odd restraint almost always makes me revert to my prior explanations. Some delicacy in me simply doesn't want to say, "They're invented things, these characters; you can't track them down like rabbits to their holes. They won't be hiding there." It's as though arguing for invention and its fragile, wondrous efficacy were indelicate, weren't quite nice. And even though arguing for it wouldn't harm or taint invention's marvels (we all know novels are made-up things; it's part of our pleasure to keep such knowledge in our minds), still I always feel queasy doing it — not like a magician who reluctantly shows a rube how to pull a nickel out of his own ear, but more like a local parish priest who, upon hearing a small but humiliating confession from a friend, lets the friend off easy just to move matters on to a higher ground.

Wallace Stevens once wrote that "in an age of disbelief . . . it is for the poet to supply the satisfactions of belief in his measure and his style." And that takes in how I feel about invention — invented characters, invented landscapes, invented breaks of the heart and their subsequent repairs. I believe that there are important made-up things that resist precise tracing back, and that it's a blessing there are, since our acceptance of them in literature (acting as a substitute for less acceptable beliefs) suggests that for every human problem, every insoluble, every cul-de-sac, every despair, there's a chance we can conjure up an improvement — a Des Moines where previously there was only a glum Abilene.

Frank Kermode wrote thirty years ago, in his wonderful book *The Sense of an Ending,* "It is not that we are connoisseurs of chaos, but that we are surrounded by it, and equipped for coexistence with it only by our fictive powers." To my mind, not to believe in invention, in our fictive powers, but instead to think that all is traceable, that the rabbit must finally be in the hole waiting, is (because it's dead wrong) a certain recipe for the williwaws of disappointment and a small but needless reproach to mankind's saving capacity to imagine what could be better and, with good hope, then, to seek it.

I Am a . . . Genius!

THOM JONES

As a fiction instructor at the University of Iowa, I was often asked by my students what it takes to devise a "breakthrough" short story or novel. Something to skyrocket the writer to fame and fortune, set the literary world aglow, win a ton of prizes, and guarantee the author a rich and prosperous future. I was a student at the Workshop myself back in the seventies, and it was a question I had dwelled on like a Zen koan. I used to think about it so hard my brain started smoking. I was Smokin' Thom Jones. Did I smoke cigarettes? No, but I was Smokin' Thom Jones. I smoked, smoldered, and fumed so hard I had to duct-tape ice cubes alongside my temporal lobes to prevent my whole head from bursting into flames, luxurious, gorgeous, flowing chestnut locks and all. It was the most acutely awful taxing of my brain that I had ever put it to in a voluntary fashion. And what did I come up with? I came up with zip. No miracles, just commonplace notions. I figured that not only did you actually have to write to become a writer, but

21

there was probably also a trick to the whole affair. Possibly there was a secret mystical society you had to join. At the least, I imagined that it had something to do with giving the right people "blow jobs." Beyond that, I was clueless. While other Iowa writers were hanging out at the Mill or the Foxhead, my fingers were blistering the keyboard five hours a day, seven days a week. I was just another greaseball from Aurora, Illinois, but I had my dreams. I believed. And I churned out one boring novel after another. The all-consuming urge to write novels began years before, when I was just a kid reading comic books in the back of my grandmother's grocery store.

Like most of the people reading this piece, I was subjected to the gulag of the American school system — not the light-duty mainstream but the maximum-security variant of such. It was a Missouri synod Lutheran school, where educational training was presented not as an opportunity but rather as a sentence to be served — a grim fourteen-year term that made Turkish prison seem like a lark and Kaspar Hauser's early incarceration an idyllic haven of uninterrupted bliss.

I tuned out in passive/aggressive style and earned very low marks. From browsing at pictures in my geography texts, I knew there were "born-free" kids in exotic parts of the world who were accorded instant adulthood. Instead of going to school, they might herd goats near the Kyber Pass, slog through sun-torched mosquito days in Burmese rice paddies, mash cassava down in the tropics, or, way up in latitude 87, where it was cold enough to freeze the balls off a brass monkey, make mukluks out of sealskin. They looked like very happy kids. They were smiling, and there wasn't an ambiguous shit-eating grin in the bunch, no smile that implicitly said, "I had to dish out seven hundred blow jobs to land this gig — suck every cock on the North Pole — but *here I am,* brother. Now ain't this . . . *real fine?*" Judging by that grin on your face, Nanook, I would say it's mighty fine indeed.

There I was at the age of reason, a *seldom* smiler — an *on-rare-occasions-only* smiler —knowing that it was theoretically possible to steal away from my bedroom one night and reemerge as a fair-eyed nomad on camel caravan in the Sahara or as an aboriginal on walkabout through the deserts of western Australia, far from the influence of crass materialism and the soul-withering zone of capitalistic imperialism that were part and parcel of the Eisenhower fifties.

The Lutheran elementary school was run by stern, joyless, second-generation German authoritarians, a Paraguay in the Midwest where crowd control was maintained by repressive conditioning and the iron fist of fear. My defense against this bullshit turn of fate was rebellion. I was a regular little James Cagney in those days.

I was an evildoer of the first order, a recidivist troublemaker who spent many long lunch hours in the principal's office (P-Block), surreptitiously drawing comics while the other students were allowed to exercise out on the "yard." My skills as an artist were rudimentary, but my ability to capture the essential horrors of Aurora, Illinois, was Hogarthian. Yes, dear reader, I was a genius even then!

On paper my wit was rapier-sharp, and the students who were privileged to view my work were known to fall down laughing or even piss in their pants. Yet when these "subversive" documents found their way into the hands of the authorities, I drew even more time in P-Block. The school's headmaster gave my mother the name of a "head doctor," and I was sent to see him. He thought my comics were piss-in-your-pants funny, too, and would sit in his office pounding his fist against his thigh as he read them, roaring with laughter. He would have to blow his nose and dab his eyes after these convulsions of mirth. Then he would remember he was a psychiatrist and would say, "Your problem, my young friend, is this: you are a stubborn individualist. You want to go it alone in the ant colony of society, and that just isn't possible. Most likely you will end up dead at an early age, or in prison. Already you are addicted to comic books; you even make your own. While they are funny, the themes emerging from them are the product of a disturbed mind. Why don't you join the Boy Scouts and get a little fresh air or something?"

I said there were two things I hated to do: get up before four P.M. and go outside.

He shook his head and said, "If that's the case, you might as well shoot yourself and get it over with now. You're in for a lot of pain and heartache, my little buddy, for you are going to find this planet a cruel and brutal place."

Each month when my grandmother received a new shipment of comics at her store, by the strictest self-imposed rationing schedule, I found myself with three days of pure reading pleasure. I wasn't one of those geniuses who were reading Vladimir Nabokov when they were six. I was reading Little Lulu. What I had seen passed off as literature was tedious and dull. Few of the literary offerings presented to us in school made for pleasant reading. They were sheer drudgery. James Fenimore Cooper comes to mind. And the poem *Hiawatha*.

That all changed when I happened upon a copy of *Huckleberry Finn*. I liked Mark Twain and attacked his whole body of work. Then one thing led to another. As an omnivorous reader of comic books, I easily accomplished the transition to reading books of all kinds. My favorites were works of fiction inhabited by characters of alienation. I prowled the glass-floored balcony of the Aurora public library, reading such authors as Steinbeck, Dickens, Somerset Maugham, Jack London, and Kenneth Roberts for no reason other than information and pleasure. My criminal mind was not bent on self-improvement, but reading did have a side benefit: it did not lead to pregnancies, hangovers, beatings, or arrests. By high school I was reading John Updike and Kingsley Amis — hardly a precocious feat, unless you think of Aurora in terms of that awful gold pit they've got in the Brazilian jungle, and imagine the shantytown culture that flourishes around it. All Aurora had going for it was a Carnegie-vintage library. It was otherwise a town devoid of color.

At the library I made the acquaintance of Salinger, who influenced me greatly, and, if I remember correctly, it was Salinger who suggested that being an author of fiction was the most noble occupation of all. Hemingway, who came from not-so-distant Oak Park, Illinois, was America's larger-than-life writer at this time. But though he wrote of things that fascinated me, like war, bullfighting, and boxing, I was never a diehard Hemingway fan. I did not dispute his authority; I just liked other writers better — Nelson Algren and James Jones, for instance. Jones was the one author I ever sent a fan letter to (I received a gracious response). I loved William Styron, John Dos Passos, and Norman Mailer. I loved Joyce Carol Oates, who did not strut and swagger but instead put out a prodigious amount of really good work. I was not a snob. I expected that I would spend my life working in one of the many factories in Aurora, Illinois. But my God, what hellholes those factories were! As my high school graduation approached, I let my subscription to Ace Comics slide past its renewal date. I didn't require pictures any longer; I was addicted to words.

✳   ✳   ✳

Since none of my friends were readers, I found my own way. *Lucky Jim* had a great impact on me. There was Alan Sillitoe with *Loneliness of the Long-Distance Runner* and *Saturday Night and Sunday Morning*; *Alfie* by Bill Naughton; *The Luck of Ginger Coffee* by Brian Moore; *Poor Cow* by Nell Dunn; *Room at the Top* and the whole body of work by John Braine. I read Flannery O'Connor, Carson McCullers, Theodore Dreiser. A fellow I knew at a warehouse job handed me a copy of *Vandover and the Brute*, a lesser novel by Frank Norris. *Vandover* instantly soared to my top-ten list. This was almost immediately surpassed by Par Lagerkvist's *The Dwarf*. My new reading buddy belt-fed real beauties to me: Stendhal's *The Red and the Black*; Jules Reynard's *Pol de Carrot*; V. S. Naipaul's *A House for Mr. Biswas*; Flaubert's *Madame Bovary*; and *Revolutionary Road* by Richard Yates.

I finally escaped the factories of Aurora and went to the University of Hawaii. Through a stroke of luck, I got a small apartment in an exclusive Manoa Valley subdivision by working as my landlady's gardener. There were royal palms off my lanai, and gardenia trees that blew fragrant breezes into my apartment each night. I signed up for my first course in creative writing, and with the trade winds blowing off the heat of each day, I pounded a Royal standard typewriter late into the night. Just as I had once found remission from the existential chasm of despair in the act of writing comics, I now found the same relief in writing fiction. *Esquire* and the *Atlantic Monthly* asked for rewrites on the first two stories I wrote. These were fixes I didn't even attempt since I felt I was light-years beyond them. I was already hard at work on a novel.

Ultimately I entered the writing program at Iowa, where a friend put me onto Hubert Selby's *Last Exit to Brooklyn*, a book that was to influence me profoundly. After Iowa I took my first trip to Europe and began to hunger after travel. I worked at an assortment of writing jobs and found them meaningless and debilitating. Any thoughts I had of becoming a real writer were extinguished soon after I joined the American work force. When I returned to Iowa to teach, I saw my students face their own graduations with a dread of the real world that bordered on panic. It was perceived as something that could suck you into its vortex and never let you go. It was a Venus's-flytrap that ate out your soul.

But life gives you many chances. After getting fired from a job as a newspaper editor in 1980, I wrote another unpublishable novel. I didn't even send it out. I got drunk and burned it.

I was drinking heavily at the time and counteracting this destructive pastime with twenty-mile runs, three-mile swims, three-hour weight-lifting sessions. I was still boxing, in spite of my epilepsy. There was a good angel perched on one shoulder and a bad one on the other.

When I ran out of money, I took a job as a night janitor at a school, where I had a pool, a weight room, a library all to myself. It was a great thing. I could rush through my area in a few hours and after that I was free to pursue whatever pleasures that struck my fancy. I was still addicted to compulsive exercise and it was for this reason that I had taken the job. One night, with a case of beer at hand, I did ten thousand sit-ups in sets of five hundred. It was easy, although I think it wrecked my back forever. In those days I could do thirty-five chin-ups, press 138 pounds behind the neck, and curl 125 pounds in reps of eight. I could pick up the entire stack of weights on the Universal machine. Weight lifting merely requires a doggedness bordering on obsession. After two years of this, nearly every joint in my body was injured. Drinking killed the pain and tedium of it, but long-term sprains would force me into weeks of recuperation. I kept on drinking. My hand-to-mouth action was never impaired, and the drinking got out of hand. There were close calls. I had to open up the school and was often drunk by then. My partner on the graveyard shift was a pot smoker, and by dawn we looked like a pair of Mission Street bums. Our eyes were like two balls of fire. There were Visine bottles everywhere you turned, and the hangovers were like bad mescaline trips. Ultimately the drinking pushed me into type 1 diabetes, and I had no choice but to stop. Stop on a dime, bro! From the first, sobriety did not seem like a very friendly place. I could accomplish only a small amount of physical work and would then be forced to lie on the floor for a time to recover from these small exertions. I would maybe get up, look in the mirror to see one pupil fully dilated and the other a pinpoint. I think they call it Horner's symptom, evidence of an ongoing stroke. My heart would flutter like a Hong Kong chicken suffering bird flu. I would go down to the welding shop and inhale pure oxygen until my sickly, racing pulse sank back into the double-digit area. The man of ten thousand sit-ups now barely had the strength to get through a single night of work. I switched over to the second shift to ensure that I would not fall off the wagon — there were too many people around then for me to get away with drinking. Also, if I fell down dead on the second shift, I was reasonably certain that my body would be found and my family notified.

Friday was the worst of days since every week feeds a janitor a furious succession of psychic blows. The students become more and more restless, and by Fridays, they are wild. Also, Friday was the night I would empty the bag on my commercial vacuum cleaner. In less than a week it would accumulate ten or fifteen pounds of dust. It was necessary to shake it into the Dumpster, but hair and fibers fallen onto the carpets caused the bag dust to adhere together into Velcro-like clumps. To avoid breathing in the dust particles, I would hold my breath and reach elbow-deep into the bag to pull out the dirt. It was like working in a flour factory. By the time I had the bulky stuff pulled out, I would be covered with filth, and as often as not, my fingers would be sliced from the pins, paper clips, and used hypodermic syringes that waited for my hands like Cracker Jack prizes in the compacted dust. It was exasperating. Just a complete motherfucker.

And I still wasn't finished. Under the cover of darkness, I repaired to a fence by the agriculture shop, where I would beat the bag against a fence post. This would clear the bag of the finer dust particles. I looked like a maniac chopping logs. I hacked and slammed the bag, and with every faceful of dust, the madder I got. Each bag-blow against the fence released huge gusts of filth into the atmosphere. Once, on a football night, I unleashed a facsimile of the Bikini Island atomic mushroom cloud, watched it rise five hundred feet into the air, and then soar over the football field, where the game was in progress. I heard the crowd gasp collectively in awe. It was a rainy night, and up near the klieg lights, some thousand yards away, the sinister dust ball hovered like the wrath of God — like impending doom.

Since I knew this would draw an immediate investigation, I hastened back into the building and casually resumed my routine. When a pair of cops came inside and asked me if I had been "out back" recently or seen anything strange, I said no. I lied again when the vice principal came inside and said people were complaining because every car in the parking lot was covered with a thick brown-and-gray paste having the consistency of cold gravy. I gave him a quizzical look and said, "Well, maybe Mount Saint Helens blew again."

"No," he said. "I remember *that*, and this is worse. Far worse!"

I looked at him like, "Hey, man, don't get all bent out of shape. You should have *my* fucking job."

I didn't know how many more Friday nights I had left in me. Once I offered another janitor a hundred dollars if he would dump my bag, and he refused. I considered other employment options, but it occurred to me that I wasn't very good at anything. I had hated every job I'd ever had.

Then one day, watching television, I saw Wile E. Coyote chasing the Road Runner across a cartoon desert. Cartoon New Mexico, I figure. I was hoping that he would catch the stupid and annoying bird and rip its head off. But then, in the middle of the chase, the coyote came to a screeching halt, stepped out of the cartoon, and walked toward the audience with a wry, self-satisfied grin on his face. His footfalls ka-flop ka-flop ka-flop, cartoon style. No big hurry here. He acted like he had all the time in the world. When he was finally in place, he pulled his shoulders back, looked into the camera, and said, just as cool as you please, "Allow me to introduce myself. Wile E. Coyote . . . *genius.*"

"Genius," he said. Genniiee-us. *Genieuz.* Maybe that's just another word for perseverance. Wile E. Coyote, no matter what else you might say about him, was not a quitter. I mean, if you keep plugging at it, you *might* get it. If you quit — pow, it's over.

Maybe it was my comic-book past — those lost years of happiness — that caused me to be affected so deeply. Wile E. Coyote reinvigorated me with hope. I made up my mind to take another stab at writing. At the time I was reading and rereading some very good writers, including Raymond Carver, Tobias Wolff, Robert Stone, Michael Herr, Richard Price, Larry Brown, and Cormac McCarthy — immaculate writers, immortals. I decided to forget trying to imitate any of them. Part of a writer's style is always imbued with the styles of the people he reads, but to the extent that such a thing was possible, I determined to write for myself alone. I would write the sort of material that pleased me, and this meant dwelling on life's absurdities. I bought a Macintosh computer. Because of my work schedule and diminished health, I wrote stories. You can write a short story in a sitting, say on a Saturday afternoon. With a draft done and the mood, atmosphere, and tone of the piece captured in the first stroke, I didn't have to try and pick up the voice again and sustain it through further adventures — all I had to do was rewrite and polish. It was fun from the very beginning. Va-room! Va-room! No more lying on the floor before the TV Saturday afternoons waiting for hangovers to burn off for Thom; I was writing. Self-discipline became my middle name. Before the Mac, I had never written more than three drafts of anything. Now I was a rewriting ace. My first computer-written piece was "Rocketman," a story about professional boxing. I went through something like thirty drafts and then I sent it to Jon Jackson, an Iowa pal and a writer who had earned a living from writing almost from the day he left the Workshop. Jon knows a lot about boxing, and he liked the story. He showed it to Richard Ford, who thought Joyce Oates might like it for the *Ontario Review*. No oral sex was asked for or given. I got a nice note from Ms. Oates, one of my great heroes. It was the first personal note I'd received since *Esquire* and the *Atlantic* wrote me in Hawaii back in the sixties. I made some changes and returned the story to the *Ontario Review*. Ultimately, it was turned down, and I was overcome by a tsunami wave of self-pity. The Voice of Discouragement spoke to me from one of my Friday-night dust clouds: "You ain't got it, man. You might as well go and buy a case of beer. You're just a greaseball. A janitor. Aurora, Illinois. Shame on you!"

I told Jon Jackson I couldn't write any better than that. He said,

"Thom, look, you wrote one of the best goddamn boxing stories I ever read. But remember this: editors don't want to *buy* your stories. They get tons of stories. *You have to write something that's so good they can't reject it.* This isn't about connections or whom you know. It's about the text. Nine times out of ten, a good magazine will print a first-rate story by an unknown before they run a second-rate story by a marquee name."

"They will?" I said.

I still remember Jackson's exasperation. "Thom!" he said. "For Christ's sake!"

His words were golden. I felt like Grasshopper in *Kung Fu*, getting some big-time insight. Suddenly acceptance wasn't about me; it was about the text. I wasn't so sure I could overcome my low self-esteem, but I truly believed I could write something fresh, original, unlike anything anyone else had ever written — something *sui generis*. Jackson had effectively severed the connection between my talent and my personal self-perceptions. I said, "Why didn't you tell me this shit twenty-five years ago?"

I felt like a *genieuz* again. A genius with a difference. Writing straight from the heart, I sat down and composed "The Pugilist at Rest" in a single sitting. Three days later I wrote "I Want to Live," and so it went. One afternoon my then-agent, Candida Donadio, called me up three times in rapid succession: first to report a sale to *Harper's*; thirty minutes later another sale, to *Esquire*; and then, fifteen minutes after that, yet another, to the *New Yorker*. Three in an afternoon. She said, "Thirty years in the business, and I've never seen that happen. Never."

As it turned out, all three of the magazines hit the newsstands in the same month, and passing through an airport I saw them on a magazine rack — all three in my frame of vision. I had been in the slicks frequently since the publication of "Pugilist," but I did not live in New York and was virtually unknown there. People were saying, "Who the fuck is this guy?" To the reading public it seemed like overnight success, but fiction writers often mature at a glacial pace. I was slower than most. I was sometimes on the verge of agreeing with Stanislavsky, who said, "They are most happy who have no story to tell." After getting lost and being found time and again, the writers who don't quit discover the ecstasy within the process of the work itself. They discover the sublime joy of seeing things come together to produce an artistic whole. You read books and love them and someday hope to have the talent and vision to write your own. It doesn't matter who you are or where you come from. In fact, many of our best writers come from the streets. From places like Aurora, Illinois. You can be a greaseball off the streets, so long as you are a greaseball who knows how to put things together. Fame or money might follow, but they are never the primary event. I had a lot of students tell me they were going to cop out and write screenplays or genre fiction to "make a shitload of money." And my reply was always the same: You don't just toss things off and make money. You have to write with your heart and soul. Do you think Willie Mays played center field for the Giants just so he could become rich and famous? Or do you think maybe he played it because he loved the game? Loved it so much he would have done it for free?

Someday Wile E. Coyote will prevail. Not because he wants a bird sandwich, but because he has a burning desire. He will pay the price. He will go the extra mile. And one day he will find the right plan. I know he will. That wolf is a *genieuz*.

Some for Glory, Some for Praise

JAMES SALTER

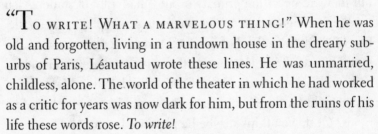

"To write! What a marvelous thing!" When he was old and forgotten, living in a rundown house in the dreary suburbs of Paris, Léautaud wrote these lines. He was unmarried, childless, alone. The world of the theater in which he had worked as a critic for years was now dark for him, but from the ruins of his life these words rose. *To write!*

One thinks of many writers who might have said this, Anne Sexton, even though she committed suicide, or Hemingway or Virginia Woolf, who both did also, or Faulkner, scorned in his rural town, or the wreckage that was Fitzgerald in the end. The thing that is marvelous is literature, which is like the sea, and the exaltation of being near it, whether you are a powerful swimmer or wading by the shore. The act of writing, though often tedious, can still provide extraordinary pleasure. For me that comes line by line at the tip of a pen, which is what I like to write with, and the page on which the lines are written, the pages, can be the most valuable thing I will ever own.

The cynics say that if you do not write for money you are a dabbler or a fool, but this is not true. To see one's work in print is the real desire, to have it read. The remuneration is of less importance; no one was paid for the samizdats. Money is but one form of approval.

It is such a long time that I have been writing that I don't remember the beginning. It was not a matter of doing what my father knew how to do. He had gone to Rutgers, West Point, and then MIT, and I don't think in my lifetime I ever saw him reading a novel. He read newspapers, the *Sun*, the *World-Telegram*, there were at least a dozen in New York in those days. His task was laid out for him: to rise in the world.

Nor was my mother an avid reader. She read to me as a child, of course, and in time I read the books that were published in popular series, *The Hardy Boys* and *Bomba, the Jungle Boy*. I recall little about them. I did not read *Ivanhoe, Treasure Island, Kim*, or *The Scottish Chiefs*, though two or three of them were given to me. I had six volumes of a collection called *My Bookhouse*, edited by Olive Beaupré Miller, whose name is not to be found among the various Millers — Mrs. Alice, Henry, Joaquin, Joe — in *The Reader's Encyclopedia*, but who was responsible for what knowledge I had of Cervantes, Dickens, Tolstoy, Homer, and the others whose work was excerpted. The contents also included folktales, fairy tales, parts of the Bible, and more. When I read of writers who when young were given the freedom of their fathers' or friends' libraries, I think of *Bookhouse*, which was that for me. It was not an education but the introduction to one.

There were also poems, and in grammar school we had to memorize and then stand up and recite well-known poems. Many of these I still know, including Kipling's "If," which my father paid me a dollar to learn. Language is acquired, like other things, through the act of imitating, and rhythm and elegance may come in part from poems.

I could draw quite well as a boy and even, though uninstructed, paint. What impulse made me do this, and where the ability came from — although my father could draw a little — I cannot say. My desire to write, apparent at the age of seven or eight, likely came from the same source. I made crude books, as many children do, with awkward printing and drawings, from small sheets of paper, folded and sewn together.

In prep school we were poets, at least many of my friends and I were, ardent and profound. There were elegies but no love poems — those came later. I had some early success. In a national poetry contest I won honorable mention, and sold two poems to *Poetry* magazine.

All this was a phase, in nearly every case to be soon outgrown. In 1939 the war had broken out, and by 1941 we were in it. I ended up at West Point. The old life vanished; the new one had little use for poetry. I did read, and as an upperclassman wrote a few short stories. I had seen some in the Academy magazine and felt I could do better, and after the first one, the editor asked for more. When I became an officer there was, at first, no time for writing, nor was there the privacy. Beyond that was a greater inhibition: it was alien to the life. I had been commissioned in the Army Air Force and in the early days was a transport pilot, later switching into fighters. With that I felt I had found my role.

Stationed in Florida in about 1950, I happened to see in a bookshop window in Pensacola a boldly displayed novel called *The Town and the City* by John Kerouac. The name. There had been a Jack Kerouac at prep school, and he had written some stories.

On the back of the jacket was a photograph, a gentle, almost yearning face with eyes cast downward. I recognized it instantly. I remember a feeling of envy. Kerouac was only a few years older than I was. Somehow he had written this impressive-looking novel. I bought the book and eagerly read it. It owed a lot to Thomas Wolfe — *Look Homeward, Angel* and others — who was a major figure then, but still it was an achievement. I took it as a mark of what might be done.

I had gotten married, and in the embrace of a more orderly life, on occasional weekends or in the evenings, I began to write again. The Korean War broke out. When I was sent over I took a small typewriter with me, thinking that if I was killed, the pages I had been writing would be a memorial. They were immature pages, to say the least. A few years later, the novel they were part of was rejected by the publishers, but one of them suggested that if I were to write another novel they would be interested in seeing it. Another novel. That might be years.

I had a journal I had kept while flying combat missions. It contained some description, but there was little shape to it. The war had the central role. One afternoon, in Florida again — I was there on temporary duty — I came back from the flight line, sat down on my cot, and began to hurriedly write out a page or so of outline that had suddenly occurred to me. It would be a novel about idealism, the true and the untrue, spare and in authentic prose. What had been missing but was missing no longer was the plot.

Why was I writing? It was not for glory; I had seen what I took to be real glory. It was not for acclaim. I knew that if the book was published, it would have to be under a pseudonym; I did not want to jeopardize a career by becoming known as a writer. I had heard the derisive references to "God-Is-My-Copilot" Scott. The ethic

of fighter squadrons was drink and daring; anything else was suspect. Still, I thought of myself as more than just a pilot and imagined a book that would be in every way admirable. It would be
evident that someone among the ranks of pilots had written it, an
exceptional figure, unknown, but I would have the satisfaction of
knowing who it was.

I wrote when I could find time. Some of the book was written
at a fighter base on Long Island, the rest of it in Europe, when I
was stationed in Germany. A lieutenant in my squadron who lived
in the apartment adjoining ours could hear the typewriter late at
night through the bedroom wall. "What are you doing," he asked
one day, "writing a book?" It was meant as a joke. Nothing could
be more unlikely. I was the experienced operations officer. Next
step was squadron commander.

The Hunters was published by Harper and Brothers in late 1956.
A section of the book appeared first in *Collier's*. Word of it spread
immediately. With the rest I sat speculating as to who the writer
might be, someone who had served in Korea, with the 4th Group,
probably.

The reviews were good. I was thirty-two years old, the father of
a child, with my wife expecting another. I had been flying fighters for seven years. I decided I had had enough. The childhood
urge to write had never died, in fact, it had proven itself. I discussed it with my wife, who, with only a partial understanding of
what was involved, did not attempt to change my mind. Upon
leaving Europe, I resigned my commission with the aim of becoming a writer.

It was the most difficult act of my life. Latent in me, I suppose,
there was always the belief that writing was greater than other
things, or at least would prove to be greater in the end. Call it a

delusion if you like, but within me was an insistence that whatever we did, the things that were said, the dawns, the cities, the lives, all of it had to be drawn together, made into pages, or it was in danger of not existing, of never having been. There comes a time when you realize that everything is a dream, and only those things preserved in writing have any possibility of being real.

Of the actual hard business of writing I knew very little. The first book had been a gift. I missed the active life terribly, and after a long struggle a second book was completed. It was a failure. Jean Stafford, one of the judges for a prize for which it had been routinely submitted, left the manuscript on an airplane. The book made no sense to her, she said. But there was no turning back.

A Sport and a Pastime was published six years later. It, too, did not sell. A few thousand copies, that was all. It stayed in print, however, and one by one, slowly, foreign publishers bought it. Finally, Modern Library.

The use of literature, Emerson wrote, *is to afford us a platform whence we may command a view of our present life, a purchase by which we may move it.* Perhaps this is true, but I would claim something broader. Literature is the river of civilization, its Tigris and Nile. Those who follow it, and I am inclined to say those only, pass by the glories.

Over the years I have been a writer for a succession of reasons. In the beginning, as I have said, I wrote to be admired, even if not known. Once I had decided to be a writer, I wrote hoping for acceptance, approval.

Gertrude Stein, when asked why she wrote, replied, "For praise." Lorca said he wrote to be loved. Faulkner said a writer wrote for glory. I may at times have written for those reasons, it's hard to know. Overall I write because I see the world in a certain way that no dialogue or series of them can begin to describe, that no book can fully render, though the greatest books thrill in their attempt.

A great book may be an accident, but a good one is a possibility, and it is thinking of that that one writes. In short, to achieve. The rest takes care of itself, and so much praise is given to insignificant things that there is hardly any sense in striving for it.

In the end, writing is like a prison, an island from which you will never be released but which is a kind of paradise: the solitude, the thoughts, the incredible joy of putting into words the essence of what you for the moment understand and with your whole heart want to believe.

That's What Dogs Do

AMY HEMPEL

‚Äî‚Äî‚Äî

W‚Äãhy do I write? I treat this question differently today than I would have years ago, when I started to write. Then I would have said that it was an act of seduction, that sentences were "my lipstick, my lingerie, my high heels." I would have said, before I knew better, that I wrote to settle a score. In fact, the answer does not require years to change; it changes throughout the course of a single day.

Morning. Trying to train a dog is a central part of my day. So is trying to say something in a new way. But as Tom Waits said to Mark Richard about trying to make it new on another kind of keyboard, "Your hands are like dogs, going to the same places they've been." One of the tenets of successful dog training is to wait to issue a command until the dog is paying attention. If the dog is distracted, first *tune in* the dog. In Immy Humes's film *A Little Vicious,* the poet and animal trainer Vicki Hearne makes the cryptic, assured pronouncement, "You can train a dog if you've read the right poems."

There's no sport in making me blush. A stranger on the street can point to his wrist and ask for the time and I, aflame, will give it. Whether from a font of deep shame, or metabolic misfire, this response is sometimes fetching, I suppose, but more often annoying (in the seventies, when megavitamin therapy was popular, I overdosed on niacin and stayed bright red for days). Yet I don't blush when I'm with dogs, and I don't blush when I write. I take it, then, that these two activities answer a related question: Where in your life are you most yourself?

The girls' school I attended abolished its mandatory uniform the year I enrolled, but I kept the tradition alive, dressing four days out of five in navy blazer and box-pleated skirt rolled over at the waist to hike it past the dress-code length. Today, I sometimes wear that blazer over another uniform — my writing togs, sweats from the Gap, the store whose premise is, as Eve Babitz put it, "Style is no longer in style." The blazer is a reminder of the time I realized the message was not "Look at me" but "*Listen* to me."

Thus attired, I watch a TV feature on the fashion designer John Galliano. In it, a friend of his recalls the way he used to wear his clothes, in particular a shearling jacket Galliano wore upside down so that the collar was at his waist and the tail stood up to create a portrait neckline. And I thought, in a kind of simultaneous translation, I have done that, too. I have stood a story on its head and started at the end. Galliano is shown putting a leather biker jacket on a pale blond Ukrainian bride. Again, I have done that. I have dressed a delicate subject in hard, tough prose. And the reverse: described in lyrical language something ugly, something bad. Used a genteel voice to describe violence, an angry voice to take on the harmless. I mix leather and lace on the page.

WFUV not coming in, forced to listen to an oldies station. With a nod to Jeff Foxworthy, You might be a writer if . . . you gag at the Dan Hill lyric "I'm just another writer/Trapped within my truth."

Afternoon. A conversation with novelist Jim Shepard, who reminds me that we talked about this nearly twenty years ago, when we agreed that many writers shared a dissatisfaction with the normal channels of communication, a lifetime of other methods' (hand puppets!) not working very well. That, and the incentive — Hey! I took off my diaper and smeared it all over my head, and they're paying me for it!

To combat grief. Recall looking for a lost dog, calling a ranger in Maine, and the ranger's saying, "I'll look in the place I hate to look," meaning the printout of dogs found dead on the roads, and my thinking: That is my job, too, to look in the place I hate to look.

Writing is as close as I will ever come to achieving the kind of self-regard that was available to my brother at the age of ten, when he composed the shapely and authoritative English theme: "Why I Am My Favorite Person."

I once interviewed a writer who had been the college teacher of one of my literary heroes. I heard my own quest echoed as the teacher remembered this writer's early efforts: "He was a gargoyle-maker looking for a cathedral." The writer has since built enduring cathedrals that make others want to do this work, too. You want to do the thing that unglues you. You want to unglue another. In an old radio interview, James Baldwin tells Studs Terkel that what breaks the heart brilliantly about a Bessie Smith song is the way the line that follows "My house fell down" is "I can't live there no more."

I was walking home from the Latin School in Chicago after algebra class. I walked through Lincoln Park in that summer of 1968 and stopped to listen to a wild-haired man with galvanizing energy teach the "snake" method of eluding the "pigs" during a demonstration. This was days before the start of the Democratic convention, and the man was Abbie Hoffman. As I watched, Chicago police appeared and attempted to break up the meeting. I may have told friends that my eyes were stung by the tear gas the police employed. I *may* have? Of course I did. It was story-making — I'd been too far away, and that was the problem — an attempt to connect myself to history, if only from the schoolgirl sidelines.

The pleasing assonance of *macintosh*, *gabardine*, and *scab*, a trio of words my brothers and I made each other chant as little kids, words that — go figure — always inspired mirth.

A dog owner asks in exasperation, "Why does my dog *do* that?" And the trainer says, "Because he's a dog, and that's what dogs do."

Evening. Finding the proof, for myself, of Mark Doty's observation about the shaping forces of one's life "becoming the lens through which you see as opposed to the thing at which you are looking."

The poet John Rybicki wrote, "Our bodies are anchors thrown down by angels." How does one anchor the dead? With words.

Words, in the middle of the night, *are* people. *Comestible*, for example, is the late Christopher Coe, as applied to a "tasty specimen" in *Such Times*, the novel he stayed alive to finish. During his first hospital stay with AIDS, he phoned to say a man he didn't know had stopped into his room and asked if he was Catholic. When Christopher said no, the man excused himself, saying, "Have a better day." "Why can't I have a *good* day?" Christopher demanded, and the man told him he wouldn't have a good day until he got to Heaven. "You use it," Christopher said to me, "if I don't get a chance to."

Sanity isn't free.

Many years ago I worked as a crisis counselor with a volunteer organization. As part of the training, we counselors were made to do an exercise the point of which is lost to me now. We faced each other in pairs and waited for the signal to begin. "No, you can't." "Yes, I can." Back and forth, dozens of times, that was all we said to each other. One person saying, "No, you can't," and the other saying, "Yes, I can," until one of the partners broke. In no time I was blushing furiously (of course I was). I asked to change partners. The exercise enraged me. Which was probably the point: Could we hold our own in the face of this kind of recalcitrance? I was never *No-you-can't*. I was always *Yes-I-can*. You see where I'm going with this.

Crop circles have long held my attention. This phenomenon, which was first seen in the English Downs and later spread to the American Midwest, features large circular patterns — intersecting or contiguous perfect circles — that appear overnight in fields of wheat or oats. The success of these designs can be seen only from above, from a plane, say, flying over the field. Are crop circles supernatural imprints, or the work of human hoaxers? Night-vision cameras set up in fields in an attempt to explain the phenomenon have recorded no activity, though in the morning there have appeared immense and elaborate circles. In England, at least, folks have confessed to sneaking into fields to effect these transformations, but I was happier when they remained a mystery. I think *writing* is like swinging a scythe in the dark and finding in the morning, if you're lucky and looking from the right angle, a mysterious, well-formed pattern has emerged.

I could claim any number of highflown reasons for writing, just as you can explain certain dog behavior as submission to the alpha, or even a moral choice. But maybe it's that they're dogs, and that's what dogs do.

Stories

PAT CONROY

FIRST, MY CREDO.

A novel is the greatest act of passion and intellect, carpentry and largess, that a human being can pull off in one lifetime. From the very beginning, I wrote to explain my own life to myself, and I invited any readers who chose to make the journey with me to join me on the high wire. I would work without a net and without the noise of the crowd to disturb me. The view from on high is dizzying, instructive. I do not record the world exactly as it comes to me but transform it by making it pass through a prism of fabulous stories I have collected on the way. I gather stories the way a lepidopterist hoards his chloroformed specimens of rare moths, or a sunburned entomologist admires his well-ordered bottles of Costa Rican beetles. Stories are the vessels I use to interpret the world to myself. I am often called a "storyteller" by flippant and unadmiring critics. I revel in the title. I bathe in the lotions and unguents of that sweet word.

Many modern writers abjure the power of stories in their work, banish them to the suburbs of literature, drive them out toward the lower pastures of the lesser moons, and they could not be more wrong in doing so. But please, do not let me mince words in this essay in which I offer an explanation and apologia for why I write. Fear is the major cargo that American writers must stow away when the writing life calls them into its carefully chosen ranks. I have been mortally afraid of the judgment of other writers and critics since I first lifted my proud but insecure head above the South Carolina marsh grass twenty-five years ago. Some American writers are meaner than serial killers, but far more articulate, and this is always the great surprise awaiting the young men and women who swarm to the universities, their heads buzzing with all the dazzle and freshness and humbuggery of the language itself. My great fear of being attacked or trivialized by my contemporaries made me concentrate on what I was trying to do as a writer. It forced me to draw some conclusions that were my own. Here is one: The writers who scoff at the idea of the primacy of stories either are idiots or cannot write them. Many of their novels could be used in emergency situations where barbiturates are at a premium and there has been a run on Unisom at the pharmacies. "Tell me a story" still comprise four of the most powerful words in English, words that are intimately related to the complexity of history, the origins of language, the continuity of the species, the taproot of our humanity, our singularity, and art itself. I was born into the century in which novels lost their stories, poems their rhymes, paintings their form, and music its beauty, but that does not mean I have to like that trend or go along with it. I fight against these movements with every book I write.

Good writing is the hardest form of thinking. It involves the agony of turning profoundly difficult thoughts into lucid form, then forcing them into the tight-fitting uniform of language, making them visible and clear. If the writing is good, then the result seems effortless and inevitable. But when you want to say something life-changing or ineffable in a single sentence, you face both the limitations of the sentence itself and the extent of your own talent. When you come close to succeeding, when the words pour out of you just right, you understand that these sentences are all part of a river flowing out of your own distant, hidden ranges, and all words become the dissolving snow that feeds your bright mountain streams forever. The language locks itself in the icy slopes of our own high passes, and it is up to us, the writers, to melt the glaciers within us. When these glaciers calve and break off, we get to call them novels, the changelings of our burning spirits, our lifework.

I have always taken a child's joy in the painterly loveliness of the English language. As a writer, I try to make that language pitch and roll, soar above the Eastern Flyway, reverse its field at will, howl and reel in the darkness, bellow when frightened, and pray when it approaches the eminence or divinity of nature itself. My well-used dictionaries and thesauri sing out to me when I write, and all English words are the plainsong of my many-tongued, long-winded ancestors who spoke before me. I write because I once fell in love with the sound of words as spoken by my comely, Georgia-born mother. I use the words that sound prettiest or most right to me as I drift into that bright cocoon where the writer loses himself in the silks of language. When finished, I adore the way the words look back at me after I have written them down on long yellow legal sheets. They are written in my hand, and their imperfect shapes thrill me. I can feed on the nectar of each work I write, and some are salt-rimed with the storm-flung Atlantic on them, some mountain-born, writhing in laurel, but each with a dark taste of my own life fresh upon it. What richer way to meet the sunlight than bathing each day of my life in my island-born language, the one that Shakespeare breathed on, Milton wrestled with, Jane Austen tamed, and Churchill rallied the squadrons of England with? I want to use the whole English language as the centerpiece of a grand alliance or concordance with my work. I see myself as its acolyte, its spy in the college of cardinals, its army in the field. I try to turn each sentence into a bright container made of precious metals and glittering glass. It is the carrier and aqueduct of the sweetest elixir of English words themselves. I build these sentences slowly. Like a glassblower, I use air and fire to shape the liquids as they form in my imagination. I long for that special moment when I take off into the pure, oxygen-rich sky of a sentence that streaks off into a night where I cannot follow, where I lose control, when the language seizes me and shakes me in such a way that I feel like both its victim and its copilot.

Story and language brought me to the craft of writing, then passion and my childhood provided both the structure and the details. When I was busy growing up on the Marine bases of my youth, my mother cast a spell on me that I found all but unbreakable. Peg Conroy was rough-born and southern-shaped, and I heard the stories of her Depression childhood so often that I have never been able to throw off the belief that I've known poverty inside and out from a very early age. Each night of my boyhood, my mother read to me, and I still hear her voice, lovely beneath soft lamplight, whenever I sit down with a pen in my hand. It was my mother who told me she was raising me to be a "southern writer," though I have never been sure that she knew what that meant. My sister Carol Conroy listened to that same voice and heard those same stories, and her book of poetry, *The Beauty Wars*, was published by Norton in 1991. Part of my childhood that is most vivid to me was being chief witness to the shaping of an American poet in the bedroom next to mine. My sister and I grew up stung by the consequence of language in my mother's house.

My father, the Chicago-born Donald Conroy, brought the sensibilities of Augie March and Studs Lonigan to the cockpits of the fighter planes he flew over target areas along the coastal South. My father was a pure man of action; he thought books made handsome furniture, but I never saw him read one. The strongest Marine I ever knew raised me up to manhood in a house that had the feel of a gulag to it. When I first read *The Iliad* in high school, I had no problem placing my father in the midst of those glittering spearmen who sat by their confreres in the shadows of poor, besieged Troy. When I wrote *The Great Santini*, I learned things about my father's military career that took me by surprise and have made me proud to this very day. Although I still believe he was a bad father to his seven children, I should like to think that my country was a far safer place because men such as my father patrolled the American skies. You would not have liked to be an enemy soldier when Don Conroy lowered his flaps and caught you moving across his field of vision with his Corsair loaded with napalm.

I was born a warrior's son, and this is a vital piece of evidence in my biography. My father treated his children like an unruly platoon that took overly long to shape up. He raised me to be a fighter pilot like himself, and that is what I had planned to do before I was waylaid by literature. Yet my books have the feel of some invisible though embattled country, where the field artillery is always exchanging rounds between chapters. Like all battlefields, my novels fill up with smoke and noise and the screams of the wounded and the answering calls of medics low-crawling through the blasted, cratered fields with their canteens and their morphine ready. My father taught me the way of the warrior at the same time my mother was turning me into a wordsmith.

War itself was a fundamental reality in my household, and my father was called to battle the way other fathers were called to distant cities for sales conferences. Civilian fathers sold shoes or life insurance while my father wiped out battalions of North Korean regulars by setting them on fire. As a father, Don Conroy carried a few shortcomings into the task of fathering, and I never thought he could tell the real difference between a sortie against the enemy and a family picnic. My parents taught me everything I needed to know about the dangers and attractions of the extreme. Even today, the purely outrageous to me feels completely natural. My novels reflect the absurdity and the exorbitance of a house in which the fully unexpected was our daily bread. My father once wiped out a dozen tanks working their way toward Marine lines in Korea, and my mother's hobby was collecting poisonous snakes. It is not my fault I was raised by Zeus and Hera, but my books mirror the odd, hothouse environment of my astonished childhood. All writers are both devotees and prisoners of their childhoods, and of the images that accrued during those early days on earth when each of us played out the mystery of Adam and Eve in our own way. My mother's voice and my father's fists are the two bookends of my childhood, and they form the basis of my art.

My parents taught me many of the exigencies and pitfalls of character. My father seemed prehistoric in his simplicity, a one-celled carnivore with a violent, unpredictable temper. Living with him was like being perched in a village near Vesuvius. He made life seem dangerous, but he made me alert and vigilant, and he wore the city of Chicago like a bad tattoo on his character. I still watch my back when I enter the Chicago city limits.

We seemed to move every year, but the South was carry-on luggage with my mother. She hailed from a testy, improvident South. The Battle of Atlanta was actually fought along the grounds where I was born and along the road where my mother brought me home to my grandmother's house on Rosedale Road. From my earliest days, my mother taught me to hate with all my heart William Tecumseh Sherman, the leader of the invasion force that had left the South bleeding and prostrate as he cut his wake across a bereft, helpless land. Many years passed before I began to realize that it was my father, not Sherman, whom my mother had been talking about. Peg Conroy thought she was teaching me history when in fact she was delivering my first instruction in metaphor.

If my father's birthplace had been rural Georgia, and my mother had come up in South Chicago, I am positive that I would be known as a writer out of the Chicago School this very day. My mother was multiformed, hydra-headed, an untamable shape-shifter whose love of miscellany was a kind of genius. The women in my books all share an air of mystery, an unwinnable allure that I trace back to my inability to figure out what made my mother tick. When I try to pin down my mother's soft, armor-covered spirit, when I fix it on a slide beneath a microscope, I can feel it all becoming immaterial before my steady gaze. The colors rearrange themselves and the cosmetology of her womanhood reverses itself. My hunt will always be for my mother. She could not give me herself, but she gave me literature as a replacement. I have no idea who she was, and I write my books as a way of finding out.

Although I was trained in the way of the Marine Corps and brought to manhood in the backwater South, my mother had possession of the keys to the kingdom of art. She turned me into an insatiable, fanatical reader. It was her gentle urging, her hurt, insistent voice, that led me to discover my identity by taking a working knowledge of the great books with me always. She wanted me to read everything of value, and we looked like bibliophiles or book thieves when our family returned from libraries during my youth. My mother taught me to outread my entire generation, as she had done hers. I believe, and I think fairly, that I have done that — that I have not only outread my own generation of writers but outread them in such a way that whole secret libraries separate us. I started this solitary voyage in high school, thinking it would give me an advantage over every single rival when I later began the strange business of writing novels. I have tried to read two hundred pages every day of my life since I was a freshman in high school because I knew that I would come to the writing of books without the weight of culture and learning that a well-established, confidently placed family could offer its children. I collected those long, melancholy lists of the great books that high school English teachers passed out to college-bound students, and I relied on having consumed those serious litanies of books as a way to ease my way into the literary life.

Even today, I hunt for the fabulous books that will change me utterly and for all time. Great writing sticks to your soul the way beggar's lice adheres to your pants cuffs after a walk through untended fields. I find myself happiest in the middle of a book in which I forget that I am reading, but am instead immersed in a made-up life lived at the highest pitch. Reading is the most rewarding form of exile and the most necessary discipline for novelists who burn with the ambition to get better.

Here is what I want from a book, what I demand, what I pray for when I take up a novel and begin to read the first sentence: I want everything and nothing less, the full measure of a writer's heart. I want a novel so poetic that I do not have to turn to the standby anthologies of poetry to satisfy that itch for music, for perfection and economy of phrasing, for exactness of tone. Then, too, I want a book so filled with story and character that I read page after page without thinking of food or drink because a writer has possessed me, crazed me with an unappeasable thirst to know what happens next. Again, I know that story is suspect in the high precincts of American fiction, but only because it brings entertainment and pleasure, the same responses that have always driven puritanical spirits at the dinner table wild when the talk turns to sexual intercourse and incontinence.

When an author sets the table right, there will be no need to pass either the foie gras or the barbecue because the characters will grab me by the collar. They will spring to life so fully developed, so richly contained in the oneness of their own universe, that they will populate the cafés and verandahs and alleyways of a city I will never want to leave. Few things linger longer or become more indwelling than that feeling of both completion and emptiness when a great book ends. That the book accompanies the reader forever, from that day forward, is part of literature's profligate generosity.

All through my life I have told myself — no, ordered myself — to read more deeply, read everything of consequence, let the words of some new writer settle like the dust of silica into the ledges and sills of my consciousness. When I find myself engaged in the reading of some magical, surprising book, I ask myself these questions: Can I match this depth? Can I incorporate this splendid work, ingest it whole into my bloodstream, where it can become part of my thinking and dreaming life? What can this writer do that I can't? Can I steal the genius of this writer and learn all of the unappropriated lessons, then turn them into something astonishing that flows out of me because I was moved by the originality and courage and eloquence of another writer? Very early on, I set up for myself the endless task of reading and incorporating books of large and exuberant vision. By reading these luminous works, I learn the shy secrets of my craft, but I also gain some idea of the novel's fertility, its free-flowing immensity. In the middle of reading a life-changing book, I feel like that grain of sand, that famous irritation in the tissue of a healthy oyster, and I can feel the pearl beginning to form around me. I welcome the silvering, then the hardening as I ingest the sheer beauty of another writer's language. I let myself be taken by, then lost in, the maze and wizardry of a gift not my own. I allow the subsuming to take place, then the transfiguration. I await the aura of wealth and mother-of-pearl handed over to the passionate reader. It is communion, and it is religious in nature. I ask a great deal of a book: astonishment, transformation, art, and nothing less. When I write a book, I move with all the magic of language toward a fixed star, offering a present of my troubled, violent spirit, and I wish to leave the reader with everything.

When I first sat down to write these books, I had to teach myself how to go about it. I called upon that regiment of beloved writers, living and dead, who had written the books that had changed the way I looked at myself and the world. I promised myself that each novel would seem like a world unto itself. I wanted a specific gravity, changeable weather, a real geography that could provide a starting point for a mapmaker's art. I wanted the atmosphere of the novels to feel like the one I had breathed in as a boy when I found myself in the grip of a mother-haunted imagination to which I owed both fealty and homage. I demanded living trees with actual names, flowers growing in their proper seasons, characters who spoke their minds, who lived as free men and women outside of my jurisdiction. My city of made-up people would live their own complex lives without my permission or my intrusion into their own sovereignty. I wanted my fictional world to feel like the one I had grown up in, with no whitewashing of the horror that stood in the doorway of any given human moment. All my rivers had to be clean enough for the cobia, the herring, and the shad to swim upstream to spawn, because I was going back to my own sources to find the secrets of the world. I desired to be one of those writers who always followed the creek bed to that source, that clear pool where the mother's roe floated in still water above the glittering pebbles.

Nothing lazy would ever enter my books. I try to write down every word with caution and a sense of craft, as though I were carving hieroglyphics on the tomb of a well-loved king. Writing is both hard labor and one of the most pleasant forms that fanaticism can take. I take infinite care in how a sentence sounds to me. I rise out of the oral tradition of the American South, and words have to sound a certain way if they're to come out right.

In my first years, my identity as a writer was drawn toward amplitude, fullness, and extravagance. I worshiped those writers who made me feel sated, coddled, spoiled with all the excess that too much attention and love can provide. The overreachers called out my name, and I responded with great zeal. I longed for writers to take me to the absolute crests and limits of their talents, but

I did not want them to leave out the grand tours of the abysses and spiritual Death Valleys they encountered along the way.

But since I have tried to read everything, I have also found myself falling for the seductiveness of economy, the telling of a story with swiftness, velocity, and even severity. Exactness is a virtue in even the most word-possessed writer. There is enormous power in stating something simply and well. Action sequences always require the straight line in the presentation, the most solid, sequential phrases, and the punchiest, most telling Anglo-Saxon sentences. Action brims and stirs. There is delicacy, craft, and restraint in all this, as in the making of a dry martini. But sometimes a lot more is required. Then you must go inside yourself to find the lift-off into the dark side of language's many rooms. When you have made a new sentence, or even an image that works well, it is a palace where language itself has lit a new lamp. It is why a writer sits alone, fingering memory and shaping imagination during all the lost, solitary days.

As a writer, I have tried to make and remake myself over and over again. I try to notice everything, and if I take the time to write it, I would simply like to write it better than anyone else possibly could. If I am describing the Atlantic Ocean, I want to make that portion of the high seas mine forevermore, and I do not want the reader daydreaming about Herman Melville's ocean while getting a suntan on poor Conroy's. I try to be athletic and supple with my talent. I train it, urge it on, drive it to exceed itself, knowing in my bones that I need to be watchful about slippage, weariness, and running on empty. The safe writers have never interested me, do not excite a single shiver of curiosity within me. I can read five pages and know I am in the hands of a writer whose feet are yawningly and cunningly placed on safe ground. Safety is a crime writers should never commit unless they are after tenure or praise. A novelist must wrestle with all the mysteries and strangeness of life itself, and anyone who does not wish to accept that grand, bone-chilling commission should write book reviews, editorials, or health-insurance policies instead. The idea of a novel should stir your blood, and you should rise to it like a lion lifting up at the smell of impala. It should be instinctual, incurable, unanswerable, and a calling, not a choice.

I came to the writing life because my father's warplanes took off against me, and my mother's hurt South longed for her special voice. Nothing is more difficult for a writer to overcome than a childhood of privilege, but this was never a concern of mine. To experience a love that is too eloquent sometimes makes for a writer without edges or karats or facets. I have drawn long and often from the memory book of my youth, the local and secret depository where my central agony cowers in the limestone cave, licking its wounds, awaiting my discovery of it. Art is one of the few places where talent and madness can actually go to squirrel away inside each other.

I have used my books as instruments to force my way into the world. It was with surprise and wonder that I discovered that the same elemental, dangerous chemistry that moves through the volcanoes of the earth also moved through me. Through words, I learned that life and art can be raised to a fever pitch, to sacramental levels, that ecstasy itself is within easy reach for all of us, but the secret is in knowing it is there and when to reach for it. I want always to be writing the book I was born to write. A novel is my fingerprint, my identity card, and the writing of novels is one of the few ways I have found to approach the altar of God and creation itself. You try to worship God by performing the singularly courageous and impossible favor of knowing yourself. You watch for the black wings of fighters writing messages in the skies over the South. Your mother plays with snakes and poison and raises you to tell the stories that will make all our lives clear. It all congeals and moves and hurts in the remembering.

I can ask for nothing more.

Writing and a Life Lived Well
Notes on Allan Gurganus

ANN PATCHETT

THERE ARE MAYBE TWENTY different stories and all of them are true.

I write because as a child I had such a hard time making my letters, remembering which direction the *S* was supposed to face. I had a painful time with spelling, punctuation, wicked contractions. I sat at my tiny desk at six and seven and eight and made nearly indecipherable marks, fishhooks and barbed wire. I was one of those kids. I struggled. I lost things. When papers were finished, they were crumpled into coat pockets. I was so poor at the form of writing, the physical act of pencil to paper, that I knew instinctively the secret to survival was in the content. Be funny, be clever, and you will scrape by. Cleverness, once learned, can be the stairs that take you down to more interesting places.

The nun who collected those papers, who tortured me for my stupidity, I write for her. Even as a child I wanted to write for revenge, to show them all, but especially this particular nun, that I had been misjudged.

A story that must be told quickly to avoid melodrama involves an especially bad car accident my sister and I were in. I remember waking up in a hospital, eight years old (this is true), and thinking, Now I can be anything, so I'll be a writer.

"And the life I live now's an extra life," Frost said, "I can waste as I please. . . ."

I write because I think my mother should have been a writer. She wrote wonderful poems. I write because my father lived on the other side of the country when I was growing up, and we wrote long letters to each other. He missed us and we missed him terribly. I made a habit of storing up my life and writing it down for him. I write because of my father's strong, clear handwriting.

There is more, but any of these reasons is enough. I said it to whoever asked, "Ann, what do you want to be?" I felt like I was picking my answer out of the air, but it was always the same answer. I always and only wanted to be a writer. I have often wondered whether, if I had said "a fireman," or "an opera singer," I would have then barreled toward those professions with such complete single-mindedness.

If there had been a supportive nun and naturally good penmanship, if there had been enough money for my father to call more often and therefore he never wrote to me, would I write? I wrote after school, during school. While my girlfriends danced and dated, I sat and wrote. Every ounce of gangly energy I had went onto paper. I sprawled. I mass-produced.

I went to college and took a writing class, and the next year I took another one.

It was in that class, the second one, that everything changed. Now we go from maybe twenty possible reasons why I became a writer to the one certain, definite reason: I write because Allan Gurganus taught me to.

Sixteen years ago, Allan was thirty-four, the age I am now. I like to say I knew Allan Gurganus before he was Allan Gurganus. This was long before *Oldest Living Confederate Widow Tells All*. He wasn't famous to the general public yet, but at Sarah Lawrence, in Westchester County, and, I imagine, in most of Manhattan, he was famous. He moved in an unmistakable cloud of celebrity. He had what must have been the best office on campus, with a fire-place and French glass doors leading out onto a garden, which in the spring was full of heavy French tulips and dogwood trees. He wore linen trousers in the spring. The chairs beside his desk were deep and dark and full of pillows. There were copies of Chekhov and a framed black-and-white picture of John Cheever. There were drawings he had done, postcards from exotic friends in equally exotic places, a large crazy quilt on the wall made out of satins and velvet. When he walked into a room, we stirred, we leaned toward him. Everybody did. Allan, young, with a handful of well-published stories, was as dazzling to us as Chekhov or Cheever themselves would have been.

How he looked (wonderful), his impeccable taste, how people spoke to him and spoke of him, have nothing to do with writing, but everything to do with my being a writer. No one made a bet-ter impression than Allan, and as I was eighteen at the time, an age when one is most susceptible to appearances, I was deeply moved. This was what it would be like to be a writer, this was how it would look. Yes. Heaven. Sign me up. Our text for the class was the collected stories of Isaac Babel, which are still here on my desk.

The class, a weekly fiction workshop that lasted two semesters, had fourteen people in it. I remember each of them. I remember their stories in a way I cannot remember stories from any other class I have taken or taught since. The deal was as follows: we were to write a story a week, every week, until it was over. For a while there were assignments, the most skeletal nudges toward plot: write a story about an animal; write a fairy tale; write a story from the point of view of . . . and so forth. Then even those little starters fell away and we were out there alone, typing. I am respectful of people whose college careers consisted of classes I was (am) unfit to audit — inorganic chemistry, advanced statistics, upper-level Greek — but I would say the best of them would have struggled under this particular load. Ninety percent of what I know about fiction writing I learned that year. Write it out. Tell the truth. Stack up the pages. Learn to write by writing. Slowing down was for later, years later. Learn the sea by sailing it. We were not writing for keeps, we were writing out our mistakes, finding our strengths by stumbling over them in the dark. We were to keep going at all costs. To miss a week was to have two stories due, which was a little like taking in a mouthful of water when you were doing your best not to drown.

At eighteen, I had already spent a good ten years dreaming about the job I wanted. I came to Allan's class with no small amount of motivation, ambition, not for fame but for real ability. What I lacked was skill. I had no habits, and writers are people who desperately need habits to fill up their days. Allan's habits were based in vast quantities of reading and writing, reading and rewriting. He was somewhere between Balanchine and Cus D'Amato. We danced until our feet bled, punched until we could no longer bob or weave. He would call us "Dearest" and "My Angel," but the standards didn't bend to meet our needs. He seemed to expect of us what he expected of himself.

Although it never occurred to me at the time, I have wondered in every class I have since taught, What must he have been thinking of, assigning so much work? Every week a maelstrom of stories, and he responded to each generously in brown fountain pen, giving nuts-and-bolts advice of the kind you'd never get from an editor, about how to actually make a story better. There was an enormous generosity in him. I don't have children, but I believe that people parent in response to their own parents, being either like them or as unlike them as possible. When I teach, it is in response to Allan's teaching. I try to find that level of generosity within myself, and never come close. He took us on a field trip to the Cloisters. He had a black-and-white class portrait taken for which he wore a dark, double-breasted blazer. He read to us. It was the first time I heard Raymond Carver's "Shall We Dance." The first time I heard anything of *Lolita*. One week he read to us from a book of conversations with Joan Crawford, how she sat at her kitchen table and wept over a failed dinner party. Sometimes he read us stories of his own. Those were the moments I remember most vividly. I remember long passages of things he read that I never saw again. Why do I write? Because the person I wanted to be came down and sat with us from time to time and showed us what he was working on, as if to say that what we were doing was all the same thing.

Allan and I have been in irregular touch over the years, but we are not friends. Allan is my teacher and I am his student, and no amount of time will change that. I send him Christmas cards. He has written me letters of recommendation. When I sold my first story to the *Paris Review*, he sent me two dozen white roses, which meant more than the publication itself. I have never written to please Allan. I'm not entirely sure if he's read my books or liked them. I mail him copies just the same. I do not wish to write like

Allan, though I greatly admire his work. He never taught us to mimic. I recognize the fact that he has had hundreds of students, some of them very successful, most of whom would have been glad to write this essay. Mentors are extremely hard to come by. The ones who are generous might not really have anything to teach you. The ones who are brilliant often prefer to keep their brilliance to themselves. To have received some genuine guidance in my life, to have received it at a time when I was capable of listening in a way I probably no longer am, was a great gift. In the end, the lesson retold in its most basic form was this: write with great truthfulness; work harder than you thought possible; have passion, enormous, sweeping passion. Give it first to your work. Let your work have all of the passion it requires, and whatever is left, put into your life. What is left varies greatly for me from year to year.

Writing, for me, is bound up completely in my quality of life. There is much about writing a novel that weighs me down, as if I am having to live two lives, my own and the one I create. But in writing I have purpose, I'm doing the thing I was meant to do. When I'm not writing — and I can go for long stretches without it — things are easier. But this life lived only for myself takes on a certain lightness that I find almost unbearable after a while, as if everything has become a moderately entertaining sitcom.

Last summer I was driving to Cape Cod and stopped off in North Carolina for a wedding. I called Allan and told him I would be passing through the town where he lived and hoped that I could see him. He said that he was leaving for Paris, but that he wanted me to come and spend the night in his house anyway. "I'd love to think of you here," he said.

And so I went. It is a very small town, and he was sitting on the front porch when I arrived. For Allan, there is still a great deal of passion left over after he has given his work everything it requires. There is passion for his friends, for his rambling gardens, and for his house, which is very much like a novel itself and would take a novel's number of pages to describe with any sort of justice. We sat in his kitchen for an hour before it was time for me to drive him to the airport in Raleigh. We talked about business and books and people we both remembered. He recounted the plot of the story I had written as a submission to get into his class sixteen years before. As far as I know, he is the only person who ever saw it. I never worked on it again and threw my copy away. "I liked that story," he said. "I knew when I read it that you'd do well."

How could he remember? What had he seen? When I came back to his house, I was glad to be alone. I could wander around the house and study the murals he had painted on the walls, soldiers with mighty horses on the second floor, Pompeii in the downstairs front room. It took me half the night just to look at his books. It took me all of the morning before I left to take in the garden.

I went back to his house again that same summer. I was in North Carolina for the filming of a movie and was invited to Allan's fiftieth-birthday party. It was the kind of party I had often imagined but had never actually seen. All of the women and some of the men came in wide-brimmed hats and danced barefoot in the grass when the jazz combo played. There were candles in the trees. There were testimonials. Allan moved among us, covering his own lawn in circles, telling jokes, taking everyone's hand. Each guest was made to feel that he or she was his secret favorite, the one he was most delighted to see. These were not students, for the most part, not people he had taught to write, but they were people whose feelings for him were not dissimilar to my own. We had all learned something from Allan, the expansiveness of his

, the reckless generosity. When it was dark, there was still champagne and then there were fireworks. Most of the guests had gone home by the time my friend Lynn Roth and I went to find him to say good-bye. Lynn had come with me; she was a screenwriter for the film. She had never met Allan before. When he walked us to the door, she told him that he had the most remarkable quality of life she had ever seen.

"And, my dear," he said, taking her hand, "I never for a moment imagined that it would be any other way."

Let me add this to the list: in my mind, sixteen years ago, Allan Gurganus made the distinct and permanent association between writing and a life lived well, a life that would stand for compassion, generosity, and grace. I do not mean to say there is no suffering; everyone knows about that. There is suffering in every life. There is more, perhaps, when it is your business to see it. But there can also be great beauty. If that's the way you want to play the cards, all of the struggle and loneliness of the job can be made into joy. We chose this, after all, we write because we wanted to do it more than anything else, and even when we hate it, there is nothing better.

Easing My Heart Inside

TERRY MCMILLAN

I NEVER WANTED TO BE A WRITER. As a kid, all I ever dreamed of was living in a house with central air and heat and a toilet that flushed. My mother *told* me I was going to college — no ifs, ands, or buts about it — and that I need not be concerned with "having anybody's babies" until after I had a degree in my hand. As a result, I was too scared to have sex during high school, when all my friends were having it, so I took to reading instead. Got my first job shelving books at our local library and spent many $1.25-per-hour hours hiding in the 700 and 900 sections.

This is where my dreams began to turn outward. I started traveling all over the world. I flew with Amelia Earhart. Sat with the Brontës. Rode in a sleigh in the snow with Robert Frost. Touched and smelled green with Thoreau. John Steinbeck fooled me with that story that wasn't really about mice: I thought he could've been black. James Baldwin frightened me when I saw his dark face on his book jacket: When did black people start writing books? I wondered. And then there was *Bartlett's Quotations*, which blew my young mind because it was like this dictionary of thought on all kinds of topics that I used to lie awake at night and ponder but never had anybody to talk to about. I didn't know then that I was already lonely. I couldn't share my feelings, and I knew no one really cared what I felt or thought.

But then I went to college, and my reading became a little broader, and one day this guy whose name I still can't remember broke a major portion of my heart and I found myself sitting on my twin-size bed in this tiny college apartment and I was in a coma for like four hours because I was unable to move (although I didn't try) and finally when I felt the blood flowing through my body again something hit my brain and exploded and I jumped up without knowing where I was going or what I was about to do and I grabbed a pen and a steno pad and began to write these words down one two three ten at a time and I wasn't even thinking about what I was doing because it happened so fast and I didn't realize until I was out of breath and four whole pages were filled with these words and I exhaled a deep sigh of relief and exhaustion but I suddenly felt better but then I panicked because when I looked at these words it sounded and looked like a poem and I knew damn well I didn't write this shit because I had never written anything before in my life.

And that's how it started.

This writing stuff saved me. It has become my way of responding to and dealing with things I find too disturbing or distressing or painful to handle in any other way. It's safe. Writing is my shelter. I don't hide behind the words; I use them to dig inside my heart to find the truth. I guess I can say, honestly, that writing also offers me a kind of patience I don't have in my ordinary day-to-day life. It makes me stop. It makes me take note. It affords me a kind of sanctuary that I can't get in my hurried and full-to-the-brim-with-activity life.

Besides that, I'm selfish. And self-absorbed. But I've discovered that writing makes me less so. It has made me more compassionate. In fact, that's what I've always prayed for: to have more compassion. For everybody. I've learned that every human being has feelings, despite the fact that sometimes I have my doubts and people think no one understands how they feel and that no one could possibly feel the same way. It's simply not true. Shock shock shock.

I'm also nosy. And I want to understand why I do some of the things I do and why we're so stupid, and in order to come close to empathizing I had to learn how to get under someone else's skin. Writing has become my *under*.

If I understood half of what I did or felt, I probably wouldn't waste my time writing. But I like the probing. I like being scared sometimes. I like worrying about the folks I write about. I want to know if everything's gonna turn out OK for them. I want to show what can happen when we err, and when we "do the right thing," because as they say, no matter what you do, sometimes, "shit happens." I like how we handle the shit when it does hit the fan. Especially when we throw it in the blades ourselves.

I just want to pay attention. To the details of everyday life. I want to be a better person. I want to feel good more often. I want to know, when I don't, *why* I don't. Writing gives me this.

Chekhov said, "Man will become better only when you make him see what he is like." This is what I'm trying to do when I portray African-American men and women behaving "badly." I'm not trying to "air dirty laundry"; I'm just trying to get us to hold up a mirror and take a long look. Most of us don't think about what we do, we just act and react. Many of us don't reflect or wonder what larger issues are really at stake in our lives.

Writing is helping me mature. As long as I'm not bullshitting myself, the act itself forces me to face and understand my flaws and weaknesses and strengths, and if I'm honest — really fucking honest — then writing is like a wake-up call. I become my own therapist. Because nobody knows me better than me, and if I do my job, I can ease my heart inside another character's until I feel what he or she feels and think the way he or she thinks. When I'm able to become, say, a chronic liar — using lies as a way to defend myself — then I know I'm on the right track because I can write about someone whom I do not in real life respect or admire but whom I've come to understand. Writing has taught me not to be so judgmental. I usually write about people I don't necessarily favor, who do things I would never dream of doing, and therefore I sort of have to make myself undo my own sense of thinking and being. It can be exhilarating, freeing, a real eye-opener, and painful as hell.

Maybe I'm weird, but I want to know what it feels like to die. To have your heart broken. Why people hurt each other intentionally. Why folks lie. And cheat. What kind of person can kill another person and sleep at night? What does a man feel when he beats his wife? How does she stay with him? How do children learn to hate? What is a good parent? What's it feel like to discover that you are gay when you're twelve? Why do some people not have the capacity to forgive? How long can I hold a grudge? And why are some people nicer and more likable, more responsible than others?

I could go on and on. But the bottom line is that I didn't make a conscious decision to become a writer. I never did it for the money. I never did it for fame. Who knew? Who ever knows? I think somehow the craft chose me. The words have given me ownership and a sense of security. Writing is the only place I can be myself and not feel judged. And I like it there.

Why the Daily Writing of Fiction Matters

RICK BASS

I LIVE IN A REMOTE VALLEY deep in the woods, and I must confess that when I go into town and encounter someone who asks where I live and what I do, for the longest time it was not entirely with pride that I would tell him or her I was a writer, and a thing I especially did not enjoy admitting was that I was a fiction writer. It seemed to me to be like answering, "Oh, I breathe," or "I'm a yawner," or "I look at air a lot." Hunch-shouldered over a one-dimensional sheet of paper, scowling and frowning at the patterns of ink, sometimes laughing, I might as well have answered, it seemed to me then, "I'm invisible" or "I don't do anything."

For a long time there was a shadow to my movements, and to my life, that asked, How real is this thing that I do? Writing was invisible and airy enough, vaporous an act as it was — one trafficked in ideas as one might traffic in smoke, or scent, or memory — but then even worse, it seemed, was the writing of fiction:

invisible ideas about things that had never even happened. A layer of the invisible laid crossways on another layer of the invisible: a grid, a subworld, of nothing. The black hole into which one disappeared for three, four, five hours a day, where everything was within arm's reach and where it all moved very slowly. Even in those rare moments when the pen raced full tilt across the page, left to right, the hand took roughly ten to fifteen seconds to traverse that eight-inch span.

It's such a slow world down there — the invisible second basement below the invisible first basement — that when you emerge, blinking and pulse-stilled, later in the day, and walk up the path from your writing cabin to your real life in your real house, even the most mundane movements of the earth seem to split your mind with onrushing speed. Simple conversation, thought, numerical gymnastics, even a seemingly easy task such as making a phone call or peeling a potato — anything of the regular nature of the world conspires to race past you like a Roger Clemens fastball; you open your mouth to respond, you raise your hand, but by that point the world has moved again. The electric sight of a butterfly dancing over tall green grass causes your brow to furrow, and you watch it with a thing like exhaustion. Things were so slow and controlled just a few minutes ago, back in your writing! Very carefully, then, you begin to ease back into humanity. You walk carefully, as if on ice, disbelieving, perhaps, if your immersion or submersion has been deep enough, that this is the real world, or rather, that you have any business in it.

You make a conscious commitment to try to enjoy the physicality of that part of the day that's left. You can't help but think (even if only with your body, like a kind of echo) about the world you're trying to remake, or protect, or attack, or celebrate — the one you left behind. And when you have a good day, a good *phys-*

ical day, in that second part of the day, you sometimes feel like a traitor when you encounter joy or pleasure, or anything else deeply felt.

— Which brings me, I think, to the reason writing is important (the reason any kind of art is important), and especially fiction writing. Art is an engagement of the senses; art sharpens the acuity with which emotions, and the other senses, are felt or imagined (and again, here, it challenges reality: What is the difference between feeling happy and really *being* happy? What is the difference between imagining you can taste something and really tasting it? A hair's breadth; a measurement less than the thickness of a dried work-skein of ink on paper).

The reading of good writing can engage the senses, can stretch them and keep them alive in the world — that is, sensate, rather than numb. Above all, in the reading of good fiction, the reader is called upon not only to believe in the thing being described, but to feel it deeply even while knowing full well on some conscious level going in that *it ain't true* — that it's made up. This is a double stretching, one that can require of the reader's mind an extraordinary suppleness. I think that almost everyone would posit that this is a good thing. To put it bluntly, I remember a football coach's arguing with some players whom he wanted to begin lifting weights. They were afraid of becoming muscle-bound and losing their speed and flexibility. The coach was desperate, spitting flecks of saliva in his inarticulate rage. Finally he understood how to explain it: "It'll make you faster and *more* flexible," he said. "You can stretch muscle. You can't stretch fat."

Fiction, by its very nature — being about a thing that, at best, at its most realistic, has not quite happened that way *yet* — is about a stretching and widening of borders, about options and possibilities of energy and character. Near a story's end, of course, as in life, all this possibility funnels into only one seemingly foregone, inescapable conclusion, but in the beginning, anything is possible — anything can be woven out of the elements at hand.

Good fiction, to my mind, breathes possibility, which is to say also that it breathes a kind of diversity, into every assemblage of characters, energies, and ideas. Reading it makes our minds supple, able to go two ways with equal strength rather than just one way: to consider the "real" but also equally to consider and feel the life of the story we're reading.

Fiction has always mattered because of its ability, its mandate, to reach across the borders and boundaries of reality, to give one the feeling, with each paragraph read, of new territory — but if you believe, as I do, that despite the stitchwork lacing of fiberoptic cables and such, the world is becoming more fragmented and more brittle, then anything that retains the ability to leap across those ever-encroaching and constricting borders is only going to become more important, particularly as we, the hungry, benumbed mass of us, continue swelling at the seams, funneling toward a conclusion that has felt inevitable all along: what my liberal friends call a loss of cultural diversity and what my right-wing friends (way right) call "one world order."

My beloved valley — the Yaak Valley of extreme northwestern Montana — is but a perfect example of and metaphor for every other finely crafted and specific system that is breaking down or being swallowed whole and assimilated, made general (and hence weak). The Yaak is the wildest place I've ever seen — ice-carved twelve thousand years ago into a magic little seam between the Pacific Northwest and the northern Rockies. It's a land a writer could love easily, a showcase of giant predators — grizzly bears, black bears, wolves, wolverines, golden eagles, coyotes, bald eagles, mountain lions, lynx, owls, bobcats — consuming big prey such as moose, deer, elk, even caribou.

Almost everything eats something else up here: so much tooth-and-claw, so much tension and remaking, so much chase and pursuit — so much like a writer stalking and following a story. Even the insects in the old-growth forests up here are largely carnivorous, consuming each other rather than preying on the forest itself, in which case they would devour the very thing that gives them nourishment.

If the forest in the Yaak, with its seething, *specific* characters, its incredible richness of diversity, and hence possibility, is so very much like the mind of a fiction writer, then understand, too, that the politics and human influences on the valley, the corporate designs on it, are also so very much like the mind of generalized, homogeneous, world-merge society. You do not need to be a scientist — or a reader or writer of fiction — to take a walk in the Yaak and know that, beautiful and mysterious though it is (seething with mosquitoes and black flies and steamy summer rain), the forest stands at the edge of some kind of loss.

Giant square and rectangular and triangular clearcuts are carved out of the valley yearly, stamped onto the sides of the steep mountains, baking and drying to arid lifeless moonscapes, on land that was previously a rich, diverse jungle. Roads rip through these old, secret corridors, old, secret paths of wolves and grizzlies, bringing light and heat into a place that was previously cool and dark.

Everything in the Yaak is being cut off from every other thing. The roads and clearcuts reduce the living, pulsing whole into a series of isolated, machinelike parts. William Kittredge has said, "As we destroy that which is natural, we eat ourselves alive."

In the face of such loss, such pain, one can enter shock. Numbness becomes a defensive mechanism, as does denial.

Fiction can be like a salve or balm to reverse this encrustation. Like sweating on a good hike, or building a stone wall, it can reengage the senses. It can reconnect isolated patches, islands of dulling senses and diminishing imagination, diminishing possibilities.

The other day, I was in my cabin working on fiction through a long green summer morning. Earlier a lion had caught a fawn, and the fawn's bleats had shaken me, as had, when I got up and went out to investigate, the sight of the lion leaping up from its hiding spot in the willows and running away. After that, it was a slow day for me, one in which I had trouble focusing. I've been using mostly analogies of lateral movement in discussing the travels on which fiction takes you, as if it were some horizontal surface along which you moved when going from the physical to the imagined; but I think it can also be described as travel along a vertical path. It often feels as if you were descending from the rock world, the real world, into the imagined one; and on a good day as if you could slip down into that chute, that shaft, into the below-place, easy as pie, like some subaqueous diver weighted with lead ankle wraps, or like some scientist suited up in an iron bathysphere: a quick descent, a gentle bump on the bottom, and you're there, and you can begin writing. Other days, though, it is as if you were full of air and could not sink beneath the surface — and certainly, on that day I heard the squawling and got up from my desk and walked out and flushed the lion up from out of those willows, the day turned raggedly (though wonderfully) into one of those days on which there can be no escape from the deep physical, no journeying across that gap into the deeply imagined. It was perhaps like being caught in a leghold trap.

I kept trying — working on a sentence, scratching it out. Trying it from another angle, scratching it out.

It was like a joke. My cabin's right at the edge of a vivid green marsh, full of life and rot. A south summer wind was blowing hard, sweeping laterally across the marsh, flattening the tall grass and slamming mountain-scent in through the open screened windows as I tried to descend, still juiced from the lion and juiced, too, now, from this, the incredible gusting wind, and the scents it brought, and all that green, green waving light. A wall of thundercloud came moving up the valley, rising like some wave larger than anything seen at sea, and it rolled in over the marsh and brought hail and then slashing rain, a drumming, shouting sound against my tin roof, deepening, in all that moisture, the smells of the marsh, crushing flowers, releasing the scent of wild strawberries after the sun came back out; and I had to just sit there, pen in hand, and float on the surface, unable even to get my head beneath the water.

Is there a story — are there stories — so important to tell that you could descend beneath this fury, such a day's *tempest*, find them, and deliver them to the reader? *Yes*; I believe there are.

Are such stories as real as the storm-lash itself — those precious few stories? *Yes*. Or *maybe*. *Yes*.

And then the kicker is this: in passing from the real to the imagined, in following that trail, you learn that both sides have a little of the other in each, that there are elements of the imagined inside your experience of the "real" world — rock, bone, wood, ice — and elements of the real — not the metaphorical, but the actual thing itself — inside stories and tales and dreams. You write a sentence about a hawk's swooping on a swallow and have no sooner finished it and looked up than you see feathers falling from the sky.

But still, for the most part, each resides in its own country: the real and the imagined; the actual and the possible. And it's important to keep the path, the trail, between the two open; important to keep the brush at least somewhat beaten back, to allow relative ease of passage between the two. Which brings us finally to the notion of why the daily doing of it is important — the writing of fiction, if that's what you do, and to a lesser extent, the reading of it. You've got to keep the grass worn down between the two worlds, or you'll get lost as shit; and sometimes you get a little disoriented, even with daily passages and explorations of the two further territories. You can't help but remember what Faulkner is alleged to have said when asked whether he wrote daily or only when the inspiration hit him. It's said he replied that he wrote only when the inspiration came, but that he made sure it came every morning at ten o'clock sharp when he sat down at his desk.

Another of these kinds of smart sayings I remember is one in which some prolific writer was asked how he'd managed to publish so many books. He said that it was quite easy: a page a day equaled a book a year. I've been working on my first novel for over twelve years now, and such statements give me encouragement and remind me that it's not just books that are important but also the sentences within them. It should be an obvious realization, but its implications become clear only when you do the math. The present draft of my novel is about 1,400 pages, which parses out to approximately one paragraph a day over those twelve years. The novel is, of course (I hope), nothing so boring as one paragraph from each day of my life over that twelve-year span, but rather a paragraph per day of a parallel and imagined life — which, after a dozen years of daily entering into and exiting from it, can make a writer increasingly a little goofy and also a bit tired, as if he or she were working one long stretch of double overtime, or had two families, or two lives.

We write fiction, I think, for very nearly the same reasons that we read it: to sharpen our senses and to regenerate those dead or dying places and parts within us where the imagination has been lost or is trying to be lost. Pine trees lose their needles every three years, and bears enter the earth, the dream-world, and float in sleep for five or six months at a time, but we humans are fragile and almost hairless, shivering on the earth, and our cells are dying and being reborn daily; we must eat often, and sleep nightly, pulled out each day by the sun. Almost all of our rhythms are compressed into parameters of one single earth's rotation. It is the rhythm into which we have evolved; it fits our bodies, physically, and it fits our minds and our imaginations. We can accumulate the days and their imaginings and then craft and create things beyond a day's work, but the days are our basic building blocks — a day's work is like a paragraph. To leave too many gaps in the thing being crafted or imagined, to work too erratically, is to run the risk, I'd think, of weakening with gaps and absences of rhythm the foundation and structure of the thing one is attempting to make real, or attempting to make be felt as deeply as if it *were* real.

That famous advice of Hemingway's is repeated often, about how a writer should leave a day's work slightly unfinished and at a point where he or she knows something of what will be in the next paragraph, to help facilitate the ease with which the rhythm may be resumed the next day. The descent of the bathysphere, vertically, or the morning trek into the woods, horizontally. The passage from here to there. The practice of staying supple rather than becoming brittle.

The daily doing of it is nothing less than a way to rage against constriction and entrapment, fragmentation and isolation, the poisonous seeds of our monstrous success in terms of our biomass and our effect upon the world, but at this cost: the erosion of the individual, the erosion of the specialist, the unique, the crafted.

The stories we tell in fiction — stories of warning or celebration, stories of illustrative possibility — are important. When the shit really hits the fan for a civilization, artists can become more important than ever, in helping to bend a culture back to another direction, away from the impending and onrushing brick wall.

I believe this. I believe that by crossing the path back and forth enough times, as if weaving something, fiction can become as real as iron or wood; that it can rust, rot, or burn; that it can nurture and nourish, or inflame. I believe that it can decide actions and shape movements, sculpt us more securely or intelligently (as well as more passionately) into the world, just as the continents on whose backs we are riding sculpt our cities, towns, and cultures.

I believe fiction can heal things, and I think we would all agree, now more than ever, that we can use some healing, and that we need it daily.

Phobia and Composition

RICK MOODY AND
MARGARET F. M. DAVIS

<table>
<tr><td>1</td><td>2</td></tr>
</table>

My Account: I always hated swimming lessons. This was on Weed Beach (in Darien, Connecticut), on the Long Island Sound. In recollection, Weed Beach feels oily, overcrowded, hemmed in symbolically by its proximity to New York Harbor and by the crowds from Rowayton and Darien who sought refuge there. I took after Mom's dad,

My Mom's account: Thirty-five years after the fact, that period of your language acquisition is recalled as a swirl of housepainting, house sale, being pregnant with your younger brother, your paternal grandparents moving from Boston to the area, your father quite ill with mononucleosis. Trying to be a "good" wife and mother to three children at age

F. M. Flynn — publisher of the *New York Daily News* — in some ways: left-handedness, redheadedness, tendency to sunburn. Thus, at the beach, I was always lacquered with various solvents to keep me from burning, and I was always burning anyhow. And then peeling. My brother nicknamed me Glue Factory.

But the worst part of the beach was swimming lessons. My sister and brother, on either side of me, were gifted swimmers, would spend hours in the flat calm of the Sound splashing and paddling. Not so with me. During my penultimate lesson (as I reconstruct it), with some teenage guy on holiday from a boarding-school or Ivy League swim team, it was decided that it was past time for me *to learn to float.* However, I was smart enough to know that rocks sank, that naval vessels plunged to the inky bottom of the seven seas, that only necromancy or supernatural powers would en-

twenty-six, a good sister, a good daughter (and daughter-in-law), was pretty exhausting.

No comes to mind as a possible first word: when you were about nineteen months and I was boiling everyone's underwear every day (Dwight had contracted a staph infection, so we all had to lather up with special soap EVERY day and go to elaborate lengths to prevent further infection . . . all this, and only one bathroom in the house), the enforcement of strict routine was stressful for us all. During this time, you developed the first of many bouts of strep throat, and around 2:00 A.M. you had a 104.5-degree fever. The doctor told me to give you alcohol sponge baths, since you would throw up the liquid aspirin. Never have I felt so much like a torturer, while you cried and cried and quivered, saying, "No more, no more!"

It was soon apparent that books were tremendously appealing to you, and I would put

able a person to traverse the surface. Furthermore, the basic human trust required for this (or other aquatic operations) was, as I saw it, unwise.

Nonetheless, the blond instructor persuaded me to lie out straight in his arms, as though I were an offering to Poseidon, and then, according to his secret knowledge, he began to remove his large hands, inch by inch, claiming that *if I held in a deep breath*, I would float upon the lazy swells. I would bob.

This was ludicrous. This was entirely contraindicated by *my personal investigations of the physics of suburban environments, the physics of tennis balls and leaf piles and rock-skipping and aggressive retrievers*, and so forth, and I began to scream and to clutch at the guy like some *Titanic* rescuee, though the water would barely lap at my waist. I fled back to my towel and would swim for no man or woman for a good five years thereafter.

Meredith on one side of me and you on the other and read most often from a big anthology of nursery rhymes and stories (I can show you the book). She would become bored after about fifteen minutes, but you would sit and listen as long as I had time to continue.

Somewhere around nursery-school age you liked to pretend that you were a different boy with another name (I can't remember the name). During this early period (and for some years to come), you deferred to Meredith on most things. I was thankful when she was in school all day, since it gave you some space from her always being "in charge."

Since we lived so close to Long Island Sound, we were around the water a lot in the summer. As you got older, you played at the edge but had no interest in getting your face in the water or learning strokes. You were pretty thin and got blue fast . . . who would find that fun? But later, when boats

In the single digits, I was sick a lot. I don't remember much about it, except the feeling of having two ear infections at once (this you don't easily forget), and, later, an Easter weekend in bed, after a tonsillectomy.

In general, I wasn't good with strangers. I avoided social events. My parents devised exercises for me, to improve my mettle. E.g., my mother sent me into a dry cleaner's in town to pick up my dad's shirts. The symbolism here is rich: *entrusted with the uniform of Dad's capitalist endeavor.* Moreover, I always really loved the smell of dry-cleaning chemicals. As well as the naphthalene of my grandmother's enormous closets (she had already confined herself to her bedroom by the time I was old enough to know her), in the pristine corridors where her things were stored in the house she shared with my grandfather.

Anyway, I went into the dry were the activity, your dad and I agreed that your learning to swim was absolutely vital. I sensed that you wanted to learn, but fear overtook you; after your uncle Jack died, we all went to Fort Lauderdale with my father for a ten-day February vacation . . . you were four and a half; you may remember flying on the private jet. I think your dad was mortified by how terrified you were of the water. Even your grandfather couldn't coax you into the pool for more than a few minutes.

When you were about five and we moved to Ironwood Lane, we met some people nearby whose daughter was giving swimming lessons. We signed both you and Dwight up for lessons twice a week. It was a generally chilly summer, with many rainy days. The lessons weren't really consistent (and in truth I think the teenager probably wasn't a very good teacher). Dwight made steady progress, but the girl told us

cleaner's, and it was forested with shrink-wrapped garments in a way I've always found inspiring, and I was feeling somewhat hopeful, until I saw *the dry cleaner himself* — an older man, in the predictably starchy professional uniform of the early sixties — thronged with brusque and affluent women looking for restitution in the matter of spots or stains or shrinkages.

I was paralyzed. Unable to proceed with my important mission. I suppose the specific problem had to do with *making my needs clear to this benevolent dry cleaner*, viz., making sure that my father's shirts were starched, proffering the ten, accepting the change. But surrounded by so many clamoring housewives, this was impossible for me. I slunk back outside to the car, made a weak excuse, and was reprimanded by my mother and induced to return tearfully to the store, with her, to stand patiently while the process of ex-

she was stumped as to how to get you over your sense of panic when you were asked to float along without a board. You complained when we talked about it, in that way that kids will, looking off into the distance and shuffling their feet. . . .

It was sad, but as far as your dad was concerned, you weren't allowed to quit until a day when he and I came to watch a lesson. You went into the water, made some tentative attempts to follow instructions, and then really got hysterical. I think I pulled you out, wrapped you in a towel, and we cut the whole lesson short, your dad then saying you wouldn't be coming back. I have a memory of him in a black mood in the car, driving home, saying, "What a waste of money!"

You also seemed to catch any germ that was floating about, and gradually it seemed that your tonsils and adenoids were the main target, becom-

change (legal tender for shirts, folded, in brown wrapping paper) took place, amid virtuosic pleasantries of the sort that I would never master. *See how easy it is?*

(This phobia reappeared in my twenties, when, in Hoboken, the only dry cleaner near me was given to a repartee overstuffed with flatteries. I'd beg my girlfriend to go in there for me, was utterly intractable about it, and in this way fell again into one of my many novel anxieties: *fear of dry cleaners.*)

Meanwhile, I was devouring the F. W. Dixon oeuvre. *The Hardy Boys and the Sunken Treasure,* etc. I also liked Encyclopedia Brown, who, like his coevals the Hardys, spent his pubescence solving neighborhood mysteries. I could never actually identify the criminals in these thrillers myself, and I didn't particularly give a shit who was responsible anyhow, but I admired the inventiveness of the crimes. I wanted to

ing chronically enlarged and swollen.

By the end of that kindergarten year, you had missed just about half the school days, and the doctor scheduled you twice for your tonsillectomy in the spring, but every time the date approached you'd get another cold and the date would have to be postponed. (I should interject here that it was in March of this year that my mother died, just eighteen months after Uncle Jack. She'd been hospitalized for about two weeks, and I'd been driving down to Westchester every other day.) Finally, the doctor said the only way to break this cycle was to hospitalize you for three to four days, load you up with medication, and do the surgery on the fifth day.

You couldn't seem to understand why all this was necessary, and you were very nervous about going. The first day went pretty well, but you got very annoyed at having to stay in bed. The nurses wouldn't allow you

be Encyclopedia Brown, of course, but I was actually getting pretty lousy grades in school. I got an X on Miss Rydell's history test in fourth grade, an original, new, *lowest possible grade* (she made clear to me), far lower even than the usual D. Mostly, my scholastic ambition was to avoid the anger of my teachers, and thereby the anger of my parents. Miss Rydell, however, was from Texas and had a thermonuclear temper (which she had visited upon my sister before me).

I loved television. I would watch reruns of old comedies all day long, and was also especially attracted to anemic science-fiction programming like *Lost in Space* and *Star Trek*. I was busy watching television, in fact, while my parents divorced. I remember nothing about their parting — beyond a particularly forlorn closed door in the living room one night, or a harsh exchange to walk around. You'd ask about when you were leaving, and I'd tell you that you'd be coming home right after the operation. I recall being agitated at not being permitted to walk you down to the surgery. . . .

You were in awful pain when we brought you home. Our job was to do just about anything to keep you from crying a lot, because this would just irritate your throat more, making the pain worse. During that summer we bought the Ironwood Lane house and we were really preoccupied with that transition, which I believed would solve everyone's problems (that's how stupidly naive I was, at age thirty).

Physically, you improved remarkably. You certainly seemed happier. You were very successful at school and had some good friends. I still sensed that you were fearful of the rough-and-tumble that most of your peers (and your

on my father's sailboat — and I guess that's because it was essentially redundant (to my knowledge, my parents never once embraced in front of me). Furthermore, I was oblivious to the division of their property, and the Mexican legal proceedings, because I was preoccupied with much more traumatic news concealed within this calamity: *We were going to move.*

This was heartrending not only because I was sick at the idea of walking into a classroom full of strangers, but also because I had recently begun *going steady* with Susan Ward. In proof thereof, I had kissed the sleeve of her denim jacket, its smudged and musty arm registering indelibly upon the scroll of my lifelong infatuations. We played four-square together. We spoke awkwardly and hastily in the shadows of oaks. Eventually, like a consumptive nineteenth-century lover, I told her of *my immi-*

brother) readily enjoyed. There was a subtle but perceptible undercurrent of anxiety. There were nightmares and sleepwalking (in that scary way where you couldn't seem to hear us talking to you but you managed to walk downstairs). When we carefully woke you, you were terrified and disoriented.

As you learned to read, you also learned to write with frightening ease and lucidity. We considered you extremely bright and destined for great things, as long as your "stamina" held up. Simmering in the back of my mind was Gramma's story of her brother Albion, who had been overseas in World War I, and when he came back was constantly ill and kept to his room for the rest of his brief life. In short, I was concerned that a certain hypersensitivity (and propensity to cry easily) would handicap you.

Your father and I knew that

nent departure from Darien forever, believing that this would immortalize our bond. It didn't register much. However, I was happy to find in my limitless grief that James Taylor had written his morose "Fire and Rain" about her: *Suzanne, the plants they may put an end to you.* I didn't know what this botanical and eschatological riddle meant, of course, and the name of James's beloved was only an approximation of the name of my angelic Susan Ward, yet I believed, based upon this evidence, that my loss, my dislocation, *was as big as the Billboard Top Forty.*

I started at a new school. And then, a year after, I started at another. And we moved. And we moved again. And we moved yet again. And again. By the end of this hot streak of suburban addresses, wherein the Allied Van lines and their x-large corrugated cartons became routine, I became so disoriented that I planned my associations around the in-

you three would pick up on signals of trouble between the two of us, so by some unwritten agreement we simply didn't talk much, except late at night in red-faced whispers. We learned each other's "hot" buttons and also learned when to use this ammunition to best effect. We all know what happens when people suffer this too long: they become numb. What we did was go out A LOT. And drink A LOT. Your dad spent many evenings in New York City. Since he was mildly depressed most of the time, I became so as well.

I'm sure you all intuited the tension, though Meredith and Dwight say they never suspected any problems (I can't remember when or how the subject came up in the last five years, but it did). Here's my oblique prose, trying not to say that I think I was more psychologically preoccupied with myself than with monitoring the impact of a gathering storm. There was no trust between

evitability of leaving. In eighth grade, at the infernal Saxe Junior High School of New Canaan, local citadel of social repression and conformism, I actually kept a calendar *on which I counted off the days until we would pack up anew.* I started counting in the hundreds, crossing off the days, all the way down to zero.

I gave up trying to talk to people. I gave up trying, in speech, to address the spot where my childhood melancholy — whether it was situational or congenital — had formed itself into a little keloid bauble. I suppose this indicates a predestined selection in the choice between spoken word and silent scrawl, between *parole et langue*. I had phobias. I had conversation fear. I thought of conversations as the places where people stuck in their penknives. I trusted few. I kept my mouth shut. And I practiced writing. Writing was about improbably languid and slothful tempos, about relax-

your dad and me, on any level. How can I assess what impact that had on you three? At this point there weren't any obvious indicators of your adult difficulties . . . as best I can see.

Changing schools: this whole period after the divorce was really chaotic for me, too. I tried and tried and tried to find a way to get your dad to move out, so that your lives wouldn't be so additionally disrupted, but since he thought I really had "lost my mind," right up to the day we signed the papers I'm sure he thought I would relent and remain with him. His constant refrain was, "You're going to ruin the children. . . . This is all a totally selfish move on your part. I never have, never will want, a divorce. Go ahead, have an affair, just don't break the partnership." Even now, not many days go by that I am free of this guilt. How to put a good face on it? When I felt like the spaceman, Keir Dullea, sailing through the

ation and torpor, about meditative silence, about stillness, about music — like the music of my mom, in our mostly empty house on Valley Road in New Canaan, plunging into the sad opening movement of the "Moonlight Sonata" on an old upright.

One of the last things my family did together was go to see 2001: A Space Odyssey. Must have been at the Darien Playhouse (what did they think of it there?). The film was so beyond me, at eight years old, so disturbing, so baroque in its exposure of complex ideas, that it singlehandedly created in me the ambition to use my imagination: HAL's struggle against the astronauts, those guys in the Cro-Magnon culottes juggling animal femurs, the Pan Am moon shuttle. I pestered my parents with questions on the way home: *If there's an edge to the universe, what's beyond the edge? If there was a moment*

black void in a tiny, soundless capsule?

You did have trouble making new friends after that time, but it didn't appear to bother Dwight in the least. . . . His troubles were delayed. At this point, I also realized I'd better get some additional income, and that meant I wasn't around as much. Still, you continued to perform in school in an above-average fashion. I'll mail you all the relevant report cards. I don't remember any major blowups, beyond your forgetting to let me know where you were going and when you'd be home (in those days, one could allow ten- and twelve-year-olds to bike around a two-mile radius without worrying that they might be kidnaped or molested). Of course, there was a lot of back-and-forth between my house and your dad's.

With your writing, our aim was to expand vocabulary and fluency by encouraging as much reading as you would

in which the universe was created, what was before that moment? Other kids in Fairfield County had the Presbyterian Church, or the Church of the Pop Warner Football League, but I was baptized in the murky font of the imagination, and I'm grateful for it. Once I was through with my Ur-texts, with Kubrick's film, with *The Odyssey*, with *Alice's Adventures through the Looking Glass*, I was never going to law school. And thus Banana Flair first smudges ruled notebook paper, in 10/71, or thereabouts, in this genuine excerpt from my juvenilia: "I *really* wonder about dinosaurs. I know about millions of kinds. Ones that are 50 ft. high. I wonder if I'm the biggest machine in the world, a curiosity machine, one big hunk of it" (italics in original).

Afraid of strangers, afraid of telephones, afraid of strangers on telephones, un-

happily tolerate. You were in a family where this was as natural as breathing. Books were positively revered by my parents, too. When I was about three or four years old, a major house renovation took place, and during that work, large bookcases were added everywhere — in the old living room, in my room, and in Jack's new room. People read all the time. Someone was always reading TO me or reading WITH me. It seems to have been my major occupation, as I look back on the years before age nine or ten. No matter what excessive pile of Christmas or birthday presents came my way, books were always included. But I don't remember being able to talk about my reactions with anyone in the family, and perhaps just barely, superficially, with my best pals.

Anyway, the stage was set. Your father and I concentrated more on Meredith's reading because she was having so much trouble with concentration and

comfortable on airplanes, in crowds, afraid of public speaking, afraid of open spaces, of confinement, of women, daylight, heights, *people*, and so on. Afraid.

I came to write, therefore, because I was too timid to be a raconteur, because the giddy freedom of imagination (as it is rendered in language) was best and most comfortably practiced, for me, alone, away from the tempests of schoolyard bluster. I wondered why I was made this way, sure, when the contrary seemed the norm for other people, and it was on this question that I first concentrated my energies, as writing often compels itself toward *unspeakable* (Donald Barthelme's word) interrogatives, things that can't, inside the Foul Pole of everyday life, really be *said*, or are ignored because of the kind of responsibilities they entail, as those words *I Love You* are pretty hard to say (I don't say them

focus. But you would very quietly pick up many of the books she had and polish them off. In your case, I'm reminded of an article on the pianist Yvgeny Kissin, who was described as only becoming really animated and dynamic when he was playing, having spontaneously learned music before he could talk. I think you learned that exquisite pleasure of abandoning oneself to a fictitious world at a very early age. . . .

By the time you were perhaps eight or nine years old, you spoke of wanting to be a writer. . . . Since I couldn't get my own act together in this area, I was determined to do what I could, at an early stage of your growth, to motivate and supply what "tools" I could discover that might help you see this as a definite path.

I think I've about exhausted what memory I have on this topic. I feel awkward and embarrassed about trying to describe your shyness . . . strange!

enough to the writer in the next column over, for example), until eventually the process of considering these questions is itself enough, as distinct from the entrapment of answers — leaving behind, in the sheer music of questions, in medias res, as Montaigne says, "some idea of my habits and opinions."

Which is not to say that I don't see you as being reclusive and depressive: I just don't understand where "shy" fits in. Are shy people phobic? Was it the alcoholism and its concomitant handicaps that make you shy? You ask how I recognize you, then . . . as a beloved son, in whom resides a lot of my own sad history.

Secret Agent

DENIS JOHNSON

I'M REMEMBERING A TIME in Chicago. Down around Jefferson Street, some ways below the Loop. I couldn't even guess how far below now, twenty-one, -two, -three years later. This was the very bad wino district around 4:00 A.M. People without soul or spirit slept against walls or right in the gutter, as they'd been warned they might someday if they kept on . . . and they'd kept on. This dark morning I'd come here to find work in the day-labor gangs the state employment people formed on weekdays, but I sensed I'd be living here, too, someday, and I observed electrically and sadly my future all around me, people with dull faces nodding like toys and fingering the tatters of their clothes and exploring their lips with their tongues. Soon one place opened for business in the neighborhood, a giant tavern with big windows and no name — just a white marquee running the whole length of the building, reading SHOT AND A BEER 25¢. I recall it now, this place, as an island of horrific light. It was illuminated inside with fluorescent ceiling lamps and jammed with people who moved around as if they were all on fire. I didn't go in. A bum woke up in the gutter right beside where I stood looking from across the street. He felt in the waist of his pants and came up with a pint bottle, half full. He tipped it up, and it gurgled steadily until he'd emptied it all down into him. I was only twenty-four or -five, but already I could have told you how important it tasted. And the people who kissed the feet of Christ could have told you how it tasted. I saw everything there in the gutter — the terror and the promise. Later I spent the morning in the smoky Day Labor Division with better than a hundred men who'd learned how not to move, learned how to stay beautifully still and let their lives hurt them, white men with gray faces and black men with yellow eyes. I worked the rest of the week in a factory without ever comprehending exactly what was manufactured there, and at night I'd get drunk and shut myself in a phone booth and call the woman in Minnesota who'd broken my heart. The calls were full of laughter and dreams because I was happy to be working and even happier to be drunk. Eventually she relented, said she'd join me in Chicago, in the streets, by the lake, in the parks — it seemed as if this city had been built and had waited its whole history for somebody feeling as good as me to step into it and make it live. What was I going to do with all of this? Where could I make my monument to these simple triumphs and these complicated sorrows?

I heard on the BBC today a news report from a torn-up African nation, and I recognized the reporter's voice — I met her down there some years back. As I listened to her describe the deteriorating situation in those eerie surroundings, I remembered how much she enjoyed being in the thick of things. It occurred to me that I know what it's like at the hotel she's staying in, because I've stayed there, too. I'm acquainted with her favorite cab driver, the one she uses all the time in that town, and I've been to the U.S. Embassy there, which she describes now as pocked with bullet holes. I've seen many U.S. embassies pocked by bullet holes, and in fact I cowered behind the embassy in the country just east of the one she's now reporting from one afternoon while it was attacked by rebels, and I heard their bullets whizzing by as they tried to pock my head with holes. Thinking about all this, it occurs to me how many of my most boyish boyhood dreams have come true.

I wanted to be a Spy, a Secret Agent. To get in undetected, to deal with inscrutable forces in exotic worlds, and get out unscathed. Then I became too old to allow myself to want that anymore. I required myself to tell people I wanted something less fantastic. I told them I wanted to be a writer.

And eventually I became a free-lance writer traveling to these unhappy places full of danger and chaos. The others, the real journalists, the regularly employed, they sneer at me. I'm a cheap adventurer. I'm taking up space among people who have to be there. But in my story they're a pack of lemmings who don't care about the truth or the feeling or the sights and sounds or the faces and the voices — only about the stock images, the stock phrases, the news that's making everybody tired.

I'm not here to get the news. I'm making a story. I get in any way I can, and I stand in a burning city, revolted and ecstatic, inhaling the dust of old murders, the stench of corpses, not just satisfying naive childhood yearnings for adventure but pursuing some deeper vision of howling chaos — engaging in the same pursuit, in fact, as these maniac boys destroying everything with their weapons. This is what I'm here to do — to be one character in the middle of it all, a person both exonerated and ashamed.

And all I have to do to gain entry to this world is claim that I'm a writer. And the only one I have to convince of that is myself.

As I came to accept my role as profoundly different from theirs, instantly the other journalists began to tolerate and even to welcome me. I'm here only to enjoy one of the great freedoms, that of having no choice but to trust the moment and everyone in it; I'm here to taste the giddy joy in understanding that any other moment is utterly inaccessible, and that this one belongs to these strangers who may help you or kill you, these Third World guerrillas or jungle denizens or this character in sunglasses who resembles Peter Lorre and claims to have powerful friends in the Junta. . . . I'm making a story. And I get to be in it.

I stopped in for breakfast at Jean's Home Plate Café this morning, a little reluctantly, because Jean had complained that she was going blind the last time I was in there, and a biopsy was scheduled, something about her left eye. I've always liked her, and she's always had scraps for my dog, Harold, and insisted on going out to my truck herself to feed him, but now, if she were truly ill, like very much so, like with fatal cancer, our friendship would deepen beyond her fondness for Harold and my admiration for her biscuits and gravy. So I went to the Home Plate this morning not only for breakfast, but also to pass through the doorway of a mild form of fear and greet her. But her son was cooking, not Jean. "Where's Jean?" I said. "She passed away last night," he said. It wasn't her left eye but her lungs that killed her. He told me about the details. The guy beside me pointed out the telephone and the electric fan he'd bought for Jean. I also had details, for instance, about how she fed my dog. I almost turned down the breakfast, but her boy was there to cook in her honor, and so in her honor I ate. We talked about elk hunting and about Fort Lewis outside of

Tacoma, Washington, and other things — you know how it is, all those universes going on while one blanks out. It seemed strange to suddenly remember my girlfriend two hours earlier with her little boy, wrapping a piece of tape backward around her hand to sop up the albino dog hairs off his black Dracula suit. It's Halloween. Yellow leaves lay all over the dark pavements as I drove home to write this. It's what I do. Jean's son is a cook. So he cooked today. The children will be children, the people will be people, all things even down to the smallest will be as they are this day after Jean's death.

The Lousy Rider

ELIZABETH GILBERT

━━

1

WHEN I LIVED OUT WEST, I knew a cowboy named Hank. I admired him a great deal. He was a drunk, and he was belligerent, and when he spoke it was mostly through curses. He could not really articulate himself otherwise. For instance, he called every inanimate object "the bitch," as in "Give me the bitch," instead of "Please pass me the sugar." I once brought Hank a thermos of coffee while he was saddling his horse at dawn. He set the thermos on the ground, where he kept accidentally tripping on it and kicking it over.

"Fuck!" he finally shouted in frustration. "I'll just drink the bitch!"

I liked Hank so much. I was in Wyoming because I wanted to be a professional cowgirl and because I wanted to be a tough character. I wanted to be just as tough as Hank, so I hung around him all the time, imitating him.

"Fuck!" I'd shout, at the slightest provocation. "Fuck! Bitch!"

Hank wasn't given to tender moments of reflection, but one afternoon we were riding our horses along a mountain pass and — quite out of nowhere — he said to me, "You're a really good rider, you know."

I was so pleased. I blushed, in fact, because it was the best compliment I had ever received, and from the most unlikely source.

"Are you serious, Hank? You really think so?"

"I wish I was as good a rider as you," he said. "You're just a natural."

Now, Hank was one of those people who rode before they walked, so this was really saying something. This was actually the best moment of my life.

"That means so much to me, Hank," I said.

Hank was quiet for a long time, and then he said, "It's true. I wish I could express myself the way you do."

There was a long beat.

Then I asked, "Sorry, did you say that I was a good rider? Or did you say that I was a good *writer?*"

Hank laughed. "I said *writer!*" he shouted. "Fuck! I said you were a good goddamn *writer!*"

I was devastated by this misunderstanding — I already knew I could write; I wanted to *ride* — but to Hank it was a major laugh riot. "You really thought I wanted to ride like you? You really thought *I* would call *you* a natural rider? Ha!"

"Ha," I said, weakly.

"You're a lousy rider," he said. "But you're a goddamn good writer."

Not immediately thereafter, but very soon thereafter, I gave up on being a tough cowgirl and moved back East, where I began writing again. We are, after all, what we are. And sometimes, when we are trying to find a calling, it is helpful to confirm that we are not really very good at anything else.

2

My husband — who is not a writer — dreamed one night that he was one. In this dream he was a journalist on assignment, and his job was to cover a massive convention of police officers. The convention was held in a major arena, and when my husband the "journalist" stepped inside, he saw uniformed cops everywhere. He took out his notebook and tried to think of a good lead for his article. He thought and he thought. And then he wrote this sentence: "I walked into a sea of blue."

In his dream, my husband knew this was a lousy, cornball lead, but he couldn't think of anything better. He stared and stared at the cops, but this was the very best he could come up with. *I walked into a sea of blue.* He gazed at his notebook, depressed. Still asleep, my husband had a big revelation.

Gosh, he thought. I could never be a writer.

Now, I kept a diary as a child. I started it in second grade, and I kept it up with pretty good discipline. For the most part, my diary was a dry chronicle of my schedule ("Today I went to piano lessons. Yesterday I went to gymnastics"), but sometimes an event would occur that was actually worth *writing* about, and then I would rise to the occasion. One winter's day, my parents took me sledding after an ice storm, and it was very exciting and it really got my seven-year-old pulse racing, so I wrote about it in my diary. I described my sledding adventure this way: "Let me tell you, it was like riding a Thoroughbred that just got stung by a bee."

I remember writing that sentence. I remember sitting back and reading it over, gazing at my diary. I remember my revelation, too, which went something like this: Hey, that's not bad at all.

3

There are some excellent writers in my family, and everyone is a good storyteller. My great-grandfather was the best. He once wrote a letter to my uncle beginning, "I have just received a missive from that well-known illiterate your father, whose only use of the mother tongue is to order more hay for the pathetic assemblage of quadrupeds he insists on calling horses."

He could really turn a phrase, and so could his children. His only daughter was my grandmother, who was a famous wit (she once told me that Poughkeepsie was the Indian name for "Place Where Vassar College Is," and said of an irritatingly upbeat neighbor, "Every time that goddamn woman sees me in the grocery store, she has an orgasm"). My father was her favorite child, and she indulged him to an extreme because he was such a wisecracker. When he got married, my grandmother told my mom, "I should have laughed at him less and beat him more. I'm terribly sorry, Carol, but he's all yours now."

Then I was born, and I soon started telling stories, too. When I was in fourth grade, I came home from my first day of school and did such a riotous imitation of my flaky young hippie schoolteacher that my dad had to wipe tears of laughter from his eyes and blow his nose into his napkin. I grotesquely exaggerated every detail of this perfectly decent woman while my parents laughed and laughed, egging me on. It evidently never occurred to them that they should try to instill in me some respect for my elders. God bless them, they just thought I was entertaining.

Now they are proud of me because I am officially a writer. Despite all the good writers in my family, nobody else had ever done it officially, and this is all a pretty big deal. When I called my father at work to tell him that my first short story had been accepted for publication by a famous national magazine, he shut his office door and wept. He said, "I'm so proud of you! And to think that I knew you when you were just a babe in swaddling clothes!"

4

When my husband was a teenager, he wanted to be a magician. He studied magic on his own and learned how to do goofy tricks with handkerchiefs and doves. He performed for Girl Scouts and nursing-home inhabitants in his small Ohio town. He used to tell me stories about this, and I thought they were the funniest and saddest stories in the world. He showed me pictures of himself, all skinny and redheaded, brandishing his magic cane, and he was so earnest in the photographs that it would make me laugh and cry to see them. I think the laughing-crying stories are the best kind, so I became consumed with the notion of writing about a gawky teenage kid from Ohio who desperately wants to be a magician. I thought the whole topic was beautifully tragic.

I had been working on that story for a few months when I ran into an old friend, and she got to telling me a story herself. She told me about how her father's beloved cat had disappeared several months earlier. Apparently this event caused her father to lose his mind with grief, and he eventually became convinced that his nice neighbors had stolen his pet. He went utterly mad with delusion and paranoia. He stalked and threatened the nice neighbors for months and finally attacked the nice neighbors, and then had to be hauled away to a mental ward. In the end, though, someone discovered that the nice neighbors really *had* had the man's cat the whole time. They actually had stolen it. Nobody knew why. Too late this information emerged, because my friend's father's life had already been ruined.

An interesting story. A true story. And some freakish neuron in my system told me to combine it with my story of the gawky teenage magician. The freakish neuron had a sweet, reassuring voice that said, "Trust me, just do it." But by this point, the gawky-teenage-magician story had taken some strange twists of its own. The gawky teenager had became a brilliant middle-aged Hungarian immigrant who — though not a magician himself — owned a magic club and was obsessed with the lost arts of skilled European conjurers. Also, he was a murderer and an ex-con. He lived in a big house with his daughter, who was a talent-free aspiring magician, and with his brother-in-law, who was North America's greatest living sleight-of-hand artist. What had happened to the skinny kid from Ohio? I do not know, but he was nowhere to be seen.

So I gave the Hungarian immigrant a cat, had the cat disappear, and had the Hungarian become convinced that the nice neighbors had stolen the cat. The Hungarian went mad, and stalked and threatened the nice neighbors, and had to be hauled off to a mental ward. And the nice neighbors really *did* have the cat the whole time. Surprise! And I worked day and night on that story, but it just wouldn't come together. The stolen cat made no sense. The story made no sense. Why would a murderous Hungarian magic enthusiast lose his mind over a cat? Why would anyone? I wished I had never listened to the freakish neuron in the first place.

And then one day I was sitting in the New York Public Library, struggling with my work, when it struck me. I sat up in my seat and exclaimed loudly, "It's not a cat! It's a rabbit!" Of course it was a rabbit! It had to be a rabbit! What animal would be most treasured by a family of magicians? What is the traditional pet of magic? Not a stupid cat, but a rabbit. A rabbit! A rabbit! A rabbit!

I really wrote that bitch then.

The action all fell into place, into perfect order, and it was sad and funny, just as I had hoped it would be, back when it was still a story about a gawky teenage magician from Ohio, but it was *better* this way. The lost rabbit was a beautiful tragedy; the Hungarian's madness was heartbreaking; the neighbor's betrayal sickened the conscience. To me, the ending felt so correct and so appropriate that it seemed to bend over backward to kiss the beginning. How excited was I? I was so excited that I almost started barking in the New York Public Library. I almost started chasing my own tail because — let me tell you — it really *was* like riding a Thoroughbred that had just gotten stung by a bee. To write like that? Even for one hour? It really *was* like pulling a rabbit out of a hat. It really *was* like walking into a sea of blue.

Writing

WILLIAM VOLLMANN

> The way of thinking that you reproach is the sole
> consolation of my life.
>
> MARQUIS DE SADE,
> prison letter to his wife

I WRITE THIS BY HAND, with swollen and aching fingers.
Sometimes the ache oozes up to my shoulders, sometimes only to
my wrists; once or twice I've felt it in my back. Poor posture, they
say, or "repetitive stress injury," or possibly carpal tunnel syn-
drome; when for a price of five hundred or a thousand dollars they
administered electric shocks to my hands and arms to determine
the relative health of my nerve sheaths (the current made my
limbs jerk, in obedience to the highest laws of galvanics, and a
premedical spectator laughed), I was told that my case was either
moderate or severe. Subject to respites occasioned by voyages or
stints of block-printing, I have woken up with pain, and slept with
pain, my sweetly constant mistress, for seven years now, ever since

my thirtieth birthday. While there have been times when I could not close my hand around a water glass or turn the pages of a book, mostly this pain is an unobtrusive companion, a chronic irrelevance when I am loving my work, a chronic warning when I am not, in either case acknowledged and respected for having so steadfastly guested me, but rarely listened to: pain gives always the same advice, the wisdom of prudes and legislators, to stay within the limits. This pain of mine certainly does. Pain's advice is also that of my own heart, which used to tell me when I was in elementary school that if I could only escape the chalkboards and inky desks, running away into sunny fields of milkweed, I would find my destiny. If I weren't writing, who knows what brighter life I would find? My pain respects me, being in no wise related to the shouting tyrant endured by puking heroin addicts in withdrawal, burned children, soldiers gassed or shot in the stomach. When I think of them, I love my pain more for being so undemanding, for letting me do almost everything I want to do. Yes, I worry sometimes about future damage, having met old ranch hands whose hands were but blackened hay-baling hooks. Writing is bad for me physically, without a doubt, but what would I do if I stopped?

The nights of sleepless excitement are almost reduced to memories now. They possess me but once or twice a year. I no longer feel, as I did at seventeen or twenty, that I am an ecstatic vessel bubbling over with words — words gushing from my hands like sparks, forming at my will or beyond my will in armies upon paper and screen, the letterforms themselves beautiful, the combinations of words likewise beautiful to eye, ear, lips, and heart. Now I feel instead that the tale is a block of darkness that I chip away at deliberately until I begin to glimpse tiny stars within; I seek to unveil as many of these as I can, leaving just the right amount of darkness behind them to make them shine the brighter by contrast, protecting them from the day. I labor where before I played. In part this change is due to the pain in my hands. But another reason is that what once came easily would now come *too* easily. The thrill of writing, as of pure animal sexuality, derives from newness. Following newness faithfully must bring us farther and farther out of school, until the milkweeds loom around us. The difficult way is the way that I want to go. I write less and less for "success," though for financial reasons I will always try to write for publication. I write to discover the universe and to discover myself. My writing is thus, for me, a deeply selfish act. Very often, what I discover infects me with sadness, even with anguish. This voyage that I am taking into the block of darkness leaves me night by night more alone.

Example: I am on the verge of concluding a long essay on violence that it has taken me sixteen years to write. My three American commercial publishers have all turned it down, mostly unread. I am sad about this to the extent that the middling advance (thirty thousand dollars, say, spread over two or three years, if I was lucky) and the minor increase in "recognition" that publication might have brought me would have benefitted my career — that is, enabled me to continue writing in comfort. That is why I will try some academic presses now. I am also sad because I love books as objects, and it would be a pleasure for me to hold my finished work in my hands. I am otherwise indifferent. I am fortunate enough to make money writing elsewhere. If the manuscript remains unpublished in my lifetime, I will entomb it somewhere, out of respect for what I learned in the writing, but without much regret. For the secret (which actually is no secret, since you who read this either know it in some sense already or will never know it) is this: Writing is an intense joy, as faithful as pain, as beautiful as love; making beauty is love, is making love; and that is what writing is.

Every joy that I have ever experienced, even the most physio-logical, ultimately reaches me as aesthetic. Whether writing is knowing or whether it is singing, the love remains, the joy, the daring, the exaltedness when one approaches, at however far a re-move, perfection. Shake the greatest art ever, and dross will come out. But honest effort for its own sake is beauty. If the writer is tal-ented and lucky enough, then the result may be beautiful, too. (I use the word *lucky* advisedly. We credit Petrarch's genius alone for his sonnets. But what if he had never met his Laura? Can we credit him for her existence, or for the effect that she had on him?) If the result is beautiful, then others can see it and feel it. But look through a camera at a face or a landscape, and you may see the perfection of it even if you fail to trip the shutter, or if you set the wrong f-stop. Write a bad poem, and you still may have seen God or gained enlightenment at the feet of the devil.

Sometimes I sit by the ocean in southeast Asia, or walk toward a subarctic horizon glittering with crowberries, and I think: This is enough. I am here; I have seen this; to the best of my capacity, I have known this. This is beautiful. And then I let it go. The per-ceiving is all the writing that I feel called upon to do. And other times I awake from a terrifying or dazzling dream, and I know that if I don't write it down now, its filmy coherence will rupture into a million shrinking droplets, like certain kinds of ink trying to dry upon acrylic. After all, so what if I forget that dream? How many faces, flowers, and rivers have I forgotten? Maybe they've sunk into me, and I draw from them without knowing it, or maybe I simply have the sense that I could only mar any conception I have of them by trying to translate it into groups of letters. But the dream calls to me, cries out for me to save it. Or a story comes into my head. Or the voice of someone who loves me speaks to me. Or an idea, an inhuman crystal, attacks me with its colors, just as strange ores and fossils attack the rockhound, their possibilities overruling his tranquillity so that he must take up his hammer and get on his walking boots.

How can I possibly have the effrontery to believe that any of this will be significant to you? When I go into a museum I see the clusters of tender, avid, or dutiful faces around the fad-pieces of the moment; and then at unpredictable intervals an unknown work will catch somebody's soul (or maybe his feet will get tired); and surrounding these hang the crucified legions of the unregarded. Which category will the books I write be placed in? How can I know, and how does it depend on me? Does what I write seem beautiful to me? That is all that I can know and count on, and it is enough. But if it seems beautiful to you, too, I am grateful. I like to please people. I like to be, as ticket collectors say, "validated." I like to make a living.

But I'm beginning to wonder whether someday I ought to prove my love. De Sade proved his in prison. Homes without bookshelves, people who don't mind *le mot juste* but will settle for any old approximation, readers without enough time to finish a short story — these signs of the times, like the pain in my wrists, which at the moment nibbles at my palms, all remind me that my days are numbered. How long will this world continue to support my easy life? I believe in my sincerity; I believe that I am willing to suffer for the sake of the word; but the pain in my hands is only a promise, not a demonstration like de Sade's ranting and masturbating behind the prison door, refusing to renounce his terrifying lusts, or Hans and Sophie Scholl's going to the scaffold for writing anti-Nazi pamphlets, or Joan of Arc's eloquently defying the inquisitors who will burn her. How can I prove myself? How can I love more? For now, the answer is to keep writing, whatever happens, to try to do better, to go where I must, listening to joy. De Sade, the Scholls, and Joan didn't choose to be afflicted, and I hope never to be tested as they were. I know that I love what I do. I hope that my life (for which I give thanks) glides on and on, and that like a good prostitute, I can continue to convert joy into cash.

For the Money

MARK JACOBSON

Wʜᴀᴛ ᴏᴛʜᴇʀ ʀᴇᴀsᴏɴ could there be? For my soul? Gimme a break. Maybe Stephen King doesn't write for the money. Then again, he has a lot of money. So why shouldn't he write for the money?

I write for the money. Sure, there are other, subsidiary reasons. Sometimes writing gets my rocks off. My spiritual rocks, my data rocks, my attention-to-craft rocks, my pet rocks. Sometimes a writer can be like a blues musician: you be playing that same riff over and over again and sometimes truth jus' seep out. After all, modes of human expression being highly circumscribed in their ability to convey various forms of information, it makes sense that certain truths can be revealed only by writing. This may be the true value of writers, since they write so much more than non-writers, therefore making them likelier to discover truths accessible only through typing. Indeed, if every writer has within himself that famous tribe of monkeys which, given enough time and paper, would come up with all the great works of the world, there's no limit to the Truth a writer might unearth in his lifetime. Writers are just chockfull of potential Truth.

Still, there is no more perfect answer to the why-we-write question, no more compelling reason to write, than: *for the money*.

Almost all of my favorite writers wrote for the money. Someone once asked Philip K. Dick, certainly one of the greatest novelists of the twentieth century, why he wrote, and he said, "The two thousand dollars," which is how much Dick got for most of his paperback sci-fi novels. Two thousand dollars for *The Three Stigmata of Palmer Eldrich*, two thousand dollars for *Time out of Joint*, two thousand dollars for *Martian Time-Slip*. Two thousand bucks for masterpieces! But then again, two thousand bucks bought a lot of amphetamines in those days, and since Dick liked to speed while writing, that two thousand dollars probably enabled him to make another two thousand dollars and another two thousand dollars after that. So it was a good investment. Besides, how else was Philip K. Dick going to make two thousand dollars — being a plumber? *Martian Time-Slip* was probably the only book he could write at that particular time, and two thousand dollars was what they were paying. Take it or leave it, Philip K. Dick.

Me, I'm no Phil Dick, but I've got the same problem. How else am I going to make the two thousand dollars? I'm a writer, and if they're paying two thousand dollars, that's what they're paying.

Since I quit cabdriving, in 1974, I haven't made a penny doing anything else except writing. No other money comes in. Plus, I'm stubborn. The only work I'll do is write. I won't do anything else. No teaching. No little woodshop in Vermont where I lovingly refurbish antique guitars. I make a living by writing. This way, when people ask me what I do, I say write, and that's that.

There's some Oedipal angle here, now that I really go deep-dish on this why-I-write deal. I do it to dis Dad, not that he deserves it, much. The incident in question dates back to eleventh grade, when my parents paid for a course that might improve my SAT scores, which were shockingly low for someone of Jewish extraction. Part of the deal was a "college/career-counseling session" attended by my father and myself, during which I was to be advised which institution of higher learning would most maximize my meager prospects.

"What do you plan to do for a living?" the counselor asked.

"I thought I'd be a writer," I replied, unexaminedly.

It slithered out, a surprise even to myself. After all, I didn't seem the type. I wasn't one of those sickly, bookish Southern boys left home from the hunting trips and football games. I grew up in Flushing, Queens, and if I read at all, it was the Hardy Boys, DC Comics, *Mad* magazine, and the occasional Quentin Reynolds biography of some figure like General Custer. Words themselves had little seductive quality to me, except maybe the words of a stray high school girlfriend saying, "OK, I'll do it." Never one to wear long, flowing Irish knit scarves on the Q17 bus, I had no romantic attachment whatsoever to the writer's life, no burning need to tell anyone beyond my friends how I felt about anything.

The reason I told that phony career counselor that I'd make my living as a writer had mostly to do with a snide comment issued by my tenth-grade English teacher. He'd never liked me, preferring to dote on the smart girls with their perfectly tortured interpretations of *Catcher in the Rye*. Not that I'd done much to warrant his attention. I'd been messing up, not handing in assignments, failing tests. Then the class was assigned a theme entitled "Yesterday Afternoon." As it turned out, my previous day had been spent at the Polo Grounds, the ancient, decaying ballpark where, in 1962, the home-team New York Mets would lose 120 games. On that particular afternoon, Marvelous Marv Throneberry, a player of legendary incompetence, hit a triple. Or at least it seemed like a triple, in the sense that Marv was standing on third base. Too bad he missed second base. First, too. So I wrote about that, and the teacher, probably one of those proto-intellecto baseball snobs in the making, liked it.

"Finally," he said, "something you're good at."

Finally something I was good at . . . funny what you take to heart. From that moment on, I thought I'd be a writer.

Dad did not see it this way. "No one makes a living being a writer," he interrupted. "He'll be a teacher," my father, a teacher himself, said to the career counselor.

Poor old Dad, he was an artist, a beautiful carpenter. But he grew up in the Depression, son of immigrants, and he knew a Jew couldn't make a living carving pieces of wood. So he became a shop teacher and bored himself silly watching the same snotty teenager make the same crappy bookshelf for forty years. Maybe that's why I decided to make my money, such as it is, as a writer. Unshackled from an immigrant sense of limitation through the unstinting labor of my mother's and father's civil-servant careers, I wanted to show that their labors had not been in vain. That I was a real American, someone without a ceiling. Rather than defy my father's wishes, the very act of my making a living as a writer would avenge his hemmed-in life.

So what's it been like, writing for money? Well, it's got its ups and down. Ins and outs. When you've got only one employee in your little-ass company, when responsibility cannot be delegated, the hours can be long, the road rough. Especially for the midlist guy, which, up to now, is the kind of guy I've been. As a midlist guy, you come to understand the exact value of your writing.

The first piece of writing I ever sold was a magazine article about underground discotheques. It was 1973; I was driving a taxi at the time and kept taking gay men to run-down warehouses on the West Side of Manhattan. One night I got invited inside. Beyond the gray steel door was a fabulous party in a huge room, an updated speakeasy. Sure, I'd been up to the Apollo, but I'd never seen so many blacks and whites dancing together, for sure not these kind of blacks and whites. There was something about it that struck me as news. So I hung out a bit, wrote an article about the scene. A friend said I could sell the piece to the *Soho Weekly News*, an Ur-sort of downtown paper that paid ten dollars. But the editors hated what I wrote and sent me into the drizzle on Broome Street. Then another friend said to send it to *New York* magazine, which sounded impossibly straight, but worked. They bought the story and gave me a thousand dollars. It was the exact same piece, now one hundred times more valuable.

It's something that always blows my mind: the price. How much things are supposed to be worth. After all, writing is a business like any other, subject to prevailing market factors. Every word I write, every notion I have, however half-baked, is for sale. I'm trying to make a living here, you understand? I'm a little idea factory, so why shouldn't every minimeme sprung from my ever-fecund brainpan cost somebody something? To this end, I've cut down on my pot smoking. Smoking makes me talk, spritz, tell jokes and stories, offer unsolicited cultural critiques, make political judgments, extend narratives. I heedlessly spew these potential gold mines into the idle ozone. This is bad commerce, a shot in the foot of personal intellectual copyright. Out here in the info jungle, asset protection is paramount. Loose lips sink ships. In paranoia there is profit.

I wish I could stick to these highly reasonable credos, exercise a little self-discipline. Then I wouldn't have to write for the money. I'd be rich. I could write for the love of the language, things like that. Except I get rattled. Every time the boiler blows, or a child's mouth opens for orthodontia, or they tow away my car, I sweat. That's when I make the usual pronouncements about how I have to get organized, how I've got to act more like I'm running a small business, get Andrew Tobias's *Managing Your Midlist Money* on the computer. I go global then, sizing up the market so as to give my little economic engine every advantage in the current postmodernist landscape. For instance, I have diversified over the years, expanded into new forms. After twenty years as a journalist, I became a novelist, published a few of those books. I'd never even written (much less published) a short story before, but it's good to have more weapons in the old quiver, so to speak. Flexibility furthers. This creative switch-hitting is ideal for me, psychologically speaking. When I get sick of everyone, I write novels, and when I get sick of myself, I write journalism; it's a fifty-fifty thing, depending on whom I happen to hate more at the moment, me or them.

At this juncture it might be useful to include A Note on the Movies, seeing that any writer in this day and age who says he writes "for the money" cannot afford to ignore the sucking pull of Hollywood's massive cash machine. Duh, but do I have to mention that magazines don't pay that well (never more than fifteen thousand dollars for months of hard work)? As for novels, my standard line is: I was looking for a lower-paying profession than journalism, so I took up novel writing. But as a movie (re)writer, I once lucked into a situation where I made thirty-five thousand dollars a week (for three weeks) revamping one of the worst pictures ever shot. Numbers like this addle the mind. In fact, the price paid to movie writers has probably done more to alter the face of American narrative than any other factor. I mean, if you've got a story that might actually play as a movie, don't you owe it to yourself to try to make it a screenplay? And if that story isn't exactly suited to films (anyone with a modicum of cultural literacy can tell the difference between a tale told better as a novel, short story, movie, comic book, etc.), wouldn't you be tempted to crush it into the movie form anyway?

What are your choices for this perfect movie story? Write it as a novel, thereby spending two years on something that should take only three months? Or throw it away? The scrap heap of twentieth-century narrative is heavily laden with such tales misfiled into the wrong form. But what do you want *me* to do about it? I'm a midlist guy! I'm not taking responsibility for the demise of American storytelling. No way. I mean, fuck those Hollywood guys anyhow. Corporate jerk-offs, I don't care how much they're paying.

I just bring this up as a sample of the omnipresent difficulties facing the writer-for-hire. Reflexive antiauthoritarian personality traits can interfere with clear thinking. I may write for the money, but there's only a certain amount of money (not so much, alas) available to the sort of guy/writer I am. As a midlist guy, I accept the vagaries of my particular talents and tolerances.

I understand that plans go awry. My most recent plan: to turn out a 227-page (about) novel every year and half, build a little audience, make a living that way, until I die. Unfortunately, my most recent book, the great, criminally overlooked comic masterpiece *Everyone and No One*, published by Villard, seems to have come and gone without even having the chance to gather dust on the Barnes and Noble shelves. This is no reason to be discouraged, I tell myself. Audiences are not built in a day; amid the thick rain of books flying out of the publishing-industry thresher, things get lost. Even if the book just blew, well, that's fine: the plan was to keep on writing, not to care if they weren't all gems.

Still, when you write for the money, you've got to protect yourself. Weigh the long run and short run. So here I am, typing this little missive from my new cubicle at *New York* magazine, the semivenerable, midlist-accessible entity where my first work was published twenty-five years ago. It's cool. Journalism's got its various rhythms, and I've always been partial to weeklies. The short lead time cuts down the space for editorial meddling. Plus, they offered me a health plan. In the free-lance world you don't ask the second question when they offer you a health plan. Besides, it never hurts to get out of your room, learn a new thing or two while planning the next opus. Except that's the hassle, when you're in journalist mode. All the junk they sling at you out there, life's own scuzzy blizzard of cognitive dissonance: baseball players one day, tantric Buddhists the next. Some of it sticks to you, leads you down another two-month detour from the source of the fictional grail. But that's what they pay me the mediocre bucks for.

Why I Write

STEPHEN WRIGHT

ALL WORK and no play makes Jack a dull boy.
All work and no play makes Jack a dull boy.
All work and no play makes Jack a dyll boy.
Alll work and no play makes Jack a xdull boy.
All work andno play makes jack a dull bit.
All work and no oplay makes Jack a dull boy.
All work and no play makes jack a doll boy.
all work and no play makes jack a dull bot.
Awl work and no play makes Jack a dull Bog.
all work and noplay mokes jack a dfil boy.
All work and no play makes jacka dull boy.
All work and no play makes jackk a dull boy/
all work and no play makes jack a dull boiy.
all work and no play makes Jack a dull boy.
All work and no play makes Jack a dull joy.

all work andno lay makes jack a dull boy.
All work and no playmajk a dull boy.
all work and no play makes jack a dull boiy.
alll work and no playt makes jACK a dull boy.
all work and no play makes kacj a dull noy.
all work and no play makes jack a diull voy.
all work and no playmakes ack a dull boy.
All work and no play makes Jack a dull boy.
All work and no play makes Jack a dull boy.
All work and no play makes Jack a dyll boy.
Alll work and no play makes Jack a xdull boy.
All work andno play makes jack a dull bit.
All work and no oplay makes Jack a dull boy.
All work and no play makes jack a doll boy.
all work and no play makes jack a dull bot.
Awl work and no play makes Jack a dull Bog.
all work and noplay mokes jack a dfil boy.
All work and no play makes jacka dull boy.
All work and no play makes jackk a dull boy/
all work and no play makes jack a dull boiy.
all work and no play makes Jack a dull boy.
All work and no play makes Jack a dull joy.
all work andno lay makes jack a dull boy.
All work and no playmajk a dull boy.
all work and no play makes jack a dull boiy.
alll work and no playt makes jACK a dull boy.
all work and no play makes kacj a dull noy.
all work and no play makes jack a diull voy.
all work and no playmakes ack a dull boy.
All work and no play makes Jack a dull boy.

All work and no play makes Jack a dull boy.
All work and no play makes Jack a dyll boy.
Alll work and no play makes Jack a xdull boy.
All work andno play makes jack a dull bit.
All work and no oplay makes Jack a dull boy.
All work and no play makes jack a doll boy.
all work and no play makes jack a dull bot.
Awl work and no play makes Jack a dull Bog.
all work and noplay mokes jack a dfil boy.
All work and no play makes jacka dull boy.
All work and no play makes jackk a dull boy/
all work and no play makes jack a dull boiy.
all work and no play makes Jack a dull boy.
All work and no play makes Jack a dull joy.
all work andno lay makes jack a dull boy.
All work and no playmajk a dull boy.
all work and no play makes jack a dull boiy.
alll work and no playt makes jACK a dull boy.
all work and no play makes kacj a dull noy.
all work and no play makes jack a diull voy.
all work and no playmakes ack a dull boy.
All work and no play makes Jack a dull boy.
All work and no play makes Jack a dull boy.
All work and no play makes Jack a dyll boy.
Alll work and no play makes Jack a xdull boy.
All work andno play makes jack a dull bit.
All work and no oplay makes Jack a dull boy.
All work and no play makes jack a doll boy.
all work and no play makes jack a dull bot.
Awl work and no play makes Jack a dull Bog.
all work and noplay mokes jack a dfil boy.

All work and no play makes jacka dull boy.
All work and no play makes jackk a dull boy/
all work and no play makes jack a dull boiy.
all work and no play makes Jack a dull boy.
All work and no play makes Jack a dull joy.

Everything Else Falls Away

LEE SMITH

———

In the Appalachian Mountains, where I grew up, stories come as easy as breathing. Maybe it's something in the water, or something that seeps out from those storied heights themselves, rough jagged mountains that held our little town like a jewel in the palm of a giant hand. But I am more inclined to think it has to do with who your people are, and how you first hear language. In my own fortunate case, it was that slow, sweet southern cadence I will always associate with stories; and all those first stories were told by people who loved me.

My mother, a home-economics teacher from the Eastern Shore of Virginia, could make a story out of thin air, out of anything — a trip to the drugstore, something somebody said to her in church. My father liked to drink a little and recite Kipling out loud. He came from right there, from a large family of storytelling

Democrats who would sit on the porch and place twenty-five-dollar bets on which bird would fly first off a telephone wire. They were all big talkers.

An only child, I heard it all. I was always around the grown-ups, always in the presence of the story.

Every day after school, I walked downtown to my father's dime store, where I got to take care of the dolls, type on a typewriter, count money, and talk to the salesgirls. Viola, back in piece goods, always hugged me; Betty always asked me if I'd been saved yet; and Mildred, my favorite, who wore bright-red spots of rouge on her cheeks and presided over the candy counter, whispered the *craziest* things in my ear. I spent hours upstairs in my father's little office, observing the whole floor through the one-way glass window in my powerful omniscience — *Nobody* can see me! I witnessed not only shoplifting but fights and embraces as well.

Often I'd go to visit my grandaddy in his office at the courthouse across the street, where I'd get the lowdown on who was in jail, who had shot his brother, who was getting married or in debt or out of a job, or had set his house on fire just to collect the insurance money.

Back at home, my mother held forth in the kitchen — we always had company — drinking coffee and smoking Salems and discussing the lives of her friends or the lives of the stars, with equal interest. She and I pored over the *National Enquirer* together. My father read newspapers, magazines, and sometimes history. Although neither of them read novels, they received the Reader's Digest Condensed Books, which I devoured, and they also encouraged me to go to our fledgling library.

This soon got out of hand. I became a voracious and then an obsessive reader; recurrent bouts of pneumonia and tonsillitis gave me plenty of time to indulge my passion. After I was pronounced "sickly," I got to stay home a lot, slathered with a vile salve named Mentholatum, spirit lamp hissing in the corner of my room. I'd read all day and sometimes all night long, under the covers with a flashlight.

But I did not read casually, or for mere entertainment, or for information. What I wanted was to feel all wild and trembly inside, an effect first produced by *The Secret Garden*, which I read maybe twenty times. The only boy I ever loved more than Colin, of *The Secret Garden*, was Johnny Tremaine, in Esther Forbes's book of that title. Other novels that affected me strongly were *Little Women*, especially the part where Beth dies, and *Gone with the Wind*, particularly the scene where Melanie dies. I often imagined I was dying myself, and planned many funerals. I also loved *Marjorie Morningstar*, *A Tree Grows in Brooklyn*, *Heidi*, and books like *Dear and Glorious Physician*, *The Shoes of the Fisherman*, and *Christy*. My all-time favorite was a book about Joan of Arc named *God's Girl*, especially the frontispiece illustration picturing Joan as she knelt and "prayed without ceasing for guidance from God," whose face was depicted overhead, in a thunderstorm. Not only did I love Joan of Arc, I wanted to *be* her.

I was crazy for horses and saints. I read all the Black Stallion books, of course, as well as all the Marguerite Henry books.

"By the way," my mother mentioned to me one day almost casually, while I was being sick in bed and she was straightening my covers, "you know, Marguerite Henry stayed at your grandmother's boardinghouse on Chincoteague Island while she was writing that book."

"What book?" I sat right up.

"*Misty*," Mama said. "Then she came back to write *Sea Star*, and I think the illustrator, Wesley Dennis, stayed there, too. Cousin Jack used to take him out on a boat."

I couldn't believe it! A real writer, a *horse* writer, had walked up the crushed-oyster-shell road where I had gone barefoot, had sat at the big dinner table where I'd eaten fish and corncakes for breakfast; had maybe even swung in the same wicker porch swing I loved.

I wrote a novel on the spot, on eight sheets of my mother's Crane stationery. It featured as its main characters my two favorite people at that time: Adlai Stevenson and Jane Russell. In my novel, they fell in love and then went West together in a covered wagon. Once there, they became — surprisingly — Mormons! Even at that age, I was fixed upon romance, flight, and religion, themes I would return to.

What did my parents think of this strange little girl who had come to them so late in life, when they had become resigned to never having children? Well, because of that fact, they spoiled me rotten and were simply *delighted* by everything I did, everything I showed an interest in. I believe if I had told my mother that I wanted to be, say, an ax murderer, *she* would have said, without blinking an eye, "Well, that's nice, dear," and then gone out to buy me an ax.

Although my parents might *say* — as they did, later — that they wished I would just stop all that writing stuff and marry a surgeon (which is what a daughter really *ought* to do, of course), the fact is that they were so loving that they gave me the confidence, and the *permission*, early on, to do just about anything I wanted to do. Now, decades later, I realize how unusual this was, and how privileged I have been because of it. Now I see this issue — permission to write — as the key one for many women I have worked with in my classes, women who have begun writing later in their lives.

Anyway, in spite of what I have told you, my childhood was not entirely a happy one. No writer's childhood ever is. There was my father's inexplicable sadness; there was my strange uncle Tick; there was a scary little neighborhood "club" we formed, which did bad things. There was a lot of drinking. There were nervous breakdowns, as they called them then, and hospitalizations and long absences and periods of being sent to live with distant relatives. I started dating boys, and almost married one. I got "sent away" to school. Things turned very confusing.

But I kept on writing stories. By the time I got to college, I was writing them, I believe, for the reason I have done so ever since: simply to survive. My belief is that we have only one life, that this is all there is. And I refuse to lead an unexamined life. No matter how painful it may be, I want to know what's going on. So I write fiction the way other people write in their journals.

My husband has been heard to bemoan my lack of self-knowledge. He envisions our respective psyches like this: his is a big room in a factory, brightly lit. He's got uniformed guys in there carrying clipboards and constantly working on all his problems, checking gauges and levels, in day and night shifts. He's always monitoring their work, reading their reports. He sees *my* mind, by contrast, as a dark forest with no path, where huge beasts loom up at you suddenly out of the night and then disappear, only to return again and again and again.

Maybe so. But when I read what I've written, I know exactly what those beasts are.

In 1980, for instance, I wrote a novel named *Black Mountain Breakdown*, about a girl named Crystal Spangler, who is so busy fitting herself into others' images of her (first fulfilling her mother's beauty-queen dreams, then altering her image to suit the various men in her life) that she loses her own true self and finally ends up paralyzed: "Crystal just lies up there in that room every day, with her bed turned catty-corner so she could look out the window and see Lorene's climbing rambler rose in full bloom on the trellis if she would turn her head. But she won't. She won't lift a finger. She just lies there. Everybody in town takes a fancy to it." The townsfolk feed her Jell-O, brush her hair, read *Reader's Digest* out loud to her. The most terrifying aspect of her condition is that "Crystal is happy . . . as outside her window the seasons come and go and the colors change on the mountain." When I wrote that, I was in a marriage that should have ended years earlier, something I'd been unable to face or even admit; later, reading these words over, I finally understood how I'd felt during the last part of that marriage. I was able then to deal with its inevitable ending, and move on with my life.

No matter what I may *think* I am writing about at any given time — even majorettes in Alabama, even a gruesome long-ago murder, or country music — I have come to understand that it is all, finally, about me, often in some complicated way I won't come to understand until years later. But then it will be there for me to read, and I *will* understand it, and even if I don't know who I am now, I will surely have a record of who I was then.

Writing is also my addiction, for the moment when I am writing fiction is that moment when I am most intensely alive. This "aliveness" does not seem to be mental, or not exactly. I am certainly not *thinking* while I write. Whatever I'm doing is almost the opposite of thinking. Especially during the prewriting phase, when I am simply making up the story and imagining its characters, and during the first couple of drafts, I feel a dangerous, exhilarating sense that anything can happen.

It reminds me of a woman I interviewed in eastern Kentucky several years ago when I was writing a novel about serpent-handling believers. An hour earlier, I had seen her lift a double handful of copperheads high in the air during a religious service. Now we faced each other across a little formica table in a fast-food restaurant, drinking Cokes and eating fries. I asked the obvious: "Why do you do this, when it's so dangerous? You could die any time." She merely smiled at me, a beautiful, generous smile without a trace of irony.

"Honey," she began, "I do it out of an intense desire for holiness." She smiled at me again while that sank in. "And I'll tell you something else, too. When you've held the serpent in your hands, the whole world kind of takes on an edge for you."

I could see that. For I had once been the girl who embarrassed her mother so much by rededicating her life over and over at various revivals, coming home dripping wet from total immersions in those stand-up pools from Sears that they set up in the little tents behind the big tents, or simply in the fast-flowing creeks that rushed down the mountainsides.

And the feeling I get when I'm writing intensely is much the same.

For me, writing is a physical joy. It is almost sexual — not the moment of fulfillment, but the moment when you open the door to the room where your lover is waiting, and everything else falls away.

It *does* fall away, too. For the time of the writing, I am nobody. Nobody at all. I am a conduit, nothing but a way for the story to come to the page. Oh, but I am terribly alive then, too, though I say I am no one at all; my every sense is keen and quivering. I can smell the bacon cooking downstairs in my grandmother's kitchen that winter morning in 1952, I can feel the cold linoleum floor under my bare feet as I run down the hall, I can see the bright-blue squares of the kitchen wallpaper, bunches of cherries alternating with little floral bouquets. Sun shines through the frost on the windows, almost blinding me; my granddaddy's Lucky Strike cigarette smoke still hangs in the air, lazy blue, though he is already up and gone, has walked the bridge across the river to the old stone courthouse where he will work all day long as county treasurer. I love my granddaddy, who always wears a dark-blue suit and has a figure like Humpty Dumpty's. I do not so much love my grandmother, who tells me not to be a tomboy and not to start sentences with "me and Martha." "Say, 'Martha and I,'" she directs, moistening her lips with her tongue in a way I hate. I wish my mother would get out of the hospital so I could go home. I don't see why I can't stay with Daddy, anyway. I could make us peanut butter sandwiches for dinner, and cut the crusts off.

See what I mean? I am *there* now, and I want to stay there. I hate to leave that kitchen and come back to this essay. Writing an essay is like pulling teeth, compared to writing fiction. It is an intellectual exercise rather than a sensory experience.

All my senses are involved when I am writing fiction, but it is *hearing* that is most acute. This has always been true. I can see everything in the story, of course — I have to see that kitchen in order to walk through it, and the icy river in order to get my grandfather across the bridge. I make a lot of maps before I start writing, scotch-taping them up on the wall. But I am not a visual person in real life. I never know how high to hang pictures, for instance, or where the furniture should go. None of my clothes match. It was *words* I loved first, remember, words and sentences and music and stories, the voice that comes out of the dark when you're almost asleep, sitting in somebody's lap on somebody's porch, trying to keep your eyes open long enough to hear the end of the story.

So a story always comes to me in a human voice, speaking not exactly into my ear but somewhere deep inside me. If I am writing from a first-person point of view, it is always the voice of the person who is telling the story. If I am writing from a third-person point of view, it is simply the voice of the story itself. Sometimes this voice is slow and pondering, or tentative and unsure. Sometimes it is flat and reportorial: just the facts, ma'am. Sometimes it's giggly, gossipy, intimate — a tale told over a Coke and a cigarette during a work break at the Piggly Wiggly. Sometimes it's sad, a long, wailing lament, telling and retelling again and again how he done me wrong. It can be furious or vengeful: "I hated him from the moment I first laid eyes on him, hated him instinctively, as if I knew somehow what he would do to our family. . . ." It can be a meditative, authoritative voice, told as if from the distant past or from a great and somehow definitive distance (I confess that ever since we moved into this old house where I work in an upstairs study looking out over the town, this has happened more frequently!).

Most thrilling, of course, is when it is a first-person voice telling a story of real urgency. At these times, all I have to do is *keep up*; I become a stenographer, a court secretary, a tape recorder. My biggest job is making sure that I have several uninterrupted hours whenever I sit down to write, so this can happen. Whenever a story like this is in progress, it is so exciting that I will do almost anything to get those hours: break appointments, call in sick, tell lies. I become a person on drugs, somebody in the throes of a passionate affair. I'll do anything to get there, to make it happen again. I know I can't ignore the voice, or waste it. I may be a fool, but I'm not *that kind* of fool.

Since the writing of fiction is such a physical and personal process for me, I have to write in longhand, still. I have to write with a pen or pencil on a legal pad. I can't have anything mechanical between my body and the page. Later, I'll type it on my little typewriter again and again and again, as I revise. I buy these ninety-nine-dollar typewriters three at a time from Home Depot and run through them like crazy. I always keep a couple stockpiled; I'm terrified that they'll quit making them. Later, I will get somebody who's a better typist than I am to put it on a disk, for publishers that expect to get it that way.

Here's what I don't understand about composing on a computer: I'm really messy when I write, and often jot down three or four words before I hit upon the right one. So I mark all the others out and go on writing, but I want to *keep* them all, all those words I thought about first and then discarded. I want to keep that paragraph of description I marked out, and that earlier section about how Ray drowned the dog when he was nine, because I might change my mind later on. The story, at this point, is organic, living, changing; anything can still happen, and probably will. This is true up until the very moment when I put it into its little coffin, usually an old typewriter-paper box, and mail it off. Then it's dead, they're all dead, all those people who have been my familiars, who have lived under my skin for weeks and months or years, and I am no longer writer, but murderer and mourner, more alone in the world.

Writing is a source of strength for me, too. I had barely begun a novel named *Fair and Tender Ladies* — intended as an honest account and a justification, really, of the lives of so many of the resourceful mountain women I'd grown up among, women whose plain and home-centered lives are not much valued in the world at large — when my beloved mother went into her last illness, a long and drawn-out sequence of falls, emphysema, and finally heart failure. This period coincided with another catastrophic illness in our family; I spent two years sitting by hospital beds. I don't know what I would have done if I hadn't been writing that novel. I worked on it a bit every day; it was like an open door to another world, another place for me to be for a little while.

Its heroine, Ivy Rowe, grew stronger and stronger the more I needed her. Every terrible thing in the world happened to her — extreme poverty, too many children, heartbreak, illness, the death of a child — but she could take it. She hung in there, so I did, too. Ivy made sense of *her* life through writing a constant stream of letters, to her children, to her friends, to her sisters — especially to her favorite sister, Silvaney, even though she had died young and would never read most of them. Near the novel's end, Ivy burns all her letters, and it is finally my *own* voice as well as hers that concludes:

I gathered them up and took them back to the firepit, where we used to lay the kettle to boil our clothes when I was a girl, it has taken me several trips as I move so slow now. I cleared out the snow in the firepit and took my big old kitchen matches out there and burned the letters every one. Now and then I would stop and look all around, but you know how quiet the land lies in the snow. . . . The clouds hung low and dark and puffy. My breath hung in the air. The smoke from the burning letters rose and was lost in the clouds. . . . With every one I burned, my soul grew lighter, lighter, as if it rose too with the smoke. And I was not even cold, long as I'd been out there. For I came to understand something in that moment which I had never understood in all these years.

Those letters didn't mean anything.
Not to the dead girl, Silvaney, of course — *nor to me*.
Nor had they ever.
It was the *writing* of them that signified.

The Nature of the Fun

DAVID FOSTER WALLACE

‒

THE BEST METAPHOR I know of for being a fiction writer is in Don DeLillo's *Mao II*, where he describes a book-in-progress as a kind of hideously damaged infant that follows the writer around, forever crawling after the writer (dragging itself across the floors of restaurants where the writer's trying to eat, appearing at the foot of the bed first thing in the morning, etc.), hideously defective, hydrocephalic and noseless and flipper-armed and incontinent and retarded and dribbling cerebro-spinal fluid out of its mouth as it mewls and blurbles and cries out to the writer, wanting love, wanting the very thing its hideousness guarantees it'll get: the writer's complete attention.

The damaged-infant trope is perfect because it captures the mix of repulsion and love the fiction writer feels for something he's working on. The fiction always comes out so horrifically defective, so hideous a betrayal of all your hopes for it — a cruel and repellent caricature of the perfection of its conception — yes, understand: grotesque because *imperfect*. And yet it's yours, the infant is, it's *you*, and you love it and dandle it and wipe the cerebrospinal fluid off its slack chin with the cuff of the only clean shirt you have left (you have only one clean shirt left because you haven't done laundry in like three weeks because finally this one chapter or character seems like it's finally trembling on the edge of coming together and working and you're terrified to spend any time on anything other than working on it because if you look away for a second you'll lose it, dooming the whole infant to continued hideousness). And so you love the damaged infant and pity it and care for it; but also you hate it — *hate it* — because it's deformed, repellent, because something grotesque has happened to it in the parturition from head to page; hate it because its deformity is *your* deformity (since if you were a better fiction writer your infant would of course look like one of those babies in catalog ads for infant wear, perfect and pink and cerebro-spinally continent) and its every hideous incontinent breath is a devastating indictment of *you*, on all levels . . . and so you want it dead, even as you dote on it and wipe it and dandle it and sometimes even apply CPR when it seems like its own grotesqueness has blocked its breath and it might die altogether.

The whole thing's all very messed up and sad, but simultaneously it's also tender and moving and noble and cool — it's a genuine *relationship*, of a sort — and even at the height of its hideousness the damaged infant somehow touches and awakens what you suspect are some of the very best parts of you: maternal parts, dark ones. You love your infant very much. And you want others to love it, too, when the time finally comes for the damaged infant to go out and face the world.

So you're in a bit of a dicey position: you love the infant and you want others to love it, but that means that you hope others won't see it *correctly*. You want to sort of fool people; you want them to see as perfect what you in your heart know is a betrayal of all perfection.

Or else you don't want to fool these people; what you want is you want them to see and love a lovely, miraculous, perfect, already infant and to be *right, correct*, in what they see and feel. You want to be terribly wrong, you want the damaged infant's hideousness to turn out to have been nothing but your own weird delusion or hallucination. But that'd mean you were crazy; you have seen, been stalked by, and recoiled from hideous deformities that in fact (others persuade you) aren't there at all. Meaning you're at least a couple of fries short of a Happy Meal, surely. But worse: it'd also mean you saw and despised hideousness in a thing *you* made (and love), in your spawn and in certain ways, *you*. And this last, best hope, this'd represent something way worse than just very bad parenting; it'd be a terrible kind of self-assault, almost self-torture. But that's still what you most want: to be completely, insanely, suicidally wrong.

But it's still all a lot of fun. Don't get me wrong. As to the nature of that fun, I keep remembering this strange little story I heard in Sunday school when I was about the size of a fire hydrant. It takes place in China or Korea or someplace like that. It seems there is this old farmer outside a village in the hill country who worked his farm with only his son and his beloved horse. One day the horse, who was not only beloved but vital to the labor-intensive work on the farm, picked the lock on his corral or whatever and ran off into the hills. All the old farmer's friends came around to exclaim what bad luck this was. The farmer only shrugged and said, "Good luck, bad luck, who knows?" A couple days later the beloved horse returned from the hills in the company of a whole priceless herd of wild horses, and the farmer's friends all come around to congratulate him on what good luck the horse's escape turned out to be. "Good luck, bad luck, who knows?" is all the farmer says in reply, shrugging. The farmer now strikes me as a bit Yiddish-sounding for an old Chinese farmer, but this is how I remember it. But so the farmer and his son set about breaking the wild horses, and one of the horses bucks the son off his back with such wild force that the son breaks his leg. And here come the friends to commiserate with the farmer and curse the bad luck that ever brought these accursed wild horses onto his farm. The old farmer just shrugs and says, "Good luck, bad luck, who knows?" A few days later the Imperial Sino-Korean Army or something like that comes marching through the village, conscripting every able-bodied male between like ten and sixty for cannon-fodder for some hideously bloody conflict that's apparently brewing, but when they see the son's broken leg, they let him off on some sort of feudal 4F, and instead of getting shang-haied the son stays on the farm with the old farmer. Good luck? Bad luck?

This is the sort of parabolic straw you cling to as you struggle with the issue of fun, as a writer. In the beginning, when you first start out trying to write fiction, the whole endeavor's about fun. You don't expect anybody else to read it. You're writing almost wholly to get yourself off. To enable your own fantasies and deviant logics and to escape or transform parts of yourself you don't like. And it works — and it's terrific fun. Then, if you have good luck and people seem to like what you do, and you actually start to get paid for it and get to see your stuff professionally typeset and bound and blurbed and reviewed and even (once) being read on the A.M. subway by a pretty girl you don't even know, it seems to make it even *more* fun. For a while. Then things start to get complicated and confusing, not to mention scary. Now you feel like you're writing for other people, or at least you hope so. You're no longer writing just to get yourself off, which — since any kind of masturbation is lonely and hollow — is probably good. But what replaces the onanistic motive? You've found you very much enjoy having your writing liked by people, and you find you're extremely keen to have people like the new stuff you're doing. The motive of pure personal fun starts to get supplanted by the motive of being liked, of having pretty people you don't know like you and admire you and think you're a good writer. Onanism gives way to attempted seduction, as a motive. Now, attempted seduction is hard work, and its fun is offset by a terrible fear of rejection. Whatever "ego" means, your ego has now gotten into the game. Or maybe "vanity" is a better word. Because you notice that a good deal of your writing has now become basically showing off, trying to get people to think you're good. This is understandable. You have a great deal of yourself on the line, now, writing — your vanity is at stake. You discover a tricky thing about fiction writing: a certain amount of vanity is necessary to be able to do it all, but any vanity above that certain amount is lethal. At some point you find that 90-plus percent of the stuff you're writing is motivated and informed by an overwhelming need to be liked. This results in shitty fiction. And the shitty work must get fed to the wastebasket, less because of any sort of artistic integrity than simply because shitty work will cause you to be disliked. At this point in the evolution of writerly fun, the very thing that's always motivated you to write is now also what's motivating you to feed your writing to the wastebasket. This is a paradox and a kind of double bind, and it can keep you stuck inside yourself for months or even years, during which period you wail and gnash and rue your bad luck and wonder bitterly where all the *fun* of the thing could have gone.

The smart thing to say, I think, is that the way out of this bind is to work your way somehow back to your original motivation — fun. And if you can find your way back to fun, you will find that the hideously unfortunate double bind of the late vain period turns out really to have been good luck for you. Because the fun you work back to has been transfigured by the extreme unpleasantness of vanity and fear, an unpleasantness you're now so anxious to avoid that the fun you rediscover is a way fuller and more large-hearted kind of fun. It has something to do with Work as Play. Or with the discovery that disciplined fun is more fun than impulsive or hedonistic fun. Or with figuring out that not all paradoxes have to be paralyzing. Under fun's new administration, writing fiction becomes a way to go deep inside yourself and illuminate precisely the stuff you don't want to see or let anyone else see, and this stuff usually turns out (paradoxically) to be precisely the stuff all writers and readers everywhere share and respond to, feel. Fiction becomes a weird way to countenance yourself and to tell the truth instead of being a way to escape yourself or present yourself in a way you figure you will be maximally likable. This process is complicated and confusing and scary, and also hard work, but it turns out to be the best fun there is.

The fact that you can now sustain the fun of writing only by confronting the very same unfun parts of yourself you'd first used writing to avoid or disguise is another paradox, but this one isn't any kind of bind at all. What it is is a gift, a kind of miracle, and compared to it the rewards of strangers' affection is as dust, lint.

Why I Write, or Not

JIM HARRISON

Standing outside the Metropolitan Museum in New York several years ago, feeling sodden and perplexed over the Goya show, I ran into an old friend, the poet Charles Simic, whom I hadn't seen in twenty years. Among other things that we talked about, he said, "I thought I'd understand everything by now, but I don't," and I think I replied, "We know a great deal but not very much."

I'm not saying that we throw in the towel on our rational mind, one that we only had two fingers on in the first place, but with age, the processes of my own art seem a great deal more immutable and inexplicable to me. For instance, even without my eyes closed, specific ideas usually carry an equally specific visual image for me. The act of writing is a boy hoeing a field of corn on a hot day, able to see either a woodlot or, more often, an immense forest where he'd rather be. This is uncomplicated, almost banal. He has to hoe the corn in order to be allowed to reach his beloved forest. This can be easily extrapolated into the writer as a small god who has forty acres as a birthright in which to reinvent the world. He cultivates this world, but then there is always something vast and unreachable beyond his grasp, whether it's the forest, the ocean, or the implausible ten million citizens of New York or Paris. While he hoes or writes, he whirls toward the future at a rate that with age becomes quite incomprehensible. He leaves a trail of books, but he really marks the passage of time by the series of hunting dogs he's left behind. His negative capability has made the world grow larger rather than shrink, and not a single easy answer has survived the passing of years.

It is more comic than melancholy because the presumptions are so immense. No matter how much you've read, something has been left out that you aim to fill in yourself. This takes a great deal of hubris and frequently a measure of stupidity. Our large family read widely if indiscriminately, the movie theater in our small town in northern Michigan changing features only once a week. I began with the usual Horatio Alger, Zane Grey, Hardy Boys flotsam, graduated to my father's passion for literate historical novels, especially those of Kenneth Roberts, Hervey Allen, and Walter Edmonds, and then also to his taste for (he was an agriculturist) Hamlin Garland and Sherwood Anderson and Erskine Caldwell, before continuing on my own so that by nineteen my obsessive favorites included Dostoyevski, Whitman, Yeats, Kierkegaard, Joyce, Rimbaud, Apollinaire, Henry Miller, and Faulkner. Such a list might very well lead an intelligent soul to keep his mouth shut, but then a curious arrogance has always been the breastplate of a young writer's armor. At this stage humility is a hobble you can scarcely afford. The only fuel the ego receives is interior. You might wander around in a thunderstorm, hiding out and repeating *Non serviam*, but then no one has asked you to do anything, and no one is looking for you, least of all those whom you have tormented with your postures.

Despite early forays to New York, Boston, and San Francisco, my work is preoccupied with rural life and the natural world. I must say that I don't see any special virtue to this. You are pretty much stuck with what you know, and Peter Matthiessen with his obsessive preoccupation with the natural world balances nicely with a taste for the more urbane James Salter or Don DeLillo. It is the artfulness of the prose and construct I'm looking for, not someone's fungoid wisdom. Good writers seem to know that we are permanently inconsolable.

It is the mystery of personality that seizes me, the infinite variety of human behavior that thumbs its nose at popular psychologisms. Even our dreams seem to wish to create new characters as surely as we do in our fictions, and our creation of our own personalities is most often a fictive event. In creating an environment for certain of my characters, I often find myself trying to create an environment for my own soul. The perception of reality grows until it is an accretion of the perceptions of all creatures. It is a daily struggle against the habituation and conditioning that bind us and suffocate us, destroying the fascinating perceptions that characterize the best writing. You continue under the willful illusion that the world is undescribed, or else you need not exist, and you never quite tire of the bittersweet mayhem of human behavior.

Except, of course, for the fatigue brought on by our collective behavior, both political and economic, the moral hysteria we are currently sunken in. Last May without an inkling I found myself saying in a French interview that we are becoming a Fascist Disneyland. This is seeping into our fiction and poetry in the form of a new Victorianism wherein a mawkish sincerity is the highest value. At one point I thought it was simply the way academia had subsumed serious fiction and poetry, but now it seems that academia and the small presses are the only barriers against totally market-driven work, despite the other obvious middling shortcomings of the M.F.A. pyramid schema, a sad breeder of middling expectations and large disappointments.

The national mood that affects our work is naturally more complicated. An English anthropologist, Mary Douglas, once said, "The more that society is vested with power, the more it despises the organic processes on which it rests." Each year we become more like Europe, with cultural rigidity typical of an increasing population that has doubled in my own lifetime. Otherness, the primal core of our lives, the unmediated aspects of our existence, our lives and loves and deaths, the rituals we have used to frame our existence for thousands of years, can't hold up and haven't under the sodden blanket of the collective media, whether television or the Internet. There is the darkly comic vision of this media-fueled cultural blender increasing in size and power until that is all there is. A blender as big as Ohio, spewing the trash, chatter, and clutter we're all familiar with. Art is confused and smothered by the art market, literature is seen as an arm of publishing rather than vice versa. Animals are what you see in the zoos within the zoos of our lives. Certain eco-Nazis appear to think that all animals still surviving in the wild, especially grizzlies and wolves, require telemetric devices. Like politics, the *rodentia* will thrive. The majority of our population that eats beef, pork, and chicken has never known an actual cow, pig, or hen. Times change, as our parents told us, and are not the less fascinating for the colors of the grotesque.

We paint our lives as we write our work, and I'm reminded of Whitman's statement that a poet must "move wild laughter in the throat of death." I've always had a somewhat childish obsession with thickets, and I suspect this shows in my work. I like a specific density in fiction and poetry, feeling that the easily perceived is almost always valueless. I often have wondered if my somewhat Pleistocene fixation with thickets, niches, and lairs may have had its origin in the childhood trauma of being blinded in one eye, but then so what? The explanation is flotsam. It is all so wonderfully random, accidental, just as hundreds since my youth have thought my appearance to be Native American, though those genes seem unlikely in my family. We have chosen to be outcasts, and they didn't, so the identification is inappropriate. There is also the suspicion that the craving for identity is the cause of the literary disease of xenophobia. Since nearly everyone is dislocated, including writers within our current critical diaspora, the staking out, lauding, and defense of territories, an otiose form of regionalism, is even more absurd. Of course literary rages, fads, events, and quarrels don't age any better than Beaujolais or the "skinless, boneless chicken breasts" that are evidently the prime meat of our time. Metaphorically, writers are better off eating the elephant's asshole, stewed thirty-three hours with hot chilies, that I partook of in Tanzania way back when.

I used to think I was becoming quadra-schizoid by writing poetry, fiction, essays, and screenplays, but then since I don't teach, I've always had a hand in all of those forms to make a living. We would be nothing without the good teachers in our lives, but I never had any temperament for it, as universities are invariably in locales where I couldn't survive due to my lifelong claustrophobia.

Poetry comes when it will, and I've never had any idea of how to cause it. Way back during the T'ang Dynasty, Wang Wei, a phenomenal poet, said, "Who knows what causes the opening or closing of the door?" There has always been a tendency among poets in slack periods to imitate their own best efforts, but this is embarrassingly obvious to their readers. It's a bit like raping your own brain, or trying to invent a convincing sexual fantasy only to have the phone ring and it's your mother, who wonders why you're still a "bohemian" at age fifty-nine. The actual muse is the least civil woman in the history of earth. She prefers to sleep with you when you're a river rather than a mud puddle.

I wrote my first sequence of novellas in the late seventies and had some difficulty getting them published, as "no one" was writing them in those days. My own models were Isak Dinesen and Katherine Anne Porter in my search for an intermediate form. I've never been able to write a short story, which used to make me a bit nervous, as magazines kept prattling that this was the "age of the short story." I became less nervous when it occurred to me that these selfsame magazines couldn't very well publish novels or novellas, though the New Yorker did publish my "The Woman Lit by Fireflies" and Esquire printed the novella "Legends of the Fall" in its entirety. A publisher who turned the latter down suggested I increase its mere hundred pages to five hundred and then we'd have a best-seller, no matter that, unchanged, it has eventually sold quite well for twenty years. Publishers naturally have the same yearning for instant gratification as dope addicts, congressmen, and car dealers. Now, under corporate and chain-store dominance, they appear to be paddleless up a terribly real shit creek.

Novels seem to take care of themselves if you offer them up an appropriate amount of time. I've never written one without first thinking about it for years. This is probably a peculiar method, but I can't function otherwise. I just did a year's research for the second section of a novel and ended up using very little. This is what the film business aptly calls "back story," without the knowledge of which it is difficult to proceed. If a woman character is thirty-seven, you still have to figure out the nature of her personality when she was a child, even if you have no intention of using that.

I've also written more screenplays than I should have, but then I've been fascinated by movies since I was a child. Admittedly, this fascination has never been very mainstream, which has caused me problems when looking for work. I doubt if there are proportionately any more first-rate novels than good movies in a particular year, but given the intelligentsia's scorn of Hollywood, this is not an acceptable idea. I admit there is a cynicism and perfidy in Hollywood that almost approach those of Washington and are probably equal to those in book publishing, but I have also noted evidence that some of the loathing for Hollywood is a veiled form of anti-Semitism and being a mixture of Swede-Irish-English, I can say this without paranoia.

I suppose the main problem in screenwriting is that you're separated from the possible director until later in the series of drafts. This is a waste of time and money, especially since you have a good idea of a suitable director from the inception of the story. Another pronounced difficulty is that film-school graduates are definitely short on the varieties of human experience in favor of cinematic technology. Despite the fact that very bright movies tend to do well, there is a relentless and collective effort to "dumb down" the story. There is always the fear-maddened search on the part of film executives for a reliable formula story line, with inevitably sad results. On the plus side, no matter the whining, there always has been more oxygen in the West. Even Bill Gates wouldn't have done very well in Connecticut or Gotham. To be even as peripherally involved in the film business as I am, you have to have a taste for insanity and vulgarity, insecurity, hideous disappointments, spates of beauty, being fired over and over, and very good pay. It is usually a shuddering elevator far above ground, but I prefer it to intense domesticity. Yeats used to say that the hearth killed more poets than alcohol.

I've recently had the uncomfortable feeling that despite my rather harsh Calvinist will, I've had less control over the trajectory of my life than I had presumed. I suppose it's because of the semi-religious nature of the original period of the calling. Without going into the anthropological aspects, the beginning of the calling when I was in my early teens was similar to a seizure. I had abruptly given up on organized religion, and I suspect that all of that somewhat hormonal fervor merely transferred itself to what I still think of as Art, whether painting, music, poetry, sculpture, or fiction. Keats and Modigliani seemed excellent models for a life! The fact that neither of them lasted very long is a nominal consideration for a teenager. If you spend hours and hours listening to Stravinsky while reading Rimbaud and Joyce, you are fueling a trajectory that is inevitably out of immediate control. If you reread all of Dostoyevski on Grove Street in New York City in a seven-dollar-a-week room with only an air vent for a window, you are permanently at age nineteen changing the nature of your mind. In your self-drama you are building an intractably wild mind that you'll have to live with.

Of course, in geological terms we all have the same measure of immortality. The heartbeat that is your own, that you occasionally hear while turning over in bed in a cramped position, doesn't last very long. The immediate noise your book might make is woefully impermanent, and self-importance is invariably an anchor. In immediate literary history, say the last fifty years, by reading lists of prizes and remembering vaunted reputations, you see how even the grandest fame is usually written on water. News magazines for years liked to refer to Faulkner as Old Mister Cornpone; when

I was a teenager, he was far less favored than James Gould Cozzens. Finally, what happens to your work is not your concern. Thinking about it gives your soul cramps that resemble amoebic dysentery.

The mail over the years has brought me thousands of manuscripts and galleys and letters from young writers. It is possible to drown in paper, but even more dangerous is the nasty mood of feeling put-upon. Other than recommending quantities of red wine and garlic, I am without advice. The closest I can come is, Don't do it unless you're willing to give up your entire life. Despite the human-potential movement, there is no room for much else. And Einstein was on the money when he said that he had no admiration for scientists who selected thin pieces of board and drove countless holes in them. You should always want your work to be better than your capabilities, as settling for less is a form of artistic death.

I'd also rather err on the side of creating humans as more than they are rather than less. There is a whining penchant for lifting the bandage, for forgetting that a body is much more than its collective wounds. In any culture, art and literature seem terribly fragile, but we should remember that they always outlive the culture. In an age of extraordinary venality such as our own, when the government is only a facilitator of commerce, they come under a great deal of general contempt, as if every single soul must become bung fodder for greed. But then we are nature, too, and historically art and literature are as natural as the migration of birds or the inevitable collision of love and death.

The Wolf in the Tall Grass

MARY GAITSKILL

Why do I write?

1. *To satisfy a basic, fundamental need.* I think all people have this need. It's why children like to draw pictures of houses, animals, and Mom; it's an affirmation of their presence in the corporeal world. You come into life, and life gives you everything your senses can bear: broad currents of animal feeling running alongside the particularity of thought. Sunlight, stars, colors, smells, sounds. Tender things, sweet, temperate things, harsh, freezing, hot, and salty things. All the different expressions on people's faces and in their voices. For years, everything just pours into you, and all you can do is gurgle or scream until finally one day you can sit up and hold your crayon and draw your picture and thus shout back, Yes! I hear! I see! I feel! This is what it's like! It's dynamic

...ation and pure, delighted receptivity happening on the same ...eld, a great call and response.

This is true even when the pictures describe horrible, even deadly events; the children at Auschwitz drew pictures. The word *delighted* may not apply in situations like that, but the fact that children draw pictures in such unspeakable circumstances shows the depth of the need to represent. Even when it's about pain and horror, it's still a powerful act to say, Yes, I see. I feel. I hear. This is what it's like. To do so asserts a fundamental, even fierce tenacity that a person needs to survive.

When I learned to write, at the age of six, the first thing I did was write a story. It was about blue jays that courted and married. They did things real birds don't do; I made it up, and in doing so I went from basic need to something more complicated.

2. *To give form to the things we can sense but not see.* You walk into the living room where your father is lying on the couch, listening to music. You are small, so he doesn't hear or see you. His face is reacting to the music, and his expression is soft, abstract, intensely inward. It is also pained. It is an expression that you have never seen. Then he sees you and smiles, but the music still fills the room with that other expression. Another time, walking on the street, you pass a stranger whose face arrests you; in her eyes you see something that makes you think of her alone in a tenement eating a cold-cut sandwich. You think of her missing someone she once loved who didn't love her. The woman has told you something with her eyes, and you've felt it; you don't know what it is, but you have a picture of it anyway. And it's something much more than what you saw physically. A friend of mine once told me that he still remembers seeing, as a young boy, his camp counselor come out of a cabin with an expression on his face that made

my friend start to cry. It wasn't because the expression was so sad; it was because it was filled with such hope and enthusiasm, which my friend imagined becoming increasingly damaged, worn, and brittle. He didn't know that to be true; he made it up.

When I was eleven, I wrote a story about a man who woke up in total darkness. He had no idea where he was, and he was very afraid. He tried to decide if he should sit and wait for it to get light or if he should move forward. After some thought, he decided to take a step forward, and he fell down his basement stairs. It was a kid's Twilight Zone story about a sleepwalker, but it was also about what I could sense and not see: something very ordinary— the basement stairs — becomes a big, mystic problem and then the cause of a cartoon pratfall.

As an adult, I once wrote a story about a man who discovers that his daughter has written about him in a highly personal way for a women's magazine. She hasn't told him about it; he hears about it by chance. It's a ridiculous and painful situation, for this father and daughter have had a miserable relationship that they've never discussed, and now here she is discussing it publicly, in "ghastly talk-show language." The very ordinary thing — the magazine — becomes a vehicle for the awful, complex darkness into which the man falls. Except that this darkness is very rich. The daughter uses language that is banal and cloying, but she is expressing powerful feelings. Ironically, the very strangeness and indirectness of his discovery of the article allow him to take in what she says in a way that he might not have done if he had been directly approached. His first reaction is anger, but slowly, almost unconsciously, he begins to feel things he still can't see — about his daughter and about himself.

Nabokov, in his published lectures on literature, said that literature was born the day a boy came running out of the undergrowth yelling Wolf, wolf, and there was no wolf: "Between the wolf in the tall grass and the wolf in the tall story, there is a shimmering go-between. That go-between, that prism, is the art of literature." I'm not sure I understand exactly what he meant, but I think it's partly this: stories mimic life like certain insects mimic leaves and twigs. Stories are about all the things that might've, could've, or would've happened, encrowded around and giving density and shape to undeniable physical events and phenomena. They are the rich, unseen underlayer of the most ordinary moments. I get great satisfaction from plunging my hands into that underlayer.

3. *To feel important, in the simplest egotistical sense.* This motivation may not seem to have much to do with what I wrote above, but it does. Strong thoughts and feelings about what you see and feel require a distinct point of view and an ego. If you are frequently told that your point of view is worthless, invalid, or crazy, your ego will get really insulted. It will sulk like a teenager hunched in her room muttering, "No one ever listens. No one cares. One day, they'll see!" To make them all see — i.e., see how important I am — was once a big part of why I wrote stories. As a motivation, it's embarrassing, it's base, and it smells bad, but it's also an angry little engine that could. It will fight like hell to keep your point of view from being snatched away, or demeaned, fighting even when there's no apparent threat. The only problem is, the more your ego fights, the smaller your point of view gets. For a while, I needed to take great pains to make myself feel safe, to the point of extreme social isolation, so I wouldn't feel like I had to fight. The angry engine quieted down a bit, and I began to learn about other points of view.

4. To reveal and restore things that I feel might be ignored or disre-garded. I was once in a coffee shop eating breakfast alone when I noticed a woman standing and talking to a table of people. She was young but prematurely aged, with badly dyed hair and lined skin. She was smiling and joking, but her body had a collapsed, defeated posture that looked deeply habitual. Her spine was curled, her head was slightly receded, and her shoulders were pulled down in a static flinch. She expressed herself loudly and crudely, but also diffidently. She talked like she was a joke. But there was something else to her, something pushing up against the defeat, a sweet, tough, humorous vitality that I could almost see running up her center. I realized that if I hadn't looked closely, I would not have really seen this woman, that I would not have seen what was most human and lively in her. I wondered how many people saw it, or even if she herself saw it. I thought of her when I wrote about a character named Patty, an aggressively promiscuous girl with a "nasty sense of humor" who repeatedly sets herself up to be rejected and brutalized. To me the character is affecting, not because she is a victim, but because her victimization comes about from her terribly misguided efforts to assert herself — from the sweet, tough, humorous vitality that goes un-recognized even by her and is grossly misused. The male charac-ter who shares the story with her, John, is someone who rather blindly mistreats her and realizes too late that he's sorry for doing so. His attempts to make amends to a stranger are so ham-fisted and inappropriate that they look like a grotesque come-on. The story ends in apparent futility and embarrassment. But John's bumbling effort harbors a very pure impulse: he is finally at-tempting to confront his own cruelty and to forgive himself for it. Even if he doesn't know it, the attempt is like a tiny bud of sorrow and compassion in him, and because it is so small and new, it's easily missed.

That kind of small, new, unrecognized thing is very tender to me, and I hate it when it gets ignored or mistaken for something ugly. I want to acknowledge and nurture it, but I usually leave it very small in the stories. I do that because I think part of the human puzzle is in the delicacy of those moments or phenomena, contrasted with the ignorance and lack of feeling we are subject to.

5. *To communicate*. To write about the kind of moments I've described above and to have people read what I've written and understand it is deeply satisfying. To read well is an act of dynamic receptivity that creates a profound sense of exchange, and I like being on both ends of it. In Saul Bellow's early novel *The Victim*, he describes his beleaguered protagonist on the way to a funeral parlor where his young nephew's body is being prepared for burial. He is walking through a working-class neighborhood:

> The heat of the pavement penetrated his soles and he felt it in the very bones of his feet. In a long, black peninsular yard a row of scratchy bushes grew, dead green. The walls were flaming coarsely, and each thing — the moping bushes, the face of a woman appearing at a screen, a heap of melons before a grocery — came to him as though raised to a new power and given another quality by the air; and the colors, granular and bloody, black, green, blue, quivered like gases over the steady baselines of shadow. The open door of the grocery was like the entrance to a cave or mine; the cans shone like embedded rocks.

This passage is a raw beauty (one among many in this book) that is as important as anything that happens in the book's plot. It opens life up down to the pit; when I read that, I can't ignore how extraordinary it is to be alive.

6. *To integrate; to love.* One of Nabokov's early novels, *Laughter in the Dark*, has an apparently simple, almost hackneyed plot: a foolish, wealthy, middle-aged man (Albinus) falls in love with a vulgar, heartless sixteen-year-old girl (Margot). She and her lover, Rex, proceed to destroy Albinus and his family in a ruthless, ultimately grotesque fashion. On the face of it, it's a soap opera, but what makes it extraordinary, aside from the beauty of the prose, is the author's gift for inhabiting every energetic strain of his breathing animal creations. Rex and Margot are absolutely evil, but they are also full of fierce life, wit, and supple, eel-like charm. Nabokov can step inside their cruelty and vitality almost as if it were an electrical current, then step out again and enter the much slower, cooler ambiance of their poor stooge Albinus, or the person of Albinus's bland, taffy-sweet wife, and emerge again, all in a flash. His expanded and detached sensibility can hold them all in a state of dazzling and organic movement, which is a mimicry of life's truth in the deepest sense. The ability to do this requires a great understanding of and regard for life that is, I think, a kind of love.

Sometimes when I write stories, my original impetus is small in the sense that it's personal. I'm perplexed or upset about something, and I need to address or unravel it, so I write about it, literally or metaphorically. It's the same kind of egotistical engine I mentioned earlier; it's got a lot of forward drive. But as I write the story, something happens. The drive is still there, but I lose interest in it because I'm noticing other things, and I'm no longer sure

I want only to go forward. John, in the story about Patty and John, is not a person I would like in real life. But on intuition, I told the story from his point of view. Once I inhabited his body, as he sat on an airplane, "rolling a greasy peanut between two fingers," I could feel how he'd gotten to the point where it seemed right to mistreat Patty. That didn't make it right, but it was impossible not to feel for him — or perhaps simply *feel* him — and thus see the story more deeply.

In another story, a lonely, middle-aged woman who has just learned of the death of an abusive former love goes to a party, gets drunk, and brings home a callow young man. The encounter goes badly, and when morning comes she is alone in bed with her unhappy memories. The situation is desolate, but it's also funny, ugly, tender, mean, affectionate, phony, and genuine all at once. At the very end, she hears her neighbors outside her window discussing the bonnets they're going to wear to the Easter parade. The situation may be bleak, but life is still outside the window, lively and mobile.

What I'm describing is a kind of integration because it requires holding many disparate elements together in a fluid mosaic: the middle-aged woman's self-wounding sexuality is present with her desperation, as well as her humor, her pain, her self-possession, and her compassion. John's brutish dullness is present with his sensitivity, his cowardice, his ineptness, and his strength. When I start writing a story, I don't feel like I'm integrating anything; I feel like I'm marching through mud. But at least some of the time there comes a moment when I feel I'm carrying all the elements I've just described and more in a big, clear bowl. It doesn't feel like I'm containing them. It feels like I'm bringing them into being and letting them be, exactly as they are. My perplexity and upset may still be there, but they are no longer the main event. I feel sadness because much of what is in that bowl is sad. But because of that tender sadness, I also feel humility and joy and love. It's strange because much of what I write about does not seem loving. But to write it makes me feel love.

Rent Retards the Revolution!

DARIUS JAMES
(AKA DR. SNAKESKIN)

WHEN THIS VOLUME'S EDITOR, Will Blythe, first telephoned and asked "Why do you write?" I paused in the middle of the sentence I was composing on my PowerBook, adjusted my Lt. Uhuru headset telephone, and thought for a moment. Finally, I said:

"I write because I can't *paint*."

"Good opening line," he said, encouraging.

"Maybe," I said, dubious — knowing, since "all writing is rewriting," that first sentences are usually trashed.

"There's five hundred bucks in it," he said.

Five hundred dollars would appeal to me only if there was a quick turnaround between the time I delivered the piece and Little, Brown's accounting department sent a check. But that wasn't going to happen, I knew. Publishing houses and record companies take their precious time about paying anybody anything (royalty statements are a great source of amusement for the published author. For example, my last book has a cult following in countries it hasn't even been *published* in [we're talking radio, TV, newspaper, fanzine, and Web-site coverage]. And yet, the last statement I received from my publisher said it earned . . . what? *Twenty-two dollars?*). By the time Time Warner parted with its money, and I actually held it between my fingers, the check would have instantly evaporated in the face of mounting debts. Gone in a puff of smoke. *Poof!* So money wasn't a temptation for this particular exercise.

"And you'll be in the company of writers like Norman Mailer," he added.

Norman Mailer? What had I read by Mailer? "The White Negro"? When was that published? In the fifties? Around the time of *Deer Park*? And it wasn't even one of his "fuggin" novels. It was an essay about how if white people really wanted to be "hip," they had to act like psychotic Negroes. Or some silly shit like that. The only thing I have in common with Mailer is that we're both from Long Branch, New Jersey (in fact, my father claims that when he was a child, he used to sell empty pop bottles to a man he believed was Mailer's dad, suggesting he brewed backyard 'shine). Being seen between the same covers as the Pugnacious Norm was not an enticement for me, either.

Frankly, I was reluctant to take on another assignment. I was under deadline for a long-term commission I had accepted, and I was anxious to return to my novel.

"Y'know," Will began, sensing my reluctance, "I was rereading *That's Blaxploitation!*, and I really thought it was a good book. I mean, there's a lot of really good writing there."

Why did he have to say that? Money and the allure of possible prestige weren't going to corral me into an exercise that would be of no value other than to remind me of the original reasons I do this shit in the first place. But I'm a sucker for flattery. Appeal to my vanity, I'm your friend for life.

"OK, I'll do it," I said, "but I've got this thing to finish first. I should be done by next week."

Will didn't realize that he would not only be acting as editor, but would take on the role of dentist as well, pulling this essay out of me as if he were pulling teeth. The "thing" I had to finish dragged on for another six months.

During those six months, I realized that much of what I write has little to do with why I write. And as I thought more and more about this, I found myself asking, with no small amount of cynicism and disgust, Why *do* I write? And why do I write *now*?

Up until the age of eighteen, I planned to be a painter (or a soldier in the overthrow of the American government, whichever came first — the bullet or the paintbrush). Throughout childhood, I was exposed to the worlds of painting and sculpture by my father, a trained painter/sculptor himself. My father taught me how to see creatively. And taught me what it meant to be a painter.

Painters were iconoclasts, people of defiant and singular vision, who were misunderstood and outcast by society. But it was these same "outcasts," these people who were deemed "insane" by the conventional social order, who created works of precious and substantial beauty. That, my father said, was a meaningful and worthwhile thing to do. So I painted.

But I also wrote. As a child, at age eight, my earliest writings were scripts for the monster movies I shot in a nearby woods with my wind-up 8mm camera. Later, since I also wanted to act, I wrote plays. My more "serious," purposeful writing grew out of the emotional crisis of teenhood. Then, confused by questions concerning identity, drugs, sex, authority, the hypocrisy of the

American mainstream, I wrote because I felt powerless and writing gave me a voice, words allowed me to define the world, they provided me with secure ground to stand on. I wrote to understand my battles, to clarify my thoughts, to make clear who I was, who I was going to be.

I also wrote to understand my rage. Now, looking back, I could attribute it to a number of things, like my mother's early death, or institutional racism; but for the purposes of this essay, I am going to focus on the salient details of one key primal incident.

One night in 1959, when I was four years old, and in the care of a neighbor while my parents were away at work, I rushed out of the apartment, down the stairs, and out into the street. When I turned my head to look back, I was knocked out of my shoes by a speeding car and flung forty feet through the air. The accident left me paralyzed, brain-damaged, and in a coma.

At the hospital, the doctors explained to my parents that there was nothing they could do. I was going to die.

But then my great-aunt Amelia Nixon appeared at my bedside. And in the company of a hougan priest (or "jackleg preacher," as my father called him), she prayed over my small and battered body. I revived after four days.

In my comatose state, I had a tunnel-of-white-light experience. I have vivid recollections of ascending upward through a cloud of fog, draped only in a gown of silver mist. And, quite abruptly, descending back down to earth.

"It wasn't my time to die," I said upon opening my eyes. "So God sent me back." Apparently, once I floated to wherever I was drifting, some weird white place that echoed with deep bass voices singing spooky Negro spirituals, I made a "cross-my-heart-and-hope-to-die"–type promise to whoever was in charge of controlling matters of Life and Death, and was sent back (and given the number of Satanists I count among my friends, I'm sure that's one broken promise I'm gonna pay for BIGTIME!!).

Needless to say, my recovery was a miracle. The doctors were amazed, my parents were grateful, and in spite of the medical prediction that I would be dead by the age of ten, I grew up to be a shiftless, no-account bohemian writer.

But supernatural intervention aside, I was still paralyzed and unable to walk. One night, after weeks in the hospital, frustrated by my bedridden state, I climbed out of my bed, shimmied down its leg, and began to crawl in an attempt to regain my ability to walk.

A nurse found me on the floor. She began screaming at me, calling me names, her face red and distorted with anger (it was a face I would see on teachers, principals, etc., over and over and over again throughout my childhood). The nurse then picked me up, dropped me on the mattress, and trapped me under a mosquito net tied to the bed's four corners.

As I fought against the netting, screaming in stark terror, a blond-haired boy whose head was wrapped in bandages because he had been kicked by a horse sat in my room and *laughed* at me.

The humiliation, confusion, terror, and overall helplessness I experienced in that situation were at the core of the feelings of powerless and voiceless rage I needed to understand and control in teenhood. And it was writing that helped me bring those feelings into perspective. I found power in words. I discovered I could call things into being with words. Writing was my form of magick, in Crowley's fullest sense of the term.

It was while attending the Educational Center for the Arts, a high school devoted to the "creative arts" in New Haven, Connecticut, that I made the decision to switch from painting to writing. I was in drawing class one afternoon, studying the line of a drawing I had done, and I realized that if I had to rely on painting for my livelihood, I was going to starve to death. For reasons that were intuitive instead of logical, I felt I would have a better chance of surviving as a writer. There was no concrete reason for feeling this; it was a vision I accepted on faith. Additionally, I could write without betraying the values and aspirations my father had instilled in me as a child.

More important, I had discovered, through writing, that I was able to transport myself into a wholly consuming imaginative world, one that affected all five senses, and was able to bring back the imagery and raw experience of that state and describe it in vivid and exacting detail. This was something I was unable to achieve through my efforts in painting. I was, however, able to achieve a similar transport as a result of the acting classes I attended in my high school.

Writing, acting, and painting taught me an important lesson: all art is interrelated, and writing is adaptable to a variety of expressive mediums. Writing does not necessarily involve the published word.

As this was the seventies, the other element in all of this was that psychedelic chemical of schizophrenic fun, LSD. I found I could re-create an acid trip I had taken, simulate it in words on paper, and have a reader experience similar sensations. This, actually, is the reason I write: the answer buried inside a platitude reeking with the rancid stench of patchouli oil:

"Revolution begins with a change in consciousness."

My writing is dedicated to fomenting that change. Writing should detonate in your brain like a strong dosage of acid, exploding in an abundance of color, attacking all that is accepted as sacred and true, rearranging, changing all sense and sensibility. Writing should dump the jigsaw puzzle of reality on the ground. Let the reader put the pieces back together again.

None of this answers why I am cynical. Or why I feel disgusted. When I ask myself, Why do I write? the question is superseded by another: What does writing mean to New York publishing?

I grew up influenced by publications like Paul Krassner's *Realist*, *Ramparts*, the *Evergreen Review*, and *Avant Garde*, and publishers like Grove Press under Barney Rosset and Fred Jordan. For me, it was the last really daring period in American publishing. Writers were actually allowed to write then, to write freely and challenge their readership with provocative ideas. That situation really doesn't exist anymore.

Now, once a manuscript leaves a writer's hands for those of a commercial publisher, it becomes a product to be marketed and sold. It means little more than that. And the really sad part is, publishers have proved themselves to be *poor marketers*. How is it that a publisher can spend $150,000 on a writer's advance, and once the book is published, no one ever knows it exists?

Magazines are no better. Intelligent journalism is truncated into demographically dictated copy to justify occupying space purchased by corporate advertisers. It appears to me that severe restrictions have been placed on the published word.

And in the midst of all this, I continually find myself torn between the demands of writing that fulfills my original, acid-inspired intent. And grinding out bullshit for slick, no-brain publications to pay the rent. Rent keeps winning out. *And it's retarding the revolution!*

So why do I continue to write at all? Why do I continue to suffer through the frustration and heartbreak? As the late Michael O'Donoghue once said, "It beats digging ditches!"

The War We Can't Win, We Can't Lose, We Can't Quit

BARRY HANNAH

I ALWAYS EXPERIENCE a mild depression whenever I type up what I have written. This act seems redundant. The work has already been done. I adore the praise of the public, no mistake. But the primary motive must be unpublic. Much more, I'd guess, the inner journey of the imagination itself. There is the ecstasy. The rest is simply good. Some money, a little fame. Not to be rolled over like scuttling claws by the sands of time. Et cetera.

I write out of a greed for lives and language. A need to listen to the orchestra of living. It is often said that a writer is more alive than his peers. But I believe he might also be deader than his peers, a sort of narcoleptic who requires constant waking up by his own imaginative work. He is closer to sleep and dream, and his memory is more haunted, thus more precise.

I write to live, and I write to share. The Original Creator's version seems random and fascistic, but there are enough consistencies, if you wait and watch for them, to give remarkable tales. You must wake up terribly to catch them, even though what you produce may be close to dreams.

My life seems precious, even though often sad, and crammed with mystery. My past seems a fine gray, like good old movie rain. I forget almost nothing. Even when I was a drunk I recalled too much, and hence was forced to relive events in an agony of shame. Friends and confederates are often astounded by what I remember of certain afternoons an age ago — weather, dress, music, mots. A blessing and a curse. I feel superior to nobody because of the gift, and in other talents I rank very low. I do not rate myself highly in thought, for instance. I find life too vivid for thought, really. Thus I go about preaching, of course, that thought is overrated.

I see them pass still, the little old tiny-headed women of Clinton, Mississippi, in the fifties, in their giant cars on the brick streets. Or on their porches or at their azalea beds scolding dogs, then me; nestled in the pews and bobbing heads in the aisles of the church. Bringing in their covered dishes to church suppers. They established the tone of my world. All of them dead or ancient beyond years now. They observed and accounted. I fled them, I was a creature of the night, a little sinner. Or was I only paranoid, like the biblical thief who fleeth when none pursueth? Those days when they were big, these women, in my youth. But now I see their replicates in my grown town, don't I? I always wanted to explain to them how they didn't know how it was, they hadn't the faintest. I picked up the rhythms of scripture for my tales, I'm certain, but it was mystery and sin that had me. I was not the echo for the voices of the tiny-headed women. Was not antiphonal to their voices. I was the dreadful opposite voice to whatever they asserted, the polar howling wretch. In Baptist songs I always liked where you were a wretch or a worm, or just as I am, helpless.

But many of the women were kind, too kind, to me. Mrs. Bunyard in the third grade, why she encouraged my tales and lies, so long as I wrote them down. Even at the same time she made us wash out our mouths with hard soap for swearing, or even for finding any humor in the term *jackass* at all. This was in the good days when teachers listened patiently to your explanations, then beat hell out of you with a holed board. Fiction is work, and I suppose there would be no fiction in the Garden of Eden until the apple and the Fall. Begins the mystery of evil, or of the Other. And the making of books of which there is no end, as warned in Ecclesiastes.

Another kind woman, Mrs. Ashley, was the object of an early mystery, such things as I have been obsessed to declare. I have never written about this, but there was a boy — M., I'll call him — in the Royal Ambassadors with us. He was one of us, I insist. Mrs. Ashley was ward for us boys of the church. One day she took us to the circus in Jackson. M. did not go with us. But while we were away, he attacked Mrs. Ashley's bedroom. Trouble of the brain, a sudden cyclone of it. M. destroyed many items, both costly and worthless. He did not steal. He simply wrecked the place and left it so. There was no explanation. He was not jealous of the circus; he could have gone. But he chose not to. He was a silent, tall boy with wide gray eyes. Nobody recalled his saying much at all, only a mutter or whisper every now and then when he was pressed. Nothing was done to him, but he sank off the town map. He disappeared into the scandal. I cannot even remember his reappearance, though I know he still came to church and school. But he was erased from our eyes by his pathology. Nobody wanted to look at him. The fury hidden in M. We looked away, ashamed for him. Where is he now? What is there to say for him? What is his story? What is it, M.? Please deliver. No. So I'll write one for you, pal, these many years from you. It still matters. And there at the center, kind little tiny-headed Mrs. Ashley, who loved all her boys. And M., this was the thing. He was one of us, he was no stranger.

The Furies turned up the volume of our own inner voices, it is told. Such was their punishment. These voices want both definition and deliverance. So I write to both record them and free myself of them. Once you are into the life of writing, you are never really rid of the inner voices, and they are certainly not all your own. They will exhaust themselves for a time, but then there will be another siege and you have to sit down and do something about it.

Even as a Baptist Christian woman, my mother told yarns. She would be telling about events when I had accompanied her, and I would know that what she told had not happened. I believe she was completely unconscious that she was enlarging on the truth. Otherwise she would know I could shoot her down, as an eyewitness. I think it was the Irish in her. To my father I owe a sense of diction. I never heard my father make a grammatical error. He was an insurance salesman and then a banker. His customers were Jews and blacks as well as the usual whites. People trusted him. He would not lie, and he never importuned. I don't believe he had a sales pitch at all. Because of Depression poverty at home, he had been unable to finish at the university. He loved knowledge and good language all the more for that, and read a book a day when he retired, a solid and respected success. He told me once about the dog and the robin at a service station in Forest, Mississippi. The dog adopted a wounded robin the owner had in a box under the counter. He licked and nuzzled the robin. The robin was almost well after two weeks and began hopping around the station, not quite able to fly yet. Then the dog, ever faithful to his friend, began playing with it. Unintentionally, he killed the robin. Then the dog was very sad. The men of the station, too, were in black grief. My dad told me this story in a faraway voice full of tenderness and wonder. There was no moral. The whole thing had been both wonderful and terrible. Whatever kindness there is in my work I owe to my parents and to the unflagging love of my brothers and sister, who all told tales and gave me the world. I was spoiled rotten, late babe that I was, and inherited great pieces of their lives before me.

I have evermore been amazed by bursts of kindness in improbable times, the warm hand in dire straits.

But it was an eruption of vileness unprovoked by anything beyond local ennui that marked my first public art, and it was theater. I still remember the complete happiness of making that tape. Reel-to-reel recorders were avant-garde where we lived. Four pals and I set about enacting a wrestling match with commentary, with a few jokes about prominent parochial fools — the Dead Deacon, the Choir Hag, Minister Masturbo, Butt Ream Rob, the Renegade Cheerleader. This was high adolescence, a valedictory to high school, and we had wild fun making it in the instrument room of the band hall. But the tape fell into the principal's hands. He announced over the public address system to the entire student body that something had fallen into his hands, as he put it. It was so corrupt that it had shaken his faith in Youth In Our World. It was a sad, sad artifact, a thing that would crush, just crush the parents of the offenders if they knew. He paused. Was he weeping, or just stringing out the fear? Cold chills took me. This seemed the end, expulsion. But nothing was ever done. Over and over I recalled my contribution to the tape, where the Dead Deacon "was kicked in his giant balls just aflappin' out of his trunks there. . . . He seems to be, oh, no . . . he's vomiting out . . . what . . . waves, I tell you . . . of turnip greens . . . my holy God!" There was no redeeming theme. It was no dreadful sermonette. It was just dreadful. But it was precious, I tell you. It was my art. And it was out there in the hands of the public. Many years later the principal, in his senility, drove down a sidewalk and into a store in a remote town. When I heard this I immediately thought of our tape.

Then to correct the tape, a fantasy, with Upont, I'll call him.

Upont was from St. Louis, and even at eighteen he looked seedy. He had big whiskered cheeks, a slouch, and the waist of a man deep into middle age. He played third-chair trumpet in the marching band, and even his cornet was nasty, green, brown, and splotched, leaking saliva at the spit valve. But he was one of us. He had a nasty wit and a big-city accent we'd hardly heard, so that even the mildest comments from him sounded cynical and decorated with slime. Actually, we thought he was fairly wonderful, and he hung with us in the room, the cafeteria, vespers, there at the college. I guess it was a college. They called it a college. Very Christerly. Conscious of the far mission fields but not of the world.

I was at the local movie house on the big hill, and there was some commotion in the lobby. Small children coming down the stairs to the balcony and pointing upward from where they'd fled. I went up there and in the front balcony seat was Upont with his arm across the shoulders of a small local boy. The boy was frozen there as Upont whispered in his ear and then fastened a tongue on his cheek. The boy just sat staring ahead. This was the thing, just as Upont was the thing. He was one of us, he was Youth In Our World. I cannot forget his utter obliviousness, his helpless tonguing of the child, his whispers. Children around them had fled with little howls of alarm, baffled nausea, signs of throwing up. Upont was heedless, too deep and gone into it. And the boy was allowing it. He seemed fascinated by it all. A first in our time, in our town. It could not be. One of us. It took Mrs. Moddy, one of those tiny-headed women, who ran the movie house, to separate them. I was so wretchedly astonished that I just hung there, mouth open, then quickly fled out the doors and down the hill, lest I be connected to Upont. When I saw my pals in the dorm room I could hardly speak. There seemed to be no straight narration to the event. Grave new world. This was no fantasy, no tape.

Upont was "withdrawn" from the college, as the books have it. We did not much discuss him, but he was still in the room with us. The voices began in my head, and never have I set Upont down in print until now.

The fact is, in a real way, Upont's passion was more sublime, even in its horror, than was our wrestling skit, which was only teenage filth. And the child, this is what kept me going. Just sat there, tongued, whispered to, fascinated. He was ready. You had to gather Upont was a pro. He could spot them. And who could know whether this illicit tenderness might one day proceed to a cyclone of destruction, as with M.'s strange afternoon. Even homicide, I discovered later.

I must get this right.

Must tell it for all of us.

Especially those bright and hungry pals I ran with in school, always my best audience, forever.

It is clear now I had no real stories through college, though I was bragged on by my poet teacher and even accused of plagiarism by another old-bat teacher who wrote verse for greeting cards. My work was bursts of expression that imitated content and charmed others. The fact is, I wanted to write long before I had anything to say. I don't find this condition at all unusual in young writers, good or bad. A sort of attuned restlessness. Often it is simply an overriding need to talk. A sort of transcribed logorrhea, worse than decent gossip. I've taught these people, forever blasting away in high-volume, wretched detail, solidly in love with their own noise. I must say, I was never infatuated by my own voice. It was the ideal inner voices that took me, and they came from everywhere, especially Hemingway, Joyce, Henry Miller, and later Flannery O'Connor. Like many Mississippians, I shied away from Faulkner, who was at once remote and right there in your own backyard, the powerful resident alien. Having read a little of him, I sensed I would be overcome by him, and had a dread, in fact, that he might be the last word. That I would wind up a pining, third-rate echo, like many another Southerner. Then T. S. Eliot, especially "Prufrock." But the earliest great howler who made me want to make the team was the badly forgotten Dylan Thomas, whose voice seemed available everywhere in English departments in the fifties and sixties. It seemed to me a fine thing to get drunk and just start being Welsh and crowing surrealism, as I perceived it. Put that against the sullen bitchery of Holden Caulfield, which charmed almost everybody my age, and you would be cooking. Miles Davis might one day shake your hand. He was God, and that would be very nice.

On a pier in the early sixties, Bay St. Louis, with a fine-looking girl who was dumping me but being pleasant about it, I accidentally declared myself. The brown waves of the two-rivered bay of the Gulf of Mexico were lapping against the piling, and we were alone. Maybe she wanted me to hurt a little, come to think of it. She was in a two-piece red, white, and blue swimsuit, blond hair on her shoulders that broke your heart. She was a smart girl from Millsaps College, but from a poor family in an old gray board house. Her father stamped the price on cans at the grocery. Her mother was frankly mercenary. I was in the running when I was premed, very hot. Then it became known I had changed to English major, and I was cold. Nancy, however, thought this needed a polite farewell, because she did like me. I was in street clothes and she was near nude. But what will you *do*? she asked me. I had no idea. I had no interest in teaching, only in my stories and wretched Beat poems. But I blurted, "Protect the King's English," just to be ironic, hip, careless. I felt like a very mocked knight at the time, a sad punk, really, but what I said is what I have tried to do all these years, even when I had nothing much to say. The language still strikes me as a miracle, a thing the deepest mind adores. At its best, when you lose your arrogance and are least self-ish, it can sing back to you almost as a disembodied friend.

I think of those moments in Faulkner, Beckett, and Holy Scripture when the words seem absolutely final, bodiless, disattached, as out of a cloud of huge necessity. My desire is to come even closer to that team — to be that lucky, to be touched by such grace. I do believe that as you write more, and age, the arrogance and most of the vanity go. Or it is a vanity met with vast gratitude, that you were hit by something as you stood in the way of it, that anybody is listening. When you are ashamed and revising your comments to old girlfriends of thirty years ago, you might be shocked to find out you really have nothing much better now than what you said in the first place. This is what I would tell her now: I want to say good stuff.

I finally had a real story at age twenty-three up in Fayetteville, Arkansas.

This followed a near–religious conversion tedious to everybody but me, I'd guess. I'll only say that I became more committed to people who could never tell their own stories and that I was no longer ashamed of being from the most derided state in the union.

Another time I was fishing one Saturday afternoon with my father, my nephews, and my small oldest son, Po, who was afire with Jimi Hendrix at the time. We were catching big bass, all of us up and down the dam, with minnows on cane poles. My father sat there in his lawn chair with his vodka and his cigar, king of the hill. All the nephews, his grandchildren, were rushing to bait his hook as he presided there. I had a novel out after enormous work. It had been celebrated widely, though it sold nothing, and I was a whole man. The sun went behind a cloud and the wind went up, and we were almost dark, in a sudden chilly breeze, a momentary violent change almost as if to another, northern geography. In July, out of the heat, it seemed pure magic, and it felt wonderful. I knelt there consumed by a decision. A huge bass suddenly grabbed my line. I went into a spiritual ecstasy. My family was all around me, we were in heaven. You could cut the joy with a knife. We all felt it, though nobody spoke. This is it, this is it, my life! To say good stuff, like this. To say it, maybe so well they won't forget. This is it. Thanks to God. Later, before his death, my father told me he had never had a better day. He caught a seven-pound bass, the family record. But that's not what I mean, son, he said. The other day my son, out of nowhere, asked me, "Dad, do you remember that day on Elwood Ratliff's dam?"

Twenty years ago I was out in the woods alone. The weather was clear and very cold, but felt good. I had a Pall Mall in my hand and I walked into an old abandoned cabin of the Roosevelt era. Inside the cabin was just a bit warmer than out. A dusty tin bed with a thin mattress on brown springs. I wanted to light the Pall Mall very badly, but I waited awhile for the dark. The hairs of a feral dog lay in a circle on the planks in front of the hearth. In the last grip of faint grays, I lit the cigarette, and the smoke felt exquisitely good inside me. I knew I was pledged to something. This lonesomeness, this cold lost place I would soon warm up. Nobody knew where I was, nobody. It wanted to be lived in here. I knew life would be sad but quite fine then. I felt a hum of joy in my head. Like some old muttering conquistador stumbled up with a flag to ram the staff into God knows what mud.

Forever afterward I would crave abandoned rooms in lost places, me with my pencil and paper. I would mount a small country here. The frame was already there, you were not really a conquistador, let's not kid our girlfriends. But you would warm up and put something in this hole. It might leak a little bit, but it would be yours.

From all my military readings I have gleaned the comment most pertinent to me and the gals and pals desperately given over to the writing life. The writer meant Korea and Vietnam, but he put his truth to the exact same glory and grief of our efforts: "It's the war we can't win, we can't lose, we can't quit."

I'm waiting, however, for the future priest to be kicking around shards of our old cabins. He finds some pages: My God, it's paper, ancient paper. He bends over, holding the cigarette pack–sized computer to his shirt pocket so it won't fall out.

Poor devils, the old scribes, jabber jabber, yadda yadda, he says.

But wait, this is pretty good.

Collecting Myself

TOM CHIARELLA

I CAN'T DO MUCH of anything, except write.

I have no jump shot. I can't balance my checkbook. Small machinery puzzles me. I have no nose for news. Cooking bores me. I don't concentrate on physical tasks very well. I can't stack cans, lift weights, or knead bread. I'm lousy with small details. Can't cut a square corner on a true piece of lumber. I don't proofread well. I like cameras, but I take shitty pictures. I enjoy certain paintings but have no heart for museums. Money? Forget it. I'm not good with money.

I'm not particularly strong. Running hurts me, and I'm dreadfully slow. I'm an OK driver, but I doze off after long distances. I fancy myself a dancer, but I've noticed that my partners must be very drunk to enjoy my lead. I'm not photogenic. I'm wildly afraid of heights and don't much like the dark. I have quick hands but no muscle memory. At work, I bungle the routine stuff and bear down to dig myself out of holes when things pile up. I do not sleep well in the summers.

The things I *can* do are embarrassingly useless. I can walk a long way, but I have to talk to myself along the route, telling fantastic lies, carrying on imaginary conversations with long-dead historical figures in which I convince them to make different choices, thus changing history. I must look like a schizo-phrenic. This embarrasses me. I can drink a lot of liquor, but since my thirtieth birthday, the headaches have become wildly punishing. I have never, to my memory, vomited, but my insides often ache, making it hard to predict from day to day what my mood will be. I have passed a kidney stone and am obsessed with the likelihood that I'll pass another. I am a reasonable car-toonist, but I can't draw the same character twice. I can post-up in basketball, which doesn't help me much since I can't jump. I used to be able to hit a baseball, too, but the skill abandoned me when I needed it most — in the clutch, when-push-came-to-shove, whatever. Suffice it to say, once I could hit a baseball. No more.

That said, I'm fat, overly impressed by wealth, and can re-member by name only nine of the thirty-two classes I took in col-lege. I never finished *Moby-Dick*. I can't play casino blackjack — not for long periods of time, anyway, and not when I'm drinking. I'm a reasonable poker player, but I've never played high stakes, so who's to say? Every putt I've ever made in golf has been a mat-ter of pure luck or overwhelming fear, and I play a lot of golf. My penis is on the short side. My grades in school were marginal, and even so I cheated on tests in high school, college, and graduate school. I've never hit another man square or fair, except my brother, and only when he was much smaller than me. Someone else does my taxes. My father buys my stocks. I do mow my own lawn, but it looks better when other people do it. My mother taught me to like gardening, but from year to year my perennials remain clumped and fisted; my annuals never flourish beyond the edges of their pots.

In short, I do a lot, but I don't do it particularly well. Indeed, there is nothing I do well. But I write. I always will. Everything I've done — all that I have survived, the things I've learned, what leaps I have forced upon myself, the choices I've made, the mistakes I've brought upon myself — all of it has come through writing. For me, writing is neither therapy nor solace. It heals no wounds. By itself, it teaches no lessons. It takes me by the nose but leads me nowhere. Still, the only way I get anywhere at all is by writing, so I persist.

Barring the above, I'm not such a terrible loser. Whatever paradoxical glimpses of myself I lend to the world in my everyday life — the loafer, the achiever, the guy with the reasonable touch around the greens, the choke-artist with the putter, the friend, the husband, the father — were all learned by writing. Notice that I did not say by telling stories, I said by writing. Any clown can tell stories. The "storyteller" — that school-visiting, self-aggrandizing, grant-grabbing, tie-to-the-past-claiming performance artist manqué, that scab-picker of the written word who populates the innumerable festivals of art and academe — knows nothing of the chill pleasure of writing. The private blackness. The close-your-eyes-and-render. The inward turn. The improvisation of the storyteller is the shallow end of the creation pool. The storyteller rambles for the village, stumbles forward merely to witness the effect of the tale upon the audience, a loathsome voyeur to himself. The writer is another breed. The writer hoots only to himself, hems without the titter of an audience, employs only the percussion of his heart to keep at it.

It is the most lonely industry. Alone. Crouched. Slouched. Slogging. I write with my own self, no one else. What I love about life — the delicate web of ice in a cocktail glass, the wet roiling soil of spring, the surprising hands of my children — is completely disconnected from the act of writing. You know this stuff: images, fragile, ethereal, distinctly imported from the land of the living. But these things occur to me only when I write. I grab them up. I write to collect the world. Otherwise I stumble through it, nothing more.

About a year ago, I had a car accident. I had been running errands. Allergy shots. Bank deposits. Tire inflations. Prescription refills. At one point I bought two boxes of wine and some beer and set them in the front seat of my Honda. I drove off to drop them at my friend's house for a party we were having later that night. Upon arriving at his house, I realized I had forgotten the ice.

As I was heading back to town, a kid in a hepped-up Mustang plowed into me from the left. All I can remember now — the plume of smoke, the serpentine slice of his tires against the blacktop, my sad little cry of fear ("Not that!") at the moment of impact — is mere snatches. As I write about it, it occurs to me that the impact was thick and juicy, about what it would feel like to hit a cow as hard as you could with a wooden baseball bat, both cruel and unusual. Still, the savage movement of my little car, which spun 540 degrees, struck me as strangely pleasurable. Afterward, the fact of my own survival made me giddy.

But the impact threw my legs across the front seat, into one of the boxes, shattering most of the wine bottles and drenching me in midrange Chardonnay. Thus, pulled from my car, I had a story to tell. Right away. People pressed me for details. Soon the cops were there, wanting to know everything. Why wouldn't they? I was a state trooper's wet dream. I smelled like wine, I couldn't keep my balance, and I'd just been involved in a high-speed collision.

I told them what I could, which was very little. Nothing came together. I knew my name. I knew where the stop sign was and had a clear sense of the mechanics of the collision. Point-A-to-point-B stuff. I relayed what I could. Even then, pinpricked by glass shards, bleary and whiplashed, I was thinking what I always think, not just in moments like this, but in every moment, on every day: I'll survive. I'll write about this. Then I'll know what's happened to me.

This is my first shot at it. It is probably not wise, as there are lawsuits in the offing, depositions still to be made; in situations like this they tell you not to say anything, not to put anything in writing. But really, what else can I do?

Ask a transvestite, "Why are you a transvestite?" and he'll tell you, "Because I wear women's clothes." At least a smart one will. Take his word for it, too. Other transvestites you ask will giggle or take a swipe at you, justify or shrug. Ignore them. They're not talking about themselves. They're responding to you and your reaction to them. The first one, the smart one, is talking about himself, about what he does and why.

I write. The longer I live, the more convinced I become that I cultivate my truest self in this one way. I pay more attention when I'm writing, and I hear myself most clearly when I'm writing. Don't get me wrong: I love to talk. Haggling about a file cabinet at the office, gassing on about the Redskins or spinning ice in my glass while recounting a movie plot, I can jabber with the best of them. But it just ain't me. Not all of me, anyway. The clearest me, the only version of me that I hear, is the one that's writing. If I'm not doing it now, I should be. Otherwise I'm just picking up more crap, starting up something I'll never finish, buying something I don't need, or reading something I couldn't give a shit about. So I write. There's nothing else for me.

Why She Writes

JAYNE ANNE PHILLIPS

THE SHORT ANSWER

I DON'T KNOW WHY, and I hope I never find out.

GUILD MEMBERSHIP, OR WORKING THE HOLE

I admit I'm given to magical thinking (as though thinking should be anything else), and I would never actually demand of myself an answer to the question. What do I know about myself? Enough to know very little. I wouldn't claim, as a celebrated writer once did, that "whatever is good about me is in the writing, all the rest is shit." The same writer was asked if he had any friends or intimates who weren't writers. "Why would I want to?" he responded — a response I understand and quietly applaud. I think of literary writers as members of a guild of outcasts, a species, through time, of the gifted handicapped, regardless of their success. You see, there really *is* no success — in terms of the writer, as opposed to the work. For the writer, the work is never what you thought it would be, or what you hoped. Sometimes it's better; if the writing is any good, it struggles free of you, and the feeling of being inside it just as it moves away is so brief; a sensual visitation, the brush of His hand. You, on the other hand, are never free, or off the hook, it is never done, writing is a process, book to book, finished piece to abandoned fragment, dream to compulsion, every failure linked to its luminous twin star. Ah, the hook with its gleaming prong, the abyss with its deep, narrow slit, its dark that plummets forever! There is the divided consciousness, the sense of leading a double life, depending on how "normal" the writer appears to be, or tries to appear to be. People have said to me, "You wrote that? You look too normal." You should look *different*, is the implication, you should have four arms or glow in the dark, so we can tell you from the rest of us at a glance and not be fooled. Writers drive cars, hold jobs off and on, raise children, climb mountains, and take out the garbage, but very few have retirement plans. Retirement from what? Thinking? Being? We try to handle our habit (William Burroughs: "I was working the hole with the sailor and we did not do bad"). We go off the rails and lose the job or screw up our relationships, then we pull it together, patch it up, but all the time, while we apologize, castigate ourselves, resolve to do better, the process of writing goes on, the secret reserve is honed and moving, moving toward writing, into writing, until death cancels all.

Double Life, Then and Now

Maybe back then, the expatriates in the cafés of Paris, Jack Kerouac when he was off with the boys instead of living with his mother, Colette with her diaries and lovers, Katherine Anne bedecked in emeralds, maybe they were writers all the time, every minute, the interior life *was* the life. That's like the writer turned inside out, for all the world to see — not a pretty prospect, and not so brave, finally. Much harder to wear the white dress and smuggle notes through the hedge, live on the slim word delivered through the mails from a like mind, drive the carpool, and much riskier, too, because writing might vanish altogether. Writing, never truly fastened up by props, always threatens to flicker out, like the one flame that keeps you breathing, guttered in the draft. Yet writing will not desist. There is no question of stopping. You can be like Rimbaud and stop actually writing the words, but you can't stop wanting to write, needing to; you can't stop leaning toward language. And frankly, if you do stop, nothing will mean anything ever again, and you'll watch all you love, everything you've ever wanted to save, all you need to invent, do a long, slow fade. You must try: commit to the magical, the invisible, while life itself keeps going, doing one thing while you save yourself for another — the writing. So you stand there with one foot in the pit, in the black hole that sucks its own energy into an alternate dimension. Light is inside it, far inside, blinding light. The light starts as glimmer, like phosphorescence on a fly's wings, and bent color, like the bronzy reflections in an oily puddle, and gets brighter, bigger, hotter. You zip on the asbestos suit, deep inside the black slit, and walk through flames. It's not about personality or strength or weakness; the writer may require a cork-lined room, fall down drunk daily, or be a perfectly lovely person. It's about writing. The instant the protection of language falls away, there is the odor of singed hair. Fall back! Fall back! And begin a renewed approach. We're in control of our rituals. We're in control of a repetition of discipline, of sitting in the chair. When something works, it may feel like the strike of lightning or a solar storm, but it's never a sustained climate. The writer can't make it happen, or make it happen again. Deep into a poem, a story, a novel, through practice and the honing of instinct, the writer can begin to follow the work, descend with it, a brain in a diving bell, breathing through a tube.

Open Veins

Despite membership in the guild of outcasts, writers do, by quirk of fate or sex or addiction or parenthood, become intimate with *others*, with those who don't originate from the planet of words and language. *Other* things do happen, but we don't know what they are until we write about them, or think about them in words, or remember them in phrases. Experience, more real than words, vanishes. Intimacy is transitory, but its effect lasts as long as consciousness regards it. Words float memory, awaken desire; words do pull people in, even demanding, haunting words, because language is, finally, a matter of survival. *Mama. I want. Yes. No. Stop. Go.* And more. Human beings can't live without the illusion of meaning, the apprehension of confluence, the endless debate concerning the fault in the stars or in ourselves. The writer is just the messenger, the moving target. People love turning their backs on writers, as they will, repeatedly, turn their backs on themselves. Inside culture, the writer is the talking self. Through history, the writing that lasts is the whisper of conscience, and history regards individual voices in various ways at various times according to the dictates of fashion, whimsy, values, politics. The guild of outcasts is essentially a medieval guild existing in a continual Dark Age, shaman/monks, witch/nuns, working in isolation, playing with fire. When the first illuminated manuscripts were created, few people could read. Now that people are bombarded with image and information and the World Wide Web is an open vein, few people can read. Reading with sustained attention, reading for understanding, reading to cut through random meaningless-ness — such reading becomes a subversive act. We're not talking detective books, romance, cookbooks, or self-help. We're talking about the books writers read to feel themselves among allies, to feed themselves, to reach across time and distance, to hope.

Nature and Nurture

The writer is, first, genetically predisposed to write, and second, born into a constellation that nurtures her. That constellation is composed of fixed stars that move through time in concert with one another: the mother, the father, the brothers, the sisters, who-ever comprises one's primal family, one's first universe. Whether present or absent, the father and mother first function as magnetic poles, polar opposites, counterparts, North Star, the tip of the Southern Cross. That universe is characterized by relationship and history: the unresolved childhood dilemmas of the mother and father, the passion and/or lonely distance between them, the dashed expectations that may find new life in relationship to the child of the union, the child who takes the place of the counter-part, the child who becomes the parent, the child who becomes the confidant, the child who becomes . . . there are endless varia-tions. But the child who evolves into a writer is the child in the process of becoming, who moves into position, who receives the bad and the good, who notices, who listens, who remembers, who saves, and he or she first does so for the sake of the loved one, the giant who shines such light and casts such shadow. Recognition is burden and blessing: the child is recognized as special, presented with truths or secrets, told stories. Promises are spoken or simply evolve. The writer is not the child who is ignored, or the one simply indulged. More often, the writer is one to whom much is given or entrusted, verbally or spiritually, the one of whom much is expected, the one with whom a bond beyond death is forged. The child is amply influenced, chameleon-like, perhaps, able to leap points of view in a single bound, possessed of a permeable identity. The die is cast. If the child survives, is educated, encounters teachers in books and schools, in streets, on corners, he or she begins to write, becomes an outlaw early on. The giant who first embraced the child may stand back aghast. The writer's first affinity is not to a loyalty, a tradition, a morality, a religion, but to life itself, and to its representation in language. Nothing is taboo. The writer will go anywhere, say anything to get it said; in fact, the writer is bent on doing so. The writer is bent.

TORTURED AND TANTALIZED

Ego enters in, but writing is far too hard and solitary to be sustained by ego. The writer is compelled to write. The writer writes for love: for lost love, perhaps. The writer lives in spiritual debt to the someone or something who needed saving, who first passed on the talisman — language, the gold key in the palm of meaning. Writers of literature don't write for gain or attention or praise, though they'll take all that when they can get it. There are exceptions, but even "successful" writers, when their incomes are averaged out over a working lifetime, do well to make a postman's salary, without the benefits. There are teaching salaries, but teaching shoots writing in the head. Sometimes the writer lives on afterward, blinking to say what he wants. But it's like when you stop smoking: the writer quits teaching, and the lungs pick up in ten weeks, the brain relearns its functions. The writer is an autonomic nervous system, a heart that won't stop pumping. The writer dreams selectively, more attentive to the conversation going on behind him than to the one in which he is engaged. The writer is probably ADD; she values her deficits and often leads with them. The writer is a good mom; he feeds the baby and then forgets where he left it. She's a stalwart soldier; her weapon is in good repair, but she keeps mixing up borders, crossing into occupied territory. They both cook for the troops. They take in strays, recognize wandering souls. Good Buddhists, they ring the bell when it's time to sit. Their practice involves silence, focus, white space, waiting. Alone yet postcoital, associatively drenched, they arrange small, two-dimensional symbols in endless combinations. The avatar is inside the word; there will be an audience soon. Awake, asleep, in every moment of being, the writer stands at the gate. The gate may open. The gate may not. Regardless, the writer can see straight through it.

In Silence

ROBERT STONE

W HEN I BEGAN TO THINK UP stories, as a child, it was because stories were my greatest childhood pleasure. I also found
that in an environment where it was very difficult to gain approval, I could get some positive reinforcement from storytelling.

My interior world felt like confusion, a source of fears and un-
requited aspirations and disappointment. But it was also, as far as
I could determine, where joy originated, and hope for and fantasies of a different, better life.

I made a few discoveries in the earliest stages of my reading that
I never quite got over. One was that a story could be knit together
in such a way that it completely dominated the mind's eye and ear
and became an alternative reality. Certain books and tales
seemed to accomplish this more effectively than others. It was like
the difference between a good trick and an indifferent one.

I also found that a story did not have to end happily to be satisfying. That even stories that made you feel like crying, or did make you cry, like Andersen's or Wilde's fairy tales, provided a certain comfort. They were almost scary to read, because you knew that they would end in your tears. Yet the satisfaction, paradoxical but undeniable, was as intense as that to be had from any funny story. After a while I realized that their secret lay in the fact that they made the world less lonely. Almost every way one felt, it seemed, could be made into a story. About then it occurred to me that stories were about recognizing the way things were. In other words, they were about truth, and truth was important.

Very early on, I thought that the ability to combine character and incident with a measure of that truth was a very fine thing to be able to do. When I was a child, there was a children's card game called Authors that featured writers like Whittier and Dickens, Longfellow and Poe. Although I can't now recall any of the rules of the game, I remember thinking that these characters with their chin-whiskers and feather pens must be great men indeed. (We believed in Great Men then.) There were, as I remember, no women writers in the game, which seems almost impossible now. But I never doubted the stature of these old-fashioned gents. I had a certain sense of what they had done for a living, and I had even read some of their work.

Whittier's "Snowbound" was, I think, the first and most vivid poem I can remember, my first favorite. Like most people, I remember poetry first.

> The sun that brief December day
> Rose cheerless over hills of gray
> And, darkly circled, gave at noon
> A sadder light than waning moon.

And "The Rime of the Ancient Mariner," which I read before I could comprehend its argument but the lines of which haunted me:

> Like one, that one a lonesome road
> Doth walk in fear and dread,
> And having once turned round walks on,
> And turns no more his head;
> Because he knows, a frightful fiend
> Doth close behind him tread.

That got to me.

I thought writing was a great thing to do, and I wanted to do it, too. I was unhandy and unartistic. I could not draw anything but stick figures, or fashion base materials into the shape of something greater. But I loved language; I loved its tricks and rhythms and ironies. Although I had been taught there was a time to keep silence, I thought there were times when the world, in its loneliness, required something other than the vast silence in which we labored. I knew no other way of not being alone in the world than through language.

Eventually the silence came to seem to me like an absence of something that must somehow be invoked. I knew only writing, that message in a bottle, with its artificial sounds and mimicked speech and tropes, as a means of invocation. I knew only narrative as a way of making sense of causality. Silence could be an enemy, a condition to which we had been consigned and to which we must respond. Because I respected the silence, however cold and alien and hostile, I wanted to make that with which I tried to answer it worthy of its terrible majesty.

Who Is That Man Tied to the Mast?

MARK RICHARD

Say you have a "special child," which in the South means one between Down's and dyslexia. Birth him with his father away on army maneuvers along East Texas bayous. Give him his only visitor in the military hospital his father's father, a sometime railroad man, sometime hired gun for Huey Long, with a Louisiana Special Police badge. Take the infant to Manhattan, Kansas, in winter, where the only visitor is a Chinese peeping tom, little yellow face in the windows during the cold nights. Further frighten the mother, aged twenty, with the child's convulsions. There's something "different" about this child, the doctors say.

Move the family to Kirbyville, Texas, where the father cruises timber in the big woods. Fill the back porch with things the father brings home: raccoons, lost bird dogs, stacks of saws and machetes. Give the child a sandbox to play in in which scorpions build nests. Let the mother cut the grass and run over rattlesnakes, shredding them all over the yard. Make the mother cry and miss her mother. Isolate her from the neighbors because she is poor and Catholic. For a playmate, give the child a mongoloid girl who adores him. She is the society doctor's child and is scared of thunder. When it storms, she hides, and only the special child can find her. The doctor's wife comes to the house in desperation. Please help me find my daughter. Here she is, in the culvert, behind a bookcase, in a neighbor's paper tepee. Please come to a party, the doctor's wife sniffs, hugging her daughter. At the party, it goes well for the nervous mother and the forester father until their son bites the arm of a guest and the guest goes to the hospital for stitches and a tetanus shot. The special child can give no reason why. Further isolate the family in the community.

Move the family to a tobacco county in southside Virginia. It is the early sixties, and black families still get around on mule and wagon. Corn grows up the backs of houses, even in town. Crosses burn in yards of black families and Catholics. Crew-cut the special child's hair in the barber shop where all the talk is of niggers and nigger lovers. Give the child the responsibility of another playmate, the neighbor two houses down, Dr. Jim. When Dr. Jim was the child's age, Lee left his army at Appomattox. When Dr. Jim falls down between the corn rows he is always hoeing, the child must run for help. Sometimes the child just squats beside Dr. Jim sprawled in the corn and listens to Dr. Jim talking to the sun. Sometimes in the orange and gray dusk when the world is empty the child lies in the cold backyard grass and watches thousands of starlings swarm Dr. Jim's chimneys. At age five he feels like he is dying in a gloomy world.

Downstairs in the house the family shares is a rough redneck, a good man who brought a war bride home from Italy. The war bride thought the man was American royalty because his name was Prince. Prince is just the man's name. The Italian war bride is beautiful and has borne two daughters; the younger is the special child's age. The elder is a teenager who will soon die of a blood disease. The beautiful Italian wife and the special child's mother smoke Salems and drink Pepsi and cry together on the back steps. They both miss their mothers. In the evening Prince comes home from selling Pontiacs and the forester father comes home from the forest and they drink beer together and wonder about their wives. They take turns mowing the grass around the house.

The company the father works for is clearing the land of trees. The father finds himself clearing the forests off the old battlefields from the Civil War. The earthworks are still there, stuff is still just lying around. He comes home with his pockets full of minnie balls. He buys a mine detector from an army surplus store and the family spends weekends way, way out in the woods. One whole Sunday the father and the mother spend the day digging and digging, finally unearthing a cannon-sized piece of iron agate. The mother stays home after that. On Sunday nights she calls her mother in Louisiana and begs to come home. No, her mother says. You stay. She says all this in Cajun French.

The little girl downstairs is named Debbie. The special child and Debbie play under the big tree where the corn crowds the yard. One day the special child makes nooses and hangs all Debbie's dolls from the tree. Debbie runs crying inside. Estelle, the big black maid, shouts from the back door at the special child to cut the baby dolls down, but she doesn't come out in the yard to make him do this, and he does not. She is frightened of the special child, and he knows this. If he concentrates hard enough, he can make it rain knives on people's heads.

Maybe it would be best if something is done with the special child. The mother and father send him to kindergarten across town where the good folk live. The father has saved his money and has bought a lot to build a house there, across from the General Electric Appliance dealer. Because he spent all his money on the lot, the father has to clear the land himself. He borrows a bulldozer from the timber company and "borrows" some dynamite. One Saturday he accidentally sets the bulldozer on fire. One Sunday he uses too much dynamite to clear a stump and cracks the foundation of the General Electric Appliance dealer. The father decides not to build in that neighborhood after all.

In the kindergarten in that part of town, the special child feels like he is on to something. There are records the teacher he calls Miss Perk lets him play over and over. When the other kids lie on rugs for their naps, she lets him look at her books. During reading hour he sits so close to her that she has to wrap him in her arms while she holds the book. The best stories are the ones Miss Perk tells the class herself. About the little girl whose family was murdered on a boat and the criminal tried to sink the boat. The little girl saw water coming in the portholes, but she thought the criminals were just mopping the decks and doing a sloppy job. Miss Perk tells about the car wreck she saw that was so bloody she dropped a pen on the floor of her car for her son to fetch so he wouldn't have to see the man with the top of his head ripped off like he had been scalped. On Fridays is show and tell, and the special child always brings the same thing in for show and tell: his cat, Mr. Priss. Mr. Priss is a huge, mean tomcat that kills other cats and only lets the special child near him. The special child dresses Mr. Priss in Debbie's baby-doll clothes, especially a yellow raincoat and yellow sou'wester-style rain hat. Then the special child carries Mr. Priss around for hours in a small suitcase. When the mother asks if he has the cat in the suitcase again, the special child always says No mam.

Miss Perk says the way the other children follow the special child around, that the special child will be something someday, but she doesn't say what.

The father and the mother meet some new people. There is a new barber and his wife. The new barber plays the guitar in the kitchen and sings Smoke smoke smoke that cigarette. He is handsome and wears so much oil in his hair that it stains the sofa when he throws back his head to laugh. He likes to laugh a lot. His wife teaches the mother how to dance, how to do the twist. There is another new couple in town, a local boy, sort of a black sheep, from country folk, who went to Asia to be a flight surgeon and is back with his second or third wife, nobody knows for sure. At the reckless doctor's apartment, they drink beer and do the twist and listen to Smothers Brothers albums. They burn candles stuck in Chianti bottles. The special child is always along because there is no money for a baby-sitter, and Estelle will not baby-sit the special child. One night the special child pulls down a book off the doctor's shelf and begins to slowly read aloud from it. The party stops. It is a college book about chemicals. In two months the child will start first grade.

At first, first grade is empty. Most of the children are bringing in the tobacco harvest. The ones who show up are mostly barefoot and dirty, and sleep with their heads on the desks all day. A lot of them have fleas and head lice. Most of them have been up all night tying tobacco sticks.

At first, first grade is incomprehensible to the special child. Of course that is the alphabet, what do you want me to do with it? What do you want me to say about it? What do you want from me? The child wants to get to the books, but the books are for later, the teacher tells him. You must learn the alphabet first. But the child has learned all that already: Miss Perk taught him the letters perched in her lap at her desk while the other children napped, and he taught himself how they fit together to make words sitting close to her as she read from children's books and *Life* magazine. The special child thought the tobacco children had the right idea, so he put his head on his desk and slept through the A's and B's and C's.

He won't learn, he doesn't learn, he can't learn, the teachers tell the mother. He talks back to his teachers, tries to correct their speech. He was rude to kind Mr. Clary when he came to show the class some magic tricks. You better get him tested. He might be re-tarded. And he runs funny.

The special child is supposed to be playing at the General Electric Appliance dealer's house with his son David. The son has a tube you blow into and a Mercury capsule shoots up in the air and floats down on a plastic parachute. The special child may have to steal it, but first he decides to go to visit Miss Perk's. Maybe she has a book or something. Miss Perk does not disappoint. She is glad to see the special child. She tells him that the Russians send men up in Mercury-capsule things and don't let them come back down. She says if you tune your radio in just right you can hear their heartbeats stop. She says if you ever see a red light in the night sky, it's a dead Russian circling the earth forever. Can I come back and be in your school, Miss Perk? No, you're too big now. Go home.

Back at the General Electric Appliance house, there's nobody home. It is too far to walk home, so the child lies in the cold grass and watches the gray and orange dusk. At dark, his life will be over. There's a gunshot off in the clay field a ways away, and something like a rocket-fast bumblebee whizzes through the air and thuds into the ground beside the special child. He stays real still. There's not another one. The child is beginning to learn that things can happen to you that would upset the world if you told about them. He doesn't tell anyone about the thing that buzzed and thumped into the ground by his head.

Y'all should do something with that child, people say. The mother takes the child to Cub Scouts. For the talent show, the mother makes a wig out of brown yarn, and the special child memorizes John F. Kennedy's inaugural speech. They laugh at the child in the wig at the show until he begins his speech. Afterward, there's a lecture on drinking water from the back of the toilet after an atom bomb lands on your town, and everybody practices crawling under tables. For weeks afterward, people stop the child and ask him to do the Kennedy thing, until finally somebody shoots Kennedy in Texas and the child doesn't have to perform at beer parties and on the sidewalk in front of the grocery store anymore.

The mother starts crying watching the Kennedy funeral on the big TV the father bought to lift her spirits. She doesn't stop. The mother won't get out of bed except to cry while she makes little clothes on her sewing machine. She keeps losing babies, and her mother still won't let her come home. The father sends for the mother's sister. They pack a Thanksgiving lunch and drive to Appomattox to look at the battlefields. It rains and then snows and they eat turkey and drink wine in the battlefield parking lot. The mother is happy, and the father buys the special child a Confederate hat. After the sister leaves, the mother loses another baby. The father brings the special child another beagle puppy home. The first one, Mud Puddle, ran away in Texas after the father drove it from Lake Charles, Louisiana, to Kirbyville, Texas, strapped to the roof of the car. He had sedated it, he tried to convince people who were nosy along the way. When they got to Texas, there were bugs stuck all in its front teeth like a car grille. When the dog woke completely up, it ran away.

This dog, in Virginia, the special child calls Hamburger. The mother cries when she sees it in the paper sack. Maybe we need to meet some more friends, the father tells the mother. OK, the mother says, and wipes her eyes. She always does what her husband tells her to do.

There's the big German Gunther with the thick accent and his wife, who manage the dairy on the edge of town. They have a German shepherd named Blitz who does whatever Gunther tells it to do. The special child is frightened of the vats of molasses Gunther uses to feed the cows. The child is more interested in the caricatures down in the cellar of Gunther's old house. Gunther's old house was a speakeasy, and someone drew colorful portraits of the clandestine drinkers on the plaster wall behind the bar. They look like people in town, says the special child. It's probably because the cartoons are the fathers of people in town, says his father.

Gunther's wife finds the special child lying in the cold grass of a pasture watching the sun dissolve in the orange and gray dusk. You shouldn't do that, she tells him. If an ant crawls in your ear, it'll build a nest and your brain will be like an ant farm and it'll make you go insane.

Later on, Gunther falls into a silage bin, and his body is shredded into pieces the size a cow could chew as cud.

The timber company gives the father a partner so they can reseed the thousands of acres of forests they are clear-cutting down to nothing. Another German. The German knows everything, just ask him, the father says. The German and his wife have two children the special child is supposed to play with. Freddie is the boy's name. Once, when the special child is spending the night, a hurricane comes and Freddie wets the bed and blames it on the special child. After that, the special child breaks a lot of expensive wind-up cars and trains from the Old Country.

From the helicopter the father uses to reseed the forests farther south, you can still see Sherman's march to the sea, the old burnage in new-growth trees, the bright cities that have sprung from the towns the drunken Federal troops torched. Yah, yah, dat iz in der past, says the German, you must let it go.

The father and the German are in North Carolina cutting timber in the bottom of a lake. The dam to make the lake isn't finished yet. The father and the German have become good friends. Sometimes they do their work way back in the deep country away from company supervisors and sometimes they walk through empty old houses on land their company has bought for timber rights. In the attics they find rare books, old stamps, Confederate money. One day eating lunch in the bottom of the lake, the father and the German figure how much more timber has to be cut before the water will reach the shore. They say, You know, if you were able to figure exactly where the shoreline will be, and buy that land, you could make a small fortune.

On the weekends, the father and the German break their promise to take their families to Indian caves they have found and have picnics and ride everybody around on the bush motorcycles they use to put out forest fires. Instead, they spend every extra hour of daylight cutting sight lines with machetes, dragging borrowed surveying equipment and measuring chains around the edge of the empty lake.

The money they give the old black sharecropper for the secret shoreline is all the money they can scrape out of their savings and their banks. The old black sharecropper accepts the first offer the father and the German make on the land left to him by his daddy.

Most of the shoreline property they buy from the timber company, but they need an access road through the old black sharecropper's front yard, past his shack. Everyone knows the lake is coming, but the father and the German don't tell the black sharecropper the size of their shoreline purchase, just as he doesn't tell them he has also eyeballed where the shoreline will appear and is going to use their money to build the state's first black marina, with jukeboxes and barbecue pits, right next to their subdivision. He doesn't tell them they just gave him the seed money to build Huff's Marina and Playland.

Twenty acres of waterfront property, two points with a long, clay, slippery cove between them when the dam closes and the lake floods. The German gets his choice of which half of the property is his because he was somehow able to put up 10 percent more money at the last minute. He chooses the largest point, the one with sandy beaches all around it. The father gets the wet, slippery claybank and muddy point. The father tells the mother it is time to meet some new friends.

Meet the American Oil dealer, the one with the pretty wife from Coinjock, North Carolina, a wide grin, and a Big Daddy next door. Down in the basement of his brand-new brick home, on a brick mantel, the oil dealer has a little ship he put together in college. Most people, if they are even guessing, foot up near the fire, glass-leaning with bourbon, take the little model to be a Viking ship. It is not a Viking ship, even though the little fur-tunicked men seated at both rails pull oars beneath a colorful sail. Who is that man tied to the mast? asks the special child. Upstairs the adults play Monopoly in the kitchen and drink beer until the father drinks a lot of beer and begins to complain about Sherman's march, and Germans, and it is time to go home.

Later on, the special child is guarding his house with his Confederate hat and wooden musket while his mother and father are at the hospital having a baby. The oil dealer drives over in his big car and spends the afternoon with the special child. He has a paper sack full of Japanese soldiers you shoot into the air with a sling-shot and they parachute into the shrubbery. He shows the special child how to make a throw-down bomb with matchheads and two bolts, but best of all, in a shoebox he has brought the special child the little ship off the brick mantel and he tells him who Ulysses was. It is a good story. The only part of the story the child does not quite believe is that somehow Ulysses was older than Jesus. He doesn't say anything to the oil dealer because the oil dealer is being nice, but he will have to ask Miss Perk about this later.

Here's some pieces that have come off the ship over the years, the oil dealer says. There are a couple of Ulysses' men in his shirt pocket. Thank you, says the child. The child spends the weekend at the oil dealer's house with his wife and children waiting for his mother and father to come home from the hospital empty-handed again.

More bad luck. The people at the dam the father calls the idiots keep turning the knobs on the water back and forth. One day the father and the German take their families on a surprise picnic to look at their waterfront property, and from a hill above their land they can see the lake, way down there over miles of mud. Then one day they come back and find Mr. Huff sitting on the front porch of his sharecropper's shack surrounded by water. All y'all's land under water, says Mr. Huff. Ain't nothing you can do about it. Man came round and said so. Said it's in your deed. The father and the German go to see a lawyer. Mr. Huff is right.

One night while his mother is fixing supper, bad luck starts for the special child. He is in the living room, where he saw an angel pass through on Easter morning, watching the Three Stooges with the sound turned down real low because the Three Stooges upsets her. It is a good Three Stooges. It is the one where Moe and them run back and forth up and down some train cars and stuff happens and there's a lion loose out of the baggage car, but the best part is when Moe keeps stubbing his toe on somebody's little suitcase every time he runs past it until finally Moe opens the train door and throws the little suitcase off the train into the night, and Moe just doesn't stop there, he keeps throwing suitcases off the train, all by himself, he just keeps throwing people's suitcases off the train in the middle of the night until he looks around and sees that he has thrown everything off the train he possibly could, and then he can relax and be himself again and not be angry. The child has seen this Three Stooges before, but this is his favorite. The only problem this night watching it with the sound turned down real low while his mother cooks supper waiting for the father to come home, the only problem is that partway through the show, the child hears a truck just outside slam on its brakes and blow its horn and he hears a dog yelp and he hears cars slow down and people getting out and men talking and somebody going around the neighborhood knocking on doors and asking Whose dog is that and he hears the people downstairs answer the door, he hears Prince say Yeah, he thinks he knows whose dog it is, and he hears Prince call up the staircase to the mother she might want to come down 'cause it looks like a dog looking like their dog got hit by a log truck, and the mother says Oh no, and comes in where the child is watching Moe start to throw the suitcases from the train with the sound turned down real low, and she says We'd better go see about Hamburger, but the child does not move from the TV he is kneeling so close in front of, and the mother has her coat on now and says Did you hear me? Hamburger just got hit by a truck and still the child does not move, does not make movements to get up even though he loves his dog and if it is true that his dog is dead then he will want to die as well, but the child kneels in front of the TV and concentrates on Moe throwing the suitcases off the train, because deep inside him he knows that he can concentrate really hard, like when he learned the Kennedy speech, like when he stepped on a copperhead and the snake would not bite him even though it should have, the child knows that if he can only concentrate hard enough that Moe will keep throwing everything off the train forever and time will stand still and he will never have to die because he will not have to go downstairs and see his dog twisted and smeared across the street and hear somebody, maybe the nervous log-truck driver, maybe Prince himself, make a joke about what his dog's name used to be and what the dog is now.

He never goes downstairs, even though he concentrates in his mind to make the story continue forever and the news comes on and his mother appears up from the street and looks at him in a new way like maybe what some people and teachers say about him is true and maybe they ought to have him tested.

The father comes home late that evening after hand-digging a firebreak almost by himself down in some cornpone county where the rednecks came out to watch the fire burn a stand of company pine. For about eighteen hours the father and a pulp-wood contractor and his pimply son worked to turn a fire that sometimes stood fifty feet high in the trees over their heads and flanked them a hundred yards on either side, sometimes closing. It was good not having to think about his life savings underwater or his sad wife and her lost babies or his strange son or Sherman's march, digging, shoveling, trying to breathe. The father can barely climb the steps up to the top of their house. All he wants is a drink and a hot soak. He has recently started sipping whiskey rather than the beer. His hands are raw and his back and shoulders ache. In the last hours the fire lit a turpentine stump and about a hundred snakes spat themselves up out of the ground and flowed like a stream over his boots. His nerves are still a little jangly.

Up at the top of the stairs stands his special child hardly able to catch his breath from crying so hard and not wanting to wake his mother. The special child clings to his pants legs by the pockets and tells him he wants to die because his dog Hamburger is dead, isn't there something his daddy can do about it, and all the father can do about it is pet the boy's head and go back downstairs, get the fire shovel out of the back of his truck, and hope he has enough strength to bury what is left of the little dog in the corner of the cornfield out back of the house.

Here is some more luck the German and the father have. One day they are driving the German's Volkswagen bus up a cliff road to check on some land the company is clearing. A log truck loaded with company logs comes around a corner in the middle of the road. The German also always drives in the middle of the road. In the collision the flat-fronted bus folds forward and the German's legs are pinned and broken in several places. The father is luckier. He raises his arms to his face in time to protect it as he goes through the windshield. In his luck, he flies through the windshield, and then over the cliff. He goes over the cliff and lands on some railroad tracks at the bottom. Luckily, the train is late that day. They find his eyeglasses perfectly balanced on a train rail, unbroken.

Here are some of the people who comfort the family: Dr. Jim's wife on the one side of the house. The other next-door neighbors, the Shorts, and next to them, the Longs. The special child has always thought it would be nice to live between them. Down the street a whole block of Misses — Miss Laura, Miss Effie, Miss Robert, and Miss Henrietta, who used to be a Mrs. until her husband had a heart attack and died the first time they had sex, everyone said. Down the next block, another, older block of spinsters, bitter children of the Reconstruction too old to come out to bring food but send Negro maids with bags of bad fruit from trees in their yards. The barber and his wife come, and the doctor with his third or fourth wife, and Prince and his Italian wife are always there. The father, laid up with a broken leg, busted head, split ribs, and ripped arm, teaches his son to play chess on a little folding set he has from college. The mother sits at the foot of the bed and watches. They all wait for the oil dealer to come. The oil dealer always brings a paper sack of cold beer and ice cream and silly jokes.

You ought to meet my cousin Ruth Ann, the oil dealer tells the mother. She's a lot of fun and she has a daughter they said ought to be tested, too.

The special child has never seen a movie before. He is stunned. *Misty of Chincoteague*, on a mile-high drive-in screen. In Ruth Ann's Rambler she drives fast down the middle of the highway, her and the mother in the front seat, the two special children in the backseat. Christie, the other special child, with impossibly tangled red hair, says, Actually, *Misty* is for babies. Christie says if the special child liked *Misty* so much then he ought to come over and watch *The Invisible Man* on TV on Saturday. She says she knows how to make the house dark even in the afternoon and make it scary. The special child is still hung over from concentrating on *Misty*. It was almost better than Moe throwing suitcases from the train. While he is thinking this, Christie says to her mother that she is going to vomit. Ruth Ann keeps her Rambler going fast down the middle of the highway talking a mile a minute to the mother and says for Christie just to do it out the window. Lean way out and try not to get any on the car.

The special child holds Christie's legs as she leans way out and vomits. It feels like she might crawl all the way out if he does not hold her. He wraps his arms around her legs and presses his face against her bottom. When she is through he pulls her in the window; her red hair is a solid mess of tangles. The special child helps clean her mouth and face of popcorn and 7-Up with an old black slip that for some reason is crumpled up on the floorboard of the backseat of Ruth Ann's rambling car.

When the father is feeling better and up on crutches he decides to drive them down to Louisiana and the mother packs that day even though they won't be leaving for a week or so. He says they will have a vacation, visit some battlefields on the way down, make a long trip out of it. He will borrow a car from the company, a gray sedan with a two-way radio in it.

Before they leave on their vacation, the school invites them to have the special child tested on the first Saturday after school closes for the summer. First grade is over. Bring good pencils.

When the special child shows up with the mother for the testing the mother is glad to see Ruth Ann there with Christie and Christie's cousin Lynn. They are all three going to be tested together. Most of the test is written and is fun, but some of the test is with a witch. The witch has cards and blocks and boxes of gears. Once during the testing, Christie has to vomit. Lynn doesn't even care that Christie has to vomit. Christie is always vomiting. That is one reason she is being tested.

The closer they get to Louisiana on their vacation, the madder the father gets. Maybe it is all the battlefields. Maybe it is all his broken places. Maybe it is all his land underwater. Maybe it is all the driving time he has to think about everything, driving on the roads before there are interstates between Virginia and Louisiana. Maybe it is going home. Maybe it is because everybody thought he would go real far in life and thinks he should be there now, him near the top of his class in chemical engineering at Rice, the people at NASA wanting him bad, and then in his senior year him switching to LSU and forestry so he could be out in the woods by himself all the time. Maybe that is underneath it all, riding in a hot car over asphalt and tar with a trembly wife and special son for days. Maybe he just doesn't like people at all, maybe that's it.

At the mother's mother's house in Louisiana, they have spicy chicken and rice and beer in coolers in the kitchen and black coffee and fried bread and brothers coming in off shifts in the oilfields and refineries to see their big sister, the brothers tossing the special child up in the air and taking him out back to see how they are putting a stock car together. Cousins and uncles and aunts come over all speaking French and Uncle Comille with his pigeons and Buddy with his five sons. Only the mother's father sits a little away from things at the table playing solitaire and smoking unfiltered cigarettes. In his life he has been a miner, a baker, a rigger, a cowboy, a pipefitter. To make ends meet, he now drives a mowing tractor at a golf course, bringing home buckets of old golf balls he runs over. Maybe now he is tired.

It is quiet across town at the father's mother's house. You can hear the grandfather clock on the back gallery ticking all through the house. Dinner will be at high noon. There are no brothers or sisters. One cousin, somewhere. Big Bill, the father's father, lets the special child, his only grandchild, sit in his lap and play with his Shriner's ring and with his warts. Before high-noon dinner of turkey and dumplings Big Bill has a shot glass on either arm of his chair, one filled with bourbon, the other with ice water. The special child likes the moments in between the drinks when the body he is slumped against relaxes and the warm deep breath blown out down on the top of his head smells sweet.

The father's mother is a big woman from Sumrall, Mississippi, who was used to more than her husband has provided over the years. He had been away a lot on Huey Long's Special Police force and then on the railroad, and when he came home he would go away on the weekends hunting and fishing with his best friend, a Jew, Dr. Goldsmith. The father's mother did not like Huey Long, and she does not like Jews. She had a pet Negro growing up named Scrap. When Big Bill takes their laundry in to the black part of town, he often stays all morning, listening and talking and eating fried-oyster po'boy sandwiches. Since Big Bill retired and came home for good, he mostly stays in his shop in the garage putting people's clocks together for them. The big clock at the nuns' convent is always stopping, and when he goes over there to fix it, they feed him lunch and make him stay all day.

On a side trip to New Orleans the women go shopping with the father along to watch their bags and Big Bill takes the special child to Jackson Square to feed the pigeons. It is hot and Big Bill takes the child to some bars off Bourbon Street to get out of the sun and to meet some friends of his from the old days. In the bars are friendly people with parrots on their shoulders, big laughing bartenders in white shirts and black bow ties who give Big Bill his two shot glasses and the child ginger ale colored with maraschino cherry juice. Big Bill lets the child sit on his lap on his bar stool while they watch the street go past the open barroom doors.

Up on a glass shelf in one of the bars they go into to get out of the sun that afternoon, the child sees a wind-up toy lit from underneath with green and red lights. The bartender takes it down and winds it up and sets it on the bar. A little monkey in a fez plays the drums nodding his head and kicking his feet. It is like Moe throwing luggage, like Misty swimming off Chincoteague: so long as that monkey keeps playing the drums and nodding his head and kicking his feet, time stands still for the special child. Wind it up again, wind it up, can we wind it up again please sir?

Come on Snort, Big Bill calls his grandson, and Big Bill takes them out of the bar and onto a streetcar out to Audubon Park. A lady in her bathrobe on the streetcar has a plastic flower in her hair and carries a long piece of wrought iron tipped like a spear it looks like she has pulled out of someone's fence. She asks Big Bill for a dime and he gives her a dollar. Where you going? she asks. I'm taking my grandson to the zoo. Well, say hello to my uncle, says the lady. He works at the zoo? asks Big Bill. He's locked up in the monkey house, says the lady. He's a monkey's uncle. Well, we'll say hello, says Big Bill, we're on our way to the monkey house. My boy here seems to like monkeys.

It's incredible, the monkey house. A big castle surrounded by a moat with millions of monkeys playing with themselves like humans and shouting at the tourists and sometimes flinging a handful of poo-poo at the people leaning over the rail.

I want to stay here all day, says the special child. OK, says Big Bill, we will, and they stay until it is time for them to go.

On their way out, the child sees a man walking around the monkey house. The man is picking up trash with a nail on the end of a stick. He carries a big burlap sack slung over his shoulder for the stuff he finds. He doesn't even have to bend over to pick it up because he has the nail on the end of the stick.

Is that that man's job? the child asks Big Bill.

Yes, says Big Bill, that's what he does.

He gets to walk around the monkey house all day with a nail on the end of a stick finding stuff? wonders the child.

Yes, says Big Bill.

In the storeroom off the back gallery of Big Bill's house the child finds lots of treasures. There are *National Geographics* from the very first year. The child mostly likes the castle, ship, and monkey issues. He finds his father's helmet from when his father was in the army. There is one thing he finds that he likes a lot better than the *National Geographics*: a box of old photographs of blown-apart people and horses and snow. When he pulls it out and asks about it, they take it away from him, and on his later visits the box of photographs is gone.

In the First World War, when Big Bill was a young man enlisted from deep within the bayous to fight the Germans, some officers took him into French towns with them because he spoke a kind of French, this kind of French being his first language, English an annoying clutterance later. The officers liked Big Bill and Big Bill became not only their interpreter but an ambassador of sorts, because Big Bill got along well with the French people they met and the French people liked Big Bill and made allowance for the coarser Americans, his army superiors.

As a gift, an officer had given Big Bill a simple box camera. With the simple box camera, Big Bill took dramatic photographs of his friends struggling and dying with their horse-drawn artillery in the heavy snows of the Argonne Forest. The only happy photograph was taken by a stranger on the returning troopship, showing a very thin Big Bill and two other soldiers, all who were left of the cannonade they had been.

Here's something you can play with, the grandmother tells the special child. She sets an old Royal typewriter on the dining-room table. Write me a letter, write me a story. The child tries to type the story of Misty of Chincoteague in several sentences. It takes most of the afternoon.

When it is time to go back to Virginia, the mother cries and begs to stay at her mother's house. Here, take some food I am making for you for the trip, the mother's mother says, ignoring her crying. The mother's mother cooks spicy food and fries up some bread and this makes the father angry because he hates when his clothes smell like fried bread. The child is afraid he will have to return to Virginia with his father by himself. They have a big going-away barbecue for the mother, and her brothers tie her up in the backyard and wash her hair for her with the hose until she says uncle. Everybody laughs except the father, who watches from the garage where the stock car and tools are, sipping beer. When the child tries to save the mother one of his uncles sets him on top of the garage roof and later makes him ride a pony.

Sometimes, on the ride back to Virginia, because the company gray sedan with the two-way radio looks like an unmarked police car, the father drives up behind people he thinks are driving too fast and flashes his lights and makes them pull over, then he speeds off. He stops doing this when in Georgia he accidentally pulls over an unmarked police car and the state trooper is very angry at the father. Later on, in North Carolina, the father seethes and speeds faster.

It had been so hot while they had been away in Louisiana that the candles the mother had stuck in the Chianti bottles were drooped over on the mantel.

There is a lot of mail. There is a letter from the invention company where the father has sent an invention. It is an invention for hooking up a device onto a kite string that can send things up to the kite and then release them so they can float to the ground. The father got the idea watching the special child trying to slingshot his Japanese parachutists as high as he could in the backyard. The father tried to explain the idea to his brothers-in-law in

Louisiana and they were polite about it but you could tell they didn't understand why anyone would want an invention like that, an invention that sounded, even to the special child as his father explained it, like something a little childish. Right on the spot, the brothers-in-law took some pipes and welded together a cannon that would shoot old golf balls about a hundred yards. You can take it back to Virginia with you, they told the child when they were leaving, giving him the cannon, and they said good luck to the father about his invention, even if they didn't understand it. When the father gets home from Louisiana, the invention company doesn't understand the invention and they don't want it, either.

In the mail are the test results. One test result says the mother is most likely pregnant again. The other test result says the child is eligible for a special school if the father can afford it.

The father goes down to check on his underwater property. While he and his family were away in Louisiana, the idiots at the dam finally adjusted the water levels on the lake just right. The shoreline is exactly where he and the German predicted it would be. In the lowering fluctuations of the lake, all the German's beautiful sand has washed along the father's shoreline and blanketed his property with long, broad beaches. Where the German's beautiful beaches had been were ugly slick stretches of slippery red clay corrupted through and through by the black roots of drowned trees. Dat iz in der past, you must let it go, the father tells the angry German, and the German and his family move away.

In the fall the special child starts second grade. His second-grade teacher is Miss Caroon. Miss Caroon has seen his test results, so she lets him spend as much time as he wants reading *The Box Car Children* and Mark Twain in the cloakroom while the other children struggle with Dick and Jane and Baby and Spot. Miss Caroon lets him wear his father's army helmet in the classroom if he wants to, and she lets him try to pass off the wad of Confederate money he always carries. At Thanksgiving when he draws the Pilgrims coming to the New World in a Chinese junk greeted by Indians selling Live Bait and Cold Beer, she hangs his picture on the wall with all the rest without extraordinary commentary.

Miss Caroon gives the children in her class a list of words from which to make a story. In the stories the class turns in, dogs get up on the furniture when they aren't supposed to, or someone finds a coin. From the special child she receives "The Ancient Castle," in which a Good King goes away to conquer an enemy and while he is gone an Evil King comes and lays siege to the Good King's castle. The Evil King's men scale the walls and some of the Good King's favorite men are shot full of arrows and beheaded. Just when all seems to be lost, everyone looks up and sees a brilliant flash of light on a distant hill. It is the sun shining off the Good King's shield. The Good King and his men come and slaughter the Evil King and all of the Evil King's men. The people in the Good King's castle are so happy they have a huge banquet and feast on roast duck and turkey. After they have eaten all they can eat, they begin singing the Good King's favorite songs. Miss Caroon reads the child's story out loud to the class. She especially likes the last sentence in the story, and takes her time sounding it out: "And the singing went on for days."

Miss Caroon hands back the stories and the child receives an A-minus because he misspells *Ancient* in the title. This is a very good story, she tells the child. When his mother comes to visit on Parents' Day Miss Caroon tells her that her son is a special child, that he could be a writer someday if he wanted to be one. The mother shakes her head sadly and tells Miss Caroon the truth. She has to tell Miss Caroon that all the child wants to be when he grows up is the man who walks around the monkey house all day with a nail on the end of a stick.

Notes on Contributors

RICK BASS is the author of eleven books of fiction and nonfiction, including *The Watch*, *Oil Notes*, *Winter*, *The Ninemile Wolves*, *The Book of Yaak*, and most recently, *The Sky, the Stars, and the Wilderness*. A new novel, *Where the Sea Used to Be*, will be published soon. He grew up in Texas and now lives with his family on a remote ranch in Montana.

TOM CHIARELLA teaches English at Depaux in Greencastle, Indiana. Alfred A. Knopf published his collection of stories, *Foley's Luck*. His textbook on writing dialogue (*Writing Dialogue*, first published by Writer's Digest Books in 1996) has just been issued by Story Press.

PAT CONROY is the author of *Beach Music*, *The Prince of Tides*, *The Great Santini*, *The Lords of Discipline*, and *The Water Is Wide*. He graduated from the Citadel in 1967.

MARGARET F. M. DAVIS was born in Mount Vernon, New York. A lifelong New Yorker with an avid interest in literature, she lives and farms part-time in Virginia.

RICHARD FORD won the Pulitzer Prize for his fifth novel, *Independence Day*. He is also the author of *A Piece of My Heart*, *The Ultimate Good Luck*, *The Sportswriter*, and *Wildlife*, as well as a story collection, *Rock Springs*, and three novellas collectively entitled *Women with Men*.

Mary Gaitskill grew up outside of Detroit. She is the author of the collections *Bad Behavior* and *Because They Wanted To* and the novel *Two Girls, Fat and Thin*.

Elizabeth Gilbert has published a collection of stories entitled *Pilgrims*. Her fiction has appeared in *Esquire*, *Story*, the *Paris Review*, *GQ*, *Ploughshares*, and the *Mississippi Review*. In 1996 she was awarded the New Discovery Prize. A contributing writer to *GQ*, she lives with her husband in New York City.

Barry Hannah lives in Oxford, Mississippi. He is the author of many works of fiction, including *Geronimo Rex*, *The Nightwatchmen*, *Airships*, *Ray*, *The Tennis Handsome*, *Captain Maximus*, *Bats out of Hell*, and, most recently, the story collection *High Lonesome*. He has been honored by the American Academy of Arts and Letters for his achievement in fiction.

Jim Harrison is a poet and a novelist whose books include *After Ikkyu and Other Poems*, *Julip*, *The Woman Lit by Fireflies*, *Dalva*, *Legends of the Fall*, *Farmer*, *Selected and New Poems*, *The Theory and Practice of Rivers*, and *Wolf*. He lives with his family on a farm in northern Michigan.

Amy Hempel teaches in the Graduate Writing Program at Bennington College. Her most recent book is *Tumble Home*, a novella and stories. She is also the author of *Reasons to Live* and *At the Gates of the Animal Kingdom*. Her work has appeared in *Harper's*, *Vanity Fair*, and *The Quarterly*.

Mark Jacobson has published two novels, most recently *Everyone and No One* (Villard). His first novel, *Gojiro*, was published in 1991. He has been a staff writer and contributing editor at *New York* magazine, the *Village Voice*, *Rolling Stone*, *Natural History*, and *Esquire*. He lives with his family in Brooklyn.

Darius James is the author of *Negrophobia* and *That's Blaxploitation!*, both published by St. Martin's Press. He lives in Brooklyn.

Denis Johnson is a poet and fiction writer living in northern Idaho. His works include the collection *Jesus' Son* and the novels *Already Dead*, *Resuscitation of a Hanged Man*, *The Stars at Noon*, *Fiskadoro*, and *Angels*. His several volumes of poetry have been collected in *The Throne of the Third Heaven of the Nations Millennium General Assembly*.

THOM JONES attended and taught at the Iowa Writers' Workshop. He is the author of the collections *Cold Snap* and *The Pugilist at Rest*, which was nominated for the National Book Award. His stories have appeared in *Esquire, Harper's*, the *New Yorker*, and other magazines. He lives in the state of Washington.

NORMAN MAILER was born in 1923 in Long Branch, New Jersey, and grew up in Brooklyn, New York. He published his first novel, *The Naked and the Dead*, in 1948. He won the National Book Award and the Pulitzer Prize in 1968 for *Armies of the Night*, and was awarded the Pulitzer Prize again in 1980 for *The Executioner's Song*. His most recent book is *The Time of Our Time*.

TERRY MCMILLAN is the author of *Mama, Disappearing Acts, Waiting to Exhale*, and *How Stella Got Her Groove Back*. She also edited *Breaking Ice: An Anthology of Contemporary African-American Fiction*.

RICK MOODY grew up in Connecticut and now lives in Brooklyn. His most recent novel is *Purple America*. His works also include *The Ice Storm, Garden State*, and *The Ring of Brightest Angels Around Heaven*, the title story of which won the *Paris Review*'s Aga Khan Prize. He is the coeditor, with Darcey Steinke, of *Joyful Noise: The New Testament Revisited*. His fiction and essays have appeared in *Esquire*, the *New Yorker, Harper's*, and *Grand Street*.

ANN PATCHETT is the author of three novels, *The Magician's Assistant, Taft*, and *The Patron Saint of Liars*. She is originally from Los Angeles and now lives in Nashville.

JAYNE ANNE PHILLIPS has published two novels, *Machine Dreams* and *Shelter*, and a number of short-story collections, including *Counting, Sweethearts, Fast Lanes*, and *Black Tickets*, the last of which was nominated for a National Book Critics Circle Award. She grew up in West Virginia.

MARK RICHARD received the PEN/Ernest Hemingway Award for best first work of fiction for his collection *The Ice at the Bottom of the*

World. He is also the author of *Fishboy*. His stories have been published in *Shenandoah*, *Harper's*, *Esquire*, and the *New Yorker*. He was born in Louisiana and raised in Texas and Virginia.

JAMES SALTER is the author of *A Sport and a Pastime*, now published by Modern Library. His other works of fiction include *Light Years*, *The Hunters*, *Solo Faces*, *The Arm of Flesh*, and *Dusk and Other Stories*, which won the PEN/Faulkner Award. His most recent book is the memoir *Burning the Days*.

LEE SMITH grew up in the mountains of Virginia and lives now in North Carolina. She has published nine novels, including *Oral History*, *Fair and Tender Ladies*, *The Devil's Dream*, and *Black Mountain Breakdown*. She is also the author of three short-story collections: *Cakewalk*, *Me and My Baby View the Eclipse*, and, most recently, *News of the Spirit*.

ROBERT STONE has just published his sixth novel, *Damascus Gate*. His first, *A Hall of Mirrors*, won a William Faulkner Foundation Award. *Dog Soldiers* received a National Book Award. He is also the author of *A Flag for Sunrise*, *Children of Light*, and *Outerbridge Reach*. His first collection of stories, *Bear and His Daughter*, came out in 1997. He lives with his wife in Connecticut and travels widely.

WILLIAM VOLLMANN recently completed a book about the nature of violence. His works of fiction include *You Bright and Risen Angels*, *The Rainbow Stories*, *The Atlas*, and three volumes of his "Seven Dreams" series: *The Ice-Shirt*, *Fathers and Crows*, and *The Rifles*. He makes his home in California.

DAVID FOSTER WALLACE is the author of the novels *Infinite Jest* and *The Broom of the System*. He has also published a collection of essays, *A Supposedly Fun Thing I'll Never Do Again*, and a volume of short stories, *Girl with Curious Hair*. The recipient of a MacArthur fellowship, he lives in Bloomington, Illinois.

JOY WILLIAMS's novels and short-story collections include *State of Grace*, which was nominated for a National Book Award, as well as *The Changeling*, *Breaking and Entering*, *Taking Care*, and *Escapes*. Her stories and essays have appeared in *Esquire*, the *New Yorker*,

Harper's, and the *Paris Review*. She is a recipient of the Mildred and Harold Strauss Living Award for her fiction.

STEPHEN WRIGHT is the author of three novels, *Going Native*, *M31: A Family Romance*, and *Meditations in Green*. He lives in New York City.

New Fiction in Paperback

VIKRAM CHANDRA ↜ *Love and Longing in Bombay*

"Richly inventive and confident . . . filled with passages of surprising magic."   —Michael Frank, *Los Angeles Times*

"Exquisite. . . . At the heart of each story is a mystery that keeps you reading."   —Chitra Banerjee Divakurini, *San Francisco Chronicle*

MARTHA COOLEY ↜ *The Archivist*

"Martha Cooley has given us something valuable and rare—a thoughtful and well-written first novel, suffused with intellectual and moral integrity."   —Brian Morton, *New York Times Book Review*

"It is rare and gratifying to read a novel about people who take literature seriously, who practically live and die by books. . . . *The Archivist* is a memorable achievement."   —Steven Moore, *Washington Post Book World*

HELEN DUNMORE ↜ *Your Blue-Eyed Boy*

"A meditation on the past and loss and how we cope with who we become. . . . Dunmore writes gracefully and has an excellent sense of place."   —Mark Lindquist, *New York Times Book Review*

"Uncommonly satisfying. . . . Reading Helen Dunmore is like sitting down to a feast."   —Phyllis Richardson, *Los Angeles Times*

TONY EARLEY ↜ *Here We Are in Paradise*

"Tony Earley does the practically impossible. . . . These stories are both incredibly funny and effortlessly convincing."   —Louise Erdrich

"Earley has a wonderful gift for deep observation, exact and wise and often funny."   —Ellen Currie, *New York Times Book Review*

 Available wherever books are sold

New Fiction in Paperback

ELLEN GILCHRIST — *Flight of Angels*

"Readers will find the penetrating intellect, deep compassion, and dark sense of humor that mark Gilchrist's best work and place it among the best writing coming out of the South—or anywhere else, for that matter—today." —Ron Carter, *Richmond Times-Dispatch*

KATE JENNINGS — *Snake*

"The chapters in *Snake* are short, vivid bursts of imagery, anecdote, insight. . . . You can easily read the entire book in one sitting—and only upon standing be struck by how much pity and terror you've consumed." —Michelle Huneven, *Los Angeles Times Book Review*

"A stunning narrative . . . clearly the work of a powerful imagination." —Carol Shields, *New York Times Book Review*

THOM JONES — *Sonny Liston Was a Friend of Mine*

"Jones's genius is served up in its purest form yet." —Michael Upchurch, *Seattle Times*

"Thom Jones's world is as atmospheric as a song by Bob Dylan or Leonard Cohen or Tom Waits. . . . Spending time with Jones's battle-worn eccentrics and disenfranchised misfits leaves you feeling bruised but also elated." —Kate Sekules, *Salon*

RICK MOODY — *Purple America*

"Hilarious and heartbreaking. . . . John Cheever belonged to midcentury, while Rick Moody is a chronicler of the middle class for the millennium. . . . A breathtaking book." —Janet Burroway, *New York Times Book Review*

"Extraordinary. . . . Moody's prose dazzles." —Andy Solomon, *Chicago Tribune*

 Available wherever books are sold

New Fiction in Paperback

ANITA SHREVE ✑ *The Pilot's Wife*

"An absorbing, inventive tale rendered in fine, original prose."
— Mike Snyder, *Houston Chronicle*

"Gripping. . . . You won't want to stop turning the pages once Kathryn has opened her door."   — Georgia Jones-Davis, *Washington Post Book World*

MARLY SWICK ✑ *Evening News*

"An affecting novel . . . utterly palpable and real. . . . It possesses both the psychological suspense of Sue Miller's bestselling *The Good Mother* and the emotional acuity of Alice Munro's short stories."
— Michiko Kakutani, *New York Times*

"A courageous book, evincing, for most of its duration, an impressive and riveting intensity. . . . A remarkable performance."
— Donna Seaman, *Chicago Tribune*

DAVID FOSTER WALLACE ✑ *Infinite Jest*

"The next step in fiction . . . edgy, accurate, and darkly witty. . . . Think Beckett, think Pynchon, think Gaddis. Think."
— Sven Birkerts, *Atlantic Monthly*

"A virtuoso display of styles and themes. . . . There is generous intelligence and authentic passion on every page."   — R. Z. Sheppard, *Time*

JAMES WILCOX ✑ *Plain and Normal*

"Wilcox is a master of comic detail, with a grasp of the bizarre and the eccentric that frequently leaves you rolling on the floor."
— Peter Kurth, *Salon*

"Trenchant and witty. . . . The funny bits are as funny as some of the best of Woody Allen, and this in itself makes the novel anything but plain and normal."   — Karen Karbo, *New York Times Book Review*

 Available wherever books are sold

HONEYED WORDS—
AND TEMPTATION
SWEET AS SIN

"Perhaps you are part of the reason I am here," Peregrine said. "Sweet Sara," he whispered, caressing her slender form as if his hands could meld them into one flesh, "you are as rare and lovely as the treasures of the Silk Road."

Unbuttoning her jacket, he slipped his hand inside. Gently he squeezed the soft, fluid weight of her breast. "You are like gold and amber and ivory that have been warmed to wondrous life."

Sara gasped as her shy acceptance changed to fierce response. In the tumult of her senses she was shameless, and passion burned in her blood.

Finally she broke the kiss and made herself focus on Peregrine's dark, craggy face. His green eyes were misty with passion, and this time there was nothing enigmatic about him. He wanted her. And, heaven help her, she wanted him. . . .

SILK
AND
SHADOWS

by

Mary Jo Putney

AN ONYX BOOK

ONYX
Published by the Penguin Group
Penguin Books USA Inc., 375 Hudson Street,
New York, New York 10014, U.S.A.
Penguin Books Ltd, 27 Wrights Lane,
London W8 5TZ, England
Penguin Books Australia Ltd, Ringwood,
Victoria, Australia
Penguin Books Canada Ltd, 10 Alcorn Avenue,
Toronto, Ontario, Canada M4V 3B2
Penguin Books (N.Z.) Ltd, 182–190 Wairau Road,
Auckland 10, New Zealand

Penguin Books Ltd, Registered Offices:
Harmondsworth, Middlesex, England

First published by Onyx, an imprint of New American Library,
a division of Penguin Books USA Inc.

First Printing, December, 1991
10 9 8 7 6 5 4 3 2 1

*To Estill, who wanted a book
that was all her own.*

Prologue

England, 1839

HE CALLED HIMSELF PEREGRINE, the wanderer, and he came to London for revenge.

It was dusk as the *Kali* drifted up the Thames, her goal a berth at the Isle of Dogs. The air was thick with the rank scents that occur where water meets land, and too many people live in too little space.

Peregrine leaned against the foremast, watching the lights of London flicker on and listening to the water splashing softly under the bow. An onlooker would have thought him casual, but the relaxation in his lean figure was a product of years of discipline, a habit of pretense so long established as to be second nature. He had learned early that it was safer to let no one know the true state of his mind and heart; over the years he had become so adept at dissimulation that he himself did not always know how he felt.

But tonight he had no doubts about the nature of his emotions. This bland, civilized English darkness concealed his enemy, and that knowledge burned triumphant in his veins. He had waited a quarter of a century for this moment, when the time was right to extract a slow and exquisitely painful blood price for what he had suffered.

The flame of hatred had been fired when he was a boy of ten, and over the years he had tended it with black, bitter care. Waiting and preparing for his revenge had been a strange mixture of pleasure and pain. He had wandered the face of the earth, acquiring wealth in many ways, honing mind and body until he was a more deadly weapon than any knife or rifle, learning how to survive and prosper in any land, among any people. Every skill, every golden coin, every sharpening of wit and hand, had been treasured as another step toward his ultimate goal.

And now all his preparations had led to this: London, called the greatest city on earth, with its wealth and squalor, snobbery and noble ideals.

He left the routine of docking and regulations to his captain, preferring silence and the voluptuous ecstasy of anticipation. From a distance he had already begun to spin his web about his prey. Now he would weave the final threads himself, learning the best and subtlest torments to apply. Peregrine wanted his enemy to know why he was being destroyed; he wanted to be close enough to see fear and fury grow, and to glory in the ultimate destruction.

When they had cleared customs, Peregrine sent a message to Lord Ross Carlisle, who was important to his plans. Then he waited. The man known as Peregrine—warrior, wanderer, rich beyond avarice, hero to a mysterious people who lived beyond the bounds of British law—was good at waiting. But very soon, the time for waiting would be over.

Chapter 1

THE MESSAGE reached Lord Ross Carlisle quickly, and he boarded the *Kali* within two hours. As the tall, rangy Englishman swung onto the ship's deck and into the pool of lantern light, Peregrine watched from a vantage point in the shadows.

It had been two years since they had last seen each other, and he wondered how strong the bonds of friendship would prove to be here in England. It was one thing for the younger son of a duke to fraternize with an adventurer of dubious background in the wilds of Asia, quite another to introduce such a man to his own circle. The two men could hardly have come from more different backgrounds, but in spite of that, there had been surprising harmony of mind and humor between them.

Even near death in the mountains of the Hindu Kush, Lord Ross had been unmistakably an English aristocrat. Now, gilded by lamplight and wearing garments whose price would feed a Kafir family for a decade, he looked like what he was: a man born to the ruling class of the greatest empire the world had ever known, with all the assurance of his kind.

Peregrine pushed himself away from the mast and stepped forward into the circle of light. "I'm glad my message found you at home, Ross. Good of you to come so quickly."

The two men's gazes met, exactly level. Lord Ross's eyes were brown, an unexpected contrast to his blond hair. There had always been competition as well as friendship between them, and the undercurrents of this meeting would not be simple ones.

"I had to see if it was really you, Mikahl." The Englishman offered his hand. "I never really thought I'd see you in London."

"I said I would come, Ross. You should not have doubted me." In spite of the wariness in the atmosphere, Peregrine gripped the other man's hand hard, surprised at how much pleasure he felt at this reunion. "Have you dined?"

"Yes, but I'd welcome a glass of that superlative brandy you always seemed to have."

"We stopped in France especially to replenish my stock." Peregrine led the way below decks. As they entered the sumptuous owner's cabin, he glanced speculatively at his companion. Lord Ross was the very image of the languid English aristocrat; had he really changed so much?

Giving way to mischievous impulse, Peregrine decided to find out. Without warning, he spun on his heel, driving his right elbow at the other man's midriff with a force that could have felled a half-grown bullock. It should have been a crippling blow, but it wasn't.

With lightning swiftness, Ross grabbed Peregrine's arm before the elbow could connect. Then he bent and twisted, hurling his host halfway across the cabin with one smooth, continuous motion.

As he crashed down on his right shoulder, Peregrine automatically tucked his body and rolled, coming to rest on his back by one of the paneled bulkheads. In a serious fight he would have ricocheted back into action, but this time he lay still on the carpeted deck and caught his breath. "I'm glad to see that civilization hasn't made you soft." Then he grinned, feeling as if the two years' separation had just vanished. "You didn't learn that throw from me."

Cravat and hair no longer impeccable, Ross laughed out loud, his face boyish. "I decided that if you really did come to England, I'd best be prepared, you old devil.'' He extended his hand to help his host up. "Pax?"

"Pax," Peregrine agreed as he took Ross's hand and vaulted to his feet. He was pleased to find that the bonds of friendship still held, and not just because the other man would be useful. "When you came on board, you looked so much like an English gentleman that I wondered if you had forgotten the Hindu Kush.''

"If I looked like an English gentleman, you looked like an oriental pasha who couldn't decide whether to welcome me or have me thrown in your dungeon.'' Ross examined the cabin, which was a blend of Eastern and Western luxury. The oak desk was certainly European, but the thick carpet was one of Persia's finest, and two benches were padded and covered with velvet, then heaped with embroidered pillows like Turkish divans. A suitable setting for a man of the East who had chosen to move into a larger world.

Ross settled on one of the divans and crossed his elegantly booted legs. He still had trouble believing that his enigmatic friend was in England, for like the falcon he was named for, Peregrine had seemed a creature of the wild places. Yet oddly, though he wore loose Asiatic robes and his black hair was longer than an Englishman's, he did not look out of place. As he opened a cabinet and brought out a decanter of brandy, he moved with the calm assurance of a man who would be at home anywhere.

"On shipboard, it would be the brig, not the dungeon.'' Peregrine poured generous amounts of brandy into two cut-glass goblets. "But since we have broken bread and shared salt, the laws of hospitality are inviolable.''

Ross accepted a goblet with murmured thanks, then cocked his head to one side thoughtfully. "You've been practicing your English. There's still a trace of accent, but you now speak as fluently as a native Briton.''

"I'm glad you approve.'' As Peregrine sprawled on

another padded bench at right angles to his guest, he gave a faint, sardonic smile. "I've a fancy to become a lion of English society. What do you think of my chances of success?"

Ross almost choked on his brandy. "Why on earth would you want to play such social games?" he asked, surprised out of his usual tact. "Lord knows that most British aristocrats are a boring lot. It doesn't seem at all your style."

"Does that mean you do not wish to introduce me to your friends and family?"

Ross's eyes narrowed at the barb lurking in the other man's deep voice. "You know better than that, Mikahl. I owe you a considerable debt, and if you are fool enough to wish to enter what is called 'society,' I will do what I can to assist. Winning superficial social acceptance requires only money and an introduction, and you will have both. Just bear in mind that no matter what you do, you will always be seen as an outsider."

"No society totally accepts a man not born into it," Peregrine agreed. "However, I do not seek to be clasped to the provincial bosoms of the British aristocracy. It will be enough to be tolerated as an exotic and amusing pet."

"Heaven help anyone who thinks you are domesticated," Ross said, amused. "But I can't imagine why you wish to waste your time on people who think Paris is the edge of the world."

"To see if I can do it, perhaps?" Peregrine tilted his head back and drained his goblet. "In truth, society as such does not interest me. But while I am in England, I intend to," he paused, seeking the right phrase, "to settle an old score."

"Whoever he is, I shouldn't like to be in his position," Ross murmured. "Is he anyone I might know?"

"Quite possibly."

Peregrine visibly weighed whether to say more, a catlike gleam in his vivid green eyes. In spite of his fluent English and a breadth of knowledge that a Cambridge scholar could envy, his expressions and gestures subtly marked him as foreign. Ross suspected that he would never truly understand how the other man's mind worked; it was one reason that Peregrine was such a stimulating companion.

At length Peregrine said, "Given the tangled relationships of the British upper classes, the man I am interested in might be your third cousin or godmother's son or some such. If so, I will not burden you with any more knowledge, but I ask that you not interfere in my quest for justice."

Unwilling to commit himself without knowing more, Ross asked, "What is the man's name?"

"Charles Weldon. The *Honorable*"—there was a slight, ironic emphasis on the title—"Charles Weldon. I imagine you have heard of him, even if you are not personally acquainted. He is one of London's most prominent businessmen."

Ross frowned. "I do know him. Recently he was made a baronet, so he is now Sir Charles Weldon. Strange that you should say that about cousins. We are not related, but oddly enough, he has just proposed marriage to one of my cousins, and she intends to accept him." He finished his brandy, his frown deepening. "My favorite cousin, as it happens."

"I did not know that he was to take another wife." Peregrine poured more brandy for both of them, then sank back in his seat, one leg folded beneath him with un-British fluidity. "I gather that you do not approve. Do you know anything to Weldon's discredit?"

"No, he is widely respected. As the younger brother of Lord Batsford, he moves in the highest circles of society, even though he has made his fortune through trade and finance." Ross considered a moment, then said slowly, "Weldon has always been perfectly affable on the occasions when we have met. I can't explain why I find him disquieting. Perhaps he is *too* affable."

"Is your cousin in love with him?"

Ross shook his head. "I doubt it. He is easily twenty years older than Sara, and she is not of a romantic disposition."

Peregrine gave a faint smile. "Since the lady's heart is not engaged, will you object if her betrothal comes to naught?"

Ross thought of the uneasy feeling Weldon gave him, and the dark whispers that sometimes touched the man's name, hints too vague to be called rumors. "Can you assure me that Weldon deserves the doom that is hovering over him?"

"I promise you that he has earned anything I might do, and a good deal more," Peregrine said, his voice soft and dangerous.

Ross believed him. Peregrine might be an enigma whose mind worked in mysterious oriental ways, but Ross had always found him to be honorable. "To be honest, I'd welcome an end to Sara's betrothal, as long as she is not injured by your actions."

"I have no desire to injure the innocent." Peregrine leaned back against the embroidered-silk cushions. "Tell me more about your cousin."

"She is Lady Sara St. James, the only daughter of the Duke of Haddonfield. Our mothers were twin sisters, two Scottish beauties of modest birth. When they came to London, they had no fortune but their faces." Ross sipped more brandy, savoring the complex flavor. "It was fortune enough. They were called the 'Magnificent Montgomerys' and both became duchesses, setting a matrimonial standard that every ambitious mother in Britain has tried to match ever since, without success."

"How old is your cousin?"

Ross did a rapid calculation. Sara was four years younger than he . . . "Twenty-seven."

"Rather old to be still a maid. Is she uncomely?"

Ross laughed. "Not at all. Twenty-seven is not such a great age to be unwed in England, you know. If Sara

had ever shown willingness, she would have been in-
undated in suitors, but she has had no desire to marry.''

Peregrine's dark face was contemplative. ''I should
like to meet Lady Sara soon. But first I must be polished into the semblance of an English gentleman.''

Ross inspected the other man. ''Easily done. Tomorrow I'll take you to my tailor and barber. I warn
you, fashionable English clothing will be much less
comfortable than what you are wearing. But don't let
yourself become too polished—a trace of the exotic
will make you more interesting, for society craves
novelty.'' He thought a moment more, then smiled
mischievously. ''I shall introduce you as a prince.''

Peregrine's brows drew together. They were thick
black and more than a little diabolical. '' 'Prince' is
not the best translation of *'mir.' ''*

''Since there is no precise English equivalent, prince
will do very well. To be a prince will earn you more
respect, even though no foreign title could possibly be
as good as an English one,'' Ross explained. ''Prince
Peregrine of Kafiristan. You will become a sensation.''

Particularly among jaded society hostesses, Ross
added with silent amusement. It was going to be very
interesting to set this particular Asiatic hawk among
the English society pigeons.

Lady Sara St. James was walking in the garden behind Haddonfield House when she heard masculine
footsteps crunching on the gravel on the far side of the
holly hedge. He was early.

Her fingers brushed uncertainly over her dark blond
hair, then dropped when she became aware that she
was behaving like a nervous female. While she was
entitled to be nervous when waiting to accept an offer
of marriage, she knew that Sir Charles Weldon's chief
interest was not in her appearance. If spectacular
beauty had been his primary goal, he would have
looked elsewhere, but what he wanted was a wellborn
lady who would be a gracious hostess and a step-

mother to his daughter. Sara was amply qualified for those roles, so it wouldn't have mattered if her hair was mussed. But, of course, it wasn't.

Wryly she decided to give Weldon what he was looking for, so she stopped and contemplated a lily in an impeccably ladylike pose. Then a familiar teasing voice called out, "Sara, where are you? I've been assured that you are lurking around here somewhere."

Artifice vanishing, she spun about and extended both hands to her cousin. "Ross! What a pleasant surprise. Did you bring the latest chapter of your book for me to read?"

He clasped her hands, then bent over to place a light kiss on her cheek. "I'm afraid to show it to you. Perhaps it was a mistake to interest you in oriental studies, for you have become entirely too critical a reader."

Sara gave him a concerned glance. "I'm sorry—I thought you said my comments were useful."

"That's the problem," he said with feeling. "You're always right. By this time you know more about Asia and the Middle East than most men in the Foreign Office. It would be easier if you were wrong, because then I could ignore your criticisms." He grimaced. "The next chapter should be done next week. It was easier to make the journey than to write about it."

Seeing that she was being teased, Sara relaxed. "I can't wait to see the next chapter. This will be your best book yet."

"You always say that," Ross said affectionately. "You're my best supporter."

"And you're my window on the wide world." Sara would never see the sights her cousin had, but his letters and journals had been the bright spots during her dark years. In fact, she had been the one who first suggested that he write about his travels. His first two books had become classic accounts of remote parts of the world, and the book he was working on now should be equally successful. "But I warn you, I'm expecting an important caller very soon."

"Anyone I know?"

Sara wrinkled her delicate aristocratic nose. "Charles Weldon is coming to receive my official acceptance of his offer. Even though all the actors in this play know what the result will be, it's considered proper to speak the lines anyhow."

"Actually, I came today to speak to you privately about this engagement." Ross regarded her narrowly. "Are you accepting Weldon against your will? Surely my uncle is not coercing you."

"Of course not, Ross. Don't let that splendid imagination run away with you." She tucked her hand under his elbow, and they began strolling along the garden path, her cousin shortening his long strides to adapt to her limp. "My father is encouraging the match, but there's nothing sinister about it. Since the Haddonfield title and entailed property will go to Cousin Nicholas, Father has decided that it is his duty to see me settled in my own household with a husband to take care of me."

"And you agree with him?" Ross asked skeptically. "Since Uncle Haddonfield will surely leave you most of his personal fortune, you'll be a very wealthy woman. If you feel the need of male protection, you can live with me." He gave her a hopeful glance. "Can I persuade you to do that? That great mausoleum I inherited is far too large for one person."

"I'd rather live in a rose-covered cottage surrounded by cats." Sara laughed. "I would quite enjoy that, you know, but I'd become so dreadfully eccentric that you would be embarrassed to admit to the connection."

"Never," he declared. "We both inherited our share of idiosyncrasies from the Magnificent Montgomerys. I shall move into the cottage next to yours and surround myself with piles of Asiatic texts. You and your cats will wander over for tea, and I will quote Turkish poetry to you." Then his whimsical tone turned serious. "Sara, do you love Charles Weldon?"

She glanced up at him in surprise. "Of course not,

but I think we will rub along very well. It's no sacrifice to marry Charles—he is intelligent and well-bred, and we know what to expect of each other. It will please Father to see me wed, and I'd rather like a child of my own.''

"And you will have a civilized marriage where you will each go your own way much of the time."

"Exactly," Sara agreed. "That is one of the things that commends Charles to me. I don't think I should like a husband who was underfoot all the time."

Her cousin shook his head sadly. "What a cold-blooded creature you are, Sara. Have you never wanted to be in love?"

"From what I've seen, it's a cursed uncomfortable state." She squeezed his arm, adding softly, "I should have thought that you had been cured of believing in love matches."

Ross gave her a wry smile. "Once a romantic, always a romantic. It's a fatal affliction, I think. You always did have far more sense than I."

They came to a bench set in a small sunny glade, and he guided her to it so they could sit down. Traffic sounded faintly in the distance, but they were so surrounded by greenery and floral scents that it was hard to believe that the garden was in the heart of London. "If Weldon withdrew his offer or was run over by a carriage, would you repine?"

"If he withdrew his offer, I would be a little relieved," she admitted, then gave her cousin a stern governess stare. "However, I don't wish to see him run over, so you are *not* to push him under a carriage in the belief that you are rescuing me."

"I have no homicidal intentions," he assured her. "I just wanted to understand how you feel about this marriage."

"I appreciate your concern," she said, affection warm inside her. Their mothers had been very close, as twins often are, and Ross and Sara had been raised almost as brother and sister. They had always brought their secrets and sorrows to each other, shared their dreams, and gotten into trouble together.

More often than their mothers realized, it was one of Sara's mischievous ideas that got the cousins into trouble, though Ross always insisted that it was his duty as the male and the elder to take the more severe punishments for their crimes. In a world that thought Lady Sara St. James was a consummate lady—boringly so—Ross was the only one permitted to see her more unruly impulses. If she had had a real brother, she could not have loved him more. "You mustn't worry, my dear. Charles is a perfectly respectable man, and we shall do very well together."

Her cousin nodded, apparently satisfied, then changed the subject. "A friend of mine has just arrived in London, and I think you would enjoy meeting him. His name is Mikahl Khanauri, but he is called the Falcon among his own people. Since his own title is unpronounceable by British tongues, he is calling himself Peregrine, after the peregrine falcon. Prince Peregrine of Kafiristan. To the best of my knowledge, he is the first Kafir ever to visit Europe."

"Impressive." Sarah knit her brows as she invoked her memory. "Kafiristan is in the Hindu Kush mountains beyond the North-West Frontier of India, isn't it? Several years ago you wrote that you intended to travel into the area, but it was months until your next letter. By then you were back in India, and you said nothing about the trip to Kafiristan."

"I may be the only Englishman who has visited there." Ross's face lit up, the passionate scholar showing through his gentlemanly facade. Like Sara, his conventionality was only surface deep—but they both had excellent surfaces. "The Kafirs are remarkable people, unlike any of the other Himalayan tribes. It would be interesting to know their history—there is the most amazing jumble of races and languages in central Asia. In appearance and customs, Kafirs resemble Europeans more than they do their Muslim neighbors. Perhaps they are a Germanic tribe that went east instead of west—they claim to be descendants of Alexander the Great and his men.

"The Kafir languages are the damnedest ones I've ever come across, every valley with a different dialect. The tribesmen are wild as hawks, and they love personal freedom more than any other people I have ever met." He gave his cousin a laughing glance. "Even the women are allowed to roam about at will, once their chores are done."

"Clearly they are people of great good sense," Sara said serenely, refusing to rise to her cousin's bait. "Your friend Peregrine is a Kafir nobleman?"

"There is no aristocracy in the British sense, but he was a man of great influence among them, a *mir,* which is the Kafir term for a chief." Ross bit his lower lip thoughtfully. "I never grew proficient enough in the language to be sure, but I had the impression that Peregrine was not a native son of Kafiristan. There was a suggestion that he came from somewhere farther west, Turkestan perhaps. Or perhaps his father was a wandering Russian who impregnated a Kafir woman and then left. I never asked about his background, and he never volunteered the information."

Intrigued, Sara asked, "How did you come to meet him?"

"He saved my life. Twice, in fact."

When Sara frowned and opened her mouth for another question, her cousin shook his head. "Believe me, you don't want to know any more than that."

"Ross!" she said indignantly. "You can't possibly make such a statement without explaining it."

He chuckled. "The first time he saved me was just after I entered Kafiristan. I had fallen afoul of a group of chaps who misliked my foreignness, and they immediately began debating the best method of effecting my demise. While my understanding of what they said was imperfect, the gist was most unpleasant.

"At a critical point in the proceedings, Peregrine

happened along and was invited to join the fun. Deciding that it would be inhospitable to allow his friends to flay me alive, he challenged my chief captor to some sort of gambling game. As I recall, the stakes were about twenty guineas worth of gold against my life. When Peregrine won, I became his property. He saved me again when he was escorting me back to India. We were attacked by bandits, and I was cornered by two of them when I had run out of ammunition. He intervened to even the odds.''

Sara shuddered, knowing that behind Ross's light words lay the specter of a hideous death. ''How many other times have you been nearly murdered in your travels?''

''I said that you wouldn't want to know.'' Ross put his arm around her shoulders for a brief, reassuring hug. ''You needn't worry when I am out of the country. If only the good die young, I will always come home to England.

''At any rate, after winning me at gambling, Peregrine took me back to his village and patched me up. Come to think of it, he probably saved my life again by keeping the local quack away from me. When I had recovered enough to take an interest in my surroundings, I was amazed to learn that my kind host spoke very decent English. He was also the cleanest Kafir I ever met, which is one reason why I think that he was born somewhere else.''

Ross paused meditatively. ''Perhaps his cleanliness is what made his coloring seem fairer than that of his fellows. Hard to say. Once I saw a Kafir lad who had fallen in a stream, and he was pale as an Englishman, but within a week or two he was back to normal. But I digress. During the months I was Peregrine's guest, we became friends. He has a remarkable mind, shrewd and quick, and he never forgets anything. Europe fascinated him. He asked questions constantly, absorbing every word like a sponge.

''He must have put what he learned to good use,

because when our paths crossed again two years ago in Cairo, he had left Kafiristan and become a very wealthy trader, with interests throughout the Orient. He mentioned that someday he intended to make an extended visit to England, and here he is.'' Ross gave Sara a smile of cherubic innocence. ''A simple enough tale.''

''Your tales always raise more questions than they answer,'' she commented, her eyes twinkling. ''But even if your prince is a savage with gold earrings and a dagger thrust through his beard, I will be glad to receive him because of what he did for you.''

''I was hoping you would say that, for if you receive him, everyone will. But Peregrine is not a savage, though I'm not sure he is precisely civilized, either. He is a remarkable man—not like anyone you have ever met.'' Ross started to say more, then shook his head. ''I should let you draw your own conclusions. May I bring him to your garden party next week? It would be a suitable occasion to introduce Peregrine to a small slice of London society. Less overpowering than a ball.''

''Of course he is welcome. I look forward to meeting him.''

Before Sara could say more, Sir Charles Weldon appeared. She suppressed a guilty start; in the pleasure of talking with her cousin, she had forgotten that Charles was due.

Ross rose as the other man approached, and they shook hands. ''Good morning, Sir Charles. I imagine it is my cousin you have come to visit, so I will take my leave.''

Weldon smiled genially. ''Very tactful of you, Lord Ross. Indeed, I am most anxious to speak with Lady Sara.''

As Ross disappeared from sight, Weldon took Sara's hand and bent over to kiss it. As he did, she examined him approvingly. Even though he was near fifty, her future husband was a fine figure of a man, tall and powerfully built, with the air of understated confidence that success brings. There was only a scattering of gray in his light brown hair, and the lines in his face just made his appearance more distinguished.

Weldon straightened, his expression intent. Clasping Sara's hand, he asked softly, "You know why I have come, Lady Sara. Dare I hope you will give me the answer I have been praying for?"

She felt a touch of irritation that he was going through an amorous charade over what was really a practical arrangement. No doubt he thought romance was what she expected. As Ross had remarked, Sara was a cold-blooded creature; most women would have preferred the soft words. Smiling, she said, "If the answer you have been praying for is yes, you are in luck."

When he heard her reply, his pale blue eyes filled with such fierce triumph that for the first time Sara wondered if his heart was engaged as well as his head. The thought made her uneasy. She was prepared to be a dutiful wife, but if he wanted passionate response, he was doomed to disappointment.

The hint of dangerous exultation vanished so thoroughly that it must have been imagination. Weldon pulled a small velvet jeweler's box from his pocket and flicked it open with his thumb. The box contained a ring with a diamond so large that Sara drew in her breath in surprise as Weldon slipped it onto her finger. It was a jewel fit for royalty or a really superior courtesan.

"It's magnificent, Charles." Sara turned her hand, admiring the shimmer of blue fire in the diamond's depths. The stone's natural color was enhanced by the small sapphires that encircled it. Rather gaudy and not at all her style, but very lovely. "Though perhaps a smaller stone would have been better."

"You don't like it?" he said with a slight edge to his voice.

Concerned that she had hurt his feelings, Sara glanced up with a quick smile. "The ring is lovely, but the stone is so large that I shall cost you a fortune in ruined gloves."

He smiled back as he sat down next to her. "I want you to cost me a fortune. You are the best, and you deserve the best."

This time it was a hint of possessiveness that made Sara uneasy. Becoming betrothed was making her over-sensitive. There was no particular mystery to marriage; it was a state most women entered, and once she became more accustomed to the idea, she would no longer start at shadows. She turned the engagement ring on her finger. "You guessed the size exactly right."

"I didn't guess. Your maid gave me the correct size."

"Was that necessary?" Sara asked, not at all pleased to learn that her future husband had engaged in a form of spying.

"Audacity is a necessary ingredient to success, my dear, and I have been very successful." He paused for dramatic effect. "I have just learned something that you might consider another betrothal gift. Your husband will not be a commoner for long—I am going to be created a baron within the next year. I will call myself Lord Weldon of Westminster. Has a nice roll to it, don't you think?" He smiled with vast satisfaction. "While becoming a baroness is a step down for a duke's daughter, this is only the beginning. I will be at least an earl before I die."

"I would be perfectly content to marry plain Mr. Weldon," Sara said gently, "but I am very pleased that you will be recognized for your achievements." In fact, she thought rather cynically, he was being rewarded less for his undeniable accomplishments than for giving large amounts of money to the Whig party. But since being made a peer was obviously important to him, she was glad for his sake.

He put his hand over hers. "We must set a wedding date, Sara. I would like the marriage to take place in about three months, perhaps the first week of September."

"So soon?" she said uncertainly. "I was thinking in terms of six months or a year."

"Why should we wait so long? We are neither of us children." Weldon's face changed, real tenderness coming into his eyes. "Speaking of children, Eliza wants the wedding to be as soon as possible so she can come live with us. Though she is fond of her aunt and uncle, she says they lack dash."

Sara smiled. Weldon's love of the eleven-year-old daughter of his first marriage was the trait that had convinced her that he would make an amiable husband. "I'm so glad Eliza approves of me. She is such a darling. Did no one ever tell her that stepmothers are supposed to be wicked?"

"Eliza has too much good sense to believe fairy tales." Weldon turned to Sara, his eyes intense. "Tell me that you will marry me in September. I don't want to wait."

He was right—there was no good reason for a long engagement. "Very well, Charles, since that is what you wish."

Weldon drew her into his arms and sealed their betrothal with a kiss. Sara had guessed that this was coming and prepared herself. She had reached the age of twenty-seven with little experience of kissing, much less what came after. As his powerful arms pulled her against the starched linen of his shirt, she decided that his embrace was not so bad, though rather engulfing. Perhaps in time she would come to enjoy kissing. Then his tongue slipped between her lips into her mouth, and she stiffened.

Immediately he released her, his breathing uneven. "I'm sorry, Sara," he said apologetically. "For a moment I forgot myself. I did not mean to offend your innocence. That must be saved for our wedding night." There was a hungry, possessive look in his eyes as he cupped her cheek with one hand.

Once more Sara felt a faint thread of alarm. Once more, she suppressed it.

Chapter 2

PEREGRINE TURNED in a slow circle, scanning the drawing room of his newly acquired suite in the Clarendon Hotel. It was a rather overpowering example of European luxury, replete with gilt furniture, heavy moldings, and mediocre paintings of landscapes and dying animals. Personally he thought the room would be improved by replacing the overstuffed chairs with cushioned divans, but the place would do well enough for the time being.

Kuram, his Pathan servant, entered the drawing room, resplendent in white turban and red silk tunic. "Mr. Benjamin Slade to see you, Excellency."

The man who followed Kuram's heels was short, slightly built, and had thinning hair. He was a man who would be easily overlooked, unless one noticed the shrewd gray eyes. Bowing, he said, "It's a pleasure to welcome you to London, Your Highness."

Peregrine grinned as he shook hands with his visitor. "You and Kuram certainly seem to be enjoying my princeliness, Benjamin. It is not how you behaved in India."

Slade permitted himself a small smile. "To be a prince enhances your status in London. Even in private, I think it a good thing to maintain the formalities."

"Doubtless you are right. Care for some tea?"

Slade accepted the offer. While Kuram went to order refreshments, the Englishman brought his employer up to date on matters of business.

Peregrine had met Benjamin Slade five years earlier in Bombay. A lawyer by training, Slade had served the East India Company loyally for a decade before being dismissed in a cloud of scandal. After some quiet investigation, Peregrine learned that Slade's business acumen had helped make his superior, a Mr. Wilkerson, a wealthy man. His reward had been to be made a scapegoat for Wilkerson's embezzling.

Benjamin Slade had been an embittered and desperate man when Peregrine paid a call and offered him two things: a job and revenge. Slade had accepted both. Within a month, new evidence came to light that destroyed Wilkerson's career and sent him to prison. While the lawyer knew that the evidence must have been manufactured, he made no protest, for justice had been done. A month later, Slade took ship for London to become Peregrine's British business agent. In the intervening years he had served his employer brilliantly, in ways both orthodox and unorthodox.

After receiving an overview of recent business developments, Peregrine leaned back in his chair and crossed his long legs. "I wish to make a splash in the London social scene, so you must find me a fashionable house. Something worthy of a prince."

Slade nodded. "To rent or to buy?"

"Either. If no suitable property is available for lease, buy one. I would also like you to look for a country estate within two hours' drive of London. Besides an impressive house, there must be enough land so that it can be farmed profitably."

His agent's eyebrows went up. "Do you intend to stay in England indefinitely?"

"That remains to be seen. As a matter of principle, I want the property to be a decent investment in its own right, as well as good for entertaining." Peregrine paused while Kuram set down a tea tray between the men, then continued, "The information you have gathered on Sir Charles Weldon was a useful begin-

ning, but I want you to explore his business dealings
more deeply.''

Slade nodded, his face expressionless. "Certainly.
Can you give me an idea of what are you looking for?''

Peregrine's answer shook the lawyer's careful control.
"Good God," Slade gasped, "what you are suggesting
is unbelievable.''

"Unbelievable, perhaps, but not impossible," Peregrine murmured. "The fact that it is unbelievable
would be Weldon's best protection. While I have no
evidence, my instincts tell me that if you look in the
directions I have indicated, you will discover something. I rely on you to find the needle in the haystack,
Benjamin, and to do it with the utmost discretion.''

The lawyer nodded, still stunned. "If it is there, I
swear that I shall find it.''

Peregrine sipped his tea, satisfied. A vital thread
was about to be spun in the web forming around Sir
Charles Weldon.

The unpredictable English weather had cooperated
to make Lady Sara's party a success, and the colorful
dresses of the female guests were like flowers strewn
across the sunlit garden of Haddonfield House. Food,
drink, and conversation, mankind's basic entertainment, were all plentiful. As voices and laughter rang
through the summer-scented air, footmen circulated
among the guests with trays of drinks and gentle strains
of music emanated from an invisible chamber quartet.

Having just arrived, Peregrine and Lord Ross stood
at the edge of the garden, their height giving them an
advantage in viewing the guests. As the Englishman
made low-voiced comments about what could be expected of the event, Peregrine listened with only half
an ear. Though his face was calm, internally he vibrated with anticipation. Today, after twenty-five years
of waiting, he would meet his enemy face-to-face.

Narrowing his eyes against the sun, Ross said, ''I

don't see Weldon yet, but he will certainly be here before the afternoon is over. Will you recognize him?"

"I will recognize him," Peregrine said softly. Even in the darkest circle of hell, he would know Weldon. There was a slight chance that the recognition would be mutual, though Peregrine had been only a boy of ten at their last meeting. The possibility added a savory dash of uncertainty to the upcoming encounter.

Revenge would be less satisfying if Weldon were an unknowing victim. But that would not happen, for eventually the Englishman would realize that he was prey and would strike back. The final battle would be fierce, for Weldon was on his own turf, with vast resources at his command.

If by some freak chance Weldon managed to destroy his stalker, he would still die himself at the hands of an assassin activated by Peregrine's death. Not a sportsmanlike action, but Peregrine had little use for the English concept of sportsmanship, which was a luxury for men who were not in danger of losing anything of real importance. No matter what happened, Weldon would die, after what he valued most had been taken from him. The only major variable was whether Peregrine himself would survive, and that was not a vital question.

Ross's voice interrupted his musings. "Are you ready to be introduced to some of your fellow guests?"

Peregrine gave him a lazy smile. "You cannot imagine how much irony there is in the fact that I am here in London, about to be plunged into the heart of respectable English society."

"You make yourself sound like a dagger," Ross said dryly. "Perhaps I can't fully appreciate the nuances, but I see that you find the situation vastly amusing."

"Indeed," Peregrine murmured. Glancing across the crowd, he asked, "Which of the lovely ladies is my hostess?"

"Look for the most beautiful blonde." Ross scanned the crowd, then nodded in the right direction when he found her. "There's Sara, under the tree on the far side of the garden, the one talking to the little girl."

Just as Peregrine's gaze located the woman, a plump man bustled up to Lord Ross. As his friend turned to the newcomer, Peregrine studied Lady Sara St. James. At first glance she was a disappointment, for he would have guessed that Weldon would choose a wife of stunning beauty as well as noble birth. Perhaps there were no eligible duke's daughters who were also beautiful.

Ross's cousin was rather small, slim, and simply dressed in a cream-colored gown. Her hair was pulled back over her ears into a demure knot on her neck, and was of a shade Peregrine considered too dark to be called blond. In spite of her cousin's description, she was definitely not a woman to bring a roomful of men to awed attention.

Lady Sara had her arm around the shoulders of a pretty flaxen-haired girl of ten or eleven years. The child glowed with the pleasure of attending an adult party. Turning her face up, she said something that caused the older woman to laugh and give the girl a gentle push toward the refreshment table.

As the child danced off, Lady Sara stepped from under the tree into the sunshine, her face still lit with laughter. And when she did, Peregrine caught his breath, suddenly transfixed.

Sara St. James was not stunning, or even vividly pretty, for prettiness was just another fashion that changed as quickly as the English weather. But in the bones of Lady Sara's face, the serenity of her expression, there was a wise, timeless beauty that would be honored in any age, by any race of earth's children. A sibyl of the ancient Greeks would have had such a countenance. Haloed by the sun, her hair was thick dark honey shot with amber and old gold, as luxurious as antique silk. Now he understood why Ross had called Lady Sara beautiful and blond, for there was no single, simple word that would describe her coloring. Or her.

Peregrine smiled and silently saluted his enemy's taste, for Weldon had, indeed, chosen a wife of rare beauty and breeding. Separating Ross's cousin from her betrothed was going to be a most rewarding endeavor, for it would save the lady from a vile husband, deprive Weldon of one of the trophies of his success, and be stimulating sport for Peregrine as well.

Since Ross was having trouble escaping his acquaintance, Peregrine decided to make his way to his hostess on his own. Like a trout into water, he slipped into the crowd. A footman with a tray of filled goblets went past, and Peregrine deftly captured one. A sip identified a fine French champagne, chosen to go with the mounds of fresh strawberries featured on the refreshment tables. He stopped and sampled a berry, discovering that champagne complemented the flavor perfectly. These English aristocrats knew how to live well, even if it was an artificial little world they inhabited.

Numerous oblique glances followed his leisurely progress, but most guests were too well-bred to stare openly. Probably they were just curious at the sight of an unfamiliar face in their usual circle. He knew there was nothing amiss with his appearance, for he had run the gauntlet of tailor, boot maker, and barber, and knew himself to be a very fair approximation of an English gentleman.

The only person who looked at him directly was a glorious golden-haired creature of mature years who gave him a warning look when his gaze lingered too long on her equally glorious young daughter. Seeing her determination to keep the wolf from her lamb, Peregrine offered his most disarming smile.

After a surprised moment, the mother smiled back, though she stayed close to her daughter. Wise woman. Peregrine estimated that the girl would be worth five hundred guineas in the Tripoli slave market, and the mother would probably bring two hundred in spite of her age. He grinned inwardly, imagining the reactions

of the people around him if they could read his
thoughts. That plump, aging dandy would be over-
priced at five pounds.

While he was alert to everything about him, most
of his attention was focused unobtrusively on Lady
Sara as she performed her duties as a hostess, saying
a few words to one guest before moving on to another.
It had not been immediately obvious, because she was
slight while Ross was tall and strongly built, but as
Peregrine came closer, he saw how much the cousins
resembled each other. The handsome, masculine
planes of Ross's face were refined to delicate feminin-
ity in Lady Sara, and the cousins also shared clear
brown eyes and well-defined brows and lashes that
contrasted dramatically with their fair hair.

But there was a subtler similarity, a quality more
mental than physical that was hinted at in Ross, and
rather stronger in Lady Sara. It nagged at Peregrine,
a faint shadow that he recognized but could not quite
define.

Then, when their paths finally intersected and he
came face-to-face with his hostess, he knew what
haunted her eyes in that particular way. Lady Sara St.
James's calm, sibyl face had been shaped and molded
by pain.

As soon as Sara saw the tall, black-haired man, she
knew that he was Ross's newly arrived friend. Then
she had questioned her conclusion, wondering why she
was so certain. His skin was dark, but no more than
that of a weathered farmer, his craggy features were
not noticeably foreign, and his superbly tailored black
clothing was quintessentially British. Nonetheless, she
was sure that he could only be Prince Peregrine of
Kafiristan.

It was the way he moved, she decided, fluid and
feral as a predator, wholly unlike the way a European
walked. She saw how women watched him covertly
and was not surprised, for there was something about

the Kafir that would make women spin foolish fantasies about sensuous savages who were really nature's noblemen, untrammeled by civilization. Sara smiled at her own foolishness, then lost sight of the prince as she talked to one of her father's elderly cousins.

Then, quite suddenly, the currents of the party brought her face-to-face with Prince Peregrine. Sara tilted her head up as she opened her mouth to welcome her guest, but her voice died unborn as his intense gaze caught and held hers. The prince's eyes were a clear, startling green, a color unlike any other she had ever seen, a wild, exotic reminder that this was a man raised under different skies, by different rules. The unknowable green depths beckoned, promising . . . promising what?

It would be easy to drown in those eyes, to throw propriety and honor aside, and count the world well lost. . . . Shocked and disoriented by her thoughts, Sara swallowed and forced her mind back to reality. Extending her hand, she said, "I am your hostess, Sara St. James. Surely you are Prince Peregrine?"

His black slashing brows rose in mock despair. Taking her hand, he said in a deep resonant voice, "It is so obvious? And here I thought I was wearing correct native dress. Perhaps I should sell the tailor to the tin mines for failing me." He had a faint, husky accent, and his pronunciation was slightly overprecise, but otherwise his English was flawless.

Sara laughed. "It is not British custom to sell people to the mines, as I'm sure you know. Besides, your tailor is not at fault. There is an old proverb that clothes make the man, but that is only a partial truth. What really makes a man is his experiences, and your face was not formed by an English life."

"Very true." The prince still clasped Sara's hand. His own hand was well shaped and well groomed, but had the hardness that resulted from physical labor.

Abruptly Sara remembered a demonstration of electricity she had once seen, for she felt as if a powerful current was flowing from him to her. It radiated from his warm clasp and those unnerving green eyes, and made her disturbingly aware of his sheer maleness. Perhaps an arduous mountain life had made the prince so lithe and strong, so attractive that she wanted to run her hands over his body, feel his muscles, draw him close. . . .

It took all of Sara's training in graciousness not to snatch her hand back. The blasted man must be a mesmerist! Or perhaps the resemblance was to a cobra hypnotizing a rabbit. She took a deep breath, telling herself not to be fanciful, the prince was merely different from what she was used to. Ross had once told her that Asiatics stood closer together than Europeans when they conversed. That was why she was so aware of the man's nearness. Disengaging her hand from his, she took a step back. "Local custom permits kissing a woman's hand, or perhaps shaking it, but the rule is that the hand must be returned promptly."

His mobile features fell into lines of profound regret. "A thousand apologies, Lady Sara. I knew that, but forgot. So many things to remember. You will forgive my occasional lapses?"

"I can see that you are going to be a severe trial, Your Highness." Sara hoped her voice sounded normal. Her hand still tingled where they had touched, and she felt abnormally sensitive, like a butterfly newly emerged from its cocoon. The flowers smelled sweeter, the music sounded brighter, the air itself pulsed with promise. "Where is my cousin? I can't believe he was so rag-mannered as to leave you to your own devices."

"On the contrary, his manners are too good. He was waylaid by a tedious fellow who is obsessed with the subject of what prince would be a fit consort for your little Queen Victoria."

Sarah nodded. "Mr. Macaw. He is very difficult to escape."

"It is simple to get away from such fellows," the

Kafir pronounced. "It is only necessary to be rude. Civilized manners are not at all an asset, you know."

"You and I could have some truly splendid arguments, Your Highness." Sara tried to look severe, but the corners of her mouth curved up and betrayed her. Though the prince was alarmingly attractive, he was also Ross's friend, and it seemed natural to treat him with informality. "What a pity that I am the hostess of this party, and can't spend the next hour convincing you that manners are essential to smooth the rough edges of life. Shall we find my cousin? Being overcivilized, I can't bring myself to abandon you in the midst of strangers."

The prince glanced across the crowd. "No need to search, for Lord Ross has finally escaped the dreaded Mr. Macaw."

A moment later, Ross reached them. "Sorry to have left you stranded, Mikahl."

"No matter," the prince said. "Your cousin had no trouble identifying me. She has been instructing me in manners, but fears it a hopeless task."

Ross smiled. "If Sara will consent to be your mentor, you could have no better guide to local customs."

Peregrine looked hopeful. "Will you mentor me, Lady Sara?"

She laughed. "Mentor is not a verb, but if you wish, I will be happy to advise you." More seriously, she continued, "Ross said that you saved him from two dangerous situations. I cannot do as much for you, but I will do whatever I can to make your stay in England a rewarding one."

With equal seriousness, he replied, "I am most grateful for your kindness. May I call on you tomorrow morning? I have many questions that I dare not ask Ross, for he has too little respect for society to give reliable answers."

"While I, conventional creature that I am, can always be counted on to know what is proper," Sara said wryly. "By all means call on me. After all, how can you enjoy the pleasures of outraging London if you do not know what is considered outrageous? I look forward to furthering our acquaintance.''

Ross broke into their banter. ''Sara, Sir Charles has just arrived, and should be with us in a moment.''

She raised her gaze to look for her betrothed, but from the corner of her eye, she saw that the prince was also watching Weldon's approach. Since his face was profoundly still, why did she feel that silent lightning crackled around him?

''Sorry I'm late, my dear.'' Weldon bent to kiss Lady Sara's cheek, but Peregrine was interested to note a slight withdrawal on the part of the lady. No, it was not a love match, though the two exchanged easy greetings like a long-married couple.

Peregrine studied his enemy with hungry eyes. The years had been kind to Weldon, and he looked like what he was: a distinguished man of breeding and wealth. In his youth, charm and good looks had masked his true nature, and on the surface those qualities were still present. It took an astute eye to interpret his face correctly, but as Lady Sara had said, it was experience that made a man, and a lifetime of evil had engraved subtle lines of cruelty in Weldon's countenance.

Lady Sara's soft voice cut across his thoughts. ''Charles, let me introduce you to Prince Peregrine of Kafiristan. He is newly arrived in England, and is probably the first man of his people ever to visit Europe. Your Highness, Sir Charles Weldon.''

''I hope your visit is an enjoyable one, Your Highness.'' Weldon offered his hand with unthinking social ease. Then his gaze met Peregrine's and his expression changed, casualness giving way to puzzlement. ''This is your first visit to England? I have the feeling we have met before.''

As Peregrine accepted his enemy's hand, for a moment his vision darkened as the bonds that restrained his rage came perilously near to bursting. It would be easy, so easy to pull out his dagger and thrust it between Weldon's ribs. The Englishman's heart blood would surge hotly over Peregrine's hand, crimson retribution for the past. He would live just long enough to be told why he was dying. . . .

With a fierce internal oath, Peregrine reined back his madness. Yes, executing Weldon now would be easy, but it would be too quick and painless a death. Besides, assassination would send him to the gallows and ruin Lady Sara's party.

Once more in control, Peregrine shook his enemy's hand with a pressure just short of inflicting pain, then released it. "Have you visited India, Sir Charles? Perhaps we met there, though I do not remember such an occasion."

At the sound of Peregrine's deep, accented voice, Weldon's expression cleared. "No, I've never been to India, and we have not met before. It is just that your eyes are such a distinctive color. I've only seen eyes so green once or twice before." After a brief hesitation, he added under his breath, "Once."

"Green eyes are not unusual among my father's people," Peregrine said smoothly. Then he offered the bait that would draw his enemy to him. "I am pleased to meet you, Sir Charles. Your reputation in the City of London is very high. I am interested in investing in this country. Perhaps, if you have the time, you would be so kind as to advise me?"

Greed overcame any disquiet Weldon might have. "Delighted to be of service. Perhaps we can dine at my club soon?"

"That would be my greatest pleasure." Peregrine found secret satisfaction in the fact that all his comments were double-edged.

As they set a date later in the week, the flaxen-haired girl who had been talking to Lady Sara earlier materialized between her ladyship and Weldon, and regarded the foreigner curiously.

Weldon said, "Prince Peregrine, this is my daughter Eliza."

"A *prince?*" The girl's blue eyes rounded with delight.

"Indeed I am, Miss Weldon." Peregrine's research had included Eliza Weldon. The girl's mother, Jane Clifton, had been the daughter of a rich city banker, and her inheritance had started Weldon on the path to wealth. The heiress had died three years ago, when her daughter was eight. Eliza had her father's good looks, but if she had also inherited his warped nature, that fact was not visible. She was just a pretty, uncomplicated child, impressed at meeting foreign royalty.

"Eliza, make your curtsy to the prince," Lady Sara said.

The girl dropped into a painstakingly correct curtsy. As Peregrine returned a deep, formal bow, he wondered idly what would become of her. No doubt Eliza had relatives who would see to her upbringing when her father was gone.

Lady Sara said, "If you will excuse us, Charles and I must speak with someone who has just arrived. I hope to see you again soon, Your Highness."

As Lady Sara turned and walked away, Peregrine saw that she walked with a slight hesitation, not quite a limp. Perhaps that had something to do with the ghosts of old pain that he saw in her eyes? He could ask Ross, but it would be more interesting to discover the truth on his own. No man or woman was civilized all the way through, and it would be intriguing to discover what untamed currents lay beneath the lady's calm surface.

As they made their way toward the bishop who was going to marry them, Charles remarked, "Interesting fellow, that prince. A friend of Lord Ross's, I assume?" When Sara nodded, he asked, "Is Kafiristan an Indian state?"

"No, it lies beyond India, in the mountains of the

Hindu Kush,'' Sara explained. ''The land is very wild and virtually unexplored by Westerners.''

''He must be an unusual man to leave his mountains for the wider world,'' Charles murmured. ''I gather he's wealthy?''

''Quite fabulously so, according to Ross. Apparently he started with a substantial fortune, and has multiplied it by trading throughout the Orient.''

''The prince seemed taken with you, Sara. Encourage the acquaintance. He could be a valuable man to know.''

''I have already agreed to advise him.'' Sara's voice was cool. It was one thing for Ross to ask her to sponsor his friend, another to have her future husband order her to cultivate a potential investor. But Charles wanted a gracious hostess who would enhance his status in the worlds of business and society; she could hardly object when he asked her to play that role.

Chapter 3

THE MORNING AFTER her garden party, Sara was just finishing a late breakfast with her father when the butler entered, a bemused expression on his face. "Your ladyship, you have a visitor. He claims to be some sort of prince."

"Good heavens," she said blankly. Then she laughed, feeling suddenly buoyant. "Father, would you like to meet the gentleman I was telling you about?"

Disapproval showed on the Duke of Haddonfield's cool aristocratic face. "Doesn't he know what proper calling hours are?"

"Obviously not. However, since everyone seems to want me to educate him, he soon will." Sara drained her coffee cup, then followed the butler.

The prince was looking out one of the windows when she entered the drawing room. Sara paused a moment to admire the way his dark, well-cut clothing emphasized his broad shoulders and lean body. One could only hope that more Kafirs would find their way to England.

Then he turned and gave her an enchanting smile. "I hope the time is not inconvenient? You did give me permission to make a morning call."

She smiled and offered her hand. "I forgot to mention that morning calls are made in the afternoon."

As he straightened from bowing over her hand, the prince raised his thick black brows. "Morning calls occur in the afternoon? That is not logical."

"You must not expect society to be logical, Your Highness," Sara commented, then added the reminder, "The hand?"

"Ah, yes, it must be released." His green eyes sparkling, the prince relinquished Sara's hand.

"Why do I have the feeling that you are using your foreign status to be outrageous?" she asked, trying to sound severe.

"I have no idea. Perhaps you have a naturally suspicious mind," he replied, brimming with innocence. He thought a moment. "I could return this afternoon to make my morning call, but doubtless at that time your house will be full of others who are calling to express thanks for your estimable party. In such a crowd, you would have no time to correct my errors. That being the case, you should let me take you for a drive now, so you will have ample time to educate me."

Sara eyed him admiringly. "I see why you are such a successful merchant. You could sell sand to a Bedouin." Before she could say more, the door opened and a line of three maids entered, each one carrying a huge vase of white roses.

As she stared at the parade of flowers, Peregrine said, "Roses are an acceptable token of gratitude for a hostess?"

She nodded, rather dazed. "Yes, though usually the quantity would be smaller. Much, much smaller."

He smiled, the tanned skin crinkling around his eyes. "But I had an exceedingly good time, many roses' worth." The maids having set the flowers on various tables and withdrawn, he moved to the nearest vase and pulled out a single blossom. His gaze holding hers, the prince inhaled the flower's fragrance, then offered it to Sara. "White roses, for sweetness and purity. There are not enough in London to do you justice."

Bemused, she accepted the flower. It was at the perfect moment of expectant bloom, just beginning to open, a faint blush of pink at the heart of the ivory petals. Impressive how he managed to make every gesture extravagant and romantic. She really must convince him to restrain himself, or every female he met would think she was being courted.

Sara inhaled the delicate scent of the rose and sighed. It would be a crime to constrain such charm. Perhaps she should be training Englishmen to emulate the Kafir rather than vice versa.

Before she could decide where to start her lecture on propriety, her father entered the drawing room. In his early sixties, the Duke of Haddonfield was only average height, but he carried his spare frame with such dignity that he commanded attention anywhere.

Sara made the introductions as the two men regarded each other speculatively. Peregrine's manners blended ease with deference to the other man's greater age, and after a few minutes of conversation her father's reserved expression thawed to affability. From there, it was a short step to the duke encouraging Sara to take advantage of the fine weather to go driving with the prince in Hyde Park.

As Peregrine assisted Sara into his curricle, she remarked, "I am beginning to believe that you are a fraud, Your Highness."

Surprised by his sudden sharp glance, she explained, "You may be a stranger to London, but you must have moved in European circles in India and the cities of the Middle East. Obviously you know perfectly well how to behave yourself when you choose to. You did an excellent job of turning my father up sweet."

He grinned. "Turn up sweet? I do not recognize that expression."

"It means to charm someone into viewing you favorably, a practice at which you excel," she explained. "It is all right to do it—in fact, it's the essence of social success—but don't use the phrase in polite society. It's a little vulgar."

"Noted," he said agreeably. "You are right, I am not without experience of Western customs, but still, London can be rather overpowering to a first-time visitor."

Sara doubted that the prince found anything over-powering, but didn't pursue the point. They traveled in amiable silence as the prince deftly threaded through the heavy commercial traffic. Eventually she said, "You drive very well. Is that a skill you learned in your mountains?"

"No, there are neither roads nor carriages in Kafir-istan. In fact, the average trail would make a goat think twice about attempting it. That is why the tribes have kept their independence—the land is very nearly im-possible to invade." Without changing his tone, Per-egrine continued, "When I met you, I thought your countenance had been shaped by pain. Did you suffer some serious accident, or a long illness?"

Lady Sara gasped. "One of the things you must learn is that personal questions are considered rude," she said in a suffocated voice. "If people wish you to know more about their lives, they will volunteer the information."

"Also noted." A quick glance sideways showed that her face was pale. He pulled the horses to a stop to allow cross traffic to go through an intersection. "Is that slight hesitation in your step a result of whatever happened to you?"

"You're incorrigible," Sara snapped. Then she ex-haled with a faint sigh. "Very well, if you must know. There's no great mystery about it. I had a riding ac-cident when I was eighteen, just after my first London Season. I had made that jump before, but this time I wasn't paying proper attention. My horse hit the wall, then fell on top of me. She had to be destroyed. It would have made sense to do the same to me, but of course they couldn't. At first the doctors thought I'd die, then they said I would never walk again."

"It was a long recovery?"

"Years. I'd still be in a wheelchair if Ross hadn't come back to England and said he would not allow me to loll about and pretend to be an invalid. With his teasing and encouragement, I regained the knack of walking.'' Her voice caught before she added almost inaudibly, "Then my mother began to die."

"And you, honorable daughter, would have nursed her to the end. Now I understand why you did not have the time to marry before now.'' Some quality in her silence caused him to glance over and see how rigid her mouth was, and he guessed that there was more to her story. "Was there a man before the accident?"

Her brown eyes raw and vulnerable in her stark face, Lady Sara turned to glare at him. "Do you read thoughts, or have you been asking about me?" Then her gaze faltered and dropped. "Though almost no one knew about that part of it."

Guessing how much it must hurt her to reveal so much of her inner emotions, he looked away and concentrated on guiding the curricle around a dray filled with kegs. "I did not read your mind or spy on you. I am merely good at conjecture. If you had had a Season in London, you would have had many suitors, and at seventeen or eighteen it is natural to fall in love.''

"Natural, and foolish.'' She shrugged her slim shoulders. "Since we were both young, there was no formal betrothal, just an understanding between us. After I was injured . . .'' She stopped, then said after a moment, "Of course he did not want to be tied to a cripple.''

"You are hardly a cripple," Peregrine remarked. "What a fool the boy was. To cast a jewel away for a slight flaw, when it is flaws that give character to beauty."

"You must not say such things," Sara said in a choked voice. "They are too personal. It sounds . . . it sounds too much like flattery or courtship.''

"I but speak the truth, my lady," he said meekly, "but if I am distressing you, I will find some unarguable boring topic. How about horses? These hired job horses do not please me. Where might I purchase better ones?''

Her voice easier, Lady Sara said, "The best place

is Tattersall's Repository, just south of Hyde Park Corner. Most of the best horses are sent there for auction. Besides having a reputation for honest dealing, it is very fashionable. Perhaps Ross can take you this afternoon. During the summer, Monday is the only sale day, so if you don't go today you will have to wait another week for the next one.''

"We are almost at Hyde Park Corner now. Which direction should I turn?''

Sara pointed. "Tattersall's is down to the left, off Upper Grosvenor Place, but you can't go there now. Or rather, you can, but I can't.''

When they reached the corner, Peregrine turned the curricle in the direction she indicated. "Why can't you go there?''

"Tattersall's is almost a gentlemen's club,'' she explained. "Everyone important in racing belongs to the Subscription Room. Men go there to settle gambling debts, see friends, and tell boring hunting stories. It's definitely no place for females.''

Peregrine pulled the curricle over to the side of the road so he could give her his full attention. "What would happen if you went with me? Would you be stoned?''

"Of course not!''

"Is there a law against it, and you would be arrested?'' he asked with interest. "Sent to Newgate, or put into *purdah* and never allowed out again?''

"Neither.''

"Then what is the problem?''

"It is just not done,'' she said, exasperated at his obtuseness. "Everyone would stare and be scandalized.''

Just how deep did Lady Sara's conventionality run? Unable to resist finding out, Peregrine said, "If you do not wish to come, I will not force you. But do you truly care what others think?''

She opened her mouth to reply, then closed it without speaking. After a long moment, she said, "The only

opinions I really care about are those of my friends and
family. But obeying the rules makes life simpler.''

"Simpler, perhaps, but so much less interesting.
Have you never wondered what men do in their cherished male sanctums?''

Lady Sara began to laugh. "You're impossible,'' she
gasped. "I will never succeed in educating you in the
ways of London society. Instead, you are going to corrupt me.''

Peregrine smiled down at her. Today she wore a
daffodil-colored morning gown that brought out gold
flecks in her wide brown eyes. A most charming and
original woman; she must not be allowed to fall into
Weldon's clutches. "Sweet Sara,'' he said softly, "will
you let me corrupt you?''

Her laughter died away and for a moment she looked
startled, as if wondering whether his comment covered
more than just the present situation. Then she smiled
back. Peregrine's greatest advantage was that apparently it had not occurred to the lady that her cousin's
friend could have improper designs on her.

"I should love to see Tattersall's. Turn right there,
just beyond St. George's Hospital. And for heaven's
sake,'' she added with a touch of asperity, "remember
to call me Lady Sara.''

It was still early by the standards of the fashionable
world so Tattersall's was quieter than it would be later
in the day. However, every man in the establishment
turned to stare when Sara and the prince entered the
main courtyard.

"You were quite right.'' Peregrine's low voice
brimmed with amusement. "Such shock at the sight
of a female. One would think these gentlemen had
never seen one before. And I thought British society
was supposed to be liberal. I am reminded of rural
parts of the Ottoman Empire, where modest Turkish
farm women wear veils when they feed roosters, to
protect themselves from the danger of a male gaze. Do

you suppose the gentlemen would be happier if they wore veils to protect themselves from your fatal glance?''

"What would make them happier was if they blinked and I was gone. Perhaps they fear that I am Medusa and the sight of me will turn them to stone," Sara said, unable to repress a smile at her companion's irreverence. "Or, since at least half of the men here are relatives or acquaintances of mine, their shock might be that Lady Sara St. James is doing something so improper. It would be more understandable if I were an opera dancer."

She glanced around with interest, determined to take advantage of this opportunity to see a masculine holy of holies. The famous yard had enough space for dozens of horses and carriages, and was surrounded by a covered arcade where horses could be shown in bad weather. Nodding toward the arcade, she added, "It looks rather like an equine cloister, doesn't it?"

"Justly so," he agreed. "There are some splendid beasts here. You said it was an auction house. If I wish to buy, can I do so immediately, without waiting for the auction?"

"I think so," she said uncertainly. "At least, if you are willing to pay a top price."

"Which I am. What better way to establish myself as a fabulously wealthy foreigner, with great style and little sense?" He glanced down at her, a wicked gleam in his green eyes. "Besides, while you are carrying this off with great aplomb, I shouldn't think that you wish to stay too long."

What a perceptive prince he was, Sara reflected. While she was capable of pretending the same confidence she had in her own drawing room, she didn't really enjoy being the target of so many scandalized eyes.

As they crossed the yard to where a number of carriage horses were tethered, Sara saw a middle-aged man with a proprietorial air emerge from inside the building. Mr. Tattersall, she presumed. His eyes widened at the sight of her, but before he could react, another man whispered something in his ear, probably explaining that she was a duke's daughter.

After that, the proprietor ignored her. Wise man. While Sara's relatives and acquaintances might not approve of her presence, it was likely that some of them would object to her being thrown out. After all, as Peregrine had said, there was no law forbidding her presence. Poor Mr. Tattersall. Caught on the horns of a dilemma, he prudently chose to do nothing.

"Do you see anything you like?" Sara asked.

After an encompassing survey, Peregrine said, "There," and led her over to a pair of perfectly matched bays.

For the next several minutes, the prince communed with the beasts in a rippling foreign language while he ran his hands over them in a comprehensive check. Sara stayed in the shadows a discreet distance away. An old groom, who had watched her entrance with great appreciation, sidled over and murmured, "Your friend's got a good eye for 'orseflesh, milady. That's the best pair we've 'ad in weeks. Wouldn't be 'ere still 'cept the owner's been 'oldin' out for a long price."

Mr. Tattersall came over to Peregrine and introduced himself, then commenced a discussion. Talking horseflesh eased the man's expression, though periodically he gave Sara a hunted look, clearly wishing her somewhere—anywhere—else.

Within ten minutes, the pair of bays had demonstrated their paces and a deal was struck that cheered Mr. Tattersall greatly. "I think I can warrant that Lord Hatfield will be most pleased with your offer, Your Highness," he murmured. Then, his business instincts prevailing over his desire to get the female out of his establishment, he continued, "Might you be interested in acquiring any other horses today? A team, perhaps? You'll find none better matched anywhere. Perhaps a hunter or riding hack?"

"Perhaps," Peregrine said, taking Sara's arm again. "Mr. Tattersall, are you acquainted with my most charming guide, Lady Sara St. James? It was she who said that your establishment was the place to come for horses."

Resigned, the proprietor bowed to her and muttered a greeting. Then he took them for a tour of the available stock. Peregrine dismissed all of the teams with a single eloquent glance, and most of the riding horses were rejected just as swiftly. Then they came to the last loose box, which contained a large stallion of so pale a gray that it appeared almost white.

"I own this horse myself," Mr. Tattersall said proudly. "Today he will be going up for auction. Splendid, is he not? He is of the line of Eclipse. His sire was . . ."

Peregrine cut the proprietor off with a quick gesture of his hand. "Bring him out."

A groom led out the young, high-spirited stallion. As it tossed its head, pulling at the halter, Sara nervously stepped back out of the way. Peregrine didn't notice. His face rapt, he circled the stallion, once more talking in the language he had used before. Soothed by his sure touch and hand, the gray steadied and watched him, bright-eyed with interest.

Sara thought that the prince would request that the horse be saddled and put through its paces. Instead, he took the reins from the groom and, with one lithe movement, swung onto the stallion's bare back.

"You will permit me?" Taking off his hat, the prince flipped it to Tattersall with a snap of his wrist. Then, under the stunned eyes of the proprietor, the grooms, and the gentlemenly clientele, he leaned forward over the stallion's neck, kicked it in the ribs, and they went bolting across the yard and out of Tattersall's Repository like silver lightning.

Having had time to become accustomed to the Kafir's ways, Sara was slightly less stunned than the rest. Presumably her companion would return when he and the horse had ridden off their high spirits, but meanwhile Sara felt uncomfortably conspicuous.

Then, to her relief, a familiar voice drawled, "My eyes say that it is you, Sara, but my mind flatly refuses to believe it. Pray clarify my confusion."

Sara turned to see the stout, good-natured figure of a distant cousin, Sir Wilfred Whiteman. "Believe your eyes, Wilfred." She offered her hand. "How are you today?"

"Prospering, my dear." He bowed gracefully. "Who is your energetic companion? A Red Indian from the American frontier? I understand that they prefer to ride without saddles."

She shook her head. "He's a friend of Lord Ross's, Prince Peregrine of Kafiristan. He rides well, doesn't he?"

"That he does," Wilfred replied with unfeigned respect.

Sara smiled inwardly; if the prince wanted to become an instant legend, he was going about it very cleverly. Fashionable gentlemen like Wilfred might be startled by his actions, but in an approving way. Even Mr. Tattersall looked indulgent after his shock wore off, though he handed the prince's hat to a groom.

For ten minutes or so, Wilfred amused Sara with scandalous gossip. Then Peregrine trotted in on the stallion, both of them looking vastly pleased with themselves. "Magnificent, Mr. Tattersall," he said as he reined the horse in. "What is your price to sell him before auction?"

The proprietor's eyes narrowed as he speculated how much an ignorant foreigner might be willing to pay. "A thousand guineas."

"Done."

Sara almost laughed at Tattersall's expression when he saw that he might have gotten much more for the horse. However, she did not waste much sympathy on him; a thousand guineas was probably more than Mr. Tattersall could have gotten at auction.

Then Peregrine rode over to Sara. His wavy black hair, which he wore a little long, was tangled from the wind, and he looked untamed and splendid and free, not at all like an Englishman. "His gaits are like silk, Sara." He extended one hand to her. "Come, ride with me."

Sara felt the blood drain from her face. She looked up at him helplessly, knowing that he did not understand what he was asking. Then, as their gazes caught and held, his expression changed. He saw too much, damn him. His green eyes compelling, he said so softly that no one else could hear, "Trust me."

She wanted to turn and run. Instead, before she could think too much about what she was doing, she took a deep breath and clasped the prince's hand. Effortlessly he lifted her onto the stallion, turning her in midair so that she landed crossways in front of him, her legs resting against his left thigh.

He waited a moment for her to settle herself. Then, as she convulsively clenched the gray mane, he urged the stallion out into the street. It took only a few moments to trot through the traffic of Hyde Park Corner and bring them to the park proper.

Peregrine turned the horse into the wide lane called Rotten Row, which was nearly empty at this hour, then put the stallion into a canter. At first the lack of a saddle made Sara's fear infinitely worse. Terror held her rigid, and she bounced against the horse with bone-rattling force. But gradually her fear began to subside, for the prince's warm, hard body held her more securely than any saddle. As she relaxed against him, she felt all the subtle movements he used to guide and control his mount.

As Peregrine had promised, the stallion's gait was sweet and smooth. Sara began to soften into the rhythm of the horse's motion. As her body remembered and her fear ebbed away, she began to enjoy the almost forgotten touch of wind against her face. It had been so long. . . .

"Are you all right?" he asked quietly.

She nodded. "Now I am."

"You have not been on a horse since your accident?"

"No. The usual advice is to remount as soon as possible after a fall, but I couldn't, not for years. And by the time I had recovered physically"—she shuddered— "I couldn't make myself do it. I'm such a coward."

"On the contrary, sweet Sara, you are very brave. Are you not here, defying custom and riding the wind like Pegasus?"

"The credit for that belongs to you, not me," she said dryly. Her mind seemed split in two. On one side was the knowledge that she was behaving in an utterly irrational fashion by riding bareback through a London park with a wild man. Her father would be shocked, her friends disbelieving.

Yet at the same time, she felt as if her actions were completely natural. The mysterious prince had been born on the opposite side of the world, raised with values and customs that were completely alien to hers. Yet no man but Ross had talked to her as directly as Peregrine did, or seen as deeply into her. Ross was very nearly her brother, but what was Peregrine?

Sara's fingers tightened in the stallion's mane as she had a disquieting realization. From the beginning she had noticed how attractive the Kafir was—no woman could fail to notice—but her admiration had been dispassionate. Though Peregrine was splendid and beautiful and masculine, that knowledge had had no personal relevance to her. She was the daughter of a duke, respectably betrothed, of sober mind and habit. Yet here she was in the arms of a man who was in most ways a stranger, and she was reveling in the experience. There was a profound sensuality in their closeness, in the way their bodies moved together in time with the stallion's. It was the greatest physical intimacy she had ever had with a man. What would it be like to have still greater intimacy?

Though Sara had never considered herself a prudish woman, the direction of her thoughts made her blush. What a shameless creature she was becoming! Thank heaven the prince thought of her only as Ross's cousin. Though he had been kind about her disability, he did not seem like the sort of man who would be attracted to a plain woman who was no longer young. But he seemed willing to be friends. That would be more than enough.

Peregrine turned to go back. "Will you ride again now?"

Without his comforting presence, it would be difficult at first, but still Sara nodded her head. "Yes. I have missed riding. I don't want to continue missing it."

"There was a pretty little sorrel mare back in the yard, a fine ladies' mount. Shall I buy it for you?"

"No!" she said sharply. "I couldn't possibly accept such a gift from you."

"What would happen if you did?" he asked with his usual air of curiosity. "You would be disgraced? Ostracized? Refused admittance to the queen's drawing rooms?"

As they halted at the edge of the park and waited for traffic to thin, Sara swiveled about and gave him a steely glance. "This time you will not be able to coax me into relenting. I neither need nor desire that mare, nor will I accept such a gift from you. Is that clear?"

He blinked. Then a wide, slow smile spread across his face. "Perfectly clear, your ladyship. I know when to yield to a superior force."

Laughing, they rode back to Tattersall's. Lady Sara delighted Peregrine with both her open mind and her occasional stubbornness. While his primary goal was to separate her from Weldon, he hoped that he would also be able to coax her into his bed. It would be a rewarding experience for both of them.

Chapter 4

THE DAY AFTER his excursion to Tattersall's, Peregrine met Sir Charles Weldon for dinner at the City of London Club. Benjamin Slade had said that this particular club was one where leaders of commerce mingled with the top men in government and society; Rothschilds rubbed elbows with prime ministers. Even without that explanation, Peregrine would have known why Weldon patronized the place, for the lofty, dignified building reeked of money, power, and genteel ruthlessness.

In the days since their first meeting, Peregrine had tempered and buried his fury, and now he could meet his enemy with complete composure. In fact, he found the situation stimulating, like playing chess or some other war game. Weldon's objective was simple: to convince a foreigner to invest money. Peregrine's goal was much more complex; he wanted to foster a spurious friendship with his enemy. Then he would be in a better position to know Weldon's weaknesses, and to exploit them.

They spoke of trivialities over the lavish and lengthy dinner, then withdrew to a quiet corner of the smoking room and settled down in leather-upholstered wing chairs with port and cigars. "If you want to invest in this country, Your Highness," Weldon said as he trimmed the end of his cigar, "I don't think you can do better than to put your money in railroads. Within the next decade, they will revolutionize modern society. Great fortunes have already been made in railway companies, and more will be made in the future."

"Great fortunes have also been lost," Peregrine pointed out. An important move in the game was to prove that he was not a rich fool fit only for fleecing. "A couple of years back, there was something of a mania for railway stocks. Then the bubble burst and most of the prices collapsed. Too many small, badly managed companies were fighting each other, building duplicate tracks, wasting their capital, promising service and profits they couldn't deliver."

Weldon raised his brows, a respectful look on his face. "I see that you have studied the subject. Yes, the industry is currently in a state of reorganization while investors wait and see, but capital is accumulating. In another two or three years, there will be an outburst of investment and building that will make the last mania look tame. For those with the courage to invest now, there will be great profits."

"Perhaps." Peregrine took a small sip of his port. "Is there a particular railway or project you have in mind?"

"The London and Southampton," Weldon said immediately. "Southampton is one of the most important ports in the country, and a railroad connecting it with London can't help but be successful. Part of the line was constructed before the company failed last year for lack of funds. Now most of the shareholders are desperate and will accept virtually any offer for their stock. It won't be hard to accumulate a controlling interest. After that, enough new capital will have to be raised to finish building the line, but when it is complete, the L & S will be the most profitable railroad in Britain."

Elaborately casual, Peregrine knocked ashes from the tip of his cigar. "If the company is a guaranteed winner, why couldn't the present board attract new investment?"

"A very pertinent question," Weldon replied. There was a subtle shift in the atmosphere as he began to realize that this was a meeting of equals. "The fact is, investors have been wary of the London and South-ampton because there has been a problem with law-suits about the amount of compensation paid for taking rights-of-way. There is one particular landowner who was a ringleader in filing the lawsuits. However, I have reason to believe that he is now willing to be more reasonable.''

''I assume that you are looking for other investors to join you in buying up a controlling interest in the com-pany, and you would become chairman of the board?''

''Exactly. Immodest though it sounds, I assure you that no one else can turn the L & S around as well as I,'' Weldon said. ''Why, would you prefer to be chair-man yourself?''

''Not at all. I have no interest in the daily operations of a business. I prefer to concentrate on finance and leave management to others.'' Peregrine leaned back in his chair. ''I agree that there is great profit to be made in railroads, *if* one chooses the right companies. I'll need to study the figures and learn more about the legal situation before making a commitment, but I find your proposition most interesting. May I prevail on you to send the relevant information to my man of business?''

Weldon's eyes gleamed. ''I was hoping that you would say that, so I brought a summary with me.'' He reached inside his jacket and pulled out a folded sheaf of documents. ''If you want more detail, send me a list of questions.''

''Very good.'' Peregrine tucked the papers away. Now for a subject that was even more interesting. ''I have a favor to ask of you, Sir Charles. Not concerning business, but pleasure. All great cities have places where gentlemen may find . . . shall I say discreet, sophisticated entertainment?''

He paused to sip his port. ''Unfortunately, the best establishments are difficult for a stranger to find, and often admittance is impossible without a personal in-troduction from an existing patron. While my friend Lord Ross Carlisle has been most helpful, he is too much the scholar to be well-informed on this subject. I assume that a man of the world like you can direct me to someone more knowledgeable about such things.''

Weldon could have disclaimed personal knowledge, or referred Peregrine to another man. Instead, a different kind of gleam came into his eyes, part calculation of the benefits of performing this kind of favor, and part something else, something dark and avid. "I would consider it a privilege to take you on a tour of the best establishments, Your Highness. London offers everything a man could desire, from simple peasant fare on the streets to the most exotic epicurean delights.''

Peregrine released a mouthful of cigar smoke. His enemy had taken the bait. Something valuable was sure to result. "It will be interesting to see if what London offers will seem exotic to a man who has known the pleasures of the Orient.''

From the way Weldon's pale blue eyes narrowed, he was irritated by the suggestion that London vice might be inferior. "I will match the amusements of London against any other city in the world. For the right price, anything can be found here. *Anything.*'' He ground out the stub of his cigar and stood. "By the end of the evening, you will concede that I am right. Come.''

They took Weldon's closed carriage, which Peregrine was interested to note was dark and anonymous, with no coat of arms or other identifying marks. As they rode through the dark streets, Weldon said, "Under English law, it is illegal for a man to earn money from prostitution, but not for a woman. That is why most such establishments are run by females.'' He pulled a periodical from a side pocket of the carriage and handed it to his guest. "This might interest you.''

The magazine was called *The Exquisite.* Peregrine opened it and saw that under headings such as "Venus Unveiled,'' it contained descriptions of women. He skimmed several pages, seeing phrases such as: *a delicate blonde, as elegant in her manner as any lady born, but most robust in her performance;* and *dark-haired, full-figured, an expert in the best French techniques.* "Interesting," he commented. "A catalog of courtesans."

"Exactly. It describes most of the better grade of Covent Garden ware and is updated regularly. There is also a listing of night houses, which are taverns where such women can be met. Common streetwalkers are not allowed in. If you want to try one, the best is Kate Hamilton's in Princes Street, but the places I am taking you tonight provide better quality and service."

"You are too kind." Peregrine leaned back against the velvet upholstery. It promised to be a most intriguing evening.

Their first stop was a conventional brothel, unusual only for the lavishness of its furnishings. They were admitted by a hulking porter who looked like a pugilist past his prime. After accepting a warm welcome, Weldon asked if Madame de Maintenon was available. Immediately they were ushered into the presence of a tall woman of middle years. The madame was heavy, her red hair of a shade not found in nature, and her smooth complexion from a paint pot, but she still had a coarse prettiness. Peregrine guessed that she had been a beauty in her glory years.

After greeting her, Weldon said, "My friend is new to London, so I knew that he could do no better than to meet you."

Madame de Maintenon looked Peregrine over with frank appreciation. In a voice that sounded more of the East End than Paris, she said, "Pleased to meet you, my lord. If you'd like to see my girls, just take a look through here."

She drew aside a brocade drapery and gestured toward several small circles of glass set into the wall at different heights. Peregrine stepped to the highest peephole and looked through into a sumptuously furnished drawing room where half a dozen young women sat or reclined in skimpily cut, translucent dresses that left no doubt as to their profession. The system was like that in certain Asian eateries, where the customer could choose his dinner from fish swimming in a large tank.

"The girls are inspected by a doctor every week," the madame said briskly. "Wine and a fine supper are included in the basic price. Special rates if you want more than one girl at a time, unless it's a busy night. Then they're full price. We also offer the best costume shows in London."

"Costume shows?"

"The girls dress up and do a bit of acting," she explained. "Most clients find the costumes very amusing. Governesses, schoolgirls, dairymaids, harem ladies, duchesses, women dressed to look like your mother . . . we can provide most anything." She cocked her head to one side thoughtfully. "You're foreign, aren't you? If you're Catholic, you might want to try the nun show—it's particularly popular with papists. We have one gent who likes a shepherdess, complete with sheep, but for something special like that, we need a day or two of notice."

She gave a raucous laugh. "One of my girls can make herself up just like the queen, so if you've a fancy to roger Her Royal Highness, here's your chance. I guarantee that Lisette knows things Victoria never thought of."

"I have no doubt of that." Peregrine wondered how Queen Victoria would react if she knew that her subjects were guilty of such lèse-majesté. "Very intriguing, Madame de Maintenon."

"What would you fancy, my lord?" she asked hopefully.

No doubt being called "my lord" was part of the service, like the wine and the fine supper. Dropping the brocade drapery, he replied, "Tonight I am just acquainting myself with what is available. I shall stay longer on my next visit."

They took their leave and returned to the carriage,

where Peregrine said, "An excellent establishment of the more conventional type, Sir Charles. Now, what of the more exotic delights you mentioned?"

Weldon laughed. "Not easily impressed, are you? Very well, I shall introduce you to some of the more unusual houses. Shall I include the city's best homosexual brothel in the tour?"

Even though he had expected this, Peregrine's hands curled into fists, the nails gouging his palms. Grateful for the carriage's concealing darkness, he said evenly, "That isn't a primary interest of mine, but it would be useful to know at least one such establishment for possible future use."

The next stop was Soho, at the lavish house of a lady who went by the name of Mrs. Cambridge. Dressed in clinging silk and trailing fur, she proudly displayed her collection of whip thongs, leather straps, needle-pointed cat-o'-nine-tails, currycombs, and much more. Her birch rods were stored in water to keep them supple, and the rooms were decorated with elegant vases full of stinging nettles that could be used if the customer wished. As the lady stroked a thong, she said cheerfully, "Many a dead man has been brought back to life with these."

The lady's pièce de résistance was an apparatus called the Cambridge Chevalet, which she had designed herself. A cross between a rack and a freestanding ladder, it was padded and could be adjusted to a man's height. When the customer was strapped in place for his punishment, holes in the rack allowed a scantily clad assistant to caress him in appropriate places. Mrs. Cambridge personally administered all punishments, but had employees of both sexes if customers preferred to do the whipping themselves. Men whose interest in the subject was strictly academic could watch for a modest fee.

Peregrine's personal opinion was that life inflicted quite enough pain and only a damned fool would pay for the privilege of experiencing more, but there was something rather touching about Mrs. Cambridge's pride in her work. When they left, he kissed the lady's hand and solemnly assured her that he had never seen a craftswoman with more respect for the tools of her trade. Charmed, she insisted on giving him a copy of a flagellation classic called *Venus Schoolmistress, or Birchen Sports*.

After stopping at a sporting establishment whose principal claim to fame was that the girls played cards and billiards in the nude, Weldon produced two black half masks for their visit to the homosexual brothel. They arrived just in time to witness a mock marriage. Under a lace veil, the "bride" was a strapping mustachioed fellow who looked like a grenadier sergeant, while the "groom" was a languid society gentleman half a head shorter.

Waiters wearing frilly aprons and nothing more circulated with trays of champagne. His skin crawling, Peregrine found a quiet spot where he could sip his goblet and watch his host circulate among the "wedding party."

He was congratulating himself on how well he was controlling his distaste when someone came up behind and caressed his arm. Peregrine whirled, his expression so fierce that the other man fell back with a stuttered apology. It took Peregrine a moment to master himself enough to offer a contrite nod intended to convey that his reaction had been surprise, not loathing. Probably he was not successful, for the man quickly disappeared into another room.

Fortunately Weldon suggested leaving after about half an hour. When they were in the carriage again, he said, "I have saved the best for last. If you are not interested yourself, I hope you will not mind waiting while I am engaged."

"Of course not. You have been very generous with your time, and I can hardly be less so." In a tone of bored curiosity, Peregrine went on, "Which of to-

night's activities would an English gentleman expect
a wife such as Lady Sara St. James to emulate?''

There was palpable shock in Weldon's gasp. His
contempt for ignorant foreigners obvious, he said,
''No English gentleman would expect a lady to behave
like the creatures we've seen tonight—a considerate
husband would not inflict himself on a gently bred wife
more than once or twice a month. Many men approach
their wives only for the sake of having children.''

''If that is how English gentlemen think,'' Peregrine
said dryly, ''brothel owning must be a very profitable
business.''

After a cold silence Weldon said, ''If it is a business
you wish to enter, remember that in England it's illegal for a man to live off the earnings of prostitution.''

''As I said earlier, I have no interest in the day-to-
day running of any business, even one so deliciously
decadent,'' Peregrine said lazily. ''That was merely a
general observation. Now, what is this last treat that
you have saved for me?''

''An establishment that specializes in young virgins.
I would advise wearing the mask again when entering
and leaving.'' Weldon smiled, his teeth a pale flash in
the darkness. ''Regular brothels are largely ignored,
but reformers sometimes kick up a dust about houses
like this one. It is wise to be discreet.''

After a moment he spoke again, his words surging
with excitement. ''There is nothing quite so stimulating
as a virgin. Knowing that one is the first to see, to
touch, to possess . . .'' He stopped, then gave a self-
conscious laugh. ''But I'm sure that you are as familiar
with that pleasure as I. Isn't the Muslim paradise a place
where a warrior is promised a harem of ten thousand
virgins whose maidenheads regrow every night?''

''So they say, though I know of no one who can
attest to the truth of that.'' Peregrine was not surprised to learn that Weldon considered their last stop
the high point of the evening; brothels specializing in

virgins and children were the dregs of the prostitution trade, despised even by other brothel keepers.

He donned his mask as the carriage rumbled to a halt. When he climbed out, his nostrils flared at the familiar, distinctive smell of the docks. This was one of the most dangerous sections of the city. After Weldon knocked on the door, a small panel slid open, and they were inspected before being granted entry. There was still another burly porter of the dangerous-looking type that seemed to be standard in London brothels.

This house's madame, Mrs. Kent, was a tall, sinewy woman with a thin mouth and cruel eyes. After greeting Weldon with familiarity, she said, ''I've exactly what you like tonight, my lord.'' She glanced at Peregrine, then shared a meaningful look with Weldon. ''And something special for your friend as well.''

Weldon turned to his guest. ''Be my guest tonight. I insist. You will not regret it, for there is not another house in London that can match the delights of this one.''

Peregrine hesitated, knowing that more was at stake than simple debauchery. Touring the fleshpots together had taken the two men beyond a business relationship into a tenuous illusion of intimacy. Peregrine had hoped for that because it would bring him closer to his enemy. But now Weldon wanted a companion in wickedness, and to refuse the offer would cause his enemy to withdraw to a more formal distance, probably for good. ''That is most gracious of you,'' Peregrine said in a warm tone that disguised his aversion. ''I accept with pleasure.''

Mrs. Kent said, ''I will be with you in a moment, my lord,'' and led Weldon away. As he waited alone in the drawing room, Peregrine realized how silent the house was, even the street noises failing to penetrate. The walls must be insulated to muffle sounds inside the building.

Slowly Peregrine turned in the middle of the room, his neck tingling with disquiet as he absorbed the atmosphere of Mrs. Kent's house. Though it was usually danger that roused him to such heightened awareness, what he felt now was not threat but pain and despair. It reminded him of a blood-drenched pass in the Hindu Kush, a place of ambushes and old bones.

Deliberately he suppressed his reaction. Mrs. Kent's house was just another step on the long road to vengeance. He could, and would, do whatever was required to carry him further toward his goal, even if that meant deflowering a young girl to win Weldon's trust. Not an admirable deed, but at least he would do it more carefully than the average brothel patron would.

A few minutes later Mrs. Kent returned and led Peregrine upstairs, the burly guard following. Stopping in the middle of the corridor, the madame said as she opened a door, "A lovely child, my lord. I'm sure you'll be pleased with her."

Just inside the room, he stood silent and watchful as the door closed behind him. A branch of candles on the mantel revealed that the room was furnished with sleazy luxury, red being the predominant color. The bed was a massive four-poster that dwarfed the slim figure lying on a scarlet counterpane.

The girl rolled her head on the pillow and looked toward him silently. She appeared to be about thirteen, with an exquisitely pretty face and flowing blond hair. Her white muslin nightdress was ruched and ribboned like an infant's christening gown, probably a deliberate attempt to make her appear even younger than she was. His face expressionless, Peregrine lifted the branch of candles and carried it to the bedside table.

The girl's wrists were tied to the bedposts with sashes that had enough slack to allow her some movement. Her gaze was fixed on his face, her huge eyes bleak in the candlelight. Yet she did not look quite the way he expected a virgin on the point of being ravished to look. Perhaps she was drugged, or perhaps she did not understand what was going to happen.

He frowned, trying to read her expression. There was trepidation and resignation, but surprisingly little fear. While Peregrine had never patronized an establishment such as this one, he had a fair idea of what went on in such places. Perhaps, after all, he would not have to do what was expected. His voice very low, he asked, "Is there a spy hole?"

The girl's eyes widened, her gaze involuntarily flickering to a mirror fastened to the wall near the door. Peregrine crossed the room to examine the mirror, and discovered a glass-covered spy hole hidden among the decorative whorls. He pulled out his handkerchief and draped it over the decorations, then asked the girl, "Are there any others?"

Resignation gave way to wariness as she tried to decide if his odd behavior might be dangerous. After an uncertain moment, she shook her head, but Peregrine spent another few minutes checking other possible peephole locations. When he was satisfied that they were private, he untied the sashes, releasing her wrists, then sat on the foot of the bed, as far from her as possible. "You're a fake virgin, not a real one, aren't you?"

"How did you know?" she gasped as she sat up with a jerk.

"Merely a good guess," he murmured, grateful to learn that raping a terrified innocent would not be necessary this evening.

The girl huddled against the headboard, her flaxen hair spilling over her shoulders, fear in her eyes. "Please, sir, don't complain to *her,*" she begged. "I'll do anything you want, anything at all. Just don't tell *her* I didn't do you right."

Having met Mrs. Kent, Peregrine had no doubts about the *"her"* that was pronounced with such fear and loathing. He raised one hand. "Peace, child, I'll not complain to your mistress, nor do anything else that you don't want. In return, will you tell me what goes on in the house?"

She scrutinized his face, as if wondering if he were some kind of spy, before finally nodding. "If that's

what you want, sir. But promise you won't tell *her?*''
She was surprisingly well-spoken, though the sound
of the London slums was in her voice.

"I promise." Casually Peregrine folded his arms
across his chest, wanting to look unthreatening so the
girl would talk more freely. "Do you play the role of
tender virgin very often?"

"Aye, two, three times a week," she said matter-
of-factly. "I expect you know how it's done—vinegar
steam for tightness, then a bit of sponge soaked in
blood. Most men never know the difference, especially if you twitch and cry enough."

"What's your name?"

"*She* calls me Jennifer, but I was Jenny Miller at
home."

"Were you stolen from your family?"

Jenny shook her head. "Sometimes they snatch a
girl off the streets, but mostly it's not necessary, since
girls can be bought so cheap. My pa sold me for five
pounds. Mrs. Kent said that's the most she's ever paid,
but she thought I was pretty, worth keeping and using
over and over."

"Are most of the girls professional virgins like
you?"

"No, there are only two others like me. The real
virgins are usually girls who agree to come here just
once and do it for a guinea, or their parents sell them
for the one night. Some men with a clap think a virgin
will cure them, so they usually get girls like that, ones
who won't be staying. *She* says it would be bad for
business if her regulars were diseased." Jenny was
beginning to relax, the tension going out of her small
body. "Sometimes she sends in men who like a girl
who looks young but is 'old in sin.' Doing that is more
work than playing virgin."

"How long have you been in the house?"

Jenny shrugged her slim shoulders. "Years—three
or four maybe. *She* keeps a record to make sure that
the same man doesn't get me more than once. There

was bloody hell to pay one time when she made a mistake, till she convinced the gent I was the younger sister of the first one he'd had.''

In three or four years, at perhaps fifty guineas per episode, Mrs. Kent must have made a fortune off the child. ''How old are you now, Jenny?''

''Seventeen, I think. Maybe eighteen.''

''Really?'' he said in surprise. ''You look much younger.''

''Aye, that's why I'm so valuable,'' she replied with acid humor. ''But it gets harder and harder for me to look like a little girl, even with clothes like these. I'm afraid that soon I'll be sent to a regular house, where I'll have to do more men in an evening than I do now in a week. That'll be hard.''

Peregrine could see that under the shift, her body was more that of a woman than a child. Even beribboned gowns would not disguise her much longer. His mouth tightened. A prostitute could earn much more than a shop girl or mill worker, and for some women prostitution was a brief, profitable interlude before they moved on to more respectable lives. But for a girl who was virtually a slave, the future was bleak. He wondered if Jenny thought the security of being cared for was worth the price she had to pay. ''Would you be allowed to leave if you wanted to?''

''Not bloody likely,'' she said bitterly. ''Even if I could escape, I've nowhere to go. Won't go home, the only reason Pap didn't use me himself was because he knew I was worth more untouched. Working the streets is worse than this, and going into service can be pretty bad. My older sister was a housemaid, worked fifteen hours a day, and every man there had his way with her as well, till she died trying to get rid of a babe.''

Not surprisingly, it did not sound as if Jenny was happy with her present state. Obviously leaving was a topic she had considered, and with an impressive degree of common sense. ''Is there something you would rather do if you could have your wish?''

Her delicate face became wistful. "I've always thought it'd be nice to be a lady's maid. They get to work with pretty things, and they're important belowstairs, not like a housemaid. I'd like to work for a lady who was young and fashionable, and who would give me her gowns when she was done with them. Maybe someday I'd marry a handsome footman." She thought a moment, then added vehemently. "One that doesn't drink like Pap."

Her eyes met his, eagerness lighting up the clear blue depths. "Why are you asking? Do you want me for a mistress? I'd be a good one, I know everything a man likes. Or . . . or I can be a virgin every night if that's what you fancy."

"I'm not looking for a mistress, and if I was, I prefer women that look like women, not children," he said curtly, irritated at himself for inadvertently giving her ideas when he had only been indulging his curiosity.

Jenny's small face was a painful mixture of hope and pleading. "Please? I swear you'd not regret it."

Peregrine sighed. London was full of girls like this one; many were in worse straits, selling their scrawny bodies in doorways, prey to any man who wanted them, hoping for a coin in return. They were like the sands of the sea, endless, unnumbered, living and dying like mayflies.

His early life had been a ruthless course in survival, and he had quickly learned that compassion was a dangerous luxury. He had seen every possible degree of degradation and suffering, and knew better than to waste his time with rescue or reform. If he chose, he could help this girl, but what was the point of saving one little whore? It would make no difference to that vast, endless, tragic horde of broken children.

But as Jenny stared at him with great stark eyes, he knew that it would make a difference to her.

Usually Peregrine was deliberate in his actions, capable of infinite patience when necessary. But sometimes he felt a powerful, irrational impulse, and when he did, he always obeyed it. He felt such an impulse now. While he was no savior, it was not against his principles to lend a hand if doing so would not interfere with his other goals. And he owed someone a good deed. "I don't want you for a mistress," he said brusquely. "But if you really want to leave, I can give you a place to stay and help you find a job that will support you."

Jenny's breath caught, as if she had not believed that he would respond to her plea. "Oh, I want to leave," she whispered, "I surely do. But *she'll* never let me just walk out of here."

Peregrine thought a moment. He could probably buy the girl's freedom if he wanted to, but stealing her away from Mrs. Kent would be both cheaper and more satisfying. Besides, he preferred stealth as a matter of general policy.

"Is this always your room?" After she nodded, he continued, "I'll come tomorrow night, between two and three o'clock in the morning. I'll throw pebbles against the glass. If you are alone and ready to leave, open the window and I'll throw up a rope."

"I'm not sure I can lift the sash," she said uncertainly. "It's painted shut."

He stood and went to the window. When he pushed aside the layers of heavy, opaque draperies, he saw that she was right. Probably the window had not been opened in years, possibly decades. Taking the concealed knife from his boot, he slid the blade around the edge of the window frame, then tried to lift the lower sash. His arms strained until he feared that the glass might shatter. Then the sash suddenly broke free and surged upward with a raucous, grating noise.

Leaning out, Peregrine saw that a dark, noisome alley separated the brothel from the building next door. All the brothel's windows were heavily curtained, so it was unlikely that anyone would look out and see that an inmate was escaping. He counted windows so that he would know the correct one when he returned, then he had Jenny lower and raise the stiff sash to be sure she could manage it alone.

Anxiously she said, "If I'm not alone when you get here, will you wait for me?"

"For half an hour or so. If you still can't leave, I'll come back the next night, and the night after if necessary. The rope I toss up will have knots every foot and a half or so. Do you think you will be able to climb down without a problem?"

"I'll manage," she said tersely.

Deciding that he had been with the girl long enough to make it seem that he'd done what was expected, Peregrine crossed to the door. "I'll go now. I assume that you will make the sheets look convincing so that your mistress won't be suspicious of what has happened—or rather, what hasn't happened?"

Jenny gave him an indignant glance. "Of course I will. I know a lot more about this kind of thing than you seem to."

"I defer to your greater experience," he said, amused. Then his slight smile faded. "You are sure you want to leave? You know nothing of me. I might be a worse monster than Mrs. Kent."

She shrugged. "Aye, you might be. But it's a risk I'm willing to take. There's no future for me here, and I may never have another chance like this."

"You're a brave girl."

"Or a stupid one," she answered with cockney tartness. In the subdued light she looked like a child ready to be put to bed by her nurse, but the expression on her small face was thoroughly adult. Peregrine smiled, glad that he had obeyed his impulse. The girl was intelligent and resilient, and she deserved a chance to forge a better life for herself. He guessed that she would make good use of her opportunity.

Later that night, after a sated, self-satisfied Weldon had dropped his guest off at the Clarendon Hotel, Peregrine sat up until he had recorded all the details of his night's tour. The names and addresses would prove useful to Benjamin Slade's investigations.

Chapter 5

IT WAS RATHER SMALL as fashionable balls went; there was still room to draw a deep breath, for which favor Sara was duly grateful. After she and Charles arrived, they had worked their way through the crowd, greeting friends and acquaintances. Then he had found her a quiet seat, half-concealed behind a potted plant, and they had enjoyed a glass of punch together.

As Sara drained the last of her cool drink, Charles asked, "Are you comfortable here, my dear? If you don't mind being left alone, I'd like to go to the card room for a while."

Sara handed him her empty punch glass. "Go and enjoy yourself. When I feel the need for company, I will have no trouble finding it."

"Admirable Sara." He touched her cheek with possessive fingers. "I am the most fortunate of men, for you will make the best of wives." Then he turned and disappeared into the crowd.

Pleased by the compliment, Sara watched his broad back retreat, thinking that her betrothed looked wonderfully distinguished in formal evening wear. Then her gaze went to the dancers crowding the floor as her mind drifted back to her own first Season. Though she had always had a serious turn of mind, she had enjoyed her first foray into adult society, and had laughed and danced and flirted as much as any of the young girls before her now. It seemed a lifetime ago.

The ballroom was warm, so she spread her fan and absently wafted cool air toward her face. On the far side of the room, she caught a glimpse of Ross and Prince Peregrine. She had talked to both men briefly earlier. Then Ross, with his usual thoroughness, had taken his friend off for further introductions.

As she watched the Kafir critically, Sara decided that he no longer needed a guide to London society, if he ever had. He moved among the British aristocracy with utter confidence, and they in turn accepted him, at least on this social level. Indeed, society had welcomed him; at the moment no less than three beautiful women were listening raptly to his every word.

Sara snapped the ivory sticks of her fan shut, feeling stifled by the heat of massed candles and active bodies. To the left, French doors led out to a wide balcony, so she slipped out for some fresh air. The balcony was blessedly cool and empty, and she inhaled deeply, enjoying the fragile scent of the garden below after the heavy atmosphere of the ballroom.

Her body swaying to the rhythm of the music, Sara watched the dancers inside, their bodies abstract blurs through the translucent draperies. Since her accident, watching was the closest she came to dancing.

Turning her back on the ballroom, she looked up at the full moon, which gilded Mayfair with silver serenity. There was no point in envying those who could still dance; it was more productive to consider her wedding plans. There was much to be done, and most of the work would fall on her own shoulders. Aunt Marguerite, Ross's mother, would help, but that was not the same as having a mother of her own to take charge of the event.

Caught up in planning, she did not hear the French doors open and gave an unladylike jump when a deep voice said in her ear, "Is playing truant proper behavior at a London ball?"

She whirled, her heart pounding from surprise even though Prince Peregrine's soft, accented voice was instantly recognizable. "It is acceptable to slip away for fresh air, but not to startle other guests out of their wits," she said severely. "You could give a cat lessons on silent stalking."

"On the contrary, I once took stalking lessons from a cat." He smiled reminiscently. "A snow leopard, to be exact."

Black-haired and dark-garbed, he belonged to the night, as intensely alive as he was irresistibly attractive. No, not irresistible; Sara was a woman grown, in control of her emotions. "Did you stalk the leopard, or did it stalk you?"

"Both, in turn. At the end I could have killed it, but could not bear to. It was too beautiful." He chuckled. "Don't tell anyone I said that—I don't think noble savages are supposed to be so sentimental."

Sara considered his remark. "You may be many things, but savage is not one of them. A savage knows nothing of the rules of civilization. You know them, I think, but do not always choose to follow them."

"As usual, you are uncomfortably perceptive," he said after a moment. "But enough of seriousness. Will you dance with me?"

"No, thank you." She looked down and smoothed a wrinkle from the lace trim of her low-cut bodice. "I do not dance."

"Do not dance, or cannot dance?"

"Do not," she said shortly. Then, fearing that she sounded rude, Sara glanced up and added, "I could probably manage most of the steps, but I prefer not to invite the pity of old friends who remember that I was once graceful."

"In that case, you are a perfect partner for me," Peregrine said, his velvet voice coaxing. "I have had some instruction in European dancing, but have not yet dared my skills in public. Come, we can dance gracelessly together."

Before she could protest, he drew her into waltz position, his right hand at the waist of her turquoise silk gown, his other hand clasping hers, a correct twelve inches between them. As they began moving to the

music, she said with amused resignation, "I can't believe that there is anything you don't dare."

"To dare is the last resort. I prefer arranging matters so that the outcome will not be in doubt."

Though the prince did not dance with the unthinking
ease of long practice, he had been well taught and his
natural physical grace compensated for minor flaws in
technique. Sara could not say the same for herself.
Though she tried to relax, she was rigid and awkward,
convinced that disaster was just a step away.

Her fears were confirmed when she stumbled on a
turn, her weak leg unequal to the sudden shift of
weight. But instead of a humiliating fall, there was
only a slight irregularity in their progress as the
prince's strong clasp carried her through the moment
of weakness. He smiled down at her. "Was that so
bad?"

Sara did not answer out loud, just tilted her head
back and laughed. Now she relaxed, her body soft and
pliant as she yielded to his lead. When Peregrine had
taken her up on his horse, he had freed her of the fear
of pain. Now he was freeing her again, this time of
the fear of making a fool of herself. Why had she let
pride prevent her from dancing? The risk of being
thought clumsy was a small price to pay for this pleasure.

As they swirled across the flagstones, he said teasingly, "I'm disappointed in you, Lady Sara. I expected gracelessness. Instead your dancing is the equal
of any other lady here."

"You were also flying false colors, Your Highness,"
she retorted, "for you could be giving lessons, not
receiving them."

"Not quite, but I thank you for the compliment."

As they spun across the rectangles of light cast by
the French windows, the sheer sensual pleasure of
dancing filled Sara's being. In the months and years
after her accident, she had done her best to detach her
mind from her body as the only way to survive the

endless pain. Now, in the joy of the waltz, her spirit and body were one again for the first time in a decade.

They had finished one dance and were halfway through the next before she became aware that another, more focused joy was growing inside her. She was intensely conscious of Peregrine's nearness. In spite of her gloves, she tingled where they touched. He was so strong, so attractive, so close. . . .

Too close, the distance between them was less than half what it should be, at this rate she would soon be pressed against his broad chest. And shamelessly Sara wanted that to happen. She wanted to raise her face to his and discover if there was more to kissing than she had yet experienced, she wanted to feel his body moving against hers.

In the darkness her face flamed as she realized that once more she was falling under the spell of his compelling masculine presence. The man was dangerous, and he wasn't even trying to be. She stopped and released him. "I must catch my breath. I am unaccustomed to so much exertion."

She sat down on a stone bench by the railing and opened her fan, needing to cool her burning face. Her temperature problem was not helped when the prince sat down beside her. Though he was a respectable distance away, he was still too close for comfort, for she could feel the warmth of his body radiating through the cool evening air.

"Clearly dancing, like riding, is another activity that should be part of your life again," he remarked.

"I think you are right." Sara's smile was rueful. "You are an alarming person, Your Highness."

His glance was narrow-eyed. "Why do you say that?"

"Because you have the power to change lives, quickly and casually. Certainly you keep changing my life."

He shrugged fatalistically. "Life always changes, it just changes faster sometimes. Are you not to marry soon? If you do that, nothing in your life will be the same.''

With a sudden shift of subject, Peregrine motioned toward her fan. ''I have heard that ladies use these to communicate with gentlemen. Do you know how that is done?''

''The language of the fan?'' Her mind flashed back to her school days, when an older girl had demonstrated the gestures to Sara and her best friend Juliet. ''It originated in Spain, I think, where young men and women were much more strictly separated than here.'' Remembering the females who clustered around the prince, she added with a touch of dryness, ''These days, there are easier ways to send a message, but perhaps there will be an occasion when you will need to understand some of the language. Let me see if I can remember any of it.''

She thought for a minute. ''Bear in mind that it is not only the fan that speaks, but also the eyes and the whole body.'' She opened her fan. It was an elegant trifle of black Spanish lace mounted on carved ivory sticks, a gift from Charles.

Letting the fan rest against her right cheek, she said, ''This means yes.'' She moved it to her left cheek, ''And this means no.'' Then she drew the fan across her eyes, accompanying the movement with a soulful look. ''This means 'I'm sorry.' ''

The moonlight disclosed a gleam of amusement in Peregrine's eyes. ''Can anything more complex be conveyed?''

Since an active performance would take Sara farther from his disquieting presence, she stood and crossed the balcony. ''Carrying the fan in my left hand like this means that I desire to make your acquaintance.''

''Better,'' he said approvingly. ''But since we are already acquainted, what might come next?''

''If I carry the fan in my right hand in front of my face, it means 'Follow me.' '' Walking toward him, she demonstrated, then turned away and cast a coy glance over her shoulder as if to see whether he was following.

Obligingly the prince stood and moved after Sara. She turned toward him and opened her fan very wide, accompanying the action with a burning gaze. "This means 'Wait for me.' "

"What am I waiting for?" he asked with interest as he stopped three feet away from her.

Sara drew the fan across her forehead, then hissed melodramatically, "We are watched!"

Peregrine glanced at the French doors. Inside the ballroom, another waltz was in full swing, the lush music flooding the night with sound. "Fortunately not," he said in a conspiratorial whisper as he turned back to her. "Apparently no one else feels the need for fresh air. Does the fan have anything to say when two people are finally alone, or do we now rely on words?"

"Some ladies are too shy or proper to say what they wish." A mad impulse drove Sara to do what she would never have dared do openly. Folding her fan, she touched the handle to her lips. "So this means 'Kiss me.' "

She did not believe he would accept her playful invitation, so when he stepped toward her, her heart leaped in panic. He was overpowering, almost frightening, in his strength and masculinity, and she nearly retreated, but did not. Instead she waited, half appalled at her brazenness, half aching to experience the result.

He lifted her chin with one finger, his intense gaze holding hers for an endless moment. Sara knew it was her last chance to retreat to respectability, but once more she stood her ground, waiting and wanting. Slowly he bent his head until his lips touched hers. His kiss was warm and subtle, as gentle as a butterfly wing, yet it moved her in wholly unexpected ways.

Her mouth worked against his, wanting more, yet when he responded, she drew back, shaken. She had wondered what his kiss would be like, and had found not an answer but more questions. Dangerous questions . . .

Breathlessly she said, "Carrying the fan in my right hand like this means 'You are too willing.' "

"Can one be too willing?" he asked softly. He bent forward again and brushed his lips against the sensitive skin between her eye and hairline. At the same time he drew his fingertips down her throat, then across her bare shoulders in a delicate, profoundly erotic caress.

Sara gasped. For the first time in her life, she experienced the sweet, melting female desire to yield to a man, to give herself to him as fully as she had when they waltzed, to follow wherever he led. Yet to surrender to desire would be utterly wrong. Bringing the fan up between them, she waved it briskly back and forth, sending cool air toward both their faces. "Fanning rapidly means 'I am betrothed.' "

"So you are," he murmured. His lean figure was silhouetted against the French doors, and she could not see his face. "More's the pity. Do you love your future husband, Lady Sara?"

She hesitated, as uncomfortable with his question as she had been with his kiss. Obliquely she said, "Twirling the fan in the right hand means 'I love another.' " But she could not bring herself to demonstrate that particular gesture.

When Peregrine's thoughtful glance drifted to her motionless right hand, she added with a hint of acid, "Twirling it in the left hand means 'I wish to get rid of you.' " Transferring the fan to her left hand, she gave it a quick swing.

"Do you really wish to get rid of me, sweet Sara?" He gave her a slow, intimate smile. Though he did not move a muscle, she felt as if he was reaching out to embrace her. His attraction was so powerful that if she surrendered to it, she would be drawn straight into his arms.

Unthinkable! She was a lady of mature years and steady temper, not a giddy girl. After a short, fierce mental struggle, Sara raised the fan and let the black lace rest against her left cheek. "No, I do not wish to be rid of you." Then she dropped her hand so that the fan hung by her side. Her gaze cool and level, she said, "This means that we are friends. No more."

"Dare I hope no less?" he said gravely. "I did not wish to offend you."

Perhaps it was dangerous to be his friend. Yet what had he done but give her the lightest and most harmless of kisses? The problem was not with him, but with her. She raised the fan and rested it against her right cheek in the gesture of assent. *Yes, I will be your friend.*

"Good." He nodded toward the ballroom, where there was a temporary lull in the music. "Are you prepared to dance again, this time in front of other people?"

As he spoke, the alarming current of attraction cut off as abruptly as a snuffed candle. For a moment Sara wondered if her wits had been wandering and only just returned. Once again the prince was just a man; admittedly a remarkably appealing one, but resistible. She sighed with relief. She had been suffering from no more than a few moments of moon madness, and now she was recovered. "I am game if you are, Your Highness."

He held the French door open for her and she went inside, blinking at the glittering light refracting through the prisms of the chandeliers. On the far side of the room she saw Charles, looking surprised and not pleased by the sight of her with Prince Peregrine. Then she dismissed the thought as the music struck up again, and the Kafir led her into another waltz.

This dance was as delightful as the previous one, and was unaccompanied by perilous longings. When the music stopped, Peregrine bowed to her, a picture of propriety. He, too, must have suffered from moon madness on the balcony, and was now recovered. "You must brace yourself, Lady Sara. Every man in the room will now wish to partner you."

Even as she laughed, Ross appeared by her side. "I've come to claim my cousin, Mikahl."

As the music struck up again, Ross swept her into

another waltz. His voice full of teasing affection, he said, ''Sara, you wretch, why would you dance for him and not for me?''

''He didn't allow me time to decline his invitation,'' she explained. ''Then, once I started dancing, I realized that I didn't want to stop.'' As Ross deftly steered them away from imminent collision with another couple, she went on, ''He has persuaded me to ride again as well.''

Her cousin gave a soft whistle of astonishment. Better than anyone save Sara herself, he knew how much pain and fear lay behind her light words. ''How did he do that?''

''I'm not quite sure,'' she admitted. ''He just makes things seem . . .'' she searched for a word, ''possible.''

His eyes intent, Ross said, ''You like him?''

''Very much.'' Just how much, she would not admit. ''As you said, Prince Peregrine is not like anyone else.'' Then Sara grinned, relaxed as she was only with Ross. ''I think that's just as well. I don't think London could survive too many like him.''

Besides being the handsomest man in the room, Ross was a superb dancer, and Sara felt as safe in his arms as she had in Peregrine's. Later, with other partners, she had a few minor problems, once stumbling with all the awkwardness she had feared, but she did not let the incident spoil her pleasure in her rediscovered ability.

She danced every dance for the rest of the evening, and by the time they left, she was in a state of happy exhaustion. As Charles took her home in his carriage, she rested her head against the soft leather upholstery, half asleep.

''You seemed to be enjoying yourself, my dear,'' Charles said as the vehicle began rumbling along the cobbled street. ''I did not realize that your crippled leg would permit dancing.''

Sara was too much in charity with the world to take

offense at his tactlessness. Mildly she said, "Neither did I. It was Prince Peregrine who persuaded me to try."

"Ah, yes, the Kafir prince." A note of disapproval sounded in his voice. "I saw that you spent time alone with him on the balcony. I'm surprised at you, Sara."

"It was chance, not prearrangement, Charles." Fully awake, Sara raised her head from the seat back. "What do you suspect I was doing out there with him?" She was not used to having her actions questioned, and the lingering sense of guilt she felt at her shameless behavior was drowned by irritation at his tone.

"Of course I know that you would never behave improperly, my dear," he assured her, clearly surprised at how she had interpreted his remark. "But one must be wary of appearances. He is a foreigner, after all, and of dubious morals."

"You yourself suggested that I cultivate his acquaintance," she pointed out acerbically. "Have you changed your mind about wanting to do business with him?"

"Not at all. We had dinner last night, and he is most interested in a proposal I made. I have hopes that he will join me in a promising venture." After a pause, Charles continued, "But I have . . . heard things that suggest that he is not an appropriate companion for a female of refinement."

"Really?" she asked with interest. "What kind of things?"

"I would not sully your ears with such stories," he said stiffly. "But he is not a man whom you should be alone with."

"The prince is Ross's friend, and I have found him to be very gentlemanly," she said, making no attempt to conceal her irritation. "Unless you can be more specific about his shortcomings, I have no intention of cutting the acquaintance."

"I will not have my wife defy me, Sara." Though

Charles's voice was low, the darkened carriage pulsed with barely restrained fury.

"I am not your wife yet, Charles." Sara was startled by his anger, which seemed out of proportion to the cause. "And if you are going to be unreasonable, perhaps we should reconsider marriage. We may not be as well suited as we thought."

"No!" He stopped, then swore a quiet oath under his breath. Choosing his words carefully, he said, "Forgive me, my dear. I do not wish to seem unreasonable. But Asiatics are an encroaching lot. Since they keep their own women secluded, they assume that the greater freedom of European women means immorality. While the prince is an excellent man in his way, I am concerned that he might misinterpret your well-bred ease of manner as license." His voice softened and he took her hand. "You are very precious to me. I can't bear the thought of that—that foreigner offering you insult."

Sara was silent, letting her hand rest passively in his. Is that how the Kafir saw her, as a wanton Western woman who might be available for dalliance? Her mouth tightened. The notion was an unpleasant one, but of no real importance, for Peregrine was merely a passing acquaintance, a brilliant shooting star who would soon be gone from her life.

What *was* important was the question of her marriage. If she wanted to withdraw from the betrothal, now was the time to do it, before wedding plans were set and invitations sent.

A husband had the right to expect his wife to submit to his wishes and desires, which was one reason why Sara had never had a strong desire to marry. Did she really want to put herself in the power of Charles Weldon? A man like Ross, with humor and an open, questing mind, would make a far more congenial husband. Perhaps the fact that she had never found a man like her cousin was the real reason she had never married.

While Charles was wealthy, well-bred, and handsome, he was cut from more conventional cloth. There was very little humor in him, and though he had traveled widely in his youth, his experiences had merely confirmed his belief in the superiority of all things British rather than broadening his mind. Moreover, tonight's irrational display of anger hinted that he might be a more difficult husband than she had bargained for.

After a brief, intense period of thought, she gave a wry smile. Charles's protectiveness was irritating and unnecessary, but it was well-intentioned. And this marriage meant so much to her father; she remembered how earnest the duke had been when he urged her to accept Weldon's proposal.

Concerned by her long silence, her betrothed squeezed her hand. "Sara? Please say that you forgive me for my temper."

"There is nothing to forgive, for I know you spoke from concern. But in the future, remember that I am quite capable of dealing with male impertinence." That kiss had been a result not of Peregrine's impropriety, but her own. It would not happen again. "But, Charles, perhaps we should discuss what we will expect of each other when we are married."

He released her hand. "What do you mean?"

Sara paused to collect her thoughts. "I'm not a young girl—I have been mistress in my father's house for years now, and am used to some measure of independence. I need room to breathe. If you cannot accept that in me, you might be happier with a more conformable wife." When he didn't answer immediately, she added, "If that is your choice, I will release you from our betrothal. I don't want you ever to regret having chosen me."

"Your sense of honor does you credit, Sara," he replied, his voice rich and soothing. "You are exactly what I want in a wife, for I value your maturity and experience. But while I am willing to grant you considerable independence, surely you admit that in some things a woman must accept her husband's guidance? It is a man's duty to protect his wife from the sordid side of life.''

Sara was not sure that she agreed, but his moderate tone calmed the doubts his spurt of anger had raised. She had made too much of what was a brief spat between two tired people. As the carriage drew to a halt in front of Haddonfield House, she said, ''Then it seems we understand each other—if you will forgive my independence, then I will forgive your temper.''

''Excellent.'' He helped her from the carriage, then escorted her up the wide granite steps, holding her arm solicitously.

To Sara's surprise, as they waited for a servant to admit her, Charles pulled her close and kissed her. This was not like the rather messy embrace he had given her on their betrothal. It was more like the light kiss Peregrine had given her on the balcony. Yet she experienced nothing like the reaction she had felt then. Indeed, she felt nothing at all.

As his carriage drove away from Haddonfield House, Weldon's trembling hands clenched and unclenched, mute testimony to his fury. It was true that Lady Sara St. James was exactly what he wanted in a wife. Her enormous dowry would be very useful and, while her appearance was rather subdued, she had a refined beauty that would do him credit. Her cool, passionless nature aroused him, and he was generously prepared to overlook the fact that she was crippled.

Most important of all was her birth and breeding, which would help him attain the rank he had desired for so long, the rank denied him because he was a younger son. But how *dare* she defy her future husband! He was appalled by the willfulness she had shown tonight. It was not at all what he expected of a lady. He must appease her until they were wed, but then she would learn the folly of opposing him. A gentleman's wife was to be cherished and protected;

in return, she must be obedient to his will, in all things. And Lady Sara would be, very soon.

Ironic that their disagreement had been over a filthy, immoral foreigner. He knew better than to think that a lady of Sara's refinement would behave improperly with a man who was little better than a savage, a man who had boldly requested a tour of the London flesh-pots. On that tour, he had shown his baseness. An Englishman knew how to separate the sacredness of the marital relation from the profane lust one felt for prostitutes, but the prince—if indeed he was a prince—had proved that he had no such understanding. God help the wife of a beast like him, for she would be used like a whore.

Tonight had confirmed Weldon's belief that Lord Ross Carlisle was a bad influence on Lady Sara. It was he who had asked his cousin to befriend the Kafir, and doubtless he encouraged her in other immodest behavior. After the marriage, the intimacy between the cousins must be severed. It would be wrong to cut the connection entirely, for Lord Ross was the son of a duke, but it would be made clear that his lordship was not welcome in the Weldon house. Lady Sara would obey her husband in that, as in all other things.

Weldon took out his handkerchief and wiped the perspiration from his face. Knowing that he would not sleep tonight unless he found release, he rapped on the roof of the carriage to get his driver's attention, then gave orders for a new destination.

The carriage turned toward Soho, to Mrs. Cambridge's flagellation establishment. She had a brother and sister there, twins, both of them very pretty. He would punish them for Lady Sara's sins. Weldon smiled into the darkness. It would be a most satisfying end to the evening.

Chapter 6

RESCUING JENNY MILLER from the whorehouse turned out to be a simple business. After leaving the ball, Peregrine had returned to his hotel and changed from formal evening wear to something equally dark but more anonymous.

Earlier in the day, Peregrine and his servant, Kuram, had made a discreet scouting expedition around Mrs. Kent's brothel so that no time would be wasted in finding the correct place. Kuram had also arranged to hire a hackney for the night. The vehicle was like a thousand other London carriages, and it would take a discerning eye to notice that the dusty horse was much better quality than would usually be found at such work.

Peregrine let Kuram drive while he himself rode inside the hackney, thinking about Lady Sara St. James. She was a constant surprise to him, unlike any other woman he had ever known. Besides her intelligence and quiet courage, she had the same directness that Lord Ross did. That quality meant she should be easy to manipulate, because those who are naturally direct do not usually assume others to be devious.

It would be an interesting challenge to end Lady Sara's betrothal in a way that would be easy for her and painful for Weldon. But instead of considering ways and means, he found himself thinking back to the kiss they had shared. When she had responded with a potent blend of innocent wonder and sensuality, he had realized that underneath her proper exterior and inexperience was a passionate woman.

Over the years, Peregrine had learned that he could attract a woman's attention and interest by sheer force of will. It was a matter of concentration, of focusing all his intensity and desire. When he made the effort, even the least receptive females became very aware of him, while the most susceptible could be lured to his hand like a trained hawk.

Fortunately, Lady Sara had proved to be very susceptible indeed. Even when he made no special effort, there was a powerful current of attraction between them, but when he had consciously set out to capture her interest, she had softened and opened like a flower. If they had not been in a public place, he would have been delighted to continue what they had begun. Though she had demurred, he did not doubt that she could have been easily persuaded to change her mind.

But her innocence bothered him. While he had promised Ross not to hurt her, innocents were notoriously fragile. That was why he preferred to avoid them. Even though Lady Sara was twenty-seven and levelheaded, there was a strong likelihood that she would suffer some emotional bruising as a result of being caught between Peregrine and his enemy.

Peregrine's expression hardened. He would rather not betray Ross's trust, but even his own promise would not be permitted to come between him and his goal. While it would be regrettable if her ladyship's delicate sensibilities were injured, any damage he inflicted would be trifling compared to the disaster that would befall her if she were to become Weldon's wife.

He dismissed her from his thoughts as the hackney rumbled through an alley they had scouted earlier in the day. Kuram stopped the carriage just within the alley's mouth, so that horse and vehicle were hidden in the shadows. If there was any pursuit, they would be able to pull away quickly.

Peregrine lifted the coil of rope he had prepared

earlier and slung it over his shoulder, then climbed out of the carriage and made his shadowed way to Mrs. Kent's unsavory establishment. At this hour, the shabby street was empty, though drunken shouts and laughter came from a tavern that he passed.

The upper half of the brothel was washed by moonlight, which made it easy to count windows. Two floors above street level, second window from the rear. Having no desire to forage in a stinking London alley, he had brought his own pebbles. He drew one from his pocket and threw it against the dirty glass. After a minute passed without response, he tossed another.

He was about to throw a third pebble when the window moved upward in a series of jerks. A small blond head appeared and looked down warily. Peregrine stepped into the moonlight so that Jenny could identify him. After she waved in recognition, he tossed the end of the rope up to her. She missed the first time, and the line made a scraping sound as it slithered down the brick wall, but no one looked out to see what was happening. In this neighborhood, any such sounds would be attributed to rats.

On the second attempt she caught the rope, then disappeared inside. Wanting to keep it simple, Peregrine had tied a loop on the end of the line so it need only be dropped over a bedpost.

After a minute Jenny reappeared with a small, shapeless bundle of belongings. When it had been lowered to her rescuer, she climbed up on the windowsill. Even from twenty-five feet below, Peregrine could see the fear on her face, but without hesitation she turned and began inching her way down the rope.

She was small and agile, and with the aid of the knots he had tied in the line every eighteen inches she came down without serious difficulty. There was a touchy moment when a muffled cry sounded from the room below the one that had been hers. Jenny's head was level with the room's windowsill, and she froze for a moment, probably thinking of all that had happened to her within the brothel's walls. Then she continued her painstaking descent.

When she was within his reach, Peregrine set down the bundle and reached up to catch the girl by the waist. Her small body was icy cold and shaking. After setting her on the ground, he asked softly, "Are you all right?"

Nodding, she picked up her bundle, but her trembling didn't stop. He pulled his coat off and wrapped it around her. "It's just a block to the carriage."

She nodded again and followed him out into the street. Unfortunately, it was no longer empty, for three drunken sailors had spilled out of the tavern and were making their way down the middle of the road, clinging to each other and singing discordantly. Peregrine and Jenny would have to go around them to reach the hackney. He took the girl's arm with his free hand. "Don't worry, it will be all right," he said under his breath. "Just stay close and keep walking."

" 'Ey, mates," the tallest of the men called out. "Look at that pretty little night bird." He leered at Jenny. "Come with us instead, sweetheart, you'll earn three times as much."

She glanced up fearfully, and the bright moonlight clearly revealed her exquisite features. With her long blond hair and gaudy harlot's gown, Jenny looked like a sailor's dream.

At the sight, another of the men, a hulking creature of ox-like proportions, gave a bleary whistle. "Aye, she's a beauty." As the three drunks began closing in on their prey, he said coaxingly, "Le'me see you better, sweetheart."

Steel in his voice, Peregrine said, "The lady is with me."

"Aw, she's no lady, any damn' fool can see that," the tall man scoffed. With bleary good humor he continued, "Don't be a dog in the manger, mate. What do you say we all four share her?"

As Jenny made a small, desperate sound, Peregrine

moved between her and the drunks. ''I say *no*. She is mine.''

The sailors' good nature tilted to anger. ''Don't say we di'n't ask polite,'' the ox-like man growled. Without warning, he leaped forward, his hands reaching for Peregrine's throat.

Unhurriedly Peregrine stepped forward and caught his assailant's right wrist. With one smooth movement, he twisted the arm into a position where the elbow was in danger of being broken backward. As the man howled, his two comrades jumped to his aid. Peregrine spun his captive around and hurled him into the other two sailors.

Five seconds after the brawl started, the three drunks were lying in the filthy street like toppled nine pins. The tall one started to scramble to his feet, but a kick in the belly took the fight out of him. None too gently, Peregrine prodded the ox-like man in the ribs with the toe of his boot. ''Find yourself another woman, and make damned sure she's willing. If you take one that isn't, I may hear of it and come looking for you.''

The sailor's eyes were murderous, but he contented himself with filthy oaths rather than renewing the fight. Taking Jenny's arm again, Peregrine guided her to the waiting hackney.

Jenny glanced at Kuram, who sat on the driver's box in mustachioed menace. His gesture toward being inconspicuous was to wear a dark turban rather than a light one. ''Why didn't he come help you?'' she asked Peregrine.

Kuram answered himself in his heavily accented English. ''Was not necessary.''

She glanced up at her rescuer, then gave a little smile. ''No, I reckon not,'' she murmured as she climbed into the hackney.

Once the carriage was moving, Peregrine produced a small flask of brandy. ''Have some of this. You need it.''

Silently she obeyed, choking as the fiery spirits

seared her throat, then handed the flask back. "If I'd ever thought of working the streets, that lot of scum would've changed my mind."

"Good. A streetwalker's life would make Mrs. Kent's nasty little house look genteel by comparison. You can do better than that." He heard the rustling of fabric as she pulled his coat tighter around her. "You don't have a cloak?"

Bitterly Jenny said, "*She* wouldn't waste money on outdoor gear for someone who was always inside."

"No, I suppose she wouldn't."

There was silence for several more blocks. Then she blurted out, "I didn't think you'd come."

"Your life has not been one to inspire trust," Peregrine said, unoffended. "But as you see, I did what I said I would."

"But why?" she asked, bewildered. "Why are you going to such trouble for someone who is nothing to you? I don't even know your name."

"I'm called Peregrine, and I'm not going to much trouble. This is an easy chance to do good without effort."

She refused to drop the topic. "God only knows how many other men came to me. Some were better than others, but no one else ever wanted to help. Why did you? What do you want?"

Her last question revealed why she needed a genuine answer, so Peregrine tried to recall just why he had offered to help her escape. Though he had acted on impulse, there was usually a reason for his impulses. "When I talked with you last night, I saw that in spite of everything, you are not damaged beyond repair. I think you are one of the rare ones with the strength to escape squalor and build a better life."

His gaze drifted to the girl's huddled, shadowy figure, but it was not Jenny Miller whom he saw. "You remind me of a lad I once knew, a lad who also endured a great deal without being destroyed. But strong though he was, if someone had not helped him, he

might never have been able to go beyond mere survival,'' Peregrine said pensively. "To answer your earlier question, I want nothing from you except your
word that someday, if your help can turn someone's
life around, you will give it.''

"Were you that lad?'' Jenny asked curiously.

Clever child. Ignoring the question, he gave her the
flask again. "Have more brandy. Your teeth are still
chattering.''

She took another swallow, managing this one without coughing. "Where are you taking me?''

"To the home of a man who works for me. He will
look out for you until you're ready to be on your own.''

"Does he know . . . what I am?''

"He knows that you've been in a brothel, but that
is what you did, not what you are.'' Peregrine's voice
was edged. "Remember that.''

"I'll try to.'' She handed back the flask. "Will he
expect me to . . . ?'' Her distaste made it clear what
she meant.

"No, he won't.'' He gave a faint smile. "Unlike
me, he's the honorable sort.''

Wisely she didn't comment.

Benjamin Slade's substantial town house was on a
quiet street in Westminster. It took only one knock to
bring him to the door. "I'm glad to see you made it
here safely,'' Slade said as he let them in. "Come into
my study. We can talk there.''

The study was comfortably furnished in a masculine
style, with oak paneling and leather-covered chairs.
Slade had been working as he waited, for the room
was well lit and the desk strewn with papers. As he
closed the door behind them, Peregrine said, "Mr.
Slade, meet Miss Miller.''

Jenny gave him a startled glance. "No one's ever
called me Miss Miller before.''

"You will become accustomed to it,'' Benjamin
said. His gray eyes widened as he saw his new house-

guest in the light. Peregrine's message had prepared him for Jenny's presence, but not for her ethereal beauty. After a moment he remembered his manners. Gesturing to a pot warming over a spirit lamp, he asked, "Would you like some tea, Miss Miller?"

When she nodded, he poured her a cup as if she were a duchess. "If you are hungry, have some cakes. Or if you would like something more, I can see what's in the kitchen."

"Oh, no thank you, Mr. Slade, this will do very well," she said nervously as she sat down and stirred her tea.

Peregrine watched the ritual with amusement. The British used tea to renew inner strength the same way other societies used God. Apparently tea was as effective as religion, for Jenny's strained white face was taking on color as her natural resilience reasserted itself.

"I'll help myself to something stronger if you don't object, Benjamin," he remarked. With his host's nod of permission, he poured himself a small glass of brandy. Taking a seat, he continued, "I didn't mention it in my note, but the man you are investigating is the one who introduced me to the house where Jenny was working." He pulled a folded paper from the inner pocket of his coat. "Here are several other establishments for you to look into: addresses, specialties, the names the madames use. Jenny was in the house at the top of the list."

The lawyer sat down and poured tea for himself. "I thought there must be some connection between the investigation and your finding Miss Miller." Cold anger showed on his face as he scanned the page, and under his breath he muttered, "Despicable."

"Merely merchants catering to sins as old as time," Peregrine said cynically. After a swallow of brandy, he added, "It would be very interesting to know if Mrs. Kent is the true owner of that house."

"She isn't," Jenny said through a mouthful of cake.

Both men's heads turned toward the girl. Peregrine asked, "You know who the real owner is?"

She swallowed the last of the cake. "Aye, a rich bloke, the sort who acts like he wouldn't know what a whore was if he found her in his teacup."

Peregrine glanced at Slade and saw that the lawyer shared his excitement. Perhaps a vital witness had dropped into their hands. "Can you describe him more fully?"

"He's maybe fifty, but takes care of himself. Light brown hair, so gray doesn't show in it much." She glanced from one man to the other. "About midway in height between you and Mr. Slade, not fat but well fed."

"You'd recognize him again if you saw him?"

Her delicate features hardened, and she did not look the least childlike. "I'd recognize him all right," she said softly. "He was the first man who ever took me, and he wasn't very gentle about it. Even though he preferred real virgins, he came to me regularly as well. He was one of the nasty ones."

"How do you know this man is the owner, not a customer?" This time it was Slade who asked.

"I used to hear things around the house," she said vaguely.

Peregrine suspected that the girl had become an expert at sneaking and eavesdropping. It was a means of survival he understood perfectly. "Do you remember what was said?"

"Couple of times I heard him talking to Mrs. Kent about the amount of money the house was bringing in. Once it wasn't enough, and he was sort of threatening her, polite-like, saying maybe she was keeping too much for herself. Made my skin crawl." Then, with satisfaction, she added, "Must've made *her* skin crawl, too, because she was kind of quiet for the next few days."

"Do you know the man's name?" Peregrine asked. She shook her head. "Not his real name. He made

Mrs. Kent and me and the other girls call him 'Master.' "

The only thing that kept Peregrine from giving an exultant war whoop was the likelihood that the neighbors would summon a constable. He had thought it was a mild impulse of charity that had led him to offer aid to Jenny Miller, but a much deeper instinct must have prompted him. "There is a chance that someday the owner will be arrested for his crimes. If that happens, would you be able to identify him, perhaps testify in court? If you do, I will guarantee that neither he nor Mrs. Kent will harm you."

Jenny's light blue eyes glowed. "Even if you didn't protect me, I'd do it—I'd do anything to hurt that bastard. He's the sort who'd rather die than have people know what he's really like, so a trial would be worse than a flogging." She gave a wicked laugh. "And I can identify him right enough. I can give a description that will make a judge blush."

"Good girl. It probably won't come to that, but I'm glad you're willing." Peregrine doubted that Weldon would ever be brought to trial for his crimes—there were so many other interesting possibilities for his enemy's destruction—but if it came to that, Jenny would be invaluable. "In the meantime, you need to rest and prepare for a new life. Mr. Slade will see that you get a new wardrobe, for one thing."

"Good," she said vehemently. "Then I can burn the clothing *she* made me wear."

He suppressed a smile. Jenny was definitely a kindred spirit. For all her look of spun-sugar fragility, she would make a dangerous and implacable enemy. "You said last night that you would like to become a lady's maid. If that is your choice, perhaps an experienced maid can be hired to teach you what you need to know. Would that be possible, Benjamin?"

The lawyer nodded. "I see no problem. After you're trained, it shouldn't be hard to find you a decent job."

Jenny turned her face away to conceal her embarrassing tears. "Thank you," she whispered. "Thanks ever so much."

Her rescuer stood, dark and enigmatic. "Don't give me too much credit. You'll do all the hard work yourself." As he donned his hat, he said, "If you need to speak to me, Mr. Slade knows how to find me. Sleep well, Jenny."

She watched as he bade farewell to his employee and left. He was a strange one and no mistake. When she'd first seen him, with his devil's green eyes that looked right through her, she'd been right worried. Even after what he'd done for her, he made her nervous, though that wasn't the same as being scared.

When Mr. Slade returned, Jenny said, "Where does Mr. Peregrine come from? When I first saw him, I thought maybe he was Irish, until he opened his mouth, but I never heard an accent like his. Not that it's much of an accent," she qualified, "but he doesn't speak like anyone I've ever heard."

"He's Prince Peregrine, and he comes from a wild place in Asia that most people have never heard of," the lawyer answered. He cocked his head on one side. "You speak very well yourself. Better than . . ." He stopped.

"Better than you'd expect a whore to talk?" she supplied helpfully, then watched with interest as he flushed.

"Yes. I'm sorry, I didn't mean to insult you, but . . ." He ran an exasperated hand through his thinning hair.

"No insult to say I'm a whore, I was one," she said, taking pity on his embarrassment. "*Was*. Never again."

He gave her a half smile. "You're an unusual young woman."

"I talk better than any other girl that was ever in the house, and I can read and write, too," Jenny said proudly. "When I was little, there was an old lady lived in the building next door. Miss Crane was a teacher, but she'd come down in the world, which is why she lived in my neighborhood. I used to run errands for her and clean her rooms when her rheumatism was acting up. In return, she taught me things. She liked teaching, and I liked learning. She had lots of books, and she let me read them at her place, where it was quiet.''

''Is Miss Crane still alive?''

''No, she died in her sleep one night. After she was gone, Pap sold me. I think maybe it was her that stopped him from doing it sooner. He was sort of scared of her.''

The lawyer shook his head, bemused. ''Once I thought that my life was a hard one, but I see that I didn't know what I was talking about. While you are my guest, use the library whenever you like.'' As she struggled to suppress a yawn, he added, ''Time for bed, Miss Miller. Come along now.''

Her eyes narrowed. Even though Peregrine—fancy him being a prince!—had said Mr. Slade wouldn't try to bull her, it sounded suspiciously like he expected her to warm his bed.

Uncannily, he guessed what was in her mind. ''You'll sleep alone, tonight and every other night. From now on, you're Miss Miller, a respectable young cousin of mine who has fallen on hard times, and is staying with me until a situation can be found.''

He hesitated a moment, then sat at his desk and pulled a strongbox out of a lower drawer. After unlocking it, he took out several bills before putting it away. Jenny's eyes widened when he handed her the money. It was twenty whole pounds, enough to live on for months. Confused, she looked up at him. ''If you don't want me to sleep with you, why are you giving me money?''

''So you won't feel trapped here,'' he said. His gray eyes were so kind that she wanted to cry again. ''I hope you won't run away, both for your own sake and in case we need you to build a case against the man you called 'Master,' but I want you to know that you're not a prisoner.''

Her gaze went to the drawer where he'd put the strongbox. ''Aren't you afraid that I might run away with your money now that I know where it is?''

He raised his brows. ''Should I be afraid?''

She swallowed hard, then shook her head. Quickly she bent over to slip the bills into her small bundle, not wanting him to see her face. She didn't know why he trusted her, but since he did, she'd die rather than take a coal from one of his scuttles.

As she picked her bundle up and followed her host upstairs, she marveled at what a strange night it had been. First Prince Peregrine and now Mr. Slade; she hadn't known men could be so nice. But then, she supposed, the nice ones didn't go in for ravishing little girls, so she'd never had the chance to meet any.

In his way, Mr. Slade was even more surprising than the prince. Peregrine was one-of-a-kind, anyone could see that right away, but because she'd known from the first that he didn't want her, it wasn't a surprise that he'd kept his hands—and other things—to himself.

But Mr. Slade did want her, she'd seen that straight off. Even so, he hadn't tried anything. And he even gave her money so she could leave if she wanted to! Amazing. He wasn't the sort anyone would notice at first, or even second, glance, but there was a lot more to the bloke than she'd thought.

Her room was clean and pleasant, and looked like it hadn't been used much. It could hardly have been more different from the whorehouse red room she'd lived in for years, and she liked it straight away. So tired from the aftereffect of nerves that her hands were clumsy, Jenny washed up and put on a shift to sleep in. As she slid between the cool sheets, she told herself that she'd be damned if she'd ever again wear one of those ruffly baby girl nightgowns—she hadn't even brought one with her.

Even though she was exhausted, she didn't let herself go to sleep right away. Very deliberately, she thought back over her years in the whorehouse, from the one time she really was a virgin and the man who called himself "the Master" had raped her, right up until earlier tonight, when she'd been terrified that the fat sot wouldn't leave, and she wouldn't be ready if Peregrine really did come back for her. But he had come, and her old life was over now. *Over.*

She'd never forget, no, nor forgive those who'd abused her, but she wasn't going to turn into a self-pitying slut, either. For some reason, she'd gotten lucky. She wasn't going to waste it.

The next day, Sir Charles Weldon received a terse note from Mrs. Kent, informing him that his favorite and most profitable whore had run away. He swore viciously and crumpled the message, then burned it. He'd made a fortune off Jenny Miller, and had always enjoyed her himself. She was a good little actress, and in spite of all the men she'd serviced over the years, she had a quality of innocence that had never failed to arouse him.

Probably the little slut had persuaded a customer to make her his mistress, and she was gone for good. His fingers blackened as he crumbled the ashes of the burned note. If he ever came across Jenny Miller again, he'd make her rue the day she had decided to run away from him. And he would enjoy every moment of her punishment.

Chapter 7

MISS ELIZA WELDON tossed a handful of shredded bread into the water, then laughed in delight as a dozen ducks and one swan hurled themselves raucously forward to grab a share.

Sara laughed along with her. After a splendid session of shopping and eating ices, she and her future stepdaughter had decided to visit Hyde Park to enjoy the afternoon sun. When Sara learned that Eliza had never had the pleasure of feeding ducks, they had stopped to buy bread at a shop. Throwing fragments from her own chunk of bread to the squawking, evergrowing flock, Sara said, "There is something very satisfying about feeding ducks."

"I think it is because they are so enthusiastic. It makes one feel wanted." Eliza's cheeks were rosy and wisps of flaxen hair curled charmingly from beneath her bonnet as she gave Sara a shy sideways glance. "I'm glad that you and Papa will be married so soon. I can hardly wait to move in with you."

Since her mother died, Eliza had lived with the family of Charles's older brother, Lord Batsford. Sara had thought that the arrangement was an agreeable one, but perhaps there were hidden problems. "Are you unhappy living with your aunt and uncle?"

"Oh, no," Eliza said, surprised at the suggestion. "They treat me just like one of their own. I'll miss them when I leave, but I want so much to live with Papa." Her blue eyes were wistful. "I've never understood why he wouldn't keep me after Mama died. Sometimes I've wondered if he was ashamed of me.''

''Of course not!'' Shocked, Sara put her arm around the girl's shoulders. ''What gave you an idea like that?''

''He's so handsome and clever and important.'' Head down, Eliza carefully ripped off more bread and tossed it to the ducks. ''There's nothing special about me. I'm just a girl.''

''You think that your father would have preferred a son?''

''Isn't that what all men want?'' Eliza said with a show of nonchalance, as if only one answer was possible.

Sara frowned. No doubt the girl had once overheard adults lamenting the fact that Charles's wife had not born him a son, and had been agonizing over the casual words ever since. ''Back in the days when a man's land had to be defended by the sword, sons were very useful, but now it doesn't matter so much. My father once said that it would have been nice if he'd had a son to inherit the title, but only if the son was in addition to me, not *instead* of me. I know your father feels the same way.''

Eliza looked up, wanting to believe. ''You really think so?''

''I know so,'' Sara said reassuringly. ''Your father has told me how much he is looking forward to having you again. But he's a very busy man, and he knew that after your mother died, you'd be lonely. That's why he agreed when your uncle offered to take you in. He thought you'd be happier with the company of your aunt and your cousins.''

''Sometimes there is too much of it!'' Eliza remarked, her face brighter. ''There are six of them, and only one of me.''

''But you'll miss them after you've moved. It's lucky that you aren't going far.'' Sara caught the girl's gaze with her own. ''Never forget that your father loves you very much—more than he does me or anyone else.''

Eliza's first expression of happiness was replaced by anxiety. "If that's true, do you mind dreadfully?"

"Not at all. Love isn't a competition, nor is it like a pot of tea, with only a certain amount to give away before it's all gone. Men love their wives and children in different ways. Perhaps love for a child is stronger because the child is part of you." Sara chuckled. "I sound like such an authority, don't I? Rather silly when I've never had either child or husband."

Eliza wrapped her arms around Sara's waist in a quick hug. "But soon you'll have both."

"Yes, and I'm so lucky to start with a grown daughter. If I have a baby, it will be years before we can go shopping together!"

They were both laughing when a deep voice said, "Are these private ducks, or can I ask for an introduction?"

Turning from the water in unison, the two females discovered Peregrine dismounting from the mist gray stallion he had bought at Tattersall's. He had been riding along Rotten Row, which at this point was only a few yards from the little lake. Though today he was in proper riding gear, he had disdained a hat and his wind-tousled black hair gave him a rakish air. Definitely a sight to warm the heart of any female. Certainly Sara's heart—or something in that vicinity—warmed at the sight.

With a sigh of delight, Eliza sank into a curtsy deep enough to honor the queen herself. It was an even better curtsy than the first time she had met the prince; Sara suspected that the girl had been practicing. Not that Sara could fault Eliza's judgment, because Peregrine looked more worthy of royal honors than any member of the House of Hanover ever had.

"These are public ducks," Sara replied with a smile. "They're a disorderly lot, so you'll have to introduce yourself to them. They've no respect for rank."

"Ducks are nature's own democrats," the prince agreed. "Miss Weldon, did you know that it is possible to lure ducks onto land by laying a trail of bread from the water?''

"Really?" Eliza immediately began coaxing ashore the braver—or greedier—waterfowl. Soon she was leading a waddling entourage down the bank of the Serpentine.

"Well done, Your Highness." Sara stroked the velvety muzzle of his horse. "With Eliza surrounded by quacking ducks, you and I can converse in perfect privacy if you wish."

"What a devious mind you have, Lady Sara," he said, giving her a wounded look. "Do you think I am always so scandalous that I must enlist ducks to protect the tender ears of innocence?"

Sara was fascinated by the way frivolity overlaid the prince's natural intensity. He had the dashing corsair appearance of a Byronic hero, yet he could tease about ducks. "I expect that when you want something, you will use whatever comes to hand, even greedy water birds."

He stilled, as if her words struck him in an unexpected way. Then he glanced at Eliza. "She's a pretty child."

"Yes, she favors her father in looks, but I'm told her disposition is more like her mother's. Charles adores her."

"Really?" Peregrine cocked his thick brows quizzically. "He doesn't strike me as the sort to be a doting father."

"You don't know him very well." Seeing that Eliza was out of bread, Sara called out to the girl, then tossed her own half loaf over so Eliza could continue playing Lady Bountiful.

"Perhaps not, but I am trying to remedy that lack. An interesting man, Sir Charles." The gray stallion shied as a duck fluttered too close, and the prince ran a calming hand down the animal's neck. "Though I've nothing very scandalous to say, I do have a favor to ask of you, Lady Sara."

When she gave him an inquiring look, he explained,

"I want to buy a country house, and my lawyer has found a possible property called Sulgrave. It is down in Surrey, and I am going to view it tomorrow. I hope to persuade you to come with me."

Sara hesitated, knowing that it was not a wise idea to be alone with the Kafir for an extended period of time because of the odd effect he had on her. After the kiss at the ball, she should have been embarrassed to see him today, but she wasn't. Instead she was pleased. Too pleased.

Peregrine turned the full force of his potent charm on her. "Please? I have no idea what an English country house needs to be suitable for entertaining."

Charles would disapprove of her jaunting off for a day with "a foreigner of dubious morals." But Charles had not been reasonable on the subject of Prince Peregrine, and she had no intention of catering to the prejudices of her betrothed. "I'll be happy to give my opinion if you want it."

"Splendid," he said warmly. "Is ten o'clock a convenient time for me to call for you?"

"That's fine." After a moment's thought, she added, "If you're agreeable, I'd like to ride rather than go by carriage. I've just had a horse sent up from the country and tomorrow will be my first chance to take her out."

His brows drew together. "It will be a long ride for someone who has not ridden for a decade."

"True," she admitted, "but on my head be it."

He grinned. "It won't be your head aching at the end of the day, but if riding is your preference, your wish is my command."

A squeal of distress from Eliza saved Sara from having to think of a clever retort. They looked up to see that the girl had lured a swan ashore, then tried to touch it. Swans are notoriously evil-tempered, and this one had spread its wings and begun chasing Eliza, neck extended and hissing malevolently.

"Oh, dear," Sara said, half laughing, half concerned. "An angry swan is alarming even for an adult, and can be terrifying to a child. Will you rescue Eliza?"

"Of course." Peregrine handed the stallion's reins to Sara and went to the girl's aid, ducks flying in every direction as he cut through the flock. The swan swiveled its long neck and started for the intruder, then reconsidered when he clapped his hands together and barked out a sentence in a foreign language. After one last hiss, the bird hopped into the water and settled down, flicking its tail feathers angrily.

Peregrine turned to Eliza and bowed. "Having slain the dragon, have I won the princess?"

Her face was flushed, but after he spoke, she regained her lost dignity. "You have won my heart forever, brave knight." As they walked to where Lady Sara waited with the horse, Eliza asked, "What did you say to the swan?"

"That if it did not cease and desist, it would end up as the centerpiece of a banquet," he said promptly.

From the way the girl's blue eyes were shining, perhaps he had won a little of her heart. He looked away, thinking about what Lady Sara had said. If Weldon really was devoted to the child, Peregrine would have to find some way to use that against him. Lady Sara was quite right; when he wanted something, he would use whatever—or whoever—came to hand. He could think of no reason to be more merciful to Eliza Weldon than her father had been to a thousand innocents like Jenny Miller.

The next morning Sara breakfasted with her father. "I'm going riding to the country today," she said, pouring another cup of coffee, "but I should be home by late afternoon."

"Riding?" her father asked, so surprised that his newspaper drifted down into a dish of coddled eggs.

Sara stirred milk into her coffee. "Yes, I've decided that it's time I took up riding again. I've missed it."

His stern features relaxed into a half smile. "Like

your mother, you have a talent for saying important things in an offhand way.'' His smile faded. "Are you sure this is wise?''

"Probably not,'' she admitted, "but I'm going to do it anyway. I've had Pansy brought to town. She's a nice, placid lady, perfect for someone who hasn't been on a horse for years.''

"Are you going with Sir Charles?''

"No, Ross's friend, Prince Peregrine. He's asked me to advise him on a country house he is considering buying.''

The duke frowned. "I'm not sure that I like the idea of you going riding alone with this foreigner.''

Sara sighed. Except for Ross, aristocratic Englishmen really were an insular lot. "The prince is perfectly respectable,'' she said, though in fact she was not entirely sure of that. "Charles himself encouraged my acquaintance with him.'' Though not recently. She gave her father a teasing smile. "What's the point of being a duke's daughter if I don't sometimes defy convention? While I am no rebel, I am well past my salad days and have been going out unchaperoned for years.''

Her father's frown deepened for a moment. Then he shrugged. "If your future husband doesn't object to the company you keep, my dear, I suppose I have no right to.'' Lifting his paper again, he added, "Enjoy your ride.''

As she went up to dress, Sara didn't doubt that she would enjoy herself. The important thing was not to enjoy herself too much.

Promptly at ten o'clock, a footman summoned Sara. She checked her appearance in the mirror. The rust-colored habit was a decade old and rather outdated, but it still fit perfectly, and the sweeping sleeves and full skirts made her small waist appear even smaller. Would her wild Kafir prince admire her appearance?

She turned away from the mirror, telling herself that she had no business wanting to be admired by a man other than her affianced husband. Then she smiled a little at her priggishness. She was human, after all, and what normal woman did not want to see admiration in the eyes of an attractive man?

She went into the hall and down the curving stairs, her left hand holding her wide skirts and her right gliding down the polished banister. The prince waited below, his green eyes focused intently on her. Momentarily Sara faltered, painfully conscious of her limp. Then she continued her descent. He was quite aware of her weakness, so there was no point in trying to conceal it. But as she reached the marble floor and greeted him, she realized that at that moment, she would willingly trade all her practical common sense to be flawless and beautiful.

"Good morning, Your Highness," she said, offering her hand. "Do you never wear a hat?"

"As seldom as possible," he replied as he took her hand. "Except during a blizzard, hats should be worn only by lovely ladies like you. That confection on your head now, for example." He touched the curling plume with one finger. "Most charming."

"You are coming along very well in the art of flirtation." Then, as she tried to tug her hand free of his, she said, "Unfortunately, you have forgotten the rule about letting go of ladies' hands. Your memory seems highly selective."

He chuckled as he released her. "You have found me out, Lady Sara. As a sundial marks only the sunny hours, I prefer to remember only what suits me."

"Really?" she said, suddenly wistful. "How pleasant it must be to forget the bad times."

His humor evaporated. "It would be pleasant if it were possible," he said as he escorted her outside. "But alas, selective memory is a goal I have not yet achieved. The evil hours are always more memorable."

She glanced at his strong profile, and wondered what his evil hours had been like, for even at the prince's most playful, there was always a dark edge to him. But probably she would never know what had made him the man he was; while he had been able to read her easily from the first time they met, she still had no idea what went on in his mind.

When they reached the stable yard behind the house, Peregrine surveyed her chestnut horse, unimpressed. "For this you refused that lovely sorrel mare at Tattersall's?"

"You must not criticize Pansy." Sara stroked the mare's Roman nose. "While she is not showy, she has been my very dear friend for many years."

" 'Not showy' is a staggering understatement." He laced his hands together to assist Sara in mounting. "This is not a horse, it is an animated sofa, broad and soft and shapeless."

Sara had feared the moment when she first mounted again, but now laughter dissipated her tension. Clever of him to distract her. "Unkind but true. Pansy *is* as comfortable as a sofa, though she also has good stamina. That's why she is a perfect choice for someone returning to riding after years away."

For a moment longer the prince stayed by her stirrup, watching her face keenly. She liked the way he was solicitous without fussing. After she gave an infinitesimal nod to let him know that she had gotten past the worst part, he went to mount his own horse.

Sara's right leg was the bad one, and she could feel the strain in muscles and joints as she adjusted her thigh over the pommel of the sidesaddle. By the end of the day she would have shooting pains from hip to knee, but it would be worth it. Being on horseback again restored confidence that she had not even realized was gone, and she laughed with sheer exuberance.

Peregrine wheeled the gray stallion, a magnificent man on a magnificent horse. "Are you ready to brave the dangers of the London streets, Lady Sara?"

"Lead on, Your Highness," she said, saluting her companion with her riding whip.

As they trotted into the street side by side, Sara was pleased to learn that her riding skills had survived ten years of disuse. Effortless balance, the subtle control of reins and body, were still as natural as breathing. Still, it had been wise to start with dependable, placid Pansy, though she could not prevent a sigh of longing as she admired the gray stallion's silken elegance. "What have you named your horse?"

"Siva," the prince replied, slowing his mount to let a delivery cart cross in front of them.

"Shee-va?" she said experimentally, trying to get the vowels exactly as he had pronounced them. "What does that mean?"

"Siva is one of the gods of the Hindu pantheon," he said. "That aspect of the divine that rules destruction and regeneration, to be exact."

"Goodness! That is a lot of symbolism for a horse to carry," she said. As he laughed, she continued, "Though I suppose only humans worry about the weight of intangibles. Are you a Hindu? I had assumed you were Muslim."

"No, I'm neither Hindu nor Muslim. Kafiristan is an island of paganism surrounded by a sea of Islam. To a Muslin, a kafir is an unbeliever, which is where the name Kafiristan comes from."

"What do you mean by paganism?" she asked cautiously. "Or should I not ask?"

"Ancestor and nature worship," he explained. "Quite a lot of gods of all types. Wooden statues of the ancestors stand outside Kafir villages. Very colorful, not unlike the statues of war heroes that the British are so fond of putting in parks."

Sara laughed, and laughter was the theme of their ride across the river and through southern London. They had reached the rolling hills of Surrey, and subsided into amiable silence before Sara realized that she had done most of the talking, and the subject had been her life. Artful comments and questions from Peregrine had led her to talk about her childhood, her accident and slow recovery, even her relationship with Charles.

She gave her companion an exasperated glance. She

had voiced thoughts that she had never before spoken aloud, but apart from the fact that she now knew that Kafirs were pagans, she knew no more about Peregrine than she had at the beginning of the ride. And now that she thought of it, she did not actually know if he subscribed to the religious beliefs of his people, for his attitude had been rather detached.

Sara sighed and rubbed her aching leg. Her companion was certainly a master of gaining information without giving anything away about himself. But while the idea that the prince knew much more about her than vice versa made Sara a little uncomfortable, there was no harm in it. Obviously he hadn't been raised in the English tradition of reserve and restraint, and he asked questions to satisfy his natural curiosity about a country and people that must seem very strange to him. And nobody had compelled her to answer; it was just that the man was diabolically easy to talk to. Perhaps it was because she knew he did not see things as an Englishman did.

As they neared their goal, Peregrine's formidable curiosity turned to the country they rode through. His gaze probed and assessed everything they passed, and he spoke only to ask Sara an occasional question.

Finally she said, "You are studying Surrey the way Wellington must have watched the field of Waterloo. Do you expect wild tribesmen to attack us?"

He gave her a startled glance, then chuckled. "Not at all. It is just that I have never seen rural England. I sailed up the Thames at night and have been in London ever since."

He gestured at their surroundings. "I had not realized what I was missing. England is like a vast garden, where everything has been designed to please the eye."

She followed his gaze, and for a moment saw her country with fresh eyes, as he must see it. The lush grassy lane they followed was bounded by low, flower-strewn hedges. Beyond lay a quilting of neat fields whose crops colored them in shades from pale gold to vivid green. The square Norman tower of a parish church punctuated the horizon, and above floated the mysterious, hazy blue ridge of hills called the North Downs. And it was not just the eye that was pleased, but all the senses, for a murmuring of insects and bird song soothed the ear, and scents of healthy growing things wafted through the air.

Sara caught her breath, feeling as if blinders had fallen from her eyes to reveal heart-stopping serenity and loveliness. "You're right, England is rather like a great garden. Did you know that Ross's estate, Chapelgate, is only about a half hour's ride from here? Because I know the area well, I was taking this beauty for granted." She smiled at her companion. "Thank you for making me see this for the wonder it is. But doesn't Surrey seem very tame compared with the mountains you grew up with?"

"While it is tame, it is also very . . ." he hesitated, "very appealing. Surprisingly so."

As she spoke, they rounded a curve and came upon the iron gates of Sulgrave. A pull at the bell eventually produced a gatekeeper, who let them in after the prince showed his authorization from the lawyer handling the property sale.

The house appeared only in glimpses as they cantered up the winding, tree-lined drive. Near the top of the road there was finally a clear view, so they reined in their horses. The manor was set on a gentle rise, and its red brick glowed with warmth in the noonday sun. The house was long and low, not grand but well proportioned and rich in classical detailing.

Sara turned her head to make an approving comment, then held her tongue. Peregrine was staring at the house with an intensity best described as hunger, as if he had caught a glimpse of his soul's desire. It was fortunate that the seller was not present, or the price would have doubled, for Sara had a powerful suspicion that no inadequacies of kitchen or drainage would prevent the prince from buying Sulgrave Manor.

Sensing her gaze, he turned his head, his brief fierceness veiled. "What do you think of the house?"

"It's very handsome. About two hundred years old, isn't it?" When he raised his brows in question, she said, "Those curving Flemish gables are the clue. They were very fashionable in the mid-seventeenth century."

"I knew you would be invaluable today. I would not know a Flemish gable from a Grecian temple."

"I'm surprised that the agent handling the property did not come with you to explain everything," she remarked as they started their horses forward again.

"He wanted to, but I preferred to see the place without him peering over my shoulder and telling me what to think."

"That would have been an exercise in futility on his part," Sara said with amusement. "It seems to be a working estate, not just a house. Why is it being sold?"

"The property was owned by an elderly widower," Peregrine explained. "His heir lives in America and has no desire to return to England. I'm told that the house needs refurbishing, but is basically sound. Besides the home farm, there are several tenant farms, about two thousand acres all together."

They followed the drive around the house to the stables. Though no farm workers were in sight, the yard was well kept and there was a pleasant scent of fresh hay. Peregrine dismounted in front of the stables' open double doors. After tethering the gray stallion, he came over to help Sara down from her horse.

Her right leg had progressed from pain to numbness, and she had to use one hand to lift her leg over the pommel. Sara clenched her teeth as she slid into the prince's grasp, but she was not prepared for the shaft of pure agony that blazed through her thigh and hip. She gave an involuntary cry as her right leg buckled under her, and she began falling.

Instantly Peregrine caught her, pulling her tight against him. "Your leg isn't working?"

She nodded, biting her lip to keep from crying out again. He turned her so that her back was against him. Then he wrapped his left arm securely around her waist and leaned over to massage her thigh, his fingers kneading deep into the cramped muscles.

Sara was unable to prevent herself from moaning as waves of agony pulsed through her. "I'm sorry," she said, on the verge of tears. "I didn't think it would be this bad."

"No need to apologize," he said, his deep voice calming. "If you did not demand much of yourself, you would still be in an invalid chair. This time you just asked too much."

Under his expert ministrations, the pain began subsiding to a bearable level. Sara's breathing steadied, though she was grateful for her companion's solid support.

After he had massaged away the worst of the pain, Peregrine moved his hand down to her knee and began working his way upward. His touch was lighter as his hand moved back and forth across her thigh with slow, thorough strokes. Sara began to feel sensations that were more than the recovery of abused muscles and joints; even through the heavy layers of riding habit, her body tingled under his probing fingers as pain was replaced by pleasure.

When he reached the top of her leg, stroking from her hip around to her inner thigh, warmth uncurled deep inside her, and a longing she had never known and did not understand. Sara inhaled, shockingly aware of the intimacy of what he was doing. As the mysterious warmth expanded through her body, she wanted to melt back against him, limp and receptive. Instead she pulled away, saying, "I think I can walk now."

Peregrine caught her arm, steadying her as she put weight on her right leg. Sara faltered but managed to stay upright, waiting for the renewed pain to subside before she tried another step.

"You are a glutton for punishment, your ladyship."
Before she could protest, he swept her up in his arms
and carried her into the stables.

While Sara had always been conscious of his
strength, before it had been a recognition of the mind.
Now she was aware with every fiber of her being. She
was shaking when he set her down on a bench inside
the stable. Physical pain was not the problem, for she
had survived a great deal of that in her life. Far more
disabling was her helpless, involuntary reaction to his
virility.

Oblivious to her mental turmoil, Peregrine said,
"With a little rest you should be able to walk, but you
won't be riding back to London today."

"I'm sorry to cause so much trouble." She looked
down, unable to meet her companion's gaze.

"Don't apologize. This is merely a nuisance, not a
disaster. I'll ride down to the gate house and tell the
gatekeeper to hire a carriage and driver to take us back
when we are ready." He touched her cheek. "Isn't the
pain more tolerable than the fear of pain was?"

She nodded, arrested by what she saw in the clear
depths of his vivid green eyes. Usually Peregrine was
enigmatic, veiled in mystery, but for an instant he let
her see deeper. And when he did, she saw a man who
knew all there was to know about pain.

That insight helped her master her disordered emotions, and she managed a faint smile. "Remarkable
how much you understand."

"Not remarkable in the least." He straightened. "I
will be back in a few minutes." After bringing Pansy
into the stables, he swung onto Siva and trotted out of
the yard.

When the prince was out of sight, Sara leaned her
head back against the wooden wall and closed her eyes,
feeling weak and foolish. She had been hurting, and
the prince had helped her with kindness and efficiency.
And because she was vulnerable and grateful, she had

responded with that intense physical awareness of him. It had been a momentary aberration, no more.

Determinedly she turned her attention to her throbbing leg. Tomorrow she would hardly be able to get out of bed, but as she cautiously prodded her thigh, she decided that no permanent damage had been done. In a few days she would be back on Pansy. At first she would ride only to the park and back, but in time, she vowed with grim determination, she would be able to ride twenty miles without a second thought.

Lifting her head, she saw that a tabby cat had materialized a yard away, sitting on its haunches and acting as if it had been in the same spot for hours. Amused by its world-weary air, she said, "Well, Furface, did you see me make a fool of myself?"

Taking that as an invitation, the feline made a flying leap onto her lap. Sara winced as it landed on her aching leg, but she couldn't resist the way the cat bumped its head against her ribs in a demand for attention. Scratching the velvety throat, she asked, "Did you see the man who might be your new master? You had better catch mice well for him, because I don't think he will tolerate idlers in his employ."

The cat turned around twice in her lap, then curled up and gave her a smile of imbecilic pleasure as it began purring. There was something very soothing about a cat. In addition, the creature made a good substitute for a warming bottle.

After a few minutes, Sara sighed and put the indignant cat back on the floor. Then she stood and began making her slow way through the stables, her right hand skimming the wall for support. It was easier to concentrate on the mundane business of walking than to think about the man whose casual touch could change her into a woman who was a stranger to herself.

Chapter 8

AFTER SENDING the gatekeeper to arrange for a carriage, Peregrine remounted Siva and rode back to the house, taking his time as he reconsidered his strategy. He had intended to make a major move in his campaign to detach Lady Sara from Weldon today.

From the beginning she had been attracted to him, though she was both too innocent and too ladylike to act on her interest. He had moved slowly, careful not to alarm her until he was sure that she was ripe for seduction. Not that he was sure he would allow matters to go that far, for seducing a noble English virgin was likely to cause complications he didn't need. But he suspected that Sara's attachment to her betrothed was not a very deep one, and a little judicious lovemaking should help persuade her that marriage would be a mistake.

However, while Peregrine had confidence in his skills, a woman who was in pain was a poor subject for seduction. He should have insisted that they come by carriage, but he had admired her courage and determination. He still did, even though her desire to come on horseback had produced a result that would balk his plan for the day.

Once more he stopped at the top of the drive and regarded Sulgrave Manor with brooding eyes. Buying a country estate had merely been part of his plan to establish himself in English society, with the added benefit of providing an excuse to be alone with Lady Sara. It had been a surprise, and not a pleasant one, when he had reacted so strongly to his first sight of the manor. It was dangerous to want something so much, because desire and affection made a man vulnerable.

After a minute he flicked the reins impatiently and continued on. He was making too much of this. Sulgrave was just a house, albeit a handsome one, and available at a bargain price. Perhaps someday, in that dim future beyond the accomplishment of his mission, he would be free to glory in pride of possession. In the meantime, buying the property was just another step toward his goal.

To his surprise, he found Lady Sara walking with reasonable ease, though her limp was much worse than usual. As he dismounted and led Siva into the stables, he said, "You recovered quickly."

"Practice improves all skills," she said dryly. "Were you able to persuade the gatekeeper to order a carriage?"

"Eventually. He was reluctant at first, until it occurred to him that I might be his next employer. Then he became most obliging." After tending the horses, Peregrine suggested, "Would you like to wait in the gardens while I go view the house?"

"I didn't come all this way to watch butterflies. I'm looking forward to seeing the inside of the manor." Taking his arm, Sara added, "Though my guess is that you will buy Sulgrave even if it is less than perfect for entertaining."

He glanced at her, not best pleased. "Am I that obvious?"

"Not usually. This time you were."

She leaned on his arm more than usual, but showed no other sign of distress. Perhaps he might achieve today's goal after all; he would let events be his guide.

The lawyer had given Peregrine a key that let them in a back door. Lady Sara pronounced the kitchens hopeless, saying that they must be completely redone with modern stoves and ovens, and even an inexperi-

enced male eye could see that she was right. But apart
from the kitchens, the house had no drawbacks. Most
of the chambers were large and well proportioned,
with richly carved ceilings and moldings. The dining
and drawing rooms were gracious, the library magnificent, and there were other chambers that could be
used for activities such as music and billiards.

Their exploration of the ground floor ended in the
hall, where exquisite antique mosaics were embedded
in the floor. Peregrine knelt and brushed his fingers
over the abstract floral pattern. "The lawyer told me
about these mosaics. They were discovered in the ruins of the old Roman town of Silchester."

"The house is superb," Lady Sara said, her gaze
lingering on the mosaic. "A great deal of cleaning and
redecorating will be required, but when you are done,
Sulgrave should suit your purposes exactly. Does the
furniture come with it?"

He stood, brushing dust from his hands. "Yes, the
heir does not want the bother of selling it separately.
Am I right that many of the pieces are very good quality?"

She nodded. "Yes. Some things will need refinish-
ing, and others are not worth keeping, but if you like
the styles of the last century, you'll have a good start
on furnishing the house."

"I hope that you will also lend me your advice about
decorating," he said. "Are you ready to see the upstairs?"

As she gave the stairs a calculating look, Peregrine
found himself very aware of her profile, the pure line
of face, throat, and breast, like the ancient sibyl she
had first reminded him of. Suddenly he wanted her
with a fierceness that shocked him. Shaken, he took a
deep breath, knowing that too much desire could play
havoc with his plans. When he was sure that touching
her would not make him act like a lust-crazed youth,
he leaned over, scooped her up, and began climbing
the carved oak stairs.

"You are a little too quick to sweep me off my feet, Your Highness," Lady Sara said rather breathlessly as she clung to his arm. "I could have climbed the stairs on my own."

"No doubt, but the price of proving it would have been too high. Show some consideration for your ill-used leg."

She tilted her head back to look at him. "Ladies don't have legs, they have limbs. 'Legs' are considered indecent."

"Indecent?" he said as he set her on her feet at the head of the stairs. Solemnly he lifted the hem of her riding habit a few inches and examined her booted ankles. "I see nothing indecent."

"Behave yourself, Your Highness." Laughing, she batted the skirt from his hand. "I didn't say that female legs *were* indecent, but that the word is *considered* indecent. It is another English absurdity."

"One of many," he said, offering his arm again. "But do not think I am ungrateful for your efforts to educate me. One must know the rules before one can properly break them."

"You, sir, are incorrigible," she said as she took his arm.

"But never dull."

Lady Sara gave him a wry half smile. "True. But it is possible that you could give dullness a good name."

He chuckled. "May I return the compliment by saying that you accomplish the even more formidable task of making respectability seem interesting?"

In perfect charity, they worked their way through the upper floor. It proved equal to the ground level, with fifteen spacious bedchambers. Bathrooms and water closets needed to be updated, but when that was done, the accommodations for house parties would be ample and luxurious.

Last they investigated the long gallery that ran across the back of the house. It was an attractive room, with fireplaces at each end and large casement windows with padded, built-in seats overlooking the garden. After studying some of the gloomy portraits, Sara asked, "Are the portraits also part of the sale?"

"No, the paintings are to be shipped to Canada." After examining one, his mouth quirked up. "I could use some respectable ancestors, but I find these a boring lot. Perhaps I shall commission a painter to do a new set for me."

He glanced across the gallery, his smile fading. Releasing Sara's arm, he crossed the room for a better view. It took a minute to unlatch the casement. Then he threw the sashes wide and leaned out, bracing his hands on the sill and balancing with one knee on the window seat. Below him lay the English countryside in all its aching beauty, the misty hills rolling to forever, and he reacted to the sight with the same intensity as when he had first seen Sulgrave. He temporarily forgot his companion, and it was a surprise to hear her voice at his elbow.

"This house sings to you, doesn't it?" she said softly.

"I suppose that is as good a way as any of putting it." He tried to understand why, and couldn't. Probably he would not have explained even if he did know the reasons. Instead he said, "You are an English aristocrat, born and raised to this kind of life—the richness, the beauty, the peace, the chance for justice. You can't appreciate how much it means."

"Probably not." The window-seat cushion shifted as she sat at the other end. "But you were a rich man in your own country, and Ross said that Kafiristan has its own matchless beauty. Does this mean more to you?"

"Not more, perhaps, but it is different." Peregrine turned and sat on the window seat, only two feet of space separating him from Lady Sara. She was cool and self-possessed, except for the warmth in her grave brown eyes. Sara St. James, as much a woman as she was a lady. She had left her riding hat downstairs, and the slanting sunbeams touched her hair to molten gold.

Something twisted deep inside him, and again he experienced the surging, uncontrollable desire he had felt downstairs. It was not just her serene beauty, nor her quiet strength, that aroused him, though he admired both.

Perhaps it was her Englishness—like Sulgrave, like England itself. She represented a way of living that now, against all probability, lay within his grasp. He did not know if it was a life he wanted, nor would he have the leisure to decide until he had finished with Charles Weldon. But in the meantime, there was no denying Lady Sara's allure.

It took all his willpower to remain still. He yearned to touch her, to call forth her latent passion, but not yet, not when his own desire threatened to cloud his judgment. Better to talk, to weave a web of words until he was in control again. "Kafiristan is a poor country, unbelievably poor. It is not even really a country, just a collection of related tribes. It didn't take much wealth to be a great man there."

"But Ross said you were very rich. How . . . ?" Sara stopped, faint color appearing across her high cheekbones.

"I gather that it is rude and un-English to ask about a man's money? No matter, I am not easily offended," he said, amused. "The source of my fortune was not in Kafiristan. Have you ever heard of the Silk Road, the ancient trade route from China to the Mediterranean?"

"I've heard of it, but no more than that."

"For perhaps two thousand years, caravans carried goods between the East and West, from ancient Cathay to imperial Rome. Silk and jade, spices, gold, and amber, and a thousand other things passed through many different hands, and were carried by every kind of beast used by man." Unconsciously his voice took on the compelling rhythms of the storyteller.

"Traders risked bandits and disease, but far worse were the natural hazards of mountains and deserts. Perhaps the most dangerous part of the journey was Chinese Turkestan. There, in the fiery, blasted heart of Asia, lies a desert called the Takla Makan, a wasteland of shifting, treacherous dunes three hundred feet high, surrounded by the tallest mountains in the world. It is a desert that makes Arabia seem tame by comparison, a place where the *kara-buran,* the black hurricane, can bury whole caravans with no trace of man or beast ever seen again."

"You speak as one who has been there and survived."

He nodded. "The Silk Road skirted the southern edge of the Takla Makan, and cities grew up at the scattered oases. Once they shimmered with wealth and power, but several centuries back, most of the cities died, and the sands of the desert reclaimed them. I am not sure why, though the development of sea routes must have had much to do with it. There are many legends about the lost cities—tales of how heaven destroyed them for their wickedness, warnings of the demons that guard the buried riches."

Her eyes widened as she guessed where his story was leading. "You found one of the lost cities?"

He nodded again. "Yes, a city called Katak by a Kirghiz herder who told me a tale that had been passed from father to son for many generations. Katak lies amid the salt marshes of Lop Nor. Finding it was hard, locating its lost riches harder yet, but the greatest dangers lay in taking the treasure away across the sands and mountains."

"I gather that you did not fear the demons?" She shifted position, unconsciously drawing a little nearer to him.

"They were not the demons of my people, and hence had no power over me." Peregrine's gaze drifted, remembering. "Luckily I was also able to convince my friends of that. We made three journeys from Kafiristan to the lost city of Katak, each time bringing back gold, silver, and works of art. As the leader, mine was the largest share, and that became the basis of my fortune. I came down from the mountains into India and learned the ways of the merchant, investing and trading until I had great wealth even in European terms.''

Lady Sara's head was tilted to one side, her expression dreamy with imagination. ''A fascinating and romantic tale.''

''Only in retrospect,'' he said dryly. ''At the time it was exhausting work and appalling discomfort, punctuated by occasional spells of heart-stopping danger.''

''Ross has said the same thing about his travels. Real adventurers like you and him must think drawing-room romantics like me are rather silly.'' A trace of wistfulness showed. ''Listening to travelers' tales is the closest I shall ever come to such exploits.''

''There are people who want only to be titillated or confirmed in their prejudices. I do not waste my time on them. But I would never think you silly, for you listen with your spirit as well as your ears.'' He gave her a conspiratorial, self-mocking smile. ''Don't tell others how I made my fortune, though. I prefer to be mysterious.''

''You are very good at that,'' she said with demure mischief.

Peregrine caught her gaze with his. The tension of pain was gone, and Lady Sara was rapt and receptive. The time had come to woo her. He concentrated with all the strength of his will, using his power to attract, spinning an invisible net to draw her to him. Her lips parted, uncertain, expectant, as she felt the increasing force between them.

''What drives you, Mikahl?'' she asked softly, using his name for the first time. ''What makes you different from the rest of your people? Why have you mastered so many skills, why have you crossed the world to come to this small, damp island where most men are too narrow to appreciate all you have achieved?''

''Ever since I was a child, I have known that my destiny lies in England.'' It was the truth, though not a truth Lady Sara was in a position to interpret. More than that he would not, could not, reveal. Continuing with another half truth, he said, ''Perhaps you are part of the reason I am here.''

He raised one hand and traced the elegant bones of her cheek and jaw with his fingertips. She stared at him, her lips parted and great eyes helpless with question and longing. Moving closer, he gave her the lightest of kisses, touching only her face, feathering across her forehead and the fragile skin around her eyes until their lips met.

At first it was a still, gentle kiss like the one they had shared at the ball. Then he opened his mouth and instinctively she mirrored his movement. Though a small shock of surprise ran through her as the kiss deepened, she did not withdraw. Instead she responded with innocent, questing enthusiasm.

Peregrine had thought that his desire was safely banked, but the taste of her tentative, yearning mouth made passion flare with white heat, needy and demanding. If Sara had been a woman of experience, he would have stopped at nothing to sweep her along with him into a fast, furious, heedless mating.

But she was not experienced, and he retained just enough control to refrain from doing what might frighten her. Wrapping his arms around her slim waist, he drew her close, needing to feel her body against his. Sara came willingly, her restless hands sliding under his coat, her mouth as hungry as his.

He leaned back against the wall, drawing her along so that she lay half-sprawled across him, breast to breast, her thighs bracketing one of his in a simulation of lovemaking that made him want more. Cradling the soft curves of her buttocks, he pulled her tight against his groin. Her hips pulsed against him, and he responded with frustrated pleasure, mentally cursing the layers of heavy fabric between them.

Over the years, Peregrine had survived and prospered by learning to seize what fortune offered, and now he discarded his earlier plan of limiting what happened today. Sara might be inexperienced, but she was a woman grown, well past the age of consent. Teaching her the joys of the flesh would not only be deeply pleasurable, but would serve his larger goals as well.

"Sweet Sara," he whispered, caressing her slender form as if his hands could meld them into one flesh, "you are as rare and lovely as the treasures of the Silk Road."

Unbuttoning her jacket, he slipped his hand inside, mentally cursing the blouse, petticoat, and corset that still separated them. Gently he squeezed the soft, fluid weight of her breast. "You are like gold and silk and ivory that have been warmed to wondrous life."

Sara gasped as his words dissolved the intoxicated delight that held her in thrall. Though not unaware of what she was doing, all normal constraints had vanished when she discovered the headlong urgency of desire. As she yielded to that urgency, shy acceptance had changed to fierce response, and in the tumult of her senses, she had been shameless.

But now passion no longer clouded her judgment, though it still burned in her blood. She broke the kiss and made herself focus on Peregrine's dark, craggy face. His green eyes were misty with passion, and this time there was nothing enigmatic about him. He wanted her. And, heaven help her, she wanted him.

She pushed herself off his lap and slid across the window seat so they were no longer touching. "No," she said, her voice raw. "I'm sorry, this is wrong, I can't do it."

After a startled moment, he sat up and wrapped one arm around her waist, pulling her close again while he lifted her face to his. Murmuring, "But of course you

can do this. See how easy and right it is?'' He drew
her into another drugging kiss.

For a moment her resolve thinned to snapping point.
Then she jerked away and stood, almost falling in her
awkward haste to put distance between them.

"It may be easy," Sara said unevenly, "but it isn't
right, because I am promised to another man." She
backed half a dozen feet along the wall, using it to
steady her precarious balance. "I have dishonored both
him and myself."

Peregrine's wavy black hair had fallen across his
forehead, and his chest was heaving, as if he had been
running. As Sara looked at the harsh planes of his
face, for a moment she was frightened. They were
alone in the house, and she was completely at his
mercy. Even an English gentleman, raised to the same
notions of honor as Sara, might be dangerous under
these circumstances, and a man from an alien culture
might decide that Sara deserved whatever he chose to
do to her.

"My behavior gives you every reason to be angry,
but please . . ." Her voice broke; even more than fear,
she felt shame.

He looked away for a moment, and she saw a faint
shudder run through his powerful frame as his fingers
tightened on the edge of the window seat. When he
turned to her again, his eyes were clear and the sense
of danger had passed. But as Sara began to relax, she
recognized a subtler danger, for once more she felt his
mysterious, potent attraction, as if an invisible current
was reaching out to draw her back to him.

Sara's willpower almost broke. She wanted to walk
straight into his arms and surrender to passion, and
she knew that if he embraced her, she would yield
utterly. But to her infinite relief, he did not move from
the window seat, and she offered a swift inward prayer
of thanks that he did not know how much power he
had over her.

"You have not married Weldon yet, and perhaps you

should not do so,'' he said coolly. ''Do you react that way to his kisses?''

''That is none of your business.'' Sara flushed. ''Besides, marriage is not about passion. It is about trust, about mutual values and respect.''

''Don't forget mutual property,'' he said, his tone ironic. ''You are a considerable heiress, and Weldon's businesses are less prosperous than they appear.''

She inhaled deeply, trying to steady herself amid a maelstrom of emotions. ''Charles is no fortune hunter, but even if he were, it would not alter the fact that I am pledged to him. By my actions, I have already betrayed him unforgivably.''

His expression became even more satiric. ''If you think that the modest kisses we just exchanged are unforgivable, why not finish what you have begun? Not only would you enjoy the experience, but you would also have something worth feeling guilty about.''

Modest kisses, indeed! Her flush deepened as she remembered the wanton way she had twined around him. Thank heaven for complicated clothing; if she had been wearing one of the flimsy dresses of the previous generation, they would have been coupling before she had had time to realize what was happening.

''I behaved badly to you as well as disgracing myself, and you have every reason to be angry,'' she said, raising her chin, ''but don't mock me. It is unworthy of you.''

His expression changed. ''I was not mocking you,'' he said gently. ''But I do think you are making too much of a momentary lapse. You are a lovely woman, I kissed you, and you enjoyed it. That is not such a great sin.''

''Perhaps that was trivial to you, but it was not to me.'' Merciful heaven, what had been a ''momentary lapse'' to him had been one of the most shattering experiences of Sara's life. She rubbed her damp palms on her skirt, then leaned against the wall, needing the support because her leg was throbbing badly again.

Remembering something Charles had told her, she said, "Englishwomen have great freedom compared to women elsewhere, so I suppose it's natural for you to suppose we are immoral. But that isn't true."

He raised his dark brows. "No? I have seen considerable evidence to the contrary."

"Perhaps it would be more accurate to say that Englishwomen are neither more nor less virtuous than those of any other race," she said, recalling uncomfortably the women who had fluttered around him. "Certainly chaste behavior is valued."

"But your countrywomen do have more opportunities to be unchaste than women in most societies." He stood and in two steps closed the distance between them, stopping so near that she felt warmth radiating from his body.

"However, fascinating though this discussion is, we are going rather far afield. It never occurred to me that your morals are deficient. You radiate integrity, Lady Sara. It is one of the things I find attractive about you." He reached out and cupped her face in both hands, his long fingers gentle and sensual along her too-sensitive skin.

She knew he was about to kiss her again, and when he did, she would yield, for her whole body yearned for him. Physically she was ripe for the plucking, and they both knew it. But honor was not yet dead, not quite. Her voice breaking, she pleaded, "You know I cannot resist you, but please . . . please stop. Don't ruin me for the fleeting pleasure of conquest."

He became utterly still. "Is that what you think? No, Sara, my motive is not simple conquest." His hands dropped away. "Nor do I want to ruin you. You deserve better than that."

"Then what do you want?" she asked, flattening herself back against the wall when he reached out to her again.

This time he did not caress her, just tucked a loose wisp of her hair behind her ear with a curiously intimate gesture. "The answer is very simple. It is you, yourself, that I want. No other woman will do."

She shook her head, feeling helpless and confused. With an Englishman, such words might have been a prelude to a declaration of love, perhaps even an offer of marriage, but she was sure that that was not what Peregrine meant. Despairingly she said, "I don't understand you at all."

Before he could reply, a loud knocking echoed through the house. They both tensed at the sound. "That must be the driver with the carriage," the Kafir said after listening a moment. "He is in front of the house. I will tell him to come around to the rear, since that is the only door for which I have a key."

The prince turned away, and Sara released her breath shakily, realizing that she had hardly been breathing. While he entered a front bedroom, opened a window, and called down to the driver, she walked as quickly as she could to the main staircase.

Clinging to the banister for support, she was just starting her descent when Peregrine rejoined her. For a moment she feared that he was going to carry her downstairs, but he correctly interpreted her warning look.

"So fierce!" he said with amusement. "Don't worry, sweet Sara, you are safe from me."

"The correct form of address is Lady Sara. I have not given you leave to be informal." Suddenly furious, she stopped and glared at him. "This is all a game to you, isn't it? I wish we had never met, for you have turned my life inside out, and it means nothing to you."

"This is not a game, and it is not meaningless to me." He stopped two steps below and turned to face her, his brief humor vanished. For once completely serious, he asked, "Can you honestly say that you have not benefited, at least a little, from my 'turning your life inside out'?"

Sara thought of how he had led her through her fears

to the heady freedoms of riding and dancing. And there had been a different, more dangerous freedom when she had discovered passion in his arms, a freedom that could quickly lead to disgrace and subjugation. She closed her eyes for a moment, and wearily rubbed her temple with her free hand. "Yes, I have benefited, and I am not really sorry to have met you," she said quietly. "But I can't see you alone in the future. Don't call on me, or ask me to ride or drive with you, because I won't accept."

"You do not trust me?" His eyes were level with hers, the green depths fathomless, impossible to read.

"No," she said bluntly. "Nor do I trust myself. I will not risk another episode like this one."

There was a long pause before he spoke. "Of course I must assent to your wishes, Lady Sara." His eyes darkened, something subtle and dangerous moving in the depths. "For the time being."

It was a long, tiring ride back to London. Sara was intensely grateful that the prince chose to ride Siva rather than join her in the small hired carriage. Spending two hours in close proximity, where every jolt might knock her against him, would have been more than she could bear. Even so, it took all of her strength to maintain her composure.

When they arrived at Haddonfield House, he behaved with impeccable politeness, returning Pansy to the stables, escorting Sara into the house with a strong impersonal hand under her elbow, and taking his leave after thanking her for her invaluable assistance. Even the stiff-rumped Haddonfield butler, who watched, did not notice anything amiss.

Sara had just enough endurance left to climb the stairs to her room without aid, though it was a slow, painful ascent. Thank heaven her father was out for the evening. Sara's sour-faced maid, Hoskins, made several acid comments about having warned her ladyship not to try to ride, and only subsided when Sara forcefully told her to hold her tongue.

Blissfully free of her riding habit and corset, Sara would have preferred to lie down and fall into exhausted slumber, but from experience she knew that she would feel much better in the morning if she soaked in a long, hot bath. Besides, there was something else she must do.

After sending Hoskins off to draw the bath, Sara seated herself at the dressing table and stared at her reflection as she drew the pins from her hair, freeing it to fall around her shoulders. It was time to face some unpleasant facts, and looking at the mirror would make it harder to be dishonest.

For she had been profoundly dishonest; from the moment she had seen Prince Peregrine, she had lied to herself over and over and over, denying how much he fascinated her. She had believed herself impervious to his dangerous allure, and that self-deception had led her to today's humiliating scene at Sulgrave.

She ran her fingers through her thick hair, loosening it and easing the tension in her scalp. A pity that her mental tension could not be eased so simply. The cheapest trollop in Covent Garden would have been more honest than Lady Sara St. James had been. Ignorance was no excuse, for she had made a point of educating herself about what happened between men and women, her best teacher being an uninhibited cockney maid. Yet in spite of her knowledge and worldly experience, she had walked straight into a situation that could have ruined her, because in her secret heart, she had wanted passion more than honor.

Sara had assumed that she was too refined, or too cold, to succumb to such folly. Obviously she had been wrong, though she could not blame herself for wanting to yield to passion now that she had experienced its awesome power. If she had felt such desire for Charles, she would have welcomed it as an extra blessing for their marriage. But instead, on the eve of her wedding, she had become infatuated with another man. And, humiliatingly, he was a man with no special interest in her.

Though Peregrine had said that she was the only woman he wanted, she discounted that as the tactful lie of an experienced seducer, in the same league as the fool's gold compliments he had given her. "Gold and silk and ivory, warmed to wondrous life," indeed! As she looked at her reflection in the mirror, she saw a small female of unremarkable appearance, overserious and—she forced herself to think the word—crippled.

Oddly, she had believed Peregrine when he said that he did not want to ruin her, and that he was not interested in her simply as a conquest. The thought made her smile faintly, for there was nothing simple about him. But she could think of only two other reasons why a handsome prince would choose her above the beautiful, experienced women he had met in London society, and neither reason was flattering.

Possibly it was her rank that attracted him, making her more alluring than her modest physical attractions warranted. Far more likely, her real appeal was that she was fool enough to make herself available. She had put herself in a position where the Kafir had reason to believe that she would accept his advances. Then, after acting like a wanton, she had retreated like a nervous schoolgirl. He could have humiliated her at the least, ravished her at the most, and she was grateful for his restraint.

No doubt she had Ross to thank for that, because the friendship between the men seemed the most likely reason that Peregrine had not taken advantage of her foolishness. Pray God that Ross, Charles, and her father never learned what had happened today. Her cousin might understand, or at least be tolerant of her weakness. But her father and her betrothed would be profoundly, and justifiably, appalled by her behavior.

Convulsively Sara buried her face in her hands, no longer able to face her image in the mirror. Even if the men in her life never learned what she had done, she could not escape the worst punishment of all: the knowledge that she had failed to live up to her own standards of right and wrong. She had thought herself a virtuous woman, but clearly her virtue was merely a result of never having been tempted.

Fortunately for Sara's composure, Hoskins returned to say that the bath was ready. Numbly Sara walked to the bathroom, stripped off her green velvet robe, and lowered herself into the large tub. The steaming, rose-scented water came up to her chin, and her aching muscles reacted with a relief so intense that it was nearly pain. It was pleasure almost as acute and sensual as what she had experienced in Peregrine's arms.

Exasperated, Sara tried to banish her unruly thoughts, but without success. Immodest though it was, she could not deny her taut, yearning awareness. Hesitantly she opened her hands and stroked down her torso, her palms gliding over her smooth feminine curves. Her skin was satin-sleek under the hot water.

Peregrine's hands were long-fingered and dexterous, hardened by work, yet gentle, so gentle. What would it be like to feel those strong hands on her bare flesh? The thought made her shiver with embarrassing longing, but she wasn't embarrassed enough to stop thinking and wondering.

Consideringly she cupped one breast. It was soft and almost weightless in the water. Remarkable things, breasts; men were intrigued by them, and even through her heavy clothing she had nearly melted with pleasure when he touched her there.

Her hand skimmed lower across her ribs, along the curve of her waist, then lower yet, toward parts of her body for which she did not even have a name, but which pulsed with yearning. As her fingertips brushed curling gold hair, she had a vivid image of his dark hand in the same place. A few short hours ago, she had been pressed against him, their loins straining together . . .

She blushed violently and withdrew her hand, but the thought of Peregrine touching her intimately was not the major cause of her discomfort. The real problem was knowing that in her mind and emotions, she had been—was still—disloyal to the man she had promised to marry. She doubted that Charles had lived a chaste life since the death of his first wife, but that did not excuse Sara's failing.

Deliberately she studied her right thigh and traced the ugly, twisting scars left by the surgeons. There had been infection, and they had wanted to amputate her leg, but her condition had improved while they were still trying to decide if the operation would be more likely to kill or cure her. The scars were part of her, along with all the limitations they represented. It would be well if she remembered that.

The water was beginning to cool. With a sigh, she took the bar of French soap and began lathering, then stopped because the slick pressure was stimulating improper thoughts again. Damn Peregrine for invading her mind and imagination so thoroughly!

Her mouth grim, Sara asked herself another difficult question. She had faced her self-deception and had acknowledged her physical attraction to the mysterious Kafir. While she was fascinated by him, she was reasonably sure that his interest in her was minor and fleeting. But what if things were different? What if she were not betrothed to Charles, what if Peregrine asked her to marry him? What would she do then?

The last shreds of her control vanished, and she began to cry, hopeless tears that stung her eyes and rolled down her face into the cooling water. And she didn't even know why.

Chapter 9

IT WAS LATE EVENING, not quite full dark, as Peregrine rode to Benjamin Slade's home for what should be a very interesting meeting. But instead of thinking about business, his mind kept turning to Lady Sara St. James, as it had done repeatedly in the last week. He still could not understand why he had restrained himself the afternoon they had gone to Sulgrave. He had desired her with overwhelming intensity, and she herself had been three-quarters willing. One more kiss and she would have surrendered completely. Yet he had stopped.

Perhaps it was because of his promise to Ross, perhaps because of the desperate vulnerability in Lady Sara's eyes as she begged him not to continue. Much as he wanted her, he had found himself unable to do something that would make her despise herself afterward.

The trouble was that he liked the blasted woman, liked her intelligence and humor and wise, gentle spirit. He also could not avoid a certain grudging respect for the fact that she tried to live up to her principles of right and wrong. Such principles were the luxuries of people who had led easy lives, but they were not without a certain charm.

His mouth curled with self-disgust as he considered the repercussions of his moment of misguided restraint. It would have been far kinder to have tumbled her. By now he knew Lady Sara well enough to be sure that her conscience would have driven her to break her betrothal if she had been intimate with another man. Weldon would have lost his rich, highborn wife, Peregrine's goal would have been enjoyably achieved, and the lady herself would have been much better off in the long run.

Because Sara's own desire had been aroused, she would have been too honest to put all the blame on her seducer, and in the aftermath she would have suffered from guilt and self-reproach. But she would have been saved from Weldon, and it would not have been long before she came to terms with her lapse from virtue, for she had too much common sense to punish herself forever.

He had been a softheaded fool, and he and Sara would both end up paying a high price for his weakness. The betrothal *must* be broken, but since she would not see him except in a crowded social setting, he would have to find another way to achieve his end. The vague plan in the back of his mind was thoroughly dishonorable, but he would resort to it if necessary. And next time, he would not let Sara's honest, accusing brown eyes keep him from his purpose.

Benjamin Slade settled his reading glasses on his nose with lawyerly precision and lifted a paper from one of the files stacked on the desk in front of him. "Following your suggestions, I have compiled a remarkable dossier on Sir Charles Weldon. I would not have believed a gentleman could be guilty of such wickedness and hypocrisy had I not seen the evidence myself."

He paused and peered over the top of his glasses. "Bear in mind that there are two categories of evidence here. Some of it is so conclusive that any judge or jury in Great Britain would be convinced. However, there are other crimes that Weldon is surely guilty of, but where the evidence will not stand in court."

"I understand the distinction," Peregrine said, lounging back in his chair and crossing his legs. "It is neither necessary nor possible to prove all his crimes. I just want to know that we have enough to hang him." Correctly interpreting Slade's doubtful expression, he added with a humorless smile, "I speak metaphorically. Frankly, I think hanging is too good for Sir Charles Weldon."

Slade blinked. Then, surprisingly, he said, "I'm inclined to think you are right." His gaze returned to the paper in his hand. "To summarize, Weldon owns all the brothels you listed. He also appears to own several other brothels and two or three illegal gaming hells, though I can't prove it in most cases because the transfer of money is in cash, with minimal records. Except for Mrs. Kent's house, he seldom makes a personal visit to his own bawdy houses, preferring to channel funds through intermediaries. The most important of these is a man called Kane, who lives in Weldon's household and is described as a personal secretary."

Peregrine nodded. "That doesn't surprise me. I met Kane a couple of times. Silent and dangerous, not at all deferential, and looks like a former soldier."

"He could be. I have been unable to learn anything of his history before he began working for Weldon some fifteen years ago." Slade set one paper down and lifted another. "While Kane's background is mysterious, his criminal talent is vital to Weldon's illicit businesses. He collects money, terrorizes anyone who doesn't cooperate, and generally keeps things running smoothly. Each brothel has at least one guard who has been recruited from the London underworld and who reports directly to Kane. Rather like a private army. Overt violence is committed either by Kane or one of the brothel guards, which makes it difficult to connect Weldon directly with criminal activity."

The lawyer gave a slight, satisfied smile. "However, I have been able to acquire some useful affidavits. For example, in the case of Mrs. Kent's appalling establishment, Miss Miller not only overheard Weldon and

Kent discussing his ownership, but she herself saw money change hands and will testify.''

Peregrine smiled, amused. Jenny might have seen what she claimed, but he considered it more likely that she had made the incident up as a way of getting back at Weldon. Better not to mention the latter possibility to Benjamin, who might be shocked at the prospect of someone lying under oath. Peregrine was less scrupulous; all he cared about was that if the girl lied, she would do it convincingly, and he suspected that she would. As he knew from experience, it was hard to be overconcerned with the niceties of the law when one has lived outside it. ''I imagine that all this information has cost a fortune in bribes.''

''I prefer not to use the term *bribe,*'' Slade said blandly, ''but, yes, substantial amounts have been expended. You did give me the authority.''

''I'm not complaining. Spend whatever is necessary.'' Though Peregrine seldom smoked, he leaned forward and took a cigar from the box on his host's desk. ''Were you able to establish if Weldon is involved with those ships I told you to investigate?''

Slade nodded, his gray eyes like chipped ice. ''I was. The ownership is indirect, and I had to follow a convoluted trail through several sham companies. However, because of the laws and government registrations involved, his guilt can be proved beyond doubt, unlike most of the brothel ownerships.''

As exultation surged through him, Peregrine trimmed the end of the cigar. So he was right—his enemy was as evil as expected, and stupid or arrogant enough to leave a trail for anyone clever enough to know where to look. ''What about Weldon's legitimate businesses?''

''Though he has a reputation for wealth and success, the reality is rather different. He's undeniably clever, but too often rash. If it were not for the income from his illegal enterprises, he might have gone bankrupt some time ago.'' The lawyer opened a new file. ''In the last eighteen months, he has made a number of bad decisions and is now overdue on repaying several personal loans. The bank holding his paper is nervous, but assumes he will recover soon. It helps that Weldon recently announced his betrothal to an heiress, Lady Sara St. James. They will marry quite soon. Perhaps you have met her at one of your social affairs? She's the only child of the Duke of Haddonfield.''

"I've met her." Eyes narrowed, Peregrine lifted the shade from the candle lamp and lit his cigar. "What would it do to Weldon's financial situation if the betrothal ended?''

Slade's brows rose. "It certainly wouldn't help him. Do you have reason to believe the marriage will not take place?''

"I'm sure it will not." The prince drew in a mouthful of smoke, then slowly exhaled it. "You may drop a few discreet hints in financial circles that Lady Sara, who is a woman of taste and perception, is in the process of reconsidering her decision to marry Weldon.''

The lawyer regarded him thoughtfully. "I have a feeling that the less I know about that, the better. Rest assured that soon it will be known that Weldon might not receive the financial settlement he is planning on. Of course, he can find another heiress, but these things take time, even for a handsome man with a distinguished reputation.''

Peregrine tapped the cigar on the edge of the glass ashtray and watched the charred tobacco fall off. "Once the marriage is in doubt, do you think that the bank holding Weldon's loans might be interested in selling them to someone else?''

"Quite possibly. But if you buy Weldon's loans, you will take a heavy loss if he doesn't recover.''

"I don't care," Peregrine said brusquely. "I want those loans. Buy them through that dummy company you set up so that my name isn't associated. Now what about the L & S Railway?''

"Taking it over is the cleverest thing Weldon has

done in years,'' Slade said, unable to withhold an approving nod. ''The financial community is very excited about the new management and the company's prospects. When new stock is issued next week, it should sell quickly. You'll make a good profit on the money you invested.''

''Did you find out the true story on the legal problems Weldon told me about?''

''I was coming to that.'' The lawyer gave him a reproving look for his impatience. ''As you know, the parliamentary bill that incorporates a railroad says that the company can take the land it needs in return for proper compensation. The original L & S management was undercapitalized to begin with, so they tried to appropriate land for less than a fair price. Not surprisingly, a number of landowners filed suit for more money, led by a yeoman farmer in Hampshire named Jethro Crawley. There was considerable bitterness between the company and the landowners.''

Slade peered over his glasses. ''This is where it gets interesting. Though it isn't commonly known, Crawley dropped his lawsuit after a mysterious fire on his farm. A most unfortunate incident. Someone died, I believe. After Weldon took the railroad over, a number of the other landowners settled their cases for amounts of money not much greater than they had been offered in the first place.''

Peregrine thought about it. ''Do you think that Crawley was the victim of arson, and most of the other landowners decided to take what money they could get rather than risk the same thing happening to them?''

''It is certainly a possibility,'' Slade agreed. ''I thought I'd go down to Hampshire this week and talk to Jethro Crawley, see if I could learn what really happened.''

''I want to do that myself.'' Peregrine drew in a mouthful of smoke, then blew out several perfect smoke rings. ''If he hasn't formally signed over the railroad right-of-way to the L & S, perhaps he will sell it to us instead. It would have to be done through another dummy investment company, so Weldon won't know who is behind it until it's too late.''

''Then what?'' Slade said, looking alarmed.

Peregrine's eyes gleamed. ''Weldon will find himself with a new lawsuit on his hands, possibly accompanied by criminal charges that the railway has been brutally intimidating innocent landowners. Wouldn't the newspapers love that? It would make a lovely scandal and probably bring construction of the railroad to a halt again.''

Slade frowned. ''You've invested a sizable fortune in the L & S. If you mean to block construction, it will be very expensive for you and a lot of other people as well.''

''No matter.'' Peregrine cut the lawyer off from further warnings with a chopping motion of his cigar. ''Have we anything else to discuss tonight?''

''The seller of Sulgrave is eager for a quick settlement, so the sale should be closed within a week.''

''The sooner the better. Have you had any luck at finding a suitable Mayfair town house?''

''An excellent furnished house on Park Street is available for rent. It belongs to a nobleman who is going abroad for a year. It's expensive but very elegant. Do you want to look at it?''

Peregrine shook his head. ''If you think it is suitable, just go ahead and rent it. I am weary of hotel living.'' He gazed absently at the bright coal on the end of the cigar, remembering another item of unfinished business. ''How is Jenny Miller?''

Slade's eyes warmed. ''You would hardly recognize the girl. She's amazingly quick—understands and remembers everything she's told. Her East End accent is almost gone.''

Peregrine heard a faint sound at the door of the study, as if a mouse had brushed by. Gesturing for Slade to keep talking, he set his cigar in the ashtray, then rose and crossed the room on soundless feet.

The lawyer watched in puzzlement as he continued, "I've found a woman who was lady's maid to a countess. She is willing to train Miss Miller in the skills required for such a position."

Peregrine threw the door open and was unsurprised when Jenny almost fell into the room. Her eyes widened with terror at being caught. She made a small, desperate sound and whirled away, but he caught her arm and turned her to face him.

The girl looked her true age now that she was dressed as a woman, not a child. In her demure chignon and modest blue gown, she might have been the daughter of a successful lawyer or doctor, or even a vicar. Hard to believe that such a pretty, respectable young lady had spent years imprisoned in a brothel.

Mildly Peregrine asked, "Were our voices loud enough for you, or should we repeat what was said?"

"I didn't hear anything," she protested, trembling in his grip. "I was just coming down to see if Mr. Slade might like me to make him a cup of tea, like I usually do in the evenings."

"That's true," Benjamin put in. "Don't frighten the child. There's no harm done."

Ignoring the interruption, Peregrine said, "Don't lie to me, Jenny." He escorted her into the study. "I've heard you rustling at the door almost since I arrived. Have a seat."

Nervously the girl perched on a straight-backed chair. She glanced at Slade, who smiled reassuringly, then looked up at Peregrine, who towered over her. His gaze holding hers, he said, "I'm sure that you are excellent at spying and eavesdropping, and those skills have helped you survive. I'm equally sure that you won't stop any time soon. I don't really object, but I want your solemn promise that you will not use anything you learn against me or my friends. Also, if you ever hear something I might be interested in, you will inform me of it. Is that clear?"

Her eyes widened. Then she nodded. "I promise.

I'd never do anything to hurt you or Mr. Slade. I—I just like to know what's going on. All those spy holes in Mrs. Kent's house could be used in both directions, and I was small enough to get into places she'd never think to look, I learned a lot that way."

"No doubt," he said dryly as he picked up his still-smouldering cigar. "Do you have any requests, comments, or complaints to make before I leave?"

"Oh, no." She shook her shining blond head emphatically. "Mr. Slade has been ever so good to me. These last few weeks have been the best of my life. I'm looking forward to learning how to be a lady's maid. I'll be a good one."

"I don't doubt it." Dismissing her from his mind, Peregrine took a last pull at his cigar before stubbing it out. "Do we have anything else to discuss, Benjamin?"

"No." The lawyer handed over a thick folder. "Here are complete details of everything I summarized tonight. I trust you'll find them interesting."

The prince accepted the folder, bade them both a polite good night, then left. After the door closed behind him, Jenny shook her head. "He's a strange one, he is. Seems to hear and know everything, and never does what you expect. Makes me nervous as a cat on a griddle."

"That's a rather tactless way to refer to your benefactor, though I must admit that I know how you feel," Slade said with a faint smile. "But if you don't cross him, you couldn't ask for a better employer or friend."

"I honest to God wouldn't want him for an enemy," she said with a shiver. Then she smiled at the lawyer, her delicate face lighting up with sweetness. "I'd much rather have you for a friend. You don't scare a body to death." She stood. "Would you like me to make you a cup of tea?"

"I'd like that very much." As she brushed by his chair, Slade half raised his hand, then let it drop, but his longing gaze followed her out of the room. Then he turned to his papers, his mouth tight. He had done many difficult things for his employer, but he had never realized that the hardest task would be turning a whore into a young lady.

Crawley's farm was solid and unpretentious, the stone buildings mellowed with years and weather. The only whimsical note was the thatched roof of the house, where a reed fox chased three reed chickens along the ridgepole. But the thatch was old and ragged, and the fox threatened to topple from the ridgepole, just one of many subtle signs of neglect, as if the farm had fallen on hard times.

No one was in sight, so Peregrine dismounted and knocked on the door. After a lengthy wait, it was opened by a middle-aged woman. Her round face had been designed for cheerfulness, but there were haggard lines around her mouth, and anxiety in her eyes when she found a gentleman on her doorstep.

"Mrs. Crawley?" Peregrine asked. When she nodded, he continued, "I want to speak with your husband. Is he available?"

"Aye," she said reluctantly. "Should be behind the stables."

"Thank you." He touched his hat and was starting to turn when a little girl peered around her mother's skirts, only to be pulled hastily back and the door closed. Something was definitely wrong at Crawley's farm.

Unhurriedly Peregrine made his way across the farmyard to the stables. The right side of the yard was bounded by the charred ruins of the barn that had burned the year before. The stone walls could be salvaged and the barn rebuilt, but that would be an expensive proposition, and there was little money in evidence around him.

Behind the stables, Jethro Crawley sat on a mushroom-shaped staddle stone, painstakingly repairing a broken harness with strips of new leather. As Peregrine approached, the burly farmer looked up, his hands becoming still and his eyes wary. Brusquely he asked, "What do you want?"

"I want to talk about the lawsuit you filed against the L & S Railway."

"I got nothin' to say to you." Crawley's gaze went back to the harness, and he stabbed a heavy needle through a hole punched in the leather.

"Once you didn't mind talking about the subject. You spoke to a couple of dozen landowners, convincing them that the railroad was not offering a fair price. Then there was a fire here, and suddenly you dropped your lawsuit. Without your leadership, all the other litigants settled quickly. I've been wondering why."

Crawley stood, fury in his blue-gray eyes. And under the anger was fear. "I don't have to answer that, you bastard. You and your kind have done enough to me. Now get off my land!"

"Not until you've talked to me." Peregrine's tone was unperturbed, but he watched the farmer alertly and was prepared when the man swung the harness at him, the leather straps cracking like a whip.

Smoothly he stepped aside, then grabbed Crawley's wrist in an iron grip. As the farmer tried unsuccessfully to free himself, Peregrine said softly, "It was Weldon, wasn't it?"

The farmer's resistance collapsed. He licked his lips, then asked hoarsely, "How do you know so much?"

"I made it my business to know." Releasing Crawley's wrist, Peregrine stepped back, though he did not relax his watchfulness. "Weldon is my enemy as well as yours. If you will tell me what happened, perhaps I can help you get some of your own back."

The other man sat down on the staddle stone again, his shoulders bowed and his hands restlessly kneading the leather straps. "I had taken out a mortgage, and used the money to buy my oldest son land in

Canada. Then the L & S decided to take a big chunk
o' my farm. With less cropland, it would be harder
to pay off the mortgage, so I filed a suit askin' for
fair compensation. Without it, there was a chance I
might lose everythin'.''

Crawley swallowed hard. ''Then that fellow Weldon and his secretary Kane came and suggested that
it might be better if I accepted the money offered. I
refused, o' course, I needed the money and all I
wanted was a fair price. Weldon said that was a pity.
I'll never forget his eyes—like a snake's. He never came
back here, but after that things began to happen. My
sheep were poisoned, and I lost almost the whole flock.
I had a small herd o' milk cows, and one night some
bastard shot half o' them. And then . . .'' His voice
choked, and he stopped talking.

''That was when the barn burned?'' Peregrine
prompted.

The farmer nodded. ''The barn and the granary
both. It was arson, no question, but there was no sign
of who'd done it. Most o' the corn harvest had just
been stored, which meant we didn't make any money
at all last year, but that wasn't the worst.''

A spasm of pain crossed his weathered face. ''My
second boy, Jimmy. There was something wrong with
him. He was simple, and his face was sort o' squashed,
not natural. But a sweeter-tempered lad you never met,
and he was wonderful with the animals. It hurt him
somethin' terrible when the livestock were killed. My
wife and I had always known he'd never be able to take
care of the farm on his own, so we figured we'd leave
the property to my third son, Will, who'd look after
Jimmy when we were gone. But now . . .'' He stopped
speaking, his face stark.

''Jimmy was the one who died in the fire?''

The farmer nodded. ''It has been real dry, and the
thatch on the barn went up like tinder. Jimmy heard
the plow horses screamin', and he went to get them
out. I didn't see him in time to stop him. The roof

beam caved in on him." Fiercely he shook his head, trying to deny the tears that showed in his eyes. "A few days later I got an unsigned letter suggestin' that since I have a wife and two more children at home, it would be wiser to drop the lawsuit. So I did."

The callous threat confirmed that Weldon was behind it. Peregrine felt murderous rage sweep through him, but he kept his fury tightly controlled. "Have you officially accepted the railroad's money and signed the rights over to them?"

"Not yet." Crawley spat onto the ground. "That should happen in a couple o' weeks. Then I'll get the money, though it's no more than half what the land's worth."

"Did you consider going to the law about what was done, perhaps the local magistrate or your member of Parliament?"

The other man gave him a look of intense disgust. "Sure as apples fall from a tree, Weldon's the one who had my stock killed and my barn fired, but I haven't a single damn' shred o' proof. How far do you think I'd get, accusin' a rich man like him?"

"Probably not very," Peregrine admitted. "What about selling the farm and going somewhere else?"

"I thought o' everythin'." Crawley spoke compulsively, as if needing to release what had been bottled up inside him. "But with the mortgage, I'd not get enough out of this place to start up again. Besides, this land's been in my family since good Queen Bess was on the throne—how could I run away? So I'll take the money and hope it's enough to keep goin'. It'll take years to rebuild the barns and the livestock, and pay off the mortgage. With a couple o' bad years in a row, we could still lose everythin', but I don't see any choice."

He took off his shapeless hat and ran one hand wearily through his grizzled hair. "I dunno, maybe there's somethin' else I can do, but I dunno know what. Seems like the heart went out o' the place when Jimmy died."

"Nothing will bring your son back," Peregrine said quietly, "but if you want it, I'll give you the chance to rebuild this farm to what it was, and to hurt Weldon at the same time.''

The farmer raised his head, startled, then gave his visitor a long, hard scrutiny. His features firmed up as his native shrewdness displaced the despair that had weighed him down. At length, he said just one word: ''Why?''

''Because I am going to break Charles Weldon.'' Peregrine's voice was soft and implacable. ''And you can help me do it.''

Their gazes locked and held, until Crawley said, ''What do you want me to do?''

''Sell the right-of-way to me, and I will reinstate the lawsuit against the railway. I will pay off your mortgage and give you two thousand pounds besides. Then I want you and your family to vanish, perhaps visit your son in Canada. When Weldon is no longer a threat, you can come back and start rebuilding, probably in time for next spring's planting.''

The farmer's brows went up. ''What's the catch?''

''There is a chance, slight but real, that Weldon will defeat me. In that case I'll be dead,'' Peregrine said dispassionately. ''If that happens and you dare not bring your family back here, at least you'll be able to sell the farm more easily and profitably than you can now, and can start again somewhere else.''

For the space of three heartbeats, Crawley was still. Then he laid the ox harness on the ground and stood, offering his hand. ''Mister, you've just bought yourself a right-of-way.''

As he shook the farmer's work-hardened hand, Peregrine permitted himself a smile of satisfaction. Another thread had been added to the web. Soon, very soon, it would be time to catch his prey. But first, he must remove Lady Sara St. James from Weldon's grasp.

Peregrine lifted a decanter and glanced at Lord Ross Carlisle, who sat on the other side of the gleaming mahogany table. ''I know that port is what gentlemen are supposed to drink after dinner, but I avoid it whenever possible. I'm having brandy. What is your preference? My new butler seems to have provided every known form of spirits."

Ross smiled. "Brandy will do nicely. I've never been that fond of port myself."

Peregrine had moved into his rented town house the day before, and having Ross to dine was a quiet celebration of being out of the hotel. As he poured brandy into two stemmed glasses, he reflected on the irony of the fact that in the last few weeks, he had seen almost nothing of Ross and Sara, whom he liked, but had spent large quantities of time with the man he loathed.

It was time well spent, for Sir Charles Weldon was coming to look on Peregrine as friend and trusted business associate. Under cover of "friendship," the Kafir had stalked the Englishman, learning details of Weldon's business and personal life, and what his enemy valued.

Peregrine found perverse, decadent pleasure in the fact that he could laugh at Weldon's jokes, while under the surface hatred simmered and hissed like hell's own fires. While making light, witty comments, he visualized Weldon writhing under slow, infinitely painful oriental tortures. He bought Weldon dinner at the hotel, and poured wine as he prayed that his enemy would know the ultimate bitterness of betrayal. It was all profoundly satisfying, and perhaps a little mad, but Peregrine found dark satisfaction in every moment.

Oblivious to his host's thoughts, Ross accepted his glass of brandy. "Except for not liking port, you have adjusted to English society very thoroughly." He gestured at the ornate dining room. "You seem to have been born to this."

Peregrine's mouth quirked up. "You know better than that."

"It certainly is different from your house in Kafiristan," his friend agreed. "All those people and animals coming and going as they pleased. I never did understand exactly who most of them were, or how they were related to you.''

"I didn't always understand, either. Kafir households are both hospitable and complicated, and most of those people were in no way related to me." The prince took a sip of his brandy. "Is your book going well? I haven't seen much of you lately."

Ross made a wry face. "I doubt if writing a book ever goes *well*, but progress is being made. Sorry I've neglected you, but after the first fortnight, you didn't seem to need assistance."

"No need to apologize, you're not my nursemaid. And you're correct, I have had no problems. Many hostesses enjoy having a tame barbarian in their drawing rooms," Peregrine said with sardonic humor. "Besides, I would not want to separate you from your work when the Muse is cooperating."

"It would be more accurate to say that the Muse and I are engaged in a tavern brawl, with the Muse striking mostly illegal blows. If my publisher wasn't demanding the manuscript weekly, I'd have given up by now," Ross said feelingly. "And there are distractions ahead because my mother persuaded me that it's my duty to give a ball in honor of Sara and Sir Charles. It will be held at my country place, three weeks before their marriage. The invitations haven't been sent yet, but I hope you will be able to come and stay a few days. The house will be full for the first time in . . ." He paused to consider. Then his eyes went opaque. "For the first time in a number of years."

With difficulty, Peregrine masked the elation that raced through his blood. Fate had just given him the last thread for the web. "Will the guests of honor be being staying with you?"

"Yes, along with my parents and some others." Ross chuckled. "My mother is doing most of the work, so I really have no right to complain of the nuisance."

"I'll be delighted to come and meet your parents. They live mostly in the country, don't they?"

His friend nodded. "Yes, my father is near eighty now. His health is good for a man of his years, but he prefers to avoid traveling. However, he's prepared to make the effort for Sara's sake. She's a great favorite of his."

"Lady Sara is a remarkable young woman." Peregrine's tone was carefully neutral. "I understand why she is so dear to you."

Ross's expression became serious. "Obviously you have had no success in persuading my cousin to end her betrothal."

"I have not yet given up hope of changing her mind." Idly Peregrine swirled the brandy in his glass. He had seen Sara several times at social affairs, had danced with her twice. It had been surprisingly hard to treat her as a mere acquaintance when there had been so much more between them. He had wanted to make her laugh, he had wanted to kiss her, and he wanted to finish what they had begun at Sulgrave.

If Sara wanted the same, she had shown no sign of it. She had been perfectly, sweetly polite, and as remote as if he were a complete stranger. Every inch a lady, to his regret. With irritation, he swallowed the rest of his brandy, then poured more. She was a distraction and a means to an end, no more, and he should not waste time thinking about bedding her. "I doubt that Lady Sara is deeply attached to Weldon, but I think she feels honor bound to marry him."

"That's Sara," Ross said ruefully. "Honorable to a fault. She would bend over backward to give the devil a fair hearing. If you have good reasons why she shouldn't marry him, it would be better to tell her directly so she can decide for herself."

It had never occurred to Peregrine to tell the simple truth, but after his initial surprise, he considered the possibility before discarding it. "I don't think that would work. Weldon's crimes are too appalling, too vicious—there is an English word. Heinous, I think?— too heinous for an honorable person to believe. I have been gathering proof, but so far, most of what I have is abstract, a matter of complex financial records rather than a true picture of the suffering he has caused. Not enough, I fear, to persuade your cousin to break her betrothal.''

''You're probably right.'' His friend frowned. ''Is Weldon really so dreadful? I find him disturbing, but it's hard to believe he is quite the monster you describe.''

''He is worse than you can imagine, and you have seen much more of the world than Lady Sara,'' Peregrine said bluntly. ''Even you, who have some cause to trust my word, have trouble accepting that Weldon is evil. Since that is so, how can I convince an honest innocent like your cousin?''

''I take your point, though it would be easier to believe if you were more specific about what Weldon has done,'' Ross observed. ''However, you obviously don't want to say more, and I assume you have your reasons. But about Sara—you said you have not given up hope.''

Peregrine looked into his friend's eyes and began to lie. ''I may soon have an incontrovertible piece of evidence. If so, I would like to present it to Lady Sara in the presence of you, her father, and Weldon. That way, Weldon can speak in his own behalf, and you and Haddonfield will be there to ensure that he does not try to coerce her. Will you help me?''

The other man gave a long, measuring look. ''That seems fair. If it comes to that, I'll do whatever I can to help.''

Peregrine raised his glass in a half salute. ''To Lady Sara's best interests and future happiness.'' Then he downed the rest of the brandy. He was not interested in the pallid English concept of ''fairness''; what he wanted was to see Old Testament justice visited on Charles Weldon. And one way or another, he would separate Sara from her betrothed—even if the price was Ross's friendship and Sara's reputation.

Chapter 10

"YOU DANCE VERY WELL, Lady Weldon."

As they swung in time to the music, Sara laughed up at her partner. "I'm not quite Lady Weldon yet, Charles, but soon. Are you enjoying yourself?"

"Very much." Her betrothed smiled back. He was splendidly handsome in formal evening dress, the touch of silver at his temples adding to his distinguished appearance. "It's very gracious of your cousin to give this ball for us."

"Most of the credit must go to Aunt Marguerite," Sara said. Briefly her gaze went to the tall, golden-haired figure of the Duchess of Windermere, who stood on the far side of the glittering ballroom and viewed the results of her work with calm satisfaction. Though over fifty, in the soft chandelier light she still had the beauty that had captivated a duke. Sara felt a familiar pang of regret that her own mother, who had so resembled Aunt Marguerite, was not here to see her daughter marry.

The duchess saw Sara's glance and sent a smile, which Sara returned affectionately before the figures of the waltz turned her away. "Even though Aunt Marguerite voluntarily renounced the fashionable world to stay with her husband in Norfolk, she does like re-emerging occasionally to prove that no one can entertain quite as elegantly as she."

"She does it very well," Charles agreed, clearly relishing the idea of being related to the duchess by marriage. "But you will be even better."

"If you want me to be a grand hostess, I'll do my best." Sara was pleased at how well she and Charles had been getting along in the last weeks. The tension at the beginning of the summer had melted away after she had stopped seeing Peregrine.

The music ended and partners separated. Weldon said, "What lucky man is your next partner?"

"You are *très galant* tonight, Charles," she said teasingly. "As it happens, I want no partner for this dance. I knew that by this time I would be ready to catch my breath and visit with Great-Aunt Sylvia. I haven't seen her for months."

Charles gave a mock shudder. "I will let you do that on your own. I've always found the dowager countess to be most alarming. I'll join you later for the supper dance."

"Until then." Sara smiled before turning toward the card room, where her great-aunt was likely to be found.

Her smile faded as she moved across the ballroom, exchanging greetings and accepting good wishes from other guests. She could not help but remember another ball, where Prince Peregrine had coaxed her into dancing again. Since the trip to Sulgrave, he had been all too willing to abide by her prohibition against seeing him privately. They had met casually at parties and balls, almost as strangers.

She had been grateful, of course; without the prince's disturbing presence, her normal equilibrium had returned. She had ordered her trousseau, sent wedding invitations, gone to Charles's house with Eliza to plan redecorating the girl's room, and calmly accepted her betrothed's chaste, respectful kisses when he brought her home after social functions.

But whenever she saw the Kafir, something secret and sorrowful tugged deep inside her. His behavior confirmed what she had suspected: he had made advances because she was available, and turned his attention elsewhere when she proved unwilling. Because he had taken the time and effort to guide her through her fears, she had thought there was a special friendship between them, but obviously she was wrong. As unthinkingly as a child plucking flowers, he had changed her life, then moved on. And because she had gained so much from knowing him, she had no right to feel anger or regret.

Tonight she had seen the prince only from a distance. He had arrived late and immediately been surrounded by eager women. She wondered if any were his mistresses. Perhaps all of them were; harems were popular where he came from.

She must stop thinking such things, she told herself as she stopped to greet Lord Batsford, Charles's pleasant, undistinguished older brother. Peregrine had no place in her life, and he never would. Never.

Peregrine made his way toward Ross across the ballroom, politely refusing to allow anyone to deter him from his path. Ever since arriving in England, exultation had coursed along the edges of his consciousness, but now it surfaced like a hidden river reaching for the sun. The time had come. Tonight he would strike the first direct blow against Weldon, though his enemy would not recognize it as the opening salvo of a war. Like a warrior going into battle, Peregrine felt heightened awareness, a sharpening of wits and senses that would enable him to turn whatever happened tonight to his advantage.

Ross saw his approach and came to meet him. Pitching his voice below the music and chatter, he asked, "Have you found the proof that you wanted?"

"I believe so." Peregrine studied Ross, knowing that the Englishman was one of the most unpredictable elements in what would happen tonight. He would not take kindly to the knowledge that he had been played for a fool. Well, for Ross's sake he would make the attempt to persuade her with words. "I'm going to ask Sara to come to the library and listen to what I have

to say. Give me half an hour to try to persuade her to
end her betrothal. If neither of us has emerged after
thirty minutes, bring Weldon and Haddonfield to the
library.''

Ross's golden brows arched up. ''You want to do
this now, in the middle of a ball?''

''So English, worrying about a scene,'' Peregrine
murmured. ''In fact, that is one reason tonight is perfect. With the house full of people, the principal players in this little drama will do their best to suppress
undignified reactions. Much more tidy. Besides, the
sooner this business is done, the better.''

''That I agree with. Very well, half an hour. The
library is a good choice. You should be undisturbed
there.'' Ross's eyes narrowed. For a moment, the formidable man who had survived some of the world's
most dangerous places was visible through his gentlemanly facade. ''I just hope you know what you're doing.''

Peregrine gave a brief, feral smile. ''I do.''

Then he went to find Lady Sara. The music had
started again, and she was skirting the edge of the
ballroom when he intercepted her. Tonight she wore
an amber silk gown trimmed with blond lace, and its
luxurious simplicity suited her perfectly. In the aftermath of dancing, she glowed with rosy warmth, and
the deep décolletage exposed an enticing expanse of
delicate curves.

Surprised at his sudden appearance, Sara glanced up
at Peregrine without the cool reserve that she had
maintained since Sulgrave. He caught his breath, unexpectedly moved by her closeness, and by the pleasure of once again seeing the essential Sara St. James
revealed in those clear brown eyes. Once more he
thought of a sibyl, a timeless beauty, simultaneously
wise and innocent, and he wanted her with blazing
intensity.

But now was not the time for such thoughts, for

desire had little to do with what would happen next.
"Lady Sara, I must speak with you alone."

"What . . . ?" She halted, puzzled and wary.

"I do not ask this lightly." For a moment he was
distracted by the way her burnished gold hair was
drawn back in shining waves, revealing the flawless
bone structure beneath her creamy complexion. Forcing himself back to the business at hand, he said,
"There is something very important you must know."

Her cool reserve back in place, she studied his face
before saying, "Very well. We can go out on the
patio."

Feeling her resistance, he focused his will and issued the silent command, *Come with me.* Aloud, he
said, "The library would be better. What I must say
should not be overheard by others."

Sara had sworn not to be alone with the prince again,
but his green eyes and deep voice were compelling.
And she was also curious, wondering what he could
have to say that required such secrecy. As she wa-
vered, Peregrine took her elbow.

She almost jerked away at the intensity of her reaction, for even his light, passionless touch aroused
her, reminding her why she had decided to keep her
distance. But there was nothing of the seducer about
him—heavens, what could he do during a ball in her
cousin's house?—so she allowed herself to be guided
from the room.

The library was on the opposite side of the house,
and the sounds of music and voices vanished when
Peregrine closed the door. Faint illumination came
from two lamps, and he turned up the flames before
facing her. "Perhaps you should sit down," he suggested. "What I am going to say will come as a
shock."

She sat at one end of the long leather-covered sofa,
her hands clasped in her lap. Her primness was a direct reaction to the Kafir's dark, dangerous allure. He
stood a dozen feet away, balanced lightly on the balls

of his feet like a fencer. Sara felt no physical threat, but something in the atmosphere made her uneasy, like storm clouds rolling across a dusky sky. "What is this vital issue you must speak of, Your Highness? I should not absent myself too long from a ball that is in my honor."

The silence stretched as he regarded her with brooding eyes. Abruptly he said, "This will not be easy for you to believe, but try to listen with an open mind. Lady Sara, you are betrothed to a man who is evil, corrupt in ways beyond anything you can imagine. You must not marry Charles Weldon."

Sara was so surprised that her mouth fell open. She did not know what she had expected, but it was not this. "Ridiculous!" she exclaimed. "Do you really expect me to believe that?"

"You should." There was a raw power in him that she had not seen before, and she realized that he had discarded the veneer of civilization to reveal the fierce mountain warrior. "Do you know how his first wife died?"

"Jane Weldon tripped and fell down the stairs, I believe," she said slowly. "A tragedy, but I fail to see the relevance."

"She told her husband that she was leaving him, taking Eliza, and going back to her family. The next day, she died—at her husband's hands."

Sara stared at him, feeling a stirring of anger. "This is utter rubbish. There was never talk of a rift between Charles and his wife, nor was there any suggestion that her death was anything but an accident. I will not sit and listen to your absurd accusations." She got to her feet. "I would advise you not to say such things to anyone else, or you run the risk of being charged with slander."

"Don't go yet, Lady Sara." He raised one hand commandingly. "I have just begun."

Reluctantly Sara sat down again, her hands clenched around her folded fan. There couldn't possibly be any truth in Peregrine's charges, but having agreed to listen, she supposed she should hear him out. If she could show him how wrong he was about Charles, it could prevent trouble for her betrothed.

"A housemaid heard Weldon and his wife shouting on the landing moments before the accident. Then there was a scream, and the sound of a falling body," Peregrine said. "The maid was the first one on the scene, but Weldon was gone, and his wife was already dead of a broken neck. Weldon came home an hour later, claiming he had been at his office."

Sara felt a faint, chilling finger at her nape. Could Charles possibly have been so angry that he had given in to a brief, violent impulse? Feeling disloyal for even thinking it, she asked, "If a crime was committed, why didn't the girl report it to a magistrate?"

"Because Weldon had her kidnapped and sent to a brothel," Peregrine said harshly. "After several months she died there, but not before she told another girl what had happened. I have an affidavit sworn by the second girl, but it is hearsay evidence and inadmissible in court."

"And since the original housemaid is dead, the story is impossible for Charles to refute." Sara shook her head, utterly unable to reconcile the prince's accusations with the dignified, familiar man she had promised to wed. "That is why hearsay is not evidence—there is no way of determining the truth."

"If that was the only charge against Weldon, perhaps one could give him the benefit of the doubt, but there are dozens of such incidents." He gave a deeply cynical smile. "Isn't there an English expression, no smoke without fire? Weldon is surrounded by the smoke and fire of hell itself, and I'm going to see that he burns."

Sara's eyes narrowed as his words triggered a flash of insight. "This has nothing to do with me, does it? It is about Charles. I thought you were his friend, but I was wrong. You hate him," she said softly. "Every time you and I have been alone, you have made some oblique remark against Charles. Because I would not listen, you have invented this parcel of lies. It will not work, and I will not stay here to listen to you slander an honest man.'' She stood and walked toward the door, but she had to pass Peregrine to do so.

He blocked her path and caught her by the upper arms, his clasp light but implacable. ''Yes, I hate him, but that does not mean that I am lying.'' His eyes blazed like green fire. ''Weldon is corrupt to the depths of his black soul. He is the prince of hypocrites, infinitely dangerous because he pretends virtue while performing the most despicable deeds.''

Sara's belief in her betrothed faltered briefly under the force of the Kafir's conviction. Then she shook her head. ''Charles has been a friend of my father's for a dozen years. Why should I believe your unsupported word against him?''

''When I am a foreigner, and he is an English gentleman? Indeed, why should you believe me?'' His voice dropped, became rich with intimacy. ''Don't you know the answer to that, Sara?''

His grip loosened as his hands skimmed down her arms in a sensual caress, then went around her waist. When he bent to Sara's upturned face, she tried to pull away, but he would not release her. ''Believe me, Sara,'' he said huskily. ''I am many things, most of them bad, but in this I tell the truth. Charles Weldon is evil.''

She shivered as his lips touched a sensitive spot below her ear, then made a leisurely journey down her throat. ''Weldon delights in destroying innocence,'' he murmured, the subtle touch of his breath another caress. ''I won't let you become another of his victims.''

As he kissed the juncture of throat and shoulder, his forefinger traced the curve of her ear. Sara gasped as melting sensations flowed and shifted deep inside her. How was he able to evoke such a reaction when she had not known herself capable of feeling it? From the beginning she had been aware of his mesmerizing allure, but never had it been this shatteringly strong. She felt immersed in a river of fire that dissolved her will, leaving her helpless.

"Stop doing that," she said weakly, wanting to push him away but unable to summon any resistance.

His embrace tightened, pulling her against the hard length of his body. As he stroked and shaped her back and hips, igniting wants and wishes, he said, "You wish me to stop? All you have to say is that you don't desire me."

"I—I can't say that I don't want you, but don't think that you will change my mind with kisses when words didn't work." Without conscious volition, she reached up and slid her hands around his neck. Her fingers brushed under his silky black hair before linking over the taut, masculine muscles. "And you can confuse me, but I will never be so confused that I will forget that I promised fidelity to another man."

"I know that, sweet Sara, and I value your maddening, incorruptible sense of honor," he said, his voice as soothing as his hands were not. "But though I cannot seduce you, for a few moments I want to hold you close, no matter what you believe, no matter what the future brings."

His words unleashed a rush of longing, doubt, and confusion, somewhere between dream and nightmare. The sin was in wanting one man when she was pledged to another, but she could not deny her desire. So if the sin was already committed, why not continue doing what she so much wanted for just a little while longer? Knowing that the house was full of people would keep her from losing what remnants of sanity and morality she still had. "I know this is wrong," she whispered, her eyes clouding with desire and despair, "but for just a moment more, because there can never be another time . . ."

Decision made, Sara stood on tiptoe so her mouth

would reach his, and kissed him with the fierceness that he had taught her. Her eyes closed, and her hands tightened convulsively on his shoulders at the first touch of tongues.

Peregrine had guessed at her potential for passion, but even so he was startled by her intensity. As his own desire flared out of control, he forgot why he had brought her here and what would happen soon, forgot everything but her yielding body and painful honesty. He had not been so aroused since he was a lustful boy. Ah, God, she was sweet, with all the dangerous fire of innocence. And dangerous Sara certainly was, for she dimmed his sense of mission.

The thought helped restore his control. Breaking the kiss, he guided Sara's pliant body back to the sofa and lowered her onto the leather as waves of amber silk spilled around her. Then he lay on his side next to her, their bodies meeting in a full-length embrace, one of his knees between hers.

She squirmed against him, burying her fingers in his hair and pulling his head closer as he spread one hand across the smooth, bare flesh above her décolletage. She was as sleek as her own silk but far warmer, and she shimmered with response, her breathing quick and rough. He slid her dress off her shoulder and kissed the tender curve revealed. Dancing had left her skin flavored with delicate saltiness, and a sweet floral fragrance from her loosened hair mingled with the musky scent of leather.

His hand glided under the neckline of her gown, beneath the constraints of corset and chemise, and molded the soft warmth of her breast. Her nipple instantly tightened when his fingers found and teased it, and he felt the rapid beat of her heart under his palm.

In a distant corner of his mind, he admitted that he was glad that words had not changed her mind. He had wanted an excuse to do this, and not just because passion was a surer way of separating Sara from his enemy.

He tugged her gown still lower, baring the gentle swell of her breast. Then he took the dusky nipple in his mouth, delighting as it grew harder yet under the pressure of his tongue. As Sara moaned softly, once more he came perilously close to losing himself in desire, even though he knew it was a self-indulgent mistake.

The clock in the back of his mind was warning that the half hour was almost over, and he knew that he must conceal this lovely curving breast again. In just one more moment he would . . .

The squeal of the opening door hit with the impact of icy water. They both looked up to see the horrified faces of Ross, the Duke of Haddonfield, and Sir Charles Weldon.

Chapter 11

It was a moment from hell, time suspended and saturated with emotion. Sara gave a choked cry of dismay, her slim figure going rigid as stone. Peregrine swore softly. While he had intended to compromise her, he hadn't meant her to suffer the additional shame of being discovered half-undressed. Under his breath he said, "I'm sorry, Sara."

Instantly changing from lover to warrior, he yanked her gown back into place. Then he sat up and pulled Sara to a sitting position next to him, his left arm protectively around her.

The three intruders seemed frozen by the unexpected scene. The duke was appalled and unbelieving at the sight of his virtuous daughter in the throes of passion, while Ross glowered with a fury that must be rooted in the suspicion that his friend had deliberately deceived him.

But Peregrine noted Ross and the duke only in passing, for most of his attention was on Charles Weldon. His enemy's expression of shock, disbelief, and annihilating rage was everything Peregrine had ever hoped for, and he exulted in the sight. The first blow had been struck—but not the last.

Then the moment shattered. As Ross closed the door to give them privacy, Weldon fixed his furious gaze on Sara and snarled, "You filthy, *disgusting* little slut!"

Though Peregrine could feel Sara trembling under his arm, she did not try to avoid the accusing eyes of her betrothed. "I'm sorry, Charles," she said, her voice unsteady. "I did not mean to hurt you."

Her apology inflamed him rather than mollified him. "Instead you meant to betray me behind my back." Weldon exploded across the room, his expression murderous. "My God, to think that I believed you were pure, a genuine lady. But you're just another little whore. I'm going to . . ."

Peregrine stood and stepped in front of Sara, but it was Ross who stopped Weldon, grabbing the older man's arm. "Control yourself! I don't care how outraged you are, you can't take it out on a woman half your size."

Weldon spun against the restraining grip, and for a moment seemed on the verge of attacking Ross. Then common sense put a fragile check on his madness. He glared at Peregrine, who stood only a yard away. "I told Sara to stay away from you, that you couldn't be trusted, and the little slut pretended to be shocked at the very idea of you touching her," he said viciously. "How long has she been spreading her legs for you?"

"Enough!" Ross said sharply. "I know you are shocked, but I will not let you speak of Sara that way."

Weldon shook Ross's hand from his sleeve and turned to the duke, who watched gray-faced and silent. "Your little cripple didn't know when she was well-off, Haddonfield. If she had been able to keep her legs together, I might have made her a countess some day. Fortunate that I discovered what she is in time."

"You have reason to be angry, Charles, but you are making too much of this. Sara was just kissing him. Girls on the verge of marriage are often curious about other men. That doesn't mean they will not become virtuous wives." The duke's voice was almost pleading. "There is no reason to end your betrothal because of an innocent experiment."

"*Innocent experiment!* Her dress was half off—if we had come in five minutes later, they would have been coupling! I wouldn't marry her if she was the last female on earth.'' Weldon's handsome face was distorted with malevolence. ''You'll both regret this—after I tell people what happened tonight, you won't be able to buy the doxy a husband even if you throw in your title and whole fortune.''

His seething gaze went back to Peregrine. ''I knew it was a mistake to have anything to do with a filthy savage. You're no better than an animal, not fit to be allowed near decent women.''

''Not a savage—a barbarian. Savages know nothing of civilization. We barbarians know what civilization is, though we may have a low opinion of it.'' Peregrine's tone was distinctly ironic. ''But of course a civilized, honorable English gentleman like you would know nothing of savagery or barbarism, would he?''

Weldon's blue eyes flickered, as if wondering whether the remark had deeper meanings. Then his gaze narrowed. ''To think that I did you the honor of treating you as a friend.''

''Were you treating me as a friend?'' Peregrine asked with interest. ''I thought it was my money that attracted you.''

For a moment it appeared as if Weldon would attack him, but, to Peregrine's regret, his enemy thought better of it.

''You belong in the gutter,'' he snarled. Then he spun around and stalked out of the library, slamming the door with ear-numbing force.

In the strained silence that followed, the duke turned to his daughter, who still sat on the sofa, her hands knotted in her lap. ''I am appalled by your conduct, Sara. I would never have believed that you could behave so wantonly when you were betrothed to another man. What have you to say for yourself?''

Sara flinched as if he had struck her. ''Nothing at all, Father. There is no excuse for my behavior.'' There was a tremor in her low voice. ''I'm sorry to have disappointed you.''

Ross had been standing by Sara, and as she spoke,

he put a comforting hand on her shoulder. "Don't put all the blame on Sara, Uncle Miles," Ross said. His hard stare at Peregrine made it clear what he meant.

"I do not deny that most of the fault is mine," Peregrine agreed, "though surely you noticed that Sara was not unwilling."

Ross accepted the words with cold fury as powerful as Weldon's anger and more dangerous for being controlled. There would be a reckoning between them, and soon. But not quite yet.

Haddonfield turned to Peregrine. "I hope you're pleased with yourself," he said bitterly. "For a few moments' selfish sport, you have ruined my daughter's life."

Peregrine glanced at Sara, who had not looked at him since they were interrupted. Her head turned and for a moment her stark gaze met his. In the sibylline depths of her eyes was bleak knowledge, and he knew that she had guessed that the intrusion was no accident.

Then she turned away, asking and expecting nothing of him. "The gossips will be delighted to say that prim Lady Sara is no better than she should be and deserved to be jilted, but to say that my life is ruined is an exaggeration, Father," she said, her voice under control. "It will be a nine days' wonder, half forgotten in a month. And as for marriage—I've never been sure that I wanted a husband."

"Perhaps your life isn't ruined, but your reputation is, and that's almost as bad." Haddonfield's face was set in hard, angry lines. "You'll never be received at court again. The only thing that could save you is a respectable marriage, but Charles was right—who would have you now?"

Sara's face went dead white at her father's condemnation, but she said nothing more. She had apologized for hurting those close to her, but she had too much pride to grovel or weep or beg forgiveness for what could not be undone.

Peregrine studied the taut line of her profile. If he had not seen her aching eyes, he would have thought her almost unaffected by what had happened. But he had seen, and the sight made him deeply uneasy.

This was a night of triumph, and he took avid delight in the knowledge that his enemy was suffering. The wound to Weldon's masculine pride was just the beginning; when his temper cooled, he would realize that ending his betrothal had dealt a mortal blow to his financial empire. He had not just lost a woman, he had ruined himself.

Yet now Peregrine found that his pleasure was tarnished by the sight of Sara's pain. Knowing that she was better off without Weldon, he had had no compunctions about compromising her. But he had not realized how much it would hurt her to be humiliated in front of her family, nor had he expected to be so affected by the sight of her suffering. Reminding himself that she would benefit by this night's work did not ease the strange, constricted feeling in his chest.

Sara's silk gown was rumpled and a loosened strand of lustrous dark gold hair had fallen over her bare shoulder, but she had not lost a shred of her aristocratic dignity. It was hard to decide which of his feelings was stronger: admiration for her stoic courage, or desire.

Peregrine was troubled in a way very rare to him. Yet even so, it was a complete surprise when he heard his own voice saying, ''If Lady Sara needs a husband, I would be happy to volunteer for the position.''

The stunned silence that followed rivaled the one that had occurred when he and Sara had been discovered. All three of the Britons stared at him in blank astonishment.

As startled as the others, Peregrine swiftly reviewed his rash statement. Usually he weighed decisions carefully, but sometimes he acted on pure impulse, as when he had decided to take Jenny Miller from the brothel.

Now impulse had struck again, skipping his brain entirely and going direct to his lips.

Yet even after fast, furious thought, he found that he did not regret his offer. A wife had never been part of his plans, but a wise man altered plans to suit unexpected circumstances. Marriage would help atone for what he had done to Sara, and as he watched the startled rise and fall of her breasts, he knew that marrying her would be no sacrifice.

He raised his brows, a little amused by the expressions of the other three. "When you said that Lady Sara needed a respectable marriage, Your Grace, you meant to a wellborn Englishman. While I am not that, I am very rich, which should counter some of my other failings."

The duke scrutinized his face before saying grudgingly, "I suppose you would do. If the marriage takes place soon, the gossip will die down quickly."

Ross said, a hard edge in his voice, "Is this what you've wanted all along, Mikahl?"

"No, the idea just occurred to me," Peregrine said blandly. "But now that I've thought of it, I find it appealing. Sara?"

Her voice rich with sarcasm, she said, "Your powerfully romantic proposal leaves me speechless."

Peregrine grinned in appreciation, but the duke said roughly, "You're not going to do any better, Sara. Accept him quickly, before he changes his mind."

"Better a scandal than a disastrous marriage," Ross snapped.

"It would be a mistake to decide anything tonight," Peregrine said soothingly. "Sara and I need to talk when she's had a chance to rest."

"That is the first sensible thing anyone has said," Sara replied, her tone brittle.

"May I call on you at eleven o'clock tomorrow morning?" Peregrine asked.

"Very well." She stood, tugging the gaudy engagement ring from her finger. Handing it to her father, she said, "Will you see that this is returned to Charles?" After he nodded, Sara continued, "I'm going up to my room, Ross, and I don't want to talk to anyone else tonight. Not *anyone.*" Her limp was more pronounced than usual as she crossed the library, but her spine was erect. She left without looking back.

"Uncle Miles, will you please ask my mother to take care of the guests on my behalf?" Ross asked. "I have a few things I wish to discuss with my esteemed friend."

Seeming grateful to have something to do, Haddonfield agreed, then left the room.

"You arranged that nasty little scene deliberately, didn't you?" Ross growled as soon as the door closed behind the duke. "If I didn't owe you my life, I would have already wrung your neck. Just what kind of game are you playing, Mikahl?"

"You are very quick to assume the worst. Isn't it possible that it was an accident of passion, that Sara and I were overcome by our feelings and lost track of the time?" Peregrine seemed totally at his ease, faint amusement visible on his dark face.

"No," Ross said flatly, fighting the urge to wipe the amusement off the other man's face. "That kind of accident doesn't happen to you. I've always known that you were devious, but I thought that in your own way, you were honorable. Instead you betrayed my trust and deceived me so that I became the instrument of injuring Sara. If that is your idea of friendship, may God preserve me from any more such friends."

"But the goal has been achieved," Peregrine said, refusing to be drawn. "Lady Sara is now free of a dangerous man."

"I've never liked Weldon, even less so after tonight, but I'd trust Sara to him sooner than to a scheming bastard like you." Ross took a firm hold on his raveling temper. "What you did to her tonight was unforgivable."

"It is Sara's choice to give or withhold forgiveness,

not yours." Peregrine's expression grew thoughtful. "I wonder whether she will accept my offer of honorable matrimony. My guess is that the odds are about even. What do you think?"

His flippancy about Sara's future snapped the last frail threads of Ross's control. Without warning, he swung a furious fist at the Kafir. "You bloody-minded . . ."

Luckily Peregrine had a warrior's superb reflexes, or the blow might have broken his jaw. He twisted quickly, and his shoulder took most of the impact, but before he could recover, Ross's second blow connected solidly in his opponent's midriff.

As the Kafir doubled over, Ross felt a moment's profound satisfaction in the collision of muscle and bone. Satisfaction was inevitably short-lived. Peregrine didn't bother to straighten up, just grabbed Ross's leg and jerked him off balance. Even as Ross hit the carpet with painful force, he rolled and dragged his opponent off his feet.

Both men were highly skilled in hand-to-hand combat, and they had sparred often enough to be able to anticipate each other's moves. The result was an intense, noisy, exhausting brawl. They rolled and pummeled each other back and forth across the library, smashing two wooden chairs and toppling the globe stand. Another furious exchange of blows sent Ross into a corner of the desk. A lamp tipped onto the carpet, and flames raced along the spilled oil until Ross peeled off his coat and tossed it over the blaze. As soon as it smothered, he returned to the fray with grim determination.

Peregrine avoided any blows or holds that could do serious damage, but Ross was less particular. Though he was not trying to kill, he *wanted* to harm the other man. He wanted Peregrine to feel some shadow of the pain that he had casually inflicted on Sara, and in his fury, Ross had never been more dangerous.

When both men were battered, bruised, and near the end of their endurance, Peregrine managed to pin

Ross to the floor and apply a choke hold across his windpipe.

"Enough!" The Kafir's breath came in harsh, rattling gasps. "You're never going to win, I have had twenty years' head start in fighting for my life. But if this goes on much longer, one of us will be badly hurt. I'd rather it wasn't me, and if it's you, Sara will be even angrier with me than she is now. Pax?"

Enough of Ross's fury had been burned off to make him amenable to reason. Now it was time to talk. "Pax," he agreed, his voice a hoarse rasp.

After Peregrine released him, Ross lay still for a minute, his lungs laboring for breath. He ached from head to foot, and one eye was blinded by blood trickling from a laceration along his eyebrow, but nothing seemed to be broken. Painfully he rolled to his knees, stopping when a wave of dizziness almost flattened him.

His erstwhile opponent grabbed him under the arms and hauled him to his feet, then propelled him over to the leather sofa. Ross sank gratefully back into the cushions, thinking that the damned Kafir was made of steel and weathered oak. Anyone else would be lying on the floor in a gentlemanly stupor after absorbing so much punishment.

Clinking sounds indicated that Peregrine had found the liquor cabinet. After a couple of minutes he sat on the arm of the sofa and started gently sponging the blood from Ross's face.

When the blood was cleaned off, Peregrine poured some whiskey on his folded handkerchief, then pressed it against the laceration. The stinging helped clear Ross's head, and he took the pad from the other man's hand and held it in place himself.

The Kafir had already poured two glasses of whiskey. He placed one in Ross's free hand, then settled down at the other end of the sofa. "Feel better now?"

"A little." Ross was pleased to see that Peregrine was going to have some lively bruises of his own, and even more pleased to see that his friend had dropped his maddening frivolity. Maybe now some sense could be gotten out of him. "I think it is time you were more specific about Charles Weldon's nameless vices. They will have to be impressive to justify what you did to Sara."

Peregrine slouched down, his head tilted back against the sofa, and his long legs stretched out before him. "Weldon owns a number of brothels and gaming hells, and patronizes them all," he said wearily. "His own favorite vice seems to be ravishing young virgins. He probably murdered his first wife, and he is part owner of several ships engaged in slave trading." He cocked an ironic eye at Ross. "There's more, but that should give you the general idea."

Ross was stunned into temporary silence. While he had never much liked Weldon, he had never imagined the man capable of such evil. "You can prove what you say?"

"Some of it. Not all. You can see my files if you like, though I warn you, they don't make pleasant reading."

Ross swallowed a mouthful of whiskey, welcoming its burn. Later he would want to see those files, but his friend's flat certainty was powerfully persuasive. "Are you sure about the slave trading? That has been illegal for over twenty years."

"Which is why it is very lucrative for those who still engage in it," Peregrine said dryly. "The slave ships go mainly to the West Indies and South America, where disease creates a chronic shortage of labor."

After Ross came to terms with the information, his scholar's curiosity was aroused. "How did you learn so much about Weldon?"

"I made it my business to know," Peregrine said tersely.

"That's not much of an answer. What did he do to you that makes you so determined to bring him to justice?"

"That is bloody well none of your business." Peregrine's green eyes were bright and hard as emeralds. "Now will you agree that Weldon was an unsuitable husband for your cousin?"

"You've convinced me." Ross rubbed his aching side and decided that he hadn't broken any ribs when he had crashed into the desk. "How much of this did you tell Sara?"

The Kafir tossed back the last of his drink, then rose to pour more, bringing the bottle over and setting it on the end table. "Just about his first wife's death."

"Why didn't you tell her the rest?" Ross asked. "If she knew what Weldon is like, you wouldn't have had to resort to seduction to break the betrothal. That was a despicable thing to do."

"Sara is a strong and intelligent woman, but she has led a protected life. Would she have believed that a man of her social order, a friend of her father's, was capable of such wickedness?" Peregrine hesitated, at a rare loss for words. "And it's all so . . . so sordid. I didn't want to be the one to try to explain to her just how evil men can be."

"You underestimate my cousin. Sara considers it her duty to be well-informed and is not easily shocked." Ross cautiously removed the pad from his forehead and found that the bleeding had stopped. "Why do you want to marry her? Guilt?"

"I do not believe in guilt—it is an unproductive emotion." Peregrine hesitated again. "But I do regret that Sara was hurt by what happened, even though it was necessary."

Ross sighed and handed his glass over to be refilled with whiskey. "At least in theory, marriage in this country is based on mutual affection, and for practical purposes it is until death do you part. Marrying Sara to save her from a scandal could be a disaster for both of you, especially her."

"Is this a polite English way of saying that you oppose a marriage?"

"I have grave doubts about the idea," Ross said bluntly. "Quite apart from cultural and religious differences, there is an unbreachable ethical abyss between you. About the most charitable thing I can say about your principles is that you believe that the end justifies the means."

"But of course." Peregrine raised his brows sardonically. "What other principles are there?"

"Sara believes in a higher standard," Ross said dryly. "It's called right and wrong."

"That is all very abstract. On the practical level where daily living takes place, Sara and I get along very well."

"Right and wrong aren't abstract to Sara." Ross saw from Peregrine's expression that the other man did not understand the point he was trying to make. Thank God for Sara's common sense; she would not let herself be pressured into a bad decision.

"I do have one principle," Peregrine said unexpectedly. "I try not to injure people unnecessarily."

"Not a bad principle as such things go," Ross allowed. "What bothers me is how you define what is 'necessary.' "

"Why haven't you married Sara yourself?" Peregrine asked in an abrupt change of subject. "First-cousin marriage is permitted in England, isn't it? You share the same ideas and values, and are obviously very close."

Ross ran his fingers through his disordered hair. There were several answers to his friend's question, some of which he had no intention of discussing. Choosing the most basic reason, he said, "We're too much alike. I told you that our mothers were twins, but did I mention that they were identical? As children, Sara and I both made mistakes about which mama duchess was our own. Very confusing. We grew up like brother and sister, and that is the kind of love we have for each other. In fact, I feel far closer to her than to my real brother."

"I have yet to meet your brother. Are you estranged?"

"Not exactly. Lord Kilburn is actually my half brother. He's almost twenty years older than I, and the heir to the dukedom. He and his mother's family objected to my father remarrying because more children would reduce Kilburn's inheritance." Ross shrugged. "He's already rich as Croesus, but there's no reasoning with greed. My brother keeps his distance, and I keep mine. It's better that way."

"Families seem like the very devil," his friend observed. "I count myself lucky not to have one."

Ross gave him a quizzical glance. "What about your family in Kafiristan?"

For a moment Peregrine seemed off balance. Then he said blandly, "Relatives who are five thousand miles away do not count because they can cause no trouble." He stood and stretched, wincing a little as bruised muscles complained. "I imagine that Weldon is already halfway to London, and that your guests are busy speculating about what happened under their very noses. It will be the better part of tact if I spend the night at Sulgrave. After all, it's only half an hour away."

Ross groaned, thinking of the social chaos that lay ahead. "Coward."

"True." His friend gave him a seraphic smile. "But it is also true that my absence will simplify the situation. When I call on Sara in the morning, I'll be discreet about it."

"I'll turn everything over to Mother. She'll have all of the houseguests gone by noon tomorrow, and thinking themselves privileged to be the objects of her solicitude."

Peregrine brushed his coat, restoring superficial neatness. "Am I forgiven my transgressions—not the ones against Sara, but against you?"

Ross's mouth quirked. "Does my good opinion matter to you?"

Peregrine considered. "It seems to."

Ross smiled reluctantly and got to his feet. "Then I suppose you're forgiven. But next time, why not just speak up rather than crashing around like a Greek Fury?"

"What a novel thought. It sounds quite boring." Peregrine flashed a brief smile, then left the library.

Ross sank back into the sofa, not yet ready to face the world outside. Thank God his mother was here to smooth things over. And though it had seemed unfortunate at the time, he was glad that a flare-up of gout had prevented his father from making the trip. No sense in upsetting the old boy unnecessarily.

Briefly he considered going to Sara's room to see how she was, but he discarded the idea. She had been quite emphatic about being left alone, and they had always respected each other's privacy.

He tried to imagine Sara married to his friend. On the face of it, the idea was ridiculous, but perhaps it might work. If anyone could break a wild hawk like Peregrine to the hand, it would be Sara. In her gentle way, she was every bit as stubborn as he was.

And now that Ross thought back, he realized that Sara had subtly changed since meeting Peregrine. As a girl, she had been full of bright laughter, until the accident that had nearly taken her life. It had taken discipline and indomitable will to survive and learn to walk again, and somewhere along the way, Sara had lost her capacity for joy. Perhaps, with Peregrine, she might find it again.

Chapter 12

SARA MANAGED to reach her bedroom without being observed by other guests, then dismissed her maid with the comment that she was suffering from a touch of the headache and wanted to retire early. Finally alone, she sank into the deep wing chair, drawing her legs up and pulling her dressing gown tight in a vain attempt to warm her chilled soul. She had the weak, shaky feeling common after a near-accident, and when her eyes closed, she saw horrified faces staring at her. She heard Charles's furious condemnation, and flinched away from her father's anger and disappointment.

But mostly she saw Peregrine, handsome as the devil and just as untrustworthy. He had not been surprised when they were discovered; Sara had sensed some other emotion, perhaps excitement or satisfaction, but definitely not surprise. Instantly she had known, with a certainty beyond logic, that Peregrine had arranged the interruption. Ross had looked guilty and furious as well as shocked, but it had not been Sara he was angry with. Probably Peregrine had made him an involuntary accomplice, for Sara knew that Ross would never knowingly have done anything to humiliate her.

But why in the name of heaven would Peregrine do such a thing? She couldn't believe that he would stoop to ruining her from casual malice. And while it would be flattering to think that he was madly in love with her and had arranged the scene as a desperate bid to win her, Sara didn't believe it. Peregrine had been far more surprised by his impulsive proposal than he had been by being caught kissing her.

Having made the offer, he was prepared to stand by it. But why? And God help her, what was Sara to do? While she had been attracted to him from the first, she had believed that marriage was out of the question. That had been a sorrowful thought, but it was one that she had understood and accepted.

Yet now the prince was hers for the taking, and the choice she faced was the most difficult of her life. Deciding to accept Charles had been easy by comparison, for she had had a fair idea of what marrying him would mean. But what on earth would marriage to her wild Kafir be like? Impossible to imagine.

She rubbed her temples despairingly, her fingers raking through her thick hair as she wondered what had become of the sensible person Sara St. James used to be. When she was with Peregrine, she became a different woman, one that she had trouble recognizing and didn't much approve of. She had never felt so alive in her life as in his presence, yet to marry him would surely be disastrous.

Hoping to break the circle of unprofitable thoughts before she gave herself a genuine headache, Sara wrote a short note to Eliza Weldon. After several attempts to explain, Sara settled on the simple statement that she would not be marrying Eliza's father because they had decided that they would not suit.

When Sara stopped and read her words, she realized that she would miss Eliza more than she would Charles. She would have liked to continue to see the girl, take her out for tea and shopping and confidences, but there wasn't a chance that Charles would let a ''filthy, disgusting slut'' near his daughter.

Sara picked up the pen again and wrote, *I shall miss you. Best wishes and love always, Sara St. James.* It seemed so inadequate; she bit her lip as she imagined the girl's shock and confusion at being abandoned by a woman she had already accepted as her stepmother.

Poor Eliza, an innocent victim of adult conflicts. But there was nothing Sara could do to comfort her except send this note. With luck, it would reach Eliza before her father would think to forbid the girl from receiving a letter from Sara.

It was getting cold, so Sara slid under the blankets, though she left a lamp lit. This was one night she didn't dare face the fevered uncertainties of the dark.

The next morning Sara's face and aspect were severe when she entered the small drawing room where Peregrine waited. Her reserve was a challenge, and he felt the excitement and heightened awareness that challenge always produced in him. She looked most charming in that shade of periwinkle blue, and the way her hair was parted in the center, then drawn softly back to a chignon, made him want to nibble on her ears. Perhaps there would be an opportunity for that later; he certainly hoped so.

Yes, he decided, marrying Lady Sara was one of his better impulses, and he would do whatever was necessary to persuade her of the wisdom of accepting him. But the atmosphere would have to warm considerably; she did not offer her hand or suggest that he sit down. Even the sight of his bruised face evoked no more than a lift of her eyebrows. "What happened to you?"

"Your cousin reproved me for my want of conduct," he explained blandly.

"He seems to have been very physical about it," she said with disapproval. "I trust Ross was not seriously injured?"

"He was not. We both benefited—very physical discussions are sometimes necessary to clear the air."

Chattering voices sounded right outside the door as several women walked by, and at the sound Sara tensed. "Is everyone talking about what happened last night?"

"Not yet," he said, thinking that under her surface composure, Sara was as brittle as porcelain. "I spoke to Ross a few minutes ago. Apparently Weldon left without talking to anyone. With the guests of honor and the host all disappearing from the ball, people deduced that *something* happened, but no one knows quite what. Perhaps Weldon has reconsidered and decided to maintain a gentlemanly silence.''

Sara shook her head, rejecting his offered comfort. ''Charles has a vindictive streak. The only thing that kept him from proclaiming my immorality last night was a desire to leave as quickly as possible. Half of London will know by tomorrow.''

More voices were heard, and Peregrine saw Sara tense again. ''Since the house is bustling with people breakfasting and preparing to leave, why don't we walk in the garden?'' he suggested. ''It will be private there.''

After Sara agreed, they made their escape without being stopped by any of Ross's curious guests. As they went down the marble steps that led from the patio to the lawn, Peregrine took Sara's arm. She stiffened, though she did not quite pull away. ''You're very nervous today.''

''Of course I am,'' she said crossly. ''I've never before had to discuss the possibility of marriage with a man who has ruined me, and I find the prospect taxing.''

''Perhaps, like Ross, you should assault me,'' he suggested. ''Doing so relieved his irritation considerably, and I should quite enjoy it if you did.''

She glared at him for a moment, then started to laugh. ''You really are quite impossible. What on earth am I to do with you?''

''Marry me,'' he said promptly. ''Then you can work on mending my manners at your leisure.''

''It is more than your manners that need mending,'' she said dryly, but the atmosphere was easier as they wandered through the magnificent gardens, which spanned some twenty acres and included a small, winding river. When they passed through the rose garden, Peregrine picked a white rose and presented it to his companion. "This flower reminds me of you—thorny but very beautiful, and with an irresistible scent."

Sara accepted the rose, remembering that he had given her flowers like it the day they went to Tattersall's. "You say the most outrageous things," she said, inhaling the rose's fragrance.

"It is not right to be romantic? I thought that was what women liked."

She lifted her head and gave him a level stare. "What happened last night was no accident, was it?"

Peregrine considered lying, then discarded the notion since he doubted she would believe a protestation of innocence. "No, it wasn't. As I told you, Weldon is a dangerous man. I am sorry you were distressed, but I could not permit you to marry him."

"Distressed? What a pallid word for shattering someone's life." She was not angry; her cool, ironic expression was beyond anger. "You had no right to interfere as you did."

"If you saw a child rushing out in front of a carriage, would you have no right to stop it?" As soon as he uttered the words, he knew that he had picked a poor example.

Sara's lips thinned. "That's an inappropriate and insulting analogy. I had some doubts about marrying Charles because of his domineering personality, but based on the evidence, you would be much worse."

"Do you truly regret that you will not be marrying Weldon?" He knew the answer to that question, but perhaps Sara did not.

"Don't try to change the subject," she said sharply. "The issue is not what I feel for Charles, but your contemptible behavior. What you did was wrong, no matter how noble your motives. How can I ever trust a man who is so high-handed?" Not waiting for an answer, she turned on her heel and resumed walking toward a footbridge that arched over the little river.

His long strides easily kept him apace with Sara. "I am beginning to understand something Ross told me last night," he said thoughtfully. "Your cousin said that the best that could be said of my principles is that I believe that the end justifies the means, and that you would find that unacceptable because you believe in right and wrong."

"Ross was correct," she agreed, her voice cool. "The result you wanted did not justify the means you chose to attain it."

"I thought that it did." He hesitated, choosing his words carefully because he must win her mind as well as her body. "That is a difference between us, Sara, but not an irresolvable one. I am not usually high-handed, and I do not expect you always to agree with me. If you have a conflicting opinion, I will not beat you or lock you in your room with bread and water. There will be times when you disagree with my methods, and there will be times when I disagree with your judgments. But surely we can live with the fact that sometimes we will disagree?"

Sara could do worse than marry a man who acknowledged a woman's right to her own opinions—always assuming he was sincere, which was a rather large assumption. She stopped in the middle of the small bridge and leaned against the railing, gazing at the flowing water rather than her companion. "You make that sound simple, but principles are not," she said slowly. "Differences of opinion can tear people and nations apart. And in marriage, men have the ultimate power, physically, legally, and financially. If your methods include forcing me to do things I believe are wrong, what advantage is there in my having your permission to disagree?"

"Legally a husband may have the power, but practically speaking, the situation is much more complicated. You have great personal strength, as well as a powerful family that is concerned for your welfare, and that will protect you from me, if you ever feel you

need protection. But I doubt that will be necessary—
we are talking about marriage, not war.''

"Some say there is little difference between love
and war.'' Sara turned to look at him, her voice chal-
lenging. "Why do you want to marry me? Charles was
interested mostly in my fortune and social rank. Is that
what you want, too?''

"Not particularly.'' He leaned on the railing, silhouetted against the glowing, light-drenched leaves of
the trees that overhung the river. "Wealth is a fine
thing, much better than the lack, but I have sufficient
now. If you doubt my motives, a settlement can be
drawn up reserving your fortune to your 'sole and separate use.' I believe that is the legal phrase. As to
social standing . . .'' He shrugged. "If I stay in England, it will be useful, but it is of no real importance
to me.''

"Do you intend to stay in England?'' Sara plucked
a leaf from the stem of the white rose and dropped it
in the water, then watched it whirl away. Would he
expect her to accompany him back to those mountains
at the edge of the world, to live under primitive conditions with no knowledge of the language and customs? "I'm not averse to travel, but England is my
home. I can't imagine myself in the wilds of Kafiristan.''

"Nor can I. It is a hard life and wouldn't suit you.''

Rather than being gratified, Sara was perversely irritated by the implication that she was a frail, helpless
creature. "So you will abandon me and return to your
home alone?''

He shook his head. "Perhaps I'll visit Kafiristan,
but I will never live there again.''

"You would exile yourself from your own country
and people?'' Sara said, incredulous.

"It is a hard thing to be born in a place that does
not suit one's spirit,'' he said obliquely, not looking
at her. "My birthplace was never my home. I don't
even want it to be.''

For Sara, whose spirit was as deeply rooted in English soil as any oak, it was a strange idea. Tentatively she said, "Did you know that the word Peregrine means wanderer or pilgrim?"

"I know," he said tersely.

Sara was silent for a time, thinking that his words gave her some insight into his complex nature. "Have you ever had a real home?"

"I have owned property in many places, but I don't think any of them were what you would call a home."

He glanced at her, his eyes as green as the sun-saturated leaves above his head. "I envy your sense of place. You are utterly English. I can't imagine you thriving anywhere else."

"You are right," she admitted. "Is that good or bad?"

"I don't know." He gave a faint, rueful smile. "Do you?"

"I am glad that I know where I belong, but surely I must seem boring to a man who has seen and done as much as you."

"You could never be boring, Sara," he said slowly. "You see below the surface of things. While it may not be a comfortable trait, it is an interesting one."

She turned away from the railing and continued over the bridge, wondering just what it was that she wanted from him. No one could guarantee another person happiness. Even if Peregrine should try to convince her that they would live in endless bliss if they married, she knew better than to believe him. Perhaps what she wanted was to know that he cared for her a little, enough to try to make a marriage work.

On the far side of the river, enormous efforts had been expended to make the gardens look like natural countryside, only better. After a few minutes more of silent walking, the path curved and entered a long, high wall of clipped yew. "Have you ever been in a maze?" Sara asked. "This one is at least two centuries old, probably older."

"No, I've never been in a maze. There is something very fitting about finding one now." Peregrine glanced down at her, his eyes intense. "We have been wandering aimlessly long enough. Now it is time to face the ultimate question. Will you marry me, Sara?"

Unsettled, she turned away from him again. "Before I answer, we must delve into the heart of the maze."

"I sense that there is a metaphor loose between us," he said, amused. "Or do I mean an allegory?"

Sara smiled and entered the maze, quickly whisking out of her companion's sight around a corner and leaving him to find his own way through. She and Ross had played hide-and-seek here as children, and she still remembered the correct turns.

The center of the maze was an oval clearing of short, lush grass, as soft as a living carpet. It was one of the most private spots on the estate and a favorite retreat of Sara's. This time, however, there was no relaxation to be found. She prowled the clearing, too tense to sit on the stone bench while she waited for her companion to find her.

Peregrine joined her in an impressively short time. "Are we at the heart of the maze yet?"

"Nowhere near it." She clasped her hands in front of her, trying to look composed, but her fingers twined tightly. "How can I marry a man who is in most ways a stranger, and a rather alarming one at that? For all I know, you have a wife in Kafiristan. Or a dozen wives, or concubines in half the cities of the Orient."

He shook his head, his face becoming as serious as her own. "No, Sara. I have never taken a wife, nor even considered it. While I have had mistresses in the past, there is no woman but you who has a claim on me now."

"Is that how you think of me, as an obligation to be met because you ruined my reputation?"

"No," he said calmly. "That is the advantage of my un-noble principles. I would never marry because of any abstract sense of obligation—I simply like the idea of having you as a wife.''

There was some comfort in that answer. Shifting to another subject, Sara asked, ''What about religion? I don't know what, if anything, you believe in. I was raised in the Church of England and want to be married in it. Would you object, or would that offend your own beliefs?''

''I will not be offended by an Anglican wedding ceremony.'' He regarded her with a glimmer of humor. ''As I said, the people of Kafiristan are pagans. I can talk with some understanding on Buddhism, Taoism, Hinduism, and several less-known Eastern religions, and have some knowledge of Christian theology and Jewish law as well. Twice in my life, when the alternative was to be executed on the spot, I accepted forcible conversion to Islam, but I do not consider such conversions binding.''

Startled and a little shocked by his recitation, Sara said, ''But what do you *believe?* Don't you have any kind of faith?''

''I have faith in myself, sweet Sara.'' He took two steps closer, and the familiar current of attraction pulsed into potent, irresistible life. ''And I have faith in you.''

He was so close she could touch him, and she wanted to, wanted to so much it hurt. But far more than passion, she needed understanding; she needed to feel that there existed a foundation on which a marriage could be built. Since Ross had once explained that the European concept of love was alien to Orientals, Sara doubted that Peregrine would ever speak of love, but she would settle for less. For much, much less. Softly she asked, ''What kind of faith do you have in me?''

''I believe that you will be good.'' He cupped her chin in one hand, his vivid gaze holding hers. ''I don't imagine that it will always be comfortable, but perhaps your honorable nature will improve me.''

She didn't know whether to laugh or weep. "You make me sound like some kind of medicine, to be taken from necessity rather than choice."

"Both, Sara." There was a rueful note in his voice. "You are my choice, and perhaps also my necessity."

Then he lowered his head and kissed her. At first his mouth was light, almost playful, but as she yielded, sliding her arms around him, the kiss became demanding. She responded in kind, hungry for the nourishment only he could give her. His arms around her felt so good, so right. . . .

Then she remembered why they were here, and broke away from his embrace. Nothing had been settled; it was answers she needed, not lovemaking. Her breathing unsteady, she tried to formulate questions that might elicit what she needed to know.

Before she could think of a single worthy question, he stretched his hand out to her. "Don't deny your desire, Sara." His deep voice was soft and rich, as tantalizing as the forbidden fruit of Eden. "And don't run from me. I will not harm you."

The pull he exerted was as inexorable as a river sweeping toward the sea. Involuntarily she took a step forward, then stopped. Something was wrong, for what she felt was more than desire, it was compulsion. "Stop doing that!" she burst out.

His dark brows arched. "Stop doing what?"

She stammered with embarrassment, knowing how foolish her words must sound. "Sometimes it seems as if you . . . you cast a spell over me, an enchantment that robs me of my willpower."

Rationally she knew it was impossible, but emotionally she felt that he was trying to coerce her. Perhaps he had some subtle Oriental power unknown to Europeans. "It happens whenever you want me to do something I have doubts about. I feel like . . . like a mongoose hypnotized by a cobra."

She saw that she had startled him, and briefly the magnetic pull diminished. "What a very original idea," he said, an enigmatic gleam in his eyes. "Hypnotizing people to do my bidding would be a useful skill, if it were possible. But alas, I do not think it is." As he spoke, the pull intensified, becoming stronger than ever.

Sara fought that potent attraction. To yield and go into his arms would be to give up her ability to choose, because once he embraced her, she would be lost. "Why do you want to marry me?" she asked again, shifting her eyes because his gaze weakened her resolve. "Me in particular, rather than anyone else? If not for money, social position, or guilt, is it because you want an English wife and I am convenient?"

"You are missing the most obvious reason of all." Lightly he placed his hands on her shoulders. "I want to marry you because you are you, unique and fascinating, unlike any other woman I have ever known. Isn't that reason enough?"

Then he drew her to him, and her resistance crumbled and vanished like dust in the wind. Before when they kissed, her sense of honor and obligation to her betrothal had protected her. But now that obligation was gone, and there was nothing to save her from her own dangerous longings.

Wherever he touched, her body sang in response and found echoes throughout her whole being. And while he was not offering love, did his words not mean that he cared, at least a little? Surely that would be enough?

"In the language of Genghis Khan, the word *sira* meant silk. *Sira* Sara—silken Sara," he breathed as his lips drifted from her temple to her hair. "Like the finest silk, you have a subtle, sensuous beauty that shimmers with hidden fire."

He caught her lobe teasingly between his teeth, not hard enough to hurt. The delicately judged pressure made her shiver in response, and she turned her face, seeking his mouth with hers and finding it. Her eyes closed, and her world narrowed to the hot, moist touch of tongues and teeth, of breath and taste, depths and sliding surfaces. Dimly she was aware that he was bringing her gently to the ground, lowering her onto the soft, sun-warmed turf, but reality was the dark fire of his kiss.

He warmed her even as he blocked the sunlight, lying beside her, his hard body half over hers. His hands roamed over her, deft and knowing, leisurely in their knowledge. Even through her heavy clothing, his touch aroused her. She arched her breast against his palm, wanting to feel him on her bare flesh as she had the night before. But this dress was not so easily defeated as her ball gown, and his questing hand roved lower, from breasts to waist to hips, an endless caress that roused and tantalized.

When he first touched where her thighs and abdomen joined, she flinched, momentarily grateful for the protection of her clothing. Then the warmth of his hand melted away her disquiet, as answering warmth slowly flowered inside her, and she rubbed against him like a cat being petted.

He raised her skirt and petticoats, and she felt almost naked with only the sheer muslin of her drawers between his questing hand and her yearning flesh. The delicate fabric added a rustling sensuality as he caressed her, massaging her calf, her knee, moving ever upward.

When he reached the exquisitely sensitive inside of her thighs, she gasped with fearful pleasure, breaking the kiss in her need for breath. His broad palm came to rest between her legs, motionless while she became accustomed to the intimacy. Then he began rotating his hand in a slow circle. Her breathing roughened as her inchoate longings began to focus into a swirl of sensation beneath his palm.

"You like that, don't you, sweet Sara?" he murmured. He shifted from general pressure to a delicate, more specific exploration, his fingers searing through the thin muslin.

She pulsed against him in wordless answer. When the stroking ended, she almost cried out at the deprivation before realizing that he was only pausing to untie the ribbon that fastened her drawers around her waist. She knew she should protest, but instead she shamelessly raised her hips to help, no longer knowing or caring what was proper, or what the consequences might be.

The air was cool on her heated skin when he tugged the flimsy garment off. Shyness was not yet gone, and she tensed when his fingers skimmed across the subtle, satin curve of her belly, then traced a path through the soft curls to the mysteries below. When at last he touched her bare flesh, she was startled and embarrassed at the moist heat of her response.

He held her close with one encircling arm. "Relax, sweet Sara, relax," he whispered. "Your body was made for love. Let me teach you."

At first she was unbearably sensitive, fearful of such intimate invasion. But he knew her body better than she did herself, knew exactly where and how to touch, easing her disquiet even as he inflamed her senses.

She was aware of his soothing voice, but not the words he uttered, was aware of the scratchy feel of his wool coat against her cheek, of the subtle, musky male scent of him in her nostrils. Her hips began moving involuntarily, and her breathing was ragged, desperate, as waves of need threatened to drown her.

"Yes, Sara, yes. Yield and be free." His voice was husky and uneven, and she felt a hot, hard bulge where her leg pressed against him. The last of her inhibitions were dissolved by the knowledge that he was also aroused by her. She lost control of her body entirely, crying out as shattering urgency overwhelmed her. She was falling, falling, frightened yet joyous.

In the aftermath, she felt as if she had been fragmented and was only slowly being reassembled. She lay on her side, and Peregrine held her against him, one hand cradling her head while he whispered gently in a language she did not understand. His other hand still rested on her, calming the heady throbbing of her most private parts.

She raised her head to look at him, struggling for a measure of composure. "That is what you wanted to teach me?"

"That was only the beginning, silken Sara, the first step on a road with no end." He smiled, unsteady brilliance in his eyes, and began caressing her again.

She had thought her body was sated, but he knew better. Under his expert touch, tendrils of pleasure began to coil deep inside her, first slowly, then with growing intensity. Her eyes drifted shut in blissful, wondering appreciation.

As he lowered her to the yielding turf, she heard the brushing sound of fingers manipulating fabric and buttons. Then he touched her again, his fingers sliding inside her, then spreading the delicate folds of flesh. She should have known what was happening, but she was too dazed, too disoriented by the newness and the pleasure to really understand.

Sara's discovery of her capacity for rapture resonated within Peregrine, touching chords of wonder he had long forgotten or had never truly known. When she gazed at him, warm with wanting, delicious in her openness and vulnerability, she touched his spirit as deeply as she kindled his body.

He reacted with primitive male possessiveness, overwhelmed by the irresistible need to make her his own. Intimacy was not something Sara would give or accept lightly, and if she would be his lover, she would also be his wife. He wanted her, by all the gods that men worshiped, he wanted her, and her response was irrefutable proof that she also wanted him.

He separated her legs and positioned himself between them. Though he yearned to plunge heedlessly into her sweet body, he restrained himself. His eyes closed as all his iron discipline focused on maintaining a fragile curb on unruly desire. While it was impossible to eliminate pain entirely, he pressed against her with slow care to minimize her discomfort.

The implacable pressure shattered Sara's desire, and she cried out, as much in shock as discomfort. Her eyes flew open. Above her, his dark face was sweat-sheened, and his breath came in rasping gulps. She shook her head, wanting to say no, not now, not yet, but her voice had vanished in her confusion. She caught at the hard arms braced around her, but she had no strength, and he was too deep in his own needs to notice her feeble resistance.

Abruptly the frail membrane sundered, and he slid into her moist, welcoming depths. For him, the sensation would have been paradise if he had not felt the spasm of pain that moved through Sara. "I'm sorry," he said raggedly, his lips near her ear. "There was no way that could be avoided."

His supporting arms shaking with strain, he ordered himself to be still until she adjusted to the feel of having him inside her. Though he had never done it before, he knew the technique for initiating an innocent; when she was more relaxed, he would begin to move, first slight, almost indiscernible strokes, then deeper and deeper as he led her into the dance of intimacy. But restraint proved impossible. He trembled with need, his control disintegrating until with a groan he involuntarily thrust deeper.

She made a raw, choking sound, her whole body going rigid as she whispered a tormented, "No!"

In a distant part of his mind, he heard and understood her protest, and knew that he should stop. But he could not, for passion had splintered his prized discipline, and his need was far greater than his ability to control it.

Ironically, when she twisted away in a futile gesture of rejection, her movement was the stimulus that sent him over the edge into pounding, shuddering oblivion. But even the chaotic pleasure was not strong enough to eradicate his sudden anguished knowledge that this was disaster for both of them.

As reason returned in erratic patches, he rolled to his side and laid his face against Sara's, feeling her silken cheek against his. She was shaking in his arms, and he guessed that she was crying. ''Damnation,'' he swore softly, as he gathered her closer and began stroking her back and neck. ''I'm sorry, Sara. That was badly done.''

Grimly he realized that it was an open question which of them was more upset. Because he had been drugged with desire, he had made an appallingly wrong assumption about her willingess, and while he did not think the result was quite rape, there had been a good deal less than full, informed consent on Sara's part. He had wanted to please her. Instead he had given her an unpardonably clumsy introduction to the delights of the flesh. Even as an inexperienced youth, he had never performed so badly.

He was furious with himself for what he had done to Sara, but even more furious over his ruinous loss of control. Though he had not had a woman for months, his roving life had often required lengthy periods of celibacy, so there was no excuse for the heedless, selfish passion he had just exhibited. Passion should be a man's servant, not his master, and being overwhelmed by it was profoundly disturbing.

His whole life had been built on discipline, on absolute focus. That was what had brought him so far; without it, he would be nothing. Literally nothing, for he might have died a hundred times over if it had not been for his finely honed, invincible will.

Sara stirred, and he clamped down on his bitter self-reproach. There would be time enough for analysis later; now he must try to make amends for his weakness. He lifted his head, wanting to see her face. ''Sara?''

He thought she would be upset, perhaps distraught,

and was prepared to comfort her, to apologize, to soothe her distress.

But her dark eyes were dry, and when he saw her diamond-cold sibyl's gaze, he knew that the situation was far worse than he had thought. The slim woman in his arms, who had at first yielded with such sweetness, had been transformed into one of the greatest challenges of his life.

Chapter 13

SARA SHOULD HAVE looked fragile and helpless lying on her back within the circle of Peregrine's arm, but she did not. Her quiet voice cutting with the force of a whiplash, she said, "Having compromised me, did you decide to finish the job of ruination so I would have no choice but to marry you?"

"Nothing so definite as a decision was involved." He sat up, thinking wryly that Sara might be innocent, but she was nobody's fool or victim. A lesser woman would have been weeping, ripe for soft words and reassurance, but Sara was ready to take his unworthy head off. "You might find this useful," he said, offering her his handkerchief. Then he turned away while she blotted the small amount of blood and put her drawers on again.

After Sara had adjusted her clothing, she said in a clipped voice, "Are you saying that what happened was an accident? I thought that you are not a man who permits accidents."

He knew beyond doubt that if he said one wrong word, she would refuse to marry him, and be damned to the consequences. And while it was true that he didn't need a wife—in fact, acquiring one would surely be disruptive—the idea of losing her was quite intolerable.

Uneasily he realized that she was far too intelligent and perceptive to let her judgment be blurred by easy apologies, so he would have to undertake the far more difficult task of honesty. He reached over and took

Sara's hand. "What happened was not an accident, but a mistake. Because your body was ready for love, I thought, wrongly, that your emotions were, too."

Her fingers tensed under his. Part of her wanted to snatch her hand away while the rest of her wanted to slide into his arms, to beg for reassurance that everything would be all right.

It was not physical pain that had pushed her almost to the breaking point, for there had been little of that. But she had experienced a rapid and upsetting transition from wondrous joy to being overpowered by his fierce male strength. She had hated that feeling of helplessness—yet here she was, seeking comfort from the man responsible for her distress.

Quietly he continued, "I *wanted* to believe you were willing, but I was wrong, and for that I am profoundly sorry."

Reluctantly she met his gaze, fearing that she would find veiled triumph. Instead she saw remorse and self-recrimination, and the sight disarmed much of her anger.

Considering how wantonly Sara had behaved, she could not blame Mikahl for believing that she would withhold nothing, but she was furious with herself for allowing desire to destroy her will and sense. Even more infuriating was her suspicion that he had deliberately taken advantage of her confusion to seduce her so that she would have to marry him. It was one thing to be wooed, quite another to be coerced.

But perhaps her worst fears were wrong; if she was reading him correctly, he was offering her the fragile, painful gift of vulnerability, for he was not a man who would easily admit or accept error in himself. Wanting to meet him halfway, she said hesitantly, "I did not really know what I wanted, so it is not surprising if you did not know what I wanted either."

"But it was my responsibility to know. I wanted it to be right for you, and I failed." He sighed and turned his head so that she saw only his taut profile. "Passion

makes fools of men, though it has never happened to
me before. Quite simply, I lost control because I desired you too much.'' A muscle jerked in his cheek.
''I think I hurt your spirit more than your body, and
that kind of injury is the hardest to heal. I wish that
my error could be undone, but it cannot. Have I alien-
ated you beyond forgiveness, Sara?''

She sensed that he would have sooner confessed to
murder than loss of control. From her own experience,
she knew that people were often most inept where they
cared the most. Perhaps, God willing, that was the
case here. Her fingers tightened on his. ''Not quite,
though it was a near thing.'' She smiled faintly. ''You
didn't fail entirely. Up to a point, it was . . . very
right.''

''You have a generous nature.'' He faced her again,
his thumb restlessly stroking her palm. ''Will you
marry me, Sara? In spite of my mistakes?''

Quite coolly, almost as if she were outside her body,
Sara considered the situation. In his way, she believed
he was sincere, but she also believed that whatever
impulse was driving him to offer marriage was a fleeting one. If she accepted him, she would pay a high
price for whatever joy she found, for the odds were
overwhelming that someday he would tire of England
and Sara, and leave them both.

Yet because he desired her enough to lose some of
his cherished control, and because she hoped that that
loss meant that somewhere in his heart was a frail
spark of caring that could be nourished into a flame,
she took a deep breath and said, ''Yes, I will marry
you.''

In the silence that followed, she heard a thrush
throwing its heart to the heavens in song. Then Mikahl
gave her a smile that took her breath away.

''I am so very glad.'' He did not kiss her, but
reached out with his free hand to brush back a strand
of fallen hair, the back of his hand caressing her cheek.

"I cannot promise that I will make you happy, but I swear that I will try."

"Trying is the most one can ever do." That was not a very romantic thought, Sara ruefully acknowledged to herself, but romance was singularly lacking in this odd courtship.

"How soon can we be married?" After a moment's hesitation, he added, "For practical reasons, the sooner the better."

Sara supposed that the chance that she had conceived today was slight, but given nature's perversity, it was not a gamble she wanted to take. "It is possible to marry immediately with a special license, but that would seem scandalous," she said, thinking aloud. "Three weeks would be best—that is the length of time it takes to read the banns."

"Excellent." Lithely he got to his feet, then took her hands and lifted her easily to hers. "Shall we go to the house and break the news to your relatives? I realize that it is a little late to do the proper thing and ask your father's permission, but I'm willing to go through the motions if you think that would help appease him."

Sara bit her lip, considering. "I think it will be better if I speak to him alone."

His dark brows arched. "Are you sure?"

"I'm sure," she replied. "I don't know what mood my father will be in today." Having Mikahl at her side was a tempting thought, but if the duke was still angry, there might be an unpleasant scene. And Sara did not want to enter marriage with her husband and her father at daggers drawn.

From his expression, she suspected that her new betrothed had guessed her motives, but he said only, "As you wish."

"Come for dinner tonight," she suggested. "By then, all the guests will have left, and there will be just family here."

"In other words, all the fur will have flown and the

feathers settled?'' He gave her a teasing smile. ''I promise that I will be on my very best behavior.''

''Don't overdo it,'' she said, an answering smile tugging at her lips. ''Otherwise no one will recognize you.''

He pulled on her hands, bringing her close to his chest. ''As long as you recognize who I am, sweet Sara.''

Mikahl bent for a kiss, his green eyes laughing. As she lifted her face, Sara knew she could never forget him. Even if he vanished in a puff of smoke at this very instant, he was already etched on her heart and soul for all time.

Since anyone seeing her rumpled and grass-stained self would have no doubts about what she had been doing, Sara took great care to slip into her room unobserved. She seemed to have spent quite a lot of time sneaking around lately. And to think that she had always led such a blameless life.

Without ringing for her maid, she changed to a more presentable gown and repaired the damage to her coiffure, then went off to break the news to her family. She was relieved to find that the other houseguests had left; it was quite enough to be facing her relatives without also facing the world. Characteristically she decided to start with her father, since that would be the most difficult interview.

The Duke of Haddonfield was in the library writing a letter, and he greeted his daughter with the same remote civility he would have given a stranger.

Uneasy at his expression, Sara halted just inside the door. ''Father, I've decided to accept Prince Peregrine's proposal.''

''I should hope so,'' he said brusquely. ''Marrying him is the only way to repair the damage you've done to your reputation.''

His gaze strayed to the sofa, where he had seen her writhing shamelessly the night before, and Sara flushed as she guessed his thoughts. Evenly she said, "I'm not marrying him to save my reputation, but because I want to."

Her father shrugged. He seemed to have aged twenty years since the night before. "Why are you bothering to tell me? You are of age and don't need my permission, and you've shown precious little respect for my wishes."

Sara's hands clenched, the nails digging into her palms. She should have accepted Mikahl's offer to come with her, for this was worse, much worse, than she had expected. "I was hoping for your blessing."

"It was your marriage to Charles Weldon that had my blessing." His mouth twisted bitterly. "But I will give you away at the wedding. Not to do so would cause talk."

For a hurt, angry moment, she considered rejecting his grudging offer, but the scandal would be much greater if he didn't attend her wedding. "We are going to marry in three weeks, as soon as the banns are posted."

Her father made a vague motion with his hand. "Let my secretary know the details of place and time, and I'll be there."

For a moment Sara teetered on the brink of tears or flight. Instead she swallowed, then crossed the room and knelt beside him. "I have not lived up to the standards you taught me," she said softly. "But you are my only father as I am your only child. You are angry, and you have the right to be, but please don't let us be estranged over this. I need you too much."

For the first time, his bleak gaze met hers. "You don't need me, for you have your mother's strength. When she died . . ." He sighed and glanced away. "I am not so much angry at you as at the repercussions. Perhaps this will turn out for the best, at least for you. I just don't know."

Puzzled, she sat back on her heels. "What do you mean?"

"Pray God you'll never find out." After the cryptic comment, he touched her hair for a moment. "Be off now. I will draft a new betrothal notice for the newspapers."

Sara felt troubled as she left the library. She had expected anger, and instead found a desolation that seemed somehow inappropriate to what had happened. Perhaps her father was regretting the loss of Weldon's friendship, for after last night things would never again be the same between the two men. Still, the way he had spoken at the end gave her hope that the duke would accept Mikahl in time.

Next she went in search of Ross and Aunt Marguerite. As she expected, her cousin was in his office, which had originally been a sitting room attached to his bedroom. Now Ross used it for his writing, so books, papers, and souvenirs of his travels lined the bookshelves and occasionally spilled to the Persian carpet.

Ross pushed his chair back from the desk when Sara entered, his brown eyes, so much like hers, scanning her shrewdly. He knew her better than anyone, but if he guessed what mischief she had gotten into in his garden, he didn't comment. Instead he stood and crossed the room to give her a much-needed hug. "Been a difficult day, little cousin?"

Her head against his shoulder, she nodded wordlessly, almost trembling with relief now that she could let her guard down. Strange that she was always uneasily aware of Mikahl's strength, while with Ross, who was equally tall and strong, she felt only comfort and protection.

He ruffled her hair, then released her. "Have you decided what you are going to do?"

"I'm going to marry him."

He regarded her gravely. "Are you sure that is what you want to do? Scandals can be ridden out—don't do something you'll regret just because a few people will talk."

Sara began to drift around the room. "Perhaps it is a mistake to marry him." She picked up a small brass figurine of an Indian goddess, a miniature study in sensuality, then set it down after a brief study. "But— I'm sure it would also be a mistake *not* to marry him."

"I see." Ross perched on the edge of his desk, his arms crossed on his chest. "Are you in love with him?"

"I don't know." An antique Venetian mirror hung on the wall, and she gazed into it, thinking that the words "fallen woman" ought to be written in scarlet across her forehead. But she appeared much as she usually did. She shifted her gaze to Ross's reflection, which was easier to address than his actual face. She wanted him to understand, and after a moment she thought of the one example that would explain everything. Haltingly she said, "I think that now I understand about you and Juliet."

A spasm of pain crossed his face so swiftly that Sara almost missed it. Full of remorse, she spun around, wishing she could retract her words. "I'm so sorry, Ross— I should never have said that. It's been so long . . . I didn't know that you still felt so strongly . . ." She stopped, wretchedly sure that she was making matters worse.

The moment of self-revelation over, Ross's expression was impassive again, though she saw the tension in his lean body. "That's an understanding I wouldn't wish on anyone," he said dryly, "but if that is how you feel, I suppose there is nothing you can do but marry him. And unpredictable though Mikahl is, I think you are better off with him than with Weldon."

Sara frowned. "Ross, do you know why Mikahl is so set against Charles?"

"Didn't you ask him?" her cousin asked, surprised.

She colored and looked away. "I—never got around to it. There were so many other things to—discuss. He did admit that what happened last night was no accident. I assume that he misled you into helping him?"

Ross winced. "I'm afraid so. I'm sorry, Sara."

She absolved him with a wry smile. "If you hadn't cooperated, I imagine he would have thought of something else." With a pointed glance at the cut above her cousin's eye, she added, "What did he tell you after you two had your 'very physical' discussion last night?"

"He claims that Weldon owns a number of unsavory and illegal businesses," Ross said carefully. "If true, your former betrothed is a hypocrite of massive proportions, and you are better off without him."

Sara's brows drew together. "The only unsavory, illegal businesses I can think of are brothels. Surely Charles could not be involved in anything like that!"

"Apparently he is," Ross said. "In a way, I can see how it would be easy. You and I both had the same reaction—that it is unthinkable for a gentleman to soil his hands with such sordid matters. Which is why a gentleman who is so inclined might get away with almost anything."

Sara shook her head, sickened by the very idea. "Perhaps, but I just can't believe that of Charles, who is so proper. Look how horrified he was to find me kissing another man."

"That could be hypocrisy as easily as propriety." Ross's voice softened. "Don't torture yourself wondering if it is true—you have quite enough things to worry about. When and if you decide you want to know more, ask Mikahl for the details. Devious though he sometimes is, I've found that he will usually answer direct questions."

It was very rare for Sara to refuse to face unpleasantness, but this time she seized her cousin's suggestion gratefully. Later she would be strong enough to evaluate what Ross had told her, and to wonder how Mikahl could have learned such things, *if* they were true. But not just yet. She smiled ruefully. "Who was it that said we should be careful what we wish for, because we might get it? And I was foolish enough to wish for a little more excitement in my life!"

Ross grinned. "You'll certainly get excitement with Mikahl."

"If worse comes to worst and he abandons me in favor of an Oriental harem, I'll accept your invitation to move in here and keep house for you."

"With your cats and my Turkish poetry?"

"Exactly." They both laughed, but Sara took comfort from the knowledge that with her family behind her, she would never be wholly in her husband's power. Less comforting was the knowledge that she had agreed to marry a man she did not fully trust.

Aunt Marguerite also proved to be supportive. The Duchess of Windermere was in the kitchens, ruthlessly using her charm to bully the kitchen staff into reorganizing the pantries. She looked up when Sara entered and waved a breezy hand. "Ross's housekeeper does a decent enough job, but a kitchen is never properly run in a gentleman's household. You would not have believed the state I found the stillroom in."

"Show me," Sara suggested, unable to suppress a smile. Of the Magnificent Montgomery twins, Marguerite had been the outgoing one, Sara's mother, Maria, the quiet one. Ross had told her once that his staff looked forward to his mother's visits, because it made them feel important to be the objects of a duchess's attention. And under her imposing manner, Marguerite had the warm heart and practical nature of a Scottish housewife.

When they reached the stillroom, Marguerite closed the door, then regarded her niece with bright-eyed anticipation. "Well, are you going to tell me what's going on around here?" she exclaimed. "Ross only gave me the barest outlines—there's no getting anything out of that lad when he's being discreet. Are you going to marry that glorious barbarian?"

"Yes," Sara said, thinking the description was a good one. "Do you think I'm mad?"

"Probably, but no more than any young woman in love," her aunt said cheerfully. "And if you must make a fool of yourself over a man, better a rich one than a poor one. Besides, if the truth be known, I like him much better than I do Charles Weldon."

Preferring to ignore the comment about love, Sara said, "He's coming for a quiet family dinner tonight. I imagine he and Father will talk of settlements and such things."

"If he can survive that, he's made of strong stuff." The duchess bit her lip. "You and I must sit down and make a list of everything that needs to be done, such as returning all the wedding gifts that were sent for you and Charles."

Sara groaned. "I hadn't thought that far. Why does high drama always end in tedious details? Think of all the gifts that were monogrammed with a *W!*"

"Don't feel too guilty about that—there are two other important weddings coming up this season where the initial is *W*, so the gifts will find a new home soon enough."

Sara laughed. "You're outrageous."

"Of course," her aunt said placidly. "That's why Windermere married me. Everyone said it wouldn't work, that we were too far apart in age and social position, and that I was a fortune-hunting baggage, but here we are, thirty-five years later." She sighed a little. "The only regret either of us has is that we won't get another thirty-five years together."

Sara went back to her room feeling considerably cheered, because she had had ample opportunity to see that the improbable marriage of the Windermeres was a successful one. Perhaps Sara and her mad Kafir would do equally well.

Reality intruded in the shape of her maid, Hoskins. Sara was wearily letting her hair down, preparing to take a nap, when the maid burst into the room.

Hoskins was about the same age as Sara, but her acid disposition had carved premature lines around her mouth, and she looked much older. "Lady Sara," she said, her voice quivering with indignation. "They're saying belowstairs that you're going to marry that foreigner, but I can't believe it, not when you're betrothed to a real gentleman like Sir Charles."

Sara swiveled around to face the servant. "Rumor is correct in this case. Sir Charles and I ended our betrothal, and I am going to marry Prince Peregrine instead."

Hoskins gaped for a moment. Then she said viciously, "I would never have believed that a mistress of mine would disgrace herself and me by marrying a filthy heathen nigger."

"How dare you!" Sara gasped. For a moment her vision darkened with pure rage; she had not been so angry since she had learned how the governors of an orphanage were abusing the children in their care. Then she rose to her feet, her hand tightening around her hairbrush like a weapon. "You won't have to worry about the disgrace because I am discharging you, effective this instant. I won't have an evil-minded bigot like you in my household."

"I wouldn't work for a slut like you!" Hoskins snapped back. "Fine clothes and a fancy name don't make a lady. That randy foreigner is only interested in one thing, and only a lustful bitch would want to give it to him. The very idea is disgusting to a decent female. But I'm not leaving till I get what's owed me— I know my rights."

The curse of a fair mind was that even fury couldn't make Sara forget simple justice. Wrapping herself in the icy dignity of generations of noble St. Jameses, Sara said, "You can collect your belongings at Haddonfield House the day after tomorrow. The butler will have the money owed you, plus an extra month's pay and a letter of reference attesting to your skills, though not your disposition. Now get out of my sight!"

''With pleasure. Plenty of *real* ladies have tried to hire me away from you before.'' An expression of malevolence crossed the maid's face. ''They must figure that if I can make a plain little cripple like you look good, I can do anything.'' Satisfied that she had had the last word, she whisked out the door.

Sara sank onto the stool, shaking all over. There was a remarkable similarity between what Hoskins had just said and Charles's words of the night before. In a protected life, she had seldom been exposed to such virulence, and it was not pleasant to know that soon others would be saying the same things. Though on the whole, Sara decided, better behind her back than to her face.

It was a salutary lesson on the dark currents that lay just beneath the surface of daily life. A man like Mikahl could be judged and condemned for the crime of being foreign, an English lady in the throes of passion could throw morality to the winds, and a respectable servant could have a mind that would shame a guttersnipe. Perhaps it was even possible that Charles Weldon was a whoremonger, though Sara did not really believe that.

As Sara's anger cooled, she realized with wry amusement that Hoskins's vituperation implied that the maid was female enough to notice Mikahl's potent masculinity, and prudish enough to be horrified by such interest.

Sara smiled a little as she resumed brushing her hair. By his mere existence, her betrothed sowed disruption in the minds of modest English womanhood. Certainly he had disrupted Sara's orderly life. But at least her sense of humor was still working; she would surely need it in the weeks to come.

The family dinner that evening went smoothly. Sara's father was somber, but Ross and Aunt Marguerite had enough aplomb to carry the conversation, and Mikahl, as promised, was on his best behavior. Sara found herself watching him with extra intensity, impressed at how well he blended in with her family, though there was a suggestion that he did not take aristocratic English customs quite seriously. Well, that was all right, neither did she, though such customs were undeniably part of her.

As expected, her betrothed and the duke disappeared after dinner for a time to discuss marriage settlements, and when they emerged, the duke's expression was a bit lighter than it had been. Sara hoped that meant that the men would deal comfortably with each other, even if they would never be friends.

After tea was served, Mikahl suggested to Sara that they take a turn on the patio. She agreed, feeling a need to talk to him privately. Outside, the pale moonlight reminded her of the night on the balcony when he had coaxed her into dancing. It seemed a long time ago, though it had only been a few weeks. She was a different woman, but he was the same lithe and fascinating man. That night she had thought of him as a dangerous distraction; now he was her future.

Putting her serious thoughts aside, she remarked, ''Aunt Marguerite said earlier that if you could survive this evening, you were made of strong stuff. I gather that you and my father reached some kind of truce?''

He chuckled and tucked her hand under his elbow as they strolled the length of the flagstone patio. ''He resents me deeply, but is too well-bred to be insulting. I believe that fathers always resent the men who take their daughters away.''

It was a tactful way of glossing over her father's lack of enthusiasm for the marriage. Deciding a change of subject was in order, Sara said, ''I suppose that now I should call you Mikahl, like Ross does. Unless there is another name you prefer?''

''That's fine. I have acquired a number of names over the years, but Mikahl Khanauri has been with me the longest.''

''Mi-kahl Khan-*aur*-i,'' she repeated, trying to duplicate the unfamiliar vowel sounds. "That's close to the Christian name 'Michael,' which I've always liked." She gave him a teasing smile. "Traditionally, Michael is the archangel who leads the legions of the Lord."

He laughed. "Obviously it isn't a very appropriate name, for no one would ever mistake me for any sort of angel."

As she studied his rugged face, she couldn't agree. "Don't be too sure. Michael is God's avenging arm, the patron saint of warriors. Surely warrior angels are a rowdier lot than the ones who do nothing but sing and pray and think good thoughts?"

He gave her an odd glance. "Perhaps it isn't such a bad name, if rowdiness and vengeance are allowed."

They had come to the far end of the patio, out of sight of the people in the house, and he stopped and turned to face her. "I like being betrothed, because now I can look at you as much as I like and be considered romantic rather than rude," he said, his gaze moving over her with leisurely enjoyment. "You look particularly delectable tonight, sweet Sara."

The warmth in his eyes made her feel shy, though undeniably flattered. "If so, it's a miracle. I discharged my maid this afternoon, and she left things in a rather chaotic state."

He raised his brows. "Dare I ask why you discharged her?"

She hesitated, realizing that the subject would have been better left unmentioned. "She was impertinent."

"Which means that she probably said something appalling about your choice of husbands. Doubtless it is better if I don't know just what it was."

"Doubtless." Sara's tone was repressive.

His brows drew together consideringly. "Do you have someone in mind for the position? If not, I know of a young woman who might be suitable. After a difficult start in life, she is now learning to be a lady's maid. While she has no formal experience, she is intelligent and willing.''

''In what way was her life difficult?''

''It isn't a pretty story.'' Mikahl studied Sara's face as if wondering how she would react. ''Her father sold her to a brothel when she was little more than a child, and she spent several years there.''

''I see.'' Sara was silent for a moment, thinking that this had been the strangest day of her life. Yesterday at this time, she had still been respectably betrothed to Charles. In the twenty-four hours since, she had been disgraced, seduced, re-betrothed, and now she was being offered a prostitute for a lady's maid. Her stomach knotted unpleasantly as she wondered how Mikahl had made the girl's acquaintance; could he possibly be trying to install a mistress in his wife's household? No, not that, she decided, but she would really rather not know any more. ''Send the girl to see me. If she is better-natured than my previous maid, the position is hers.''

His brows arched in question. ''As simple as that? You don't feel that you will be contaminated by her past?''

''My former maid thought she would be contaminated by me,'' Sara said dryly, ''so I think it will all even out.''

''You, my lady, are living proof that a genteel upbringing doesn't have to ruin a woman's sense or heart.''

As she smiled at the compliment, his fingers skimmed lightly over her cheek and his voice dropped, becoming husky and intimate. ''Three weeks seems a very long time to wait.''

He traced along the underside of her jaw to her throat, his touch doing strange, melting things to her insides, but this time Sara stepped away before the process could go too far. Memory of what they had done earlier hung in the air like smoke. But while he might want to repeat the experience, she had done some serious thinking during the day, and knew that she was not yet ready to do so. "That is what I want to do, Mikahl," she said haltingly. "Wait."

"I really did upset you this morning, didn't I?" he said quietly after a silence that stretched too long. "Don't worry, Sara, I can wait as long as necessary. Perhaps it is best if we not see each other between now and the wedding, except on formal occasions. That should prevent any more . . . misadventures."

She swallowed hard, intensely grateful. "You are very good to be so understanding."

His smile widened, becoming genuine. "One thing I am not is 'very good.' But I am not usually a fool, especially not twice in the same day." He tilted her face up and gave her a quick, expert kiss that sent pleasant tingles throughout her body. Then he whispered in her ear, "Now let us go inside before I am tempted to make a liar of myself."

The intensity of her relief was almost dizzying. It amazed her that a man so forceful could also be so considerate. And at that moment she finally admitted the truth to herself. What she felt for Mikahl was more than passion, more than infatuation, more than need: it was love, soul-deep and irrevocable. The realization was a soaring joy, like racing across a meadow on horseback or whirling across a ballroom in the waltz, but a thousand times greater.

His arms were still loosely linked around her waist, as if he was reluctant to let her go, so it was easy to catch his head between her hands and draw it down. His dense black hair silken beneath her fingers, she kissed him, not with passion, but with aching gratitude. Sensing something of her mood, he returned the kiss with tenderness, his arms tightening around her waist.

Sara wanted to engrave the sweetness of the moment on her heart—his look and scent and feel, the warmth of his lips, the sheer, solid reality of him. Love was a greater terror than passion, for she knew that she was mad to fall in love with someone so improbable and unpredictable. Though he desired her, he did not love her; perhaps he was incapable of returning the kind of love she wanted.

But in spite of the risks and the certainty of future anguish, she also knew that never would she regret loving him.

As a gesture to decorum, Peregrine had had Kuram drive him to Chapelgate, but for the return to Sulgrave, he took the reins himself. The Pathan lounged back in the seat, quite content to be driven by his master. When they were clear of the grounds, Peregrine observed, "You look pleased with yourself. I gather that they took good care of you down in the kitchens?"

Kuram smiled, his teeth white in the night. "Most friendly, these English girls. And most curious about wicked foreigners."

Peregrine grinned. "I know. After all, I'm marrying one."

The Pathan snorted. "A mistake to let a woman in your life. They are nothing but trouble."

"Nonetheless, I am looking forward to marriage. Winter is coming, Kuram, and nights are cold in the north." Reaching a straight stretch of road, Peregrine urged the horses into an exuberant dash that matched his own mood. "And my woman is a treasure rarer than ancient amber or Cathay silk."

"She has the quality of a fine Arab mare," the Pathan admitted, "but good women are the worst kind, and a man need not take a wife to have his bed warmed."

"You are a cynic, Kuram," Peregrine said, refusing to be affected by the other man's opinion.

Yet as he drove through the quiet country night, he found himself reflecting on the strangeness of what he was doing. For twenty-five years, personal pleasure had always been subordinated to his mission, but now that the end was in sight, he found himself impatient for the future that lay beyond vengeance. He wanted to put down roots, create a place where he belonged—and to have someone who belonged to him.

Undoubtedly it would have been wiser to wait until Weldon was destroyed, for a home and wife would be distractions. But delay might have lost him Sara and Sulgrave. Both moved him deeply, and he had learned early that one must seize the gifts of the gods when they were offered, for one seldom received a second chance. Sulgrave was like a dream home of the imagination that had been made physical in stone and earth, and Sara . . .

Ah, Sara, how could one describe Sara? She was a living symbol of his first victory over Weldon, but so much more: wit, warmth, honesty, and the quiet courage of a tempered blade. Though he regretted how he had treated her, he did not regret discovering the steely strength she had revealed in adversity.

Caring for Sara would be a pleasure, for simply being in her presence was a delight. When they were finally married, he would atone for his clumsiness, would teach her the mysteries of passion with the same care a connoisseur would use with fine porcelain. He was amazed by her willingness to accept him despite his mistakes, and he made a mental pledge that she would not regret her generosity.

As he turned into Sulgrave's long drive, he realized that all the things he had ever wanted—revenge, roots, a passionate companion—were now within his grasp. And with the confidence that carried a warrior invincible through battle, he knew that nothing and no one would deprive him of his prizes.

Chapter 14

DURING THE DRIVE to his brother's house, Charles Weldon reviewed his day with vicious satisfaction. In the morning he had visited his clubs, in the afternoon he had called on society women with notoriously loose tongues, and everywhere he had spread the news of his broken betrothal.

A pity, he mused, that he could not describe her misconduct in detail without seeming ungentlemanly, but he was a master of the innuendo, the raised brow, the suggestive glance. The story of Lady Sara St. James and her savage had been received with avid delight, for many society beauties had resented the prince for spurning their lures. Now they took feline pleasure in the knowledge that Lady Sara, who had always been above reproach, was no better than the rest of them, and perhaps a little worse.

Yes, it had been a good day. If Lady Sara's reputation was not quite ruined, it was certainly tarnished, a good first step in making her pay for betraying him. Once more his mind's eye saw the vivid image of Sara panting in that bastard's embrace. At the thought, Weldon balled his right hand into a fist and slammed it into his left palm. And to think he had believed her so pure, so well-bred! It sickened him to think of the disgrace she would have brought on his name if he had married her.

He was beginning to believe that there was no female who was worthy of trust. When he had first married Jane Clifton, she had adored him, and had been

as obedient as any man could want. She had also behaved like a lady in bed, combining a becoming distaste for the marital act with the submission a wife
owed her husband. Then one day, without warning,
she had announced that she was taking his daughter
and going back to her family, as if she had a perfect
right to leave him.

He ground his fist into his palm as he thought of
how she screamed when she fell down the stairs. It
had all been Jane's fault, for she should have known
better than to make him angry. A woman should not
defy her husband; if she did, she deserved whatever
consequences befell her.

He had taken his time choosing a second wife,
wanting one who was well-bred and attractive as well
as rich, for he was destined for great things and needed
a woman worthy of him. Sara St. James had seemed
such a woman, until she had proved that she did not
deserve the title Lady.

The knowledge of her lechery was perversely, itch-
ily arousing, and his loins had been burning ever since
he had discovered her in her shame. First thing this
morning he had sent his man Kane to Mrs. Kent with
an order to procure a virgin with Sara's slim figure
and dark gold hair. The girl would be waiting tonight,
and when he ravished her, he would close his eyes and
think of the woman he had almost married.

Someday, he swore, he would ravish Sara herself,
even though it was too late to take her maidenhead.
He reveled in the prospect of battering into her until
she pleaded for mercy.

A pity that he must let some time pass before having
her kidnapped, but it would not do to have anyone
connect him with her disappearance. In such things he
was cautious, for meticulous care and matchless cun-
ning were what made it possible to live a shadow life
under the very noses of society and law.

As always, thought of his cleverness restored his
equanimity. Most men were fools, blind to the dark

grandeur of living beyond society's narrow limits. His licit and illicit worlds complemented each other, point and counterpoint, each richer for contrast with the other.

He considered keeping Sara a prisoner for his own use, but decided that a brothel would be greater punishment. He would send her where no one would ever find her, to Brussels, perhaps. If she survived the first year, he would visit and ask if she still lusted for her heathen lover after thousands of men had vented their lust on her. All her aloof dignity would be gone, and she would beg for him to release her, but he would not, for she had degraded herself by her own unforgivable conduct.

Weldon felt a kind of sorrow when he contemplated the Kafir's treachery; he had done so much for the man, treating him almost as if he were an Englishman. The only mitigating factor was that one could expect no better from a savage. For that reason, perhaps Peregrine would be allowed to die quickly when the time came.

Unfortunately, this revenge would also have to be delayed because death would throw the Kafir's finances into disarray and endanger the L & S Railway. It was almost a pity that the company was doing so well, for it was maddening to know that Peregrine would profit from Weldon's own efforts. But his money had been essential for recapitalizing the company, so there was no way to get rid of him yet.

Thank God he'd had the foresight to arrange matters so that Peregrine had no real say in running the railway, even though he was the largest shareholder. Later, when the new stock offering was completely sold out, Weldon would find a way to force the Kafir out of the company. Meanwhile, he would look for other, subtler ways to make the savage pay for his disloyalty.

Weldon's pleasant thoughts were interrupted by his arrival at Lord Batsford's town house. He had intended to talk to his sister-in-law first, then Eliza, but his daughter must have seen the carriage, for she came racing down the stairs as the butler admitted him, her long blond hair flying.

"Papa!" she said excitedly. "I didn't expect you. Did you come to take tea with me?"

"Show more decorum, Eliza, don't run like a beggar child." As his daughter slowed down, abashed, he feasted his eyes on her. She was enchanting in a full-skirted pink dress with lacy pantalets beneath, and she had the pure sweetness of an angel. Here was true innocence; perhaps the only female a man might trust was his daughter. Batsford and his wife were dull, utterly without grace and unworthy of the title they bore, but he had to admit that Eliza was flourishing under their care.

He touched her shining hair. "I must talk to you, my dear, so let us go to the drawing room and order tea."

Several letters lay on a silver tray on the hall table, and before leading her father up to the drawing room, Eliza cast a hopeful eye over them. With an exclamation of delight, she picked up one of the envelopes. "Look, Papa, it is a note for me from Lady Sara! I recognize her writing."

"Give that to me!" Weldon snatched the letter from his daughter's hand as fury swept through him. How dare the slut write Eliza, sweet Eliza, the only truly pure female in his life! As his daughter stared in bewilderment, he crumpled the envelope and shoved it in his pocket. He would read it later to see just what kind of poison the slut was trying to put in Eliza's mind, and he would give orders to all the servants that nothing should be accepted from Haddonfield House.

"Is something wrong?" Eliza faltered.

Not wanting a servant to hear, he did not answer until they had climbed the stairs to the drawing room. As soon as the door was closed, he said harshly, "Don't ever mention that woman's name again. You must forget her, forget everything she ever told you, forget that you ever knew her.''

Eliza's eyes widened with shock. ''But . . . but aren't you going to marry Lady Sara?''

''Never! She has disgraced herself, and is not fit to be my wife or your mother.''

''But what happened? What did Lady Sara do?'' Eliza's brow creased with confusion. ''She has always been so kind to me.''

''That woman never cared about you, she was just trying to please me,'' he snapped, losing patience with the girl. ''Now do not speak of her again, Eliza, I absolutely forbid it.''

As his daughter's eyes filled with tears, he felt remorse. She was just an innocent child, the most precious being in his life. More calmly, he said, ''Sit down and I'll ring for tea.''

Eliza perched on the sofa, frightened that she might anger her father again. ''Does this mean I can't live with you?''

Weldon started to agree, then stopped. Perhaps it was time to remove his daughter from this house, for her female cousins were getting old enough to be marriageable. They were empty-headed chits, and soon they would be babbling about men, filling Eliza with improper ideas. More than that, the whole household would soon be buzzing with talk about Lady Sara. In fact, appalling thought, Sara might be able to persuade Lady Batsford to let her see Eliza; the slut had always been able to charm his brother and wife around her little finger.

No, Eliza belonged with her father, who knew what was best for her. Unlike her mother or the slut, his daughter was devoted to him, and to reward her for her devotion, he must guide her properly, ensure that no wickedness came her way. He would take her out of school and get her a governess, one who knew what was proper. ''No,'' he said decisively, ''I want you to move in with me again as soon as possible. I've missed you.''

As Eliza's face brightened, he went over and gave her a rare hug. "It will be just you and me, my dear," he said softly. Soon he must find another rich wife to give him a son, but next time he would choose more wisely. "We don't need anyone else."

"Oh, Papa, that's wonderful." Eliza returned his hug with delight. She had always dreamed that some-day her father would show that he loved her, and now he had.

When the tea tray arrived, Eliza carefully poured her father's tea, just like a proper lady, for soon she would be his hostess. As she sipped tea and nibbled on tiny iced cakes, Papa explained his plans for her. Of course he would still be busy, but finally she would have him all to herself for some of the time. She would not even have to share him with Lady Sara, though it would have been worth sharing to have Sara for a mama.

But later, when her father had gone, Eliza made a resolution. Even though Papa was the wisest, hand-somest man in the world, he was wrong about Lady Sara. They must have had some misunderstanding, like the characters in the romances she and her cousins read, but that didn't mean Lady Sara was a bad person.

In spite of what Papa had said, Eliza knew that Lady Sara had been genuine in her affection. Sooner or later, Eliza promised herself, she would find an opportunity to speak to Lady Sara. Perhaps the misunderstanding could be cleared up so Sara and Papa would resume their marriage plans?

Eliza sighed, knowing that life did not always work out as neatly as books. But even if reconciliation was out of the question, at least Eliza could talk to Sara and tell her that she missed her, and find out what was in the letter Papa had taken away.

* * *

When Jenny Miller was ushered into the morning room of Haddonfield House, her expression was not precisely fearful, for the girl had an air of resilience that implied that she was not easily frightened. But her blue eyes did show anxiety as she curtsied in front of Sara.

Subconciously Sara had expected that years in a brothel must leave some sort of mark, and Jenny's delicate loveliness was a distinct surprise. In her simple, high-necked navy gown, she looked like a schoolmaster's daughter, not a reformed prostitute.

"Have a seat," Sara said. "I don't bite."

Jenny obeyed with a quick smile. "Thank you, my lady."

"I understand that you have not worked as a lady's maid before," Sara said. "Are you sure that you will like the work?"

"Oh, yes, my lady. I'm ever so good with hair, and I love fine clothing. I know what is quality, you see, and what is flattering." Then she colored and ducked her head shyly. "I'm sorry, my lady, I can see that you aren't one who needs advice from a maid, but I promise I will take good care of your gowns, and slippers, and jewels, and linens, and everything else, and I'll always do exactly what you want."

Sara smiled at the rush of words. "Relax, Jenny, I'm looking to hire you, not buy you." Only when a strained expression touched the girl's face did Sara realize what she had said. She bit her lip. "I'm sorry, that was thoughtless of me. In practical terms, you *were* a slave, weren't you?"

Jenny regarded her warily. "The prince told you about me?"

"Not in detail. He just said that you'd been kept in a brothel against your will."

Jenny flushed scarlet. "You don't mind?"

"I mind for your sake," Sara said softly, her heart aching at the thought of what the girl must have endured—and what thousands of other girls in London were enduring still. "I can't tell you to forget the past, for the past is as much a part of us as our bones. But if you want to work for me, the subject will never be mentioned again unless you raise it yourself. None of the other servants need know."

"Now I know what a real lady is." Jenny swallowed hard, fighting tears. "If you'll have me, Lady Sara, I swear I'll be the best maid you ever had."

Making a quick, instinctive decision, Sara said, "I'd love to have you. My former maid had the temper of a pickled onion, but I think you and I will deal together very well." She rose to her feet. "Let me show you where you will be living and working."

"Wonderful!" Jenny bounded up, a beaming smile across her face. Then she hesitated. "Lady Sara, might you be wondering about how Prince Peregrine and I met?"

It was Sara's turn to blush. "I don't suppose that it's any of my business what he does before we're married."

"It wasn't what you think, my lady," Jenny said earnestly. "He came to the brothel as someone's guest, and I knew as soon as I saw him that he didn't want to be there. He didn't touch me, just asked me questions. When he found out that I didn't want to be there either, he helped me escape. He's a real gentleman, just like you're a real lady."

"Thank you for telling me that, Jenny." Sara felt a surge of happiness, not just because the girl wasn't Mikahl's mistress, but because her enigmatic betrothed had been the one to rescue Jenny from servitude. He was a better man than he was willing to admit to. "It might not be my business, but I must admit that I'm glad to know that. Now, are you ready for the tour?"

Jenny nodded eagerly and followed her new mistress upstairs to the wonderful world that was going to be hers.

* * *

Alert for the sound of Mr. Slade's key, Jenny bounced out of the drawing room to meet him as soon as he entered his house. Ever since returning from Lady Sara's, she had been waiting impatiently to give him the good news.

The lawyer greeted her with a smile. "I don't need to ask how the interview went—I can see by your face that Lady Sara gave you the position."

Jenny nodded an enthusiastic confirmation. "She's lovely, and so kind. And she's not much larger than I am, and has fair coloring, and she said that most of her clothing would look good on me, if I didn't mind wearing hand-me-downs. As if I'd mind!"

Slade laughed. "This calls for a celebration. I have no champagne, but we can toast your success in Madeira."

He escorted her into the library and solemnly poured small amounts of Madeira into two glasses. Raising his glass in salute, he said, "To Jenny—may all your dreams come true."

In spite of his genuine pleasure in her success, Slade drained the glass with a sense of melancholy. Peregrine had said that Jenny had wanted to become a lady's maid, to work for a pleasant lady whose discarded clothing would fit her, and eventually to marry a handsome footman. Now that the girl's first dreams had been realized, it was just a matter of time until the last one was. If and when a lovely girl like Jenny decided to marry, she would have her choice of husbands, in spite of her past. And they would be young, handsome men, not boring lawyers almost twenty years her senior.

Jenny had held her own glass while he toasted her. Now she raised it. "To you, Mr. Slade, for making it possible."

He was pleased but too punctilious to accept an undeserved tribute. "It is Prince Peregrine you should be toasting, for it was he who set you free."

"I surely don't mind drinking to him or his lady, but you're the one who spent time with me, showed me how proper females behave, found me a teacher, trusted me with your money, and kept saying that I could better myself.'' She poured more Madeira for both of them. ''While the prince gave me the chance, it's you who made it mean something.''

''Thank you, Jenny,'' he said gravely. ''It has been my privilege to be of assistance.''

After the toast to Peregrine and his lady, Slade asked, ''When will you begin with Lady Sara?''

''Tomorrow. She is sending her carriage for me.''

So soon? Slade sipped his Madeira, thinking that he had not noticed how dull the house was until she came to brighten it up. With her departure, his home would be bleak indeed, for darkness is always deeper after one has known light. ''Since her ladyship is preparing her trousseau, you'll be very busy.''

He hesitated, wondering if he should say more, then said simply, ''I shall miss you, Jenny.''

She set her glass down with a businesslike air. ''I want to do something to thank you for all you've done for me.''

''There's no need.'' He smiled a little. ''Since you started practicing your skills on my wardrobe, my clothing has never looked better—everything brushed, mended, and pressed.''

''That's not enough. I want to do something more— it isn't right to just take and never give.'' Stepping forward, she twined her arms around his neck and pressed her slim body against him. ''I know that you've fancied me right from the beginning, so to show my appreciation for your kindness, I'll share your bed tonight.''

For a moment, he was almost paralyzed by shock and surging desire. She was beautiful, woman-soft, fresh and sweet as an armful of flowers. And willing . . .

Willing because she was grateful. He removed her arms from his neck with more speed than courtesy, for if he did not move quickly, he would be unable to put her aside. "No, Jenny," he said hoarsely, "it is better not to do this."

"It's all right, Mr. Slade," she said, misunderstanding. "You never asked, but the doctor you sent me to said I'm clean, so you won't catch anything from me. I know all about preventing babies, too, and how to please a man."

"Jenny," he said with a touch of desperation, "this isn't necessary. You've already given me a great deal, more than you'll ever know."

She cocked her head. "You're being honorable, aren't you? But I'm no innocent, so it's not like you could take advantage. Spending the night with you wouldn't mean a thing to me."

If she had deliberately tried to hurt him, she could not have done a better job. It took a moment for Slade to regain his lawyer's coolness. "I know it wouldn't mean anything to you. That's why it wouldn't be right."

He kissed her lightly on the forehead, like an uncle. "Be happy, Jenny. You deserve it." He turned to leave the library, but stopped when she spoke.

"Can . . . can I come and visit you now and then on my half days?" she asked uncertainly. "I won't enjoy things as much if I can't tell you about them."

It would have been wiser to refuse, but he found himself saying, "I'd like that."

Then he left, thinking that it would be good to see Jenny sometimes, at least until she found her handsome footman. When she started talking about beaux, it would be time to let go. But for now, her visits would give him something to look forward to.

Long after the lawyer was gone, Jenny continued to stare at the dark wooden panels of the door as she tried to understand her sense of loss. Something had happened tonight, and she didn't quite understand what. She figured that she knew just about everything there was to know about male desire—certainly she knew that a man didn't need to care to want a woman.

But she had never known that a man could want a woman and not take her because he *did* care. There was something very fragile and precious in the idea, though she didn't really understand it. Maybe someday she would.

It was Slade's first visit to Sulgrave, and he looked around with admiration. "A very handsome place. You got more of a bargain than I realized."

Ushering his lawyer into the study, Peregrine smiled lazily. "I'm glad you approve, since you were the one who found the estate and negotiated the price. How do you manage to arrange so many things from behind the scenes?"

"It's all a matter of knowing who to ask," Slade said vaguely as he chose a seat. "Are you going to be doing any decorating or remodeling?"

"Not until after the wedding. I'm sure that Sara will want to make some changes. Only another week now." Peregrine drifted to the window and looked out. He never tired of the sight of the rolling English hills, and often rode or walked in the Downs. "Are Weldon's affairs prospering?"

Slade permitted himself a small smile as he put on his reading glasses. "Not at all. As expected, the ending of his betrothal made his bank very anxious, and I was able to buy up his debts at a substantial discount."

"Good. Notify him that if the loans aren't repaid in the next thirty days, we will foreclose on all the property mortgaged as security."

"Why not immediately?"

"Because thirty days will give Weldon more time to worry," Peregrine said in a dulcet tone.

The lawyer frowned. Even though he knew that Weldon deserved whatever he got, there was something profoundly disturbing about Peregrine's lethal pleasure in the process of destruction. Slade wondered sometimes what had set his employer on his course of vengeance, but suspected that it was better not to know. Looking back at his notes, he said, "Weldon's stock in the railway is very valuable just now. He may be able to borrow enough against that to pay off the loans."

"Only if the railway maintains its value." Peregrine turned to face the room, lounging against the window frame with arms crossed and fierce satisfaction in his eyes. "Has Weldon learned yet that Crawley sold the right-of-way to his property?"

"Not yet, but he will soon."

"When he does, it will be time to reinstate the lawsuit for greater compensation on Crawley's land, plus to file charges of criminal harassment against the company in general and Weldon in particular." Peregrine thought a moment longer. "Tracklaying has almost reached Crawley's property. In case Weldon decides to go ahead and build there anyhow, in spite of the lawsuits against the company, be ready to file for an injunction to stop construction."

Slade gave a nod of approval. "So even if he is finally ready to offer a fair price for Crawley's right-of-way, the company will be so tied up in lawsuits that investors will drop it like a hot coal."

"That's the general idea," Peregrine said genially. "With luck, that will push the L & S Railway into serious financial trouble." He began to prowl across the room. "One more matter—the barony that Weldon has been angling for. Have you made any progress toward thwarting that?"

"The matter has been taken care of. Several prominent members of Her Majesty's government have received packets of information detailing some of Weldon's more believable crimes." Slade smiled. "I doubt that anything will ever be said publicly, but it's a safe bet that Weldon's name will be quietly dropped from the next honors list, never to be considered again. If he tries to find out what happened, he will meet with polite vagueness. British politicians are very good at that.''

Peregrine laughed out loud. ''Benjamin, you're a wonder. Am I paying you enough?''

''You pay me too much,'' Slade said severely. ''I've told you that before. You really do not have a proper respect for money.''

His employer smiled. ''You have enough respect for both of us. Too much, in fact—have you never learned that money is only a tool, not an end in itself?''

Immediately Slade thought of Jenny Miller. For years, money had bought her body, but there was not enough money on earth to buy what he wanted from her. Brusquely he said, ''Money may not buy happiness, but it certainly makes misery a great deal more comfortable. Is there anything else you wish to discuss today?''

Peregrine studied him curiously, wondering what personal nerve had been touched by the casual words, then shrugged. Slade, who was a master of information gathering, was not at all forthcoming about his own private life. Probably he didn't have one. ''No, nothing else. Thank you for coming out here today.''

Slade nodded acknowledgment, then gathered his papers and left. Peregrine sat down at his desk, elation filling him. Thread by thread, the web was being completed. A pity that he could not be present when Weldon realized the full extent of the ruin facing him.

There was a secret drawer in the desk, and he opened it to take out his private file on Weldon. Soon after coming to England, Peregrine had made a list of what Weldon valued most, and it was time to evaluate the progress that had been made.

A column on the left side of the page listed *fortune, business reputation, railway, personal reputation, social standing, Lady Sara St. James, barony, daughter, life.*

Peregrine made a neat check by *fortune* and scribbled the note *private fortune gone, railway bankruptcy will ruin him.* By *business reputation,* he wrote *faltering.* Already rumors about Weldon were starting to circulate, and when the railroad crashed, his name would become anathema to the financial community.

Next to *personal reputation,* he wrote *possible newspaper exposure?* An ambitious journalist looking for instant fame might be a good channel for making public Weldon's vicious hypocrisy; when that happened, social standing and reputation would both vanish instantly.

Next to Sara's name Peregrine drew a star, for she represented his greatest success to date. Simply ending the betrothal would have been adequate; having the world know that Sara preferred a different man was better yet; but marrying her himself was pure triumph. He had entered English society, Weldon's own territory, and against all odds he had won his enemy's lady.

He wrote *gone* next to *barony,* for it sounded like Slade had taken care of that most efficiently. How long would it take before Weldon realized that the title he lusted after would never be his? Weeks at least, perhaps longer; appropriate that the misery of uncertainty would precede the pain of loss.

He frowned at the entry *daughter;* as with Sara, the trick was to remove the girl from Weldon without damaging her. The question had taken on added weight since Eliza had just gone back to her father's house. When Weldon was dead, Peregrine guessed she would return to the custody of her aunt and uncle, who were decent people. The girl also had an inheritance from her mother that Weldon couldn't touch, so her future should be secure.

But how could she be used to injure her father now? The girl had a special place in Weldon's heart; possibly she was the only person for whom he had any unselfish affection. Peregrine frowned at the list for a long time. Then an idea came to him, and a wolfish smile spread across his face.

Over the year, Weldon had been responsible for de-

stroying the lives of countless young girls; how would
he react to the news that his own cherished daughter
had been kidnapped and installed in a brothel? He
would tear the London underworld apart trying to find
her, increasingly desperate, for he would know exactly
what his protected child would be suffering at the
hands of bastards like himself.

Peregrine would not actually send the girl to a
brothel; for the purpose of vengeance, it was only necessary that Weldon *believe* his daughter was in a
whorehouse.

It would be easy. Since Eliza and Sara were friends,
all that needed to be done was coax the girl away for
a holiday with Sara while Weldon was told that his
daughter had been kidnapped. Sara and Eliza would
both be happy, and Weldon would be in hell. Absolutely perfect. It would have to be done carefully, since
Sara would not approve if she knew what Peregrine
was doing, but she would not have to know. Next to
daughter, he jotted "kidnap/brothel."

That left only *life*. He gnawed on the end of his pen.
Since the injury Weldon had done had been vicious
and personal, revenge must be equally vicious and
personal. Peregrine craved the sight of his enemy's
fear; he must administer the death stroke himself, feel
the hot splash of Weldon's blood, for nothing less
would balance the scales of the past. But marrying
Sara meant staying in England, so if Peregrine were
to personally execute his enemy, he would have to do
it in a way where he would not be detected.

He was still pondering the best method of admin-
istering death, when a knock on the door was immediately followed by the entrance of Lord Ross.
Smoothly Peregrine returned the file to the secret
drawer, closed it, then stood to greet his friend.
"Good afternoon. This is an unexpected pleasure."

There had been a flicker of curiosity in Ross's eyes
when Peregrine had hidden the file, but he was too
polite to ask about it. Instead he dropped a heavy

folder on the desk. "I've been going over the material you lent me on Weldon. For God's sake, Mikahl, why not take it to the authorities and stop the bastard now? All the evidence may not be firm, but there is more than enough to hang him."

"I have reasons for waiting." Peregrine sat down again, gesturing for Ross to do the same. "But I promise that it will not be much longer before Weldon's sins catch up with him."

"The sooner the better." Ross's lips were a tight line as he took a chair. "I've just heard that he's been slandering you and Sara all over London."

"Trying to," Peregrine corrected. "We have gone to several social affairs in the last fortnight, and while there was some whispering and curiosity at first, by the end Sara had won everyone over." He smiled with pride. "She is splendid. No one can talk to her and believe that she has an immoral bone in her body or an unprincipled thought in her head. As a result, Weldon's slander is rebounding onto himself. Soon he will find that he has less friends than he thought."

Ross's expression relaxed. "I can believe that Sara is outfacing all gossip, but how are people treating you?"

"The usual—curiosity, some titillated disapproval. But since they think it likely that marriage to Lady Sara means that I will be among them for some time, most people seem to be willing to give me the benefit of the doubt for her sake." Peregrine gave a faint smile. "I find it vastly amusing to be achieving such respectability."

Ross laughed. It was hard to see the wild Kafir in the urbane, well-dressed man in front of him—except when Weldon was mentioned. Then Peregrine's eyes held the mercilessness of the falcon he had named himself for. Ross had a strong intuition that the sooner Weldon was dealt with, the better for everyone.

* * *

"Something unexpected has happened, Sir Charles." Walter Baines shuffled through his papers uneasily, knowing that his employer was not going to take this news well. "The bank has sold your notes at a discount, and the new creditor is demanding payment in thirty days."

Weldon stared at his accountant, slack-jawed with surprise. "Why the devil would they do that? I've done business with that bank for years."

"Mmm, yes, but you've only been paying interest on the loans—the principal has been outstanding for quite some time. The bank has always trusted that you were good for the money, both because of your business success and certain other—mmm—intangible considerations. However, your personal debts have mounted to a rather substantial figure in the last eighteen months. Plus . . ." Baines coughed into his hand. "A clerk at the bank told me in confidence that the directors had become anxious because your betrothal had ended. It is well-known that Lady Sara is a considerable heiress, but now . . ." He spread his hands apologetically. "It's nonsense, of course, but you know how conservative bankers are."

After swearing a string of vicious oaths, Weldon asked, "How much money do I have in reserve?"

"Apart from a small account for daily household expenses, nothing. You liquidated everything for the recapitalization of the L & S Railway."

Weldon frowned. "Much as I hate to do it, I may have to borrow against my shares in the railway. Find a lender who will give me what I need at a decent interest rate." He thought a moment. "Incidentally, who bought the notes?"

Baines shuffled his papers again. "That isn't clear. The demand came through a solicitor who is acting on another solicitor's behalf. I couldn't learn the name of the principal."

"Find out," Weldon ordered. "Also, ask if the new

creditor will accept less than the face value of the notes—enough to make a profit on his speculation, but less than the full amount.''

"Very good, Sir Charles.'' Baines gathered his papers and left with alacrity.

Weldon sat frowning for long after the accountant's departure. What a damnable stroke of luck. In the last couple of years, he had put huge sums of money into politics, both to advance his business interests and to secure a title for himself. As a result, he had been skating on very thin ice for the last six months; if he had not had the illicit income to subsidize his legitimate enterprises, he would have been ruined.

His financial situation had been a significant factor in his decision to remarry, for Lady Sara's dowry would have put him back on his feet. But when he had discovered Sara in her wantonness, he had been too furious to think through the implications of breaking the betrothal. Christ, he should have married the slut! Not only would he have had her money, he would not have had to wait to punish her for her treachery. And if she had threatened to tarnish his name—well, he had lost one wife in a tragic accident. Such a thing could have happened again.

Briefly he wondered if the betrothal was broken past mending, and reluctantly decided that it was. Neither Sara nor her lover would be likely to forgive the things that had been said that night. It was ironic that the one wealthy man who might have been willing to help Weldon through this bad patch was Peregrine. The bastard seemed to be made of money, and he had been very free with it. But it would be impossible to ask for a loan after what had happened.

A pity that relations had grown so strained with his wife's family after her death; his father-in-law could easily have afforded a loan, but he wouldn't help. Weldon knew that because he had hinted about a loan the year before, and his father-in-law had reacted very badly. Before she died, that bitch Jane must have told her father that she was unhappy in her marriage.

Might the brothels be sold? After consideration, he decided not. They generated a good income, but their only assets were the frail ones of human flesh and secret reputation. Besides, they were not the sorts of businesses that could be easily sold.

The Duke of Haddonfield was certainly wealthy enough, but Weldon suspected that he had already pushed the duke as far as possible. Haddonfield might tell Weldon to speak and be damned if more pressure was brought to bear. Still, if worse came to worse, the duke was a possibility.

Finally Weldon shrugged and left his office for the day. The situation was difficult but not disastrous; he'd come about soon. He had better start thinking about a new wife. In the meantime, thank God for the thriving L & S Railway.

Chapter 15

SARA RETURNED to Haddonfield a week before the ceremony, profoundly grateful to be back in the country. She and her betrothed had gone into society several times in the previous fortnight and the occasions had been stressful. While no one had been overtly rude, she had been aware of the whispers and curiosity, of people studying both her and her betrothed with fascinated, avid eyes. But the effort had been successful; the talk had not blossomed into a scandal, and the St. James's name was still unsullied.

Because of the circumstances surrounding Sara's broken betrothal, she had decided to marry from her family home rather than in London. After a week of frenzied preparations, her wedding day dawned, having arrived both too quickly and too slowly. Afterward, Sara remembered her wedding as a collection of kaleidoscopic fragments. She knew she must have acted normally, for no one said otherwise, but most of the day was a blank, punctuated by occasional moments of sharp clarity.

She had been awakened by Aunt Marguerite, who came in with a tray of tea and toast. As Sara stirred milk into her cup, the duchess had said briskly, "Since Maria is no longer with us, I suppose I should do all the things mothers are supposed to do. You are not a child and are both levelheaded and well-informed, but still, there is a shocking amount of ignorance about what takes place in the marriage bed."

She cocked her head to one side. "Need I explain

what happens? Though I warn you, the description is quite ludicrous and far less appealing than the reality. Or if you feel that you have an adequate grasp of the basics, are there any special questions you would like to ask? You needn't be shy with me.''

Sara had choked on her tea and gone into a coughing fit. After recovering, she said, ''That isn't necessary, Aunt.''

The duchess studied her niece's burning face, then said with distinct approval, ''I see. Very good, my dear.''

Knowing that her aunt undoubtedly *did* see, Sara had hastily risen and rung for her bath.

The next memory was of Jenny Miller. Sara had canceled the order for the elaborate dress she would have worn to marry Charles, choosing instead a simpler gown of ivory-colored silk. Privately, she made the ironic reflection that she was not entitled to pure white.

Jenny had dressed her mistress with loving skill, making sure that every glossy fold of fabric, every fall of delicate lace, was perfect. At the end, after pinning the chaplet of silk flowers in place and adjusting the veil that fell almost to Sara's heels, the girl had unashamedly wept. ''You're the most beautiful bride there ever was, my lady,'' she whispered. ''And you'll be happy. I know it.''

Sara had wished she shared her maid's optimism.

During the carriage ride to the church, her father had been resigned, neither glad nor disapproving. As he assisted her out at the end, he had said softly, ''Ultimately we must all work out our own fate. I wish you happy, child, and I wish your mother could have been here to see you.''

If Sara had married Charles in the fashionable London church he had wanted, she would have been attended by a dozen bridesmaids chosen from both her family and his. But this wedding was to Sara's own taste rather than to please a socially conscious bridegroom, so it was held in the flower-scented parish church she loved, and her only attendant was Marguerite.

The church was filled with Haddonfield tenants and the closest St. James's relatives and friends. Peregrine had invited only two guests, a quiet London businessman and a turbaned, fierce-looking Asiatic who sat in the back row and watched the proceedings with the detached curiosity that a European might have shown to the ceremonies of African pygmies.

The processional march began, and Marguerite made her majestic way down the aisle, lending her duchess's dignity to the ceremony. Then it was time for Sara. She had been grateful for her father's arm, for being the center of attention always made her acutely conscious of her lameness. Every sight and sound was unnaturally exaggerated, even the whisper of her train as it glided over the medieval brasses embedded in the stone floor.

As she made her slow progress in step to the organ music, she noted individual faces in the crowd. Here was the steward's wife, just Sara's age and the mother of five children; there stood the head groom from the ducal stables, who had been the one who found Sara after her accident and who had wept as he carried her broken body back to the house. Jenny Miller was in the middle of a row, standing next to Peregrine's London friend. And there were scores of others, all of them beaming with goodwill. Some must have heard of the London gossip, but the duke's daughter belonged to them, and they believed in her.

It was almost noon, and the church was flooded with light. Though the sun warmed the ancient stones and scattered jewels of colored light through the stained glass windows, Sara was ice-cold, the fingers clasping her bouquet almost numb.

Her gaze went to the men who waited at the altar. Both were dressed in formal black, tall, broad-shouldered and powerful, and she thought that there could not be two more handsome men anywhere. Ross was groomsman. He must have guessed at her nerves, for he gave her an outrageous wink.

But most of her attention was on her future husband: Mikahl, dark and exotic and mysterious, the stranger whom she was marrying. She had not seen him since her return to Haddonfield.

Her father delivered her to her future husband's side and stepped back. For a moment Sara swayed. What would the vows of eternal love and fidelity mean to a man who was not a Christian? Not enough, perhaps. She wanted to marry Mikahl more than she had ever wanted anything in her life, yet if she had been steadier on her feet, she would have turned and fled the church.

Then her gaze lifted to his green eyes: gem green, cat green, growth green, the vasty green depths of a sea deep enough to drown in. When he had taken her onto his horse at Tattersall's, he had whispered "Trust me"; now his fathomless eyes held the same message. *Trust me.* She put her hand out, and he took it in his, his powerful fingers closing over hers with a warmth that radiated all the way to her chilled bones. Oblivious to local custom, he raised her hand and kissed it with melting tenderness.

She smiled at him with sudden joy, and when he smiled back, her fears began to dissolve. They turned to face the vicar, and the ceremony began.

Scattered phrases struck her: *Dearly beloved . . . Do you, Mikahl, take this woman . . .* answered with a firm baritone *I do. Do you, Sara Margaret Mary, take this man . . .* To her surprise, her own voice sounded firm and confident.

With this ring I thee wed. . . . He had had the ring specially made for her, and the gold band was a study in subtle curving surfaces, a Western symbol rendered in Oriental style.

The greatest reality was his hand clasping hers, and

his kiss at the end of the ceremony when he whispered, "Sweet Sara, sweet wife."

She had clung to him for a moment, grateful for his solid strength, and for the sense of caring emanating from him.

Then it was over, and she was Sara Khanauri, married past redemption. More fragmented images: walking down the aisle, receiving the good wishes of what seemed to be every person she had ever met, Aunt Marguerite crying happily, Ross enveloping her in a long hug that was both best wishes and a wordless promise of support if ever she needed it.

There had been a private wedding breakfast for family and visiting friends and an outdoor feast for everyone in the village. During the festivities, Mikahl was no more than an arm's length away until she went to change to her traveling dress. Then, at last, Sara was alone in a carriage with her new husband by her side, mildly bawdy jokes and shouts of laughter fading behind them.

Reality returned with a snap. Now the business of making a marriage must begin, and she felt suddenly shy. "I'm glad we were married at Haddonfield. It seems more real than a London society wedding. But I'm also glad that it's all over."

"An exhausting business, marriage," he observed, his eyes twinkling. "Can you imagine how much worse it must be for a Muslim, who may have up to four wives? Think about going through that three more times!"

"The guest lists and seating plans would be incredibly complicated," she said with a hint of smile. "Perhaps that is why the Christian church allows only one spouse at a time?"

Peregrine studied her face, seeing the tight-strung nerves beneath her composure. Sara continually amazed him. She had been heartbreakingly beautiful when she came down the aisle toward him, a cream and gold sibyl with her soul in her eyes.

Yet she had also been terrified. Not exactly of him, he sensed, or of marriage in the conventional sense, but because he was such an unknown quantity. He couldn't blame her for being alarmed by him; he was not at all an admirable person. Yet here she was, her presence an act of faith.

What made Sara willing to tempt fate by marrying him? The question fascinated him, for even though she desired him, he knew that the answer was nothing as simple as lust.

His wife's eyes shied away from his intent gaze as she absently stripped off her gloves. "Where are we going?"

"I was wondering if you would ever ask," he said with amusement. "To Sulgrave, unless you have another preference."

"Were you thinking of any particular inn to stay in tonight?" she asked. "The Black Horse in Oxford is a pleasant place, and about the right distance."

He shook his head. "Not necessary. We'll be in Sulgrave tonight."

"But surely it is too far away?" she said, surprised.

"No, it isn't." He grinned. "Shall I explain, or would you rather be surprised?"

"Surprise me."

Sara's voice was calm, but the way she toyed with her new wedding ring hinted at her tightly strung nerves. Deciding that it was time to end the formality between them, Peregrine scooped her into his arms and arranged her across his lap, the blue folds of her gown spilling around them. "Isn't this a more comfortable way to travel?"

After a surprised inhalation of breath, she said peaceably, "It's a good thing that Jenny and Kuram are in the carriage behind. They might not approve of such a cavalier attitude to our finery, after all their efforts to make us presentable."

Her voice was light, but he felt her tension. Abandoning levity, he said quietly, "Sara, when I said that

I would give you all the time you needed, I did not mean just until we were wed.''

Puzzled, she studied his face. ''What do you mean?''

''The ancient Hindus had a worthy custom,'' he answered obliquely. ''Girls were married very young to men who were much older. Since rough treatment from a virtual stranger might give a maiden a distaste for marital relations, it was recommended that the couple live together chastely at first. Perhaps ten days would elapse before the first kiss, and matters would progress slowly from there. The marriage would not be consummated until the man was sure that his bride was ready.''

Suddenly hilarity lit Sara's brown eyes. ''There is an English saying about barn doors and stolen horses. Isn't it a bit late to apply such a custom?''

He smiled, glad that her sense of humor was returning. ''The principle is valid. I pushed you too far, too fast, Sara. From now on, I will not do anything unless you are ready.''

Her brow furrowed. ''But won't that be . . . ,'' she searched for a euphemism, ''difficult for you?''

How typical of Sara to be concerned more for his welfare than for her own. ''I hope that your preference will be for days rather than months,'' he admitted wryly, ''but the future is long. It is worth giving your mind and body time to come into harmony. Do not worry about me—I will find much pleasure in anticipation.''

Sara gave him a slow smile. ''You are really quite a remarkable man,'' she said softly. ''Thank you, Mikahl.''

Then she put her head on his shoulder and settled trustfully into his embrace. One of her hands slid under his coat and came to rest on his chest, and her other arm circled his waist. As the afternoon sun found rich highlights in the dark gold of her hair, he could actually feel the tension flowing from her body.

The tension found an immediate home in him, for Sara had been right to wonder if it would be hard for him to curb desire indefinitely. As her delectable curves nestled against him, he realized ruefully that restraint would be even harder than he had thought. But for perhaps the first time since they had met, Sara was wholly relaxed with him; that was worth any amount of temporary discomfort.

He stroked the back of her neck, and she made a soft sound that was almost a purr. His wife. An amazing thought; just a few weeks ago, it had never occurred to him that he might marry. At what point had the idea of marriage gone from unthinkable to inevitable? It must have been the night he had compromised Sara, but for the life of him, he could not describe why or how his attitude had changed. No matter, he was glad of the result.

The road they traveled had a smooth surface, and in the gentle swaying of the carriage his wife slept in his arms, serenity emanating from her. As he inhaled the delicate scent of orange blossoms from her hair, Peregrine realized that he was experiencing a gentle peace different from anything he had ever known. As he slipped into a half doze, he wondered what other things he would learn from his wife.

"Wasn't the locomotive smashing, Lady Sara?" Jenny said as she unlaced her mistress's corset. "Who but the prince would have thought to hire a private carriage for just the four of us!"

"It was a wonderful idea," Sara agreed, giving a sigh of relief as the corset came off. "I can see why railroads are becoming popular—they are so swift, and for a long journey, much less tiring than a horse-drawn vehicle."

Besides hiring a luxurious private car, her clever new husband had also arranged for an elegant cold supper to be served on the trip, and two carriages had been waiting in London to take the newlyweds and their servants the final leg of the journey. And at Sulgrave, when Sara climbed from the carriage, Mikahl swept her into his arms and carried her, laughing, up the steps of her new home.

Sara sat down and peeled off her silk stockings, then wiggled her toes. "Is your own room suitable, Jenny? I didn't see the servants' quarters the one time I visited here."

"I only just had time to drop my bag before coming down to unpack your things, my lady, but it looked very nice. I like this house." Jenny began to pull out Sara's hairpins.

"So do I. Sulgrave was designed for comfort, not show." Sara gestured at their surroundings. "For instance, here in the master's suite—it must have been a woman who thought of building a private bath between the dressing rooms."

"That reminds me, I had best check the water for your bath," Jenny exclaimed. "And I'll take Furface away. I don't expect you want him underfoot tonight."

Sara chuckled at the grieved expression on the face of the tabby cat as Jenny scooped it up. It was the friendly stable feline Sara had met on her first visit to Sulgrave. According to her new husband, the beast had moved into the house the same day Mikahl had. Now officially christened Furface, the cat was clearly a permanent member of the household.

Finally alone, Sara absently began brushing her hair. It was both kind and wise of Mikahl to give her time to adjust to marital intimacy. If he had not, she would be wound as tight as a clock spring now. Instead she was relaxed, looking forward to being alone with him, but not fearing what he would expect of her.

After dismissing Jenny for the night, Sara took a quick bath, then donned an embroidered white night-gown and matching robe. The dainty muslin was almost as sheer as silk, and it whispered across her sensitive, anticipating skin. Even the weight of hair falling over back and shoulders stimulated her height-

ened senses. Her husband had tactfully disappeared to
give her privacy, but now she longed for him.

Too restless to sit or lie down, she drifted around
the bedroom, an airy chamber that by day commanded
a spectacular view of the Downs. Now three lamps
illuminated the room with a soft, romantic glow.
Though Mikahl had only lived here a few weeks, he
had already marked the room with his taste. On one
wall hung an exquisite Oriental painting of mountains,
and underfoot was the most gorgeous Chinese carpet
she had ever seen, richly colored and so thick that it
had the springy resilience of turf.

The bed, however, was English, a carved walnut
four-poster that was both sturdy and spacious. It was
a handsome piece of furniture, and Sara ran her hand
appreciatively down one polished post, then glanced
at the woven blue counterpane, which a maid had
turned down to reveal fine linen sheets.

Abruptly Sara's well-being evaporated, and her fingers tightened on the bedpost. All too clearly, she remembered the moment in the garden when trust and
pleasure had turned to pain and anger. She had felt
betrayed, overwhelmed by his strength. . . .

She took a deep breath and turned away. It had been
an unfortunate accident stemming from her confusion
and his arousal, as much her fault as his. But it was an
unpleasant memory, one that she did not want to dwell
on tonight.

A table between the windows held a small jade sculpture of a horse and a Chinese porcelain vase containing
crimson roses. Sara had expected Sulgrave to seem a
bit drab, since no redecorating had been done yet, but
Mikahl had had the house filled with brilliantly colored
late summer flowers to welcome her. The roses must
have been cut and arranged just before they arrived, for
traces of evening dew were still on them. She touched
a velvety petal. Red for passion.

With uncanny timing, her husband entered the bedchamber from his own dressing room. His dark, exotic

good looks were enhanced by a black velvet robe trimmed with intricate scarlet and gold embroidery. He was magnificent, like a visitor from some grander, more dramatic world. As Marguerite had said, a glorious barbarian, and the sight of him made Sara's knees weaken.

How did one proceed on one's wedding night, particularly an unconventional one? Uncertain about the etiquette, Sara restricted herself to the mild comment, "What a marvelous garment. I assume that it's from somewhere in the Middle East?"

He nodded. "It's one style of Turkish caftan. Sometimes I weary of Western clothing." He crossed the room to where she stood by the windows. "Was Jenny able to find what you needed? Though the butler you sent me is very capable, the household is not yet running smoothly."

"Everything was fine," she assured him. Then an amused smile came into her eyes. "Though I was surprised to see that the room next door is now a sitting room. Didn't it used to be the mistress's bedroom?"

He leaned casually against the wall, his arms crossed over his chest. The black robe made him seem even taller and broader than usual. "Do you really want to sleep alone? I will never force you to do something against your will, Sara, but I have never understood the aristocratic English passion for separate rooms. After all, sharing a bed is one of the main reasons to marry." He gave her a slow, provocative smile. "How can a bride become accustomed to her husband if she doesn't sleep with him?"

Blushing, Sara pulled one of the scarlet roses from the vase. "I don't know if I prefer sleeping alone, because I've never done otherwise, but I am willing to . . . test the advantages of sharing." Her eyes cast down, she inhaled the rose's sultry sweetness. "You have done so much today to make me feel cherished and cared for. Thank you, Mikahl."

"I'm glad," he said simply. "I want to please you in all things."

She glanced at him from the corner of her eye, inexplicably moved by the pleasure he took in pleasing her. If Sara had not already been in love with him, she would have tumbled into love on the spot. A pity that she did not dare admit to love. Instead, she returned the rose to the vase, then stepped up to him and slipped her arms around his neck. "You please me more than any man I've ever known."

Taking her embrace as permission to touch, he straightened up and pulled her close. Sliding his hands down her back from shoulders to hips, he said, "Ah, Sara, sweet Sara, it is delightful to hold you without all that female armor in the way."

"I'm equally glad not to be wearing it," she said fervently, enjoying the feel of his solid, muscular body.

For a few minutes they simply held each other, savoring closeness after the busy day. As she relaxed, Sara began to realize the humor in the situation. Her voice teasing, she said, "I suppose that most wedding nights have an established program of events, but since we intend to move with Hindu deliberation, where do we go from here?"

After a moment's thought, he said with a perfectly straight face, "Perhaps I should draw on my experiences as a world traveler to give you a combination lecture and demonstration on differing sexual attitudes. If I demonstrate anything you are not comfortable with, just say so and I will stop."

"A lecture and demonstration. That sounds very worthy and intellectual." Sara rubbed her cheek against the lush nap of his caftan, not feeling in the least intellectual.

"I shall attempt to maintain a high moral tone," he said solemnly while he stroked the underside of her chin with his knuckle. "I will begin with the fact that women bear children. That simple law of nature is the reason why it is dangerous for a woman to bestow her favors lightly, because she must find a man with the strength and desire to care for her and their children. Since the wrong man can ruin her life, girls learn early, and justly, to be wary of male intentions.''

"But women still succumb to male lures," Sara observed. "I did whenever you came near me."

"For which blessing I am duly grateful." He lifted his hand, his fingertips whisper-light across the curve of her cheek. "Western women carry two burdens: besides the fact that nature decrees that they should defend themselves against men, they must also contend with the attitudes of the Christian Church. For almost two thousand years the church has taught that the flesh is evil, though such teaching was not always successful, for desire is a fundamental part of human nature.''

"Thank heaven for Mother Nature," Sara said, interested at how clearly her husband saw underlying influences that she had never considered. She was equally interested by the fact that when he ran his finger around the edge of her ear, warm tingles spread to distant parts of her anatomy.

"When a girl has been raised to hate and fear a man's touch, it is hardly surprising if she does not become instantly responsive when she marries," he continued. "Some women are never able to overcome their fears, and both husband and wife are the losers for that.''

Sara's languid contentment abruptly vanished when Mikahl untied the ribbons fastening her robe, then peeled the filmy garment away and let it float silently to the floor.

"Too often women are uncomfortable with their bodies and do not understand their own capacity for passion." Putting his hands on her shoulders, he began massaging the hollows above her collarbones with his thumbs. "I want you to learn to love your body, Sara. Then, in time, I hope you will learn to love mine.''

Feeling overexposed in her gauzy nightgown, she said with brittle flippancy, "Some bodies are easier to love than others."

Immediately she wished that she had not spoken, for his hands stilled. Then he cupped her face and raised it so that she was looking directly into his green eyes. From his expression, she knew that she had revealed something that she would rather have kept deeply buried.

"You believe that your body is unlovable? Wrong, sweet Sara. The first time I saw you at your garden party, I was struck by your beauty."

"You don't have to lie to me—I would rather you didn't." She twisted away from his too-penetrating eyes. "My looks are average at best."

"Foolish, foolish Sara," he murmured. Leading her to the pier glass on the opposite side of the room, he stood behind her so that she saw them both full-length. Her head did not even reach his chin.

"Look in the mirror, Sara." He lifted a handful of her hair, then let it spill slowly through his fingers, the strands shining in the lamplight as they drifted down over her breast and shoulder. "Your hair is enchanting, like antique gold that has been spun into thread fit for the gods." He grinned. "Ross's hair is much the same, but for some reason on him it doesn't affect me the same way.

"And your face. You do not have the bland prettiness that will be out of fashion next year, but true beauty." He drew his hands down both sides of her face, his fingers tracing the delicate bones from temple to cheek to chin. "Whenever I look at you, I think of an ancient sibyl, wise and pure." Then, before she realized what he was about, he bent over and took hold of the hem of her loose nightgown and swept it straight up over her head.

Sara gasped in dismay, her appalled protest lost in the folds of fabric. When he had disentangled her and tossed the gown aside, she leaned over and snatched it from the floor. Blushing to the roots of her hair, she held the gown in front of her. It would have been embarrassing enough to be be naked in front of a man for the first time in her life; far worse was being forced to confront the image of her own flawed body. More than a little angry, she said, "What is the point of this?"

"The point is for you to see yourself through my eyes. If you do, you cannot help but love your body." He put his left arm around her waist and firmly locked her against him so that once more she faced the mirror.

The lush velvet of his robe was web soft against her bare back and buttocks. Against his black grandeur, Sara saw herself as a plain, colorless figure who looked foolish in her less-than-successful attempts to cover herself.

With his right hand Mikahl pressed on her arm, lowering the concealing nightgown until she was bare above the waist. "You have a lovely body, delicate and feminine. Exquisite breasts."

He cupped one, and she caught her breath as sensation flared through her.

"And such a tiny waist." His right hand lightly skimmed over her body to illustrate his words. "I think I could span your waist with two hands, but I won't try now because if I let go of you, you'll undoubtedly dive under the blankets and refuse to come out until breakfast."

Sara bit her lip, disarmed into near-laughter at his gentle teasing. Humor began to dispel her embarrassment, and her grip loosened on the protective gown. Taking advantage of her relaxation, he pushed the gown lower yet, until it covered only her legs and the area usually associated with a fig leaf.

Caressing the curve of her hip, he said, "It is really quite wonderful, the way a woman is made. Try to see that."

And for a miraculous moment, she did see herself as he did: as a creature of subtle curves, soft shadows, and smooth surfaces, mysteriously female to his intense masculinity.

Mikahl bent and kissed her shoulder, and she inhaled sharply, both moved and aroused. Then he pulled the gown from her unresisting fingers, leaving her completely uncovered.

Like a china plate smashing onto a stone floor, Sara's moment of soaring delight shattered at the sight of her right thigh. She tried to avoid looking directly at her disfigurement, even in the bath, but now she could not escape the sight. As a permanent reminder of her near-fatal accident, two livid scars twisted across her right thigh between groin and knee. One scar was from her original injury, where she had struck a jagged branch that tore her flesh and smashed the bone. The other was from the excruciating surgery that came later.

Though it was a less obvious flaw, she was acutely aware that years of favoring her right leg had left it thinner and weaker than the left. During the seduction in the garden, she had felt protected by her masses of petticoats. Given the circumstances, she had decided later that Mikahl had not noticed the scars. But now she was exposed to his eyes, and her own. With the bitterness of a decade's suppressed anger she snapped, "Do two exquisite breasts outweigh one ugly, crippled leg?"

Her question hung in the air, acrid as a witch's curse. Mikahl said softly, "Sweet Sara, beauty is not a result of mere symmetry."

Then, to Sara's disbelieving shock, he knelt at her feet and kissed the longest scar, his lips warm and tender.

"Perfection would be boring, for the greatest beauty is often flawed, always unique," he murmured, his breath warm on her sensitive flesh as his tongue traced the gnarled ridge of tissue that curved around her inner thigh to her knee. "A scar of the body cannot wholly destroy beauty. Only a scar of the spirit can do that."

His kiss was deeply erotic, sending tongues of flame licking into her intimate depths. But he was doing far more than stir her desire; his words were a gift of acceptance, of forgiveness for her flaws.

Looking down at his dark head, Sara began to shake, near collapse as a decade's worth of physical and emotional defenses crumbled. "Mikahl," she whispered. Partly as a caress, partly to support her unsteady body, she buried her fingers in the soft waves of his black hair. She wanted to say something, but had no words for what he was doing to her, so she could only repeat helplessly, "Mikahl . . ."

He looked up at her, and his grave eyes would have made her weep if she had not sworn off crying ten years before.

At the sight of her wordless anguish, her husband stood and lifted her with one arm under her knees and the other around her ribs. Then he carried her to the bed and set her on the cool white sheets, before lying down beside her and pulling her close against him.

An old, festering wound had been lanced, and Sara trembled as years of anger and self-hatred gushed forth. For a long time she hid her face against his shoulder, breathing in ragged gulps. Even to herself, she had never admitted how much she had resented her injury, or how she despised herself for the instant of carelessness that had killed her horse and crippled her.

As her shaking stopped and her breathing steadied, she became aware of mundane details like the sandalwood scent of the soap he used and the faint rasp of embroidery against her forehead. Gradually her world returned to normal, though she knew that she had changed forever, and for the better.

It was hard to believe that a few short weeks before, Sara had found Ross's closeness comforting, while Peregrine's was disquieting; the mysterious, unsettling foreign prince had been transformed to Mikahl, who was her husband, and in his arms she found solace.

Chapter 16

WHEN SARA was in command of herself again, she lay back against the pillow and asked ruefully, "Are you licensed to practice surgery of the soul?"

"No formal training, but I've had some practical experience. Do you feel better or worse for having seen through my eyes?"

"Better. For a moment I did see myself as you do, and I was beautiful. That didn't last long—but I will never feel as ugly or crippled again." She made a face. "It must seem foolish to be so upset about scars that aren't even visible to the world."

"Ah, but surely the scars are just the surface of a very deep river. They stand for the years of pain when you forced yourself to learn to walk, when it would have been so much easier to stay an invalid, and for the occasional pain you will feel for the rest of your life."

Deliberately he laid his hand on her right thigh. "The scars also stand for loss—the loss of a young man you wished to marry, the loss of riding, dancing, and all the physical freedom that the healthy young never question." Gently he squeezed her leg. "And perhaps also they are a symbol of the fact that you can't always live up to your own high standards? You made a mistake." He removed his hand and drew the blanket up to her waist. "We all do. Learn to live with it."

Sara stared up at him, temporarily stunned by his

insight. At length she said, "How do you know such things—sorcery?"

"Hardly." He shrugged. "I watch people. I try to understand them. It's a useful skill."

"An uncanny skill." Sara regarded him with curiosity mixed with some awe. "Do you understand yourself equally well?"

Mikahl looked surprised, then thoughtful. "Probably not. There is less practical value in self-knowledge."

Sara had to laugh. "You are quite incredible," she said affectionately.

"Not really," he said with a trace of dryness. "I am merely what my past has made me. It is just that no one else has such a past." His fingers drifted down her bare arm in a gentle, unthreatening caress. "Have you had enough lecturing and demonstrating for one night?"

"Actually, I find your ideas very interesting. I suppose someone from a different society can see this one more clearly. You are right that we English are often uncomfortable with our bodies." Though Sara found that she was not shy about her bare breasts, perhaps because of the admiring warmth in Mikahl's eyes.

He was still robed, probably because he did not want to alarm her with the sight of a powerful, naked male body. But she found the idea much less alarming than she had earlier. Her eyes fastened on the curling tuft of black hair visible at the throat of his caftan. "I've never even seen a square inch of bare male flesh below a man's collar."

Seeing the direction of her gaze, he grinned. "That can be remedied whenever you like."

Sara blushed a little, preferring to keep the discussion abstract, at least for the moment. "Are sexual attitudes very different in other lands?"

He propped his head up on his left hand and regarded her with lazy-lidded eyes. "Everywhere it is recognized how much power and danger there is between men and women. Often desire is condemned, but not always. Sexual customs differ enormously.''

His fingertips feathered down her throat, then across the top of her breasts. Though Sara was interested in his words, she found herself distracted by the pleasure that began humming through her.

Blandly he continued, ''There is an interesting paradox between East and West. In your country women have more freedom, so they must be taught to defend their own virtue. In contrast, in many Eastern lands women are virtual prisoners, separated from all men except their husbands. Curiously, this gives such women more freedom to be sensual.

''For example . . .'' With his middle finger, he drew slow circles around her left breast, never quite touching the nipple. ''While the early Christian fathers preached that sexual abstinence was the path to heaven, the ancient Taoist masters of China taught that nature is energy in constant, shifting motion.

''Two complementary principles are at work: the active energy, *yang,* and the receptive energy, *yin.* Yang and yin apply to all polarities: summer and winter, sun and moon, male and female. When the energies are in balance, life is healthy and harmonious. Hence, for a Taoist, sexual intercourse is a path to spiritual harmony. Man does not take, and woman give—they share their energies in a search for mutual balance.''

Sara's nipple stiffened, longing to be touched directly. Thinking that it was impossible to decide which was more erotic, his rich, deep voice or his skilled fingers, she asked, ''I assume that men are yang and women yin?''

''Excellent! You have the mind of a philosopher.'' He transferred his tantalizing attentions to her other breast. ''Though actually it is not quite that simple. Even the most aggressive man has some yin nature, and even the most passive woman has some yang.''

It was becoming difficult to concentrate on ideas, but Sara did her best. ''You must be very yang,'' she said, rather breathlessly. "Certainly you are very male."

"And you, silken Sara, are very yin—utterly and desirably female." He covered her breast with his hand, the gentle pressure both satisfying and rousing. Then, his intense gaze holding hers, he leaned over and kissed her.

His mouth was yang, aggressive and demanding, while hers was yin, receptive and yearning. Sara felt the melting desire to yield that his kisses always induced, and gladly she surrendered to the sensation.

Then, as the kiss lengthened, her energy began to change. She became more yang, wanting more of him, wanting to explore the depths of his mouth as he had explored hers. As she became more assertive, he also changed, became welcoming and receptive. And in the process, Sara discovered that to give and receive at the same time opened new vistas of delight.

Becoming dizzy from both desire and lack of air, finally she pulled her head away. Her lips an inch from his, Sara murmured, "What . . . what else do the Taoist masters say?"

"A great deal," he replied distractedly, his breathing as rough as Sara's. Deciding to abandon the lecture and concentrate on demonstration, Peregrine lowered his mouth to her breast. The instant hardening of her nipple made him lose all interest in philosophy. For a time he gave himself up to the satisfactions of tasting her delicious breasts. Now that she was wed and no longer fearing him, Sara responded without reservation, and her innocent fire was the most potent aphrodisiac he had ever known.

He almost passed the point of no return without realizing it. His whole body throbbed with urgency, and he was fumbling with the sash of his caftan before he recognized just how near disaster was. Barely in time, he mustered the last shreds of his control and pulled away.

Damnation, he had known that restraint would be

difficult, but this was far worse than he had expected.
She would not be responding so wholly if she did not
trust him to be master of himself, yet here he was, on
the verge of doing the same thing that he had done to
her before. What was it about Sara that had such an
extraordinary effect on him? Swearing under his breath
in Kafiri, he closed his eyes and ordered his racing
heart to slow to a more manageable level.

Deciding that it was time to return to a more intellectual plane, he opened his eyes and gave Sara a
crooked smile. "Human intercourse is a reflection of
cosmic balance, like the mating of earth and sky. When
men and women join, it is a solemn spiritual duty.
Taoist masters wrote books on the subject of achieving
balance."

Her eyes wide and dazed, she said gamely, "Their
books must have been very popular."

"Very." Unable to resist the lure of Sara's silken
skin, he reached for her again, moving the blanket
aside as he stroked across the subtle curve of her abdomen. Surely it was safe to touch her as long as he
remembered that he must stop. . . . "The Chinese are
very fond of poetic imagery, though many of the terms
are amusing when translated."

He laid his hand over the triangle of soft, ash blond
hair at the junction of her thighs, and felt the beating
of her blood against his palm. "The female organs,
for example, were called names such as the Open Pe-
ony Blossom and the Golden Lotus." His fingers
probed through the fine curly strands to the moist,
acutely sensitive folds of flesh below. "The Cinnabar
Cleft."

"A-h-h-h . . ." Sara's eyes drifted shut. Weakly she
said, "I . . . I've always been very fond of poetry."

"Then you will be interested to know that this"—
he located the most sensitive nub of all, and gently
began stroking it—"is called the Jeweled Terrace. It
is vitally important, for the Taoist masters believed

that a woman's yin energy is strongest when she also finds satisfaction in mating.''

Sara moaned and arched into his touch. "What . . . what is the male organ called?''

"Various things. The Vigorous Peak. The Swelling Mushroom. The Coral Stem." He racked his brain, knowing that there were many terms, but finding it difficult to remember or translate them under these conditions. "The Jade Stalk.''

That briefly penetrated Sara's sensual haze. Her brow furrowed. "Since jade is green, that sounds odd. I like the other names better.''

He chuckled. "Jade comes in many colors, including white, tan, and brown. That must be the sort of jade meant.''

Sara was feeling more yang by the minute, but even so she was surprised to find herself reaching for the sash of his caftan. "Lecture is less effective without demonstration.''

Shy but determined, she untied the sash, then separated the velvet panels and spread her hands across his chest. The dark hair tickled her palms with delicious roughness. Drawing her hands the length of his torso, she reveled in the feel of hard muscle and bone.

The coarse dark hair thickened as she moved lower until she reached the Coral Stem and clasped it between her palms. His flesh was jade smooth and very warm, hard yet subtly yielding.

When she gently squeezed, Mikahl groaned and moved against her hand. Sara was delighted to learn that she could affect him as powerfully as he affected her. As her fingers tightened experimentally, a shudder ran through him.

Abruptly he rolled onto his back so that they were no longer touching. His chest heaving, her husband said with glass-edged precision, "It is time to end the lecture, sweet Sara, for we have reached the limits of my restraint.''

He was keeping his word, but was that what Sara wanted? Realizing that her earlier trepidation had burned away like morning mist, she said, "Don't." She touched her tongue to her upper lip. "Don't restrain yourself."

He studied her expression for a long moment. "Then let us return to the Jeweled Terrace." He turned onto his side and resumed his intimate caresses, saying unsteadily, "A woman is a never-ending source of yin, and this increases her potency."

His expert touch produced waves of pleasure so intense that Sara wondered if she would dissolve. But this was not what she wanted, for he was holding himself away from her, giving without letting her give in return. She reached for him, saying, "Wouldn't it be more harmonious to join yin with yang?"

He stopped her before she could touch him, a film of sweat covering his face and throat. Deadly serious, he said, "Sara, don't think that you must do this for my sake."

Softly she said, "I don't." She grasped his shoulders and fell back on the pillows, drawing him down on top of her. "I just find Taoist theology more interesting than Hindu restraint."

"Ah, Sara, Sara . . ." he whispered. Words ceased as he kissed her, his mouth wide open on hers. Separating her legs, he moved between them, then slowly entered.

Not quite able to forget the first time, Sara tensed at the first moment of invasion. But this time there was no pain; instead, there was completion.

Enchanted, Sara rolled her hips against him, savoring the splendid new sensations of slick friction and sliding depths.

"You are a natural Taoist philosopher," he said with a choke of laughter, "but this will last longer if you slow down and move in tandem with me."

Obediently she did as he suggested, and found that the natural rhythm of thrust and response began taking on a life of its own. In the garden she had been frightened and overwhelmed by his strength, but this was different, for now they shared their energies. His strength was hers and hers was his, and in the blending was joy.

The black velvet caftan fell around them, a shadow-soft cocoon. Sara slid her arms beneath the robe and wrapped them tightly around his waist, tasting the saltiness of his shoulder against her mouth, feeling the hard flexing muscles of his hips and buttocks, sleek sweat contrasted with unexpected roughness.

Then all thought disintegrated in a vortex of demand and reward. When she cried out, he drove into her one last time, his own body convulsing around hers. And in the final, shattering moment, for an instant Sara found the harmony of the masters.

Sara drifted to sleep in her husband's arms, face-to-face, her body intertwined with his. The velvet caftan enfolded her, providing the only other warmth needed on a mild night.

She was not sure how long she slept—two or three hours perhaps. When she slowly floated up into consciousness, the lamps still burned, filling the room with soft light. Outside the window, the night sky was still cavern black.

Sleepily Sara thought what a delicious intimacy it was to sleep within the shelter of Mikahl's robe. Perhaps an Arab prince and princess might sleep side by side like this, beneath the star-strewn skies of the desert? Probably not, but it was a pleasant fantasy.

She shifted position a little, and his eyes opened just a few inches away. Greatly daring, she slid her hand down his torso, curious about what she might find.

With a lazy smile, Mikahl said, "Though woman's yin essence is inexhaustible, the same is not true of male yang essence."

She chuckled, intrigued by the way his body changed at her touch. "Perhaps not inexhaustible, but I think not yet exhausted?"

He laughed. "Many Eastern religions believe in re-incarnation—one soul living many lives. If so, you must have spent a life or two as a courtesan."

She stopped and asked uncertainly, "Should I not do this?"

"That was a compliment, sweet Sara," he said swiftly. "By all means, continue."

She gave him a mischievous smile. "You wanted me to learn to love your body, and I find that is very easy to do." An enticing idea occurred to her, so she propped herself up on one elbow. "Since you viewed my body earlier, I now claim the same privilege."

An undefinable change came over him, a subtle withdrawal without moving a single muscle. Wondering if she was imagining the reaction, Sara glanced in his eyes questioningly.

"Fair is fair," he said in a voice of absolute neutrality.

She considered retreat, but having been granted permission, she could not resist the opportunity to see all of him. Mikahl was lying on his side, so she pulled his caftan down his arm, then pushed it backward so that he was naked before her.

To her surprise, Sara saw that his complexion was almost as fair as hers. Because his face and hands were a weathered tan, she had thought him dark, but his skin looked white against the black hair that arrowed down his chest and flat stomach.

She stroked the silky hair appreciatively, then touched a round, angry-looking mark on his shoulder. "This is an odd bruise."

"You did that, my little vixen," he said with amusement.

"I did?" Then Sara remembered how mindlessly she had behaved, how frantically her mouth and hands had worked, and she blushed. To cover her embarrassment, she ran one hand down his powerfully muscled arm, thinking that he had the fitness and perfect proportions that Greek sculptors had immortalized in marble. But he was far more beautiful, for he had the supple warmth of life.

Her admiring hand paused on the side of his hip, where she found a faint, jagged mark shaped like a sprawling *W* or *M*.

It was a cross between a scar and a tattoo, and curiously she traced the shape.

His muscles went rigid under her fingers. She glanced at his face again, wondering what was wrong. She could not believe that he suffered from either shyness or excessive modesty.

Mikahl said nothing, just watched her with the wariness of a trapped animal.

Beginning to feel uneasy, Sara skimmed her hand over his shoulder and along the back of his ribs. Her fingers encountered an unexpected texture; where the skin should have been smooth over taut muscle and bone, there was roughness. She frowned, remembering that she had vaguely noticed the same thing when they were making love. Sitting up, she tugged her husband more onto his stomach. He cooperated passively.

Sara leaned over to investigate more thoroughly, then caught her breath, frozen in shock. Mikahl's back was a tapestry of crisscrossing scars, some so faint as to be almost invisible, others long, wicked ridges of gnarled tissue.

"Dear God," she whispered, knowing that such scars could only have been caused by ferocious, near-lethal whipping. She looked down into his face and saw that he watched her with hooded eyes that gave nothing away. Intuitively she knew that these scars were, in a different way, as traumatic for him as hers were for her. "What—what happened to you?"

"I was a slave." His voice was quite without inflection.

Sara swallowed hard, her gaze returning to the scars. "I don't suppose that you were very good at taking orders."

"No." The flat syllable was like a granite wall.

Faced with the reality of how unimaginably different and difficult her husband's life had been, Sara wanted

to weep for the second time that night. There was only
one possible response, and she made it with all the
growing love of her heart.

Leaning forward, she kissed the deepest scar. The
ruined flesh was rough beneath her lips.

"Perhaps, for a while, someone had dominion over
your body," she whispered, her hands and mouth tenderly moving across the obscene lines that marred his
beautiful body. "But I cannot believe that your spirit
was ever anything but free."

A spasm ran through him. Then he rolled onto his
back and pulled her down into an anguished kiss.
There was nothing playful or erotic about his embrace;
it was a desperate bid for oblivion, a desire to drown
an unspeakable past.

Before tonight, Sara would have been terrified by
his raw masculine power, but she had learned much
in the last few hours. When she had faced the pain of
her scars and her anger, Mikahl had solaced her with
tenderness. Now, if it was what he wanted, she would
solace him with passion.

It proved easy to give him what he desired, for even
though he flailed at inner darkness, he did not use her
with blind selfishness. Earlier he had taught her with
gentle caresses; now his hands and mouth wooed her
with the compelling force of molten lava.

Sara responded with all her love and all her fire, and
she was ready, more than ready, when he rolled her over
and buried himself inside her. It was primal, savage sex
in the shadow of the volcano. She met him thrust for thrust
in a wild, wordless joining, wrapping her legs around his,
wanting to give back some of what he had given her.

Such a rage of passion could not last long, and he
culminated quickly, his ragged, heart-deep groan
drawing her with him into a shuddering reality of fus-
ing flame. In the aftermath Sara lay limp, her limbs
trembling and numb, her chest heaving as she struggled for breath.

Still without speaking, Mikahl rolled to his side and

drew her into his arms, burying his face in her hair. This time when they slept, it was in the depths of exhaustion.

Peregrine woke slowly and found that he was lying with his head pillowed on his wife's soft breast, his arms encircling her. It was dawn, and the lamps had burned out. Sara still slept, her heart thumping slow and steady beneath his ear. He lay motionless, not wanting to disturb her because he needed to think through the events of the night before she woke.

What the devil had he gotten himself into? He had desired Sara and felt some sense of obligation, so he had married her without a single serious thought about the consequences.

Vaguely he had assumed that marriage would be rather like one of his brief, intense affairs. He had always subordinated sex to business; when convenient, he would indulge himself with high-level courtesans who enjoyed their work and knew better than to ask questions. Over the years, there had been a few special women whom he would see regularly, whenever he visited their cities. He had looked forward to their company both in and out of bed, and had thought marriage would be much the same: amusing, physically satisfying, and uncomplicated.

Instead, marriage seemed to involve a mutual peeling away of masks and a shocking amount of vulnerability. When he had discovered Sara's buried pain over her old injury, it had seemed natural to comfort her. Yet in some mysterious fashion, comforting her had weakened his own defenses.

In a way, his scarred back was a perverse badge of honor, an indelible reminder of what he had suffered and the vengeance he would exact. The only way to conceal the disfigurement from a bedmate would have been to limit intercourse to furtive, mostly clothed grapplings, which he had no intention of doing.

But since it had been inevitable that his wife discover the scars, why had he been so profoundly disturbed when she did?

Because he usually knew what he wanted, he seldom wasted time analyzing his own motives, but now he probed the depths of his mind, trying to learn why he had reacted with such violence.

Eventually, he decided that it was Sara's tenderness that had touched a long-buried chord. The boy who had been whipped so many years ago would have appreciated some kindness, but had known none; somehow, Sara's aching sweetness had released that child's anguish. As a result, Peregrine the man had lashed out with terrifying force.

Like an earthquake, it had been an interesting experience, but it was not one that he was anxious to repeat.

Propping himself on one elbow, he looked down into Sara's face. She looked absurdly young and innocent, her golden hair spilling across the pillow like tangled sunbeams. Yet within her slender frame was a lionhearted woman with the resilience and compassion to respond to his furious demands, even though she was the next thing to a virgin.

Perhaps he should be ashamed of how he had used her, but he had not been too distraught to notice that she had responded with eagerness. And not just with passion; she had brought her own special quality of tenderness to the encounter, and her caring had touched and softened something deep inside him.

And that was dangerous, for he could not afford softening. In the future, he must keep his guard up, keep Sara at enough of a distance that she could not slide under his skin again. But that should not be difficult; certainly the risks were not so great that he dare not allow himself to enjoy her sweet warmth.

Issues resolved, he leaned forward and gave Sara a light kiss. Her eyelashes fluttered open sleepily, and she gave him a slow, shining smile. "Good morning, husband."

He stroked her hair back from her temple. "Good morning, wife." He wondered what he should say if she asked about his period of slavery. While he would rather not lie to Sara, he surely wouldn't tell her a truth that might shatter the growing intimacy between them. Some things were best left hidden in the darkness where they belonged.

Uncannily, the deep sibyl eyes seemed to see and weigh his internal questions, and he had the absurd feeling that Sara had judged and decided that silence was better than lies.

"Let's keep the other chamber as a sitting room," she murmured, her eyes teasing. "I've decided that sharing a bed is much nicer than sleeping alone."

"Agreed." He lay back on the pillows, and pulled her on top of him for a more serious kiss. As the embrace began to develop into another energy-balancing session, he knew that he was a fortunate man to have a wife with the sense to know what things were none of her business.

Charles Weldon had several offices, but these days he spent most of his time at the L & S Railway. As managing director, he had to make decisions about everything from finance to the design of the railway carriages being built in Yorkshire.

The company secretary had learned to have a pot of tea and a newspaper waiting for him in the morning, and as he drank his tea, Weldon skimmed the headlines to see what was happening in the world. He usually skipped the society notices, but this morning his eye was caught by the word "Haddonfield," so he stopped and read the brief announcement. Lady Sara St. James, daughter of the Duke of Haddonfield, had three days previously married Prince Peregrine of Kafiristan.

Weldon's lip curled when he read it. They certainly hadn't wasted any time; he wondered if the silly bitch was pregnant. Well, the two had better be enjoying their honeymoon, because their time together was going to be limited.

Laying the paper aside, he began reading through the morning post. It was midday when the bad news was delivered by his personal secretary, Kane.

A man of few words, Kane had dropped uninvited into a chair and said tersely, "Trouble."

Weldon leaned back in his oak swivel chair. "What kind of trouble?"

"Remember you sent me to Hampshire with the right-of-way papers for that farmer, Crawley, to sign?"

"Of course—we're going to be starting construction there in a few days. What's the matter, is he still trying to get more money? The oaf should realize that he's lucky to get anything."

"Don't know what he thinks—Crawley and his family have vanished, bag, baggage, and livestock. I talked to some of the neighbors. Seems the Crawleys just up and left a few weeks ago. Didn't say where they were going or when they'd get back."

Weldon's face twisted into a scowl as he considered the implications. "Did Crawley sell the farm to someone else?"

"Doesn't seem to have."

Weldon bit his lower lip, thinking that there was something unnatural about the business, for Crawley certainly didn't have the money to go off and start again elsewhere. Perhaps the farmer had panicked and run?

After a minute's thought, he shrugged; Crawley's disappearance wouldn't make any difference to the railway. "We'll go ahead and start laying rail across the farm anyhow. Crawley isn't around to object, and no one else will know that we haven't gotten the correct authorizations. If he comes back, we make him sign, only maybe then he won't get any money at all for the privilege of being part of the L & S route."

Dismissing Kane, he returned to work. Crawley's cowardly flight was a minor nuisance, no more.

Chapter 17

MIKAHL HAD LEFT early to go into London on business, so Sara slept late, then rose for a leisurely bath. Since he would be gone all day, she was going to ride to Chapelgate and lunch with her cousin. After a fortnight of honeymoon solitude, she supposed that it was time to remember that the rest of the world existed. Then, after Mikahl had been gone for a whole ten hours, she would have the pleasure of welcoming him home.

Sara knew that she had an absurd, dreamy smile on her face, but didn't care. She was hopelessly, passionately in love, and marriage was wonderful. Admittedly there were many things she didn't know about her husband, and he had never said that he loved her. But deeds were more important than words, and his actions could not have been more tender or loving. Mikahl liked to touch, and did so with a freedom seldom seen in an Englishman. In spite of her occasional blushes, Sara loved his demonstrative nature and responded like a flower opening to the sun.

Though she knew that her present joy could not continue forever, she refused to worry about that. No matter how much pain her marriage might bring in the future, this fortnight of loving was worth any price she might have to pay. And there should still be weeks or months of happiness to come; if she was very lucky, years.

After her bath, Sara summoned Jenny to help her dress. As the maid braided her hair, Sara asked, "Now that you've had a chance to settle in, do you still like Sulgrave?''

''It's unholy quiet after London,'' the girl observed, ''but the country is pretty, and the other servants couldn't be nicer.''

Sara smiled. ''We'll be going to London again in a few days. That should save you from falling into a bored melancholy.''

''Very good, my lady,'' Jenny said demurely, her deft fingers coiling one of the braids over her mistress's left ear.

As Sara watched Jenny's elfin face, she could not help but think of the girl's sordid past. Years in a brothel, Mikahl had said. Sara had been shocked at the idea; now that she understood the profound intimacy of the marriage bed, she was even more shocked. The thought of strangers violating one's body, forcing what should be sacred, was appalling. If anything ever happened to Mikahl, Sara knew that she would never be able to share such intimacy with another man.

Impulsively speaking her thoughts, Sara asked, ''Jenny, how did you survive those years in a brothel with your humor and sanity intact?''

Jenny's hand jerked, and the hairpins she had been holding dropped from her hand and skittered over Sara's shoulder to the floor. Dismayed, Sara turned swiftly and said, ''Jenny, forgive me, I had no right to ask such a thing. I said when I hired you that you need never speak of the past again—please forget that I ever mentioned the topic.''

The maid knelt on the floor to pick up the hairpins. When she straightened, she said in a voice that was almost normal, ''It's not so bad that I can't talk about it, Lady Sara. I was mostly surprised that you asked.''

Her movements precise, Jenny wound the other plait over Sara's right ear and pinned it in place. ''I suppose I survived because in the East End, life is always hard, and if you expect the worst, you're never disappointed,'' she said reflectively. ''Having my pa sell me to a brothel was bad, but worse things happened to some of the other girls I grew up with.

"The brothel was hardest for girls who'd been raised decent. Some went kind of crazy when they found out what was going to be done to them." Jenny's face darkened. "The walls were thick, but not thick enough. Of course, a lot of those girls were there just one night because it was a virgin house. For those of us who were there longer—well, you can get used to almost anything."

"What is a virgin house?" Sara asked, having a horrible feeling that she could guess.

The girl frowned. "This isn't a subject for a lady's ears. The prince won't like that I'm talking to you about such things."

"Dear God, Jenny, how can something that you had to *live* be too harsh for my delicate ears to *hear!*" Sara felt the same cold fury as when she had discovered that the orphanage children were being abused by those who should protect them. "Anyone born with fortune or influence has an obligation to use it to try to help others. I was active with charitable work in Haddonfield, and I intend to do the same here. While I don't know if I can do anything about the evils you suffered, if I am ignorant, I will not even be able to try."

Sara gestured for the maid to sit down. "If you can bear to talk about it, I want to know. Then perhaps someday I might be able to do some good."

After a moment of hesitation, Jenny sat down and summarized the operation of Mrs. Kent's house. The account turned Sara's stomach, but she listened with grim determination. At the end, she exclaimed passionately, "What kind of men can behave so to innocent girls?"

Jenny gave a cynical smile. "All kinds. I'll bet every penny I have, some of those fancy society gents who kiss your hand at balls are customers of Mrs. Kent's. Girls, boys, any ages and combinations that a man is willing to pay for."

"Boys?" Sara asked, not understanding what the maid meant.

Jenny looked uncomfortable. "You really don't want to know that, my lady. It's downright unnatural."

Sara's lips thinned. Turning away from unpleasant facts seemed a betrayal of innocent victims. "Tell me."

Jenny complied, her blunt words describing in detail what a grown man might do to a little boy.

Sara's hands clenched so tightly that her nails left deep crescents in her palms. When the maid was finished, Sara said in a strained voice, "How can such wickedness exist so flagrantly in the heart of the greatest city in the world?"

Though Sara's words had been more for herself than her maid, Jenny replied bitterly, "Laws are made by those with power, my lady. How many of those with power really care what happens to the poor? They're the wolves, and folks like me are the sheep."

Sara sighed. "You've learned hard wisdom, Jenny. But there are a few people with power who care about those less fortunate. I'm going to make it my business to find out who does care, and to contribute what I can."

The maid looked uneasy. "You won't be telling the prince what I said? He'd be powerful irritated with me."

"No, I won't tell him." Sara gave a twisted smile. "He's a man of the world—I doubt that there is anything either you or I could say about wickedness that would surprise him." And like most men, he probably accepted that evil would always be present, and that there was no point in wasting time fighting it. And who was she, who had been pampered all her life, to criticize Mikahl for not being outraged when he had had so much to endure? It was hardly surprising if his sensibilities had been blunted.

As Jenny completed Sara's toilette, Sara thought about what she had learned this morning. While she would have liked to ask Mikahl if anything could be done to close Mrs. Kent's house, she did not want to bring his wrath on Jenny. Better to wait and learn more about the subject before she talked to her husband.

Sara knew she could not save the world. There had always been prostitutes, and perhaps there always would be. But raping helpless children was not simple prostitution: it was an unspeakable crime, and Sara would do what she could to stop it.

As Sara made her way downstairs after dressing, the Sulgrave butler heard her footsteps and came out into the hall. Gates was a long-time Haddonfield employee who had asked permission to accompany Sara to her new home. Since Mikahl was willing, Sara had been grateful to accept Gates's offer.

"Good morning, my lady," the butler said with a deep bow. "Cook wishes to know what time to serve dinner tonight."

"Probably about eight o'clock, but tell her to prepare something that won't be injured by reheating in case my husband returns later than he planned." Sara drew her riding gloves on as she stood on the bottom step. "You've done a wonderful job since your arrival, Gates. My husband said just yesterday that the household is running like a fine clock."

The butler gave a small, satisfied smile. "A pleasure to be of service. It's a small return for what the St. James family and Prince Peregrine have done for me."

Mildly curious, Sara said, "You have done as much for the St. Jameses as we have done for you, but what has my husband done? You've only just met him."

"I expect you know what it is like in the servants' hall, my lady—considerable information is exchanged. There was much discussion about the prince below stairs when it was announced that you were marrying him." Gates's smile became downright smug. "Someone had learned that he is a major shareholder in the new L & S Railway. I decided that if the company was good enough for Lady Sara's husband, it was good enough for me. So I invested my savings in the stock.''

Sara frowned. ''My husband invests in many businesses and does not expect them all to be successful. I hate to think that your savings might be jeopardized if the L & S doesn't do well.''

''But it's doing splendidly,'' he assured her. ''The value of the stock I bought has already gone up by almost half.''

''I don't know anything about finance,'' Sara said dryly, ''but surely a stock that goes up that quickly can go down just as fast. Perhaps you should sell now and take your profit.''

''It will only go higher, my lady. Railroads are the way of the future.'' He looked vastly pleased with himself. ''When I retire from service, the L & S will buy me a nice little hostelry in a south-coast town where the wind is easier on old bones.''

One of the parlor maids entered the hall, and Gates immediately returned to his impassive manner. An upper servant might talk to his mistress with some freedom, but never in the presence of his inferiors.

Sara walked to the stables, thinking that the day had certainly begun rather strangely. But her good mood was restored by the ride along the Downs to Chapelgate. She was mounted on a superb, sweet-tempered sorrel mare that her husband had given her as a wedding gift, and the day was glorious, with the tang of coming autumn. Though the world was an imperfect place, her particular corner of it could not be better.

Ross strolled down the front steps to greet her when she rode up to Chapelgate. ''Bless you, Sara. You have arrived just in time to save me from deciding whether I must throw out all of the last chapter.''

She rolled her eyes in mock horror. ''What, and deprive the world of some of your golden prose?''

''I suspect there is more dross than gold in this case.'' Her cousin raised his arms, and Sara slid down into them, then handed the mare's reins to the groom who had accompanied her.

The cousins climbed the steps together, Ross's arm around Sara's shoulder. "I don't have to ask what you think of marriage—I can see canary feathers all around you."

Sara laughed. "Marriage is wonderful," she agreed, unable to prevent a blushing smile from spreading over her face.

He glanced down, his brown eyes serious. "No regrets?"

"No regrets," she replied. "Mikahl may be complicated and mysterious, but he could not treat me any better than he does."

Her cousin sighed. "Honeymoons don't last forever."

"Of course not," she agreed. "But how many people ever know two weeks of perfect happiness? No matter what happens in the future, I will always have that." She gave him a shrewd glance. "Because you introduced him to me, you feel responsible for whether or not I'm happy. But you must stop worrying—for better or worse, the future is for me and Mikahl to work out. If I end up miserable, it won't be your fault."

"Wise words, but impossible to follow," Ross said with amusement as he opened the door. "You'll just have to stay happy to spare me from guilt."

Sara stepped into the hall and removed her veiled riding hat. "We're going up to London in a few days. The Little Season is starting, and I want to show my glorious husband off."

Ross grinned. "Does that mean that Mother has prevailed on you to go to Cousin Leticia's ball?"

"That's part of the reason," Sara admitted as she handed her hat and riding crop to the butler. "I haven't seen Letty in donkey's years, but since she is launching her daughter, I suppose I should be present. Exactly the sort of affair I hate: very large, very noisy, very boring." She smiled again. "Mikahl says that I have more cousins than anyone he's ever met, but he is very amiable about escorting me to such functions. Besides, he has business in town, I want to buy some things for the house, Father wants Mikahl to be presented at court, and there are other parties. We'll probably stay for a fortnight or so. Are you going to Letty's ball also?"

When Ross gave an exaggerated shudder, Sara said, "Foolish question. As if anyone could withstand Aunt Marguerite."

"Mother keeps muttering that I am turning into a hermit, and that it is her duty to drag me into society regularly. I'm beginning to think it's time to take another trip. Constantinople first, then perhaps down through the Levant."

Sara repressed a twinge; exploration of the world's wilder places was a dangerous business. But she understood her cousin's need to roam, and she would not try to stop him, any more than his parents did. Those who loved Ross knew that an empty society life in England would soon drive him mad.

First Jenny, then Gates, and now Ross. As Sara led the way into the drawing room, she realized that her honeymoon was over. She and Mikahl might enjoy each other just as much tonight as on the previous nights, but they were part of the world again.

Peregrine dropped his hat negligently on a table when he entered Slade's office, but his offhand manner was pure fiction. Inside, he vibrated with excitement. "Good morning, Benjamin. I was delighted to hear that the die has been cast. How is the City reacting to news of the volley of lawsuits that hit the L & S Railway yesterday?"

"The stock lost half its value this morning, and is still dropping like a stone." Slade pushed his chair back and laced his fingers across his midriff. "Investors would have been able to take the compensation suit calmly, and perhaps even the injunction barring construction over Crawley's land. But the charges of harassment of landowners and manslaughter in the death of Jimmy Crawley have terrified them. The only thing worse would have been if there had been enough evidence to have Weldon arrested outright.''

"Splendid.'' Peregrine sat down and crossed his legs casually. ''Absolutely splendid.''

''That is a downright unnatural attitude for a man who has just lost forty thousand pounds and stands to lose considerably more,'' Slade complained.

''The satisfaction it brings me is cheap at the price. Are there any other developments?''

''I understand that Hammersley's bank was about to lend Weldon enough money to pay off the notes you hold, but with the decline in value of the railway stock, I'd be surprised if the bank doesn't withdraw.'' The lawyer pursed his lips thoughtfully. ''If he wants to avoid default, he will have to go either to a friend or the moneylenders.''

''Or perhaps Weldon may blackmail someone who has been particularly indiscreet in one of his whorehouses,'' Peregrine said cynically.

''Does the idea of that bother you?'' Slade asked. ''To think that some poor devil might be crucified because of the financial pressure you're putting on Weldon?''

''A man should be willing to live by his deeds,'' Peregrine said, unimpressed. ''Only a scoundrel or a hypocrite can be blackmailed. Perhaps Weldon's death struggles will flush another few scoundrels from the shrubbery.''

The lawyer toyed with his pen. ''You've got Weldon where you want him. You've broken up his betrothal and married the woman who would have been his wife, destroyed his hopes of a title, and pushed him over the financial brink. But have you thought about the consequences if he learns that you are behind his troubles? He could be a very dangerous man.''

"I *expect* him to learn that," Peregrine said cordially. "Indeed, I want him to know. Vengeance would be less satisfying if it were blind."

The lawyer looked up sharply. "That's a cavalier attitude. What if he strikes back at you through Lady Sara?"

"Do you think I cannot protect my wife?" Peregrine said, his voice going ice-cold.

"Do you mean to keep her prisoner? In London particularly, anyone can be at risk from a marksman with a good rifle," Slade pointed out, his voice equally cold. "Can you protect her without her discovering some of the truth, or don't you care if she learns of your feud?" He scowled. "For that matter, she has already been an unwitting pawn in this lethal little game of yours—do you really care if she becomes an innocent victim?"

Pure rage swept through Peregrine. "You go too far, Slade," he said furiously, slamming his palm down on the lawyer's desk. "What's the matter, do you fear for your own precious hide?"

"Some," the lawyer said, refusing to be intimidated. "I have covered my tracks as well as possible, working through a chain of intermediaries, but a determined investigator could find me, and through me, you."

Slade pushed back his chair and tossed his pen on the desk, where it landed with a flat rattle. "You saved me from disaster in India, Mikahl, and in return I've served you to the best of my abilities. But I'm a lawyer, not a soldier, and frankly I have no great desire to be a martyr to your obsession. And what about members of your household, like Jenny Miller? Or friends of yours, like Lord Ross Carlisle? Or your wife's father? Can you protect them all?"

Furious though he was, Peregrine could not deny the wisdom of Slade's words. For too many years he had walked alone, needing to be concerned for only his own survival. But since arriving in England, he had fallen prey to a sticky web of relationships: friends, dependents, relatives by marriage.

And Sara. If Weldon wanted to hurt Peregrine, Sara was the logical target, for Weldon already hated her for her betrayal. Gentle Sara, who had only the vaguest knowledge of the evil men could do.

The thought of what Weldon might do made Peregrine's blood chill. It was time for another change of plan. "Find half a dozen men who are trained in arms to act as guards. Former soldiers by preference, men who are not easily bribed. I'll make loyalty worth their while."

But that was only a partial answer; Slade was right, it was impossible to completely protect Sara short of keeping her locked in a tower, which she would not like. And if Weldon could not get at Sara directly, he might strike at those Sara loved, for hurting Sara would hurt Peregrine. There were too many people involved, particularly since it would be best to keep this business a secret. With a sigh, he reached an inevitable conclusion. "I suppose I must end my cat-and-mouse game more quickly than I had planned."

"The sooner the better," Slade agreed.

A few minutes more were spent discussing other business. Then Peregrine left.

After his departure, Slade spent a long time staring out the window, his face dark with foreboding. He could not help but feel that his employer's carefully orchestrated vengeance might spin awry in the final phases. Peregrine might be playing cat and mouse, but Weldon was more a rat than a mouse. And a cornered rat with nothing to lose was a vicious creature indeed.

Chapter 18

COUSIN LETICIA'S HUSBAND, Lord Sanford, was very rich and very influential in Whig politics, so his oldest daughter's coming-out ball was one of the grandest events of the autumn social season. As they waited in their carriage to be dropped in front of the Grosvenor Square mansion, Sara said hesitantly to her husband, "Charles Weldon will probably be here tonight—he is related to Letty's husband."

"I'll be amazed if he isn't." Mikahl glanced out at the line of carriages before and behind them. "From what I can see, the whole of fashionable England is either inside or waiting to get in." He turned to Sara, his expression becoming serious. "Will it bother you to see him again?"

"We must meet sooner or later—London society is not large enough to avoid someone." Sara began toying with her Chinese fan, rippling the tortoiseshell sticks open and shut across her shimmering green skirt. She had wronged Charles. It was not a fact she was proud of, even though she could not regret the ending of her first betrothal. "The first time will be the worst. Later it will become easier."

"Will it help if I stay with you all evening?" he asked, his voice gentle.

She shook her head. "That's not necessary. Charles has too much pride to make a scene. Besides, I know that my father wants to introduce you to some of his old cronies."

"Publicly put his seal on his son-in-law?" Mikahl's

mouth quirked up. "I thought that sponsoring me for presentation to the queen had taken care of that."

"Father wouldn't want anyone to think that he doesn't approve of his son-in-law. The pride of the St. Jameses, you know." Sara gave her husband a fond look. "Was the presentation dreadful? All you said after was that you hadn't disgraced my father or yourself."

"It was an interesting experience, though not one I would care to repeat. There must have been at least two hundred men presented at the Levee—I felt like a camel in a caravan." He grinned. "Would it be treasonous to say that if I had met her anywhere else, I would have said that your Victoria is a wench with a roving eye?"

"It might be true, but for heaven's sake, don't say so to anyone else." Sara chuckled. "Drina is only twenty years old and has always enjoyed the sight of a handsome man. Whichever of her royal German cousins she decides to marry, it is a safe bet that he will be good-looking."

"Drina?"

"That was her childhood nickname, for Alexandrina," Sara explained. "It was a surprise when she decided to use one of her middle names when she became queen. Still, Queen Victoria has a ring that Queen Alexandrina does not."

"You did not mention that you know the queen well," Mikahl remarked with interest.

"When she was a child, I used to visit her sometimes at Kensington Palace. I was wellborn enough to be considered a suitable companion for a royal princess." Sara sighed. "Even though I'm seven years older, Drina and I became quite fond of each other. She was a sweet child. I used to feel very sorry for her because her mother, the Duchess of Kent, kept her almost a prisoner. When the duchess saw that Drina was becoming attached to me, my visits were no longer allowed."

"It doesn't sound like good training for a future queen."

"No," Sara admitted, "but in spite of everything her mother did, Drina has turned out very well. She has a mind of her own and is very conscientious. Few people know it, but when she became queen, she began to pay off her father's twenty-year-old debts out of the Privy Purse."

Her husband raised his brows. "A Hanoverian who pays her debts? Her royal uncles must be spinning in their graves. Perhaps she's a changeling."

Sara chuckled. "That is something else you had better not say in public. Drina is a good person, and she will be a good queen. She asked me to become one of her ladies, and I almost accepted, but court life is very tedious and requires much standing around, so I declined on the grounds that my leg was not strong enough. Lameness is not without its advantages."

The carriage lurched forward another few feet, then halted again. Mikahl said, "I don't know about the court, but the aristocratic social life is definitely tedious. I'll be glad to go back to Sulgrave."

"You're so patient with all this nonsense. Do you ever long for the simple primitive life?"

"Primitive does not mean simple—most tribes have social systems and rules that make London look uncomplicated." Mikahl lifted her hand and peeled back the edge of her glove so he could kiss the inside of her wrist. "Besides, if I become bored, I shall refresh myself with thoughts of those delectable black silk pantalets that I gave you earlier this evening. You did wear them tonight?"

Tingling from the touch of his lips, Sara blushed and nodded. "You have the most improper mind."

He raised his brows. "Of course. Isn't that one of the things you like about me?"

Sara blushed even more and nodded again.

"And you, sweet Sara, have the most enchanting blushes," he said with approval. "Do we have to stay very late? I would like to investigate those blushes further.''

''We needn't stay more than an hour,'' Sara reassured him, being not uninterested in the subject of the blushes herself.

Their turn had finally arrived, so they climbed from their carriage and went into Sanford House to wait again, this time in a receiving line. Lady Sanford was pleased to see Sara and positively ecstatic at meeting Sara's husband. Mikahl exerted some of his charm, kissed the hands of both Letty and her debutante daughter, and left both females glowing. Sara was used to women reacting that way to her husband; as long as he didn't glow back at them, she didn't mind.

The huge ballroom was beginning to fill. Under the sparkling chandeliers, the black-clad formality of the men provided stark contrast to the drifting flower-bright gowns of the women. Sara had a dance with Mikahl, wanting one good waltz before the room became too crowded for easy movement. Orchestra music competed with a babble of voices, and the air was filled with the mixed scents of perfumes and active bodies.

After their waltz, Mikahl dutifully went off with the Duke of Haddonfield, and Sara began visiting with other guests. But she kept a watchful eye on the crowd; if she and Charles were to meet tonight, she wanted to be prepared for the encounter.'

A group of men were clustered in one corner of the ballroom, and from that vantage point Charles Weldon saw Lady Sara and her husband enter. His mouth hardened. Much as he disliked the idea, he intended to talk to Peregrine before the night was over in the hope that a fulsome apology would persuade the Kafir to forgive the unpleasantness of their last meeting. If the breach were healed, perhaps Peregrine might lend the money needed to stave off financial disaster.

A few minutes later, Weldon's expression eased

when he saw that Lord Melbourne, the Whig prime minister, had arrived. Though the two men were not personal friends, Weldon's support for the Whig party always assured him of a cordial welcome from the prime minister.

Thinking that it was a good time to ask about his barony, Weldon made his way across the overheated ballroom. On seeing him, the prime minister said, "Good to see you, Sir Charles. Bit of bad luck about the lawsuits filed against your railroad."

Irritated at how quickly bad news traveled, Weldon waved his hand dismissively. "Spurious charges by a man deranged from the tragic death of his son. Everything will be resolved within a week. Meanwhile, since the price is temporarily depressed, it's an excellent time to buy L & S stock."

"I'll bear that in mind," Melbourne said vaguely. His eyes began scanning the ballroom. "Now if you'll excuse me . . ."

"A moment, please." Choosing his words carefully, Weldon said, "About that matter we discussed last year when you visited my estate. I've been expecting to hear about the outcome. Have you any definite news?"

The prime minister shook his head. "Drop a note to my secretary. He might have some information."

"I did." Weldon's voice was edged. "He referred me to you."

Melbourne's eyes became opaque and unreadable as he weighed his response. Finally he said, "I'll look into the matter, but I can't promise anything. The political situation is difficult just now, very difficult. The Tories are baying at our heels, and my ministry may fall within a matter of weeks. This isn't a good time to do something that could give the appearance of impropriety." He gave a quick, meaningless politician's smile. "Best to let it rest for the time being, Sir Charles. Now I really must go. There's a gentleman I must speak to."

As the prime minister vanished, Weldon stood still, numb with shock, not noticing the buffeting of the guests around him. *Bloody, bloody. hell!* He knew enough of politicians to recognize that his expectation of a barony had just received a deathblow.

In theory, the government granted honors for outstanding service to the nation; military heroes were routinely ennobled. If honors also went to men whose greatest service was their financial support of the political party in power, well, that was the way of the world.

Weldon's baronetcy had cost him twenty thousand pounds, plus other favors over a number of years. In addition, he had contributed another hundred thousand pounds to the Whigs with the unspoken understanding that he would receive a peerage in return.

A hundred thousand pounds was an enormous fortune, more than large enough to save him in his current difficulties. Now the money was gone, and there wasn't a damn thing he could do about it because—in theory—he had contributed from his love for the Whig party, with no expectation of reward.

The excuse Melbourne had given was nonsense. The Whig ministry had been weak for some time; if it *was* on the verge of falling, the Whigs would use the final hours to pass out honors with a liberal hand. That also was the way of the world.

Only after Weldon had worked through to that point did he ask himself what had gone wrong. It wasn't like a politician to alienate an important contributor; though nothing had ever been stated bluntly, Weldon had been guaranteed his barony. *What the hell had gone wrong?*

The question rapidly broadened to embrace his whole life. At the beginning of the summer, he had been on top of the world: his businesses were prospering, the title he had always craved had been within his grasp, and he had been betrothed to a highborn woman whose status and fortune would enhance his.

Now, like Job, he was seeing everything turn to ashes. His betrothed had betrayed him, he was on the verge of personal bankruptcy, and his most important business would collapse if the legal problems were not solved very soon. It was as if some malign fate had chosen to destroy his personal and public lives.

The realization that other guests were giving him concerned glances reminded Weldon where he was, so he rearranged his expression to conceal his inner turmoil. When business was bad, one must always look confident; fear would bring the jackals to gnaw on his bones.

He began to make his way along the edge of the ballroom, trying to look purposeful, when suddenly the swirling currents of the party brought him face-to-face with Prince Peregrine. There was a suspended moment while the two men looked at each other. The prince's expression was guarded, but not unfriendly.

Remembering his earlier plan to make peace with the barbarian, Weldon forced himself to smile politely. The barony might be gone, but his financial situation could still be salvaged. "Good evening, Your Highness."

"Good evening." The Kafir nodded toward the center of the ballroom. "This reminds me of a riot in Calcutta."

Thinking that the other man's civility was encouraging, Weldon said, "It certainly is a crush. The Sanfords don't do anything by halves." He put a dash of manly regret in his voice. "I owe you a considerable apology. The last time we met—well, I said some unforgivable things. Quite unforgivable."

Peregrine gave a deprecating flick of his fingers. "You were distraught. Who could blame you for speaking intemperately under such difficult circumstances? To find your woman in another man's arms—every man's greatest nightmare."

"Exactly." Weldon seized on the other man's offered excuse, even as it infuriated him. "Especially when the man is a good friend. Besides being upset for my own sake, I was concerned for Lady Sara. In her innocence, I feared that she might have fallen victim to a casual seducer. But it wasn't simple seduction, was it? The fact that you married her leads me to suppose that it was love rather than mere lust. Since that is the case, I must wish you both happiness.''

Peregrine's expression was satirical, but he said only, ''I also owe you an apology, for betraying our friendship.''

''Friendship often ends where a woman begins.'' Weldon shrugged. ''My loss is your gain. I hope that you and I can put that behind us and be friends again.''

''But of course,'' the Kafir said, a disturbing gleam of humor in his lazy green eyes. ''Incidentally, I'm curious about the lawsuits just filed against the railroad.''

Weldon's growing sense of well-being suffered a check. Trying to sound confident, he said, ''All the charges are spurious and will be resolved very soon.''

''Oh?'' Peregrine's brows raised skeptically. ''The City doesn't think so. The fall of the stock price is nothing short of disastrous. Compensation suits against a company are common, but criminal charges are rare. If they are proved, you might be sent to prison yourself.''

Weldon's voice dropped. ''Confidentially, I believe that a rival railroad group is behind this. Because they know how profitable the L & S will be, they want to cause trouble so later they can step in and claim our route. Crawley, the farmer who is accusing us of criminal harassment, has disappeared, along with his whole family. I fear foul play.''

''Indeed?'' Peregrine's brows lifted.

''You must have heard about some of the vicious things that have been done when several companies are competing for the same routes—some railroads have been forced to buy off rivals in order to stay in business,'' Weldon said, elaborating on his story. ''I would rather avoid that because it's a poor use of stockholders' funds, but in this case, buying the plaintiffs off may be the best solution.''

"One must be practical,'' the Kafir agreed.

Weldon finally reached his key point. ''Because of these legal problems and the drop in the value of the stock, the company is facing a temporary cash shortage. Might you be interested in increasing your investment? That will protect your existing stake in the L & S and repay you well later.''

Peregrine drew his dark brows together thoughtfully.

Weldon held his breath, trying not to show his anxiety. He feared that he might have moved too quickly, but the Kafir's expression was encouraging.

Then Peregrine looked right into Weldon's eyes and said pleasantly, ''I'll see you in hell first.''

Not believing his own ears, Weldon stammered, ''Wh-what?''

Obligingly the other man repeated, ''I'll see you in hell before I will save you from the disaster you so richly deserve.''

It was a moment when every impression was razor vivid. Weldon was acutely aware of the waltz music pulsing around them, the scents of sweaty bodies and heavy perfumes. A woman's wide skirt brushed his leg as she whirled by. But most of all, he was mesmerized by the Kafir's green, green eyes, which watched him with mocking malice. Weldon had never seen eyes so green.

No, he *had* seen eyes like that once before. There had been a nagging sense of recognition the first time he'd met Peregrine. When and where had he seen such eyes? A long moment of intense thought produced a shattering answer.

''Tripoli,'' Weldon gasped. He scanned the face of the man in front of him, looking for traces of an almost forgotten boy. ''No, it's impossible. You can't be . . .''

Still mockingly polite, the Kafir said, ''What is impossible—that justice has finally caught up with you? You said it was impossible then, too. One would think that the evidence of your eyes would convince you otherwise.''

The words were an echo from a distant time and place, and they instantly resolved Weldon's doubts. Suddenly everything made horrible sense, for all of Weldon's problems had begun when Peregrine had come into his life.

Suffused with fury, Weldon hissed, "It hasn't been bad luck, has it? You miserable bastard, you've been stalking me for months, persecuting me in every way possible. Lady Sara, the railroad, maybe even the barony."

"Precisely." Peregrine kept his voice level, but inside he vibrated with exultation. This was the moment he had been anticipating for twenty-five years, the moment when Weldon realized that his doom had found him. "I decided to give you a hint because I was growing weary of waiting for you to identify me on your own." And also, as he had told Slade, it was time to draw the game to a close.

Weldon's face was a study in emotions: shock, rage, and best of all, fear. Then his features hardened, the mask of a gentleman crumbling to reveal the viciousness within. "You certainly have changed." His insulting gaze scanned Peregrine from head to foot. "I would never have believed that a filthy brat like you would ever be able to ape the manners of a gentleman. For that is all you are doing: aping."

"I learned to ape gentility from an expert," Peregrine said with barbed civility.

The swelling of violins announced a new waltz, the lush music curling sensuously around the two men. Weldon's face twisted into a sneer. "How did you make your fortune? I suppose you began by selling that nice, tight little . . ."

Before the sentence could be completed, Peregrine exploded, his vision going blood crimson. His left hand shot out to seize his enemy's throat as his right balled into a fist. Through his murderous rage, he felt the pulse of the other man's veins beneath his fingers.

Then he saw the triumphant expression in Weldon's eyes, and had enough sanity left to know that he had been goaded into just such an action. Startled eyes

were being turned in his direction, and in a moment
the two men would be in the center of a scene—a scene
where Peregrine would be the villain.

Instantly he released his grip and brushed at Weldon's upper shoulder, making the gesture casual, as if
he was flicking something from the other man's coat.
The curious bystanders turned away, thinking that they
must have misinterpreted what had been briefly visible
from the corners of their eyes.

With an easy, lying smile, Peregrine said, "You'll
not catch me like that again, Weldon. You were
damned lucky—I might as easily have slit your throat
as tried to throttle you. That would have gotten me
into trouble with the law, but you would have been
quite dead." His smile widened. "A delightful prospect, except that it would be far, far too swift."

His own expression equally insincere, Weldon said,
"What do you want of me, you bastard?"

"Oh, surely you must know that, Weldon." Peregrine's smile faded, and his voice rang like tempered
steel. "In the name of all your victims, I am here to
destroy you. I have already taken away much of what
you value, but I will not be satisfied until you drink
from the chalice of death."

"You're mad," Weldon said contemptuously. "That
is the melodramatic babble of the East. This is England. In spite of the problems you have caused, I still
have power and influence that a gutter rat like you can
never match. Now that I know what you're doing, I
can defend myself against your wild schemes. More
than that, I will destroy you for your insolence."

"My wild schemes have been quite effective so far,
have they not?" Peregrine murmured, thinking that it was
bizarre but somehow appropriate that they were having
this confrontation in the midst of a crowd of revelers.

Weldon's eyes narrowed as a new thought struck
him. "The personal loans—are you the one who
bought them and is demanding payment?"

Peregrine gave a slight, derisive bow. "I have that humble privilege."

"In that case, it will give me great pleasure to default," Weldon snarled.

"Sorry to deprive you of your amusement," Peregrine said with spurious sympathy, "but the day you default, I'll have the bailiffs on you. I'll attach every bit of property you own: the town house, the Hertfordshire estate, the buildings in the City." He rubbed his chin thoughtfully. "I wonder if I can also put a lien on the whorehouses. They are illicit businesses, of course, but they are part of your assets, and I can prove you own them."

Weldon blanched. "How much do you know about me?"

"Everything," Peregrine said softly. His reply hung in the air between them. A laughing couple danced by, leaving a scent of lilies and sweat in their wake.

Weldon's eyes became feral. "Then it is war. Since you mean to ruin me, I have no choice but to ruin you first."

"You can try, but you will not succeed. Even if you manage to kill me, I will reach from the grave to bring you down."

"Bah, spare me the cheap dramatics. You have as much to lose as I do, and lose it you will," Weldon said viciously. "By tipping your hand, you have doomed yourself, for I will stop at nothing to destroy you."

"There is one line you will not cross," Peregrine said with cold menace. "If you hurt Sara, I swear that you will regret the day you were born."

Weldon gave a genuine smile. "What a fool you are. You have just put the perfect weapon in my hands. Hard to believe that a cold little cripple like her can interest any man, but since you seem to want her, the slut will pay for your crimes."

Weldon started to turn away, but Peregrine caught his wrist. "Listen very carefully. *You will not hurt Sara.* If you do, it is Eliza who will suffer for your wickedness."

Weldon's face went white. "You wouldn't kill a little girl—even you are not such a monster as that."

"Very true, I would not kill her." Peregrine's voice was soft with menace. "But you and she will wish that I had. No matter how hard you try, you will never be able to hide Eliza from me—and when I find her, I will put her in a brothel."

When Weldon recoiled in horror, Peregrine twisted his wrist with punishing force. His voice pitched below the clamor around them, he whispered, "I would send her to a virgin house first—just think, Weldon, your darling little girl being ravished by a brute like you. I think I would specify that she be given to a man looking for a virgin to cure his syphilis.

"Then I would transfer her to a specialized house—flagellation, perhaps, or one where mechanical devices are used. Not a house in England—I will send her somewhere you will never find her." He twisted Weldon's wrist again, to a point just short of wrenching the joint apart. "How long will your delicately reared daughter last, hmmm? And I will be sure that she knows she is in hell because her father sent her there."

"You filthy bastard," Weldon swore, his voice savage. "You are evil, truly evil."

Peregrine released the other man's wrist. "Like false gentility, I learned evil from a master of the art. Is it agreed—you will leave Sara alone, and I will spare Eliza?"

"Agreed. But that is the only agreement." Weldon rubbed his sore wrist, his blue eyes shimmering with mad violence. "You are going to be sorry that you ever tried your petty vengeance on me. You are no better than a common criminal, no match for me."

"On the contrary. I am no common criminal, but justice incarnate." Peregrine savored the moment, thinking that when this speech was done, he must find Sara and share his exultation with her. His voice dropped to a chilling whisper. "You have sowed the wind, Weldon. Now you will reap the whirlwind."

Chapter 19

SARA WAS BEGINNING to wonder what had become of her husband when he appeared before her, his eyes brilliant with excitement. After greeting the great-aunt with whom Sara had been speaking, he said under his breath, "Come, sweet Sara. I have found a spot where we can dance without feeling like herring in a barrel."

She laughed and took her leave of her aunt. As her husband steered her across the ballroom, she asked, "Have you found another balcony where I can give you lessons on the language of the fan?"

"Better than that."

There was an odd note in his voice, and Sara looked at him askance, wondering if he had been drinking. She had never seen Mikahl intoxicated, but he was in a strange, volatile mood. He led her from the ballroom, then turned right into a dark corridor. In the middle of the passage, he opened a door on the right and ushered Sara into a sparsely furnished reception room lit by a single lamp.

She looked around doubtfully. "Should we be here?"

"Probably not." There was a key in the door lock, and he turned it before facing Sara. "I think this must be where unwelcome visitors wait—not much furniture and all of it uncomfortable. On the positive side, there is some open space, and the ballroom is on the other side of that wall so the orchestra can be heard quite clearly." He made a deep bow. "Will my lady dance with me?"

"Of course." Smiling, Sara held her arms up in waltz position. "But I must tell you that this is most improper."

"To dance with my own wife?" He raised his brows comically as he swirled her across the floor.

"To steal away to a private room, lock the door, and hold a partner this close are all definitely improper." She relaxed in his arms, feeling that her feet scarcely touched the ground. Trust Mikahl to find a place where they could be private even though several hundred people were just a wall away. "Remember, the rule is at least twelve inches of space between partners."

"And I thought I had gotten the knack of correct behavior," he mourned, pulling her tight against his hard chest. "Truly this is a strange country."

Sara tilted her head back and laughed. "Of course this is a strange country. Two or three years ago, Lady Gough published an etiquette book saying that for true propriety, books by male and female authors must be placed on separate shelves."

"You are making that up!"

"God's own truth," Sara said solemnly, feeling deliciously pliant and yielding as they moved together almost as one body. "Unless the male and female authors are married to each other, in which case the books may rest side by side on the same shelf."

"I shall never understand the English," he said, brimming with hilarity. "But doesn't the fact that I have been presented to the queen make me wholly respectable?"

"*Nothing* will ever make you wholly respectable," Sara said with conviction. He laughed and she felt the vibrations of his amusement from her breasts to her pelvis.

Mikahl slowed their waltz until they were drifting in a leisurely circle. Then he bent his head and kissed her. Sara welcomed his mouth, for dancing aroused every fiber of her being to tingling awareness. Soon they were turning around a single point, then they stopped dancing entirely, except for the passionate rhythms of lips and tongues and quickening breath.

When the music next door ended, Sara tilted her head back and whispered, "My yin energy is very strong now."

He grinned and walked her backward until she was against the wall that adjoined the ballroom. "Splendid, for I am feeling very yang."

He pulled off his gloves and slid them into his coat pocket, then began kissing her again. This time his hands roamed over her body, teasing and caressing his way down her torso.

"My old governess was right when she warned me that the waltz is a dangerous dance," Sara said weakly as she leaned back against the wall for support.

"A wise woman, your governess." He breathed soft warm air into her ear, with devastating effect. "What else did she warn you about?" Cupping his hands around her buttocks, he pulled Sara hard against him.

Feeling fire in her loins, she replied breathlessly, "To beware of wolves in sheep's clothing."

"Is that what I am, silken Sara?"

"More like a wolf in wolf's clothing." The orchestra struck up another tune. Sara felt the music pulsate inside her body, vibrating through her slippers into the sensitive soles of her feet. "My governess would not approve of you."

"Good, for I am sure I would not approve of her." Mikahl spread his palm over her mons veneris and moved it in a slow circle. The mount of Venus, the Cinnabar Gate.

"You are quite—quite shameless." Sara felt as if she was about to burst into flame. "Please," she begged, "let us leave now—I shall go mad if we don't go home at once."

"I admit to being shameless, but it is not time to leave. At least, not yet." He bent to lift the hem of her gown, then straightened and slid his hand between her silk-clad thighs.

"A-a-h-hh," Sara breathed, her eyes drifting shut as waves of sensation pulsed through her. A good thing that this room did not have a decent sofa, or they would be on it disgracing themselves. The fabric of the black pantalets was so sheer that his warm hand might have almost been on her naked flesh.

Her eyes shot open as she realized that his deft fingers were indeed touching bare flesh, probing into her moist, intimate depths. "How . . . ?" After a moment she guessed that the pantalets must have an open seam. He had given them to her just before they came to the ball, and she had donned them quickly, not noticing.

"You devil!" Startled, her fingers involuntarily curled into his upper arms. "So that is why you wanted me to wear them. Were you planning this?"

He laughed, a rich, deep male sound of satisfaction. "Not exactly. I didn't know if this house had a place where we could be private. But if it did, I wanted to be prepared."

A small, well-bred part of Sara's mind was shocked at the sheer carnality of what he was doing. It was one thing to lie with one's husband in a bed, or even in a private spot in the garden; but to do so in the middle of a ball, where half the people Sara knew, including her father, were within fifty yards of her?

However, the rest of Sara's mind and all of her body were beyond shock, except for the shock of loss when he lifted his hand. "Shall I stop, sweet Sara?" he murmured. "Behave with propriety?"

"Don't you dare!" she gasped. "The only thing worse than being depraved is being a depraved tease."

"Very well, my little vixen. One thing I have learned is to obey my lady's commands."

There was a sound of slipping buttons and loosening fabric. He gave a sigh of relief, then put his hands beneath Sara's buttocks and lifted her, bracing her between the wall and his own solid torso. Acting more from instinct than conscious thought, Sara grasped and guided him as he slowly lowered her. She inhaled sharply at the fierce rightness of his entry.

"How does this feel?" he whispered when they were locked together, Sara's silk-stockinged legs wrapped tight around him.

"Splendid. Decadent. Quite, quite mad," she replied raggedly as she rotated her hips, feeling him deep inside her.

To her satisfaction, her movement annihilated his control, and he surged into her. "Ah, God, Sara, you are air and fire and heart's blood," he groaned, his breath roughening to match his strokes.

Sara's rustling petticoats foamed around them, and her cheek pressed into his shoulder as they melded into the ultimate dance. They were close, so close, both physically and mentally. Perhaps she should have been alarmed by her precarious position, but she was not, for she had absolute trust in her husband.

It was hot, sweet sex, made almost unbearably erotic by the knowledge that other people were so close. But they were private here and harming no one by their madness. It was an intimate universe of passion that filled Sara's heart, mind, and body, then shattered into a kaleidoscope of rapture. Her teeth sank into his shoulder, and she shuddered uncontrollably, her violent movements triggering a matching response from her husband.

Another dance ended in the ballroom, and the loudest sound was of their own panting breath and pulsing blood. The frantic tension drained from Sara like water from a spilled glass.

Gently Mikahl disengaged himself, then lowered her feet to the floor and embraced her. For long minutes they clung together, savoring closeness and regaining strength as the wall supported them both.

At length Mikahl said, "And you told me this ball would be a dull affair."

Sara gave an unsteady giggle. "I've never been to a ball quite like it." Stepping away from her husband, she accepted his handkerchief to dry herself, then began to check her appearance. "Do I look all right?"

Mikahl buttoned his trousers and straightened his coat, then brushed Sara's petticoats and skirts down smoothly. "Your gown is a bit rumpled, but no more than expected at a ball." He tucked a wayward lock of hair back into her chignon. "You look absolutely beautiful. As always."

It amazed Sara how cool and gentlemanly he could appear when just a few minutes before he had blazed with demanding passion. She knew that her own cheeks glowed with good health and bad deeds, and wondered if anyone would guess what she had been doing.

After drawing his gloves on, her husband offered his arm. "Shall I return my lady to the ball?"

The door rattled as someone tried to enter, then two gruff voices started discussing the situation.

Mikahl turned the key in the lock and opened the door to find two middle-aged men holding unlit cigars. Blandly he said, "My wife was a bit faint and needed to rest for a few minutes. But she's feeling better now, so we will leave you gentlemen to your smoking."

Then he led Sara away before the men could comment. She bowed her head and clung to his arm, barely managing to suppress her laughter until they were around the corner. "You have a rare talent for duplicity, husband mine."

"Nonsense," he replied as they reentered the ballroom. "Didn't you once tell me that social lies to spare other people from embarrassment were not only permitted but required?"

"Whoever wrote the book of proper conduct never imagined anyone like you," Sara retorted.

Mikahl paused. "I see Ross. I'd like to talk to him for a moment, then leave. Unless you prefer to stay longer?"

"To stay later would be very anticlimactic," she answered, then blushed beet red when she heard her own words.

"Sweet Sara, what a splendid double entendre," he said with delight. "If we weren't in public, I would kiss you again. But I am being very proper. I trust you will give me credit for how proper I can be." Scanning the ballroom again, he said, "Your Aunt Marguerite is by the door. Shall I meet you there after I've talked to Ross?"

Sara nodded. After giving her husband's fingers a quick squeeze, she started around the edge of the room. Proper, indeed. Mikahl could make a stone saint blush. And she loved him, dear God, how she loved him.

After the shattering confrontation with Peregrine, Weldon needed some whiskey to steady his nerves. Fortunately that could be found in one of the smaller rooms where men retreated for serious drinking. As he drank, he began to plan. Learning who his enemy was had restored Weldon's confidence, for it was easier to destroy another man than to overcome blind bad luck.

Piece by piece, a strategy emerged. The Duke of Haddonfield would probably lend enough money to repay the personal loans, for the duke would not like London society to learn what kind of man his son-in-law was. Then Peregrine must be discredited so that any accusations he made later would not be taken seriously. Weldon shook his head as he poured a second whiskey; the bastard had been a fool to tip his hand. If he had stayed in the shadows, he might have been successful, but now he was doomed.

After three drinks, Weldon decided that it was time to go home and consult Kane about what must be done. He was on his way across the ballroom when he saw Lady Sara and Peregrine emerge from a corridor on the far side of the room.

He stopped and stared, his expression darkening. From the way they looked at each other and unobtrusively touched, Weldon guessed that they had been kissing in a back room. Or even worse, for they positively reeked of sex. What a shameless slut she was.

The couple separated, Peregrine going one way, Sara the other. That was when the brilliant idea struck Weldon. He did not dare injure Sara physically, but he could tell her a few things about her precious husband: things that would humiliate the bitch and quite possibly destroy her marriage.

Best of all, he could do it with impunity, because prim little Sara would never be able to repeat what Weldon told her. It would be perfect justice in return for what Peregrine had done, with the added bonus of making Sara herself miserable.

Swiftly Weldon cut through the milling crowd, overtaking his prey just as the orchestra began again. "Sara, my dear," he said smoothly, taking her hand. "Will you dance with me?"

Sensing her reluctance, he said under his breath, "People are watching. If we have a nice, civilized waltz together, it will reduce any lingering scandal."

"Very well." Sara stepped into his arms, holding her body stiffly away from him and looking past his shoulder.

Weldon noted a slight reddening on her throat, as if a man's bewhiskered face had rubbed against the tender skin. And as he had guessed, the faint musky scent of sex hung around her. It added to his fury, but he kept his voice controlled. "Try to look as if you are enjoying yourself, my dear," he admonished. "And don't sulk. Remember, I am the injured party, not the villain of the piece."

She looked up at him, her brown eyes grave. "I know. That is why it is hard to face you. I owe you a great apology, Charles. I am thoroughly ashamed of my behavior. I have no excuse except that . . . I could not help myself."

Her words only inflamed him further. His fingers tightened on her left hand. "Wantons always say that," he said pleasantly. "It sounds better than admitting to promiscuity."

Sara's face flamed, but she did not try to defend herself.

Deciding that it was time to get down to business, Weldon said, "You know, the first time I met Prince Peregrine, I thought that he looked familiar. It's those green eyes. Quite striking. Unique, in fact. Don't you agree?"

Reluctantly she nodded.

"But while the eyes were familiar, I had trouble placing him," Weldon continued. "It has been so many years and miles that I did not make the connection. Then earlier this evening we talked, and I remembered."

He had caught Sara's unwilling attention, and she watched him intently as he guided them out of the path of another couple. "He hates me. Did you know that, my dear?"

"I know that there is something between you two," she said slowly. "But I don't know what."

"No, he would not want to admit it," Weldon said. "We met in North Africa, in Tripoli. I was making my Grand Tour. He was not called Peregrine then. God knows where he picked up that name—he's probably had a hundred names."

"He said that Peregrine is merely a translation of what he is called in Kafiristan," Sara said defensively.

"Perhaps, though he is not Kafiri, and he is a liar if he claims otherwise." He smiled down at Sara and pulled her into another turn. "Your husband is such a superb liar that anyone can be forgiven for believing him."

Sara's eyes flashed. "You go too far," she said as she tried to tug away from him. "I will not stay here to listen to you insult my husband."

"But you will stay to learn more about him, won't

you, my dear?'' Weldon said with an undertone of viciousness, keeping a firm grip so that she could not escape.

Sara quieted, wary but watchful.

Reminiscently Weldon said, ''He was such a pretty lad, and so amiable at first. We were on our way to being great friends. Our falling out was all my fault, I fear.''

''Charles, will you get to the point?'' Sara said sharply. ''What are you trying to tell me?''

''I am explaining why your husband hates me, darling Sara.'' Enjoying himself, Weldon spun the moment out. ''You see, he was a whore, and he has never forgiven me for kicking him out of my bed.''

Chapter 20

STUNNED BY CHARLES'S ACCUSATION, Sara felt the blood drain from her face. A fortnight before, she would not have understood what he meant, but Jenny's lecture had been very enlightening.

Her former betrothed gave her an ironic glance. "Do you know what that means, my dear, or do I have to explain?"

"I know what you mean," she said in a soft, furious undertone, "and I don't believe a word of it. My husband said that you are evil, and he was right. You do yourself no credit by spreading such lies."

For a moment Sara experienced an unnerving sense of déjà vu, for the scene reminded her of when Mikahl had tried to convince her of Charles's wickedness. She thrust the thought aside, to be dealt with later. Doggedly she said, "You are speaking from drunkenness—I can smell the liquor on your breath."

"Of course you don't want to believe me, Sara," Charles purred, "but that does not mean I'm lying. Did you ever notice the scar on his left hip?"

Sara tensed. "He has a number of scars."

"This one is shaped like an irregular *M*. Quite distinctive. He cut it himself with a stiletto as a proof of how much he adored me, or so he said. Personally I thought he was a little deranged."

Though Sara tried to conceal her shock of recognition, Weldon saw her flinch. He continued, "*M* for Master. He claimed that he wanted to return to England with me as my slave of love." Weldon's eyes grew dreamy. "I was rather tempted, but of course I couldn't bring him back to England. For me, your husband was just a passing experiment, a local North African custom that I felt like trying. Still, he was a lovely youth, much better-looking than he is now, and so passionate. Surely you have noticed how passionate he is?"

"You are disgusting," Sara said furiously as she tried to jerk her hand free. But Charles held her hand and waist too tightly for her to escape without making a major scene. "The fact that you know of a scar is not proof."

"Proof is hard to come by after so many years," he conceded. "A pity that I didn't keep his love letters, for you would have found them quite convincing. Almost illiterate, of course, but rather touching in their intensity and very explicit about what he wanted me to do to him. Shall I tell you more?"

Without waiting for Sara to reply, he proceeded to recite several examples, using gutter language that she barely understood. Dizzy with agitation, she stumbled on her bad leg and almost fell.

Weldon's cruel grip held her upright. "Don't faint on me, Sara," he said sharply. "Use that fine logical brain of yours. The way he hates me—haven't you ever heard that hell has no fury like a lover scorned? He used to say that I was the love of his life. I thought that was just boyish enthusiasm and would soon be forgotten, but apparently he has spent years stalking me. And now, like a lover scorned, he wants to destroy me."

Thinking of what Mikahl had said about Weldon's first wife, Sara shook her head vehemently. "No, it's not just a personal feud. He has other reasons for hating you."

"Oh? Has he given you any proof of my wickedness?" He smiled as he read her expression. "I didn't think so. So it is my word against his. Have you ever heard anyone besides him impugn my reputation? Yet what is he but an adventurer that your cousin found somewhere in Asia? He used Lord Ross to gain entry to society, and now he is using you.''

Not wanting to concede an inch, Sara said stubbornly, ''If I must choose between you, I choose to believe my husband.''

''Your husband,'' Charles sneered. ''Why do you think he married you, Sara? Certainly not for your looks. Your fortune isn't reason enough for a man of his wealth.''

''He married me because he loves me,'' Sara retorted. Though Mikahl had never said so, it was what she wanted to believe, and certainly he behaved like a man who cared greatly.

''Did he say that? Well, he's very good at telling people what they want to hear.'' Charles's mouth curled with contempt. ''What an innocent you are. Listen closely, you foolish bitch. He married you because he couldn't have me, and you were the closest he could get. He hoped that stealing my future wife would hurt me. He was wrong, of course—losing you wounded only my pride. Still, I must give him credit for imagination.''

''I knew that you were interested mostly in my birth and fortune,'' Sara said, trying to keep her voice and mind steady under Charles's stream of vitriol. ''But Mikahl is not like you. He did not seduce me, nor did my father force him to marry me. In fact, he had trouble convincing me to accept him.''

''So you had doubts even then? You should have listened to them and not tied yourself to a madman.'' Charles squeezed the fingers of her right hand until they hurt. ''Did you know that he and I talked earlier this evening? He made a number of threats about what he would do if I would not become his lover again. When I denied him, he dragged you off into another room and worked his angry frustration off on you. How does it make you feel to know that you are the receptacle of his warped desires?''

Dear God, would the dance never end? Sara felt dizzy from the spinning, almost nauseated. Though she loved Mikahl, she did not feel that she knew him well, nor did she wholly trust him. Much as she wanted to dismiss Charles's charges as pure malice, she could not quite do so.

The fact that Charles knew of the *M*-shaped scar was hardly proof that they had been lovers, but it was unusual for a man to be so familiar with another man's body. And Mikahl's reaction to her discovery of the scar had been anguished and irrational. He had used Sara physically to drown the past on that occasion; he might have done so again tonight.

The very idea made her ill, but it was undeniably true that her husband had been in a strange, wild mood earlier in the evening. An encounter that had been passionate and loving was now unbearably tainted by Charles's accusations.

But what really undermined Sara's faith in her husband was Charles's evil, all-too-convincing explanation for why Mikahl had married her. Mikahl did not need her money, he cared little for her status, and had never said that he loved her. He did desire her, but lust was not love.

Though she did not want to believe it, the way Mikahl had spoken of Charles could have been the obsessive hatred of a lover scorned. If there had once been love between the men, it was horridly possible that Mikahl had married her either for revenge or as a substitute for the person he really wanted. Perhaps both.

Charles had been watching her expression, and now gave a nod of satisfaction. "You are beginning to believe me, aren't you? Very good. Your intelligence is one of the things I always liked about you: when confronted with facts, you listen rather than have an attack of vapors. You may take comfort in the fact that your husband is undoubtedly a bigamist who will abandon you when he is ready to leave England. Then you will be free of him."

In the remote corner of her mind that was still capable of thought, Sara realized that Charles had an uncanny ability to trigger the hidden fears that her husband did not love her and would eventually leave her. But she would not admit that. "You have not given me facts, Charles," she said as evenly as she could. "Merely showed me what a vulgar mind you have."

He shook his head pityingly. "You will learn the truth, but it is already too late. By marrying him, you have ruined your life and reputation."

The music ended, and with a final flourish, he released her. After bending over her gloved hand for a mocking kiss, he said, "I would advise you not to rush home to discuss this with your dear husband—he is a dangerous man and might react very badly to your knowledge of his past. You would be wise to find excuses to spend as much time as possible away from him."

Then Charles turned and left her.

Sara stood very still and concentrated on her breathing. After a minute, her nausea began to subside. When she decided that she would be able to walk without falling, she began to make her way to the door where she was to meet Mikahl.

She would have given anything she owned not to have to face her husband until she had had time to think through what she had just been told. When Mikahl had tried to persuade her that Weldon was evil, she had not believed him. She had put the whole subject out of her mind once she and Mikahl became intimate, and had not thought about it since.

Tonight Charles's malice had been unmistakable, and it was easy to believe that he might have pushed his first wife down the stairs in a fit of rage. Nonetheless, though he had clearly been doing his best to hurt her and injure her marriage, Sara could not escape the horrible belief that somewhere in his tissue of lies was a grain of excruciating truth.

Ross was part of a group of men discussing colonial policy, and Peregrine had to wait a few minutes before he could separate his friend for a private talk. When they were alone, Peregrine said only, "The cat is among the pigeons."

Ross raised his eyebrows as he considered the statement. "You mean that you have shown your hand to Weldon."

"Exactly. I decided that it is time to bring the game to a conclusion. Weldon could be dangerous. I don't think he will threaten you, but be careful—the man is like a loose cannon on a ship's deck."

"What about Sara's safety?"

Peregrine smiled humorlessly. "Weldon agreed to one condition: he will not hurt Sara. In return, I will not hurt his daughter Eliza."

Ross frowned. "This is getting very ugly."

"It has always been ugly," Peregrine retorted. "But soon it will be over. Sometime in the next few days, I'd like to talk to you again. I'm hiring some guards, former soldiers, and it might be good if you took one. You've got frontier experience of your own, but no one can look all ways at once."

"Do you really expect matters to get that bad?"

"Expect the worst. That way you are never disappointed." Then Peregrine said good night and turned to look for his wife. With his height, he was able to see over the crowd, and his mouth tightened when he saw her dancing with Charles Weldon.

The music stopped and Weldon bowed deeply, then left his partner. Sara stood still for a moment, then turned and slowly made her way toward the door where her aunt had been earlier. Wondering what Weldon had said, Peregrine worked his way through the thick crowd. To his intense irritation, several people stopped him to talk, and it was several minutes before he was able to reach Sara's side.

His wife flinched when he touched her arm, then looked up at him with a blind, unseeing stare.

He mentally hurled an oath at his enemy, then said quietly, "I saw you dancing with Weldon. Did he threaten you? Frighten you in some way?"

She shook her head and managed a thin smile. "No, Charles had the admirable motive of showing people that we are on polite terms. I am merely suffering from a guilty conscience. As I said earlier, I knew it would be difficult the first time we met again. I'll be fine in a few minutes."

Peregrine frowned, sure that Weldon must have said something to upset Sara. But he would not ask her again until later. Taking her arm, he said, "Come, let us go home."

"We must take our leave of Letty first."

He would rather have ignored the amenities, but knew Sara would never be so rude. After scanning the room, he was glad to see that Lord and Lady Sanford were holding court by the main entrance, so making a polite farewell would not take long.

When they were almost to the Sanfords, a new party entered the ballroom, and there was a sudden flurry of surprise. The music stopped, and guests began turning toward the door. Lady Sanford dropped into a curtsy, and her husband bowed deeply.

Peregrine gave a soft whistle of surprise when he identified the new arrivals. "Believe it or not, Queen Victoria has just walked in with a sizable party of courtiers."

His comment pierced Sara's abstraction. "Drina is here?" she said, startled. She stood on her toes and craned her neck, but could not see over the heads of taller people. The murmur became a babble of excitement as everyone turned to the queen.

"She certainly is. Does the queen often come to private balls?"

"Almost never," Sara replied, "but the Sanfords are very active at court, and they are dedicated Whigs. I've heard that the queen is afraid that soon a Tory government will come to power. Melbourne is the only prime minister she has ever worked with, and she is very attached to him. Coming here might be a way of showing support for the Whigs."

"Clever wench," he said admiringly.

"For heaven's sake," Sara said, sounding more like herself, "don't say that to anyone else! What is happening?"

"Melbourne has joined her. Perhaps he knew she was coming?" Peregrine said in an under-the-breath commentary. "Now the queen is moving in this direction. She stops to say a few words to someone, then moves on. More like a politician than a Royal." Peregrine watched Victoria's progress with interest. She was tiny, scarcely five feet tall, but she certainly had great presence. She was also pretty, though she was already plump and would likely be quite stout in later years.

Since the queen knew Sara, probably she would stop to say a few words. A great honor, no doubt, but Peregrine could not help wishing he and Sara had left before the queen's unexpected visit.

Like everyone else, Weldon was immobilized by the queen's presence. It was rather like being at one of her drawing rooms. He chafed at the delay, then scowled when he saw that the queen was about to speak to Peregrine and Lady Sara. Not only was Victoria the ruler of the British empire, but was also a pure, modest young woman. Appalling to think that the queen would be tainted by contact with that imposter.

Then Weldon had his second inspiration of the night. He wanted to discredit his enemy; what better way to do so than by denouncing him in front of the most influential woman in England? He would not even have to lie; the truth was quite bad enough.

Yes, Weldon's luck had turned; once more the world was falling into his hands. He began forcing his way to the front of the group.

Melbourne and the Sanfords trailing behind her, the queen stopped in front of Peregrine and Sara. With a gracious inclination of her head, she said, "A pleasure to see you, Lady Sara." Her voice was sweet and very clear, like a nightingale.

Sara curtsied. "This is an unexpected honor, Your Majesty."

"Your husband was presented to me at the last Levee." She turned to Peregrine. "Prince Peregrine. I hope that relations between your country and mine will be fruitful."

He bowed and murmured, "As do I, Your Majesty."

As Peregrine straightened up, Charles Weldon emerged from the crowd, his eyes gleaming with triumph.

After bowing to the queen, Weldon said in a ringing voice, "I beg Your Majesty's pardon, but I must tell you that this man is an imposter. He is not a prince, not even a native of Kafiristan. He is not worthy of being presented to you."

A gasp rippled through the onlookers who were close enough to hear. Startled by this departure from protocol, Victoria turned to the man who dared interrupt her. Melbourne stepped forward and whispered in her ear, probably identifying Weldon.

With a sick feeling in his stomach, Peregrine realized that Weldon had found a perfect place to discredit him. Peregrine could try to lie his way out of it, of course, and he lied very well. But who would these staid Britons believe, an English gentleman who was one of them, or a foreigner of dubious background? The answer was obvious.

For himself, Peregrine did not much mind being disgraced, but his friends were part of this world, and they would not relish being publicly humiliated for having sponsored him. Ross and Haddonfield would feel betrayed, and justly so. And Sara, dear God, what would Sara think?

Knowing that all eyes were on him, Weldon continued, "The man calling himself Prince Peregrine of Kafiristan is an imposter. In fact he is English, the illegitimate child of a cockney barmaid." He turned to Peregrine, vicious satisfaction in his eyes. With a wave of his hand, he thundered, "And this fraud, this insolent East End gutter rat, dares try to deceive the whole of British society."

The queen's jaw dropped, and for a moment she looked like a startled young girl rather than a monarch. The room was so silent that a carriage could be heard rattling by outside. Then Victoria's blue eyes narrowed to icy slits, and her head swung around to Peregrine. An insult to royal dignity was not something she would forgive. The royal voice cold and clear, she asked, "Is what Sir Charles says true?"

Peregrine should have been thinking of the best way to escape disaster, but instead his gaze was fixed on his wife. Sara's face was pale and her wide, stunned eyes regarded him with shock. Helplessly he wondered if she believed Weldon's charges. More to the point, how she would react if she did believe?

"I have spoken to you, sir," Victoria snapped, no longer according Peregrine the courtesy of his nominal title.

He turned to the queen, wondering if he had any chance of lying his way out of this. Perhaps he should just admit the truth and be done with it, but he supposed he owed it to his friends to try to avoid disgrace.

Then another cool voice entered the conversation. "I believe that Prince Peregrine is stunned at such a wild accusation, Your Majesty."

Lord Ross Carlisle emerged into the circle of open space around the queen and bowed. With his golden hair and bone-deep elegance, he was the perfect English gentleman to counter Weldon. "Sir Charles must be jesting. I myself have visited the prince's palace in Kafiristan and seen how his people revere him."

Ross's answer broke Peregrine's paralysis. "Please excuse my slowness in answering, Your Majesty. I sometimes have trouble with your language," he said in his thickest accent. "There is some justice to Sir Charles's statement that I am not a prince, for Kafiristan does not have princes in the European sense. In Kafiri, I am called," he hesitated, "I suppose 'war hawk' is closest. My title would best be translated as leader or chief. If I stay in England, I think I will drop the title altogether, since it is not formally recognized in this country."

"I was the one who suggested that he call himself a prince, Your Majesty," Ross said. "While the translation is not exact, Peregrine was the greatest and most respected man in Kafiristan. I myself can vouch for that."

His face darkening, Weldon snapped, "Lord Ross is part of the plot to deceive society, Your Majesty. Without his help, this guttersnipe would not be able to bring his masquerade off. They are both laughing at the rest of us."

The queen's brow furrowed as she weighed Ross and Peregrine's words against Weldon's accusations.

Then Sara spoke up. "You have known me for many years, Your Majesty," she said in a soft voice that could not be heard more than a few feet away. "Do you think I would dishonor my name by marrying a man who was not of suitable rank?"

The two women's gazes met, and for a moment warmth for her old friend showed in Victoria's eyes. Perhaps she was also remembering that Weldon had been betrothed to Sara and might feel malice to her new husband. Then the queen resumed her regal formality. Turning to Weldon, she said in a voice that would cut glass, "If that was your idea of a joke, we are not amused."

Victoria inclined her head to Peregrine and Sara. "Prince Peregrine, Lady Sara. I trust we shall see you at court again soon." Then she turned and resumed her progress.

His face white with rage, Weldon spun on his heel and stormed out of the ballroom, people drawing away from him as if he was a plague carrier.

The attention of the other guests stayed on the queen and her entourage, leaving Peregrine facing Ross and Sara. His eyes filled with unholy amusement, Ross said, "You are right, Mikahl, we must talk in the next few days. Good night, Sara." Then he turned and left.

Peregrine looked down at Sara. Her face was still pale, and he could read nothing in her expression. As for himself, he felt that he would explode if he stayed at this damned ball a moment longer. "Come, we are leaving," he said roughly.

He would not have been surprised if Sara had balked, but instead she just nodded.

As Sara collected her evening shawl, Peregrine summoned his carriage. Neither he nor his wife spoke on the short ride back to the Park Street town house, but the atmosphere in the coach was thick with tension.

And with every revolution of the carriage's wheels, Peregrine heard his wife's cool, aristocratic voice ringing in his head: *"Do you think I would dishonor my name by marrying a man who was not of suitable rank?"*

Chapter 21

AFTER THE SILENT journey home, Sara was undressed by Jenny. Then she dismissed the maid and entered the main bedroom. This was one night when she might have welcomed separate chambers, but here, as at Sulgrave, the master and mistress had only one bed between them.

Sara considered crawling between the sheets and pulling the pillow over her head, but that seemed impossible in such a fraught atmosphere. Warily she sat down in a wing chair facing her husband, sure that a blazing great row was waiting to happen. She would have preferred to face it rested and composed, but rows, like childbirth, took place in their own time.

Mikahl had already undressed and wore his flowing black caftan as he stared out the window and sipped a glass of brandy. When he had made love to her at the ball, his mood had been volatile but good-humored. Now he seemed dark and dangerous, and very foreign. He turned to face Sara when she entered the room, his expression rigid with suppressed anger.

"Why are you glaring at me?" she asked, hoping to appeal to his sense of humor. "After all the different things I heard about your past tonight, I should be the one seething."

Her lame attempt at a joke failed. "So Weldon did say something appalling when you were dancing," Mikahl said grimly. "What did he accuse me of then—the same things he told the queen, or worse?"

So he was going to the heart of the trouble; Sara

would have preferred a meaningless quarrel, which could be forgotten when it was over. Talking about what had happened tonight could open a Pandora's box of her husband's dark secrets, and she was terrified that what was revealed might destroy their marriage. Taking a deep breath, she said, "Worse. Charles claimed that he first met you in Tripoli."

Her husband's body went taut as a drumhead. "What else did dear Charles say?"

Sara wanted to drop her eyes, but didn't. "He said that when he met you, you were a male whore, and the reason you hate him is that he kicked you out of his bed."

Rage sizzled through the room like St. Elmo's fire. Sara shivered; if ever she was to fear her husband, now was the time.

But he did not move or threaten her, just stared with ice in his eyes. "Do you believe him?"

"He was acting from malice, and he probably thought it was safe to be outrageous because I would be too horrified to discuss his accusations with you." She hesitated, choosing her words. "But in spite of that, I did think there was a grain of truth in what Charles said."

His voice low and overcontrolled, Mikahl said, "Of the different things Weldon said, what do you think is true?"

"I'm not sure," Sara said slowly. "I just had the feeling that what he said was not wholly invented."

The temperature in the room seemed to drop ten degrees. "If I deny his accusations, who will you believe, me or your aristocratic former suitor?"

"You are my husband," Sara said, an edge to her voice. "I would hope that I could believe you."

"But you aren't sure," he said bitterly. "What a touching vote of confidence from my own wife."

Beginning to feel angry herself, Sara snapped, "I am trying very hard to have faith in you, Mikahl, but you are giving me damned little to work with. I think it's time you told me the truth about your past.''

There was a flicker of surprise in his eyes at her unaccustomed profanity. Then he tossed back half the contents of his brandy glass. ''Surely you know all you need to know. An aristocrat like you would never dishonor your name by marrying a man who was not of suitable rank. Ergo, I must be of suitable rank, and Weldon was lying from sheer bloody-mindedness.''

''That is no answer,'' she said, exasperated. ''Why don't you answer a few questions instead of just asking them?''

Her husband banged his glass down on a table and stalked across the room to brace his arms on the wings of her chair.

''What questions do you want answered, sweet Sara?'' he said in a low, menacing tone. He loomed above her, his face a foot away, and his eyes glittering like emerald shards. ''Do you want to know if I am really a whore or a London gutter rat? What will you do if the answer is yes? Will you return to your father's house and look for a lover who is 'of suitable rank' once you learn what I am?''

Insight struck Sara like lightning. Mikahl's underlying fury was for Weldon and tonight's near-humiliation, but some of his anger was for her, and now she knew why. Amazingly, her powerful, confident husband feared that Sara would reject him if she knew the truth about his origins.

Sara raised one hand and slipped it around his neck, her fingertips caressing the tight muscles. ''I know what you are, Mikahl,'' she said softly. ''That is why I married you. But I admit that I am also curious about what you were.''

His angry expression shattered, leaving desperate vulnerability in its wake. Then he straightened and spun away, unable to face the tenderness in her eyes. He stopped at the window and stared out, showing only his broad, black-clad back. Sara felt the energy currents swirl through the room, changing tone like light refracted through cut glass.

Minutes passed before he said in an almost inaudible voice, "Most of what you've heard tonight is true."

Walking to the table that held the decanter and glasses, Mikahl poured himself another drink, his hand less than steady. "Would you like some brandy, Sara? If you want to hear the sordid story of my life, it is going to be a long night."

"Please." Sara closed her eyes with a shuddering sigh of relief, passionately grateful that Mikahl was once more the husband she knew and loved.

When he placed a glass in her hand, she opened her eyes. "The part about you being a male whore and madly in love with Charles—that is the part that is false, isn't it?"

He stared at her a moment. "Sometimes, Sara, you make my blood run cold. Why do you say that?"

"I cannot believe it of you," she said simply.

"You are quite correct—he was lying about those things." He began pacing the room, too restless to sit. "However, just about everything else Weldon said was true: I was born less than five miles from here, near the East End docks."

Sara shook her head in amazement. "So you are really English. Incredible."

"I was born in London, and spent the first eight years of my life here, but that does not make me English," he corrected sharply. "Besides, the England that I knew is very different from the world you grew up in."

From what Sara knew of the East End, she knew that he spoke the truth. Still, he was as English as she was, perhaps more so, since her privileged life was the exception rather than the rule. "Who were your parents?"

"No one you would know," he said dryly. "My mother was a country girl from Cheshire who ran away with a soldier. After he abandoned her, she became a barmaid in a London dockside tavern. My father was a sailor in the Royal Navy. He lived with her when he wasn't on duty. He had an estranged wife, so he couldn't marry my mother even though he loved her, or so my mother once told me. Perhaps it was true—it pleased her to believe it.''

''What happened to them?''

''My father died at Trafalgar when I was two years old. I don't remember him, but my mother used to say I looked just like him.'' Mikahl perched on the edge of the windowsill. ''Her name was Annie. She was rather casual but good-natured. She never complained and could always find something to laugh at.

''She wasn't a prostitute, but after my father died, she had a series of male 'friends' who stayed when they were in port and who helped with the bills. When I began to run wild, she sold the gold necklace one of her lovers had given her, and used the money to put me in a dame school. That helped keep me out of trouble and saved me from being completely illiterate.''

''What was your original name?''

''Michael Connery, after my father. He was Irish.'' His face was pensive. ''I suppose I'm not really entitled to the Connery name since I'm a bastard, but my mother called herself Mrs. Connery. I never knew what her maiden name was.''

Michael Connery. Pronounce it with a different accent, and it became Mikahl Khanauri. Sara examined her husband with fresh eyes: the height, the black hair and fair skin, the green eyes, the ability to charm the birds from the trees when he chose. ''Irish. I should have guessed,'' she said with dawning understanding. ''The first time I met you, you said that green eyes were not uncommon among your father's people.''

''Which is the truth.'' His expression was sardonic. ''You may not believe this, Sara, but I've tried to avoid lying to you.''

Sara cast her mind back over their conversations. At

length she said, "I do believe you. Thinking back, I don't recall you ever actually saying that you were Kafiri. And there were many other times like that, when my expectations shaped what you said. You certainly are a master of selective facts."

"A minor skill, but one that I excel at." His voice was self-mocking.

Sara's brows knit as she thought of a new question. "What about your accent? It is impossible to place. If I had to guess, I would have said that you speak like an Asiatic who had attended Oxford University. Certainly not like a cockney."

"After I left England, I was exposed to standard English. Then for many years I never spoke my native tongue, though I read it whenever I found an English book. I didn't want to forget the language because I always knew that I would need it again someday," he explained. "When I went to India and had the chance to speak English again, I found that my original accent had been modified by the other languages I had spoken over the years, so I cultivated the new accent as a way of covering up the cockney. I knew that when I returned to London, I would be accepted more readily as a rich foreigner than as an East End slum rat who had made good."

He smiled a little, for the first time since they had separated at the ball. "I can still speak a cockney so thick you wouldn't be able to understand more than one word in three. I think of it as another foreign language."

Sara pulled her legs up under her in the chair, tucking her blue robe around her ankles. "You said that you lived in England for your first eight years. Why did you leave?"

"My mother died of a fever. By chance one of her friends, a sea captain, was in port. Knowing that if I was turned out on the streets I'd probably end up on the gallows, he took me on as a cabin boy." Mikahl sighed, his face deeply sad. "Captain Jamie Mc-

Farland, from Glasgow. If you listen hard, you'll probably hear a trace of Glaswegian in my accent. Most of my mother's lovers thought of me as an unavoidable nuisance, but Jamie McFarland actually liked me. He would bring me small gifts from his travels and always had time to talk. He was the closest thing to a father I ever had.''

Sara had never imagined her husband as a child; he seemed too elemental, too fully formed, ever to have been small and helpless. But now his words conjured up a picture of a girl called Annie, who had followed her heart and who had given her resilience and good nature to her son. It was equally easy to envision the fatherless child who had been eager to love a man who gave him the protection and love all children deserved.

Her heart ached for him, but she guessed that it would be better to change the subject, for Mikahl hated showing any weakness. ''How did you end up in the wilds of Asia?''

His face closed. ''That is a long story, too long for tonight. The summary is that after my seafaring days, I wound up working on the caravans through Central Asia. When I was about twenty, I was captured in a raid and made a slave.''

She winced. ''That is when you got the scars on your back?''

He drank some of the brandy, his expression impenetrable. ''Some of them. It was my second stint in slavery, and most of the scars are from the first time. After about a year, I managed to escape with a fellow slave, a Kafir named Malik. Once we were free, he wanted to return to his mountains. Since I had no better ideas, I went with him.''

''And you stayed?''

He nodded. ''Yes. I liked the Kafirs a great deal. I was adopted into Malik's family. They accepted me as no other people ever had, and I found that I rather liked having a family. Even though I knew I must leave eventually, Kafiristan became my base of operations for the next dozen years.''

"Were you really made a prince?'' Sara asked curiously.

"There is no hereditary aristocracy in Kafiristan. What makes a man prominent is wealth and fighting skill. Especially wealth. After I led the expeditions to the lost city of Katak, I was the wealthiest man in Kafiristan. Ergo, I was in some ways the most prominent, so saying that I was a prince has a certain metaphorical truth.''

He sipped more brandy, his face thoughtful. "I had an odd status, rather like a favorite cousin who had come for an extended visit. I spent several months a year there, the rest traveling, making my fortune. Malik and his family always made me welcome. Largely because of me, they had become rich in their own right. They always said that their house was my house, and they meant it quite literally.''

"Where did you meet Kuram?''

"In India. He was a scout for the Indian Army. After he had a falling out with authority, I helped him escape the consequences. He felt a strong sense of obligation to me and offered to serve me as a way of repayment. Also, Kuram wanted to travel and see the world. In six months or a year, he will be ready to return home for good. When he does, he will visit Malik and his family, to assure them that I am well and that they are in my thoughts. Which they are.''

Sara leaned her head against the back of the chair. "So many things make sense now,'' she said quietly. "For example, you said that you never belonged where you were born, and you did not even want to belong there. Now I understand why.''

"No one with a choice would ever return to the poverty and violence of the East End.'' His eyes narrowed. "Any comments, now that you've heard the story of my unsavory origins?''

Not an easy question to answer. Groping for the right

words, she said, "While you have become a citizen of the world, I like the fact that you spent your formative years here in England. It makes you seem more comprehensible. Less alien."

His mouth quirked humorlessly. "Aren't you shocked to learn that you, the daughter of a duke, have been sharing your bed with a cockney bastard?"

"My life has been one shock after another ever since I met you, so learning that you were born in London isn't worth much more than a raised eyebrow," she said tartly. "The only reason I mentioned 'suitable rank' earlier was because Drina is very conscious of birth, and I wanted to say something that would convince her to decide in your favor."

His face hardened again. "She will not be amused if she discovers that a bastard commoner was formally presented to her."

Exasperated, Sara said, "Mikahl, the founder of the noble house of St. James was a cockney actress called Nellie James, who was one of the many mistresses of Charles II. She was a round-heeled wench, and Charles had some doubts about whether he was actually the father of her son. Being a generous man, he compromised by making the boy an earl rather than a duke, which is what he did for some of the sons he was more sure of."

"Really?" Mikahl asked, startled.

"Really. The first few Earl St. Jameses were notable mostly for their ability to marry daughters of rich merchants. My great-grandfather Nigel was a clever fellow who must have inherited some business ability from the maternal side of his family. Nigel developed a swamp on the edge of London into a community of expensive squares and houses, and was created Duke of Haddonfield for his efforts. He also made vast amounts of money, which enabled my father to marry for love rather than fortune. My mother came from a family of respectable, but impoverished, Scottish gentry—no grand aristocrats in that branch of the Mont-gomeries, just farmers and soldiers.''

Mikahl shook his head, his eyes gleaming with amusement. "I presume your father knows all this family history.''

"Of course, though he prefers not to dwell on Nellie James. I once found a picture of her in an old book. She was not at all a respectable-looking wench.''

"Charles probably wouldn't have liked her if she was.''

"Very true.'' Sara sighed. "Since meeting you, I've discovered that I have more than a dash of the old girl's blood in me. But think about it, Mikahl. I, too, am descended from a cockney and a bastard, as well as assorted tradesmen and farmers, so stop prickling like a hedgehog about your background.''

"A hedgehog.'' He blinked. "I stand corrected. Your ancestors sound more disreputable than mine.''

Sara smiled back at him, but the moment of levity ebbed away. "There is a great deal you haven't men-tioned,'' she said quietly. "Such as how you got from shipboard to caravan, and what is between you and Charles Weldon.''

"I know. I owe you an explanation.'' Her husband closed his eyes, a spasm of exhaustion crossing his face. "It is going to be . . . very difficult to explain. I would rather not do it tonight, though I will try if you ask it of me.''

It was a measure of how much the events of the evening had drained Mikahl that he would make that oblique request for her to be patient. Sara had also had quite enough drama for one night; more might shatter them both.

Rising from her chair, she went to her husband and slipped her arms around his neck. When he opened his eyes again, she saw that they were gray-green with strain.

Laying her cheek against his, she whispered, "Another time, Mikahl. Now let's go to bed. And tomorrow, please take me home to Sulgrave.''

He pulled her into a fierce embrace. ''Ah, God, Sara,'' he murmured, his voice unsteady, ''what have I done to deserve you?''

She did not answer, just closed her eyes and relaxed against him, profoundly grateful that they had weathered this storm.

Perhaps their marriage might have a future. In the weeks since the wedding, they had shared laughter and talk and astonishing physical pleasure. But never had Sara felt more married than at this moment.

Chapter 22

WELDON WAS IN a blazing rage when he arrived at his house. He had told the truth about the sly bastard and been humiliated for his pains, in front of the queen and the cream of London society. While Peregrine was the root of the problem, he could not have carried off his imposture without the help of Lady Sara and Lord Ross. They had told barefaced lies in support of Peregrine, and they would pay. By God, they would pay. Weldon had already intended to wreak vengeance on Sara, but now he added Ross Carlisle to the list of those who must be punished.

Though it was past midnight, he summoned Kane. Within ten minutes Kane appeared, fully dressed and showing no signs of sleepiness. Fleetingly Weldon wondered if the man ever slept, or whether he really was the passionless, blue-eyed weapon that he always appeared to be.

Wasting no time, Weldon said, "I've found that the man who calls himself Peregrine is behind all of my current problems. *All* of them. He came to England to destroy me. He must die."

"Easily done." Kane did not even blink. "When—tomorrow? And do you have any particular method in mind, or can I do whatever is easiest?"

Such ready acquiescence made Weldon pause to think the matter through. "Better to wait a few days," he decided. "I need to learn how wide a net the bastard has cast. Set watchers on his houses in town and the country. I want them in place by tomorrow morning, or rather, by this morning. I want Peregrine followed. I need to find out who his associates are, particularly the man or men who have been acting for him in the City. As for the best method of killing . . ."

He pondered. "If you take him in the country, a shooting accident would be best. If it happens in London, make it appear like a robbery that went awry. Needless to say, don't do anything that can be traced back to me. Use some of the guards from the whorehouses if you need extra help. And if Lord Ross Carlisle is with Peregrine, you can kill them both."

Kane nodded. "What about Lady Sara?"

"Don't shoot Lady Sara," Weldon said, his tone ugly. "I have other plans for her."

The Duke of Haddonfield was not surprised when Sir Charles Weldon called the day after the Sanfords' ball. It had been obvious that something dark and dangerous connected Weldon and Prince Peregrine; like it or not, Haddonfield and his daughter were now reluctant players in the same game. And the blame for that must be laid squarely on the duke's own shoulders.

When Haddonfield entered the morning room, he saw that his visitor looked strained and had a dangerous gleam in his eye. The two men had not met privately since the disastrous night at Chapelgate when Sara had let herself be compromised by Peregrine.

"Good morning, Charles," the duke said with dry courtesy. "Dare I guess that there is a connection between your visit and what happened last night at the Sanfords?"

"There's a connection, all right," his visitor growled. "What I said about your son-in-law was the truth. If your nephew and daughter hadn't interfered, Peregrine would have been exposed for what he is."

The duke sat in a straight-backed wooden chair. "I suspect that your references to *my* son-in-law, *my* nephew, and *my* daughter means that you hold me responsible for their actions.''

"If you had raised your daughter properly, she would be my wife now, and I would not have a tenth of the problems," Weldon said, sitting without an invitation. "But because she's a trollop, she married a baseborn criminal who is doing his best to destroy me."

"Indeed?" Haddonfield's face showed only aristocratic boredom, for he had learned that showing genuine feeling to Weldon gave the other man dangerous power.

His visitor scowled. "Have you fallen under Peregrine's spell, too? So much so that you don't care what he is?''

"No matter what else he might be, he is my daughter's husband, and for her sake I want to stay on good terms with him. And I must say that he is always polite, which is more than can be said of you," the duke said with a trace of acid.

"You will regret the day you ever met him, Haddonfield," Weldon sneered. "Let me tell you about how I first met your son-in-law, in Tripoli."

It was difficult for the duke to keep his face blank as he listened to the story. No doubt Weldon was embroidering the truth for malicious effect, but it was still appalling to think that gentle, well-bred Sara had married a man with such a sordid history. Haddonfield kept his thoughts to himself; he had forfeited the right to judge his daughter's actions. When Weldon was finished, the duke said only, "That is neither here nor there. Let us stop bandying insults and go directly to whatever it is that you want from me. I assume that is why you are here—because you want something?''

"I need eighty thousand pounds immediately," Weldon said. "Peregrine secretly bought up all my outstanding loans, and is demanding payment within the next few days. He has almost ruined both my personal and business finances, so no one will lend me that kind of money." He gave a mirthless smile.

"Then I thought of you, my friend and almost father-in-law."

"Were we friends?" the duke murmured. "Looking back, I feel more like I was your victim."

Weldon laughed nastily. "That is a role you relish."

Haddonfield flushed as his visitor's barb struck home.

Weldon continued, "There is still a debt between us, Haddonfield. You said you would give me Sara, and you didn't."

"I never promised to 'give you' my daughter. I said that I would encourage her to accept your proposal, which is not the same thing," the duke corrected. "Though it shames me to admit it, I fulfilled my part of the bargain. Thank heaven Sara broke the betrothal, though I wish she had done it a different way."

Weldon's eyes flashed with fury. "If you had raised her to obey her father's wishes as a daughter should, we would both have been spared a great deal of unpleasantness. However, since I'm a flexible man, I will allow you to recompense me with money. If you don't . . ." His voice trailed off menacingly.

"The world will learn a number of unappetizing things about me, and perhaps about my son-in-law as well?" the duke said, his voice ironic. "That sounds remarkably like blackmail. However, I will do as you ask this once. Just remember that while silence may be golden, it is not infinitely valuable."

Weldon's face eased, triumph coming into his eyes. "It's valuable enough." After a brief discussion to arrange the transfer of the money, he left.

Haddonfield stayed in the morning room, his gaze unfocused. There was something fitting about paying Weldon blackmail, for the duke deserved punishment. And since the money was going to Peregrine, at least it would be staying in the family.

At length he shook his head, and rose. God only knew what Peregrine was, but he could not be a worse husband to Sara than Weldon would have been.

* * *

Before leaving for Sulgrave the next morning, Peregrine visited Benjamin Slade and described the latest developments.

The lawyer's brows rose when he heard what had happened at the Sanfords' ball. "Was it wise to let Weldon know that you are behind his problems?"

"Not wise, perhaps, but essential," Peregrine said tersely. "What would it take to hang Weldon?"

Slade considered. "It would probably require iron-clad evidence that he had personally murdered someone. But I thought you were more interested in killing him yourself than in having Her Majesty's courts do it for you."

Peregrine ignored the remark, though inwardly he decided that the people closest to him were beginning to know him too well. "Of the eight guards you hired for me, I'm assigning two to you personally. Take them along whenever you go out, and make sure that they stand watch in your house at night."

Slade was taken aback. "You really think that's necessary?"

"My guess is that before Weldon comes after me, he will try to remove pressure on the railroad. If he traces the lawsuits back to you, he might decide that killing you will help him and inconvenience me." Peregrine gave a sardonic smile. "The former assumption may be wrong, but the latter is certainly correct."

The lawyer's face became shuttered. "Since you put it like that, I'll welcome the guards. Is there any chance that Weldon could eliminate both you and me, and get away with it?"

"No chance at all. I had a third set of copies made of the evidence we have on Weldon, and gave it to someone that Weldon will never connect with me. No matter what, he will be brought to justice for his crimes." Seeing Slade's expression, Peregrine continued, "Don't look so doomed—I am just taking care of all possibilities. Weldon is not invincible. He is

only a madman with a few thugs working for him.
With luck, he'll never find you, and he may do nothing
to you personally even if he does.''

Then he turned on his heel and left, his mind already on what other precautions must be taken.

Across the street, a nondescript man had already
learned from a shopkeeper who lived at that address.
When Peregrine left, the nondescript man resumed
following him.

That afternoon, a report of Peregrine's morning visit
reached Charles Weldon. By luck, Weldon's railway
secretary recognized the name of Benjamin Slade. A
few more inquiries in different directions established
that Slade was undoubtedly Peregrine's man of business. For a quiet man who worked from his home,
Slade was surprisingly well-known in the business
community. He was also respected to a point just short
of awe.

As the pieces came together, Weldon rubbed his
hands in satisfaction. Yes, luck was still on his side.
In a week, he would have closed the book on Michael
Connery, the fool who thought he could defeat Charles
Weldon.

That night, two men broke into Benjamin Slade's
town house. The intruders were in the process of starting a fire when they were surprised by two armed de-
fenders. Shots were exchanged in the darkness and one
of the intruders was wounded, leaving blood on the
floor and the windowsill. Slade arrived on the scene
in time to assist in putting out the fledgling fire, which
did no serious damage.

Considerably disquieted, the lawyer sent a message
to his employer first thing the next morning. Shortly
after lunch, Peregrine arrived at Slade's house. After
a guard let him in, Slade came into the hall to greet
his guest, and was almost smothered when Jenny Miller hurled her small self into his arms.

''When she found that an urgent message had come

from you, she bullied me until she learned what it said,'' Peregrine explained with a faint smile. "Then she wouldn't let me leave the house without her.''

"Are you all right, Mr. Slade?'' the girl said anxiously, scanning him as if looking for scorch marks.

"I'm fine, Jenny,'' the lawyer assured her. Dressed in the clothing Lady Sara had given her, the girl would not have looked out of place in the highest society. With considerable reluctance, he removed her clinging hands. Glancing at his employer, he said, "Did you wish to speak to me alone?''

"Jenny might as well come with us,'' Peregrine said dryly. "She'll just listen at the door if we try to exclude her.''

"Right you are, mate,'' she said with a defiant gleam in her eyes. Following Slade into his office, she sat next to him on the hard, horsehair-covered sofa and clutched his hand as if her presence would guarantee his safety.

As soon as the door was closed, Peregrine said, "Pack everything essential and close the house. You'll be safer at Sulgrave. It will only be for a few days— whatever is going to happen will happen soon.''

Slade frowned. "Can the guards stay here? I would rather not have my house burned down.''

"Fine, though if you leave conspicuously enough, there probably won't be another attempt.''

The lawyer gnawed on his lower lip. "How do you think Weldon located me so soon?''

Peregrine grimaced. "Probably he had me followed yesterday morning. I thought I had come early enough so that he would not have had time to arrange that. Instead, I must have led him here myself.'' He shook his head in self-disgust. "I should have known better than to underestimate him for even a moment.''

"Your guards prevented anything serious from happening,'' Slade pointed out.

"True. I was half a move ahead of Weldon this time—barely enough.'' His face was set like granite.

"I will not let my friends suffer for my lack of foresight."

"Are we friends? I thought I was your employee."

"Would you have done all the strange and sometimes dubious things I've asked of you just for money?"

"No, I suppose not."

"I didn't think so." Peregrine hesitated for a moment, for it was very hard to say what he felt out loud. "I value you, Benjamin, and I don't want anything to happen to you."

Slade looked as embarrassed as Peregrine felt. "Thank you. I appreciate hearing that." He smiled, his eyes briefly touching the young woman at his side. "My life has become so much more interesting since I met you."

Peregrine's mouth quirked wryly. "The Chinese have a curse that says 'May you live in interesting times.' I hope you don't come to think that meeting me has been a curse."

Slade was impressed when Lady Sara welcomed him to Sulgrave without so much as a hint of surprise. The lawyer thought that boded well for the marriage; a woman married to Peregrine had better be unshockable. Slade was allotted two comfortable adjoining rooms, one for an office and the other for sleeping. Right after dinner he excused himself and withdrew to his rooms, wanting to take care of the work that had not gotten done because of the break-in and move to Sulgrave.

The evening was well advanced when a soft knock sounded at the door. He invited the visitor to enter, thinking it must be Peregrine. Instead, Jenny came in with a tray and an uncertain expression. "Would you like some tea, Mr. Slade?"

He couldn't suppress his smile of pleasure. "You really shouldn't be here," he said as he rose from his chair. "It's not proper, and Lady Sara might object."

"I've finished my work for the evening, so she won't mind." Jenny set the tray down and poured two cups full. "In fact, she won't even notice. All she really sees is her husband."

"They're happy?" Slade pulled a chair out for Jenny.

She nodded as she sat down. "There's kind of a glow between them. I've never seen anything like it." Then Jenny's brows drew together as she offered a plate of cakes to her companion. "But I don't think he's telling her what's happening. That's not right—she should know because she's part of it."

"I understand why Peregrine doesn't want his wife involved. I doubt if anyone except he and Weldon will ever know the full story. He certainly isn't telling me."

"He's making a mistake," Jenny said darkly. "Lady Sara may have led a protected life, but she's not a child. She's going to be angry when she learns everything he's been up to. And it could be dangerous for her *not* to know."

"Tell him that, if you're brave enough," Slade said with a small smile. "I'm not."

"I'm not either," Jenny said ruefully. "I expect it will be all right. But there's trouble coming—I can feel it in my bones. When I heard that someone had tried to burn your house down . . ." She shuddered. "You could have died in your bed."

"But I didn't. Now I'm here and safe, and everything will be over soon."

Jenny just shook her head, her face grave. "Weldon and Peregrine—they're like two cocks fighting, and they won't stop till one or both of them are dead. And God have mercy on anyone who gets in the way."

Slade fell silent, uneasily aware that the girl was probably right. He had been caught between the two men, and it might have killed him if Peregrine hadn't thought to supply the guards.

Deciding that the conversation was too serious, he began asking questions about Jenny's life in the country. Her descriptions of a London girl's introduction to cows and harvests was hilarious, and the evening went quickly.

A clock striking midnight finally reminded Slade of the lateness of the hour. "Time for bed, Jenny. Thank you for coming—I've really missed our evening talks."

"So have I." She stood and gathered the cups and plates onto the tray, but instead of leaving, she began toying with the lid of the teapot. Not looking at him, she said, "Remember how you said that lying together should mean something?"

Slade tensed, not sure what was coming. "I remember."

She darted a quick glance at him. "If we did now— it would mean something." Her eyes flicked back to the tray. "If you still wanted to."

He swallowed hard, not sure what to do or say. This was different from the first time she had propositioned him, but he was not sure how. Then he realized. Jenny was no longer the young woman who had calmly offered her body to pay a debt. She was shy, fearful of rejection, because this time her feelings were involved.

"Oh, yes, Jenny, I want to," he said softly. "But I'm still not sure that it's the right thing to do. What about your new life and the handsome young footman?"

"I've met all kinds of men here," she said simply. "Grooms, footmen, guards, and gardeners. Most have given me the eye, and some of them are handsome, but none of them are you."

He felt that he had been given the greatest gift of his life. Beyond caring if his actions were right or wrong, he reached out and cupped her cheek, his fingers tingling at the feel of her delicate skin.

"Ah, Jenny, you are so lovely," he whispered. Then he leaned forward and kissed her, very gently. While he was not without some experience of women, he had never been a womanizer, and he knew that he was not a dashing, expert lover. But he wanted, with every particle of his being, to please this young girl who had known so little of pleasure.

Jenny's lips worked under his, slow and experimentally, as tentative as Slade himself. Then she gave a soft sigh and raised her hands to his shoulders to draw him closer. And as the night flowed on, the man with little experience and the girl with too much found magic together.

After they had made love, she began weeping. Horrified, Slade propped himself up on one elbow. "What's wrong, Jenny? Did I hurt you?"

He thought that she might draw away, but instead she burrowed against him, wrapping her arms around his chest. "I didn't—I didn't know it could be so sweet."

He cuddled her close, stroking her flaxen hair with one hand, awed that such a lovely young woman was happy in his arms. There had been moments of awkwardness, and they had much to learn about each other, but she was right: there was great sweetness between them. Quietly he said, "I know that this is too soon, but would you at least consider marrying me?"

Shocked, she drew her head back, tears glinting on her cheek in the lamplight. "Marry you?" she faltered.

Carefully he brushed the tears away with the tip of his finger. "I know that I shouldn't ask. I'm almost twice your age and not a very interesting person, but I'm rather well-off, and I swear I'll take good care of you. As my wife, you'll never be cold or hungry or bullied by anyone again."

"You're the most interesting man I've ever met," she retorted. "But you can't marry me! You're a gentleman."

He smiled, "I can marry any woman I can talk into accepting me, Jenny, though I've never wanted to marry before."

"What would people say?" she asked miserably. "Gentlemen don't marry whores. I would embarrass you."

"Don't say that! You are not a whore—you're a brave and beautiful young woman who has survived and flourished in the midst of great adversity. Like a perfect rose that miraculously has bloomed among the weeds."

She giggled. "That's not very romantic."

"Probably not. I don't have a very romantic nature," he admitted, glad she was laughing again. "Don't worry about not fitting in—you are so quick at picking up accents and manners that people will never know that you don't have the same boring background that they do."

She smiled but shook her head. "I think you're being romantic now, Mr. Slade. You don't have to marry me just because you think you should after what we've done."

"I think we've gotten to the point where you could call me Benjamin." He lay back against the pillow, pulling her head down on his shoulder and stroking her pale silken hair. "Once upon a time, Jenny, I always did exactly what I thought I should. I studied hard, worked hard, obeyed all the rules, thinking that all that sober virtue would be rewarded. I went into the East India Company, determined to make a success of myself."

He sighed, thinking of what had happened in India, and how close he had come to destroying himself from despair. "After all my hard work, I was made the scapegoat for my superior's embezzling. I lost my job, my reputation, most of my friends, and very nearly my freedom. If Peregrine hadn't come along and saved me in an illegal but very effective way, I would be in prison or dead now." He bent his head and kissed her on the end of the nose. "After that, Jenny, I no longer much cared what the world expected of me. I decided that in the future, I would please myself first. It would please me greatly to marry you—but only if that would please you as well.''

Jenny was silent, knowing that if she tried to speak, she would begin crying again. Tentatively she flattened her hand on his chest. She had known many male bodies, with indifference at best, sometimes with fear and loathing. But she had never wanted to be close to a man like this. Benjamin had a nice body, fit and wiry, not large and frightening.

Joining with him had made her feel happy, cherished like fine porcelain. She had been told that women could feel passion the same as men, but had never quite believed it. Now she did, dimly sensing that someday she would respond with more than sweetness. ''It would please me,'' she said. ''It's too soon, but maybe later, if you don't get bored with me . . .''

''I'll never get bored with you, Jenny. But I won't press you for an answer. Marriage is a serious business, and you should take time to think about it. In the meantime . . .''

He kissed her, this time seriously. And when she kissed him back, he knew that he had never felt so much a man in his life.

Chapter 23

KANE LAY FLAT on his stomach in the high grass, his spyglass trained on the two horsemen galloping heedlessly along the crest of the hill. He couldn't believe his luck. He had come out today only to scout the land around Sulgrave, yet here were the very men Weldon wanted killed, racing along without a care in their foolish heads.

While his employer might prefer to stay the execution for a few days, Kane refused to waste such a perfect opportunity. He might never have as good a chance to get both men at the same time. Weldon would be angry, but the idea did not bother Kane; the pleasure of the kill would far outweigh his employer's irritation. And Weldon needed Kane far more than vice versa.

Stealthily he crawled down from the top of his hill, staying low so that he would not be silhouetted against the sky. He smiled with contempt; considering how careless his quarry was, such precautions were probably unnecessary.

In his left hand he carried a light, ultra-accurate Prussian sporting rifle. He would work his way along the hill until he found a good ambush site. The two riders would almost certainly return by the same route that they had taken. And when they did, Kane would be ready for them.

Siva needed no encouragement to go flying along the North Downs. As they tore along the ancient hilltop trail, Peregrine leaned over the stallion's neck, the feel of the wild wind blowing away some of his restless frustration.

The two days since the Sanfords' ball had been uneasy. Peregrine studied Sara, wondering if there would be a subtle change in her behavior now that she knew about his background, but she acted exactly the same. She scarcely raised an eyebrow when he introduced Benjamin Slade as an indefinite houseguest, and she went out of her way to make the lawyer feel welcome.

Yet underneath the surface, there was an odd combination of closeness and sizzling tension between Peregrine and his wife. He knew that she was waiting for him to tell her about the missing years and his vendetta against Charles Weldon. Half a dozen times he was on the verge of speaking, yet always he shied away at the last minute.

There were two reasons why he held his tongue. One was a profound distaste for revealing what he had never told another living soul. In fact, he was not sure he could speak of it in any but the most general terms. And while he knew that he could trust Sara's compassion and generous heart, she was the last person on earth he wanted to know about his humiliation.

The other reason was that he was not sure what he wanted to do next. He must decide soon, for it was dangerous to let his enemy have the initiative. But it would be even more dangerous to act without knowing exactly what he wanted to accomplish.

For that reason, he had been glad when Ross rode over from Chapelgate and suggested Peregrine join him for a ride on the Downs. Ross knew more about the situation than anyone else; he was also the one person Peregrine knew who could understand both the world of law-abiding citizens and the twilight zone of violence, where Peregrine and Weldon were locked in mortal combat.

Siva was beginning to become winded, so Peregrine pulled the stallion back to a moderate canter. A few minutes later Ross caught up with him.

Peregrine called out, "Is that lazy hack of yours related to Sara's Pansy?"

"Those are fighting words." Ross laughed as he reined in his mount with the grace of the born horseman. "If you want to race, we can try again someday when my horse hasn't already been ridden hard. If we make it a steeplechase, I guarantee that Iskander will show his heels to that park saunterer of yours."

"Probably," Peregrine admitted. "Siva goes like the wind over a flat course, but is only a moderate jumper."

The two men turned their horses back the way they had come, riding companionably side by side. Peregrine's temporary sense of well-being began to fade. He scanned their surroundings, his brow furrowed. "We really shouldn't be out here. Too exposed. It would be very easy for a sniper to pick us off. I'm getting careless—I don't even have a gun with me."

Ross's brows drew together. "Do you really think Weldon will try to murder you outright?"

"Yes, though I think he will not want to do so just yet. It will make more sense to try to trace Slade and my business connections first." Peregrine glanced at his friend. "After the ball, I'm afraid he will come after you as well. Did you see his expression when you stepped in and vouched for me?"

Ross nodded. "I think the man is more than a little mad, and your vendetta is revealing the worst in him."

"The evil that has always been inside him is getting closer and closer to the surface." Peregrine frowned. "By speaking up, you deflected the disgrace from my head to his. Being incapable of admitting an error in judgment, Weldon will put the blame squarely on you and Sara."

"You could have talked Victoria around once you got over your shock." The path narrowed as it circled a small pond. Ross went ahead until the path widened and they could ride abreast again. "I admit I was surprised to see you thrown for a loss. After all, it was

just his word against yours, and as Sara's thwarted
suitor, he had an obvious motive for malicious mischief.''

"Perhaps," Peregrine said dryly. "But I thought
that if it came down to the word of a wellborn Englishman against a foreigner, Weldon was the one who
would be believed. I didn't expect my friends to lie
for me.''

"I didn't lie," Ross said, his expression innocent.
"I did, indeed, meet you in Kafiristan, and while it is
stretching a point to call your house a palace, it was
the grandest building in the village, and the Kafirs
thought very highly of you." After a moment, he
added reflectively, "Can't say that Sara lied, either.
It's just that her idea of what constitutes a husband of
suitable rank is considerably broader than Victoria's.''

Peregrine had to laugh. "You two are as bad as I
am.''

Ross grinned. "Were you really born in London?''

"Indeed I was." Peregrine gave his friend an ab-
breviated version of the story he had told Sara. At the
end he said, "You don't seem very surprised.''

"I'm not. Even in Kafiristan, I thought that you were
either of mixed blood or not a native son," Ross said.
"Since you came to England at the beginning of the
summer, I've come to the conclusion that you were
probably at least partially European. And if European,
why not English?''

"How did I give myself away?''

Ross pondered for a while. "Subtle things. Underlying patterns of thought that seemed more Western
than oriental. I can't be more specific than that.''

"Considering how widely you've traveled, I suppose if anyone was going to guess, it would be you.''
Peregrine's voice acquired an edge. "Does it matter
to you that I'm a slum bastard?''

Ross gave him a cool glance. "Are you proud or
ashamed of your background?''

Peregrine was taken aback. "Not ashamed. I suppose, in an odd way, I'm proud. If I had been raised in a softer environment, I never would have survived what came later."

"Then don't be defensive about what made you what you are," Ross said crisply.

That seemed to close the question of his background rather thoroughly. There was no shortage of class prejudice in British society, but it was Peregrine's great good fortune that his wife and his best friend had none.

As they rode along the trail in silence, Peregrine's gaze continued to scan the trees and hills around them, and he saw that Ross was equally watchful. At length, Ross said, "What are you going to do about Weldon?"

"I honestly don't know," Peregrine admitted. He described the break-in at Slade's house. "If the fire had been successful, Benjamin would be dead and many of his records destroyed. Weldon must die—he is dangerous to too many people. The question is how. I don't think the law would give a guaranteed result."

Ross gave him a sardonic look. "Why are you talking about the law? Aren't you going to kill him yourself?"

Peregrine glanced at the other man, his face impassive. Yes, his friends were definitely getting too perceptive. "I prefer to think of it as an execution."

"So what is stopping you?"

Peregrine's brows arched. "What, no lecture on morality?"

"I don't like the idea one damned bit," Ross said, his voice clipped, "but I don't see an alternative. It is obvious that you and Weldon are locked in a till-death-do-you-part feud, and if one of you must die, I would prefer it to be Weldon."

"If and when I kill Weldon, I intend to do it in a way that can't be traced back to me," Peregrine said, grateful for his friend's pragmatic acceptance of the situation. "But if something goes wrong, and I have to leave England—I want to know that you will look out for Sara." He stopped, then started again. "You will anyhow, but I'll feel better knowing that at least one person here understands what really happened.''

Ross's dark eyes flashed. ''So you intend to desert your wife?'' he snapped, far more angry than he had been at the prospect of his friend's committing murder.

''I didn't marry her to abandon her, but frankly, I doubt that she would come with me if I asked,'' Peregrine said, his voice cold. ''Her whole life is in England—all her friends, her relatives. How could I take her away from that?''

''You can let her make the choice for herself,'' Ross said, his voice equally cold. ''If you desert her, I swear I will track you down and make you sorry that you ever set foot in England.''

Peregrine chuckled, wanting to defuse the situation. ''You're beginning to sound like me. Too much exposure to my amoral ways is corrupting you.''

As Ross gave a reluctant smile, Peregrine continued, ''Believe me, I have no desire to flee England as a criminal, just as I have no desire to force Sara to make a decision where either choice will make her miserable.'' Besides, he thought he knew how Sara would choose—and it wouldn't be for her husband. ''I just want you to be prepared for whatever comes.''

''Try not to get yourself killed,'' Ross suggested. ''Sara wouldn't like it, and it would leave me in the regrettable position of having to hunt Weldon down myself to prevent him from injuring Sara or me.'' In a piece of massive British understatement, he added, ''Untidy.''

''Definitely untidy.'' Peregrine shook his head. ''When I came to England, I thought revenge would be a straightforward business. Instead, my life has gotten unbelievably complicated.''

Ross's mouth quirked up. ''Welcome to the real world.''

* * *

When he heard the sound of approaching horses, Kane readied himself. He had found a perfect ambush spot in a patch of broken ground and was concealed in a clump of rocks. The trail was about sixty yards away, an easy shot for an expert marksman. Like many old lanes, this one was sunken about three feet below ground level, but men up on horseback would be easy targets.

He lay on his stomach, his rifle steady in his hands. Far better to do this task himself; assistants were invariably more trouble than they were worth. The dolt Kane had taken along to the lawyer's house had been too stupid to avoid getting shot in the arm. No, this was best.

The two men rode into range. Kane spent a moment confirming that they were the right ones. He was careful about such things.

Lord Ross Carlisle was on the near side, but Kane aimed at Peregrine, for the dark foreigner was more important and also had experience that should make him cooler under fire. A pampered English aristocrat like Lord Ross would probably be too surprised and confused to take cover before Kane reloaded and shot him.

Aiming for the heart, Kane began tracking Peregrine. In just a moment, another moment . . .

Without haste, he squeezed the trigger.

If the sun had not come from behind a cloud a few minutes earlier, there would have been no warning at all. As it was, Ross saw only a brief flicker as light slid along a rifle barrel, but that was enough. Without conscious thought, he reacted with the reflexes honed in thousands of miles of dangerous traveling.

From the angle of the barrel, Peregrine was the target. And he was unaware of the danger because his attention was on a clump of trees to the left. The trail was narrow here, and the horses were so close that the two men were almost touching.

Acting from instinct, Ross shouted, "Get down!"

At the same time, he dived sideways, reaching out to shove his friend lower.

Both warning and action were a fraction too late. As Ross grabbed Peregrine's arm, a bullet slammed into his own back with paralyzing impact. As the breath was blasted from his body, he had the fleeting thought that it was ironic to have survived Bokhara and Afghanistan only to die like this among the peaceful green hills of England.

Then darkness claimed him.

Furiously Kane watched his plan go awry. The Englishman must have seen something, for he shouted and moved between Kane and his target. As thunderous echoes of the gunshot rolled across the valley, a horse screamed, and both men disappeared from view, falling between their mounts. Since the path was below ground level, Kane could not see what had happened. Both horses bolted down the path, one still screaming. Then all was silence.

As he swiftly reloaded, Kane swore under his breath. His rifle was powerful, and it was possible that the one bullet had hit both men, going through Lord Ross to strike Peregrine. In fact, that was likely, for there was no sound from where the men had fallen. But it had been sloppy shooting, and quite possibly one or both of the men were still alive. Kane would have to finish them off at close range, which would make it obvious that this was no hunting accident.

But it was too late to turn back. Every sense alert, Kane began to make his way across the ground to his victims.

The deafening crack of the rifle made it shatteringly clear to Peregrine that once again he had made a lethal miscalculation. Weldon wasn't waiting, he was going direct to the death stroke.

Peregrine could have retained his seat on the horse, but let himself be pulled off by Ross's falling body.

Fueled by self-fury, his mind raced at top speed. The shot must have come from the right of the trail, where Ross was watching and Peregrine wasn't. A single gunman or there would have been more than one shot. And Ross had taken the bullet intended for his friend.

Peregrine hit the ground hard, Ross landing half on top of him as the horses stampeded, panic-stricken by the blast of the gun and the scent of blood. Keeping his head below the edge of the sunken lane, Peregrine did a hasty examination of his friend, praying that the wound was minor. The bullet had struck in the upper left back. As he turned Ross over to see if there was an exit wound, his friend's eyelids flickered open.

"That was a bloody stupid bit of heroics," Peregrine swore in a furious whisper. "You had damned well better not die, or Sara will never forgive me."

Ross gave a ghost of a smile. His voice almost inaudible, he said, "Tell Sara that . . . I owed you . . . a life for a life." Then his eyes closed again.

Peregrine's mouth twisted savagely as he saw the brilliant scarlet stain spreading across the other man's white shirt. The bullet had gone right through him, which was good, and the wound was high enough so that possibly the lungs were not damaged. But even if the gunshot was not mortal in itself, Ross would bleed to death quickly without treatment.

Two impulses warred within Peregrine; he wanted desperately to stop the bleeding before it was too late, but he could not afford to take the time when there was a murderer within yards. If either of them were to survive, the gunman must be stopped.

The only weapon Peregrine had was the knife he always carried in his boot. It would have to be enough. He crouched below the edge of the lane, and swiftly moved fifty yards to the left. Then he peered over the edge of the lane in the direction he thought the shot had come from. There was a tumble of boulders in the right position.

He held absolutely still, listening. At first there was

no sight or sound of the gunman. Then he heard a slight rustle of grass. He could see nothing, but from the sound guessed that a single man was moving carefully from the rocks to the trail.

The ground was covered with a mixture of trees, grass, and shrubs, which prevented Peregrine from seeing the sniper, but which also provided cover for his own movement. He slid the knife from his boot, and carried it in his right hand as he crawled over the lip of the lane and began to stalk his enemy.

Staying low, he chose an angle that should bring the two men together at the brink of the lane. His progress was slowed by the dryness of the early autumn vegetation, which made it hard to move silently. Fortunately the sniper was making enough noise to cover the faint sounds of Peregrine's passage.

A few feet from the lane, the gunman stood up, presenting his back to Peregrine, who was still a dozen feet away. His rifle at his shoulder, the sniper gazed down into the lane to discover how much damage he had wrought. When he saw that there was only one body below, the gunman instantly realized his danger. He whirled around, hands tightening on his weapon, his eyes narrow and dangerous. It was Kane, Weldon's chief jackal.

Seeing Peregrine, Kane snarled, "Now I have you!"

Simultaneously Peregrine hurled himself at the other man, covering the distance in three long strides. "Not yet, you bloody murderer!"

Kane made the mistake of pausing to aim. Peregrine dived under the rifle, knocking the other man backward. The gun fired, the bullet blazing perilously close as Peregrine knocked Kane to the ground. The fight was swift and deadly. A stream of profanity pouring from him, Kane fought with every savage trick he knew, but Peregrine knew more. It took less than ten seconds to pin the other man to the ground.

A distant, rational corner of his mind said that he should interrogate Kane because the other man might know something useful about Weldon's plans. But rationality had no chance against the annihilating rage that drove Peregrine. "Die, you bastard," he swore.

Then he slit Kane's throat in the middle of a curse. Blood spurted forth, and a hoarse, gurgling noise came from Kane's severed windpipe, but he could not speak. Very quickly the flow of blood slowed, then stopped. Peregrine stood and wiped his knife on Kane's coat before he dragged the body behind some shrubbery. He took a moment to peel off his victim's coat and shirt. Then, his face grim, he went to see if anything could be done for Ross.

His friend was still breathing, though shallowly, and his face was chalk white from shock and blood loss. Peregrine had considerable experience with gunshot and knife wounds, and swiftly he improvised a bandage from strips of Kane's clothing, tying fabric pads over the wounds on both chest and back.

Having done what he could to staunch the bleeding, Peregrine stood and ran down the path in the direction the horses had gone, praying that one of the beasts was close.

Whatever gods he invoked were listening, for less than a quarter of a mile away he discovered Ross's mount. Iskander was an even-tempered beast, but he shied away from the wild, bloody human who wanted to capture him. It took too much time for Peregrine to calm himself to the point where Iskander would let him close. Finally he managed to catch the horse.

He galloped back to Ross. The next half hour was a series of disconnected, nightmarish moments: struggling to get his friend's considerable weight onto the skittish horse. Mounting behind and guiding the beast with one hand while the other kept Ross from falling. Forcing Iskander faster than a horse carrying two heavy men should have to go. And praying that his friend would still be alive when they reached Sulgrave.

Chapter 24

SARA ONLY DID needlework when she wanted to think. As she chose a new hank of green silk thread, she realized ruefully that she had done quite a lot of embroidery in the last two days. After they came back to Sulgrave, she had hoped that Mikahl would reveal the critical pieces of his missing past, but he had not raised the subject, and she was reluctant to do so herself.

There was tension in the air, like a ribbon of molten glass being drawn thinner and thinner until it must reach the snapping point. Absently Sara leaned over to scratch the head of Furface, who was curled up on the hem of her gown. Something was on the verge of happening; she had the frustrated feeling that there were things she should know, but didn't.

Her abstraction was broken when the butler entered to bring her afternoon tea. She glanced up to thank him, then stopped, her attention caught by the gray misery in his face. Guiltily remembering that she was not the only person with problems, she lowered her embroidery hoop. "Is something wrong, Gates?"

He hesitated, on the verge of denial, then said reluctantly, "You were right in your investment advice, my lady. I should have sold the L & S Railway stock when the price was high."

"It has gone down?" she said, concerned.

"Badly. In fact, the newspapers say the company is on the verge of bankruptcy." After another hesitation, he said hopefully, "Has Prince Peregrine said anything to indicate that this is just temporary, that the company will recover?''

His brief animation faded when Sara shook her head. "I'm sorry, he never talks business with me." Disturbed by the bleakness in the butler's eyes, she said, "That doesn't mean that the company's situation won't get better—just that I don't know. Perhaps you should ask him yourself.''

He shook his head, scandalized. "I couldn't possibly."

Sara understood. Gates had grown up at Haddonfield, and he could speak to her as he could not to an outsider. "I will ask my husband myself this evening,'' she offered.

"I would appreciate that, my lady." He used a linen towel to flick a speck of dust from a gleaming table. With sudden bitterness, he said, "I should have known that stocks and companies are a rich man's game. Someone like me is a fool to think he has a chance to better himself that way."

Sara watched him unhappily, knowing that the fact that Gates spoke at all was a measure of his distress. At the same time, she doubted that Mikahl was equally disturbed; since the railway was Weldon's pet project, her husband might applaud if the company was failing.

Their conversation was interrupted by a sudden commotion in the front hall. Curious, Sara set her embroidery down and hastened out to investigate.

To her horror, she found Mikahl and the head groom carrying the limp body of her cousin into the hall. Both her husband and Ross were soaked in blood. Sara clutched the door frame, dizzy with shock. "Good God, what has happened?''

Mikahl glanced up at her, his green eyes glittering with furious emotion. "Some damned fool hunter shot Ross."

She pressed her knuckles into her mouth, on the verge of fainting. "Is he—is he alive?''

"For the moment," was the grim answer. "Send for a doctor while we get him upstairs to a bed."

Sara nodded, grateful to have something to do. Turning to Gates, who had followed her into the hall, she said, "Send one of the grooms into Reigate. Have him promise the surgeon any amount of money if he will come immediately."

Gates nodded and hastened off. Sara stood for a moment, hands pressed to her temples as she tried to think what to do. Dear God, Ross couldn't die. All her life, he had always been there, laughing in the good times, helping in the bad, always caring. And now his life hung in the balance.

Realizing that her breath was becoming rapid and shallow, she forcibly clamped down on her rising emotions. Hysteria would not help her cousin, but coolness might.

After a moment her mind began to work again. Other servants had been drawn to the disturbance, so she ordered a maid to bring hot water to the patient. Then Sara herself went upstairs to the linen closet for clean sheets.

The groom had left after Ross had been put to bed. When Sara entered the sickroom, Mikhal was scowling over the blood-soaked bandage. "He's bleeding again. Can you bear to help me put a dressing on? If not, leave and send one of the servants in. I can't afford to be worried about you, too."

"I can bear it," Sara said tersely. She had remembered to bring her sewing scissors and now used them to rip a sheet into strips. When her husband lifted Ross to turn him over, she put another folded sheet beneath her cousin to absorb the blood during the messy job of changing the bandage.

"We were riding on the trail that runs across the top of the Downs," Mikhal explained as he removed the crude, earlier binding. "There was just one shot—the hunter must have run away when he realized his mistake."

"It must have been a poacher," Sara said, averting her eyes as her husband uncovered the oozing wound in Ross's shoulder.

"Very likely." He covered the bullet hole with a thickly folded pad of linen, then tied it in place with one of the long strips Sara provided. "Both horses bolted, but I was able to catch Ross's again. The head groom met us partway back. He realized something was wrong when my horse came home with a graze wound on its neck."

"Dear God," she whispered. "If the bullet had struck you rather than Siva, you and Ross might both have died there."

"But we didn't." Having covered the entry wound in Ross's back, Mikahl began winding linen strips around chest and shoulder to hold both pads securely in place. "Though I hate to think of what might have happened if I couldn't have caught Ross's horse."

The maid had delivered a basin and pitcher of hot water, and when Mikahl was done, Sara began gently sponging the blood from her cousin's bare chest and arm. Beneath his golden hair, his face was like grayed marble. It was agonizing to see a man so vital lying as still as death.

Her husband put a hand on her shoulder. "I'm sorry, Sara," he said, his voice full of helpless frustration. "I wish I had been the one hit."

"I couldn't bear that, either," she said unsteadily. "Accidents happen. Don't blame yourself."

For a moment his fingers tightened on her shoulder. Then his hand fell away. "If I'm not careful, you'll be as bloodstained as I am. I have to go out and take care of something now. I'll be back as soon as I can."

Disregarding his words and his stained clothing, Sara stood and turned into his arms, needing his strength. "Please," she said softly, "hold me for a moment before you go."

He complied, embracing her with fierce protectiveness. "Will you be all right?"

Sara felt the tautness in his body. It must have been dreadful for Mikahl to have seen Ross struck down right in front of his eyes. "I'll manage," she said. "There isn't really much to do now but wait for the doctor."

Then her husband left, presumably to change his clothing and perhaps see to his horse. Sara sat down beside Ross and resumed the task of cleaning him. It wasn't much or even necessary, but it was the only way she knew to express her anguished love.

The surgeon arrived just before dinnertime. After tending Ross's wound, he told Sara that her cousin was very fortunate to have someone available to stop the bleeding so quickly, or he would have died. As it was, Lord Ross had a broken shoulder, but no major internal injuries, and should recover if serious inflammation didn't set in. He gave her some laudanum for the pain, then left, promising to return the next day.

"Thank God," Mikahl said, his voice intense. Back from his errands, he had been sitting with Sara in the sickroom.

"Amen," Sara added, weak with relief.

"Are you going to inform his parents?"

Sara thought a moment, then shook her head. "I don't think so. Ross won't like it if I upset them unnecessarily. Unless you think I should?"

Mikahl shook his head. "They are your family, and you know them best. Now come." He pulled her to her feet. "Ring for someone else to stay with him. You are going to change into a gown that isn't bloodstained. Then I'm going to take you downstairs and stand over you while you eat. I don't want you becoming ill, too."

"That won't be necessary. Now that the doctor has seen Ross, I can tear myself away for half an hour. But I'll be back to stay with him for the rest of the night." Her glance at her husband held a hint of challenge.

"I'd be surprised if you didn't." Mikahl's face tightened as he looked at Ross's still unconscious form. "But Sara, I don't think I can bear to stay all night with you."

"I don't expect you to, my dear, nor would Ross expect it. He's no better at sitting still than you are."

Her husband pulled her into a hug, his large hands kneading the tense knots out of her neck and shoulders. "You are a very understanding woman."

Jenny came to sit with Ross while Sara and her husband ate a simple supper. Than Sara returned to her quiet vigil.

Earlier in the day, Peregrine had ridden into the Downs with a spare horse, wrapped Kane's body in a blanket, then brought it back to Sulgrave and stored it in a little used outbuilding. After darkness fell, he transferred the corpse to a nondescript cart that was used for rough work around the estate.

Dressed as unmemorably as the cart, Peregrine took his time driving into London, not wanting to reach Mayfair until after midnight. His mission to dispose of Kane's body went without complication. Another move had been made in the lethal game between him and Weldon. And during the hours of driving, he planned what to do next.

Sara was glad when Ross began tossing and turning restlessly. He did not seem feverish, and his increased activity was less alarming than his death-like unconsciousness had been. She managed to get some beef broth down him, laced with a little laudanum to reduce the pain.

She dozed off herself for a time, then awoke with a start when she heard a faint voice saying, "Sally?"

Ross had sometimes called her that when they were children. Glad that he was conscious, she leaned over the bed. "How are you feeling?"

He blinked to bring her into focus. "Like hell, if

you'll excuse the language." His voice was barely audible.

"You're excused."

He raised his right hand uncertainly toward his bandaged left shoulder. "My mind seems to have been dipped in molasses."

"Better leave the bandage alone." Sara caught his wandering hand. "You've had some laudanum, which is why you feel fuzzy. Do you remember what happened?"

"I was riding with Mikahl in the Downs." Ross frowned. "Was he hurt?"

"He's fine," she assured him. "The same bullet that hit you grazed his horse, but Mikahl wasn't touched. He bandaged you up and brought you back to Sulgrave."

"Glad he's all right." Ross's fingers moved restlessly in Sara's grasp. "If Weldon had sent two assassins instead of one, I suppose we'd both be dead."

"Weldon?" Sara said, startled. She was about to say that Ross had been accidentally shot by a poacher when her cousin's rambling voice cut her off.

"Ironic. Just before I was shot, Peregrine said it was dangerous to be riding in such an exposed place. But he thought Weldon wouldn't try to kill him yet." Ross pulled his hand free and rubbed at his forehead, trying to clear his mind. "I think the sniper was aiming at Mikahl, not me. I saw the rifle and tried to push Mikahl out of the way and got in front of the bullet myself. Bloody stupid thing to do."

Sara felt as if her heart had stopped. Carefully she said, "You and Mikahl are sure that Charles Weldon is behind this?"

"Of course. Weldon wanted to strike before Mikahl could kill him first." Then Ross's gaze sharpened. "Damnation. You don't know any of that, do you?"

"No, but you are going to tell me everything, Ross," Sara said grimly. "What has been going on?"

"Mikahl hasn't wanted to tell you," her cousin said uncertainly. "He didn't want to worry you."

"My husband has made an error in judgment," she said, her voice clipped with anger, "and you are about to rectify it."

Perhaps if Ross had not been feeling the effects of laudanum, he would have resisted. Instead, he ran his fingers through his hair. "I've thought he should tell you. How much do you know now?"

Sara thought a moment. There had been much fire and brimstone, but what had her husband actually said? "I know that Charles and Mikahl hate each other. Mikahl said that Charles is evil, and that he may have killed his first wife by pushing her down the stairs. Once you told me that Charles might be involved in illicit activities, but it seemed so improbable that I didn't really believe it. Is all that really true?"

Ross sighed, and his eyes closed briefly. Then he began a flat litany that turned Sara's blood cold: that Charles Weldon did indeed own gaming hells and whorehouses, including the one that Jenny Miller had been in; that he was part owner of illegal slave ships; that he casually gave orders that ruined lives. And that Sara's husband was determined to destroy him.

Her cousin's words painted a picture that made horrible sense, though there were still huge holes; why Mikahl hated Charles so much, for example, and just what he was doing to bring his enemy low. Sara felt like a child who had been living in a prettily decorated tent, only to have the canvas walls suddenly drop to reveal monsters in every direction. She thought that she and her husband had been building a marriage and a life together; instead she found herself on the sidelines of an impending tragedy that she didn't understand.

"Ross, do you have any idea what Mikahl is planning?" she asked, keeping her voice level so as not to disturb him.

"Don't know," he said tiredly. After a moment, he

added, "Once I came into his study, and found him looking at some papers that he shoved into a concealed drawer in his desk. Maybe there's something there. Maybe not."

"I'll take a look," Sara said.

Ross was gray with fatigue, but he was not yet ready for sleep. "You won't do something foolish, will you?"

"No. I just want to understand what is happening." Sara's brow furrowed with thought. "Will you mind if I call the housekeeper to sit with you now? She said she'd relieve me if I wanted to go to bed."

Her cousin looked indignant. "Don't need anyone here."

"Well, *I* need someone to be here even if you don't." She leaned over and kissed his forehead. "Get some sleep now, my dear. Everything will be all right."

Yet even as she gave the automatic reassurance, she didn't believe it. Sara was not sure things would ever be all right again. She waited until Ross fell asleep, then rang for the housekeeper, Mrs. Adams. After she was relieved of her duty, Sara went down to the study. There were several standard types of concealed drawers, and it did not take long to locate and open the one in Mikahl's desk. Then, her face like granite, she took her husband's secret files upstairs to read.

It was about three in the morning when Peregrine quietly let himself back into his house. He stopped to look in on Ross and was surprised to see that Sara had been replaced. Presuming that meant that his friend was doing well, he moved on without disturbing Mrs. Adams, who was drowsing in a chair.

He had thought Sara would be asleep, but she was not. Instead she was curled up in a wing chair, wearing a flowing blue velvet robe and with her dark gold hair loose over her shoulders. When he entered, she laid the paper she was reading on a pile in her lap and looked up. In the soft lamplight, her face was not that of a sibyl, but the goddess Nemesis herself.

He paused in the doorway, warning alarms going off in his head, before entering the room and closing the door behind him. "I assume that Ross is improving, or you would still be with him."

"Ross is definitely better," Sara said in a steely voice. "He was able to speak quite coherently. And because of the laudanum, he told me some very interesting things." She held up the sheaf of papers. "Would you care to explain just what you are doing to Charles Weldon, and why?"

He raised his brows in mock surprise. "I see that the honorable Lady Sara has been going through my private papers. I would not have expected it of you."

"Don't try to change the subject! If my standards of honesty are declining, it is probably because of contact with you," his wife said, her voice tight. "Just what the devil have you been doing? And how many people are you injuring in the process of trying to bring Charles down?"

"I am doing nothing to Weldon that he does not deserve," Peregrine said calmly.

Sara's brown eyes flashed. "What gives you the right to be judge, jury, and executioner, Mikahl?"

"You are too civilized, Sara," he retorted. "Anything that is moral for the law is equally moral for an individual—just as a wrong act is not made right because a government commits it instead of an individual."

"I'm not interested in your sophistry! I may be too civilized, but you are an anarchist, and your private war almost got Ross killed," she said, anger rising. "If you want to see Charles Weldon pay for his crimes, why not turn the evidence you have collected over to the authorities? It looks like you have more than enough to send him to prison for the rest of his life."

"Prison would be too easy," he replied, his voice edged. "I want him to suffer. I swore that I would take away everything he valued, and that is what I have been doing.''

She lifted the top sheet of paper, listing Weldon's tangible and intangible assets, along with notes on Peregrine's progress. "So I noticed. I see that I fall about the middle of the list, between *social standing* and *barony*. But you didn't have to go as far as marrying me—I should think it would have been quite enough to end the betrothal.''

"Ah-h-h," he said, thinking he understood, "so that is what has upset you. You are right, breaking the betrothal would have been enough to injure Weldon. I married you because I wanted to.''

He had thought that statement might mollify his wife, but he was wrong. She slapped the sheaf of papers hard against her knee. "I admit that I'm not very flattered by my position on the list, but my expectations have never been high. What appalls me is the cost that others are paying for your private war. How many people will be injured by the fact that you are driving the railway into bankruptcy?''

He shrugged. "When speculators guess correctly, they make money. When they don't, they lose. They deserve what they get.''

"It isn't just rich businessmen who are affected,'' she snapped. "Did you know that our butler invested his life savings in the company because he trusted your business judgment?''

Peregrine was taken aback. "I didn't know that. I'll reimburse him for his losses.''

"That will help him, but what about all the others who are involved?'' Sara exclaimed. "Some of the investors in the railway may be rich speculators, but there must be many others like Gates, modest people trying to earn a little hope and security.''

"They took their chances like anyone else.''

"But they didn't know that they were investing in a company that you had decided to use as a weapon.'' Her mouth was a tight line. "You have been cutting a swath like the four horsemen of the apocalypse. Deliberately ruining the railway was bad enough, but your lack of action about the brothels was unforgivable. You could have closed that ghastly place that Jenny was in, but you didn't do it.''

"I was waiting for the right time," he said defensively.

"Damn the right time!" Sara leaped to her feet, unable to sit still any longer. "You have known about the place for months, and every night of that time, girls like Jenny have been suffering at the hands of strangers."

The best reply he could make was "I helped Jenny."

"That's not good enough, Mikahl," Sara said, her voice trembling. "She is only one person. What about the other innocent people who have been suffering because you have been so determined to slowly savor every particle of your revenge?"

"The world is full of evil. Nothing I might do will change that. If I had closed down Mrs. Kent's house, another one just like it would be open a week later."

"But you could have done something that would have helped a few girls, and you didn't!" She bowed her head and pressed her hand over her eyes. "You don't even understand why that bothers me, do you? Because you can survive anything, you have no compassion for others who are less strong. You might help someone you know personally, but you have no thought for anyone else."

"Why should I?" He was beginning to feel heated, so he peeled off his coat and tossed it over a chair. "It is quite enough to be concerned with those I know. I have never deliberately harmed anyone who did not deserve it."

She shook her head dully. "The fact that you are not deliberately harming strangers does not absolve you of responsibility. Nothing that Charles Weldon did to you can justify what you are doing to others."

His anger at her criticism tilted over into fury. "There you are wrong, my innocent little wife. Whatever I do to Charles Weldon will be less than he deserves. For years, the only thing that kept me alive was knowing that someday I would make him suffer as he had made me suffer. And I promised myself that I would be close enough to savor his pain."

"And that includes putting his daughter in a brothel?" Sara said, her voice a bleak thread of sound. "When I saw that on your list, I couldn't believe that you would do it."

"Nor did I do it," he said sharply. "The idea had occurred to me, but I decided it would be enough if she disappeared for a few days, and Weldon *thought* that she had been sent to a whorehouse. He would have all the suffering without the girl being injured."

Sara's eyes widened with disbelief. "I suppose I must be grateful that you had met Eliza in person. Would you have cheerfully put her in a brothel if she was only a name to you? The fact that you could even consider doing something like that—dear God, you have turned yourself into a monster." She turned away, no longer able to look at her husband.

Peregrine caught her wrist and roughly turned her to face him. "If I am a monster, it is what he made me."

Deliberately she scanned him from head to foot. "Charles Weldon didn't ruin your life in any obvious way. You are a successful, wealthy, intelligent man. You can do and be almost anything you wish. It seems that you choose to be a monster."

Furious, he wanted to shake her. Instead, he released her wrist. "You have no idea what you are talking about."

"Then tell me," Sara said softly, her stark eyes meeting his. "What did Charles Weldon do to you? Why do you believe you are justified in committing crimes while trying to destroy him?"

Above all, he had wanted to avoid this. Yet he knew

that if he could not make Sara understand, a breach that might never heal would open up between them.

He spun away, not able to look at her. "I told you that Jamie McFarland had taken me on his ship. For two years I sailed with him, seeing the world and learning whatever eccentric thing he felt like teaching me. Then, when I was ten, the ship was captured by pirates from Tripoli."

He took a deep breath, bracing himself for what was to come. "Most of the Barbary pirates were actually corsairs who were chartered by their government. The true corsairs operated under an elaborate system where the great European trading nations paid for safe conducts for their ships. There were rules about which foreigners could be sold in the slave market, and the local consuls could reclaim any of their citizens who were captured illegally."

He stopped by the window, his shoulders rigid as he stared out into the blackness. "But there were some ships that operated outside the rules. Even though we were sailing under the British flag and should have been safe, we were attacked by pirates. Half of Jamie's crew was killed outright. The rest of us were captured and taken to an illegal slave market in Tripoli."

It had been stiflingly hot, the air thick with the stench of fear and pain. "Charles Weldon was there. He was making an extensive tour of the Mediterranean and was an honored visitor in the city. I think he came to the market from pure curiosity. Since I was a child, I was separated from Jamie and the rest of his crew, and taken to the market with a group of women and children. I saw Weldon and guessed that he might be English, so I broke away from the group and ran over to him. I said that I was English and begged for his help."

Even a quarter century later, the memory was indelible. Weldon was young and handsome, immaculately turned out in spite of the Tripolitan heat. His nostrils had flared with delicate distaste when accosted

*by the scruffy child. "So you're English. Couldn't be
anything else with that dreadful cockney accent." A
light note of amusement in his voice, he had lifted
young Michael's chin. "You're a pretty lad, though
you could certainly use a good scrubbing. I've never
seen eyes of such a color."*

*By then a guard had arrived to take Michael back
to the group. As he was being dragged away, Weldon
had said languidly, "I'll see what can be done."*

Peregrine's hands clenched convulsively, the pain of
biting nails pulling him back to the present. "Chris-
tians could not buy slaves, so Weldon arranged to buy
me through his host. As he took me to the house he
was renting, I told him about Jamie McFarland and
the others. I knew that if the British consul was notified, arrangements might be made to release them, so
I begged Weldon to contact the consul. He said he
would do it."

*Besides relief for himself, Michael was delighted that
he could do something for Jamie after all the sea captain had done for him.* "Several weeks later, Weldon
told me that he had not bothered to notify the consul.
It was many years before I was able to return to Tripoli. When I did, I tried to learn what had happened to
Jamie and the other crewmen, but they had vanished
without a trace. I'm sure that Jamie died in slavery,
though God only knows how or where. But I didn't
know that at first—I just thought I had been been saved
from slavery."

*A couple of quiet days had passed at Weldon's house.
He hardly saw his benefactor, who had ordered him to
take a bath and burn his ragged clothing. A fine Arabic
robe in his size had been supplied. There had been
fresh fruit and luxurious foods. Then, about the time
that Michael was beginning to feel bored and anxious,
Weldon had sent for him.*

*Michael had gone eagerly. He had been fascinated
by the dashing young man who had rescued him. Surely
a man with such power could have done the same for*

Jamie McFarland. Perhaps Jamie himself was waiting to take Michael away.

Instead, there had been only Weldon, mildly drunk and wanting amusement. At first Michael had not understood what the charming young aristocrat had wanted. Though uncomfortable with the way Weldon touched him, he had tried not to show it, not wanting to offend his benefactor.

When Weldon's attentions became inescapable, Michael had tried to run away. He had fought, frantic as a trapped animal, when Weldon caught him and forced him down on the divan. But he had been only a child against a grown man.

It was almost impossible to continue, for the years had not dimmed the images or the emotions. When Peregrine finally managed to speak, his voice was unrecognizable in his own ears. "I was not a whore, but he used me as one."

From the sound of Sara's horrified gasp behind him, she knew what that meant. But she could not possibly know how it had felt: the shock, the horror, the pain. And most of all, the shattering humiliation, the knowledge of wrongness, of defilement that could never be cleansed away.

"I fought. God, how I fought," he said bitterly. "Perhaps that was a mistake, for fighting excited him, but it was impossible to surrender to something so despicable. After a week or two, Weldon began to tire of fighting, so he tied me to the bed and used a whip to teach me better manners." *Weldon had enjoyed that immensely, his eyes gleaming, hardening with arousal as he slashed away, over and over, with all his strength. It had been an African whip of rhinocerous hide, supple and evil.*

"You have seen the results of his whip. I still tried to fight, but I was half-dead, so he was able to subdue me with little effort." *Weldon had also enjoyed the blood. Whenever Michael grew a little stronger, Weldon would use the whip again. Eventually, Michael stopped fighting.* "I'm not sure how long he kept me there. A couple of months, I think. I lost track of time."

As Sara walked up behind her husband, she saw that he was sweating, his white shirt clinging to his back in patches. She ached for him, for the terrified ten-year-old child he had been, and for the man who still carried mental and physical scars that would never disappear. Wanting to comfort him, she laid a gentle hand on his arm.

Lost in the past, her husband whirled around and almost hit her, his eyes jungle wild and his fists clenched. Barely in time he checked himself from striking.

For an endless moment they stared at each other. Sara began to tremble, for his furious near-violence explained more about what Weldon had done to him than words could ever have conveyed. Her mouth dry, she asked, "How did you escape him?"

"I didn't," Mikahl said bitterly. "Eventually Weldon decided it was time to continue his travels. Having no further use for me, he gave me to the local pasha with the suggestion that I be castrated. He said he was doing me quite a favor, for eunuchs could become great men in the Ottoman empire."

"Dear God, how could any man do such things to a child?" Sara said, sickened by the thought that her husband might have been emasculated for a madman's whim. The passion and closeness they had shared, the blending of energies that joined and transcended them, might never have existed. Mikahl might have died from the dangerous castration procedure.

"Weldon delights in hurting children. As a parting gift, he carved his initial on my hip and rubbed lamp-black in the wound. It pleased him that one letter could do double duty: *M* for master and *W* for Weldon. I cursed him, and believe me, an East End slum child who has spent two years at sea is an expert at profanity. I swore that someday I would find him, and make him pay for what he had done." A muscle jerked in his cheek. "He laughed at me. After he left Tripoli, I'm sure he put me and my threats out of his mind. I was just one small episode in a lifetime of evil."

"Yet against all the odds, you have achieved what you swore you would." Sara shuddered as she saw how viciously Weldon had perverted the truth when he had told her about her husband's past. Indeed, Mikahl felt a special kind of hatred for Weldon, but it was not that of a lover scorned; rather, it was the hatred of a fatherless boy who had wanted to love, and who had instead been savagely betrayed. Mikahl was right: Weldon was truly evil. "How did you get from North Africa to Asia?"

"Rather than having me castrated locally, the pasha decided to present me to the sultan in Constantinople, along with several other boys." His mouth twisted. "It's those wonderful green eyes you're so fond of. They make me memorable. I would have been infinitely better off with blue or brown."

Sara flinched, feeling unreasonably guilty for having admired the intense, magnetic color.

"The ship reached Constantinople and moored for the night before unloading," he continued. "I was able to jump overboard and swim ashore. I had learned some Arabic and Turkish by then, as well as many Muslim customs, so I was able to pass as just another street child of uncertain ancestry. Fairly soon I had the luck to find work with a Persian merchant who had no children of his own. When he saw that I was interested, he taught me accounting and business. After he died, I became a trader myself along the old Silk Road across Turkestan. The rest you know."

"It's incredible that you survived, much less that you became the man you are." Sara shook her head, having trouble grasping the enormity of what her husband had endured, and how he had transcended it. "And after all these years, you have come to England to bring Charles Weldon to justice."

"Exactly. To make him suffer, and ultimately to kill him." His low voice vibrated with emotion. "Now do you understand why my vengeance is justified?"

"I can't condone your desire to take the law into your own hands, though I can certainly understand it." Sara closed her eyes, a spasm of pain going through her. "Weldon deserves to be punished for his crimes, but what you are doing goes beyond simple justice to torture and murder."

She had the cowardly wish that Ross had not told her what was happening. But now that she knew, she could not turn her back on that knowledge. Fearing that she might faint, she sat down in her wing chair again as she rubbed her temples. "I suppose that I have no right to judge what you are doing to Weldon. But nothing—*nothing*—can justify hurting others as you pursue your revenge. That's wrong, Mikahl. No matter how much you have suffered, you have no right to hurt the innocent."

Peregrine was jarred. He had thought that once Sara knew, she would accept. "You make too much of this," he said, anger rising again. "You are condemning me for damaging a railway that might have failed anyhow, for not closing a brothel that would be in business again in days, and for considering actions that I never actually performed."

"I don't think this is something that we will ever agree on," Sara said wearily. "Go ahead and enjoy your revenge. Revel in every wicked moment of it. Kill Weldon with your bare hands."

As she watched him with great haggard eyes, the ticking of the clock could be heard, sharp and insistent as the hoofbeats of hell. Her voice a raw whisper, Sara finished, "But I cannot live with a man who is wantonly injuring innocent people."

Chapter 25

I CANNOT LIVE with a man who is wantonly injuring innocent people.

Sara's words hung in the air like smoke. At first Peregrine did not comprehend her meaning. Then annihilating rage swept through him. He strode to her chair and grabbed the arms, his fingers digging into the upholstery to prevent him from doing violence to his wife. "How dare you give me an ultimatum! Do you seriously think you can force me to tamely turn away from what I have lived for?"

She stared up at him, her eyes dark pools of pain. "There can be no ultimatum since I have nothing to bargain with." Her quiet words undercut his rage. "I know my love means nothing to you, so I have no power to force you to change. Nor do I have the right to even try. We are what we are, Mikahl. You must crucify Weldon, just as I must leave you."

Her words struck him like a physical blow. He stepped back from the chair, too numb to know what he felt. "This is the first time you have mentioned love. What does the word mean to you—some kind of superior weapon for controlling me?"

"I never spoke of love because I never thought you wanted to hear of it," she replied, bleak as dust. "I have loved you almost from the day we met, or I never would have done so many things that went against my principles."

"You seemed to enjoy them at the time," he said caustically. "Isn't that why you married me?"

She shook her head. "If you mean lust, no, that isn't why. I married you because I was in love with you—why else marry a man who I knew would break my heart?"

He stared at her, astonished. "Just how was I supposed to break your heart?"

"By leaving me." Wearily she brushed back her heavy hair. "When we married, I didn't believe it would last long. And I knew that when you left, it would hurt like nothing else I have ever known. But I wanted so much to be with you that I was willing to pay any price in future pain."

He felt as if he had somehow landed in a strange country with no familiar landmarks. "You seriously believed that I married you with the intention of deserting you?"

"Nothing so calculated as that," she said slowly. "I think you married me for a number of small reasons that together tipped the scales. I amused you. You had some regrets over ruining my reputation. You were intrigued by the thought of marrying a duke's daughter, and you desired me. Now I see that I was also a prize that you had won from Charles Weldon—stealing an enemy's woman is a classic form of revenge."

She leaned back in the chair, her face deeply sad. "But you never spoke of love. Now I understand why—with so much anger and hatred in you, perhaps there is no room for love."

"If I did not speak of love, neither did you," he pointed out, his voice brusque.

"Our backgrounds were so different that I didn't know what words of love would mean to you." A corner of her mouth curved ruefully. "And I suppose pride was part of it. It was bad enough to be sure that I would lose you. I didn't also want to appear pathetic by wearing my heart on my sleeve."

"What the bloody hell made you so sure that I wouldn't stay with you?" he exploded. "You keep coming back to that, and I don't understand why. Yes, my background is different, but I have usually been a man of my word. Did you think that marriage vows mean nothing to me?''

"After a lifetime of wandering, I couldn't imagine you staying in one place. You told me that you had never considered marriage, so I thought that when the impulse waned, it would be just a matter of time before you became restless and left.'' Sara paused, searching for words. "If I had known you were English, I might have been more optimistic about our marriage, for there is more common ground between us than I thought. In fact, there have been times in the last few weeks when I have believed it was possible . . .'' Her wistful voice trailed off.

Peregrine wanted to refute her cool reasoning, to throw it in her face and growl that she was wrong. Yet he could not, for all her reasons had a grain of truth in them. Nonetheless, the conclusion she had drawn was wrong, for his desire to marry her had been much greater than the sum of her reasons.

Feeling that he was suffocating, he untied his cravat and pulled it off, drawing it restlessly through his fingers. "That is a fascinating set of thoughts you have invented to put into my head. However, you seem to have missed a point. I have not left you, nor do I have any intention of doing so. It is you who are threatening to leave me, not vice versa.''

She buried her face in her hands, the hair falling away from her fragile nape. "Ironic, isn't it?'' she whispered. "I knew that you would break my heart. It just seems that I was wrong about how it would happen.''

"If your heart is breaking, don't blame it on me,'' he snapped. "I have tried to be a good husband, and until tonight you have had no complaints.''

She raised her head at that. "I still have no complaints—you could not have treated me better if you did love me. What I find intolerable is how you are treating the rest of the world. Because of your private vendetta, Ross almost died today.''

"Do you think I don't regret that?'' he said savagely.

"I'm sure you do, but you are still responsible.'' She looked at him pleadingly. "Don't you see how you have let your passion for revenge corrode your life and mind? Yes, Weldon behaved with appalling savagery, but was what he did to you any worse than what was done to Jenny Miller when she was put in that brothel? Your vengeance comes at too high a price, for it has cost you your soul.''

He was struck by a sudden image of Jenny as she might have looked her first night in the brothel; her childlike face mirrored everything he himself had felt as Weldon's victim.

"That is hardly an argument for sparing Weldon,'' he said harshly. "Dear Charles is the man who took Jenny's virginity. She was so pretty that he had to have her himself. Then he made her play the part of virgin over and over for whatever man had the price. He used to visit her regularly. If I gave Jenny a knife and held Weldon down for her, I think she would cheerfully cut him into ribbons herself.''

Sara's mouth twisted. "How many other Jennys suffered the same fate in the weeks you have been spinning your web around Charles Weldon? Was prolonging your revenge worth their pain?''

There was no answer he could give in return, for finally he understood why Sara was so profoundly upset. Nonetheless, she was being naive. He could not change the world's evil, but he could see that Charles Weldon paid a price commensurate with his crimes. Tiredly he said, "It was been a long and difficult day, and both of us have been half out of our minds with worry about Ross. Let's go to bed now and finish this discussion in the morning. All we are doing now is hurting each other.''

"Nothing will be different in the morning.'' Sara

stood and turned away from him. "But you are right, it is far too late to start packing. I will sleep in one of the guest rooms."

He had not believed that she seriously intended to leave. How could she, when there was so much between them?

Catching her by the shoulders, he spun her around before she could reach the door. "Oh, no, sweet Sara," he said softly. "You married me for better and for worse. There were no special clauses in the marriage service to cover philosophical differences. You promised to be my wife, and I am not releasing you from your vows. The fact that you had the mad notion that I would leave you does not justify your leaving me."

She simply looked at him, her great eyes bleak with sorrow. "This is not an Asiatic harem, Mikahl. You can't stop me if I want to leave. At least, not for long."

He opened his mouth to talk, then stopped. There had been too many words already. Instead he pulled her close and kissed her, using all his strength of will, all of his mesmerizing ability to attract, to make her yield.

For a moment Sara was stiff in his arms. Then she made a low, despairing sound and opened her mouth under his. "I love you," she whispered, her voice thick with longing. "May God forgive me, in spite of all you've done, I can't help loving you."

When her arms went around him, triumphant desire flared, for he knew that he had won. He had been a fool to argue; what bound them was beyond words and philosophy. His hands as hungry as his mouth, he kneaded and shaped her gentle curves.

As Sara moaned and pressed closer, he untied her blue robe and let it drop to the floor, then pulled her nightgown over her head. Wrapping his arms around her waist, he lifted her from her feet and carried her to the bed. Her slim, graceful body was overpoweringly erotic, and his fingers were rough with impa-

tience as he stripped off his clothing. In a lifetime of
intensity, he had never desired a woman as much as
he desired Sara now.

He lay down beside his wife and bent over to kiss
her, then stopped, shocked to see that she was crying.
As her gaze locked with his, soundless tears ran down
her cheeks, and every one scalded him like acid.

He had never seen Sara cry, not after her rough ini-
tiation to passion, not on their wedding night when he
had laid bare her hidden scars, not even when she
feared Ross was dying. But her tears were not a sign
of reluctance, for her desire was as urgent as his. She
caught his shoulders and pulled him down so that his
body pressed against hers. Then she branded her husband with mouth and nails, alternately fierce and
tender as she proved her love without words.

He had never before made love to a weeping woman,
and he used every art at his command to dry her tears
with passion. She responded without reservation, and
when he gave her the most intimate of kisses, it took
only moments to bring her to a shuddering climax.
She cried out, then lay still for half a dozen ragged
breaths, one arm thrown across her eyes.

Then, for the first time in their marriage, Sara boldly
returned the intimacy. After pressing him back against
the pillows, she used mouth and tongue to cherish what
might have been sliced away when he was a child.
With uncanny instinct, she teased and aroused, then
slowed to prolong the ecstasy.

When he was on the verge of disintegrating, Sara
lay back, then caught his arm and drew him into the
ultimate joining. As he drove into her, she whispered
his name over and over, like a broken prayer. Yet still
she wept, even as her body thrust and clashed against
his. Her tears were a potent aphrodisiac, inflaming
him to madness, urging him to fill her with passion
until there was no more room for grief.

After desire and grief had culminated in blazing rapture, they lay twined together, hearts pounding in tan-

dem. At length he wordlessly rolled to his side and pulled her close, burying his fingers in her thick, tangled hair. Sara's light breath caressed his damp skin as she drifted into exhausted slumber.

He did not allow himself to fully relax until she lay still and pliant in his arms. Finally he slept, secure in the knowledge that his wife had forgotten ever having harbored foolish thoughts of leaving him.

Sara slept for perhaps three hours. When her eyes opened, there was light in the room, and she guessed that it was a little after dawn. Mikahl lay on his stomach, one arm thrown across her waist, both protecting and imprisoning. His face was just inches away. Relaxed in slumber, his stern features became handsome and youthful. Seeing the long black lashes against his cheek filled her with tenderness.

Though she was saturated with leaden fatigue, Sara's mind was quite clear. Perhaps it would be easier if she left later in the day when he was out, but she had a frantic need to escape as soon as possible. Leaving would get no easier with time, and knowing she could not stay would make every moment agony.

Sara slid out of the bed. When her husband shifted uneasily, she slipped a pillow under his arm. He settled down again, pulling the pillow against his chest.

She wanted to kiss her husband good-bye, but did not dare for fear of waking him. They had already said everything there was to say; another excruciating argument would change nothing.

Though she loved him as much as ever, perhaps more, she knew she could not continue living with a man who heedlessly caused so much suffering. She did not believe that anything would deter him from his vengeful course, which meant that it would be impossible to ever be happy with him again—unless she blinded herself to what was right and wrong, and became someone she did not want to be.

Silently Sara turned and walked to her dressing

room, but she had to stop for one last look at the
stranger she had loved and married and lost. She wondered if she would ever see him again.

Turning, she entered her dressing room and closed
the door quietly behind her. After dressing, she began
to pack. Some of her clothing was in London, so very
little was needed.

She was almost finished when Jenny entered the
dressing room from the corridor. The maid stopped,
her blue eyes widening.

Sara touched a finger to her lips for silence. "I'm
leaving, Jenny," she said in a low voice. "Do you
want to come with me? The choice is up to you."

"You mean you're leaving the prince? Not just going to London for a few days of shopping?" Jenny
asked in disbelief.

"Exactly."

The maid swallowed but asked no questions. "Then
I had better go with you. You need someone to care
for you."

"Very well. I'll arrange for a carriage to be ready
in half an hour. You had better go pack your own things
and make any good-byes you need to."

Jenny gave her a sharp, questioning glance, then
bobbed her head and left, taking one of her mistress's
two bags.

Sara wondered if her maid had spent the night with
Benjamin Slade, but preferred not to know. It was
hardly the usual case of an innocent young maid being
seduced by an older man; Jenny was no innocent, and
Slade was no callous seducer. Sara had seen the two
talking together; in spite of the differences in age and
background, the mutual caring had been obvious. Perhaps they would be luckier or wiser than she and Mikahl.

She lifted her other bag and went into the corridor,
stopping to look in on Ross. Both he and Mrs. Adams
were sleeping. Her cousin's color was better, and he
looked almost normal again. She kissed him but he

did not wake, so she let him sleep. It seemed wrong to leave Ross without a word, but Mikahl would see that he was well cared for. Mikahl did a fine job of taking care of people whom he knew and liked.

She woke the housekeeper with a hand on her shoulder and gestured her out into the hall. There Sara explained that she was going to London and that Mrs. Adams was now in full charge of the household. Since Ross did not seem to need a full-time attendant, Mrs. Adams was free to go to her own bed, but would she first order a carriage, please?

After the bemused Mrs. Adams went off to obey, Sara went down to the study and wrote Mikahl a brief note. After putting the envelope in her dressing room, she was ready to leave the home where she had been completely happy for a handful of weeks.

Weldon's parlor maid Fanny was the unlucky person. One of her jobs was to scrub the outside steps and polish the knocker first thing in the morning, when the streets were almost empty. Yawning, she cleaned the front steps all right and tight. Then she made her way to the back door, which opened off the kitchen.

Fanny opened the door and tripped right over the long bundle lying across the back steps. She was not the quickest of girls at any time, especially not early, and she had no inkling of what she had found. Tentatively she poked at the bundle with her toe.

The blanket fell away, revealing the slashed throat and rigid corpse of Kane.

Fanny began screaming, making up in volume for what she had lost in speed. Within two minutes, most of the household had gathered in the kitchen, where Fanny was still shrieking.

Besides servants, the racket also brought Weldon, wearing a hastily donned dressing robe. Impatiently he elbowed his way through the jabbering group to learn what the problem was.

Finding the body of his right-hand man shocked him

to the marrow. He had wondered why his secretary had not returned the night before, but Kane moved in mysterious ways, and Weldon had thought little about the absence. Now Kane had carelessly gotten himself killed. What would Peregrine do next?

Weldon's paralysis was broken by the sound of Eliza's light voice. "What has happened?" she called out as she entered the kitchen. "Why is Fanny screaming?"

Weldon snapped to his butler, "Shut the silly wench up." Then he ushered his daughter out of the kitchen so she would not see the grisly sight on the steps. "There's been an accident, but it doesn't concern you, my dear."

His mind raced as he tried to come to terms with this latest event. Now that Peregrine had brought the war to Weldon's very doorstep, perhaps Eliza should be sent back to his brother's household. Yes, Weldon decided, that would be for the best. She would be safe there until this wretched business was settled.

Peregrine awoke slowly and reached for Sara, then came fully conscious when he realized that she was not there. The angle of the sun showed that he had slept later than usual, so it was not surprising that she was up already. He pulled on his caftan, then went to see if Sara was still in her dressing room. If she was, perhaps he could persuade her back to bed.

The dressing room was empty, and he turned to leave. Then he saw an envelope with his name on it propped up against the mirror of the tall chest of drawers. His skin prickling with unease, he lifted the envelope and opened it.

When he pulled out a folded sheet of notepaper, a small object fell to the carpeted floor. Before picking it up, he read the note. It said simply *Mikahl—Passion is not enough. Even love is not enough. I wish one of us were different. May God keep you and grant you peace. Love, Sara.*

Disbelieving, he read the note again. Then he numbly bent over to find what had fallen out. The gleam of gold caught his eye, and he picked up the subtly contoured wedding ring that he had had made specially for his wife.

Last night's passion had not changed Sara's mind. With a blaze of shattering, anguished fury, he realized that her tears had not meant surrender. She had wept because she was saying good-bye.

Ross was yanked from sleep by a blood-chilling howl. The sound was somewhere between an Afghan war cry and the tortured keening of Middle Eastern women mourning their dead, and it compelled instant response. Automatically he tried to get up, only to be stopped by shattering pain in his shoulder and weakness that almost sent him crashing to the floor.

As he clung dizzily to the bedside table with his good hand, he remembered the shooting the previous day, plus a few fragmentary later images: jolting along on a horse, painful probing at his shoulder, later Sara's soft voice. That explained his unfamiliar surroundings—he was at Sulgrave.

The howl had not been repeated, but now sounds of smashing and breaking came from the same direction. Could Weldon possibly have mounted some kind of attack on the house? When his head steadied, Ross lurched over to the fireplace and grabbed the poker. Then, clad only in his drawers, he opened the door and tracked the noise to its source.

It sounded like a battle was taking place in his cousin's dressing room. Cautiously he opened the door, thinking that there had better not be any real danger, because at the moment Sara's cat could whip Ross with one paw behind its back.

The scene inside the small room brought Ross to a stunned halt. Mikahl was going berserk. He had already tipped over a heavy wardrobe, and the floor was ankle-deep in delicate lady's undergarments, bruised shoes, and crushed hats.

As Ross watched, the other man shoved over the chest of drawers with an incoherent growl of fury. Then he began jerking out drawers and pitching them into the wall. The frames smashed noisily, gouging holes in the plaster before clattering to the floor. Drawers emptied, Mikahl grabbed an elegant evening gown and ripped it from décolletage to hem with his bare hands.

Ross tightened his grip on the poker, for Mikahl in a rage was a daunting sight. Raising his voice, he said sharply, "What the devil are you doing?"

His friend whirled, his eyes feral and his body poised for attack. Seeing who had entered, Mikahl checked his motion, but he still radiated violence. "Your damned cousin has left me."

Ross whistled softly. An assault by Weldon would have been more believable than Sara deserting her husband. Deciding that he was in no immediate danger, Ross let the poker sag to the floor while he unobtrusively propped his right shoulder against the door frame. "Why?"

"Because I'm a bastard who has injured innocent people without giving a damn," was the harsh answer. "Because I'm a monster who has been cutting a swath like one of the four horsemen of the apocalypse."

Ross took a moment to absorb that. "She didn't leave you because you're a bastard," he said with dry, calculated humor, "though the rest may be correct."

Ross thought that the odds were about even whether the comment would bring assault on his own head or penetrate Mikahl's mania. Fortunately, after an uncertain moment, the latter happened. Gaze sharpening, his friend growled, "What the hell are you doing out of bed?"

"I came to find out if Weldon had broken in with a party of hired assassins."

"Not yet." Mikahl smiled mirthlessly. "I think

Weldon will need to pause and regroup his forces. His chief thug, Kane, is the one who shot you, and Kane is now answering to a higher master than Charles Weldon.''

Ross's brows went up. ''What happened?''

''I had my knife, and I was faster than he was,'' his friend said with grim satisfaction. ''Someone in Weldon's household has probably found his body on the back steps by now.''

Ross gave an involuntary shiver; this was definitely an ugly business. ''What happens next?''

''I don't know.'' Wearily Mikahl pushed his disordered hair from his eyes. ''I just do not know.''

''Well, I hope you think of something quickly,'' Ross said tartly. ''If Sara went to London, will she be safe there?''

Mikahl's expression changed again. ''I'll check to see if any of the guards went with her.''

''Good idea.'' Ross's knees were slowly beginning to give way, so he said, ''Would you mind helping me back to bed before I join the rubble on the floor?''

Swearing, Mikahl reached Ross just in time to save him from collapse. The hard grip sent pain blazing through Ross's side and momentarily darkened his vision.

''Neither you nor your cousin have the sense God gave a sparrow.'' As Mikahl pulled Ross's good arm over his own neck, his voice was rough but his hands were not. After half carrying Ross back to the bedroom and depositing him on the bed, Mikahl made a quick examination of the bandages. ''Doesn't seem to have started bleeding again. Do you have the elementary intelligence to stay in bed until you're fit to get up?''

''I'll be delighted to stay here,'' Ross said, sweat sheening on his forehead, ''as long as the house isn't under attack.''

''It isn't and it won't be.'' Mikahl straightened.

"Are you going to thrash me or give me a lecture on how to treat my wife?"

"I couldn't thrash you when I was healthy, so I certainly couldn't do it now." Ross smiled wryly. "And while I have done many foolish things in my life, meddling in someone else's marriage is not one of them." At the moment, he wanted nothing more than to slide back into darkness, but he forced his weighted eyelids to remain open. "No one ever said marriage was easy, but most problems can be solved."

Mikahl shook his head. "Not this one. Once you said that I believed that the end justified the means while Sara held to the higher standard of right and wrong. That is the heart of our disagreement. I doubt that something so basic can be changed."

Ross sighed. "Don't say I didn't warn you. When Sara was a child, she fell in love with John Wesley's Rule of Conduct. Wesley founded a religious group called the Methodists, and he said *Do all the good you can, By all the means you can, In all the ways you can, In all the places you can, At all the times you can, To all the people you can, As long as ever you can.* Sara embroidered it on a sampler and made me memorize it."

"If that is what she believes, the situation is hopeless," Mikahl said acidly. "No one can live up to that."

"Probably not, but the point is to try," Ross said, his voice fading. "Why not try to compromise? I imagine that Sara is as miserable as you. Surely you can find some common ground."

"I'm not miserable, and I don't need a priggish, moralizing female in my life," Mikahl snapped as he pulled the blankets over his friend.

Ross had heard more convincing denials, but wisely he held his tongue. Instead, as he drifted into welcome darkness, he uttered a heartfelt prayer than Mikahl and Sara would find some way to heal the breach, for both their sakes.

Chapter 26

AFTER LEAVING ROSS, Peregrine made inquiries about how and when his wife had left Sulgrave. He was relieved to learn that Jenny Miller had gone with Sara, and that the maid had insisted on taking two of the guards. Thank heaven for Jenny, who understood the danger and would look out for Sara.

As Peregrine was finishing his morning coffee, another move in the game was played. A solicitor arrived with an envelope containing a bank draft from Weldon in the amount of the notes Peregrine held. He had forgotten that this was the last day for Weldon to pay. Benjamin Slade had not forgotten, of course; the lawyer would have had the bailiffs on Weldon the next morning if the notes had not been paid off. Now Weldon was safe from debtor's prison.

More interesting than the money itself was the accompanying note from Weldon. Tersely he said that the Duke of Haddonfield had been delighted to provide the money to frustrate his son-in-law's evil intentions toward an English gentleman. Doubtless the message was intended to provoke, but Peregrine was beyond being irritated by anything so petty. Besides, today he had received eighty thousand pounds, and Weldon had received Kane's corpse; Peregrine felt that he had come out ahead in the transaction.

After turning the draft over to Slade, Peregrine went out to the stables. Siva, though not seriously injured, needed time to recover from being grazed by the bullet, so Peregrine took another horse. Then he went galloping up to the Downs, feeling a desperate need for open air to sort out his chaotic feelings.

In theory, riding alone here might be dangerous, but Peregrine believed what he had told Ross earlier. Weldon's violence had always been committed at second hand, except when he was terrorizing someone smaller and weaker than himself. Now he would have to find a replacement for Kane, which would not be easy. For the day, at least, the Downs should be safe, though Peregrine kept automatic watch as he cantered along the trail.

It was hard to believe that Sara was gone. Just a few days earlier, they had ridden along these hilltops, stopping to enjoy the views, to picnic, and make love.

Fiercely he told himself that he did not need Sara. He would survive without her, as he had survived many things far worse than the loss of a woman.

He drew his horse in at the highest point on this section of the trail. The hills, fields, and scattered villages of southern England rolled away below him. It was a peaceful, prosperous land, though not a dramatic one.

Without Sara there was no reason to stay in England. He would not have to be as careful about how he killed Weldon, for after the deed was done he could leave the country forever. To be peregrine meant to be free, unconstrained by tethers and obligations. The longer he had stayed in England, the more he had become Mikahl Khanauri, but now he could return to being Peregrine, the wanderer.

The whole world would be at his feet again. The high Himalayas, where the crystal air pierced the lungs as deeply as the beauty pierced the heart. Desert nights with brilliant stars flung across the black velvet sky. Tropical islands with turquoise waters and darting fish in improbable rainbow colors.

He had seen all those things, and he did not need to see them again. None of them was Sulgrave.

What made a place worth revisiting was friends. He

would go back to Kafiristan, where Malik and his family would welcome him with joyous affection. He could stay as long as he liked and always be welcome.

But he would never be truly one of them, no matter how long he stayed.

There were friends scattered in other places, men of many races. There were also women whom he remembered with great fondness; in one or two cases, perhaps with a little love. He would also be welcomed by those who were still in the business of pleasing men who could afford them.

None of them would be *his* woman. They were wary creatures, survivors like himself, who would never give more than they could afford to lose. None would be brave and foolish enough to deliberately put their hearts in the hands of a man whom they knew would break them.

Now he understood why Sara had been terrified on their wedding day. She had not feared physical pain, but the anguish of inevitable loss. Yet still, with desperate, loving courage, she had given herself to him.

Abruptly he set the horse moving again. What had happened to him since he came to England? For twenty-five years he had been filled with absolute purpose. Every action had been measured against his ultimate goal.

But now, for the first time in his life, he was torn by internal conflict. He had found Sulgrave, the home of his heart. And Sara, ah, God, Sara. In a few short weeks she had sunk into his soul, filling cracks and pores so thoroughly that her loss made his spirit feel as if it had been stripped naked and thrown to the winds.

Summer was giving way to autumn, and the ominous rasp of dry leaves whispered along the wind. When he reached the spot where Ross had been shot, he dismounted and tethered his horse. There was a blotchy patch on the trail, easy to overlook if one did not know what it was. He went down on one knee by the dark stain of his friend's blood. *I owed you . . . a life for a life.*

Peregrine had done little to earn that loyalty. The first time he had seen Ross Carlisle, the Englishman had been a bruised and battered prisoner. He must have known that his captors were planning some particularly ugly death, but he sat calmly with his hands tied behind his back and his clothes in rags, looking as if he didn't give a damn what happened next.

His expression of cool English detachment had been unpleasantly reminiscent of Charles Weldon, and Peregrine had almost let Ross go to his fate. But he knew that a highborn Englishman might be useful in the future, so he had intervened and offered to gamble for the captive's life. There had been little risk for him; winning the game would give him the captive, while losing would cost only a handful of gold. But Peregrine had won the game, and when he took the captive home, he discovered that he had also won a friend; a friend whose mind and humor matched his own more closely than any man he had ever known.

There had been that other occasion, during an Afghan raid. Outnumbered and out of ammunition, Ross could have been killed, though his own fighting skill might have been enough to save him. Peregrine had intervened, again with little risk to himself, but at least that time he had helped from friendship rather than a cold calculation of possible usefulness.

He lifted a pinch of dry, blood-saturated soil and crumbled it between his fingertips. *I owed you . . . a life for a life.*

Ross had welcomed Peregrine, introduced him to his own friends and family, sponsored him in society, defended him in the presence of the queen. Most valuable of all, Ross had given trust, allowing Peregrine the benefit of the doubt about the justice of his mission against Weldon. And yesterday, Ross had taken the bullet intended for Peregrine. If not for him, Peregrine would be the one lying dead now, not Kane.

It had been purely a matter of luck that the bullet had not struck his friend's heart. He smiled mirthlessly as he remembered his own half-mocking comment that he did not believe in guilt, for it was an unproductive emotion. If Ross had died, no power of earth, heaven, or hell could have assuaged Peregrine's guilt.

No man could ask for a better friend than Ross. In return, Peregrine had compromised and seduced his friend's beloved cousin. Even then, Ross had tried to understand and had ultimately forgiven.

The anger and pride that had sustained Peregrine collapsed in the face of a grief more devastating than anything he had ever known. When Sara had left, he had flailed out in rage and pain, but now he was beyond that. He sank down on his knees and bowed over, his face buried in his hands and his lungs heaving with raw, anguished gasps. He did not weep, for he had not shed a tear since his mother's death; not for himself, not even for Jamie McFarland. But he rocked back and forth, shaking with violent bone-deep chills, as if racked by tropical fever.

Sara was right. He had filled his life with hate, worshipped the dark god of vengeance. And when his mission was done, what would be left inside of him? Nothing. He would be as empty as a wind-scoured ravine, a hollow core in dead stone.

He had never planned what would come after revenge; that was why the thought of dying to accomplish his mission had been unalarming. But lately he had begun to sense that there could be a life beyond hatred, beyond vengeance: a life with friends, a home, and love. Most of all, with love.

"Sara," he whispered brokenly, feeling that he had been torn in half. "Oh, God, Sara." He had thought Charles Weldon had sent him to hell, but he was wrong. Hell was not pain; it was not even hatred. Hell was to have known love, then to lose it.

The thought made Peregrine smile bitterly. He had

not lost love; he had thrown it away, which was infinitely worse.

He did not need Sara to survive. But without her, he did not much care whether he did or not.

Her note had said *I wish one of us were different. May God keep you and grant you peace. Love, Sara.* His wife had loved him fully, with tenderness, passion, and acceptance. The only peace he had ever known had been with Sara.

He had not missed love and peace when they were only words. But having experienced both, how could he live without them?

For the first time he wondered if he should, or could, abandon the mission that had been the center of his life. What could he do to bring Sara back to him?

It would be easy enough to get Mrs. Kent's evil virgin house closed; it was almost time for that anyhow. Nor would it be difficult to save the railway and its unlucky investors.

Those things were simple. The heart of the problem was Weldon. Peregrine had sworn to kill him with his own hands, but if he was to win Sara back, he would have to forgo that pleasure.

Weldon versus Sara. Death versus life. To a disinterested person, it might sound like an easy choice, but it was not. The thought of retribution was all that had sustained young Michael Connery when Charles Weldon was flaying the flesh from his back. To block out Weldon's violations, Michael had imagined a thousand slow, excruciating ways to kill his tormentor.

Over the years, the dream of vengeance had sustained Peregrine through every kind of danger; deserts that baked the marrow from the bones, hunger and disease, savage attacks, and thirst so tormenting it was madness. No matter how dark his situation, he had never despaired, for he knew he could not die before he had fulfilled his mission.

Peregrine had come to realize that, while he could kill a man in hot blood, he was not capable of deliberate, cold-blooded torture, not even of Weldon. At least, he could not perform physical torture. Thus had been born the idea of mental torture, of stripping away everything Weldon valued. It was a more sophisticated revenge than the bloody dreams of young Michael Connery, and it had been deeply satisfying to plan how to ruin Weldon's life before the final reckoning.

Only now, when his mission was half-completed, could he see the limitations of vengeance.

With a shuddering breath, he lifted his head from his hands and sat back on his heels. Scooping up another handful of earth, he crumbled it in his fist, then let the dry soil drift through his fingers. Vengeance was like dust in the wind, ultimately worthless, for the past could never be changed.

Admittedly there had been great pleasure in his campaign against Weldon. He had enjoyed taking away Sara, and the barony, and his enemy's fortune, and he had certainly delighted in Weldon's confusion and rage. But nothing that Weldon suffered in the present would save the child Michael from the savagery he had endured, and Peregrine would never be able to hurt Weldon as much as he himself had been hurt. Now that he looked at his mission a new way, he saw that vengeance could never be fully satisfying.

Even Weldon's death would not heal the wounds of the past. Scars of the body would be with him until he died, and the only balm that might heal his spirit was Sara's love.

Wearily he stood and brushed the dust from his fingers. He still craved the feel of his enemy's blood on his hands, and he wondered if it would be possible to kill Weldon without Sara learning that her husband was responsible. After a moment's consideration, he shook his head. He would never be able to deceive the woman who had seen so much of his soul, and he doubted that it would be possible for them to build a future on a lie.

With stark regret he accepted that the pleasure of

killing Weldon would come at too high a price if it meant losing Sara. He must put Weldon's fate in the uncertain hands of the law.

He could no more change what he had done since coming to England than he could change the months in Tripoli that had shattered his life. But he could change the present and the future, and perhaps Sara would give him credit for the positive things he had done. Granted, he had injured strangers as Sara had charged, but he had also helped some people as a consequence of his mission. Jenny Miller and Sara herself had benefited.

As he swung up on his horse, he prayed that his actions would persuade Sara to give him another chance. Otherwise the future stretched bleak and barren before him.

Back at Sulgrave, Peregrine immediately sought out Benjamin Slade, who was working in the room he had turned into an office. Without preliminaries, he said, "Benjamin, I want you to collect all the evidence we have on Charles Weldon and prepare to present it to a magistrate."

Startled, Slade pushed his chair back from his desk. "You are actually going to trust the law to punish him?"

"Yes," Peregrine said without elaboration. "I also want you to drop the lawsuits against the L & S Railway. Is it possible that Weldon will soon be in so much legal trouble that he will have to step out of the company?"

"I think that is a safe assumption." Slade leaned back in his chair, his eyes narrowing with thought. "What do you intend to do with the company? With some more capital and good management, it will be very successful. As the largest single shareholder, you can run it yourself if you want to."

Peregrine grimaced. "No thanks. Start thinking

about who might have the skill and experience to run the company. I'm sure you can find someone worthy."

Slade gave a beatific smile. "You can't imagine how happy I am to help you make money rather than waste it."

Ignoring the comment, Peregrine said, "Tomorrow morning, I'm going to the London house for a few days. I think you should stay there, too, at least until Weldon is arrested."

"Fine," Slade said, starting to gather his papers. "Country peace and quiet are beginning to wear. But what about Lord Ross—will you just leave him here alone?"

"Ross will be well taken care of," Peregrine said. "And when he learns why I'm going to London, he'll wish me Godspeed."

It was pure luck that Weldon happened to see Sara's return to London. His usual route between home and office ran by Haddonfield House, and he was traveling to work when his eye was caught by a carriage pulled up in front of the duke's mansion. He leaned forward in his seat and peered out the window.

Lady Sara stood on the pavement, and the pieces of luggage beside her implied that she had come to stay with her father for a few days. Perhaps the two love-birds had had a quarrel? Weldon sincerely hoped so. He was about to drop the curtain and lean back in his seat when another small figure climbed out of the carriage. He sucked his breath in with shock, then leaned forward again. Yes, by God, the second female was Jenny Miller, and she was acting as a lady's maid.

Then his carriage moved past the newcomers, and he could see no more. Weldon sat back and crossed his legs, thinking hard about what he had seen. Damnation, the little trollop had disappeared from Mrs. Kent's within a day or two of Peregrine's visit to the girl. Weldon hadn't made the connection before, but now he was willing to bet that the bastard had helped

Jenny escape. He must have made the girl his mistress, then installed her as his own wife's maid after the marriage.

It was an impressive display of gall, the sort of thing Weldon had always enjoyed. He wondered if Sara knew her husband kept a mistress under her very nose. Probably not; she was too prudish to approve, much less join the other two in a bed.

Weldon began drumming his fingers on his knee. He couldn't touch Sara without running the risk of retribution against Eliza, but Jenny Miller was fair game. He had sworn that if he ever found the little slut again, he'd make her pay for running away. And now fate had given him a perfect chance to avenge himself on Jenny and strike a blow against Peregrine at the same time.

Instead of proceeding to his office, he gave orders to return home. There he summoned Jimmons, whom he had selected as a replacement for Kane. Unfortunately, while Jimmons was the best of the brothel guards, he was to Kane what a plow horse was to a thoroughbred. Still, he was strong and he obeyed orders.

When Jimmons appeared, Weldon handed him a crude map. "I want Haddonfield House watched. Have two of the other brothel guards do it. They'll only need to watch during daylight, so they can still do their usual jobs." When his subordinate nodded, Weldon continued, "A girl who used to be in Mrs. Kent's house is there now, probably as a lady's maid. She's about eighteen but looks younger. Small and blond, very pretty. When they see her entering or leaving, they should grab her without attracting attention." As an afterthought, he added, "Tell them not to hurt the girl. She's valuable."

"Yes, sir. What we do with 'er once we've snatched 'er?"

"Take her to back to Mrs. Kent's," Weldon ordered. There he himself would punish her for running away, and for consorting with the enemy.

At first Eliza Weldon was hurt when her father said she must stay at her uncle's for a few days, but she found herself surprisingly happy to be back among her cousins. While Papa was wonderful, she didn't see much of him, and she had missed the company of other young people.

The center of the girls' activities had always been the bedroom of Jane, at sixteen the oldest daughter of the family. Eliza had hardly entered Lord Batsford's house when she was swirled upstairs by Anne, who was twelve and closest in age to Eliza. The middle daughter, fourteen-year-old Lucy, completed the party, which was organized around marzipan and gossip. Such a self-indulgent orgy was possible only when the governess was taking her half day off, and the Weldon girls were taking full advantage of her absence.

In the spring Jane would be presented to society, so most of the afternoon was spent poring over fashion books and arguing about what styles would look best on her tall brunet frame. Eliza entered into the discussion wholeheartedly, for she had missed such feminine chatter.

When the last fashion book was closed, Jane said casually, "By the way, I saw your almost stepmother today when Mama took me to Bond Street. When Lady Sara saw Mama and me, she looked as if she thought we would give her the cut direct for jilting Uncle Charles. But of course Mama would never do that to Lady Sara." Jane was about to add that her mother had said Lady Sara was better off not marrying Charles Weldon, but remembered just in time that such a thing should not be repeated in front of Eliza.

Eliza lifted her head eagerly. "How is Lady Sara?"

Jane frowned. "She looked rather tired. Perhaps she had done too much shopping. But she was very civil."

Jane's expression shifted to longing. "I wish I knew how Lady Sara manages that look of quiet elegance."

Ignoring the latter comment, Eliza asked, "Did she come up just for the day, or is she staying in town for a while?"

"She mentioned that she was staying at Haddonfield House," Jane replied. "That probably means she is here for two or three days, and doesn't want to bother opening her own house."

"I would like so much to see her," Eliza said wistfully.

Lucy gave her a stern look. "You can't. Uncle Charles had Mama tell every servant in the house that you can't have any contact with Lady Sara. Even if she called here, you wouldn't be allowed to see her." Lucy was something of a prig.

"I think that sounds positively Gothic," Anne said.

"It is because Uncle Charles's heart is broken," Jane said wisely. "Broken hearts make one do strange things. I thought I would go mad when Mama discharged Signore Carlo."

The sisters began lamenting the loss of Signore Carlo, a handsome music master, who had been banished after being caught kissing a maid. Eliza was silent. She must not waste this chance to see Lady Sara. Of course, a young lady shouldn't go out alone, but Haddonfield House was only two blocks away, and what could possibly happen in Mayfair in broad daylight?

She would slip out in the morning, Eliza decided, after breakfast and before lessons started. She'd wear her plainest dress and cloak so people would think she was just a servant. It would only take a few minutes to reach Haddonfield House. While Eliza would prefer a long visit with Lady Sara, the most important things could be said quickly. Eliza would be home before anyone missed her.

* * *

Jenny Miller found it interesting to be back in Haddonfield House. She had spent a fortnight here before Lady Sara's marriage, and everything and everyone in the place had scared her half to death, especially the butler. Now that she'd lived at Sulgrave and the prince's London house, she was a lot harder to scare. Which was good, because the other servants kept teasing her to find out why Lady Sera was back with her father rather than with her husband. But Jenny never said a word to the nosy biddies.

She wished they were back in the country, and not just because Benjamin was there. Poor Lady Sara missed her husband so much that she looked as if she'd swallowed hot coals. Of course, she wouldn't talk about what had happened, so Jenny was dying of curiosity. How had two people who were half-crazy about each other come to such a pass when they should still be on their honeymoon? It was a depressing question for a young lady who was herself considering an offer of marriage.

Having served Lady Sara a breakfast of tea and toast that wouldn't keep a sparrow alive, Jenny had a spot of tea herself. She sipped from the cup while watching out the window of Lady Sara's sitting room, which overlooked the street in front of the mansion. Partly that was because Jenny never tired of watching the fancy carriages and fancy people of Mayfair. She also couldn't help hoping that she'd see Prince Peregrine drive up, or Benjamin. Better yet, both of them.

She had just finished her tea and was about to move away, when her eye was caught by an odd little scene in the street below. A girl had just started up the steps of Haddonfield House, when a rough-looking man came by and asked her something. The girl turned to answer. Then the girl was sagging in the man's arms, though Jenny didn't see what had happened. An old hackney pulled up beside them, and the first man got in with the girl.

Jenny frowned. If this was a different part of town,

she would have been right worried about the girl, and
even in Mayfair, she couldn't help wondering if something was wrong. But the girl had spoken to the man,
so maybe she knew him.

Briefly Jenny wondered if she should tell Lady Sara
what she had seen, but decided against it. It was too
late to do anything, because the hack was already out
of sight, and it looked just like a thousand other hacks.
No point in upsetting her mistress unnecessarily, especially when nothing could be done.

Still, Jenny couldn't put the scene out of her mind.
There had been something familiar about the man,
though she couldn't place what it was. And it made
her neck prickle when she realized that the girl had
been about the same size and coloring as Jenny herself. The streets weren't safe anywhere.

The girl was mute with terror, her blue eyes huge in
her white face. After locking the chit in a bedroom,
Mrs. Kent came downstairs and scowled at the two
men who had delivered her. "That ain't the girl the
master wanted, you loobies. He's going to be furious.
What if she's some rich man's pampered daughter?"

The two men exchanged an uneasy glance. "She fit
the description," one of the men said. "I think she's
just a maid. Ain't dressed like a swell, and she was
walking alone."

Mrs. Kent considered. It was true that the clothing
was respectable, but not extravagant, so the girl was
probably a servant. Weldon would still be mad that it
wasn't Jenny, but maybe it would mollify him to know
the girl could be used in the house. She was just the
right sort, young and pretty and scared. She would be
worth at least fifty pounds this very night.

They didn't usually abduct girls—no need to—but in
this case, it would be best to keep the chit. If they let her
loose, she'd raise holy hell. Even though the girl would
never be able to find her way back to the house, it was
bad business to get the police looking for kidnappers.

Mrs. Kent sat down and wrote her employer a note, explaining that they had the wrong girl and suggesting that they keep her.

Within two hours, Weldon sent a reply saying to put the new girl to work that very night, and not to send the guards back to Haddonfield House until the next day. Mrs. Kent smiled with satisfaction, glad that a mistake had turned out so well. The new girl was exactly the type one of her best customers, a rich merchant, always asked for. She'd send the merchant a discreet note, and he'd be around this very night.

Chapter 27

PEREGRINE WAS RECEIVED politely at Haddonfield House. He hoped that was a good sign, but probably it meant nothing; Sara would never give orders for servants to be rude.

When he asked to see Lady Sara, the butler inclined his head and said, "I will see if her ladyship is in."

It was all horribly formal for visiting one's wife. One's estranged wife. Rather than taking a seat in the receiving room, Peregrine stayed on his feet, trying not to look as nervous as he felt. He wished he could speak to Sara somewhere other than under her father's roof; perhaps she would consent to go for a drive, or even go back to their house where they could talk more freely. Probably she would be reluctant to do that, for fear that he would try to seduce her.

She was right; he would try. Even though he knew their differences must ultimately be resolved with the mind rather than the body, he craved her physical closeness as an opium eater craved his drug.

When the door opened, he turned swiftly, his body braced for confrontation, but it was the Duke of Haddonfield who entered. The men regarded each other in silence. They had always been civil for Sara's sake, but there was no love lost between them.

The duke spoke first. "Sara is not in."

"Is she really out, or is that a polite excuse?"

The duke raised a brow at such bluntness. "Really out. Visiting friends, I believe. I imagine she will be back sometime this afternoon, but I don't know just when. I've hardly seen her since she arrived."

"I see." Peregrine considered waiting, but he would go mad with nothing to do for hours. Besides, Slade wanted them both to go to a magistrate to present the evidence on Weldon; with luck, a warrant would be issued for his arrest this very day, and the long nightmare would be over. "Please tell Sara I want to see her. She can send a message to me at the town house. If I don't hear from her today, I will call again."

Haddonfield gave a faint, sardonic smile. "Is that a threat or a promise?"

"A request." Then, though he knew he should not, Peregrine asked, "Has Sara said anything to you about us?"

The duke shook his head. "No, though I gather you are having problems. Would you care to enlighten me?"

"Philosophical differences," Peregrine said tersely. Deciding that it was time for a change of subject, he said, "Yesterday I received a draft for eighty thousand pounds from Charles Weldon, in payment of notes that I hold. He implied that you gave him the money primarily to thwart me. Is that true, or did he blackmail it out of you?"

The duke blanched; this was bluntness with a vengeance. For a moment his expression fluctuated between anger and guilt. Then he sighed and sat down, his face weary. "One could call it blackmail. It was equally a form of self-punishment."

"Why—for promoting a marriage between your only daughter and Charles Weldon?" Peregrine's voice was edged. "That certainly merits self-punishment."

"I knew that Charles Weldon had his little— peccadilloes, but what man doesn't?" the duke said defensively. "I thought that he would make my daughter a good husband."

"For Sara's sake, you should have made it your business to learn what Weldon is. But because he was above suspicion, it was easier and more convenient for you to wear blinders.''

Unable to refute the charge, Haddonfield's gaze dropped. "I see that now. I didn't then."

Following his intuition, Peregrine continued, ''What did Weldon know about you—are you a patron of one of his more disreputable brothels? He owns a number of them, in case you didn't know.''

"He is the owner?" Haddonfield's eyes widened with shock, his aristocratic hauteur entirely gone. "After my wife died, I felt—half-dead. No longer a man. Charles suggested going to a place where they were expert at . . . bringing men back to life. I found myself going back again and again. I couldn't stop myself . . .'' His voice trailed off for a moment. "Charles never made any blackmail threats. If he had, I would have refused. He just made it clear how much he admired Sara and hoped she would accept him. He didn't have to threaten to expose me—it was enough that he knew my weakness. As a result, I used what influence I had to promote a marriage.''

Peregrine wondered which of the whorehouses had appealed so much to the duke. A normal brothel would not have inspired such shame. Guessing, he said, "Which was it, Mrs. Kent's house for children, or Mrs. Cambridge's whipping establishment?''

The duke looked horrified. "Children? Such places exist, but surely Weldon couldn't be involved in anything so despicable.''

"He is indeed," Peregrine said dryly. "Being an English gentleman doesn't mean that there are depths to which one will not stoop. I don't think there is anything that would shame Charles Weldon.''

Haddonfield shook his head, looking ill. "What I did was shameful enough. I went to—the other place you mentioned.''

So the noble Duke of Haddonfield enjoyed whipping, or being whipped. At a guess, his preference was the latter. One could see why the duke would not wish his taste to become public knowledge. "So in return for silence about your charming little vice, you gave your daughter to a monster. May the saints preserve us from English gentlemen."

Haddonfield flinched. "I deserve your condemnation, but remember, the idea of marrying Charles was not distasteful to Sara. I swear I would have endured public humiliation sooner than let her be hurt. I did not know what he was, though perhaps I should have."

"Indeed you should." Peregrine was about to continue in that vein, for chastising his father-in-law relieved some of his restless anger. Then he abruptly shut his mouth when he realized that this conversation had similarities to his argument with Sara. He had claimed ignorance of the repercussions of his actions then, just as Haddonfield was doing now. They were both culpable. It had taken courage for the duke to admit his shameful weakness and the way he had failed his daughter, and Peregrine had no right to continue haranguing him.

Besides, if he wanted mercy from Sara, he should show it to her father. Deciding that enough had been said, he crossed to the door. "Tell Sara that she can send a message at any time, no matter how late she comes in."

The duke nodded and got to his feet. With difficulty, he said, "Will you tell Sara about . . . what I've done?"

Peregrine shook his head. "I see no reason why she should know." He hesitated, his hand on the knob. "In turn, I hope you will not encourage Sara to ask for a permanent separation."

Haddonfield said, "I will not try to come between you." After a long pause, he said, "You're a better man than Charles Weldon. A better man than I am. I hope you and Sara can resolve your 'philosophical differences.' "

"Thank you." As Peregrine left Haddonfield House, he realized that he and the duke had moved to a different level of relationship. They might never be great friends, but there was a beginning of mutual understanding. He hoped it was a good omen.

It was the middle of the day before Eliza was missed, for everyone assumed she was somewhere else. Lady Batsford thought that her niece was with the governess, while her daughters supposed that their cousin would not be taking lessons because she was only staying for a few days.

When Eliza did not appear for luncheon, more time was lost looking throughout the house. Only when it was clear that the girl was nowhere to be found did Lady Batsford confront her daughters. Her voice stern, she asked, "Was Eliza up to some mischief? If you are withholding information, I will hold you responsible for any trouble that results."

Her three daughters exchanged uneasy glances. As oldest, Jane usually spoke for all three, so she said, "Truly, Mama, Eliza didn't tell us anything." Remembering the conversation of the afternoon before, she went on, "But yesterday I told her how we had seen Lady Sara, and how her ladyship is staying in town with her father. Eliza was awfully interested."

Anne, the youngest, piped up, "Eliza has told me several times that she really wanted to see Lady Sara, to tell her that she wasn't angry with her even though her father was."

Lady Batsford bit her lip indecisively, thinking that it was exactly like Eliza to slip off to visit Lady Sara, whom she idolized. She gave a sigh of exasperation; though she was very fond of her husband's niece, there was no denying that the girl had a willful streak. Lady Sara would have brought the chit back immediately if she suspected that the visit was illicit, but Eliza had a quick tongue, and she might have convinced Lady Sara that her aunt had approved it.

Charles Weldon would be furious if he found out that his daughter had called on his former betrothed.

Better not to notify him that his daughter was missing unless she was still gone at dinner. But Lady Batsford did not expect that; likely Eliza and Lady Sara were having a fine time together. She herself thought it cruel of her brother-in-law to forbid the acquaintance, though she understood his hurt pride.

Lady Batsford was an easygoing woman, not inclined to expect the worst. It was with no real sense of urgency that she sent a note to Lady Sara to ask if Eliza Weldon was at Haddonfield House, and if she was, to please send the girl back by the end of the afternoon.

Sara was exhausted when she returned to Haddonfield House in mid-afternoon. Though she was keeping busy in the hope that activity would save her from breaking down, trying to behave normally was an overwhelming strain. Ironic that she had quite consciously chosen to marry Mikahl in the belief that she was strong enough to survive the inevitable pain. Obviously she had badly overestimated her own strength, for her present anguish was greater than anything she had ever known.

The butler gave her two notes when she came in, and Sara carried them up to her room to read. The first was in her father's hand, and she expected that he was just informing her that he would dine at his club or some such. In fact, the duke did say that, but only after writing that her husband had called and was most desirous of speaking with her. The prince had asked her to notify him when she came in: if he did not hear from her, he would call again.

A violent, debilitating chill swept through Sara, and she sat down, not feeling strong enough to stand. So Mikahl wanted to see her. She reread the note, but her father gave no hint of her husband's mood.

For a moment Sara shut her eyes, praying that Mikahl wanted a reconciliation as much as she did. If he was willing to try, surely something could be worked out? She didn't expect him to turn into a plaster saint, simply not to commit murder; to stop heedlessly wrecking people's lives.

Sighing, she rubbed her temple with numb fingers. Perhaps that *was* too much to ask of a man who had lived for revenge.

"Is something wrong, Lady Sara?" a concerned voice asked.

Sara opened her eyes to find that her maid had entered the room. "Nothing's wrong, Jenny."

Fingers trembling slightly, Sara refolded the paper. Wanting to cover her emotions, she opened the second note. She had to read it twice before the sense soaked in; then she frowned. "This is odd. It's a note from Lady Batsford, Charles Weldon's sister-in-law. Apparently Charles's daughter Eliza has been staying with her aunt, and Lady Batsford is under the impression that Eliza might have come to visit me. It isn't very far. Do you know if a little girl might have called here today?"

Jenny had been folding Sara's shawl, but at the question she looked up, startled. "What time would she have come?"

Sara glanced at the note. "This doesn't say. Sometime this morning, perhaps. I believe the butler said that Lady Batsford's message had arrived earlier in the afternoon. Do you know if Eliza came and was turned away?"

Ignoring the questions, Jenny asked urgently, "How old is the girl, and what does she look like?"

"She's eleven, a little tall for her age, and she has light blond hair," Sara said. "About the same height and coloring as you are, in fact."

"This morning when you were eating breakfast, I saw a girl on the street who looked like that. Then a couple of men took her away." Jenny's hands worked nervously on the shawl. "It seemed strange, but I didn't exactly see what happened, and they were gone before I could think of doing anything."

Sara was beginning to feel alarmed. "Do you think that the men might have abducted Eliza?"

Jenny bit her lip and nodded. "I thought there was something familiar about the bloke I saw, but I wasn't sure. But I just realized that I saw him once at Mrs. Kent's house, acting as guard when the regular one was sick."

Sara's brows drew together as she tried to puzzle out what might have happened. "It doesn't seem possible that Charles could have known that Eliza was coming here to see me. And if he did, surely he would have stopped her himself or sent a servant, not brought a man from the other side of London."

"What if it wasn't Miss Eliza they were after?" Jenny asked miserably. "You said she and I are about the same height and coloring. What if they thought she was me? I always knew Weldon would be furious that I ran away, but it didn't seem likely he'd ever find out where I'd gone. But maybe he did and sent a couple of his guards to bring me back. Mrs. Kent would know they had the wrong girl, but would probably keep her anyhow—she's always looking for new girls." The maid swallowed hard. "I wouldn't wish that on anyone, not even Weldon's daughter."

Sara stood. "Come. We must go to my husband. He will know what to do."

Neither Sara nor Jenny spoke during the ten-minute ride to the house on Park Street. Even though Sara didn't want to believe that Eliza had been taken to Mrs. Kent's house, she had a horrible intuition that was exactly what had happened. If so, the girl would not be the first innocent victim of the struggle between Mikahl and Weldon.

In spite of their estrangement, Sara did not doubt that Mikahl would rescue Eliza; though he hated Weldon, he had already decided not to punish the child for her father's crimes.

She was so sure that her husband would solve the problem that it was a shock to arrive at the house and

learn that he was not home. Neither was Benjamin
Slade, who had returned to the city with his employer.
The men had gone out together some hours earlier,
leaving no word of where they had gone or when they
would be back.

After a moment of feverish thought, Sara drew Jenny
into the drawing room so they could talk privately.
"Do you know exactly where Mrs. Kent's house is?"
When Jenny nodded, Sara continued, "Then I'll go
and bring Eliza home if they have her."

"You can't go there, Lady Sara!" Jenny said, scandalized. "It's in one of the worst parts of the city, and
it might be dangerous to go inside."

"I must go, Jenny," Sara said, her voice calm. "I
can't allow Eliza to be held captive in such a place.
She has been there for hours, and the longer she stays,
the greater the chance that something dreadful will
happen to her." She bit her lip, unable to say out loud
what might happen to the girl.

"But we don't even know if she is there," Jenny
said desperately. "Really, my lady, you mustn't go."

"I won't go alone. I'll take one of the guards." Sara
had a happy thought. "Or better yet, Kuram. Didn't
you say that he was there the night Mikahl took you
from Mrs. Kent's house?"

"I suppose he could find it, but it's just too dangerous a place for a lady," Jenny said stubbornly.

"My cloak is plain and has a hood, so no one will
know that I'm a lady," Sara said, impatient to be off.
"A brothel is in the business of making money, so I'll
take plenty of gold and ask to buy Eliza free. With
Kuram along, I'll be safe enough. But there is no time
to be lost. It's almost dinnertime, and I assume that
evening is when a brothel is busiest."

Jenny nodded with reluctant agreement. "I'll go
with you."

Sara considered the offer, for certainly Jenny knew
more about such places than her mistress. But Mrs.
Kent might recognize the girl and try to prevent her

from leaving the house. The risk was too great to take. "Stay here and explain to Mikahl what happened if he returns before I do," Sara said. "If something more needs to be done, he will know what." It was odd, Sara realized, to trust her husband to help her in spite of their estrangement. But trust him she did.

Though Jenny still looked unhappy, she agreed to stay. Kuram also had grave doubts about taking his master's wife to such a spot, but soon capitulated to Sara's urgency. Ten minutes later, Sara was heading for dockland in a small closed carriage, with Kuram and a driver outside on the box.

As the wheels rattled through the darkening streets of the city, she prayed that she would be in time to save Eliza from the horrors that Mikahl and Jenny had suffered.

Killing Peregrine was the key. Once the bastard was out of the way, Weldon could bluster his way out of any accusations that might be leveled against him. He would claim that the foreigner had forged evidence out of jealousy against a man who had been his wife's former suitor. Weldon still had enough influence to make sure that an investigation wouldn't go far.

But Peregrine would not be an easy man to kill, especially now that he was on his guard. For all his dangerous skills, Kane had already failed at the job, and Weldon was unsure where to turn next. A fire perhaps? Or find another marksman? A pity that Jimmons and the other brothel guards were no more than bullies, good at controlling unruly patrons, but no use for tasks requiring thought. Perhaps Jimmons would know another man like Kane. The trick was to make sure that the chosen tool didn't turn around and blackmail the man who had hired him.

It would be best if Weldon did the deed himself, but while he was a good shot, he had no military training or experience at calculated assassination. Not that he shrank from killing; more than once his unwilling partners had proved too weak and died under his hands. But this was different.

Weldon sighed with frustration, tired of how his thoughts were running in circles. It was evening, and he was no closer to a solution than he had been that morning. As he poured a glass of port, a startling thought hit him. Mrs. Kent had said that the captive girl was not Jenny Miller; could Lady Sara herself have been abducted? While his former betrothed didn't really resemble Jenny, she was small and blond. She also dressed simply and looked youthful for her years.

While Weldon had not planned to seize Lady Sara, he certainly wouldn't release her if fate had dropped her into his hands. He began calculating. If Sara was at Mrs. Kent's, Eliza could be sent away the next day to his hunting box in Scotland. Peregrine would never find her there. Eliza's absence would give Weldon the freedom to use Sara against her husband.

Deciding that it would be easiest to go see the captive himself, Weldon immediately called for his carriage. The trip would not be wasted even if the captive wasn't Sara, for he would use one of the girls before he returned home.

Peregrine followed Slade up the steps of his house, feeling pleased with the day's work. They had just visited a magistrate called Hanlon, a man of flinty integrity who loathed the exploitation of children. Hanlon had found the evidence against Charles Weldon very convincing and was preparing to issue a warrant when Peregrine and Slade left. Now, if there was just an encouraging note from Sara waiting . . .

Instead of a note from Sara, the two men were met by an anxious Jenny Miller.

"Thank heavens you've come back!" The girl threw her arms around Slade without stopping her rapid speech. "Eliza Weldon disappeared, and we think she may have been taken to Mrs. Kent's house; and because you weren't here, Lady Sara went to Mrs. Kent's herself to get her out.''

It took a moment to absorb the breathless speech. Then Peregrine swore to himself in Kafiri, and ushered Jenny and Slade into the drawing room for a more detailed explanation. A few questions established what had happened. It was a relief to learn that Kuram was with Sara, but going to Mrs. Kent's was still a damned fool thing for her to do. Peregrine snapped, ''How long ago did she leave?''

Jenny glanced at the clock. ''About half an hour.''

Frowning, Peregrine said, ''I'm going after her. I'll ride to get there more quickly.''

Slade frowned. ''Are you sure you'll be safe? Since you visited Mrs. Kent's once, you'll be recognized. If Weldon has alerted all his employees to watch out for you, it may be harder to get out of the place than to get in.''

Peregrine thought a moment. ''Probably not, but I might as well be cautious. Two of the guards are here; they can follow in the large carriage. If Sara and I aren't out of the house quickly, they can come in and get us.'' He glanced at Jenny. ''I don't like asking this of you, but will you ride in the carriage and show them the way to Mrs. Kent's?''

''Of course,'' Jenny replied. ''I'd go crazy waiting here, wondering what's happening.''

Slade started to protest, then stopped. ''Very well, but I'm going with you, Jenny.''

She gave her lover a fleeting, grateful glance, then looked back at Peregrine. ''Everything is happening at once, isn't it?''

Peregrine nodded. ''We just returned from a magistrate. A warrant is being sworn for Weldon's arrest, and Mrs. Kent's house will probably be closed down within the next couple of days.''

''Please, sir.'' Jenny put her hand on his arm. ''That's the law acting, but no one is going to care that much about the girls in the house, and what will happen to them. Can we take them away? One or two are probably girls I knew, and they're going to be scared to death if the police come in a raid. They can testify against Mrs. Kent later, but until then, they're better off with someone like me who knows what they've been through.''

Sara had wanted him to care about the suffering of people he didn't know, and perhaps he owed these anonymous girls something for not having acted against Mrs. Kent earlier. "Very well," Peregrine said, "do what you can for them. Benjamin, order the carriage and a horse for me. I'll find the guards and tell them what we're planning.''

A few minutes later, a pistol thrust under his cloak, he was riding through London as fast as he dared. If there was going to be trouble, he must first make sure that Sara was out of harm's way.

Weldon's hope that Lady Sara was captured died as soon as he talked to Mrs. Kent. "No, sir," the madame said emphatically. "She's just a child. Couldn't possibly be a woman in her twenties.''

"Pity," Weldon said with regret. "Is she pretty?''

"Very. Long blond hair like an angel.'' Mrs. Kent gave an approving nod. "She could be another Jenny Miller, a girl who can play the virgin over and over. Valuable.''

"We'll keep her then.'' Weldon glanced upward. "What room is she in? Someone has to be the first, so I think I'll take that pleasure for myself.''

The madame frowned. "I've already promised her to someone else for later tonight. I've a particularly good customer who likes blondes, the younger the better.''

Weldon shrugged indifferently. "He can have her second. Unless you've got another virgin in the house?''

"Not tonight. Just three of the regular girls, plus the new one. A man is bringing in two of his daughters tomorrow, just for one night." A peevish note entered her voice. "It's a lot harder running a virgin house than a regular brothel."

"Which is why you earn so much," Weldon pointed out unsympathetically. "What room is the new girl in?"

"The end of the hall, on the right."

"What's her name?"

"She wouldn't tell me. Won't do anything but cry for her father," Mrs. Kent said with contempt. "But I made her ready for her first customer." She went to her desk and pulled out a key. "Here's the key to the room."

Weldon went into the hall and climbed the stairs. Outside the new girl's room, he paused, his heart and breath quickening in anticipation. There was such ecstasy in being the first, in knowing that no one else had ever penetrated that innocent body. Amidst the frustration of his struggle with Peregrine, he needed this to restore his power and confidence. His organ began swelling to hard potency at the thought.

After turning the key in the lock, he quietly opened the door. In the room's dim light, at first he saw only a slender body and blond hair tumbling over the pillow. As usual, the girl wore a flimsy, childish white nightgown, and her wrists were tied to the bedposts.

He licked his lips as waves of desire pulsed through him, melting his fears and frustrations. Yes, he needed this. Softfooted, he crossed the room, anticipating the sweet taste of the child.

The girl had whimpered with fear when the door opened. Then she turned her head toward the entrance, a swath of lamplight falling across her childish features.

Weldon stopped dead in his tracks. Then nausea began boiling through him, along with paralyzing grief.

The child's blue eyes widened, first with shock, then with joy. "Papa!" Eliza whispered, her voice raw from weeping. "Papa, I knew you would come."

Chapter 28

IT HAD TAKEN Kuram time to find Mrs. Kent's house, for in this part of London the streets were not well marked. Sara burned with impatience, and when Kuram opened the door and said, "Here, lady," she jumped out immediately.

It was full dark now, and she pulled her hood up so that it shadowed her face. Kuram directed the driver down the block to an alley where the carriage would be inconspicuous.

Then Sara went up the steps, Kuran close behind her. There was an interminable wait after she knocked.

Finally a small window slid open in the door. "Who are you and what do you want?" a hoarse voice asked.

Perhaps some special password was required, but Sara didn't know what it might be, so she said, "I am here on a matter of business—profitable business for Mrs. Kent."

The window slid shut, and there was such a long wait that she feared they would not be admitted. But eventually the door swung grudgingly open, and she stepped inside, Kuran behind her.

Standing in a drab hall were a burly ruffian and a large, unpleasant-looking woman who matched Jenny's description of Mrs. Kent. Eyes wary, the madame snapped, "What's your business—do you have a daughter to sell?"

Disguising her revulsion, Sara replied, "I have reason to believe that earlier today a young girl was brought here by mistake. I will pay well for her release, no questions asked."

Mrs. Kent frowned. "How did you know to come here?"

"No matter." Sara waved one hand negligently, trying to look more confident than she felt. The house reeked of evil. Even if Eliza wasn't here, Sara would willingly use her money to buy the freedom of any other captive children.

The madame pursed her lips, then shot a quick, hard glance to her guard. "Come into my office where we can talk."

Sara nodded and began following the woman. She had gone only a few steps when the noise of a fight exploded behind her. Whirling, Sara discovered that the burly guard must have received a hidden signal from Mrs. Kent, for he had attacked Kuram. The two men rolled across the floor of the hall, kicking and swearing. The Pathan fought like a fury, but his opponent outweighed him and had the advantage of surprise.

Seeing the odds against Kuram, Sara scanned the hall, looking for some weapon to use on the guard. As her gaze fell on a wooden chair, Mrs. Kent seized Sara's arms in a powerful grip.

Though Sara struggled to free herself, the other woman effortlessly immobilized her. "I don't know who you are, my fine lady," the madam snarled, "but you got no business here."

Kuram managed to throw off his assailant, but the other man grabbed a stone doorstop from the corner of the hall when he fell. The fight ended abruptly when the guard smashed the heavy weight into the side of Kuram's head.

The Pathan groaned and went limp. As blood began soaking through the white fabric of his turban, Sara cried out and tried to go to him, but she couldn't break the madame's grip.

"Tie him up in the back room," Mrs. Kent ordered

the guard. "The master may want to question him, so don't kill him yet."

Sara's hood had fallen back when the women struggled. Mrs. Kent studied her captive with narrowed eyes, then gave a slow, unpleasant smile. "I'd lay fifty quid you're the older wench my master described not more'n ten minutes ago. He's going to be right pleased to see you." She twisted Sara's wrist viciously. "You'll wait in my office till he's through upstairs."

In the office the madame searched her captive with rough thoroughness, giving a grunt of satisfaction when she discovered the money hidden in the cloak. "This is a day for good things coming out of bad. First a mistake gave me a new girl for the house, and now you walk in ripe for the fleecing." Mrs. Kent pushed Sara into a heavy chair, then lashed her wrists together and tied them to one wooden arm.

Knowing that the more helpless she appeared, the more careless and contemptuous Mrs. Kent would be, Sara shrank back in the chair, letting her fear show. Looking frightened was easy, for Jenny had been right—Sara was a fool to have come here. Not only had she failed to help Eliza, her disastrous error in judgment might cost her and Kuram their lives. Worst of all, Mikahl might come and be taken unaware by the guard.

Closing her eyes, Sara forced herself to calmness. Then she began to pray.

As his daughter spoke, Weldon stood stock-still, his body chill with stupefaction. He, who always had prided himself on being unshockable, now found that the sight of his daughter's plight was like a blade thrust mortally deep into his heart.

Eliza's voice trailed off uncertainly. "Papa . . . Papa, are you all right?"

Her question snapped Weldon from his horror-struck trance into molten, coruscating rage. If it had not been for Peregrine, Eliza would never have been abducted.

Her presence in this foul place was an abomination, a corruption of the innocent for which that bastard was ultimately responsible, and for which he would be made to pay an unspeakable price.

The sight of Eliza's wide, panicky eyes forced Weldon to curb his rage. Before vengeance could be executed, his daughter must be freed. With clumsy fingers, he began undoing the sashes that bound her to the bed. "Don't worry, darling," he said in a shattered voice. "Papa's here. I won't let anyone hurt you."

Released from her bonds, Eliza sat up and leaned into her father's embrace as she shook with desperate sobs. "I was going to call on Lady Sara, just for a few minutes, but they grabbed me on the street just outside Haddonfield House," she gasped. "They had a smelly rag that put me to sleep. When I woke up, I was here and a horrible woman was touching me. She said I could never go home again. She said I would have to . . . ."

As his daughter's voice broke entirely, Weldon patted her on the back, crooning over and over that she was safe now, that her father would never let anyone harm her. When Eliza's sobs finally subsided, he asked, "Are your clothes here?"

She swallowed, then spoke with a heartbreaking attempt at bravery. "The awful woman put them in that chest of drawers."

"You get dressed while I go downstairs and make sure it is safe for you to leave." Weldon's trembling hand touched his daughter's bright hair as she gazed at him with trustful eyes.

"Yes, Papa." In her father's presence, Eliza was recovering rapidly from her terror. "I knew you would come, and everything would be all right."

Out in the corridor, Weldon leaned back against the closed door, his breath coming in ragged gasps as he struggled to suppress horrifying images of what would have been done to Eliza if he hadn't chanced to come to the house. His precious daughter would have been defiled by some filthy brute who did not recognize true innocence when he saw it.

Peregrine was behind this, but Mrs. Kent and the guards who had kidnapped Eliza were also guilty. They should have known as soon as they saw her that she was pure; they should never have laid their vile hands on her. They would pay; by God, all of them would pay.

Weldon always carried a small pistol when he came to this part of London. Now he pulled the weapon from under his coat, checked the loading, cocked it, then concealed it again. White-hot with fury, he went downstairs to Mrs. Kent's office.

When he opened the door, the madame said, "We've a visitor, sir. This female just pranced in, bold as brass. Is she the one you told me about earlier?"

The words Weldon had meant to hurl at his employee were temporarily forgotten when he saw Sara tied to the chair. Incredulous, he exclaimed, "What the hell are you doing here?"

Sara stared back, vivid shock on her face. "I might ask you the same, Charles. I refused to believe that you could be involved in something so sordid, but I see that I was wrong." A mask of cool control smoothed her expression. "I came because I feared Eliza had been brought here. Is she upstairs?"

"Yes, but she's about to leave." Weldon gave a smile of deep, malicious satisfaction. "You, however, will not." Then he turned to Mrs. Kent, his expression vicious. "The girl upstairs is my daughter, you stupid bitch. Are the two beasts who abducted her in the house?"

Mrs. Kent paled. "One went back to Mrs. Cambridge's, where he usually works. The other is here, in the back room watching the servant who came with this lady."

"For laying hands on my daughter, you must die,"

Weldon growled as he reached under his coat and withdrew a small, ugly pistol.

Her gaze fixed on the gun, Mrs. Kent gave a strangled gasp. "You can't blame me for not knowing who she was! The girl wouldn't even tell me her name."

"You should have known that she was an innocent," he said relentlessly, his finger tightening on the trigger. "Instead you treated her as just another worthless slut."

Finally believing that her master meant what he said, Mrs. Kent screamed and tried to run away, but flight came far too late. The pistol discharged, the noise deafening in the small room. The ball caught Mrs. Kent in the temple and she crashed to the floor, knocking over a wooden chair. She sprawled in an ungainly heap, her eyes still wide with desperate disbelief as the room filled with acrid smoke.

"Fortunate that this house has such good soundproofing." Weldon turned to Sara, a wild, dangerous gleam in his eyes as he reloaded his pistol. "Before I am done, you will wish that I had killed you quickly. I have some business to take care of, but I will be back soon."

He strode from the room, the door behind him not quite closing. Sara began to work frantically to loosen her bonds. Until now, she would not have believed it possible that Charles would hurt her, but now she knew that he was capable of any kind of mad violence.

She tensed as she heard a single shot in the back of the house. Had he killed the guard or Kuram? Considering how he had executed Mrs. Kent for the mistaken abduction, probably he had shot the guard and spared Kuram, at least for the moment. Weldon was mad, thoroughly, terrifyingly mad, executing others for the same crime he had routinely committed against other children.

Weldon's footsteps ascended on the stairs again. Several minutes later, two sets of feet sounded, one heavy, one light.

Listening hard, Sara heard Eliza say fearfully, "Is that awful woman gone?"

"Yes, darling," Weldon said in the soft, comforting voice of a perfect father. "You're safe now; Papa will let no one harm you. But you must be brave and ride home in the carriage alone. The driver will take you straight back to your uncle's house."

"You can't come with me?"

"No, darling, there are some things that must be done before I can leave. The people who hurt you must be punished."

Sara could have screamed, but that would do no good. Eliza could not help her, and knowing that Sara was in the brothel would put the child in an intolerable position.

The front door opened and closed. Then the house was silent for perhaps five minutes. It was odd just how quiet it was; Sara supposed that the children were locked in their rooms, and it was too early for customers. If there were any servants, they were wisely keeping away. Perhaps they had even fled.

Sara had one wrist almost completely free when Weldon returned to the house and came directly to the office. He crossed the room and finished undoing the bonds, then yanked her to her feet. Savagely he said, "We're going upstairs, where I can punish you in comfort."

Praying that she might be able to calm him, Sara said quietly, "What have I done to deserve punishment, Charles? For Eliza's sake, I risked my life coming here."

His eyes flared with renewed rage. "You have tried to corrupt her! Eliza was captured while trying to visit you. She would never have disobeyed her father's orders if not for your pernicious influence. But it is not just for Eliza that I must punish you." As he dragged Sara from the room and up the stairs, he continued, "I thought you were a lady, worthy to be Eliza's stepmother. Instead, you betrayed me for a rutting foreign bastard. Tonight you will pay for your treachery.''

Thinking it might deter him, Sara considered saying that Mikahl would arrive at any moment, but she quickly rejected the idea. If he knew that his enemy was coming, Weldon would tie her up again and wait with pistol in hand.

Weldon took her to an empty bedroom at the end of the upstairs hall, and shoved her inside. Sara staggered as her weak leg twisted, but she managed not to fall. ''Have you ever considered blaming yourself for your problems?'' she said, reckless with anger. ''Surely Eliza was kidnapped on your orders, not Mrs. Kent's.''

''She frightened my daughter. She shouldn't have done that. And the guard—he hurt Eliza. They deserved what they got,'' he said with glittering eyes. ''Now, you little whore, you will also get what you deserve.'' With one hand he pulled Sara close while with the other he fondled her coarsely, his fingers digging deep into intimate flesh.

Revolted, Sara shrank away from him, but it was impossible to avoid his probing hand. Even through layers of petticoats, she felt violated.

Weldon smiled with vicious satisfaction. ''Don't play the virtuous lady with me, Sara. You'd like this if I were the bastard, wouldn't you?'' Releasing her, he reached to turn the key in the lock. ''Before the night is over, you are going to do everything for me that you do for him.''

While his attention was on the key, Sara reached under Weldon's coat in a desperate attempt to take the pistol. Her fingers had just touched the weapon's handle when he felt her action and whirled around.

''You will regret that,'' he snarled. He untied her cloak, which slithered to the floor in heavy folds. Then he seized the neck of her gown and ripped the fabric down to her waist.

Sara raked at her assailant's face with clawed fingers, but Weldon easily slapped her hands aside. Then

he forced her to the floor and dropped down to trap
her under his solid body.

Impact with the floor temporarily stunned Sara, but
as Weldon tore at her with feral hands, she screamed
and began struggling frantically. In her naïveté, she
had thought she understood something of Mikahl's
furious need for revenge. Now that early understanding paled beside the deep, visceral rage she felt at
Weldon's abuse. But even rage was futile against her
assailant's brutal power.

As Weldon tore at her clothing, Sara made a despairing prayer for strength to survive the horror that
was to come.

Before approaching Mrs. Kent's house, Peregrine
checked the alley where Kuram had kept the carriage
the night they had rescued Jenny. Sure enough, the
alley was occupied, this time by Peregrine's own armed
and watchful driver.

Before leaving his horse in the driver's charge, he
asked a few quick questions and learned that Sara and
Kuram had gone inside about twenty minutes earlier.
Just a few minutes ago, a man and a little girl had
come out of the brothel. The man had put the child in
a waiting carriage, then returned to the house.

From the description, the people were Weldon and
Eliza, which meant that the girl was safe, but Sara and
Kuram were in danger. Peregrine swore under his
breath at the sheer bad luck that had brought Weldon
to the brothel at the same time as Sara.

Seething with impatience, he sprinted to Mrs. Kent's
house and knocked on the door. Unsurprised that no
one answered, he studied the building's facade with
narrowed eyes. The lower-level windows had always
been barred, and bars had also been installed on the
upper floors since Jenny's escape.

Frowning, he recalled from his previous visit that
the front door and lock were solid. However, he also
had a vague impression that the door frame had been

old and brittle-looking, and a lock was no better than the wood that surrounded it.

Hoping that his memory was correct, and that he didn't break his foot, he kicked the door hard, striking beside the lock. With a sound of splintering wood, the door shuddered and moved inward. After two more kicks, the lock ripped from the frame and the door swung open. He pulled his pistol out and cocked it, then entered cautiously, weapon ready.

The racket of his entrance should have drawn everyone in the house, but the building was eerily silent, with no one in sight. Peregrine looked around, puzzled. It was not too surprising that there was no sign of children or patrons, but what about Mrs. Kent? And surely there would be a guard to keep order. Soundlessly he crossed to the madame's office and looked in.

Mrs. Kent's body sprawled across the floor in a puddle of blood. Peregrine whistled softly, wondering what had happened. More important, where were Sara and Kuram and Weldon?

As he returned to the hall, he heard a muffled scream coming from upstairs. Impossible to be sure with the soundproofing, but it sounded like Sara. Three steps at a time, he raced up the stairs. A second scream led him to the bedchamber at the end of the corridor. This time he was sure the voice was Sara's.

To his surprise, the knob turned in his hand. Knowing it might be a trap, he ducked down before opening the door. Keeping low so that he would present a difficult target, he charged into the room.

At his explosive entrance, the struggling figures on the floor stared up at him, immobilized by shock. Peregrine's gaze met his wife's for a fractional moment. Relief flared in her dark eyes, followed instantly by concern. "Look out, Mikahl," Sara cried, "he has a gun!"

Simultaneously Weldon leapt to his feet and reached

under his coat, snarling, "You foolish bastard, you have delivered yourself into my hands."

Afraid that a bullet might hit his wife, Peregrine held his own fire. "Sara, get out of the way!"

As she scrambled to one side of the room, Weldon cocked and leveled his pistol. Peregrine shot first, aiming high so that he would not endanger Sara. Though the bullet only grazed Weldon's right shoulder, it did force him to drop his gun, and the weapon skidded across the floor, mercifully not discharging.

Now it was just the two of them, man to man, without firearms to lend false superiority. Peregrine launched himself at Weldon, staggering the other man with a ferocious blow to the jaw. Weldon gasped, but he had studied boxing in his youth, and old skills returned to help him block the next blow.

It was a savage, hand-to-hand struggle without rules or quarter. For Peregrine, twenty-five years fell away in an instant, and once more he was an abused, betrayed child. But the wheel of fortune had spun around, and this time all the power and all the choices were his. He pummeled his enemy's flesh with fierce joy, every one of Weldon's groans a balm to his wounded spirit.

Weldon was heavier, and he fought with the strength of madness, but he was older and softer than his opponent, and without a weapon he had no chance. After absorbing several minutes of bruising punishment, Weldon crashed to the floor, face bleeding and expression dazed.

Sliding the knife from his boot, Peregrine dropped to one knee beside the other man. "You laughed when I swore vengeance, but finally your doom has found you." His voice throbbing with hatred, he laid the razor-sharp steel on Weldon's throat and drew a thin crimson line with delicate precision. "For twenty-five years I have lived for this moment."

The touch of the blade brought Weldon back to alertness, and with a surge of defiance he sneered, "If not for me, you would be a slave in Islam or an ignorant sailor. You should thank me for spurring you to better yourself.''

At the taunt, Peregrine almost drove the knife through the other man's throat. Barely in time he stopped himself, not yet ready to send his enemy to hell. ''Do you think that Jamie McFarland would have thanked you for what you did? Or any of his sailors, who died as slaves because you would not lift a finger to help them?'' he said with ice-eyed fury. ''A pity that you will die too quickly to suffer as much as you made them suffer.''

He shifted the knife from Weldon's throat to his groin, driving the tip through fabric to rest on flesh. ''Shall I do to you what you wanted done to me, Weldon?'' he said softly. ''How long will it take you to bleed to death if I decide to kill you by castration?''

''You filthy savage!'' Weldon was no longer the urbane businessman and aristocrat. Face twisted with terror, he tried desperately to grab his assailant's weapon.

Peregrine easily lifted the knife out of his enemy's reach, then used his left fist to strike a paralyzing blow to the other man's solar plexus. As Weldon convulsed, retching with pain, Peregrine touched the knife to his enemy's eye socket. ''Shall we play a game of blindman's buff?'' he asked with mocking courtesy. ''First I will gouge out your eyes. Then every time you make a wrong move, I will slice away another part of your body. An English version of the Chinese death of a thousand cuts.''

''I am glad for what I did to you,'' Weldon spat out, glaring up at his tormentor. ''I only wish I had killed you in Tripoli.''

''It was your mistake that you did not.'' Peregrine soared on wings of fiery justice, savoring the culmination of his mission. Weldon was at his mercy, and nothing could save his enemy now.

Then Peregrine felt the pressure of someone's gaze.

In his rage he had forgotten when and where he was, but now he glanced up and saw Sara. She stood flattened against the wall, watching him with agonized sibyl eyes. Sara, his conscience and salvation.

Her expression cooled Peregrine's fury like a shock of ice water. The raw anguish that fueled his rage ebbed and was replaced by vivid memories of Sara's warmth, the touch of her lips on his ravaged back, the sweet totality of her love.

He wrenched his gaze away to stare down at the man who had been his devil and his doom. Though Peregrine's barbaric fury had subsided, he still ached to claim his enemy's life. Pushing aside the image of Sara's face, with cool deliberation he poised the knife above Weldon's body, angling first toward the heart, then the throat, then the eyes. It would be exquisitely easy and profoundly satisfying to collect the ultimate price for the other man's crimes.

But it was too late. Peregrine's wildness had passed; to kill Weldon now would be deliberate, cold-blooded murder.

Perhaps Sara would forgive her husband for committing murder. But perhaps she would not.

"Damnation!" Peregrine swore, his furious voice filling the room. For an instant he raged against the bitter knowledge of what he must do. Then he turned back to his enemy and slashed down with fluid, violent power.

Weldon had been waiting for the death stroke with the paralysis of terror, his gaze transfixed by the glittering blade. As light flashed along the descending knife, he gave a panic-stricken, animal shriek.

Weldon's wail was drowned by Peregrine's shattering war cry. Riveted by horror, Sara closed her eyes to block the sight of murder being committed for the second time that evening.

Sara was on the verge of fainting when she opened her eyes again, and it took her a long, shaken moment to believe the stunning scene before her.

Weldon still lived, ash-faced and writhing with terror. Rather than striking a death blow, Mikahl had deliberately driven the knife into the floor beside his enemy's neck.

"You are not worth killing, Weldon," Mikahl said viciously as he wrenched his blade free. "Rather than soil my blade with your blood, I shall hand you over to the tender mercies of British justice."

Knife held warily, Mikahl got to his feet, but his caution was unnecessary. Weldon was broken. Like a whipped dog, he lay cringing and submissive before his conqueror.

"Come, Sara," Mikahl ordered. "I will lock Weldon in here and send the police to deal with him."

Quickly Sara bent to snatch her cloak from the floor where it had fallen earlier, then hastened to her husband's side.

Weldon pushed himself to a sitting position, his expression incredulous at being spared. Keeping his gaze fixed on his enemy, Mikahl collected the two pistols, giving the empty one to Sara and keeping the loaded one himself. Then he backed across the room to the door. "Every scurrilous newspaper in Britain will be screaming for your blood, Weldon. Your name will become a synonym for evil and hypocrisy."

Mikahl ushered Sara outside, then pulled the key from the inside lock. "You'll hang, Weldon, for the murder of Mrs. Kent if nothing else. Perhaps your neck will break, and you'll die quickly, but that doesn't always happen. Death by strangulation is slow and painful—you can look forward to that while you rot in prison." Then he closed the door and locked it. With the windows barred, Weldon would not escape before the police came.

Still trembling with strain, Sara watched Mikahl in anxious silence, knowing that Mikahl must be furious over her stupidity in coming to the brothel. When he turned to her with blazing eyes, Sara braced herself for an explosion.

Furious her husband might be, but he did not waste time in recriminations. Instead, he swept her into a rib-bruising hug that briefly lifted Sara from her feet. She responded with frantic relief, burrowing deep into his arms and finding safety in his strength.

The embrace ended as abruptly as it had begun. As Mikhal released her, he said with surprising mildness, "Coming here was not one of your better ideas, Sara."

"I know." She brushed her hair from her eyes with an unsteady hand. "I was so afraid of what might happen to Eliza, but in the end, I did her no good."

"The girl was not seriously injured?"

"I believe she is all right—I heard them speak when Charles brought her downstairs." Sara shuddered. "I think he had gone up with the intention of ravishing the new girl. When he realized that it was Eliza, he must have pretended that he had come to rescue her. Pray God she never learns what almost happened. What if the room had not been well lit, or he had been too drunk to notice who she was?"

"But that didn't happen," he said quietly. "Eliza is safe, you are safe. And you would not be my Sara if you were not willing to risk your life to help an innocent child."

Though Mikhal's dangerous wildness had passed, his green eyes still held a strange, volatile light that Sara could not interpret. There was much to be said between them, and before she could decide where to start, they were interrupted by the sound of people entering the downstairs hall. Sara stiffened, fearing that new danger threatened.

"Don't worry," her husband reassured her. "That is two of my guards and Slade, with Jenny doubtless tagging along behind."

Sara's mouth curved ruefully. "Jenny has every right to say 'I told you so' to me."

His movements crisply efficient, Mikhal took Sara's cloak and draped it around her shoulders to cover her torn dress. Then they both went downstairs. Several minutes of chaotic greetings and explanations followed.

Directed by Sara, they found Kuram in the back room by the body of the dead guard. When he was ungagged, the Pathan cursed furiously for allowing himself to be overcome. His turban had cushioned much of the force of the blow to his head, and a quick examination confirmed that he was not seriously injured.

Her face set with determination, Jenny delved into Mrs. Kent's desk for keys, then went off to free whatever children were in the house. Before she left, Mikahl warned, "Don't unlock the room on the right at the end of the upstairs corridor. Weldon is there, and it's a good place to hold him until the police can come."

"Weldon is alive?" Slade asked, startled.

Without looking at Sara, Mikahl said dryly, "My wife doesn't approve of murder."

After a calculating pause, Slade suggested, "Lady Sara has had a difficult time of it. Why don't you escort her home while I deal with the situation here? Jenny and I will take the children back to my house. Then I'll contact the magistrate and the police, and tell them what has happened."

"Very well. Here is Weldon's gun, though you shouldn't need it. Be careful, it's loaded." Mikahl glanced at Sara, his gaze unreadable. "Come. I'll take you home." He took Sara's arm with a cool, detached hand, and silently guided her outside.

Sara's heart twisted when her husband ordered the coachman to drive to Haddonfield House. So he was going to return her to the protection of her father's roof.

She had seen ample evidence that Mikahl neither forgave nor forgot easily. As he assisted her into the carriage, Sara prayed that he would someday forgive her for having left him.

* * *

Left in charge, Slade eyed the gun thoughtfully. Then he went to help Jenny. There were three girls in the brothel, one a dark-haired child known to Jenny, the other two being strangers who had been in the house for only a short time. Since Jenny had once been one of them, the girls trusted her and gratefully accepted the opportunity to leave the house and build better lives.

It didn't take long for the children to gather their few possessions and be taken to the carriage. When they were safely inside, Slade said to the driver, "Wait for me. There is one more thing I must do."

The driver nodded, and Slade went back into the house, Jenny at his heels. "What else needs to be done?" she asked, puzzled.

"A little rough justice." The lawyer glanced down at her. "I must speak with Weldon, but you shouldn't come."

Her chin tilted stubbornly. "I want to see."

After studying her face, Slade nodded and led the way upstairs. He unlocked the door cautiously, pistol raised, but his wariness was unnecessary.

Weldon lay on the bed, his face bruised and bleeding, his expression dazed, as if unable to accept that his diabolical luck had run out. When the door opened, he sat up and glared at the intruders, but his malice was a pale shadow of his old manner. "If it isn't my favorite little whore," he said nastily. "Did you come back because you missed me?"

Jenny's eyes narrowed to angry slits. "I came back to see you broken. Someday soon, I'll spit on your grave."

Slade put an arm around her taut shoulders. "I'm going to give you more mercy than you deserve, Weldon," he said coolly. "You're doomed. If you stand trial, the scandal will follow your daughter for the rest of her life. But if you die tonight, your crimes need never become public knowledge, and Eliza won't have to know how vile her father was. Since Peregrine intends to save the railway, your daughter will even be a rich woman someday from the stock she'll inherit.''

Weldon's bitter gaze sharpened. ''That would also make things easier for you,'' he sneered. ''Well, I'm not going to take the coward's way out. Who knows what might happen in court.''

Slade shrugged indifferently. ''If you want to delude yourself that a miracle will save you, go right ahead. Your daughter will suffer, but not a tithe as much as the rest of your victims have.'' The lawyer set the loaded pistol on the dresser and withdrew with Jenny, carefully locking the door behind them.

Weldon stared at the door, then got up and limped over to pick up the pistol. Caressing the warm wood and cool steel, he turned the weapon over and over in his hands while he considered what Slade had said.

Eliza was the best thing in his life, the only pure female he had ever known. He thought of the expression in her eyes when he had found her tonight. She adored him, as a daughter should, and she would be devastated by her father's public vilification. Since she was female, Eliza would never be able to understand the irresistible allure of the dark side of life; she would come to hate the memory of her father, her innocent love destroyed by all the people who would say he had been wicked.

And if Weldon killed himself, he would deny Peregrine the pleasure of seeing him suffer. Quickly, before he could change his mind, Weldon put the pistol barrel to his temple and pulled the trigger.

Downstairs, Jenny shivered and drew closer to Slade at the sound of the shot. ''Why did you let him do that?''

''It's better this way, Jenny. No more innocents suffer, there will be no trouble for Peregrine or his lady, no chance that your reputation will be damaged.'' Slade's ice-gray eyes gleamed with chilly satisfaction. Jenny's tormentor was dead. A good lawyer could do murder without ever touching a weapon.

His expression warmed. "Since you're going to be my wife, your reputation is my business. You *are* going to marry me, aren't you, Jenny?"

"Yes, Benjamin," she replied as warmth blossomed deep inside of her. She stood on her toes and gave him a kiss of aching promise. Then, with her lover at her side, Jenny left the house of death forever.

Insisting that he was perfectly well, Kuram chose to ride the horse, so Peregrine was alone with Sara inside the carriage. Wrapped in her cloak, his wife sat in the far corner of the vehicle, not touching him. The darkness was thick with tension. Peregrine knew that he should speak, but was painfully unsure where to begin.

It was a relief when Sara's soft voice broke the silence. "Why didn't you kill him?"

Knowing how important his answer was, he hesitated before speaking. "After you left Sulgrave, I did a great deal of thinking and realized that vengeance could not alter or heal the past. Today, if I had stayed in a white heat of rage for just a minute longer, I would have killed Weldon, but the sight of you broke my anger. After that, I could not do it."

"Are you saying that you gave up your revenge because of me?" she exclaimed, incredulous.

Obliquely he replied, "After you and I had that argument, I realized that you were talking not just about right and wrong, but about choosing whether to live a life rooted in hate or one rooted in love. For too many years, the center of my life was hatred, Sara. Then I met you, and slowly, without my conscious awareness, the center shifted."

He paused, searching for the right words to convey his meaning. "If destroying Weldon meant losing you, the price was too high, for I would be condemning myself to a living death." Then, wryly, he added, "Before we married, I said that I trusted you to always be good. Fortunately I didn't know then how difficult it can be to live with someone who is always good, or I would have been afraid to try.''

''I sound like a dreadful prig,'' she said with a shaky laugh. A streetlight outside momentarily illuminated her pure profile.

''You are not at all priggish about matters that count.'' Briefly there was a smile in his voice, but he was deadly serious when he continued, ''Yin and yang mean many things. Light and dark, good and evil, even love and hate. Together, opposites make a whole. You are my heart, Sara, and your light balances my darkness. Will you come home?''

Instantly she flowed across the carriage and into his arms. ''Of course I will!'' she said joyously, her breath feather-soft against his throat. ''When you told the driver to go to Haddonfield House, I was afraid that you didn't want me back.''

With a gust of laughter, he said, ''I was trying to do the gentlemanly thing, though it went against my nature.'' The knot of tension in his chest miraculously dissolved as he pulled her onto his lap and drew her close. ''Whenever you wondered why I married you, I always said that I did it because I wanted to, and I never looked any deeper.'' He stroked a gentle hand through Sara's silky hair, which had come unpinned during her struggle with Weldon. ''After you left, I realized that my words were a coward's way of saying that I love you.''

Sara inhaled deeply. ''I didn't believe you would ever say that.'' Tenderly she lifted her hand to his cheek and caressed the chiseled plane with her fingertips. ''You've changed so much. When I first met you, you were like some exotic, alien creature, forever wild and incomprehensible. It seemed impossible that you could ever love me as I love you.''

''I started changing as soon as I met you, though I didn't realize it at first. And when I did, I can't say that I enjoyed the sensation. But the formative years of my life were spent here, and the longer I stay, the more I feel like an Englishman. This is my heritage, and I no longer want to deny it.'' His tone became teasing. ''In fact, I have succumbed to the most banal of ambitions: to become an English country gentleman and live quietly with my wife and raise children and horses.''

''There is nothing banal about happiness,'' Sara retorted. ''If life as a country gentleman is a common ambition, that is because it is a good life. But you will never be banal—there has never been a man like you, and there never will be again. And in spite of the way you deny it, you are a good man.''

''As long as you think I'm good enough,'' Mikahl said, amused. After reaching into an inner coat pocket, he said, ''Give me your left hand.''

When she complied, he slid her wedding ring onto her third finger. Then he raised her hand to his lips, and kissed it with lingering reverence. ''I want to be with you always, Sara,'' he said softly. ''To make love with you, laugh with you, be silent with you. And most of all, I want to be the man that I am only when I am with you.''

''And I want to be the woman that I am only with you.'' Sara's fingers tightened around the ring. Shyly she went on, ''If you are willing, I would like to have a wedding ring made for you—one that matches mine.''

''I would like that.'' After a thoughtful pause, he said, ''Since I intend to stay in England, perhaps I should become Michael Connery again. We can tell people that I decided to Anglicize my name for the sake of simplicity. Will you mind being Sara Connery?''

Intuitively she knew that he was not just suggesting a name change; he was accepting his past—all of it, the bad and the good. That acceptance had come from healing. Finally, after too many years, the wounded boy was whole and had become a man.

In the half-light of the carriage, Sara looked into the

vivid depths of his eyes. "I love you," she whispered as she lifted her face to his. "I'll always love you, whether you are Peregrine, Michael, or Mikahl."

Their lips touched, at first lightly, then in fierce declaration as they pledged their souls without words.

Pledge and promise turned quickly to passion, and the trip across London passed in a haze of touch and love and laughter. On reaching Mayfair, Mikahl gave orders to continue to their own town house rather than to Haddonfield House.

When they arrived home, he climbed out first and let down the steps, then caught Sara around the waist and effortlessly whisked her from the carriage. "Before I take you upstairs and make love to you," he said as he set her feet on the ground, "perhaps you should say good-bye to Peregrine, for I am a wanderer no more."

"So my hawk has become a dove?" Hair tumbled and eyes dreamy with desire, Sara caught his face between her hands. "Welcome home, wanderer, welcome home."

Author's Note

KAFIRISTAN, also sometimes called Dardistan, lies in what is now eastern Afghanistan. The Hindu Kush was one of the most remote areas on earth, and Kafiristan was not officially charted until George Scott Robertson visited in 1889. The country took its name from the Arabic "qafir," meaning "unbeliever." (Arab slavers applied the same word to the tribes of East Africa, and "kaffir" became a derogatory term for black Africans.)

As indicated in *Silk and Shadows,* the natives of Kafiristan claimed Alexander the Great as an ancestor. Some of their customs seemed more European than Asiatic, and they welcomed the first Europeans as long-lost kinfolk. (The Russians believed that the Kafirs were a Slavic tribe.)

A romanticized version of the country was the goal of the adventurers in the movie *The Man Who Would Be King,* which was based on a story by Rudyard Kipling. In 1895, Amir Abdur Rahman, the ruler of Afghanistan, conquered Kafiristan and forcibly converted the inhabitants to Islam. Since then the region has been known as Nuristan, "the country of light."

ABOUT THE AUTHOR

MARY JO PUTNEY is a graduate of Syracuse University with degrees in eighteenth-century literature and in industrial design. In 1988, she received the *RWA Golden Leaf* Award for Best Historical Novel, and the *Romantic Times* Award for Best Regency Author. In 1989 Ms. Putney won three awards for her Regency *The Rake and the Reformer.* Her novel *Dearly Beloved* received the *RWA Golden Leaf* Award for Best Historical Novel in 1990.